On *The Great Ar*

"Dr. Keith Payne has painstakingly and skillfully developed a masterful analysis of American Cold War nuclear deterrence theory to practice with insightful critique and prescriptive considerations for the post-Cold War era. Keith utilizes a vast amount of previously classified information to facilitate the comprehension of high-level key deterrence decisions. A 'must read' for defense policy professionals, scholars, and concerned citizens. "

- ADM Henry Chiles Jr., USN (ret.), former Commander in Chief, U.S. Strategic Command

"Prof. Payne provides the theories, facts, history and judgments on both sides of salient nuclear deterrence issues. And there's a stark lesson: too often we have been wrong—luckily avoiding catastrophe; we can't know the adversary so hedging is a necessity."

- Dr. Johnny Foster, former Director, Defense Research and Engineering, Department of Defense and Director, Lawrence Livermore National Laboratory

"Keith Payne's book is the first to explain convincingly how strategic ideas shaped American nuclear policy, strategy, and postural choices in the Cold War. Based solidly on newly accessible essential official records, this work tells the real story of the US conduct and misconduct of the nuclear arms competition. This is the book for which we have been waiting."

- Dr. Colin S. Gray, Professor and Director, Centre for Strategic Studies, Department of Politics and International Relations, University of Reading, United Kingdom

"*The Great American Gamble* makes a seminal contribution to our understanding of deterrence theory and the profound influence of theory on national security policy. In this definitive work, Keith Payne presents the most insightful retrospective on the development and consistency of U.S. strategic thinking across decades of Democratic and Republican administrations. Most important, his research, logic, and prospective analysis provide a wake-up call for re-thinking our deterrence and defense requirements. Put simply, if we rely on the doctrines of the past, we put at risk our future."

- Amb. Robert Joseph, former Under Secretary of State for Arms Control and International Security

"This book is an extremely important study and analysis which will enrich teachers as well as students with its balance, scholarship, and clarity of presentation."

- Amb. Max Kampelman, served Presidents Carter and Reagan as Ambassador to the Conference on Security and Cooperation in Europe, Recipient of the Presidential Medal of Freedom

"Building on his previous seminal writings, Professor Payne meticulously traces and cogently explains the development of deterrence theory and U.S. strategic nuclear policy from the mid-1960s to the present time. He provides new insights into the thinking that shaped the assured destruction paradigm that decisively influenced Cold War choices that emphasized offensive forces and deliberately rejected defenses. Of greatest importance, however, is Dr. Payne's discussion of the need for a deterrence concept that moves beyond the Cold War balance of terror to align our strategic policies and forces with the realities of the twenty-first century. Dr. Payne discusses in detail the remaining obstacles that are the product of a Cold War strategic culture based on assured destruction thinking. He addresses what still needs to be done to deter states and terrorist groups that may be armed with nuclear capabilities in the years ahead. This book should be required reading both by policymakers and in the broader strategic affairs community."

- Dr. Robert L. Pfaltzgraff, Jr., Shelby Cullom Davis Professor of International Security Studies, The Fletcher School, Tufts University, and President, Institute for Foreign Policy Analysis

"You cannot read *The Great American Gamble* and remain indifferent to the challenge posed by the post-Cold War doctrine regarding deterrence. Keith Payne painstakingly documents the history of nuclear deterrence—and nuclear assurance for our allies—and then thoroughly and dispassionately analyzes the consequences of the choices that will confront our next President. For anyone content with belief that the republic will remain secure by simply maintaining a 'stable balance of terror,' this book will be unsettling. Dr. Payne made his bones long ago in the field of nuclear deterrence, and it is in this same arena where the next President will probably make the most important strategic decisions of his presidency. The whole question of the role of nuclear deterrence in U.S. strategic policy deserves a robust national debate, and Dr. Payne's insightful, timely and exceedingly well-documented analysis in *The Great American Gamble* is a perfect place to begin. For many who read his book, it is also likely where it will end."

- Senator Charles Robb

"It is no exaggeration to say that this book is now the definitive study and explanation of American strategic nuclear deterrent concepts and the decisive influence of one school of thought on U.S. policies and programs. Dr. Payne has conducted painstaking research in the literature on the subject, including official documents previously unavailable or untapped. The book is lucid, careful, and compelling. It is essential to understanding the 'why?' of U.S. deterrent and arms control policies."

- Dr. William R. Van Cleave, Professor Emeritus and Founder, Department of Defense and Strategic Studies, Missouri State University

"The essence of the reigning strategy of nuclear 'assured destruction' was outlined to me forty years ago, with little sense of irony, by a Pentagon official: 'Weapons that kill people are good. Weapons that kill other weapons are bad.' In this superb and definitive work, Keith Payne spells out how we got here and the extreme danger of continuing to so design our strategic forces."

- The Honorable R. James Woolsey, Former Director of Central Intelligence, Venture Partner, Vantage Point

THE GREAT AMERICAN GAMBLE

DETERRENCE THEORY AND PRACTICE
FROM THE COLD WAR TO THE TWENTY-FIRST CENTURY

KEITH B. PAYNE

National Institute Press ®

Published by
National Institute Press ®
9302 Lee Highway, Suite 750
Fairfax, Virginia 22031

Library of Congress Cataloging-in-Publication Data (TK)

Payne, Keith B.
  The great American gamble : deterrence theory and practice from the Cold
  War to the twenty-first century / Keith B. Payne.
      p. cm.
  Includes bibliographical references and index.
  ISBN 978-0-9776221-6-0 (alk. paper) -- ISBN 978-0-9776221-7-7 (pbk. :
  alk. paper)
  1. Deterrence (Strategy) 2. Strategic forces--United States. 3. Military
policy--United States. I. Title. II. Title: Deterrence theory and practice from
the Cold War to the twenty-first century.
  U162.6.P393 2008
  355.02'17--dc22
                              2008024453

10 9 8 7 6 5 4 3 2 1

This book is dedicated to the military and civilian personnel of the Department of Defense. Thank you for your incomparable service to the country. It also is dedicated to the members of the Board of Directors of the National Institute for Public Policy, M. Jane Mortensen, Colin Gray, Felix Hampton and Charles Kupperman. Thank you for your unwavering encouragement and support.

Contents

Figures

Foreword

Very few books have the potential to redefine the parameters of debate in a whole subject. Dr. Payne's book is one such. But, before I explain why this work is so deep and far reaching in its argument and implications, I think it is necessary for me to say a little about the qualifications of its author.

In the first place, Keith Payne has been a student, scholar and teacher of strategic nuclear matters for more than 30 years. In that time he has written extensively about nuclear deterrence and the U.S. strategic forces' posture. As much to the point, he has written to advise responsible officials, civilian and military. Secondly, Dr. Payne has not only been a scholar and advisor of long-standing, in addition he has served as a senior official in the Pentagon, with duties focused upon the principal themes of this study. So, Dr. Payne is abundantly entitled to claim to be as expert as anyone can be in an area of national security for which, blessedly, everyone is short of actual battlespace experience. Fortunately, no-one has won any medals for the conduct of nuclear warfare.

Why do I claim that this book is so important? A three-fold answer is necessary. It provides a new organizing framework that enables us to grasp far more clearly than ever before just how and why the modern theory of deterrence developed as it did. Dr. Payne delivers a golden key to unlock many of the mysteries of strategic theoretical and public policy debate. Next, the book tells the story of U.S. policy and strategy for its long-range, "strategic" nuclear-armed forces. And of particular value, he relates this history to the course and outcome of the strategic theoretical contention. Finally, Dr. Payne actually can demonstrate, even prove, the veracity in his argument. Given the ubiquity and authority of speculation and intuition concerning nuclear deterrence as concept and as policy, it is rare to find a book that can support its claims convincingly. This work is not merely illustrated by the occasional documented anecdote; instead, it rests solidly upon official records and empirical evidence. Given the high security sensitivity of the subject, nuclear policy and strategy, it is not hard to appreciate why Dr. Payne's book truly is a landmark.

I do not wish to pre-empt Dr. Payne's text unduly, but I must advise that the true glory of this analysis is the near crystal clarity of the all too meaningful distinction he draws between the strategic ideas represented by the brilliant Harvard economist, Thomas C. Schelling, and those of no less brilliant Herman Kahn. To the best of my multi-decade knowledge, second and first hand, no-one other than Dr. Payne has succeeded in presenting 50 plus years of nuclear argument, debate, and policy, in such a way that it all makes such sense as the material allows.

Different readers will favor different strengths in this text. I will cite a few of the features of these pages that I find especially appealing and important. Dr. Payne demonstrates, not merely suggests or illustrates, the significance of strategic theoretical ideas as a true driver of policy and defense plans. Those among us who have believed that ideas merely decorate and rationalize material forces, should be humbled by the evidence presented here. Schelling's vastly speculative abstract ideas were chosen to be the footings for the construction of U.S. strategic policy and the procurement of its matching posture. It may come as something of a shock to many of us to be reminded, or simply to have it so well revealed, that neither of the principal rival theories of nuclear deterrence rested upon anything more solid than a chosen logic and intuition (i.e., native wit and guesswork). Both Schelling and Kahn were empirically challenged, as Dr. Payne shows beyond a possibility of serious doubt. Neither of them was deeply steeped in strategic history, while, of necessity, neither could draw upon historical evidence of nuclear deterrence in action. It has to be said that such experience as the superpowers had of nuclear deterrence in the late 1940s and the 1950s, was not a dominant source of inspiration for the theories of Schelling and Kahn.

Dr. Payne makes no secret of his strong partiality for the reasoning of his former senior colleague, Herman Kahn, but he is neither blind to Kahn's limitations, nor is he at all inclined to shout his opinions. The book is consistently critical of Schelling's ideas, as theory and as expressed in policy, strategy, and posture, but he does not permit this attitude to license unbalanced judgments. It also is nonpartisan politically, finding comparable lapses in the strategic thought and policies of Republican and Democratic presidential administrations. What Dr. Payne achieves is an extended reminder of just how fortunate we probably were to survive the Cold War. He rubs our noses in the unarguable fact that nuclear deterrence is all theory, and much of it is not very convincing theory at that. He reminds us that his subject actually is pervasively human. Moscow and Washington were not, are not, peopled by wholly Rational Strategic Persons, but rather by flawed human beings doing their best to cope through sometimes dysfunctional policymaking and strategy-making processes. Additional to the sometimes odd behavior of individuals and the erratic antics of supposedly orderly official procedures, there is always the opaque, but sometimes potent, influence of national cultures to pour into the witch's brew that could thwart deterrent intent. Finally, it need hardly be emphasized that Carl von Clausewitz's "climate of war"—"danger, exertion, uncertainty, and chance"—applies luxuriously to the strategic nuclear context that is Dr. Payne's subject. Mistakes and accidents can and do happen. When we consider the Soviet/Russian and U.S. strategic nuclear postures as complex somewhat interdependent systems, especially in their full political, military, human, social, and technological contexts, it is hard to resist the judgment that we are fortunate to be here today. Complex systems have 'normal accident' rates.

I commend this magnificent book for setting new standards for evidence in the most vital of fields, as well as for its unwavering course of sustained, logical argument in favor of a balanced offense and defense. Also, last but not least, I commend the work for its conclusive demolition of the mainstream of theoretical, policy, and strategy error, which we have been truly fortunate to survive—to date.

Colin S. Gray
Director, Centre for Strategic Studies
Department of Politics and International Relations
University of Reading, United Kingdom

Acknowledgements

Writing this book has been an enormous challenge—a challenge that I could not have met without great advice, assistance and support. So many people have contributed so substantially that the traditional preface "thank you" hardly does justice to their efforts. Nevertheless, it is an appropriate start. I would like to express my great appreciation to the Sarah Scaife Foundation, the Smith Richardson Foundation, and to the National Institute for Public Policy for their financial support for research and writing. Professor Colin S. Gray, Director of the Centre for Strategic Studies at the University of Reading (U.K.), a world-renowned expert on the subjects of these pages, meticulously reviewed every word in every chapter and graciously provided the generous Foreword. Encouragement and many helpful comments similarly were provided by Dr. Johnny Foster, innovative nuclear weapons scientist, former Director of the Livermore Laboratory, and Director of Defense, Research, and Engineering for the Department of Defense in Democratic and Republican administrations, and by Professor William R. Van Cleave, founder and former Director of the graduate Defense and Strategic Studies Department at Missouri State University and a world-class expert on these security issues.

Many thanks also are due to Kurt Guthe, Tom Scheber, and Dr. Mark Schneider at the National Institute, Professor Brad Thayer of Missouri State University, and Dr. Michael Altfeld at the Hoover Institution. Several graduate research assistants helped over the years with fact-finding and reference-checking: Christine Bent of Georgetown University; and Russ Roth, John Friend, Melanie Inglis, and Laura Marsh from Missouri State University. Amy Joseph endured many hours preparing each chapter repeatedly, and did so with enviable skill, patience and good temper. Finally, and most importantly, my wife Beth read and edited every page multiple times—the book would not exist without her substantive continuing technical help and moral support. I thank all of these many talented individuals who have contributed so much time and effort to this book and hope they are pleased with it.

With appropriate permissions, I have drawn from or adapted for use in this book, selected earlier writings:

Deterrence in the Second Nuclear Age (Lexington, KY: University Press of Kentucky, 1996); *The Fallacies of Cold War Deterrence and a New Direction* (Lexington, KY: University Press of Kentucky, 2001); *Nuclear Deterrence in U.S.-Soviet Relations* (Boulder, CO: Westview Press, 1981); "Nuclear Deterrence for a New Century," *The Journal of International Security Affairs*, No. 10 (Spring 2006), pp. 49-55; "The Nuclear Posture Review: Setting the Record Straight," *The Washington Quarterly*, Vol. 28, No. 3 (Summer 2005), pp. 135-151; "Action-Reaction Metaphysics and Negligence," *The Washington Quarterly*, Vol. 24, No. 4 (Autumn 2001), pp. 109-121; "Bush Administration Strategic Policy: A Reality Check," *Journal of Strategic Studies*, Vol. 28, No. 5 (October 2005), pp. 775-787; "The Fallacies of Cold War Deterrence and a New Direction," *Comparative Strategy*, Vol. 22, No. 5 (December 2003), pp. 411-428; "The Nuclear Jitters," *National Review*, June 30, 2003, pp. 22, 23-24; and, Dr. John Foster and Keith B. Payne, "What Are Nuclear Weapons For?" *Forum on Physics & Society*, American Physical Society, Vol. 36, No. 4 (October 2007), available online at, http://units.aps.org/units/fps/newsletters/2007/october/foster-payne.cfm.

The views expressed in this book are my own and are not the views of any governmental office or organization.

Chapter 1
Introduction

"There is a slow train coming up around the bend."
-Bob Dylan

"There is a slow train coming up around the bend" is a lyric from "Slow Train Coming," a 1979 song by legendary singer-songwriter Bob Dylan. In it, Dylan warns of the need to move while there is time, or risk being struck. We are in need of such a warning. There is "a slow train coming," and prudence now demands that we move. No doubt, my use of this metaphor is different from Bob Dylan's. The danger I anticipate is another surprise failure of deterrence to prevent foreign attack. There have been many such surprises in the past; the future may hold one with catastrophic consequences for U.S. society—which will be the likely target.

It is impossible to anticipate the precise timing or nature of the next failure of deterrence. It could involve chemical, nuclear or biological strikes by a state or terrorist organization. If we are fortunate, we will have the time necessary to take steps to better align U.S. deterrence strategies and forces to help prevent attack, and to deploy defensive capabilities to mitigate the consequences of an attack.

To continue using Dylan's metaphor, moving "off the track" we have been on will be a challenge; the long-familiar balance of terror formula for deterrence is thoroughly entrenched in U.S. thought and policy and, correspondingly, official acquiescence to U.S. societal vulnerability to strategic attack has a well-established place in U.S. strategic policy. Cold War deterrence theory provided an overarching rationale for U.S. policy to eschew most forms of strategic defense, first against Soviet nuclear missile attack and, subsequently, against virtually any strategic attack.

Those basic decisions were made initially in the early 1960s and early 1970s by the Johnson and Nixon Administrations, respectively. They were not overturned by any subsequent Republican or Democratic administrations during the remaining decades of the Cold War. And, with few exceptions, the theory of "stable" deterrence underlying those policy decisions continues to provide the dominant narrative about deterrence and measures of merit for U.S. strategic force acquisition.

On the strength of a particular theory of deterrence—popularly called a "stable balance of terror"— Secretary of Defense Robert McNamara expressed his belief in 1963 that the goal of establishing mutual deterrence with the Soviet Union was incompatible with significant defensive capabilities intended to limit U.S. societal vulnerability.[1] The U.S. capability to threaten nuclear retaliation against the Soviet Union, and the vulnerability of U.S. society to Soviet nuclear attack, were believed to be the basic ingredients of a "stable" balance of terror.

Correspondingly, Secretary McNamara chose to emphasize the U.S. capability to threaten offensive nuclear retaliation against Soviet society as the key metric for the U.S. acquisition of strategic forces, and to eschew significant defensive capabilities against the Soviet nuclear threat. We have since enjoyed the relative ease and convenience of strategic policies derived from an approach to deterrence that promises safety against attack without the effort and cost of providing defenses for society.

With confidence in this promise, in the early 1960s the Johnson Administration decided *not* to pursue significant measures of strategic defense for U.S. society *against Soviet attack*. Subsequently, the Nixon Administration expanded that policy choice. In contrast to the Johnson Administration's earlier decision to defend directly against Chinese missiles, the Nixon Administration essentially chose to abandon even that option by signing the 1972 Anti-Ballistic Missile (ABM) Treaty, which greatly limited development and deployment of societal defenses *against any strategic missile attack*. This rejection of significant defense against missile attack subsequently justified the elimination of most U.S. strategic defense: if society was to be vulnerable to missiles, why defend against other forms of attack? Following the Nixon Administration, and to the end of the century, there was no change in the basic condition of U.S. societal vulnerability to strategic nuclear attack.

From the early 1960s to the early 1970s, the die thus was cast with regard to the priority of the deterrence goal and the policies believed to be suitable for establishing "stable" deterrence. "Stable" mutual deterrence was to be the priority goal. As defined, the presumption was *against* the goal of defending society directly against strategic nuclear attack and the deployment of most forms of defense for that purpose. As former Secretary of State Henry Kissinger observed in this regard, U.S. doctrine from the mid-1960s onward was based on the belief "that vulnerability contributed to peace, and invulnerability contributed to war."[2] This belief reflected a curious mixture of prudent skepticism regarding the potential for societal defense and naïve hubris regarding the reliability and predictability of deterrence.

That this particular U.S. deterrence strategy essentially mandated acquiescence to U.S. societal vulnerability to nuclear attack is not news to anyone familiar with U.S. strategic policy. However, it comes as a troubling shock to most Americans: for decades public opinion surveys demonstrated consistently that the majority of Americans mistakenly believed themselves defended against nuclear missile attack.[3]

Ideas have consequences in defense policy as in other walks of life. This Cold War definition of "stable" deterrence and its translation into policy left a legacy most apparent at the time of the 9/11 attacks. The norm of U.S. societal vulnerability had become so well-established that the North American Air Defense Command (NORAD) Northeast Air Defense Sector (NEADS) could call on but a few immediately-ready interceptors. Apparently, not all of those few interceptors were armed. There is little wonder that, according to *The 9/11 Commission Report*, the absence of U.S. air defense capabilities at the time, "...led some NORAD commanders to worry that NORAD was not postured to protect the United States."[4]

That was an understatement. The lack of significant U.S. air defense capabilities was the cumulative effect of U.S. Government policy choices for almost four decades prior to the 9/11 attacks. Successive American governments had decided to forego the deployment of significant strategic defenses against intercontinental ballistic missiles (ICBMs), and to sustain only minimal defenses against bombers.

Now-declassified Department of Defense studies from the 1960s concluded that differing measures of protection for society against nuclear attack *were technically feasible*, depending on several key factors, particularly including the level of defensive programs put into place. In 1965, for example, Secretary McNamara observed in a classified memorandum for President Johnson that, "appropriate mixes of Damage Limiting measures can effect substantial reductions in the maximum damage the Soviets can inflict, but only at substantial additional cost...."[5] The choice *not* to proceed with significant damage-limiting programs was made on the basis of the particular set of beliefs embedded in, and following from, the theory of a "stable" balance of terror—including the belief that deterrence could be orchestrated to function predictably because all "rational" opponents would respond prudently and cautiously to U.S. nuclear deterrence threats.

Where To Now?

This book examines the development of deterrence theory and U.S. policy, and the related evolution of the definition of "adequacy" applied to U.S. strategic forces. Initial chapters look back at the history of that evolution as the prelude to examining contemporary and future strategic goals, deterrence strategies, and related force requirements. A thread running through this examination of theory and policy—past, present and possible future—is a focus on the nexus between the goals of deterring attack and defending against attack to limit damage directly.

The goal here is not to refight past debates about U.S. Cold War approaches to deterrence or the related rejection of significant U.S. defensive deployments. It is to look retrospectively at how a particular theory of "stable" deterrence came to dominate U.S. policy and to be regarded as the acme of sophisticated strategic thinking—how U.S. policy makers could decide repeatedly that foregoing most forms of strategic defense against nuclear attack was the preferred or only practicable policy choice. The purpose of this retrospective is to establish a basis for assessing how the theory behind that policy choice—the terms of art, metrics and underlying judgments—fares today in conditions dramatically different from those of the Cold War.

Seeking to understand the value of established theory and policy given contemporary conditions is pertinent because U.S. policy decisions will have to be made in coming months and years about whether and how to deter and defend against the emerging threats of the twenty-first century. As these decision milestones approach, it is important to understand that the balance of terror theory of "stable" deterrence continues to dominate the U.S. defense community's thinking about such subjects. Contemporary strategic policy and programmatic initiatives still are assessed by unofficial commentators and government officials alike according to aged "stable" balance of terror tenets, idioms, and related standards for U.S. strategic forces.

The expectations, definitions, norms and force metrics associated with a "stable" balance of terror are so thoroughly ingrained as the acceptable parameters of U.S. strategic policy and forces that often they are unrecognized as the product of a particular set of Cold War conditions and judgments. *These propositions about deterrence and expectations about opponents constitute the familiar and accepted Cold War narrative about strategic forces and policy that "everyone knows is true."* They remain the most powerful lodestar in the appraisals of contemporary U.S. strategic policy initiatives and strategic force programs. The question that follows, of course, is whether this accepted wisdom from the Cold War serves now to enlighten or mislead when the conditions that gave it life and apparent integrity no longer exist.

That is the critical question which this book addresses. The basic answer offered herein is that this purported wisdom from the Cold War now fares very poorly. The implications of that fact are enormous for U.S. deterrence policy and practice, U.S. strategic force acquisition, and ultimately, U.S. security.

Herman Kahn and Thomas Schelling: Competing Theories of Deterrence From Competing Expectations About Opponents and the Functioning of Deterrence

Chapter 2 traces the origins of U.S. strategic policies after the early 1960s to two different, competing Cold War schools of strategic thought led by two comparably brilliant and innovative thinkers, Nobel laureate Thomas Schelling and the late Herman Kahn. These two schools of thought started from the same Cold War context, but followed different trails of logic and judgment, and concluded with different recommended approaches to deterrence policy and U.S. strategic force requirements.

The differences separating these schools of thought included contrary expectations about how "rational" opponents behave, the priority that should be attributed to deterrence and how it functions and, correspondingly, which strategic forces the United States should acquire or avoid. Different interconnected judgments about opponent decision making and deterrence produced very different conclusions regarding the appropriate character of U.S. strategic policy and the size and composition of U.S. forces.

Schelling, for example, set forth the definition of—and recommended as a U.S. policy goal—a "stable" balance of terror with the Soviet Union. "Stable" deterrence could be orchestrated to proceed from mutual prudence born of mutual vulnerability. According to Schelling, the U.S. offensive nuclear force requirement for this "stable deterrence" could be the relatively modest level of capabilities necessary to threaten Soviet society with destruction. The purported benefit of mutual threats along this line was enticing: *in the absence of the "reciprocal fear of surprise attack" that might ignite a nuclear war,* a "stable" balance of terror could be established to provide reliable, predictable mutual deterrence. Schelling's priority, thus, was minimizing the "reciprocal fear of surprise attack" that might upset this "stable deterrence." This, according to Schelling, meant eschewing societal defenses—or as Schelling put it, "the forbidden defense of human resources"—because he believed they would contribute to the fear of surprise attack.[6] Correspondingly, Schelling viewed the ABM Treaty's strict limitations on the development and deployment of such defenses as the "high point...of successful arms control."[7]

In contrast, Kahn posited different expectations about how opponents would behave and how deterrence would function. As a result, he recommended a significantly different approach to deterrence and, correspondingly, different U.S. strategic force requirements. For the United States, Kahn specifically recommended *against* a "stable" balance of terror, per Schelling's definition. Instead, Kahn emphasized the requirement for U.S. strategic defensive capabilities to help establish *an asymmetrical and advantageous imbalance of terror* favoring the United States. Kahn believed that U.S. deterrence responsibilities demanded that U.S. strategy proceed from a position of meaningful advantage. He outlined more expansive U.S. offensive and defensive strategic force requirements for deterrence than those identified in Schelling's baseline "stable" balance of terror model. He emphasized the value of defensive capabilities both for U.S. deterrence strategy and as a hedge against the possibility of deterrence failure and unavoidable war.

An understanding of these two decidedly different schools of thought is important for an understanding of U.S. strategic policy development and force acquisition history. Although Schelling's school of thought proved the more influential in shaping U.S. policy, together they established the logic and language of U.S. strategic policy and the related debates about offensive and defensive force requirements; they presented the contending rationales and metrics applied by U.S. officials to questions of deterrence strategy, the acquisition of strategic forces, and arms control objectives. These decidedly different schools of thought— grounded in contrasting expectations about opponent behavior and the functioning of deterrence—provided the basis for differing assessments of U.S. strategic forces, particularly including strategic defenses.

Some commentators claim that, "the central debate is between those who want nuclear use to be very rare, and those who want it to be very, very rare."[8] This is a recent and relatively polite rendition of the charge that often bedeviled Kahn, i.e., that his more demanding strategic force recommendations sprang from a less restrictive attitude about the *employment of* nuclear weapons. On the contrary, the central debate has *nothing* to do with more versus less opposition to the employment of nuclear weapons. Rather, it is between competing visions of "rational" opponent decision making and correspondingly different expectations regarding how deterrence is likely to function.

Chapter 3 suggests numerous substantial, as well as some superficial, reasons why Schelling's approach to deterrence and strategic policy proved the more attractive to a broad spectrum of American audiences, including those important to the development of U.S. defense policy. Ultimately, Schelling's school of thought—its idioms, metrics and definitions—provided the dominant compass for U.S. thinking and policy. This is not to suggest that the ideas closely associated with Herman Kahn were dismissed or ignored entirely. However, the basic orientation and language of U.S. policies on strategic deterrence, force acquisition and arms control came to reflect Schelling's theoretical framework for "stable" mutual deterrence much more than Kahn's recommended asymmetry of terror and U.S. advantage.

From Theory to Bipartisan Policy

Chapters 4 and 5 move beyond the dissection of these two deterrence schools of strategic thought to describe the nexus between Schelling's formula for a "stable" balance of terror and actual U.S. policy developments from the early 1960s to the end of the Cold War. During that period, the priority strategic goal and related measures of merit for U.S. strategic force acquisition and arms control policies came to be geared toward orchestrating and preserving a "stable" balance of terror, generally in line with Schelling's definition.

In 1962, the fundamental policy choice Secretary McNamara portrayed to President Kennedy was the priority to be assigned to the different goals of deterrence and strategic defense.[9] This was a basic choice, he believed, because the measures of merit and definition of adequacy for U.S. strategic forces differed significantly depending upon that prioritization. Would U.S. strategy and force structure be designed to support as the priority goal the direct protection of U.S. society from nuclear war, or would it follow a more exclusive strategy of mutual deterrence made "stable" *by mutually severe retaliatory threats and the absence of significant strategic defensive capabilities?*

Secretary McNamara pointed to the very different strategic force requirements and measures of merit determined by that choice—differences previously reflected in the theoretical work and contrasting force recommendations of Kahn and Schelling. Secretary McNamara's own explicitly expressed preference—and the U.S. policy choice reflected in the historical record—was for Schelling's "stable" balance of terror as the overarching goal, with correspondingly consistent opposition both to most U.S. strategic defensive capabilities and U.S. strategic offensive capabilities deemed to stray too far from that goal.

There was considerable debate and policy evolution regarding how the United States should define its *offensive retaliatory threat* within a balance of terror. This debate focused on the types of offensive threats the United States should be able to make for deterrence purposes and, correspondingly, the appropriate size and character of the U.S. offensive strategic forces necessary to make those threats. By the mid-1960s, Secretary McNamara had established his "assured destruction" deterrence metric that focused on the U.S. nuclear force requirements necessary to threaten specific percentages of Soviet population and industry. Over the succeeding two decades, the officially-declared definition of adequate U.S. deterrence threats evolved and the associated U.S. strategic force requirements for deterrence expanded correspondingly.

There was, however, no effective move to deploy significant societal defenses via ballistic missile defense, air defense, or civil defense during Republican or Democratic administrations. Initiatives to do so ultimately were constrained or short-lived at least in part as a result of the continuing political power and familiarity of the basic presumption against societal defense in the logic and language of a "stable" balance of terror. Different presidential administrations and officials appear to have approached this balance of terror policy orientation with different mixtures of enthusiasm, grudging acquiescence or measured hostility—but the balance of terror's presumption against the deployment of significant U.S. societal defenses held.

U.S. Government decisions regarding strategic force acquisition and arms control policies, as detailed in numerous public and now-declassified documents—including a decade-long series of previously highly-classified memoranda from secretaries of defense to presidents—consistently reflect the fundamental goal of acquiring U.S. forces per the evolving offensive requirements deemed critical for a "stable" balance of terror. This record illustrates that the basic questions came to center on the details of offensive capabilities and planning considered necessary to preserve a "stable" balance of terror. The "paper trail" examined here reveals how thoroughly the concepts, terms of art, strategic goals and priorities, and measures of merit outlined in Schelling's theoretical narrative were integrated into U.S. policy. Most obvious in the historical record are: the priority goal of preserving "stable" deterrence via secure retaliatory nuclear threats; the presumption against acquiring "destabilizing" offensive capabilities deemed too far outside that goal; and, the presumption against a goal of direct societal defense and strategic capabilities for that purpose.

Of course, U.S. decisions for or against strategic force programs during this or any other period cannot be traced to an overarching strategic theory alone; force acquisition decisions tend to reflect multiple inputs, some wholly unrelated to strategy. For example, in 1961 famed economist John Kenneth Galbraith reportedly provided President Kennedy a decidedly partisan political evaluation of a draft booklet on the Kennedy Administration's fledging civil defense initiative: "I am not at all attracted by a pamphlet which seeks to save the better elements of the population, but in the main writes off those who voted for you."[10] Adolf Hitler cancelled the V-2 program on the basis of a bad dream he had about the missile; it took the combined efforts of Albert Speer and Wernher von Braun to get the program back on track.[11] Clearly, a variety of factors can contribute to the evaluation of programs.

Nevertheless, Secretary McNamara rightly emphasized a methodical and systematic approach to decisions about U.S. forces in general and strategic forces in particular. He sought a coherent, logical force acquisition process—free from extraneous factors—that linked U.S. strategic goals to a detailed analysis of the capabilities required to support those goals, and the acquisition of the forces thus deemed necessary. The basic conceptual framework for "stable" mutual deterrence as outlined by Schelling weighed heavily in this process.

The significance of the Cold War's balance of terror definition of deterrence and strategic force metrics to U.S. strategic force acquisition and arms control policies is *not* a new story. But the degree to which virtually *all* sides of U.S. policy debates ultimately adhered or acceded to *this formula* is not well appreciated. In the absence of a serious commitment to direct damage limitation as a priority goal and, correspondingly, to comprehensive U.S. strategic defensive capabilities, the many U.S. Cold War debates about the preferred character of U.S. strategic offensive forces and options reflected *variations on the basic balance of terror theme*, not significant departures from it.

During the 1970s and 1980s, U.S. policy regarding how best to threaten the Soviet Union for deterrence purposes evolved well beyond Secretary McNamara's 1960s assured destruction metric for U.S. strategic forces. That departure from his specific definition of requirements reflected evolving interpretations of what constituted adequate U.S. deterrence threats and planning; it did not equate to rejection of an overarching balance of terror deterrence strategy, despite frequent charges to that effect.

Many commentators clung to the 1960s assured destruction metric as the *only* possible definition of deterrence. Prominent policy or strategic force initiatives that strayed from the familiar 1960s definition of assured destruction were subject to sharp criticism: they were deemed unnecessary for security and worse than useless. Commentators in and out of government claimed them to be indicative of a "war-fighting" nuclear strategy instead of a deterrence strategy.

With the continuing absence of a serious U.S. commitment to the deployment of strategic defenses, however, U.S. survival remained in the hands of Soviet decision makers.[12] The evolution of U.S. offensive deterrence requirements did not move U.S. strategic policy beyond considerations about how best to deter within a balance of terror. Kahn's alternative prescription of finding protection in significant U.S. defensive capabilities rarely was on the table. It entered U.S. Cold War debates after the early 1960s only in occasional displays of official enthusiasm, quickly beaten back into submission by the accepted balance of terror narrative on "stable" mutual deterrence.

Alternative descriptions and explanations of U.S. strategic policy are common in the United States and abroad. One of the most popular is that U.S. strategic forces and policies were designed throughout the Cold War around the goal of acquiring "nuclear primacy" over the Soviet Union, including the strategic planning and capabilities necessary for "winning a nuclear war" with the Soviet Union.[13] This assertion, with its explicit charge of U.S. imprudence per balance of terror norms, fundamentally misses the centerpiece and reality of U.S. strategic policy for three decades: its basic continuing orientation has been along "stable" balance of terror guidelines with the corresponding practice of "self-restraint" in the expectation of "Soviet reciprocity."[14]

The now-common assertion of a supposed U.S. nuclear "war-winning" policy of "primacy" simply collapses under the weight of the unquestionable absence of a serious U.S. Government effort to deploy most defensive capabilities from the mid-1960s onward. The willful acceptance of U.S. societal vulnerability for decades betrays the profound error of the "primacy," "war-winning" explanation of U.S. strategic policy and forces. The actual available record of words and deeds demonstrates that the preeminent source of U.S. strategic policy choices from the early 1960s onward can be found in the expectations and strategic force metrics embedded in the formula for a "stable" balance of terror. U.S. strategic policies have been limited to variations well within the boundaries of that formula.

Applying Cold War Metrics and Adages to Twenty-First Century Policies and Programs

Chapter 6 illustrates the continuing contemporary use of the familiar balance of terror terms of art, adages and force metrics to judge U.S. strategic policy and force initiatives. Prominent commentators in and out of government continue to apply the same Cold War "stable" balance of terror tenets and measures of merit to contemporary questions of policy and force acquisition. As was the case during the Cold War, to do so shapes judgments about the significance of emerging threats and the potential value of U.S. policies and forces to address them—whether threats are deemed "deterrable" and whether U.S. forces are likely to be useful or wasteful, "stabilizing" or "destabilizing."

If emerging nuclear, chemical and biological threats can be countered reliably via familiar deterrence strategies, for example, new or alternative measures to deter and defend against them are unnecessary. Unsurprisingly, the application of long-familiar metrics and adages to contemporary strategic force initiatives typically produces long-familiar conclusions: those deemed to be unnecessary for deterrence, or "destabilizing" as defined by Cold War standards—particularly including strategic capabilities for damage limitation—continue to be viewed in the same negative light despite the great differences in opponents, threats and contexts.

Chapters 7 and 8, however, identify three basic reasons why the balance of terror framework should *not* be the basis for assessing contemporary strategic policy or forces: its internal logical incoherence;

the inconsistency of its most basic expectations regarding "rational" behavior with considerable historical evidence and recent findings on cognition; and, the dramatic differences between Cold War and contemporary conditions.   The potential tradeoffs now involved in continuing obeisance to the balance of terror formula are likely to be very different from those believed to be in play during the Cold War. In particular, the relationship between the goals of deterrence and strategic defense, and the priority accorded to each during the Cold War, must be reconsidered.   The set of judgments and choices that traded away the goal and capabilities for significant U.S. societal damage limitation in return for the putative "stability" of mutual deterrence cannot be considered prudent in many plausible contemporary circumstances.

Over the course of the Cold War decades we developed sophisticated concepts of strategic deterrence and came to have enormous confidence in them.   Any "rational" Soviet leader was expected to be deterred from extreme provocation by our nuclear threat.   We came to assume that the lethality of our nuclear weapons would deter Soviet leaders reliably and predictably, virtually regardless of the local conditions in Moscow. The objective condition of a "stable" balance of terror brought about by U.S. and Soviet long-range nuclear weapons was thought to ensure that, short of insanity, no leader—past, present, or future—would choose a nuclear fight.   The problem of deliberate nuclear war was considered tractable and judged to have been solved: "In U.S.-Soviet relations, the current nuclear postures have substantially solved the problem of deterring deliberate nuclear war."[15]

This belief—that a well-managed balance of terror would deter predictably, even existentially—was made possible only by the convenient simplifying assumption that Soviet leaders reliably would choose to be deterred regardless of their goals, domestic context, or how the circumstances of an attendant crisis might affect their decision making. The formula was simple and mechanistic: a "stable" balance of terror, plus rational decision makers, inevitably would produce mutual caution and deterrence; only an insane Soviet leader could choose not to be deterred in a balance of terror.

This confidence in Cold War notions about deterrence was a reflection of specific expectations about the opponent and Cold War conditions. Most of what we then believed to be true about deterrence is of questionable value now because the stakes, the opponents, the contexts, and our deterrence goals differ so dramatically from those of the Cold War. Confidence in the Cold War narrative regarding deterrence and related idioms has survived the conditions that were believed to make that confidence possible.

Why should changes from Cold War conditions make a difference in how we think about deterrence and its requirements? *It is because the details of circumstance and the opponent's local conditions—time, place, culture, ideology, religion, domestic politics, leadership decision making process, and even personality—can be decisive in determining if and how deterrence operates.* The circumstances and key local conditions pertaining to contemporary contingencies and foes are diverse and differ dramatically from those of the Cold War. Many of the sophisticated deterrence concepts we developed during the Cold War specifically to prevent Soviet aggression in a bipolar context—concepts in which we placed great confidence—are ill-suited for deterring contemporary foes.

To risk understatement, the new reality is dramatically different from the Cold War's conditions that supposedly provided "existential deterrence." Assertions about deterrence being reliable and predictable, however tendentious during the Cold War, are wholly unsupportable in this post-Cold War environment. Confident predictions about how deterrence will operate against unspecified or unfamiliar leaders, over unpredictable stakes, and in unknown or unfamiliar contexts, in reality can be little more than speculative guesses—risky grounds for making important decisions.

In the contemporary era there is an irreducible level of uncertainty surrounding the functioning of deterrence. This is not because rogue states or terrorist leaders, as a rule, should be considered irrational.[16] More importantly, in the absence of considerable efforts to understand circumstance and opponent, we are unlikely to anticipate the multiplicity of factors shaping opponent decision making or the weight of those factors. Uncertainty may be higher or lower depending on the details of the engagement and our efforts to reduce our ignorance about the opponent and context. Uncertainties may dominate, however, even following an effort to gain an understanding of the opponent.

This conclusion does not suggest that deterrence should be discarded; far from it. It does, however, explain why our contemporary assessment of deterrence strategies and strategic forces must be very different than it was during the Cold War. Then, our focus was on the Soviet Union, and we believed we knew how to orchestrate a "stable" balance of terror with relative ease and certainty; deterrence was the priority and regarded as predictably reliable. Deterrence remains important, but its functioning must be recognized now as uncertain, as is our understanding of how to orchestrate its effect and calculate its requirements.

Because we can assume no longer that deterrence will operate predictably against all "rational" foes, we lack the luxury of focusing so exclusively on deterrence as the sole or dominant goal and measure of strategic force adequacy. In recognition of contemporary deterrence uncertainties, we must seek not only to deter, but also prepare to defend our society, expeditionary forces, and allies in the unpredictable event that deterrence fails. Defensive capabilities have taken on a higher priority and potential value than during the Cold War, when the accepted tradeoff for "stable" mutual deterrence was the absence of defenses.

The point may seem prosaic, yet it is a dramatic departure from much contemporary commentary that continues to be grounded in the Cold War adage that "vulnerability contributes to peace." Some countries, including North Korea and China, voice opposition to U.S. strategic defenses on the grounds that they would upset "stability." We should recall that continuing adherence to the traditional Cold War definition of "stability" would mandate that the United States perpetuate its societal vulnerability *even when it can be mitigated.* In an era of deterrence uncertainty, however, the risk of accepting that tradeoff should be sufficient to deliver us from continued enthusiasm for, or acquiescence to, such strategic policies.

Contemporary Roles and Metrics for U.S. Nuclear Weapons and the 2001 Nuclear Posture Review: Reformation and Counterreformation

Finally, Chapter 9 concludes with a discussion of the roles for U.S. nuclear weapons in the contemporary security environment, and how those roles should affect the measures of merit applied to the U.S. nuclear arsenal. In line with the discussion in Chapter 6, it describes how a politically powerful critique of the 2001 Nuclear Posture Review (NPR) followed familiar Cold War patterns: the old balance of terror metrics and formulas were applied to the NPR, despite the fact that the review was a self-conscious attempt to reconsider the roles and value of nuclear weapons in the very different conditions of the twenty-first century. It sought, for example, to include in the measure of U.S. force adequacy the goals of *defense against selected strategic threats* and the *assurance of allies* who increasingly are concerned about the acquisition of nuclear weapons by their regional rivals. Again, however—as with other past policy initiatives that recommended standards and programmatic initiatives beyond the familiar parameters of a "stable" balance of terror and Secretary McNamara's assured destruction metric—sharp opposition followed the NPR; it was dubbed a dangerous, "destabilizing," "war-fighting" departure from the supposedly tried and true formula for "stable" deterrence. In the contemporary strategic environment, this language from the "stable" balance of terror narrative has little substantive meaning, but it retains considerable political effect.

Bob Dylan's lyric that there is "a slow train coming" should speak to us now. Our deterrence strategies will be subject to failure or irrelevance. This is not a question of *if, but of when, where, how, and with what consequence?* To claim otherwise is to suggest that the future will be far different from the past, with no apparent reason for believing it to be so. This prospect represents an unprecedented danger when otherwise minor powers and even terrorist organizations can threaten U.S. and allied societies with weapons of mass destruction (WMD). We need to move forward with a fundamental reconsideration of the U.S. Cold War deterrence framework and strategic policies. With great admiration for those theorists and policy makers who helped to bring us safely through the Cold War, and due humility regarding what more may be possible, this book is offered as a step in that direction.

Endnotes

1. Draft Memorandum for the President, Secretary of Defense [Robert S. McNamara] to the President [Lyndon B. Johnson], Subj: Recommended FY 1965-FY 1969 Strategic Retaliatory Forces, December 6, 1963, p. I-35. (Originally classified; sanitized and declassified on January 5, 1983). This and other Draft Presidential Memoranda can be found online at the Master OFOI Reading Room, Department of Defense, http://www.dod.mil/pubs/foi/master_reading_list01.html. See also, Robert S. McNamara, *Blundering Into Disaster* (New York: Pantheon Books, 1986), pp. 97-100.
2. Quoted in, "Kissinger Looks at the Future of NATO," *Congressional Record*, September 6, 1979, p. E4292.
3. See, for example, Keith B. Payne, *Strategic Defense: "Star Wars" in Perspective* (Lanham, MD: University Press of America, 1986), p. 234.
4. *The 9/11 Commission Report: Final Report of the National Commission on Terrorist Attacks Upon the United States* (New York: W.W. Norton & Company, 2004), p. 17.
5. Draft Memorandum for the President, Secretary of Defense [Robert S. McNamara] to the President [Lyndon B. Johnson], Subj: Recommended FY 1967-FY 1971 Strategic Offensive and Defensive Forces, November 1, 1965, p. 20. (Originally classified; sanitized and declassified on January 5, 1983).
6. Thomas Schelling, "What Went Wrong With Arms Control?" *Foreign Affairs*, Vol. 64, No. 2 (Winter 1985/86), pp. 221-222.
7. Ibid., p. 223.
8. Ivan Oelrich, *Missions for Nuclear Weapons After the Cold War*, Occasional Paper No. 3 (Washington D.C.: Federation of American Scientists, November 2004), p. 8.
9. See, for example, Draft Memorandum for the President, Secretary of Defense [Robert S. McNamara] to the President [John F. Kennedy], Subj: Recommended FY 1964-FY 1968 Strategic Retaliatory Forces, November 21, 1962, pp. 6-7. (Originally classified; sanitized and declassified on January 5, 1983).
10. Quoted in, Thomas J. Kerr, *Civil Defense in the U.S.: Bandaid for a Holocaust?* (Boulder, CO: Westview Press, 1983), p. 123.
11. See the discussion in, Keith B. Payne, *The Fallacies of Cold War Deterrence and a New Direction* (Lexington, KY: University Press of Kentucky, 2001), p. 70.
12. Draft Presidential Memorandum, Secretary of Defense [Clark M. Clifford] to the President [Lyndon B. Johnson], Subj: Strategic Offensive and Defensive Forces, January 9, 1969, pp. 12-13. (Originally classified; sanitized and declassified on January 5, 1983).
13. Keir Lieber and Daryl Press, "The Rise of U.S. Nuclear Primacy," *Foreign Affairs*, Vol. 85, No. 2 (March/April 2006), pp. 43, 44, 50.
14. William R. Van Cleave, "The US Strategic Triad," in, Ray Bonds, ed., *US War Machine* (New York: Crown Publishers, 1983), p. 67.
15. Joseph Nye, Graham Allison, and Albert Carnesale, "Defusing the Nuclear Menace," *The Washington Post*, September 4, 1988, pp. C1, C2.
16. The set of rogue states can shift over time. Rogue states are characterized in official U.S. public documents as brutal, corrupt regimes that reject basic human rights, violate international norms and treaties, seek weapons of mass destruction (WMD), sponsor terrorism, and are hostile to the United States. See, for example, *National Security Strategy of the United States of America* (Washington, D.C.: The White House, September 2002), pp. 13-14.

Chapter 2
Deterrence: In the Beginning

> *"...the ideas of economists and political philosophers, both when they are right and when they are wrong, are more powerful than is commonly understood. Indeed the world is ruled by little else. Practical men, who believe themselves to be quite exempt from any intellectual influences, are usually the slaves of some defunct economist. Madmen in authority, who hear voices in the air, are distilling their frenzy from some academic scribbler of a few years back."[1]*
>
> -John Maynard Keynes

Deterrence is a strategy of issuing threats to cause another to decide against an unwanted behavior, and is as old as the second chapter of *Genesis*. In the Garden, the consequence of eating the forbidden fruit was spelled out clearly to Adam: "You will be doomed to die." In this premier recorded case of attempted deterrence, the threat promised lethal consequences and presumably was credible. Eve, however, was encouraged to doubt the threat, and deterrence failed. The rest, as they say, is history.

This antediluvian attempt to deter as recorded in *Genesis* illustrates well that the free will of the target audience poses a challenge to the reliable, predictable functioning of deterrence. The party issuing the threat can control important elements of the deterrence process, including the character of the demand, the threatened consequences if that demand is not met, and the manner in which that threat is communicated. But if the side issuing threats cannot or chooses not to control the target audience's behavior directly—i.e., that audience has the freedom to choose its own actions—it is the audience and not the issuer of threats with the power to decide if deterrence will "work." Regardless of how lethal or brilliant the deterrent threat, for deterrence to work by design the audience must have the will and capability to comply with the issued demand; it must understand, believe, and fear the deterrent threat to the extent that it chooses to comply.

Deterrence is a deceptively complex process. What seemingly is the simple expression of a threat, and the subsequent decision by the target audience to yield, in fact is a process with many necessary conditions, steps and occasions for misstep. For a strategy of deterrence to work by design requires: attentive players; the expression of threat; mutual recognition, communication and understanding; purposeful decision making by the target audience based on a rational calculation of expected risks, costs and benefits, and the decision to yield to the threat; and, the implementation of that decision. The success of the strategy can break down at any point in the process.

If deterrence by threat of punishment works, it is because the threatened party agrees to yield for fear of the consequences if it does not. Punitive deterrence is a strategy that requires this degree of cooperation—cooperation grudgingly given and under duress to be sure— but, nonetheless, a strategy always reliant on a degree of cooperation. It is no simple matter for all of the necessary conditions of a successful deterrence process to be in place so that the threatened party prudently cooperates to the point of yielding.

Deterrence is not a strategy of eliminating the other party, or of directly preventing it from taking the unwanted action; those strategies may be available and necessary in the event the target audience chooses not to be deterred. But, destroying the opponent or directly controlling it are not strategies of securing its willing conciliation. In fact, it is a sure indication that deterrence was not attempted, or failed, if one must seek to control the target audience's behavior directly; it was not asked to yield or did not choose to yield, and thus had to be controlled directly.

Attempting to control an opponent directly generally requires greater effort and runs greater risks than securing its grudging conciliation via deterrence threats. That is the great advantage of deterrence; it is why approximately 2,500 years ago the famous Chinese strategist, Sun-Tzu, observed that, "achieving victory in every battle is not absolute perfection: neutralizing an adversary's forces without battle is absolute perfection."[2] Sun-Tzu was not a pacifist who opposed battle per se; his point was that the most efficient strategy is that which places the opponent in such constrained circumstances that it chooses to yield without fighting.

Although Sun-Tzu discussed military strategy, most parents understand the general principle. It is much less taxing for the parent if a child willingly chooses to obey, even if grudgingly, than to control the child's actions directly. In a broad spectrum of human interaction, strategies of deterrence promise the most efficient route to controlling another's behavior because the *other ultimately is persuaded to exercise self-control.*

As was illustrated well in Eden's garden, those who have the freedom of choice will not always choose to yield, even if the threat they face is severe. They may not believe, understand, or fear sufficiently the threat behind the deterrent; they may not prudently calculate the costs and benefits, or calculate them at all; or, they may be so motivated that, despite the threat, they are willing to take the action proscribed by the threatener.

There are many routes to the failure of deterrence strategies. Threats that, in theory, "should" deter because they seem severe and believable can fail in practice for unforeseen reasons; there is no sure formula for the predictable functioning of deterrence. Numerous historical examples reveal national leaders who willingly accepted the risk of choosing not to yield in the face of extreme threats. For example, even after the atomic bombing of Hiroshima in 1945, Japan's World War II War Minister, General Korechika Anami, called on the Japanese Supreme Council to fight on to the death rather than accept the dishonor of surrender. Under the circumstances, the War Minister declared, "Would it not be wondrous for this whole nation [Japan] to be destroyed like a beautiful flower."[3] For Minister of War Anami, conciliation was dishonorable and the preservation of honor was preferred over national survival.

This is not to suggest that deterrence cannot work; it has on many occasions in the past, and likely will do so in the future. There is, however, an irreducible level of uncertainty regarding strategies of deterrence; the threatener can never know in advance precisely if or how an individual or small group of individuals with the freedom to choose will interpret and respond to threats, especially if the circumstances are intensely stressful. That level of uncertainty may be smaller or greater, depending on many details of the circumstance, but it never disappears. This is true whether the engagement is between nations or individuals.

If the party attempting to deter is a parent attempting to train a familiar child, the uncertainties surrounding the likely effect of a parental warning—with repetition and experience—may become modest. If the threatener is the leader of one country attempting to influence the decision making of an opposing foreign leadership in unique and stressful circumstances, the uncertainties surrounding the outcome of the deterrence process are likely to loom much larger. But whether parent or president, no matter how obvious it seems to the party issuing deterrent threats that the target audience *should* yield if it is "sensible," the decision to do so remains in the hands of that target audience, and that audience, whether child or foreign leadership, may assess the situation very differently.

The historical landscape is littered with national leaders who were surprised when the chosen audience did not yield to their deterrence warnings and threats. U.S. Ambassador Paul Robinson has observed that, "when I travel through Europe, which was a battleground twice last century, I see that in every little town there is a memorial to the folly of conventional deterrence—with lots of names on it."[4]

Failures of deterrence may not reflect a lack of wit or initiative on the part of those seeking to deter. Predicting how a foreign leadership will interpret and respond to threats—what they will believe to be the most sensible response—is an uncertain business for the most astute observer. For example, shortly before the December 7, 1941 Japanese attack on Pearl Harbor, Assistant Secretary of State Dean Acheson advised the U.S. president that war with Japan was unlikely because, "no rational Japanese could believe an attack on us could result in anything but disaster for his country." At roughly the same point in history, Japanese Prime Minister Hideki Tojo informed his emperor that, "Our empire has no alternative but to begin war."[5]

Superpower Deterrence During the Cold War

Deterrence has been a tool of statecraft from ancient times through today. Discussions of deterrence strategies—successes and failures—can be found in the earliest accounts of wars and relations among tribes and nations. During the Cold War, nuclear deterrence became the centerpiece of U.S. grand strategy to contain the Soviet Union. Given the enormous, prompt lethality of nuclear weapons, they are well-suited to support strategies involving extreme threats. There is no comparable single instrument for threatening prompt physical destruction. Even a small nuclear weapon has many times the blast effect of the largest, modern conventional bomb, reportedly the U.S. Massive Ordnance Air Blast (MOAB).

Not surprisingly, every nuclear-armed country offering a rationale for possessing nuclear weapons prominently includes their value for deterrence. Deterrence is, and since the end of World War II has been, the primary rationale for U.S. nuclear weapons. During the initial decades following World War II the United States, in particular, developed sophisticated concepts for integrating nuclear forces and deterrence strategies to meet the Cold War security threat posed by the Soviet Union.

The highest U.S. security goal during the Cold War was the deterrence of Soviet attack and, correspondingly, the preeminent U.S. focus during the Cold War was the establishment and support of an effective strategy of deterrence. The United States sought first and foremost to prevent attack on itself, its allies and friends by convincing the Soviet leadership that, under any conceivable circumstances, the cost of attacking would outweigh any possible gains that might otherwise motivate an attack. Following Sun-Tzu's admonition, the U.S. goal was to place the Soviet Union in circumstances such that the Soviet leadership would choose not to attack, and to achieve this goal without employing military force against Moscow directly. This strategy of deterrence was central to the U.S. grand strategy of containment—which in its most basic terms was designed to limit Moscow's expansionism without general warfare—in anticipation of the Soviet regime collapsing in the absence of opportunities for external expansion. This U.S. and allied strategy appears to have worked and the twentieth century was spared a third world war that could have taken hundreds of millions of lives.

The explicit U.S. threat of nuclear retaliation was the chief means for presenting the Soviet leadership with prospective costs so severe that it would reliably decide against military expansion. The entire spectrum of U.S. military capabilities played a supporting role in this retaliatory threat, including short-range nuclear weapons deployed in Europe. But, it was the U.S. strategic nuclear arsenal that ultimately was thought to "ensure" deterrence by leaving the Soviet leadership to anticipate the severe costs it would pay if it ever chose to ignite the powder trail to war with the United States.

The precise character of the U.S. strategic nuclear deterrence threat evolved throughout the Cold War. In the 1960s, for example, Secretary of Defense Robert McNamara publicly expressed the U.S. nuclear deterrent threat as the destruction of 20 to 25 percent of the Soviet population and 50 percent of the Soviet industrial base. He called this, the "assured destruction" capability.[6]

During the 1970s, Secretary of Defense James Schlesinger publicly declared retaliation against Soviet economic recovery, as well as military and political leadership targets, as the basis of the U.S. "assured destruction" nuclear deterrence threat, rather than McNamara's earlier specific declared levels of societal damage. Additionally, Schlesinger called for a variety of limited nuclear retaliatory options.[7] Secretary of Defense Harold Brown later emphasized that the U.S. strategic nuclear deterrent threat would retain the capability to threaten retaliation against 200 Soviet cities,[8] but also would include the capability to threaten retaliation against Soviet military capabilities, political control centers, and war-related industry.[9]

Secretary of Defense Caspar Weinberger subsequently said that the United States had never based its deterrent on plans to retaliate against Soviet cities, and *did not* plan retaliatory options, "...to maximize Soviet casualties or to attack deliberately the Soviet population. Indeed, we believe such a doctrine would be neither moral nor prudent."[10] Instead, according to Weinberger, "...secure deterrence should be based on the threat to destroy what the Soviet leadership values most highly: namely, itself, its military power and political control capabilities, and its industrial ability to wage war."[11]

As the above brief review illustrates, through the Cold War decades *official U.S. declarations* about the types of targets to be threatened for deterrence of the Soviet Union shifted in focus from Soviet cities and industry, to military, military industry, and political targets in the Soviet Union. Despite this evolution in the expressed character of the U.S. nuclear threat, a consistent thread throughout most of the Cold War was that the United States sought to deter Soviet attacks by threatening grievous nuclear retaliation, and retained powerful strategic offensive nuclear forces with which to threaten retaliation in support of that strategy.

In the final decade of the Cold War, the Reagan Administration, routinely criticized as having abandoned deterrence in favor of "nuclear war-fighting," in fact centered U.S. strategy squarely in classic deterrence terms:

> Our strategy is simple. We seek to prevent war by maintaining forces and demonstrating the determination to use them, if necessary, in ways that will persuade our adversaries that the cost of any attack on our vital interests will exceed the benefits they could hope to gain. The label for this strategy is deterrence. It is the core of our defense strategy today, as it has been for most of the postwar period.[12]

The high priority Washington attached to deterrence was wholly reasonable under the circumstances of the Cold War. By the early 1960s, the United States possessed a powerful long-range or "strategic" nuclear arsenal, including almost 2,000 intercontinental ballistic missiles (ICBMs) and long-range bombers. And, by the late 1960s, the Soviet Union also had acquired a formidable strategic nuclear arsenal, including over 1,000 ICBMs and submarine-launched ballistic missiles (SLBMs).[13] Acute political hostility combined with these levels of strategic nuclear capability inspired great hope that mutual deterrence could keep the peace between the United States and the Soviet Union.

By the mid-1960s, the actual waging of war between Washington and Moscow carried the possibility of severe consequences for both, regardless of the details of military morale, operational skill, tactics or strategy. Various U.S. Government studies during the 1970s suggested the possibility that a relatively large-scale U.S.-Soviet nuclear war would result in American fatalities ranging from 20 million to 165 million, depending on assumptions about the weapons employed, the targets, and the level of population sheltering and evacuation.[14] The consequences for the Soviet Union may have been comparably severe, although there was some disagreement about the likely scope of Soviet casualties, resulting in part from uncertainties about the effectiveness of Soviet protective civil defense measures.[15]

Because war with the Soviet Union could have been a history-ending event for America, the deterrence of war became an imperative. Washington put a premium on strategies for deterring war and acquiring a strategic nuclear arsenal with an eye to its expected deterrent effect.

Under these circumstances, in the United States it became customary to believe that the mutual fear of nuclear retaliation cast a long shadow over the ambitions and behavior of both sides, moderating each one's willingness to provoke the other. The scope of contingencies expected to be deterred by mutual nuclear threats ranged from thermonuclear war to conventional border clashes. Winston Churchill famously pointed to the hoped-for deterrent effect that mutual vulnerability to nuclear retaliation would have upon decision making. Looking to a future world with numerous nuclear weapons, he observed in 1955, "It may be that we shall by a process of sublime irony have reached a stage in this story where safety will be the sturdy child of terror, and survival the twin brother of annihilation."[16] He had described what came to be called the "balance of terror," and the hope was that mutual terror, sustained by offensive nuclear capabilities, would deter direct attacks and other severe provocations. Mutual vulnerability to the consequences of nuclear war, it was hoped, would inspire mutual caution.

The Cold War's central characteristic of mutual vulnerability to nuclear retaliation, firmly in place by the mid-1960s, validated Churchill's comment and the 1946 observation of the noted American deterrence theorist, Bernard Brodie, that deterrence via the threat of nuclear retaliation would become the priority for U.S. security policy:

> The first and most vital step in any American security program for the age of atomic weapons is to take measures to guarantee to ourselves in case of attack the possibility of retaliation in kind. The writer in making that statement is not for the moment concerned with who will win the next war in which atomic bombs are used. Thus far the chief purpose of our military establishment has been to win wars. From now on, its chief purpose must be to avert them.[17]

As Brodie anticipated, deterrence of war would become the primary goal and strategy, and the great value of U.S. long-range "strategic" nuclear weapons came to be seen not primarily in their actual employment, but in the deterrent effect of their *threatened* employment. Their most desirable "use" was not in being launched per se, but being withheld as the ultimate threat for deterrent effect. In this sense, strategic nuclear weapons never were employed during the Cold War, but they were "used" through times of relative calm and crisis as the ultimate sanction upon which to base the strategy of deterring the Soviet leadership. Manipulating threats to deter Soviet leaders from ever deciding on war became the *leitmotif* of U.S. strategic policy: deterrence was king. It was America's premier goal and strategy, the dominant strategic noun and strategic verb.

Extending Nuclear Deterrence Coverage to Allies

In U.S. deterrence strategy, the threat of strategic nuclear retaliation was not only for the purpose of deterring a Soviet nuclear attack on the United States; far from it. Soviet and Warsaw Pact conventional forces were so powerful that, for much of the Cold War, successfully fighting a conventional war in Europe in the event of Soviet attack seemed unacceptably destructive and challenging. This argued for the prevention of war altogether as the priority goal, and the primacy of deterrence. From the 1950s through the 1980s, the United States repeatedly attempted to lead the North Atlantic Treaty Organization (NATO) in the direction of improving its conventional forces to reduce the pressure to employ locally-deployed "tactical" nuclear weapons in response to a massive conventional Warsaw Pact attack. But NATO as a whole never concluded that the basis for Western security could rest primarily on a capability to fight and win a conventional or nuclear war against the Soviet Union—the great proximate superpower. The cost of acquiring such conventional capabilities was daunting, and the prospect of fighting yet another horrific war in Europe during the century was unacceptable. Deterrence of war altogether was the preferred theme.

NATO's 1952 Lisbon Agreement, for example, attempted to move NATO strategy toward that goal of effective conventional defense by increasing its conventional forces to an extraordinary 96 divisions. Within two years that goal was abandoned as economically untenable and, by 1957, NATO had adopted the more modest—but still challenging—goal of having 30 combat-ready divisions in Europe's central region, with an emphasis on nuclear deterrence.[18]

A basic reason for the retreat from a conventional defense strategy for NATO was the widespread belief that the cost of conventional defense would be prohibitive, and that nuclear deterrence offered an efficient, affordable alternative. Official estimates of Soviet conventional military capabilities during the 1960s suggested that the Soviet Union had 140 active divisions in the European theater, and that 400 Soviet divisions could be mobilized within 30 days.[19] Given the apparent great disparity in NATO and Soviet strength, "A conventional option was automatically assumed to require major increases in defense budgets, which politicians on both sides of the Atlantic were unwilling to make, particularly since nuclear weapons were assumed to be a substitute for manpower and therefore a viable alternative."[20]

Some European leaders also argued that too much emphasis on conventional defense by NATO might actually undermine European security by signaling to the Soviet leadership that NATO was backing away from its commitment to nuclear defense and deterrence, which would create a possible opening for massive conventional attack. Nuclear deterrence was needed to prevent war because the alternatives were judged unacceptable.

The Soviet Union enjoyed a number of advantages over the Western democracies in the arena of traditional, conventional military capability—including the continuing ability to put an extraordinary percentage of its gross national product into military expenditures, and its geographic proximity to Western Europe. With regard to the latter, simple geography meant that Soviet and Warsaw Pact divisions and reserves were near or in Central Europe, while American divisions had to be deployed overseas to be "over there."

Rather than match Soviet conventional military capabilities—an arena in which the Soviet Union had seemingly unbeatable advantages—the United States and NATO ultimately chose to pursue what now is called an "asymmetric strategy." NATO chose to rely heavily on the threat of nuclear escalation and nuclear deterrence as the ultimate guarantor of Western European security. It held out the option to meet a massive Soviet conventional onslaught, not with a conventional military defense alone, but with the possibility of nuclear escalation—ultimately including strategic nuclear retaliation. NATO's locally-deployed conventional forces were intended to preclude any easy territorial grab by the Soviet Union. NATO conventional power might not be up to halting a Soviet march to the English Channel but could ensure that, if the Soviets ever considered an attack on Western Europe, any such gambit would have to be a large-scale war of uncertain duration and fraught with the possibility of U.S. nuclear escalation.

NATO conventional forces, including U.S. divisions, provided visible proof of the U.S. military commitment to European security. They were an obvious link to the U.S. strategic nuclear retaliatory threat and the possibility of an "asymmetric" NATO nuclear response to a Warsaw Pact conventional assault. In this way, NATO conventional forces played a key role in the U.S. provision of nuclear deterrence coverage for Europe. General Lauris Norstad, NATO's Supreme Allied Commander under President Eisenhower, explained this rationale for NATO conventional forces early in the Cold War: "The function of shield forces is really not to fight, not even to defend, but to complete the deterrent."[21]

Throughout the Cold War decades, the United States typically championed the improvement of NATO conventional capabilities, as noted above, not because it rejected nuclear deterrence, but to help ensure that Soviet leaders could not anticipate a conventional *fait accompli* and would understand that an attack westward was fraught with the potential for NATO nuclear escalation. Fear of that prospect was expected to deter the Soviet leadership from ever taking the gamble.

Manfred Woerner, who served as German Defense Minister and Secretary General of NATO, reflected this view in his 1971 observation that the Warsaw Pact had assembled the greatest concentration of conventional military power known in history. Consequently, "A massive conventional attack against Europe cannot either now or in the foreseeable future be warded off with conventional means alone. Deterrence in Europe is, therefore, not credible without a nuclear component. The nuclear element alone provides a chance for defense at whatever level necessary and confronts an aggressor with an incalculable risk."[22] The risk confronted by the Soviet leadership—that an assault on the West would escalate to nuclear war—was the risk that was expected to deter the assault despite Soviet regional conventional force advantages.

General Andrew Goodpaster, the Supreme Allied Commander, Europe, explained the affordability of this "flexible response" deterrence strategy to President Richard Nixon during a 1970 top-secret meeting in the White House:

> It is based primarily on the deterrent but it cannot be divorced from our actual defense capability. It is a strong deterrent based on a limited defense capability, at medium risk and medium cost. A full conventional defense capability would be a low-risk/high-cost strategy....At present, we have a high prospect of success against small-scale or limited attacks. That is important. Against a full-scale sustained attack, we have a limited capability in time.... Assured destruction [deterrence] is always the back-up which supports the other elements of the strategy.[23]

In this way, the United States extended its nuclear deterrence protection—its "nuclear umbrella"—to select allies, including NATO countries, Japan, and South Korea. The U.S. threat of nuclear escalation or nuclear retaliation was expected to help deter a broad range of possible Soviet provocations, from a large-scale conventional attack on U.S. allies to a massive nuclear attack against the United States itself.

The basic structure of NATO's security situation did not change much during the Cold War. In 1987, the U.S. Commander in Chief, U.S. European Command, General Bernard Rogers reported in testimony before the Senate: "I say to you, as I have said before this committee, that if attacked conventionally today, NATO would face fairly quickly the decision to escalate to the nuclear response in order to try to cause the aggressor to halt his advance."[24]

According to General Rogers, the basic problem and need for nuclear deterrence remained: "There is no way that nations in Western

Europe can find the resources for sufficient conventional forces [to offset Soviet conventional superiority]. The resources aren't there. And so as a consequence it's that nuclear umbrella tied to the U.S. that is the basis of our deterrent." Because of Soviet conventional force advantages, NATO's movement away from nuclear deterrence would, "make Western Europe safe for conventional war."[25]

In 1988, Supreme Allied Commander General John Galvin similarly warned that there was a threat to his capability to deter war and to defend Europe, if necessary. That threat was, "the imbalance in conventional forces between NATO and the Warsaw Pact. At this moment I can guarantee only that we can defend ourselves for two weeks against an all-out Warsaw Pact attack—then we will have to use nuclear weapons."[26]

One might question, once there was a balance of terror, why the Soviet leadership should believe a U.S. threat to escalate to nuclear war on behalf of West European allies? Escalating a regional European or Asian war into a deadly intercontinental strategic nuclear war could hardly be considered in the U.S. national interest. In fact, it might be suicidal: why should the Soviet leadership fear U.S. deterrence threats that ultimately would have suicidal consequences for the United States?

In 1962, President John Kennedy anticipated this deterrence dilemma in a meeting with his military advisors:

Our big danger is the Soviet Union is going to get in a position where they are going to have so much on us, such nuclear capabilities to deliver on us and cause us so many casualties, that we will not initiate a nuclear attack on them. And that being true, then they will use their conventional force to take whatever they want...in Europe and in Asia. That is the danger we are going to face, that I'll—or whoever is President—will not want to fire this [nuclear] weapon to stop this conventional attack.[27]

By 1970, the deterrence problem anticipated by President Kennedy had been realized. During a top-secret discussion of NATO security policy, General Andrew Goodpaster attempted to assure President Nixon regarding the lethality of the U.S. nuclear deterrent threat, "Our capability for assured destruction against the Soviets is very high." Nixon replied, "But what about the risks we would take if we do that?"[28]

Presidents Kennedy and Nixon each had posed the question that became a centerpiece of the Cold War debate about deterrence: how could an effective U.S. extended nuclear deterrent be based on an essentially suicidal threat? In the United States, this problem confronting the U.S nuclear umbrella became known as the problem of U.S. "self-deterrence." This label was a misnomer. The potential for U.S. paralysis was imposed by U.S. vulnerability to the Soviet nuclear retaliatory threat; it was the possibility that the U.S. threat of nuclear escalation meant to deter attacks on allies could itself be countered by Soviet nuclear retaliatory capabilities.

Two fundamentally different answers to this nuclear deterrence quandary became the cornerstones of two divergent and competing schools of U.S. deterrence theory.

Herman Kahn: U.S. Advantage, Credible Threats, and an Imbalance of Terror

One school of thought may best be illustrated by the brilliant theoretical work on the subject by Herman Kahn, a physicist at the RAND Corporation throughout the 1950s, and later co-founder of the Hudson Institute. Kahn was the author of the widely-noted texts, *On Thermonuclear War* (1960), and *Thinking About the Unthinkable* (1962). Other prominent, brilliant contributors to this school were Albert Wohlstetter, an influential mathematician at the RAND Corporation, and Professor Colin Gray, the most innovative and prolific of the "second wave" of theorists writing in the 1970s and 1980s. To simplify the description of this school, the following discussion focuses primarily on Kahn's work.

Herman Kahn argued strongly that offensive threats on behalf of others which ultimately would be self-destructive—such as U.S. strategic nuclear threats to the Soviet Union on behalf of NATO members in a balance of terror—simply were not reliably credible, and could not alone serve as the basis for an effective policy of deterrence. The Soviet leadership should not be expected to believe that the United States would, on behalf of its allies, deliberately initiate a nuclear war that it could not survive. Kahn believed that Soviet leaders would see an essentially suicidal U.S. threat on behalf of others as a bluff to be called. Consequently, Kahn argued that unless the United States was capable of limiting damage to itself in a nuclear war, it could not credibly threaten nuclear escalation on behalf of allies, and extended deterrence could easily fail. The U.S. capability for deterrence, according to Kahn, required U.S. capabilities for defense against nuclear attack. He warned early in the Cold War that no matter how severe U.S. offensive nuclear threats may look, "it will be irrational [for the United States] to attack and thus insure a Soviet retaliation unless we have made preparations to counter this retaliation." [29]

Sir Michael Howard, noted British military historian and analyst, expressed a similar concern about the credibility of Western deterrence threats: "Peoples who are not prepared to make the effort necessary for operational defense are even less likely to support a decision to initiate a nuclear exchange for which they will themselves suffer almost inconceivable destruction, even if that decision is taken at the lowest possible level of nuclear escalation." [30]

According to Kahn, extended nuclear deterrence based on a threat that would be suicidal if executed could be viewed as an incredible bluff, and consequently could invite challenges. In addition, such threats could provide no useful basis for actual war planning because they would be reckless to implement in the event of war. Basing deterrence on threats that ultimately would be self-destructive was folly on multiple levels: it could lead to an incredible deterrent, invite challenges, and offer no useful planning guidance following the failure of deterrence.

Kahn scorned theories of deterrence predicated on nuclear threats that could be seen as incredible because they risked national destruction. Instead, he argued that for extended deterrence to be manifestly credible, the United States must be seen by the Soviet leadership as capable and willing to escalate to ever higher levels of threatened destruction, with the credibility of the U.S. threat coming in part from the U.S. capability to defend itself against Soviet nuclear weapons and thereby survive the process of nuclear escalation. In one hypothetical example Kahn suggested that the capability to limit the loss of population to 10 percent in a nuclear war could help provide the necessary credibility for effectively extending deterrence. [31]

Kahn saw this as a particular requirement for Western security because, given Soviet conventional force advantages in Eurasia, it was the West—and the United States in particular—that would likely be placed in the position of having to threaten nuclear escalation to stop a Soviet attack against U.S. European or Asian allies. It was Washington, not Moscow, that would have to threaten initial nuclear escalation; a war that remained conventional would be to the Soviet advantage. The deterrence threat of *initiating* nuclear escalation was key to America's threatened response to Soviet conventional force advantages. Consequently, it was the United States that had to make the threat of nuclear escalation appear credible by complementing its lethal offensive nuclear threats with defensive capabilities that could protect the United States throughout any nuclear escalation process.

In a 1979 address to an audience of Europeans and Americans on the subject of deterrence, former U.S. Secretary of State Henry Kissinger echoed Kahn's critique, if not his prescription, with considerable candor: "If my analysis is correct we must face the fact that it is absurd to base the strategy of the West on the credibility of the threat of mutual suicide...and therefore I would say—what I might not say in office—that our European allies should not keep asking us to multiply strategic assurances that we cannot possibly mean, or if we do mean, we should not want to execute, because if we execute, we risk the destruction of civilization."[32]

Thomas Schelling:
The Deterring Effect of Uncertainty in a Balance of Terror

Thomas Schelling was the single most influential Western strategic theorist of the Cold War. His innovative concepts of deterrence formed the core of an alternative school of thought that fundamentally rejected Kahn's contention that effective extended deterrence required a deliberate threat to escalate to nuclear war made credible by U.S. defensive capabilities. There were, of course, additional brilliant contributors to this school, most notably academics Bernard Brodie and Glenn Snyder, and somewhat later, Robert Jervis. Like Schelling, they argued that the credibility of a deliberate U.S. decision to escalate to nuclear war was not a necessary ingredient for effective deterrence. The *chance* of nuclear escalation could provide ample deterrent effect and *any rational* opponent would fear that chance whether or not the United States also could defend itself.

An adequate U.S. extended deterrence policy, according to Schelling, did not require Kahn's vision of a credible, deliberate threat to initiate nuclear escalation; the Soviet leadership would instead be deterred by the uncertainties surrounding U.S. threats, and the attendant *chance of U.S. nuclear escalation.* "This is why deterrent threats are often so credible. They do not need to depend on a willingness to commit anything like suicide in the face of a challenge. A response that carries some risk of war can be plausible, even reasonable, at a time when a final, ultimate decision to have a general war would be implausible or unreasonable. A country can threaten to stumble into war even if it can not credibly threaten to invite one."[33] And: "Any situation that scares one side will scare both sides with the danger of a war that neither wants, and both will have to pick their way carefully through the crisis, never quite sure that the other knows how to avoid stumbling over the brink."[34]

Schelling explained why the effectiveness of a deterrence threat should not depend on whether the target audience actually believes that the threatener would choose deliberately to execute the threat if its demands are not met:

> The key to these threats is that, though one may or may not carry them out if the threatened party fails to comply, the final decision is not altogether under the threatener's control. The threat is not quite of the form "I may or may not, according as I choose," but, has an element of, "I may or may not, and even I can't be altogether sure."

> Where does the uncertain element in the decision come from? It must come from somewhere outside of the threatener's control. Whether we call it "chance," accident, third-party influence, imperfection in the machinery of decision, or just processes that we do not entirely understand, it is an ingredient in the situation that neither we nor the party we threaten can entirely control.[35]

Schelling famously labeled this approach to deterrence, "the threat that leaves something to chance."[36] According to Schelling, effective deterrence of Moscow did not necessarily require Soviet expectation of a deliberate U.S. decision to escalate to a strategic nuclear war made credible by U.S. defensive capabilities. Rather, extended deterrence could be based on Soviet fear of Washington's unpredictability, the unpredictability of war itself, and the chance that nuclear escalation would occur without Washington's intention to escalate.

U.S. non-nuclear forces deployed to an area, such as U.S. troops in Europe, could contribute to a "seamless web" of deterrence. They could compel Soviet leaders to confront the deterring possibility that a conventional war in Europe could escalate out of control. Local forces, according to Schelling, did not need to promise defeat of the Soviet Union to have this deterring effect: "What local military forces can do, even against very superior forces, is to initiate this uncertain process of escalation. One does not have to be able to win a local military engagement to make the threat of it effective. Being able to lose a local war in a dangerous and provocative manner may make the risk—not the sure consequences, but the possibility of this act—outweigh the apparent gains to the other side."[37]

In contrast to Kahn's insistence on the U.S. need for threat credibility that would follow from a U.S. capability to survive the execution of its nuclear escalation threat, Schelling maintained that the "uncertain element" of *what might happen* in response to a Soviet attack—possibly beyond Washington's control—would make extended nuclear deterrence "work." Soviet leaders would fear that the United States might not behave rationally, or in the "fog of war" might "blunder" toward strategic nuclear war even if it would not rationally, intentionally choose such a course because it would be self-destructive to do so. It might be suicidal for the United States to escalate to the employment of strategic nuclear weapons, but the threat of escalation could provide extended deterrence nonetheless because the Soviet leadership could not be certain that U.S. actions would be prudent, or precisely and tightly controlled.[38]

Glenn Snyder similarly posited that the United States could extend deterrence to Europe with the threat of nuclear escalation, despite the fact that such a step ultimately could be self-destructive because, "The Russians cannot be sure of our rationality; therefore, they face a risk that we will retaliate all-out, and they cannot afford to take that risk."[39] Late in the Cold War this thesis remained central to much Western theorizing about extending deterrence. Robert Jervis, one of the most prominent of the "second wave" of academic theorists inspired by Schelling and Brodie, concluded in 1979 that, "it is hard to imagine" that the Soviet Union would attack NATO conventionally because Soviet leaders "could not be sufficiently confident" that NATO would not escalate to nuclear weapons; Soviet leaders similarly would face uncertainties with regard to initiating a nuclear war in Europe, particularly including the risk that such a nuclear attack would "trigger the American strategic [nuclear] force."[40]

In short, according to this view, the U.S. capability to deter the Soviet leadership was not necessarily dependent on Soviet fear of a deliberate U.S. decision to retaliate with nuclear weapons. Rather, the Soviet leadership would be deterred by the possibility that U.S. nuclear escalation could follow from irrationality, or accident, or the "fog of war."

The possibility of an uncontrolled U.S. response, not the full expectation of a deliberately decided nuclear response, would be the basis for extended deterrence of Soviet conventional or nuclear attack.

Schelling and Kahn thus differed over the basic mechanism of extended deterrence and how to attach adequate credibility to the threat of U.S. nuclear escalation. Kahn sought the U.S. capability to escape from the restrictions of the balance of terror via defensive strategic forces manifestly capable of limiting the destruction which the United States would suffer in a nuclear war: if the prospective costs of escalation to the United States were lowered, the Soviet leadership should attach greater credibility to the U.S. threat to escalate. Kahn sought to use U.S. damage-limiting strategic forces to minimize the chance that Soviet leaders could doubt the U.S. deterrence threat; he wanted a deterrent that left little to chance in this regard.

Schelling suggested as an alternative that Soviet fears of the uncertain possibility of U.S. nuclear escalation could deter adequately, even in the context of U.S. vulnerability to subsequent massive Soviet nuclear retaliation. He emphasized that U.S. threats could acquire sufficient credibility from the U.S. potential for graduated escalation, including threats of limited nuclear escalation. The potential for the limited U.S. use of nuclear weapons would not be for achieving tactical military advantage, or directly limiting damage to the United States à la Kahn, but to demonstrate U.S. resolve and will to Soviet leaders and thereby highlight the risk of all-out nuclear war.[41] Threats of "limited or graduated retaliation" could provide increased credibility for the U.S. extended deterrent threat because, "The [U.S.] risk involved in a bit of less-than-massive retaliation would be a good deal less than it is now because the fear of an all-out [Soviet] strike in return should be a good deal less...the threat of limited retaliation (even on a scale that deserves the word 'massive') would become a great deal more credible."[42]

Schelling helped to explain how uncertainty and limited escalation could make otherwise incredible threats effective with his analogy of "rocking the boat." According to Schelling, "If I say 'Row or I'll tip the boat over and drown us both,' you'll say you don't believe me. But if I rock the boat so that it *may* tip over, you'll be more impressed. If I can't administer pain short of death for the two of us, a 'little bit' of death, in the form of a small probability that the boat will tip over, is a near equivalent. But to make it work, I must really put the boat in jeopardy."[43]

While Kahn sought deterrence credibility by directly reducing through U.S. defensive capabilities the risks the United States would confront in threatening nuclear escalation, Schelling identified U.S. limited or graduated nuclear war capabilities as a means of emphasizing the risks the Soviet Union would run, and thereby reinforcing the deterrent effect: Soviet leaders would see the United States as less fearful of initiating a limited nuclear escalation process, and thus the risk of provoking the United States would appear greater to Soviet leaders. Schelling's preferred alternative was intended to reinforce in Soviet calculations the possibility of initial U.S. escalation leading to uncontrolled nuclear war, and thus reinforce the deterrent effect of uncertainty on Soviet leaders.

Schelling's innovative proposition that the reliable functioning of extended nuclear deterrence could be based on the Soviet leadership's fear of the uncertain risks of nuclear escalation was a potentially significant conceptual breakthrough. The proposition was profound, and contrasted starkly with Kahn's fundamental belief that a sufficiently credible extended nuclear deterrence could follow only from Soviet belief that the United States, protected to a significant extent from Soviet nuclear retaliation, could deliberately choose to escalate to nuclear use on behalf of its allies because it could be considered prudent and in the U.S. interest to do so.

Kahn's Adequate U.S. Deterrent: An Imbalance of Terror and U.S. Advantage

The contrasting answers by Kahn and Schelling to the fundamental question, "What makes deterrence work?" may seem to be an arcane and trifling dispute over the meaning of credibility and the conditions necessary to extend deterrence reliably. The differences in their answers may be arcane, but they are far from trifling. The practice of deterrence is affected dramatically by whether Schelling's "threat that leaves something to chance," or Kahn's credibility from a threat that leaves little to chance, is judged to be an adequate basis for reliable deterrence. Schelling's thesis, if fully embraced as policy, eliminates the requirement of deploying the various offensive and defensive forces identified by Kahn as necessary to make the U.S. threat of nuclear escalation sufficiently credible to deter.

As noted above, Kahn argued that for the Soviets *to believe the U.S. extended nuclear threat*, i.e., for it to be credible, the United States had to have the capability to survive the process of nuclear escalation and the likely Soviet nuclear reply. Consequently, the United States had to be capable of limiting the damage to itself from Soviet nuclear attack. Kahn relentlessly posed these questions: If the United States could *not* survive the Soviet strike that was sure to follow U.S. nuclear escalation, why would the Soviet leadership believe that the United States would ever implement its threat? And, if the Soviet leadership could doubt the U.S. nuclear threat, how could that threat reliably provide the desired deterrent effect?

According to Kahn, "Credibility depends on being willing to accept the other side's retaliatory blow. It depends on the harm *he* can do, not on the harm *we* can do....It depends on [U.S.] *will* as well as capability."[44] That will would be lacking, and seen as lacking, Kahn insisted, if the U.S. deterrent threat offered only a process of nuclear escalation and counterstrikes that Washington was unprepared to survive: "About all an unprepared government can do is to say over and over, 'The other side doesn't really want war.' Then they can hope they are right. However, this same government can scarcely expect to make up by sheer determination what it lacks in preparations. How can it persuade its opponent of its own willingness to go to war if the situation demands it?"[45] And, "If we wish to have our strategic forces contribute to the deterrence of provocation, it must be credible....Usually the most convincing way to look willing is to be willing."[46]

Consequently, Kahn was a firm supporter of U.S. civil defense preparations to reduce the potential damage from a Soviet nuclear attack by sheltering and relocating threatened population and industry, and of air defenses and ballistic missile defense (BMD) to intercept Soviet nuclear-armed bombers and missiles en route to the United States.[47] Kahn did not contend that this protection could or had to be perfect, but that it had to be capable of reducing damage to the United States to the extent that the Soviet leadership would judge U.S. nuclear deterrent threats to be credible because the United States could risk nuclear escalation. That is, the United States had to be sufficiently well-protected that the Soviet leadership would believe that under some dire conditions the president could deliberately choose to escalate to a nuclear war because the stakes were high and the United States could survive the ensuing war.

Kahn was not interested in the least in reducing the barriers to nuclear war. To the contrary, his objective was to build the sturdiest deterrence barrier possible. To do so, Kahn insisted, the U.S. threat of deliberately escalating to nuclear war had to appear credible to the Soviet leadership and that, in turn, required Moscow to believe that the United States could choose nuclear escalation over conciliation under at least some conditions.[48]   The capability to limit damage to the United States, according to Kahn, was the key to that Soviet belief and thus the credibility of the U.S. deterrent—particularly the extended deterrent for U.S. allies.

In addition, Kahn maintained that a credible deterrent to Soviet attack on the United States itself required that the United States have the spectrum of offensive nuclear weaponry necessary to threaten different types of Soviet targets, from cities and industry to relatively small, hardened Soviet military and political targets. The latter types of targets could require that the United States possess in its arsenal many nuclear weapons with precision accuracy.

How did Kahn link this requirement for a spectrum of offensive nuclear capabilities to the credibility of the U.S. deterrent threat? In Kahn's view, the Soviet leadership might not believe a U.S. nuclear escalation threat if it could be posed *only* against Soviet cities and industry. American scruples and the near certainty of a Soviet nuclear counterreply against U.S. cities and industry could lead Soviet leaders to doubt such a U.S. nuclear threat. Consequently, Kahn reasoned that a U.S. threat only to Soviet cities and industry again might be insufficiently credible to deter the Soviet leadership under dire circumstances. Rather, the United States also needed to be capable of threatening Soviet military and political targets— while always holding a nuclear threat to Soviet cities as leverage—to give the Soviets continuing incentive to avoid striking U.S. cities. Kahn noted that, because the United States placed its highest value in its people and industry, playing a high-stakes deterrence game of threats and counterthreats to cities as the only targets would be particularly incredible for the United States.

Consequently, Kahn's insistence on *threat credibility* led to offensive requirements for nuclear deterrence that were as robust as his defensive requirements. As Kahn observed: *"At the minimum, an adequate deterrent for the United States must provide an objective basis for a Soviet calculation that would persuade them that, no matter how skillful or ingenious they were, an attack on the United States would lead to a very high risk if not certainty of large-scale destruction to Soviet civil society and military forces."*[49] That *"objective basis"* required a diversity of U.S. offensive nuclear forces to hold a range of Soviet targets at risk and defensive capabilities to limit prospective damage from Soviet nuclear strikes. Armed with such offensive and defensive capabilities, the U.S. threat of nuclear escalation could be sufficiently credible to deter because the Soviet leadership would understand that, "[the United States] might conceivably prefer to go to war rather than acquiesce on some vital interest."[50]

Two basic judgments led Kahn logically to his insistence that strategic defenses and diverse offensive nuclear forces were necessary for deterrence. First, the type of deterrence strategy necessary for the United States could proceed only from the manifest threat of nuclear escalation; and, second, the deterrent threat of nuclear escalation would be sufficiently credible to "work" reliably only if, *in extremis*, the Soviet leadership believed that the U.S. leadership could deliberately choose to execute that threat because it would be in the U.S. net interest to do so. This level of credibility, according to Kahn, could not be based on a U.S. nuclear retaliatory threat against Soviet cities and industry alone, or on the absence of the defensive capabilities necessary to limit damage to the United States. As a result, Kahn embraced strategic defenses and rejected a U.S. strategic nuclear deterrent limited to the "assured destruction" standard of offensive nuclear weapons targeted against Soviet cities and civilian industry.

In short, Kahn's belief that effective nuclear deterrence required a *credible* U.S. threat to initiate nuclear escalation put him squarely at odds with Schelling's "threat that leaves something to chance" and the type of "assured destruction" deterrent threat to Soviet cities and industry expressed by Secretary of Defense McNamara in the 1960s. Instead, he favored a threat of deliberate U.S. escalation that, in his view, Soviet leaders would be likely to believe—a threat that left little to chance.

Kahn had considerable confidence in the functioning of a deterrence policy that followed his prescription. He noted, however, that deterrence could fail and war break out regardless of the deterrence measures intended to prevent or contain it. He emphasized that an advantage of the combined offensive and defensive forces he recommended for deterrence was that they had the concomitant potential to reduce the damage to society in the event deterrence failed catastrophically despite our best deterrence efforts: "War can still occur and it is better to survive the war than not. Therefore one needs to have systems that can reduce the damage done in a war."[51] Kahn saw full compatibility between the types of capabilities he deemed necessary for an effective U.S. deterrence policy and those capabilities that could serve to limit damage in the event of war. For Kahn, the capabilities necessary for effective deterrence, and for limiting damage in the event deterrence failed, were consistent.

Kahn's ideas were criticized sharply during the Cold War. Because he wrote and spoke analytically—almost clinically—about the need for

U.S. strategic offensive and defensive forces that would enable the United States to threaten and survive a nuclear war, he was charged with being inhumane, cavalier, or even jocular about the prospect for nuclear war, and somehow in favor of war-fighting rather than deterrence.[52] Some reviews of Kahn's famous 1960 publication on the subject, *On Thermonuclear War*, were unusually sharp and even mocking. James Newman, for example, wrote in the pages of *Scientific American*, "Is there really a Herman Kahn? It's hard to believe....No one could write like this; no one could think like this. Perhaps the whole thing is a staff hoax in bad taste....This is a moral tract on mass murder: how to plan it, how to commit it, how to get away with it, how to justify it."[53] Two ostensibly religious writers descended to character assassination, labeling Kahn's work, "Satanic doublethink."[54]

Such charges against Kahn and his views were utter nonsense. There is ground to question Kahn's stipulation that for deterrence threats to "work" they must be credible in the sense of their execution being manifestly consistent with national interest, and his linking of that stipulation to the requirement for extensive U.S. offensive and defensive forces. But, there is no gainsaying that his analysis was logical and coherent, and that his driving goal was to understand how best to *prevent* war, particularly nuclear war, via deterrence.

Critics of Kahn's work often reflected little comprehension of the subject. That was perhaps best illustrated by the reply Kahn received from the editor of *Scientific American*, Dennis Flanagan, following his offer to write a rebuttal to the review by James Newman appearing in *Scientific American* quoted above. Kahn proposed to title his response to Newman, *Thinking About the Unthinkable*. Flanagan reportedly replied to Kahn: "I do not think there is much point in thinking about the unthinkable; surely it is much more profitable to think about the thinkable....I should prefer to devote my thoughts to how nuclear war can be prevented. It is for this reason that we must decline your offer to give us your article."[55]

The charges that Kahn was cavalier about nuclear war, and that his intellectual energies were devoted to something other than preventing nuclear war, reflected a wholly superficial understanding of his work; his recommendations regarding U.S. offensive and defensive strategic forces rigorously followed from his judgments about the requirements for deterrence, not from an ignorant, cavalier or jocular view of nuclear war. Kahn was deeply humane, and had an expansive wit which he applied liberally. No less than Schelling, Kahn was wholly serious in his intellectual quest to understand how best to prevent nuclear war by deterring it. Kahn understood the abiding complexities regarding the consequences of nuclear war as well as anyone, and at least as well as his critics. The source of his force structure recommendations was not a frivolous or cold-hearted attitude about nuclear war, but his basic judgment about the requirements for threat credibility and the fundamental conditions necessary to make deterrence "work."

Schelling's Adequate U.S. Deterrent: A Stable Balance of Terror

In contrast to Kahn's judgments about the basic conditions required for effective deterrence and the recommendations that logically followed, Schelling emphasized that effective deterrence could be established on the basis of the U.S. capability to threaten Soviet population and industry. According to Schelling, "Human and economic resources were hostages to be left unprotected" for deterrence purposes: "…I like the notion that East and West have exchanged hostages on a massive scale and that as long as they are unprotected, civilization depends on the avoidance of military aggression that could escalate to nuclear war."[56]

Equally important, as noted above, Schelling believed that a sufficiently effective deterrence threat could follow from the Soviet leadership's belief that there *was a chance* of U.S. nuclear escalation. Based on these presumptions about how deterrence could function, Schelling offered his own recommendations about the types of forces that would support deterrence. His prescription regarding the U.S. strategic force requirements for deterrence was far less demanding than Kahn's. For example, from his belief that effective deterrence did not need to rest on Soviet expectations that the United States could *deliberately* choose to execute its nuclear threat, Schelling concluded that, for deterrence purposes, the United States did not need to be capable of defending its cities against a Soviet nuclear attack. Because deterrence of the Soviet leadership could follow from Moscow's fear that the United States might "stumble" into nuclear war through a chaotic, out-of-control process, the U.S. nuclear threat could deter without defenses because the Soviets would fear the *possibility* that Washington would initiate a nuclear war without consciously, deliberately calculating that it could be in the U.S. interest to do so. Deterrence did not require Kahn's defenses, according to Schelling, because deterring Soviet leaders did not require that they believe Washington would consciously, deliberately choose to execute its nuclear threat.

Consequently, while Kahn viewed defensive capabilities as indispensable to a *credible* nuclear deterrent threat, Schelling viewed defenses as unnecessary for deterrence:

> The...most reasonable way that you threaten the Russians, as they threaten us—the way they kept us out of Czechoslovakia, for example—is not that they would launch thermonuclear war as the first American jeep crossed the border; but in ways that can't be foreseen, through processes not wholly under control, something would happen, escalate and lead to bigger and bigger clashes, and some day somebody would fire off some nuclear weapons....This gives the Russians pause, and gives them pause whether or not they are naked to our attack and whether or not we are naked to their attack.[57]

Further, according to Schelling, U.S. defenses for cities and industry were not simply unnecessary for deterrence; they could undermine deterrence by reducing Soviet confidence in its own capability to threaten retaliation against U.S. society—the Soviet threat in a "stable" balance of terror. Schelling contended that if the United States had missile defenses for U.S. cities, Moscow's leaders could fear that Washington would be free, to some extent, from fear of the Soviet nuclear threat, and thus could be motivated to seek the strategic advantage of executing a U.S. pre-emptive nuclear first strike against Soviet strategic forces. Washington's motivation in such an attack, in principle, would be to reduce the Soviet retaliatory capabilities to a level more manageable for U.S. defenses. This Soviet fear of a U.S. pre-emptive strike, inspired by U.S. defenses, could motivate Soviet leaders to conduct their own nuclear pre-emptive strike against the United States first—rather than wait for a U.S. first strike and cede the possible advantage of the initial strike to Washington.

Schelling emphasized that this fear of pre-emption would work against a *stable* balance of terror. The two sides, driven by the "reciprocal fear of a surprise attack," would have incentives to strike first.[58] He warned that, "Military technology that puts a premium on haste puts a premium on war itself."[59] According to Schelling, the "haste" to strike first generated by, "the fear of being a poor second for not going first," was "perhaps the main incentive" for the deliberate initiation of nuclear war:[60] "The premise underlying my point of view is that a main determinant of the likelihood of war is the nature of present military technology. We and the Russians are trapped by our military technology."[61]

 This potential immediate cause of deliberate nuclear war typically was and is called "crisis instability." Some have referred to this incentive as the desire to use weapons before they might be struck: "Use 'em or lose 'em." This idea that one side would start a nuclear war for the sake of using missiles that otherwise would be destroyed does *not* capture Schelling's more subtle point: the incentive to strike first would follow from the belief that there would be a material strategic advantage in doing so, not simply from the desire to employ otherwise vulnerable weapons, per se. If each side could retain confidence in its capability to retaliate, "there would be no advantage in jumping the gun and little reason to fear that the other would try it."[62] Schelling's logic was that if mutual destruction were the certain result of nuclear war—whether or not a side strikes first—neither would be strongly motivated to start that war: "If the gains from even successful surprise are less desired than no war at all, there is no 'fundamental' basis for an attack by either side."[63]

Schelling concluded that the potential incentive to gain a material advantage by striking first was, "the greatest source of danger that peace will explode into all-out war," and found alternative routes to deliberate nuclear war hard to envisage: "It is hard to imagine how anybody would be precipitated into full-scale war by accident, false alarm, mischief, or momentary panic, if it were not for such urgency to get in quick."[64] The very "likelihood of war," according to Schelling, "is determined by how great a reward attaches to jumping the gun, how strong the incentive to hedge against war itself by starting it, how great the penalty on giving peace the benefit of the doubt in a crisis."[65] These incentives could be caused by defensive and offensive strategic forces that might pose a threat to either side's retaliatory capabilities. Whether offensive or defensive, such capabilities could "lower the nuclear threshold" by instigating such incentives to strike first.

According to Schelling, dampening these potential incentives to strike first was the key to controlling the probability of deliberate war; securing the, "lack of temptation to deliberate surprise attack" was the basis for deterrence "stability" in the balance of terror.[66] "There would be no powerful temptation to strike first," Schelling believed, "…if each side were confident that its own forces could survive an attack, but also that it could not destroy the other's power to strike back."[67] And, "If the advantage of striking first can be eliminated or severely reduced, the incentive to strike *at all* will be reduced."[68] In this condition, "A powerfully stable mutual deterrence results."[69]

The "stability" solution was for both sides to have confidence in their respective capabilities to retaliate against the other's society, *regardless of who might strike first.* With both sides confident in their retaliatory capabilities, according to Schelling, mutual deterrence would be "stable."[70] It was not simply a balance of terror that necessarily provided effective mutual deterrence to deliberate war, but a "stable" balance of terror built on unbeatable *U.S. and Soviet* confidence in their respective nuclear retaliatory capabilities against the other's cities and industry.

In short, according to Schelling, because U.S. defensive capabilities might be more effective against a Soviet strategic arsenal that had been partially destroyed by a U.S. offensive strike, their presence could be seen as instigating dangerous U.S. incentives to strike first and, correspondingly, promote Soviet incentives to beat the United States to the first punch. Thus, Schelling argued that U.S. defensive capabilities could be the immediate cause of deterrence instability by leading the Soviets to seek a material advantage by striking first. The fear and haste generated by each side seeking to gain the advantage of striking first determined the likelihood of deliberate war and could be the proximate cause of a nuclear war otherwise unwanted by either side; it could cause "crisis instability."

Schelling contended that the basis for judging the merit of offensive or defensive strategic forces should be their capacity to establish and sustain mutual confidence in *mutual capabilities for retaliation*, and thus to work against the "reciprocal fear of surprise attack." He labeled as "stabilizing" those forces that could pose *retaliatory threats to societal targets*, and "destabilizing" those forces that could pose an offensive or defensive threat to strategic retaliatory capabilities, i.e., could threaten the mutual vulnerability to retaliation that was the cornerstone of "stable" mutual deterrence.

This categorization of strategic forces as "stabilizing" if they facilitated mutual retaliatory threats, or "destabilizing" if they might counter those threats was to be the primary basis for evaluating their merit: "Once we have identified the surprise-attack problem as the possible vulnerability of either side's retaliatory force to a first strike by the other, it becomes necessary to evaluate military strength, defensive measures, and proposals for the inspection or limitation of armament, with precisely this type of strategic vulnerability in mind."[71]

Consequently, for stable deterrence Schelling argued *against* defensive capabilities that might threaten to protect cities, and *for* mutual offensive forces that were capable of retaliation against population and industrial targets. For example, he deemed "stabilizing" those U.S. nuclear forces that were *incapable* of threatening military targets such as Soviet ICBM silos. They could pose a retaliatory threat to cities but not to strategic forces, and thus could *not* diminish the Soviet leadership's confidence in its own nuclear retaliatory threat to U.S. society: "It is precisely the weapons most destructive of people that an anti-surprise attack scheme seeks to preserve—the weapons of retaliation, the weapons whose mission is to punish rather than to fight, to hurt the enemy afterwards, not to disarm him beforehand. A weapon that can hurt only people, and cannot possibly damage the other side's striking force, is profoundly defensive: it provides its possessor no incentive to strike first."[72] The working principles here were that *mutual* deterrence was the priority, and *mutual* capabilities for nuclear retaliation against cities were the key to stable mutual deterrence. Such capabilities, therefore, ought not to be undermined by offensive or defensive strategic forces that could call these mutual retaliatory threats into question.

Logically enough, Schelling rejected as "destabilizing" offensive nuclear forces with a sufficient combination of numbers, speed, accuracy and lethality to be capable of destroying the other side's nuclear forces on the ground. "Destabilizing," in Schelling's words, "... is the weapon that is designed or deployed to destroy 'military' targets—to seek out the enemy's missiles and bombers—that *can* exploit the advantage of striking first and consequently provide a temptation to do so."[73]

Consequently, Schelling categorized strategic forces as "stabilizing" of the balance of terror or as "destabilizing," according to their technical characteristics and the specific type of threat they could reasonably pose. Nuclear forces capable only of posing retaliatory threats to cities contributed to stable mutual deterrence; those offensive or defensive forces that could threaten the other side's retaliatory capabilities undermined mutual deterrence stability because they could instigate the "reciprocal fear of surprise attack." By facilitating retaliatory threats to cities and limiting "destabilizing" forces U.S. policies, Schelling believed, could promote U.S. and Soviet confidence in their mutual nuclear retaliatory capabilities and thus help orchestrate stable mutual deterrence.

The technical characteristics of each side's strategic arsenal were key to stability, but their number could also be important. Given the immense lethality of nuclear weapons and the physical challenge of protecting cities against nuclear strikes, Schelling considered the level of U.S. strategic force capability necessary for the task of stable deterrence to be modest, especially when contrasted with Kahn's recommendation that U.S. cities be defended and all types of Soviet targets be held hostage. Schelling warned that there was nothing to be gained and much to be risked by acquiring "destabilizing" nuclear capabilities beyond the limited offensive arsenal necessary to threaten Soviet "human and economic resources." The limited number of Soviet cities and their vulnerability to nuclear threats facilitated Schelling's basic conclusion that a relatively small number of survivable, strategic nuclear weapons could be adequate for stable mutual deterrence. He noted the potential deterrence value of enhancing the "...anti-population potency of our retaliatory weapons...." and concluded that a stable balance of terror, "...is simply a massive and modern version of an ancient institution: the exchange of hostages."[74] In a thought experiment, Schelling suggested that the U.S. nuclear capability to threaten retaliation against Soviet cities with 100 secure missiles might be considered as a standard by which to judge the adequacy of U.S. forces for stable deterrence.[75]

Such a comparatively modest level of U.S. nuclear retaliatory capability is consistent with recommendations by other notable deterrence theorists and senior U.S. officials who also identified mutual threats to population centers and the chance of escalation as the ingredients for stable mutual deterrence. For example, when describing stable mutual nuclear deterrence, President Kennedy's National Security Advisor, McGeorge Bundy observed, "In the real world of real political leaders—whether here or in the Soviet Union—a decision that would bring even one hydrogen bomb on one city of one's own country would be recognized in advance as a catastrophic blunder; ten bombs on ten cities would be a disaster beyond history; and a hundred bombs on a hundred cities are unthinkable."[76]

In Congressional testimony Jerome Wiesner, science advisor to Presidents Kennedy and Johnson, stated that a U.S. deterrent threat to "deliver six modern nuclear weapons on city targets" would be more than adequate to deter "any but the most fear-driven action." He then went on to explain the relative ease of maintaining such a threat.[77]

In his classic Cold War text on deterrence, *Deterrence and Defense: Toward a Theory of National Security*, Glenn Snyder asked the pertinent question: "Would the Soviets be deterred by the prospect of losing ten cities? Or two cities? Or fifty cities?" He then provided the answer: "No one knows, although one might intuitively guess that the threshold is closer to ten than to either two or fifty...One can only guess, but it does seem likely that the Soviets would be deterred from deliberately starting World War III by an expectation of loss considerably below their World War II losses."[78]

McGeorge Bundy, with former Chairman of the Joint Chiefs of Staff Admiral William Crowe, Jr. and scientist Sidney Drell, similarly stated with confidence that, "the possibility of even a few nuclear detonations in populated areas provides ample deterrence and targeting staff should be able to make plans that produce this result against many different target sets with forces much smaller than those now in prospect."[79]

Herbert York, who served as Director of Defense Research and Engineering in the Department of Defense during the Eisenhower Administration and as Director of the Lawrence Livermore Laboratory in the early 1950s, agreed:

> Most professional analysts of the subject believe that the prospect of about one hundred thermonuclear warheads exploding over urban areas is more than enough to deter either side from starting a nuclear war....I personally believe that very much smaller numbers are sufficient to deter war; I have used numbers like one hundred only because it is customary to do so in such arguments, and because the above arguments do not hinge on whether the number is in fact one hundred or something very much smaller.[80]

Finally, Bernard Brodie observed that if a curve for "deterrence effect" from the U.S. nuclear retaliatory threat to destroy Soviet cities could be drawn, "we can surmise that the curve begins at a rather high level of deterrence for the first such bomb, and that while it moves significantly higher as the number of bombs increases beyond one, it does so at a decreasing rate. At a relatively modest number (probably well short of a hundred), the curve is closely approaching the horizontal."[81] In other words, there would be little or no additional deterrent effect available by adding U.S. nuclear capabilities beyond that required to threaten retaliation against a number of Soviet cities "well short of a hundred."

Most important is not whether Schelling, Bundy, Wiesner, York, Snyder, Crowe, Drell, or Brodie believed that an adequate U.S. nuclear deterrent could come from the capability to threaten one or one hundred cities, *but that threatening Soviet cities was deemed the basis* for U.S. deterrence strategy and the measure of adequacy for U.S. strategic forces. Because unprotected cities are extremely vulnerable to nuclear weapons and the number of Soviet cities was limited, if cities were to be the designated asset to be threatened for U.S. deterrence purposes, the question of "how much is enough" for nuclear deterrence was narrowly bounded. The answer could be addressed in principle with relatively simple arithmetic: "Enough" was that level of nuclear capability required to threaten retaliation against the most identifiable and vulnerable of Soviet targets—namely, cities. Whether Bundy's *one* city, Wiesner's six cities, or Brodie's *well short of a hundred* cities was the preferred answer, threatening cities with nuclear weapons established minimal force requirements compared to Kahn's more expansive definition of requirements.

The U.S. deterrence strategy did not have to be based on a threat to Soviet cities, per se. But, with rare exceptions, during the 1960s the capability to destroy Soviet population and industry became the metric typically identified for the U.S. side of the balance of terror, and the prevalent assumption was that Soviet policies were built around the same requirement. As Herbert York acknowledged: "We imagine them trying to deter us as we try to deter them."[82]

In contrast to Kahn's claims that extensive offensive and defensive U.S. strategic forces were necessary for credible deterrence, this prescription for a stable balance of terror was relatively easy to fill. Because secure, mutual nuclear threats to cities constituted the basic requirement for a stable balance of terror, and capabilities to defend cities were eschewed, the standard for an adequate U.S. strategic arsenal was not high: a relatively small number of secure, retaliatory nuclear weapons could be sufficient. The diverse offensive and defensive strategic forces identified by Kahn as necessary for making threats credible were regarded as unnecessary and destabilizing. Indeed, armed with his formula for stable deterrence, Schelling recommended that the United States actively oppose such "destabilizing" capabilities because they might call into question the Soviet capability to threaten U.S. society and thus incite reciprocal fears of surprise attack—ostensibly the plausible potential cause of deliberate nuclear war. Schelling's formula for mutual deterrence meant that, at the end of the day, if destabilizing forces could be avoided, preventing deliberate nuclear war was a tractable problem and orchestrating a stable balance of terror was a *relatively* easy undertaking. An easily defined set of force requirements existed, and supporting those requirements was neither overly costly nor technically challenging. Schelling outlined an affordable technical solution to the daunting political problem of Soviet nuclear power and hostility.

It was on the strength of this basic Cold War deterrence formula that many commentators in the United States came to believe with great confidence that they understood how to identify the force requirements for nuclear deterrence and, correspondingly, that the task of establishing and sustaining stable strategic nuclear deterrence could be accomplished *easily*. Professor Kenneth Waltz, one of America's most prominent international relations theorists and past president of the American Political Science Association, observed confidently that, "Not much is required to deter. What political-military objective is worth risking Vladivostok, Novosibirsk, and Tomsk, with no way of being sure that Moscow would not go as well?"[83] Professor Robert Jervis, another of America's most prominent deterrence theorists, reached the same conclusion for the same reasons: "The healthy fear of devastation, which cannot be exorcised short of the attainment of a first-strike capability, *makes deterrence relatively easy.*"[84]

Individuals from prestigious academic institutions, including those who moved in and out of senior government positions, shared this belief that the balance of terror requirements for effective deterrence were known and easily met. On this basis, for example, Herbert York claimed with confidence in 1970 that the U.S. submarine-launched strategic missile force alone (with 640 deployed nuclear warheads) "is capable of delivering far more warheads than is actually needed for deterrence."[85] Former Secretary of Defense McNamara has observed that "minimal" forces were adequate for effective deterrence—with "minimal" defined as, "forces of a size and structure that would permit the destruction of, say, a dozen rather than thousands of targets in a retaliatory attack."[86] The authors of such claims clearly were confident that they understood the functioning of deterrence and Soviet decision making so well that they could specify with considerable precision how many nuclear weapons would be adequate to ensure deterrence effectiveness. The balance of terror formula gave them such license.

Many believed the question of deterring reliably and predictably to have been answered by Schelling's basic formula. That particular answer was attractive: it promised deterrence of a spectrum of threats with easily calculable and extremely modest force requirements when contrasted to the alternative approach advanced by Kahn.

U.S. Advantage or a Stable Balance of Terror?

Kahn, in effect, recommended against a *mutual* balance of terror in the sense that the two sides should be deterred comparably. He instead sought conditions in which the United States would be *less constrained* by the fear of nuclear escalation than would be Soviet leaders and, as a result, called for U.S. offensive and defensive strategic capabilities that could both threaten the Soviet Union effectively and limit damage to the United States in the event of war. According to Kahn, these capabilities were critical to the perceived credibility of the U.S. "nuclear umbrella," and were *uniquely* important for the United States because seemingly overwhelming Soviet conventional military capabilities were adjacent to regions vital to U.S. security; it was the West that depended on the threat of initiating nuclear escalation for deterrent effect. Soviet leaders had to be convinced that, in fact, the United States would escalate to nuclear war if severely provoked. In such conditions Kahn did not believe a *truly mutual* balance of terror could be adequate for U.S. and allied deterrence needs. The U.S. capability for deterrence relied on the threat of nuclear escalation and that threat, according to Kahn, had to be made credible.

Kahn and Schelling addressed different concerns. For Kahn the causes of nuclear war included the potential for a deliberate, calculated decision on the part of the Soviet leadership to advance dearly-held goals or to change the course of an intolerable situation, *despite the attendant uncertainties* of escalation. Uncertainties might not deter; they might even push a gambling, risk-tolerant opponent toward *a decision for war*—after all, uncertainty includes the possibility that things might just turn out better than should be expected.[87]

Kahn's goal was to identify a logical mechanism for deterring Soviet nuclear or conventional attack on the United States and its allies given the realities of Soviet nuclear and conventional military power, the acute hostility inherent in Soviet ideology, and apparent Soviet political aspirations to dominate parts of the world considered vital to U.S. security. Doubtful of the West's willingness to afford abundant conventional firepower, Kahn wanted to harness the deterring effect of credible nuclear escalation threats. For this purpose, he sought a U.S. deterrence strategy based on a credible threat of deliberate U.S. nuclear escalation to deter Soviet leaders who otherwise could decide to wage war despite the uncertainties of escalation or perhaps because of them. Kahn disdained the idea that Soviet uncertainties about U.S. nuclear escalation amid mutual threats to cities could provide an adequate basis for deterrence.

In contrast, Schelling believed adequate deterrent effect could come from Soviet uncertainties about U.S. behavior in a mutual balance of terror, which he would define as "stable" *if* both sides were confident in their retaliatory nuclear capabilities. He supposed that under such conditions neither likely would be motivated to strike first because there would be little or no strategic advantage in doing so. To ensure this confidence and prevent the reciprocal fear of surprise attack—which Schelling identified as an imaginable cause of a deliberate decision for nuclear war—he recommended strongly against the very "destabilizing" strategic capabilities that Kahn insisted were necessary for U.S. deterrence purposes.

Kahn and Schelling were brilliant theoreticians; they wrote about the same Cold War and both placed great value on identifying routes to the reliable deterrence of war. In working out their respective positions, however, they maintained differing judgments about the effects of uncertainty on decision making, the basis of and need for threat credibility for deterrence, and the plausible causes of deliberate war. Ultimately, they focused their respective concepts of deterrence on essentially different problems and threats. For Schelling, the goal became establishing and maintaining a stable, mutual balance of terror that would deter reliably. The primary threat to that happy condition was the "destabilizing" effect of forces that could incite reciprocal fears of surprise attack. The clear solution, thus, was to limit or avoid such "destabilizing forces" on both sides. For Kahn, the threats to be deterred centered on the potential for nuclear or conventional war stemming from the combination of Soviet military power, political aspirations, and Moscow's potential willingness to accept risks. Given this combination of factors, Kahn concluded that *Washington had to be in the position to threaten nuclear escalation credibly and deliberately, and that a truly mutual balance of terror thus posed a net threat to Western security.* These divergent judgments about what makes deterrence "work," the effects of uncertainty on decision making, and the nature of the problem to be addressed, led to wholly divergent recommendations about the types of U.S. strategic forces deemed adequate for Western deterrence needs.

A summary of the divergent presuppositions, judgments and recommendations at the heart of the two very different schools of thought represented by Schelling and Kahn appears below:

Competing Approaches to Deterrence:
Two Schools of Thought

Schelling's Stable Balance of Terror	Kahn's U.S. Advantage
Goal: U.S. and allied security via deterrence, and if deterrence initially fails, the prevention of escalation by the re-establishment of deterrence via graduated escalation steps.	**Goal**: U.S. and allied security via deterrence, and if deterrence initially fails, the prevention of escalation by the re-establishment of deterrence; in the event of utter deterrence failure, the capability to limit damage to the United States directly and significantly.
Means: The unavoidable, overwhelming mutual deterrent effect created by mutual, secure retaliatory nuclear threats to population and industry; the specific characteristics of the two strategic forces determine the cost-benefit calculations of each side, and thus their decision making.	**Means**: The deterrent effect on the Soviet leadership caused by U.S. strategic forces capable of threatening many Soviet targets— including nuclear forces—and significantly protecting U.S. and allied targets against Soviet attack. Those capabilities determine the cost-benefit calculations of each side, and thus their deterrent effect. U.S. damage-limitation capabilities mitigate losses if deterrence fails and make U.S. threats of escalation credible.

Basis for U.S. Deterrence Credibility: Soviet fear of the possibility of uncontrolled U.S. nuclear escalation; U.S. capabilities for graduated retaliation to reinforce Soviet fears and to help re-establish deterrence effect following initial failure: a "threat that leaves something to chance."	**Basis for U.S. Deterrence Credibility**: Soviet belief that the United States could deliberately initiate nuclear escalation, if necessary, to protect vital interests; U.S. capabilities to protect population to reinforce this Soviet belief: a threat that leaves little to chance.
Primary Problem for Deterrence Success: Mutual incentives to strike first from the loss of confidence by either side in the deterring effect of its retaliatory threat.	**Primary Problem for Deterrence Success**: Potential Soviet disdain for U.S. nuclear escalation threat, given Western conventional force disadvantages and U.S. vulnerability to Soviet nuclear attack.
Immediate Cause of Problem: Reciprocal fears of surprise attack instigated by "destabilizing" strategic offensive/defensive forces that threaten the effectiveness of retaliatory capabilities.	**Immediate Cause of Problem**: Soviet conventional force advantages and U.S. vulnerability to nuclear coercion, leading Soviets to calculated decision for severe provocation.
How to Address Challenge: Minimize reciprocal fears by limiting "destabilizing" strategic forces through unilateral and/or cooperative measures.	**How to Address Challenge**: Make U.S. first-use threat credible by denying the Soviet Union any reasonable expectation that it could deter the United States from nuclear escalation following an attack on its vital interests.

Prioritization of Deterrence and Damage Limitation: Stable deterrence is a higher priority than the limited level of damage limitation feasible; significant damage-limitation efforts would be ineffective, unnecessary and destabilizing, and thus incompatible with the priority goal of mutual deterrence.	**Prioritization of Deterrence and Damage Limitation**: The goals of deterrence and damage limitation are inseparable because damage limitation is necessary for U.S. deterrence credibility: imperfect damage-limitation efforts would be valuable because deterrence may fail.
Force Recommendations: Mutual deployment of relatively small, "stabilizing," secure forces for threatening retaliation against population and industry. Mutual avoidance of "destabilizing" strategic capabilities capable of undermining either side's retaliatory threat.	**Force Recommendations**: U.S. deployment of the offensive and defensive strategic systems necessary to threaten the spectrum of Soviet targets— including Soviet nuclear forces before and after their launch— and to significantly limit damage to U.S. society in the event of war.

It is important to recognize that both schools of thought were built on the belief that it was possible to predict with some confidence how U.S. and Soviet leaders would calculate costs and benefits and make decisions and, accordingly, manipulate deterrent effect by controlling the specific characteristics of strategic nuclear arsenals. They disagreed on the preferred characteristics of those arsenals for the reasons noted above, but both posited that manipulating those forces could create predictable deterrent effect; the character of the deterrence relationship could be orchestrated by adjusting the characteristics of the strategic arsenals.

Although they differed over the problem to be addressed and, correspondingly, the preferred characteristics of the forces, each confidently presented an approach to deterrence that was technically deterministic—although, it should be noted, Kahn placed greater emphasis on the possibility that deterrence could fail unpredictably and on the value of defensive preparation for such a catastrophe.

For Schelling's stable balance of terror school, extreme confidence in the predictability of deterrence based on the technical characteristics of the respective arsenals was particularly important. The formula for "stable" deterrence allowed little room for deterrence failure because it posited a stark tradeoff between strategic defenses and the goal of mutual deterrence, and eschewed defenses in adherence to the supposed requirements for deterrence stability. That is, Schelling's school recommended sacrificing the physical protection for society against Soviet attack that might otherwise have been available because deterrence *was believed to work reliably in the absence of, but not with, city defenses*. Glenn Snyder, for example, stated explicitly that the potential value of damage-limiting capabilities was directly and inversely related to this confidence in the functioning of deterrence:

> The value of all preparedness measures intended to reduce our losses or to make possible gains in all-out war tends to decline as the probability of war declines. If we had the high confidence deterrent we have been discussing, substantially insuring against all possible Soviet incentives for a first strike, the chances of war would be very low. In view of this, it seems doubtful that the defense benefits from having forces well beyond those necessary for high confidence deterrence would justify their peacetime costs.[88]

Bernard Brodie pointed to this preferred tradeoff favoring deterrence over defense in his comment that: "...peace is better than war not only in being more agreeable but also being very much more predictable. A plan and a policy which offers a good promise of deterring war is therefore by orders of magnitude better in every way than one which depreciates the objective of deterrence in order to improve somewhat the chances of winning."[89] In short, a policy goal of physical protection for U.S. society against nuclear attack was disdained because it was thought to "depreciate" deterrence.

To eschew defenses against nuclear attack as the accepted tradeoff for establishing stable deterrence required great confidence in the predictable functioning of deterrence: enemy leaders would be deterred from deliberate attack under virtually all plausible conditions; they would be prudent and cautious in the face of uncertainties, and deterrence would protect as predicted. If not, the rejection of defenses as the price to be paid for a stable balance of terror could only facilitate an unmitigated holocaust in the event deterrence failed.

Because Kahn recommended against a symmetric balance of terror and favored U.S. damage-limiting capabilities to provide a strategic advantage for the United States, he did not confront this same tradeoff and choice between deterrence and defenses. He posited full compatibility between U.S. deterrence goals and damage-limitation capabilities and, therefore, did not place priority on mutual deterrence at the expense of defenses. As such, Kahn's approach sought to deter war, but unlike Schelling, Kahn recommended against conditions that would facilitate an unmitigated holocaust for the United States in the event that deterrence utterly failed.

Kahn, however, did not escape from potentially important tradeoffs. The tradeoff Kahn confronted involved the possibility that the offensive and defensive damage-limitation capabilities he recommended would be ineffective for the purposes he specified and would lead instead to greater net risks to U.S. security, not increased safety. When considering the potential tradeoff between the possible security benefits of U.S. strategic defenses for cities and the possible risks involved in Soviet reactions to those U.S. defenses, Kahn placed priority on the deployment of defenses as opposed to avoiding the "destabilizing" effects posited by Schelling.

The question for Kahn was whether the security value of U.S. damage-limitation capabilities for deterrence and defense was greater than the possible risk to Western security that U.S. damage-limitation capabilities might generate by inspiring Soviet incentives for nuclear pre-emption and the acquisition of additional nuclear capabilities. In contrast to Schelling's answer to that question, Kahn concluded that defenses provided a powerful U.S. advantage and a net security benefit.

These very different approaches to deterrence—based on different judgments regarding the functioning of deterrence, the fundamental problem to be addressed, and the likely behavior of the opponent—led to contrary measures of merit for the strategic forces believed in each case to determine deterrent effect. These approaches also had differing levels of appeal to most audiences—Schelling's having far greater public acceptability. The subject of the next chapter is the set of powerful reasons for that appeal.

Endnotes

1. John Maynard Keynes, *The General Theory of Employment, Interest and Money* (New York: Harcourt, Brace and Co., 1936), p. 383.

2. See, Sun-Tzu, *The Art of War*, translated by J.H. Huang (New York: William Morrow and Company, Inc., 1993), p. 48.

3. See the discussion in, Keith B. Payne, *The Fallacies of Cold War Deterrence and a New Direction* (Lexington, KY: University Press of Kentucky, 2001), p. 43.

4. Ambassador Paul Robinson, President of the Sandia National Laboratory. Personal comment to author. Quoted with permission.

5. Both quoted in, Scott Sagan, "The Origins of the Pacific War," *Journal of Interdisciplinary History*, Vol. 18, No. 4 (Spring 1988), pp. 894, 906.

6. See, Alain C. Enthoven and K. Wayne Smith, *How Much Is Enough?* (New York: Harper & Row Publishers, 1971), p. 175.

7. See the discussion in, James Schlesinger, *Annual Defense Department Report FY 1975* (Washington, D.C.: USGPO, March 4, 1974), pp. 25-45. See also, William Van Cleave and Roger Barnett, "Strategic Adaptability," *Orbis*, Vol. 28, No. 3 (Fall 1974), p. 666.

8. Harold Brown, *Department of Defense Annual Report, Fiscal Year 1979* (Washington D.C.: USGPO, February 2, 1978), p. 55.

9. See, *Remarks Prepared for Delivery by the Honorable Harold Brown, Secretary of Defense, at the Convocation Ceremonies for the 97th Naval War College Class, Naval War College, Newport, Rhode Island*, August 20, 1980. See also the discussion in, Walter Slocombe, "The Countervailing Strategy," *International Security*, Vol. 5, No. 4 (Spring 1981), pp. 18-27.

10. Caspar W. Weinberger, "U.S. Defense Strategy," *Foreign Affairs,* Vol. 64, No. 4 (Spring 1986), pp. 680-681.

11. Ibid., p. 682. See also, Caspar Weinberger, U.S. Senate, Committee on Foreign Relations, *U.S. Strategic Doctrine,* Hearings, 97th Congress, 2nd Session (Washington, D.C.: USGPO, 1983), pp. 14-22.

12. Weinberger, "U.S. Defense Strategy," op. cit., pp. 676-677.

13. See, Robert Norris, William Arkin, and Thomas Cochran, *Nuclear Weapons Databook: Working Papers* (Washington, D.C.: Natural Resources Defense Council, July 1987), Tables 1 and 2.

14. Congress of the United States, Office of Technology Assessment, *The Effects of Nuclear War*, OTA-NS-89 (Washington, D.C.: USGPO, May 1979), pp. 94-95.

15. See, for example, Eugene Wigner's testimony in, U.S. House of Representatives, Committee on International Relations, Subcommittee on International Security and Scientific Affairs, *First Use of Nuclear Weapons: Preserving Responsible Control*, Hearings, 94th Congress, 1st Session (Washington, D.C.: USGPO, 1976), p. 90. See also, T.K. Jones and W. Scott Thompson, "Central War and Civil Defense," *Orbis*, Vol. 22, No. 3 (Fall 1978), pp. 681-712; and, Central Intelligence Agency, Director of Central Intelligence, *Soviet Civil Defense*, NI 78-10003 (July 1978).

16. Winston Churchill, House of Commons, March 1, 1955, in, *The Speeches of Winston Churchill: Blood, Toil, Tears & Sweat*, David Cannadine, ed. (Boston, MA: Houghton Mifflin Company, 1989), pp. 345-346.

17. "Implications for Military Policy," in Bernard Brodie, ed., *The Absolute Weapon* (New York: Harcourt Brace, 1946), p. 76.

18. See, Enthoven and Smith, op. cit., pp. 120-121.

19. Ibid.

20. Ibid., pp. 157-158.

21. Quoted in, Glenn H. Snyder, *Deterrence and Defense: Toward a Theory of National Security* (Princeton, NJ: Princeton University Press, 1961), p. 127.

22. *Strategic Balance and the Alliance*, Eighth International Wehrkunde Encounter, February 20-21, 1971, Munich, text, pp. 8, 9.

23. Quoted in, *Top Secret Memorandum of Conversation, NATO Meeting: NATO & MBFR*, The Cabinet Room, White House, November 19, 1970, in National Security Archive Electronic Briefing Book No. 192, p. 9 (Declassified July 17, 2003). Available at, http://www.gwu.edu/~nsarchiv.

24. U.S. Senate, Committee on Armed Services, *National Security Strategy*, Hearings, 100th Congress, 1st Session (Washington, D.C.: USGPO, 1987), p. 922.

25. Quoted in, Elizabeth Pond, "A Nuclear-Free Europe?" *The Christian Science Monitor*, April 23, 1987, p. 1.

26. Quoted in, Henry van Loon, "An Exclusive AFJ Interview With: General John R. Galvin, USA," *Armed Forces Journal International* (March 1988), p. 50.

27. "New Tapes: JFK Questioned Value of Nuclear Build-Up," John Fitzgerald Kennedy Library, released February 6, 2002, available at: http://www.jfklibrary.org/pr_tape_65.html.

28. Quoted in, *Top Secret Memorandum of Conversation, NATO Meeting: NATO & MBFR*, op. cit., p. 1.

29. Herman Kahn, *On Thermonuclear War* (Princeton, NJ: Princeton University Press, 1960), p. 133.

30. Michael Howard, "The Forgotten Dimensions of Strategy," *Foreign Affairs*, Vol. 57, No. 5 (Summer 1979), p. 983.

31. Kahn, op. cit., pp. 142-143.

32. Henry Kissinger, "The Future of NATO," in, *NATO, The Next Thirty Years*, Kenneth Myers, ed. (Boulder, CO: Westview Press, 1981), p. 8.

33. See, Thomas Schelling, *Arms and Influence* (New Haven, CT: Yale University Press, 1966), pp. 97-98.

34. Ibid., p. 99.

35. Thomas Schelling, *The Strategy of Conflict* (Cambridge, MA: Harvard University Press, 1960), p. 188.

36. Ibid., p. 187.

37. Schelling, *Arms and Influence*, op. cit., pp. 104-105.

38. See, ibid., pp. 38-47, 97-98; see also, Schelling, *The Strategy of Conflict*, op. cit., pp. 188-203.

39. Snyder, op. cit., p. 116.

40. Robert Jervis, "Why Nuclear Superiority Doesn't Matter," *Political Science Quarterly*, Vol. 94, No. 4 (Winter 1979-1980), p. 624.

41. See, Schelling, *Arms and Influence*, op. cit., pp. 102-112; and, Thomas Schelling, "Comment," in, *Limited Strategic War*, Klaus Knorr and Thornton Read, eds. (New York: Frederick Praeger Press, 1962), pp. 248-250.

42. Thomas Schelling, "Surprise Attack and Disarmament," in, *NATO and American Security*, Klaus Knorr, ed. (Princeton, NJ: Princeton University Press, 1959), p. 207.

43. Schelling, *The Strategy of Conflict*, op. cit., p. 196.

44. Kahn, op. cit., p. 32. (Emphasis in original).

45. Ibid., pp. 213-214.

46. Ibid., p. 287.

47. Ibid., p. 213. See also, Herman Kahn, "The Case for a Thin Defense," in, Johan Holst and William Schneider, Jr., eds., *Why ABM?: Policy Issues in the Missile Defense Controversy* (New York: Pergamon Press, 1969), pp. 63-90.

48. Herman Kahn, "Some Comments on Controlled War," in, Knorr and Read, eds., op. cit., p. 65.

49. Kahn, *On Thermonuclear War*, op. cit., p. 557. (Emphasis in original).

50. Kahn, "Some Comments on Controlled War," in, Knorr and Read, eds., op. cit., p. 61.

51. Ibid., p. 64.

52. For recent examples see, Sharon Ghamari-Tabrizi, *The Worlds of Herman Kahn* (Cambridge, MA: Harvard University Press, 2005); and, Louis Menand, "Fat Man: Herman Kahn and the Nuclear Age," *The New Yorker*, June 27, 2005, pp. 92-98.

53. James R. Newman, "Two Dimensions of Thermonuclear War," *Scientific American*, Vol. 204, No. 3 (March 1961), p. 197.

54. Ronald Sider and Richard Taylor, *Nuclear Holocaust & Christian Hope* (Downers Grove, IL: InterVarsity Press, 1982), p. 69.

55. Quoted in, Fred Kaplan, *The Wizards of Armageddon* (Stanford, CA: Stanford University Press, 1983), p. 228.

56. Thomas Schelling, "What Went Wrong With Arms Control?" *Foreign Affairs*, Vol. 64, No. 2 (Winter 1985/86), pp. 222, 233.

57. Thomas Schelling, U.S. House of Representatives, Foreign Affairs Committee, *Strategy and Science: Toward a National Security Policy for the 1970s*, Hearings, 91st Congress, 1st Session (Washington, D.C.: USGPO, 1969), pp. 151-152.

58. Schelling, *The Strategy of Conflict*, op. cit., pp. 207-229.

59. Schelling, *Arms and Influence*, op. cit., p. 225. See also, Jerome Kahan, *Security in the Nuclear Age: Developing U.S. Strategic Arms Policy* (Washington, D.C.: Brookings Institution, 1975), pp. 272-273, 282.

60. Schelling, *The Strategy of Conflict*, op. cit., p. 231.

61. Thomas Schelling, "Reciprocal Measures for Arms Stabilization," in *Arms Control, Disarmament and National Security*, Donald G. Brennan, ed. (New York: George Braziller, 1961), p. 170.

62. Schelling, *The Strategy of Conflict*, op. cit., p. 233.

63. Ibid., p. 207.

64. Schelling, *Arms and Influence*, op. cit., p. 227.

65. Ibid., p. 235.

66. Schelling, *The Strategy of Conflict*, op. cit., p. 251.

67. Ibid., p. 233.

68. Ibid., p. 231. (Emphasis added).

69. Ibid., p. 251.

70. Ibid., p. 232.

71. Ibid., p. 234.

72. Ibid., p. 233. See also, Schelling, "Reciprocal Measures for Arms Stabilization," in, Brennan, ed., op. cit., p. 167.

73. Schelling, *The Strategy of Conflict*, op. cit., p. 233. (Emphasis in original).

74. Ibid., p. 239.

75. Schelling, *The Strategy of Conflict*, op. cit., p. 236.

76. McGeorge Bundy, "To Cap the Volcano," *Foreign Affairs*, Vol. 48, No. 1 (October 1969), p. 10.

77. Testimony of Jerome B. Wiesner in, U.S. Senate, Committee on Foreign

Relations, Subcommittee on Arms Control, International Law and Organization, *ABM, MIRV, SALT, and the Nuclear Arms Race*, Hearings, 91st Congress, 2nd Session (Washington, D.C.: USGPO, 1970), p. 402.

78. Snyder, op. cit., p. 57.

79. McGeorge Bundy, William J. Crowe, Jr., and Sidney D. Drell, *Reducing Nuclear Danger* (New York: Council on Foreign Relations Press, 1993), p. 95.

80. Herbert York, *Race to Oblivion: A Participant's View of the Arms Race* (New York: Simon and Schuster, 1970), pp. 167-168.

81. Bernard Brodie, "The Anatomy of Deterrence," *World Politics*, Vol. 11, No. 2 (January 1959), p. 177.

82. See York's testimony in, U.S. Senate, Committee on Foreign Relations, Subcommittee on Arms Control, *ABM, MIRV, SALT, and the Nuclear Arms Race*, Hearings, 91st Congress, 2nd Session (Washington, D.C.: USGPO, 1970), p. 64.

83. Kenneth N. Waltz, "More May Be Better," in, Scott D. Sagan and Kenneth N. Waltz, *The Spread of Nuclear Weapons* (New York: W.W. Norton & Company, 2000), p. 22.

84. Jervis, op. cit., pp. 617-618. (Emphasis added).

85. York, *Race to Oblivion*, op. cit., p. 202. U.S. submarine-launched warhead numbers are from, John Collins and Patrick Cronin, *U.S./Soviet Military Balance Statistical Trends, 1970-1983*, Congressional Research Service, Report No. 84-1635 (Washington, D.C.: Congressional Research Service, August 27, 1984), p. 18.

86. Carl Kaysen, Robert S. McNamara, and George Rathjens, "Nuclear Weapons After the Cold War," *Foreign Affairs*, Vol. 70, No. 4 (Fall 1991), p. 105.

87. See the discussion in, Herman Kahn, "The Arms Race and Some of Its Hazards," in Brennan, ed., op. cit., pp. 90-99.

88. Snyder, op. cit., p. 117.

89. Bernard Brodie, *Strategy in the Missile Age* (Princeton, NJ: Princeton University Press, 1959), pp. 408-409.

Schelling vs. Kahn
Possible vs. Credible

Chapter 3
The "Stable" Balance of Terror Theory of Deterrence: A Multitude of Virtues

"To understand today, you have to search yesterday."
                                        -Pearl S. Buck

The claim that it is possible to know how to prevent deliberate nuclear war in a nuclear-armed world has enormous appeal. Both Schelling and Kahn presented the prevention of deliberate nuclear war as a tractable problem via deterrence, given the proper orchestration of forces. Schelling, however, rejected as contrary to mutual deterrence "stability" the types of offensive and defensive capabilities Kahn believed were necessary for *credible* deterrence and for protecting the United States and its allies in the event deterrence failed. In return, Kahn disdained Schelling's propositions that stable deterrence adequate for U.S. needs could be based on Soviet uncertainty and mutual nuclear threats to cities. Policies built on such notions and narrow capabilities, according to Kahn, would undermine U.S. deterrence effectiveness and contribute to an unmitigated holocaust in the event of deterrence failure.

Schelling's formula for a stable balance of terror, however, was far less demanding in terms of U.S. force requirements. It purportedly provided deterrence against the route to deliberate nuclear war and thereby made security against nuclear war relatively easy. His preferred deterrence framework benefited from this and other real and apparent virtues that were, and remain, particularly appealing to diverse American audiences. Not all of the virtues discussed here appealed to all audiences, of course, but the stable balance of terror formula offered much to many.

Easily Identified and Limited Requirements, at Modest Cost

Schelling's concept of the stable balance of terror, for example, established an elegant and apparently prudent basis for setting specific boundaries on offensive and defensive force requirements and thus on the cost of strategic force programs. The balance of terror identified an avenue for preserving U.S. and allied security while simultaneously *rejecting as unnecessary and potentially dangerous* strategic capabilities beyond the modest levels said to be adequate for stable deterrence.

The number of nuclear weapons necessary to threaten retaliation against Soviet society was reasonably calculable and finite; there was little or no deterrence value attributed to additional nuclear capabilities beyond the relatively modest numbers necessary to pose such a retaliatory threat. And, defensive capabilities to protect U.S. cities against the Soviet nuclear threat were to be eschewed as unnecessary, useless and "destabilizing." Kahn's recommended greater offensive and defensive strategic capabilities could be dismissed as unnecessary "overkill" and contrary to the priority goal of deterrence.

The advantages attributed to a stable balance of terror were breathtaking: the avoidance of deliberate war with the Soviet Union with little risk, rancor or expenditure. It was claimed that mutual deterrence from a balance of terror was a technical fact of life; jockeying for strategic advantage was unnecessary and useless because mutual vulnerability and the associated mutual deterrent effect was inescapable, "imposed by available technology."[1] It "worked," regardless of politics, personalities, or even whether the two powers found the arrangement acceptable. Rather than worrying about the details of military forces—a concern which had consumed so much energy in the past—considerable equanimity could now be the rule because imbalances in numbers of weapons that did not threaten mutual vulnerability would not be helpful or hurtful with regard to the technical reality of mutual deterrent effect.

In addition, as discussed above, a stable balance of terror would allow U.S. extended deterrence commitments—including the "nuclear umbrella" for NATO allies—to be met without the U.S. damage-limiting capabilities specified by Kahn as necessary for credibility; also, it would eliminate the need for a vast buildup of local conventional firepower to ensure an effective forward defense of Western Europe. NATO did not need to purchase the costly conventional forces required to defeat a concerted Soviet conventional attack because the Soviets could be deterred from such an extreme provocation by the obvious *possibility* of U.S. nuclear escalation.

NATO conventional forces needed to be able only to hold out the prospect of a war that could escalate. Local conventional forces that were incapable of defeating the Soviet Union could still provide security by posing the deterring prospect of an uncontrollable military conflict fraught with the possibility of U.S. nuclear escalation.[2] The concept often was illustrated by the metaphor of a plate glass door—a barrier easily penetrated but the breaking of which could obviously set off a dangerous and deterring escalation process.

In the American political context wherein the competition for budgets is fierce—both between defense and non-defense outlays, and within the defense budget itself—an easily-understood theory that suggests stable deterrence and security at a relatively modest cost, including strategic nuclear and conventional forces, is powerfully attractive. The U.S. Navy, in particular, presented its fleet ballistic missiles in terms of their value for a balance of terror.

Part of the genius and attractiveness of Schelling's stable deterrence formula is that it offered an elegant methodology for answering the question, "How much is enough?" for deterrence, with easy guidelines that could be treated numerically; the potentially messy and ambiguous was made clear. The requirements for establishing and preserving stability were simple to understand and to calculate in principle: the number of Soviet city targets could be counted easily, as could the likely number of U.S. nuclear weapons needed and available for retaliation, their probabilities of arriving on targets, and their gross effects on those targets. Stable mutual deterrence to prevent nuclear war could be reduced to a simple formula involving identifiable numbers and a few obvious technical characteristics of forces.

According to Harvard professor Stanley Hoffmann, the United States has long preferred an "engineering approach" to solving political foreign policy problems.[3] This was fully reflected in U.S. hopes for a "stable" balance of terror; it promised an easily understood technical solution to a daunting and unprecedented political threat, i.e., Soviet hostility, military might, and apparent aspirations for revolution on a global scale. It promised safety from deliberate nuclear attack if the United States simply orchestrated its nuclear force characteristics properly, and complemented them with relatively modest locally-deployed forces in Europe and other vital areas.

The Appearance of Scientific Objectivity and Numeric Precision

Such calculations—while relatively simple—allowed the requirements for deterrence stability to take on the important accoutrement of "objective" quantification, rendering precise and seemingly definitive answers to complex questions. The balance of terror framework and its elaboration were not scientific in any reasonable sense of the word, but benefited from seeming objectivity, precision, and the tools of quantification. Once the simple principles of stable mutual deterrence were understood—including the need for mutual retaliatory nuclear threats against cities, the avoidance of damage-limitation capabilities, and the categorization of forces as "stabilizing" or "destabilizing"—calculations could be made and definitive-sounding conclusions about deterrence and stability delineated. For a society unaccustomed to direct foreign threats and now under the nuclear gun, this was very comforting and convenient.

Armed with the balance of terror formula, those proffering comforting conclusions needed little, if any, specific knowledge about the Soviet Union per se, including its leadership's intentions, fears, worldviews, history, military organization, access to information, values, propensity to take risks, health and other variables. Mutual deterrence was a technical matter; the how's and why's of deterrence "working" were derived not from a close assessment of the Soviet Union and its leadership, but from generalized first principles that supposedly were true by definition *vis-à-vis* any sane leadership:

- Cities were the values to be threatened with retaliatory nuclear attack for deterrence purposes;
- The fear of that threat, plus the uncertain possibility of U.S. nuclear escalation, would provide an adequate basis for deterrence in plausible contingencies; and,
- Very particular types of force characteristics could be defined as "stabilizing" or "destabilizing" because they would limit or incite reciprocal fears of surprise attack.

The players of the day were the United States and the Soviet Union, but these generalized first principles did not depend on the specific character of either. There was nothing particularly U.S.- or Soviet-specific about this approach to mutual deterrence; it "worked" because of objective, inescapable technical conditions, not because of either side's goals, values, or character. This independence of the theory from the character of the countries involved was important because it meant that individuals with little or no familiarity with Soviet history, foreign policy goals, military organizations, political structure and leadership, and forces or doctrine, could render conclusions with precision and confidence on the details of how to deter that leadership, and could identify from generalized first principles what types of forces would be "stabilizing" or "destabilizing." In fact, because deterrent effect was inescapable and technically determined, expert-sounding discussions of deterrence could be based almost entirely on first principles, leaving behind all the ambiguous, messy questions of history and psychology, and the shifting details of politics, persons, doctrines and foreign policy. Expertise on the predictable preservation of peace apparently had become the province of a theory that sounded as if it were based on the apolitical and ahistorical calculations of physics and engineering.

The first principles of deterrence under a balance of terror were both easy to master and sufficient for detailed recommendations about U.S. deterrence policy and force acquisition. They seemingly were so simple that they could be, and literally were, summarized by advocates in an illustrated children's book.[4] Substituting generalized first principles for detailed knowledge of the Soviet Union with regard to the how's and why's of deterrence allowed almost anyone familiar with the few basic balance of terror principles, and possessing even rudimentary knowledge of strategic forces, to render confident conclusions about how deterrence would operate in general, and in the specific case of U.S.-Soviet relations. Armed with the balance of terror framework, and very little additional intellectual investment, anybody could be an apparent master of deterrence theory and strategy; it provided easy entrée into the business of deterrence strategy and nuclear policy. That constituted a powerful, and powerfully attractive, framework.

Balance, Symmetry, and Objectivity: Above Politics and Anti-Communism

In addition, the stable balance of terror framework for deterrence was built on metaphors that connoted symmetry, balance, equality, and an even-handed treatment of the antagonists. The countries could, in effect, be treated as interchangeable "actors" in the formula; neither side, in principle, needed to be thought of as posing a significantly different or greater challenge to peace and stability. Mutual threats to cities would provide mutual deterrence and mutual security because, regardless of the character or aspirations of the opponents, neither could escape the deterring effect brought about by inescapable technical realities.

The potential villain in this scenario was *not* the Soviet Union or Communism, but the potential "instability" of reciprocal fears of surprise attack caused by the technical characteristics of either side's forces. Addressing that problem did not require dealing with the ideological character of the Soviet Union; rather, it was amenable to orchestrating the proper form of the balance of terror. Technical characteristics of the weapons were the immediate problem and, if adjusted properly, also the mutual deterrence solution.

Because the particular political character of the opposing parties played little, if any, role in considerations of creating and managing a stable balance of terror, there was no need for discussion of the abiding and deep political conflict or judgments about the source of that conflict. The Soviet Communist Party's brutality, seemingly intractable hostility to the West, and its drive to revolutionize the international status quo did not need to be discussed. No unflattering assessments needed to be expressed about the Soviet leadership's goals or vices; no partisanship in the titanic Cold War ideological struggle needed to be exposed. Indeed, discussions of stability often did not even refer to the Soviet Union or the United States, but to "Countries A and B." This form of mutual deterrence and war prevention could be pristinely non-judgmental because the militarism and expansionism of the Soviet system could be deemed irrelevant to war causation and the question of deterrence stability.

Other than positing some level of mutual hostility, and thus the baseline need for deterrence, the particular political character of U.S.-Soviet hostility did not count for much in the balance of terror formula. Nuclear weapons were an apolitical, technical problem and the mutual deterrent effect of the balance of terror offered a technical solution enforced by the proper juxtaposition of threats that could not be escaped whatever the character of the political context.

The stable balance of terror was separate from and above what Winston Churchill described in a House of Commons speech as: "... antagonisms now as deep as those of the Reformation and its reaction which led to the Thirty Years' War. But now they are spread over the whole world instead of only over a small part of Europe. We have, to some extent, the geographical divisions of the Mongol invasion in the thirteenth century, only more ruthless and more thorough." Churchill fully attributed the cause of these antagonisms to, "... the Communist dictatorship and the declared ambition of the Communist Party and their proselytizing activities that we are bound to resist, and that is what makes this great world cleavage which

I mentioned when I opened my remarks."[5]

The stable balance of terror formula, however, transcended all the messy, sometimes arcane, ugly, and perplexing details of Soviet history, goals and behavior. Establishing and preserving the necessary forces for a stable balance of terror may have been a challenge, but not half so daunting and disturbing as acknowledging, let alone confronting, the threat posed by a hostile Soviet regime—its expansionist aspirations, high-intensity and aggressive ideology, and fundamental militarism.[6] That goal clearly was not susceptible to an easy technical fix; a stable balance of terror, however, presented a solution that got around all of the puzzling and brutal political extremism of the Soviet Union. In fact, that subject was rendered conveniently irrelevant because the character of the Soviet Union was not the security problem to be addressed per se; it was the technical characteristics of the weapons themselves.

Such a technical conceptualization of the security problem and deterrence stability allowed the analysis of deterrence and the prevention of war to avoid discussion of the Soviet system, to be non-judgmental, objective, and removed from partisan patriotism or favoritism; it could appear scientifically antiseptic. For many, talk that focused on the Soviet Union as a malevolent political system and a military threat had been discredited as unsophisticated anti-Communism and "McCarthyism." It was considered gauche in many political and academic circles. The balance of terror could avoid all of that with its ostensibly non-partisan analysis.

Indeed, the threat to deterrence stability and the impetus to arms competition at the time frequently were said to originate with U.S. "overreactions and technological excesses."[7] The attribution of the cause of "instability" to the technical characteristics of the U.S. arsenal and U.S. policies fit well with the emerging revisionist interpretations of Cold War history, which placed blame for the Cold War largely on Washington's anti-Communism. Commentators embracing the balance of terror formula often assigned blame for "destabilizing" systems and the pace of the nuclear arms race to American "...patriotic zeal, exaggerated prudence, and a sort of religious faith in technology."[8] This was part and parcel of the "anti-anti-Communism" tenor of the times. A popular adage drawn from a political cartoon of the period was that we had met the enemy and it was, indeed, us. In this case, who was responsible for threats to deterrence stability and the arms race? It was the U.S. governing establishment: "The guilty men and organizations are to be found at all levels of government and in all segments of society."[9] The Soviet Union might be hard to influence with regard to its nuclear forces and strategy—not to mention its ideology and foreign policy goals—but that was not terribly important because it was U.S. weapons and policies that posed instability problems: deterrence stability could be established if the United States would understand and follow the enlightened policies suited to a stable balance of terror.

The balance of terror framework provided a basis for arguing against U.S. spending for strategic programs at a time of growing political activism against the war in Vietnam—particularly among university students and faculty—and against defense spending and programs in general. In fact, critiquing U.S. strategic policy along balance of terror lines allowed proponents to combine the trappings of strategic sophistication with the progressive political activism of the 1960s and 1970s. Per the balance of terror formula for stable deterrence, by the mid-1960s it was a relatively simple matter to assert with seeming knowledge that U.S. strategic force requirements had long been met, stability was secure, and Washington should not pursue additional strategic offensive and defensive capabilities lest it "destabilize" the deterrence balance.

A telling anecdote along these lines was offered by Herbert York, a senior scientist and Pentagon official during the 1950s and 1960s. He tells of a nationwide series of student strikes and meetings in March 1969 to call attention to the relationship between academic institutions and "war research." Apparently much of the discussion focused on BMD: "At M.I.T. where the idea for the meetings originated, [world-renowned physicist] Hans Bethe, spoke before a multitude of students and faculty. He started by saying, 'You're here because you're against the ABM [Anti-Ballistic Missile defense]. I'm here to tell you why you are.'"[10]

Proponents of a stable balance of terror fancied it to be politically avant-garde—a sophisticated, new direction suited to the new nuclear era—and presented it as such. The pertinent expertise in this arena was not dominated by the traditional uniformed military. It "had no clear claim to special wisdom" in such matters;[11] pre-nuclear military experience and strategy now were said to be largely outmoded. In fact, the application of traditional military measures of merit to modern strategic questions was regarded as a problem.[12] Old ideas about war and strategy no longer held because, with nuclear weapons and a stable balance of terror, national security no longer came from superior military capabilities. Having greater capabilities than the enemy, defeating the enemy, taking and holding territory, striving for military advantage, or deploying defenses for society were deemed to have little relevance to modern strategic thought.

A new nuclear age had dawned and pursuing forces intended for such traditional purposes could "destabilize" the balance of terror. Modern thought focused on stability, the symmetry of mutual threats, mutual security, "crisis management," and war-prevention through mutual, shared risk. Compared to these scientific- and benign-sounding concepts, Kahn's notions of damage limitation and strategic advantage seemed primitive.

On those occasions when appearing "tough" was still important, identifying the nuclear capabilities necessary for a stable balance of terror could sound appropriately grim. But when a more avant-garde ambience was preferable, promoting a stable balance of terror certainly fit because each side could achieve its security through deterrence without challenging the other's security; old-fashioned striving (and spending) for strategic advantage could be disdained because it actually could harm security by undermining deterrence stability. Now, simultaneous mutual security through stable mutual deterrence was the *leitmotif*. International conflict no longer need be played as a competitive zero-sum game wherein one side's drive for security would cause the other's insecurity. Now, with the minimal effort necessary to establish and sustain a stable balance of terror, both sides could ensure their security simultaneously without provoking the other.

This was the new vision of reliable security through a benign and decidedly non-judgmental process of seeking mutual security and war-prevention, albeit based on mutual nuclear threats and the vulnerability of cities to nuclear destruction. These threats, however, were the passive backdrop of technical realities, not the reflection of malign, hostile intentions. In fact, *preserving* the vulnerability of cities now reflected the purely non-offensive goals of stable deterrence. For many, this vision contrasted sharply and favorably with Kahn's alternative framework and force recommendations that appeared to be for the purpose of preparing to win a nuclear war, not deterrence, and to put the United States on the road to nuclear "war-fighting."

McGeorge Bundy illustrated the importance of these virtues of impartial, even-handed, and benign-sounding mutual restraint in his own description of the attractive qualities of a stable balance of terror: "It deters quite impersonally; no provocative threats are needed to support its power. It deters both sides at once, since the unpredictable risk of catastrophe is essentially symmetrical. It makes full and impartial use of one of the great realities of nuclear weapons: they are far more terrifying to adversaries than they are comforting to their possessors."[13] Armed with the balance of terror formula for stability, proponents could stand above apparent political favoritism between East and West, and offer impartial, definitive, quantified prescriptions for mutual security; no unseemly anti-Communism or anti-Soviet judgmentalism was needed.

Vulnerability as Technical Certainty

The stable balance of terror framework also had apparent technical virtue. No one doubted the lethality of nuclear weapons against unprotected cities, or the technical challenge of protecting cities and populations against the Soviet nuclear threat to them. The burden of showing the technical feasibility of meaningful levels of defense against a determined Soviet threat was on those, such as Kahn, who recommended such a course. Some noted experts concluded simply that, for the foreseeable future, effective damage limitation for society was infeasible at any practical price if the Soviet Union wanted to maintain a threat to it.[14] This was the modern equivalent of British Prime Minister Stanley Baldwin's famous pre-World War II dictum that, "The bomber will always get through." Now, however, this condition was deemed advantageous; the stable balance of terror framework relied not at all on the feasibility of directly defending U.S. cities against Soviet attack. The reverse was true; it made a virtue of the apparent technical impossibility of defending cities against nuclear retaliation: their mutual, unavoidable vulnerability offered the deterrence solution to their mutual, unavoidable vulnerability.

A New Lodestone for Arms Control

The "stable" balance of terror also had the important virtue of being compatible with a new approach to arms control negotiations, an approach that seemed significantly more practicable than the illusive "ban the bomb" nuclear disarmament goal of the 1950s. Rather than continue trying to find political support in Washington and Moscow for complete nuclear disarmament—which seemed a distant prospect—the goal of negotiations now could focus on "stabilizing" mutual deterrence and the arms race by limiting the numbers and characteristics of strategic nuclear arsenals per the formula for a stable balance of terror.[15] The elusive vision of nuclear disarmament could be set aside for the more practical goal of facilitating a stable balance of terror.

The logic of the stable balance of terror formula suggested to many an elegant understanding of the immediate cause of the U.S.-Soviet arms race and, consequently, the potential basis for finding a solution via arms control. "Much of the arms race—both in the procurement and in the development of weapons—may involve each side's 'over-responding' to the other's behavior. Whatever aspect of the arms race we have in mind, it is usually some kind of reciprocated military preparation in which each side's force level or development or deployment is a response to what it perceives to be the other's forces, programs and deployments."[16] The arms race apparently was not about Soviet intentions and actions to meet expansive doctrinal requirements; rather, it reflected overreactions and misperceptions. If these overreactions and misperceptions could be addressed, each side could aspire to the cooperative equilibrium point in forces offered by a balance of terror.

As noted, the pace of the arms race typically was said to be driven by U.S. strategic force initiatives which, in turn, compelled the Soviet Union to respond to preserve its nuclear retaliatory capability—its side of the balance of terror. The arms race supposedly reflected this action-reaction cycle, led by U.S. actions which drove Soviet reactions. The solution, thus, was to use arms control to limit "destabilizing" U.S. initiatives so that Moscow would not be compelled to overreact. Schelling himself identified, but did not emphasize in his own writings, the notion that the supposed engine of the arms race was this U.S.-led action-reaction dynamic;[17] many others subsequently did.[18]

The potential solution to the arms race was clear enough: stop the action-reaction cycle. Both sides could act unilaterally or in cooperation to limit or avoid altogether deployment of those types of destabilizing forces which compelled the other to react. But the primary call was for the United States to follow a more enlightened path because—again in line with then-current revisionist histories of the Cold War—the United States typically was viewed as being in the forefront with the types of forces which compelled Soviet reactions, and it was thus U.S. strategic technological challenges to the Soviet Union that needed containment. Again, this type of arms control discussion and analysis was particularly attractive in the many academic and political circles where sharp condemnation of the Soviet Union was to be avoided, while active skepticism of U.S. policies was *de rigueur*.

What type of U.S. strategic force programs drove the Soviets to react with their own new programs to protect their retaliatory deterrent? Logically enough, it was those same systems that Schelling had already identified as "destabilizing" of the balance of terror because they posed a potential threat to retaliatory forces. U.S. movement toward missile defenses and offensive forces capable of threatening Soviet military targets would compel Moscow to build more and better strategic nuclear weapons in order to preserve its side of the balance of terror. Years before the beginning of the U.S.-Soviet Strategic Arms Limitation Talks (SALT) in 1969, Schelling expressed the "hope" that, "some kind of cooperation with the Russians, or mutual restraint, formal or informal, tacit or explicit, may prove to make a significant difference in the stability of the balance of terror; and the stakes of course are very high."[19] He suggested that negotiated measures to limit the vulnerability of either side's retaliatory nuclear forces—and thus preserve the certainty of each side's societal vulnerability—could help to enhance mutual deterrence. He remarked "how different this would be from the 'ban the bomb' orientation."[20]

The goal of negotiations in this regard would not be to disarm per se, but to limit or preclude those so-called "destabilizing" strategic forces thought to inspire reciprocal fears of surprise attack, such as missile defenses and offensive nuclear forces capable of threatening the other side's retaliatory capabilities. In principle, arms control measures thereby could help produce a stable balance of terror. As quoted earlier, Schelling observed, "Once we have identified the surprise-attack problem as the possible vulnerability of either side's retaliatory force to a first strike by the other, it becomes necessary to evaluate military strength, defensive measures, *and proposals for the inspection or limitation of armament*, with precisely this type of strategic vulnerability in mind."[21] Arms control was to facilitate the balance of terror by protecting the nuclear threats posed by each side's retaliatory weapons: "Schemes to avert surprise attack have as their most immediate objective the safety of weapons rather than the safety of people.... They seek to perfect and to stabilize mutual deterrence—to enhance the integrity of particular weapon systems."[22]

In principle at least, if both sides were motivated similarly to establish and sustain a stable balance of terror, such "schemes" would not pit the two sides against each other in competitive negotiations to secure strategic advantage; both could gain equally and simultaneously from the cooperative pursuit of mutual confidence in the vulnerability of U.S. and Soviet societies. This could be their common goal. With this vision, Kahn's ideas and recommendations of U.S. strategic advantage via significant defensive capabilities represented the *common problem* to be addressed. If such "destabilizing" forces could be limited or precluded, tacitly or by formal agreement, both sides could rest confident in their secure deterrent capabilities. An equilibrium point in strategic arms could be reached once each side had satisfied the relatively modest retaliatory capabilities required for a stable balance of terror because there would be no need for the continued buildup of strategic arms. Negotiations had a new purpose with a common goal—codifying this deterrence equilibrium point in armaments possible in a mutual balance of terror.

Establishing a "stable" balance of terror as the goal of arms control appeared to offer enormous advantages. At a time when nuclear disarmament seemed increasingly impracticable, it provided the grounds for identifying what arms control could do and how to do it. Purportedly it could promote stable deterrence by limiting or precluding "destabilizing" weapons—i.e., those that could pose a defensive threat to the retaliatory capabilities of either side or would present tempting targets by being deployed in a highly vulnerable fashion.[23] Success in arms control would equate to its contribution to stable mutual deterrence, and therefore it could be defined and even quantified with equal ease. This approach to arms control seemed to offer a mutually attractive agenda because promoting the stability of the balance of terror would be mutually advantageous.

In sum, the stable balance of terror approach to deterrence was extremely attractive because it integrated a theory of arms control with the preferred formula for deterrence to produce a practicable avenue for policies that could meet severe political challenges with elegant technical solutions. The overarching goal was to advance the stability of the balance of terror, and the immediate goal was to constrain or prohibit those force characteristics that could cause deterrence instability and lead to further cycles of the arms race, i.e., "to break the action-reaction cycle." Both goals supposedly pointed toward bringing under control U.S. strategic initiatives that threatened Soviet retaliatory capabilities. If this were done, "destabilizing" U.S. strategic force initiatives would cease and the Soviet Union would not be compelled to respond: action-reaction would be replaced by inaction-inaction, and the balance of terror would come to a mutually satisfactory equilibrium point in strategic forces. In the words of Herbert Scoville, former Deputy Director of the CIA and Assistant Director of the Arms Control and Disarmament Agency, the arms race could be capped because, "...in such a climate there would be little excuse for the Russians to continue building additional ICBM sites. In a situation of stable, frozen deterrence, they would not be needed."[24]

Morally Respectable Goals and Talk

Finally, and perhaps most surprisingly, the stable balance of terror formula had apparent moral virtue. This may seem unlikely, given that its basis was in mutual nuclear threats to cities and that the primary relevant Catholic and Protestant "Just War" doctrine includes centuries-old prohibitions against the intentional targeting of civilians. For many, however, the ostensible moral problem of massive nuclear threats to civilians was subordinate to the expected effect of those mutual threats, i.e., war prevention via mutual deterrence. The consequentialist argument that the balance of terror would reliably prevent nuclear war with minimal requirements took priority over old Just War principles against deliberately threatening civilians.

In addition, the balance of terror formula provided other important advantages in the moral debate about nuclear weapons. As noted above, it provided: an easily-understood delineation of "good" versus "bad" types of strategic forces; relatively modest force requirements and associated limitations on defense spending; a perspective that appeared to be "objective" and above political partisanship; the rejection of past strivings for strategic advantage and "destabilizing" offensive and defensive capabilities; an apparent compatibility with arms control negotiations; benign, impartial-sounding terms of art, e.g., stability, mutual deterrence and security, and balance; and, perhaps most importantly, it seemed to be the antithesis to Kahn's "war-fighting" school of nuclear deterrence.

In 1983 and 1988, the National Conference of Catholic Bishops issued reports that essentially embraced much of the stable balance of terror agenda as the interim solution to the threat of nuclear war, pending the establishment of a global authority with the capability for worldwide surveillance and the power to enforce nuclear disarmament.[25] The reports included the important Just War-oriented caveat that the United States not actually plan to strike at civilian targets. And, following Schelling's intellectual lead, the bishops also argued against U.S. missile defenses and U.S. planning and capabilities for strikes against Soviet military targets.

If civilian and military targets were off the books for U.S. strategic targeting, what then, according to the bishops, would be the basis for nuclear deterrence? The bishops confidently embraced Schelling's proposition that the existence of U.S. nuclear forces could provide adequate deterrent effect because Soviet *uncertainty* would deter; that uncertainty did not depend on U.S. targeting plans. Deterrent effect would be from Soviet uncertainty regarding the *chance* of U.S. nuclear escalation, not from the actuality of U.S. nuclear planning to strike civilian or military targets. Soviet fear that U.S. nuclear weapons *could* be launched would deter, even if there were no actual U.S. plans to do so. The bishops thus fully embraced Schelling's innovative notion that uncertainty about U.S. nuclear escalation could adequately deter Soviet leaders. With a stable balance of terror built on Soviet uncertainties vice actual U.S. nuclear strike plans, according to the bishops, U.S. policy could claim moral integrity and the benefits of stable deterrence too.

An Asymmetry of Appeal: "Stability" vs. "War-Fighting"

This kaleidoscope of virtues of the stable balance of terror framework appealed to most of the pertinent audiences in the United States and Europe. To be sure, not every segment of those audiences embraced, acknowledged, or cared about each of the above virtues but, taken together, they attracted wide support. The description of a stable balance of terror seemed to show an easy way to war prevention through symmetry and balance; it provided some simple "rules of thumb" without all the costly, technically-uncertain, strategic capabilities for damage limitation required by Kahn's framework for deterrence. And, whereas Kahn seemed to dwell on how to prepare for and conduct nuclear war—including chilling discussions of the number of likely casualties and survivors if deterrence failed—Schelling focused less on the potential conduct of nuclear war and more on the possible peacetime preparations that would deter deliberate nuclear war altogether.

Indeed, the stable balance of terror theory explained the prospective cause of deliberate nuclear war and how to prevent it via practicable, morally defensible, deterrence measures. It seemed to offer an easily calculable and understandable technical solution to the potential for deliberate nuclear war without the need to point to or address the harsh realities of Soviet political hostility and military expansionism, or even to study the Soviet Union seriously. It was apolitical and mechanistic; that was part of its beauty. Its simplicity, seeming objectivity, precision of formula, and relatively low cost were enormously attractive to military and civilian audiences. Moreover, it provided an easily understood explanation of the arms race and a practicable basis for integrating arms control negotiations with the prevention of war.

Finally, both Kahn and Schelling discussed nuclear threats. But, in expressing these threats, Schelling appeared simply to identify the proper orchestration of threats to prevent war via deterrence. The threats were not "real" in the sense of being intended to serve as guidance for the actual conduct of war; they made no sense in that light. Schelling's stable balance of terror tenets seemed to encompass mutual nuclear threats as a passive, benign backdrop for *preventing* deliberate nuclear war without rancor or even much effort. They were guidelines for the prevention of war, not its conduct. Schelling said publicly that he did not want to "sound warlike"[26] and, given the generally benign, impartial language with which one could discuss a stable balance of terror, that could be avoided. The balance of terror was about equilibrium points and preventing nuclear war, not planning for war or reducing the number of fatalities should war occur.

Some proponents of a stable balance of terror took advantage of these attributes of their favored approach to deterrence in the occasionally heated polemics that surrounded U.S. strategic policy debates. They presented the policy alternatives as being between a "stable" balance of terror that would reliably and economically deter war altogether—and thus prevent *any* fatalities—and Kahn's school which supposedly rejected deterrence in favor of nuclear "war-fighting," would increase the prospects of war, instigate an arms race, and offer no worthwhile prospects for mitigating the consequences of the nuclear war it was likely to unleash.

Much of the journalistic and cinematic treatment of the subject essentially adopted this polemical characterization as a shorthand-like description of the alternatives. Kahn's recommendation of U.S. strategic advantage via damage limitation was presented as an immoral, cavalier and outmoded military prescription for nuclear "war-fighting." A representative caricature can be seen, for example, in Stanley Kubrick's classic 1964 movie on the subject—a movie that remains popular today and continues to be shown on university campuses—*Dr. Strangelove, Or: How I Learned to Stop Worrying and Love the Bomb*. According to Kahn, Kubrick discussed the subjects of nuclear weapons, deterrence and war with him, and appears to present the above-described characterization of Kahn's views on damage limitation in the movie's dialogue. In a key scene, for example, "Gen. Turgidson" presents U.S. "President Muffley" with the possibility that there could be very different U.S. casualty levels in the coming nuclear war—twenty million versus a hundred and fifty million. "Gen. Turgidson" cavalierly compares the lower level of this casualty spectrum to having one's "hair mussed," and "President Muffley" responds by equating "Gen.

Turgidson's" proposals with Hitler's mass murder.[27]

Associating Hitler's name and a cavalier view of 20 million casualties with a position closely associated with Kahn—that there could be great variation in the outcome of nuclear war—suggests the intent of the portrayal. As noted already, Kahn's examinations of the potential conduct of war were elaborations on his views about how best to deter war, *not* cavalier musings about nuclear war.

Kahn's unaffected, trenchant assessment of the subject was as innovative and brilliant as Schelling's. His and Schelling's themes, however, seemed divergent and were presented quite differently, with Kahn depicted as relentlessly reviewing nuclear war scenarios, complete with statistics about fatalities and survivors. The goal of Kahn's discussion, of course, was to provide insight into the deterrence of Soviet attack altogether; but his work included long elaborations on the conduct of war, and thus posited the possibility of a nuclear war as an intellectual construct. Both schools posited nuclear war outcomes as part of their discussions of deterrence, but Kahn focused more on conflict scenarios while Schelling focused more on the pre-war decision making and maneuvering intended to make mutual deterrence "work" reliably and predictably. The greater appeal of the latter was inevitable.

The fundamental differences between these two alternative approaches had to do with differing expectations about opponent decision making, the nature of the threat, and the requirements for deterrence. The popular misimpression encouraged by some, however, was that the distinction was in Kahn's greater willingness to countenance the employment of nuclear weapons—a mischaracterization of the distinction dividing the two schools that continues to this day.

Kahn recognized the problem endemic to his message: "This is a difficult, unpleasant, and emotional subject; the points raised are often irritating or dismaying, and many readers transfer their irritation and dismay to the author."[28] Nevertheless, he typically pursued the subject in direct, unflinching language that did indeed disturb many. His testimony before a Congressional committee in 1969 elicited this response from then Pennsylvania Congressman James Fulton: "You are putting this cold war logic of nuclear war and overkill for two peoples in such remorseless terms that it actually almost drives a person of commonsense to seek some way to escape this conclusion." To which Kahn replied, "I used to make the comment to people who said they didn't like what they called icy rationality. I would say, 'Do you prefer a warm human error, a nice emotional mistake?'"[29]

Kahn made no apologies for his conclusions and recommendations; they were the logical result of his views of how deterrence should work and how it could fail despite our best efforts to deter. In addition, whatever the prospects for successful deterrence, Kahn reasoned that nuclear war could occur and that trying to ensure the survival of more people was preferable to not doing so. It was not the U.S. Government's prerogative, Kahn would claim, to facilitate the vulnerability of its citizenry in the hope that mutual deterrence via Soviet uncertainty would reliably be "stable." And, because he believed that U.S. capabilities to limit damage would also contribute to the U.S. deterrence of Soviet attack, he favored the simultaneous pursuit of deterrence and defensive strategic capabilities—particularly including civil and missile defense.

Kahn's position required faith in the technical feasibility of limiting the damage of a nuclear war to a meaningful level and that doing so would buttress deterrence effectiveness. In contrast, Schelling's recommendation *against* programs to mitigate the damage of a nuclear war in favor of an intentional, orchestrated condition of unmitigated societal vulnerability required faith that deterrence could be made to work predictably and reliably, and that a stable balance of terror was a practicable route to that goal.

Both positions essentially were based on a mechanistic portrayal of deterrence and on intuitive speculation about prospective Soviet decision making and behavior. Neither Schelling nor Kahn marshaled much by way of evidence beyond their own sophisticated presumptions and logical extrapolations from those presumptions to demonstrate *why* their particular beliefs about the opponent, credibility, uncertainty, and the functioning of deterrence should have been considered more reasonable. Schelling acknowledged the essentially intuitive basis of at least some of his expectations about the functioning of deterrence: "You can sit in your armchair and try to predict how people will behave by asking how you would behave if you had your wits about you. You get, free of charge, a lot of vicarious empirical behavior."[30]

If put into practice, both sets of recommendations had the potential to fail catastrophically. Kahn's policy direction recommended preparation for the failure of deterrence and, to the extent that damage limitation was feasible, it was less vulnerable in principle to the possibility that nuclear deterrence was not as well-understood or predictable as expected, and might fail or function unpredictably in practice.

Chapters 4 and 5 examine how the pathbreaking conceptual work on deterrence by Schelling and Kahn contributed to U.S. strategic policy development from the early 1960s on. Of the two, it is evident that Schelling's intellectual framework and recommendations had the greater influence on U.S. declared deterrence strategy and force acquisition policy. The multitude of real and apparent virtues discussed above appears to have had an enduring impact.

— neither theory based on anything other than "intuitive speculation"!

Endnotes

1. As described in, Glenn C. Buchan, "The Anti-MAD Mythology," *Bulletin of the Atomic Scientists*, Vol. 37, No. 4 (April 1981), p. 13.

2. Thomas Schelling, *The Strategy of Conflict* (Cambridge, MA: Harvard University Press, 1960), p. 199.

3. See, Stanley Hoffmann, *Gulliver's Troubles, or, The Setting of American Foreign Policy* (New York: McGraw-Hill for the Council on Foreign Relations, 1968), p. 146.

4. See, Herbert Scoville and Robert Osborn, *Missile Madness* (Boston, MA: Houghton Mifflin, 1970).

5. Winston Churchill, House of Commons, March 1, 1955, in, *The Speeches of Winston Churchill: Blood, Toil, Tears & Sweat*, David Cannadine, ed. (Boston, MA: Houghton Mifflin Company, 1989), pp. 339, 343.

6. For a discussion of the security problems posed by "high-intensity aggressive ideologies," see, Yehezkel Dror, "High Intensity Aggressive Ideologies as an International Threat," *The Jerusalem Journal of International Relations*, Vol. 9, No. 1 (1987), pp. 153-172.

7. Herbert York, *Race to Oblivion: A Participant's View of the Arms Race* (New York: Simon and Schuster, 1970), p. 234.

8. Ibid.

9. Ibid.

10. Ibid., p. 199. The same occasion is presented in, Donald R. Baucom, *The Origins of SDI: 1944-1983* (Lawrence, KS: University Press of Kansas, 1992), p. 42.

11. Alain Enthoven and K. Wayne Smith, *How Much Is Enough? Shaping the Defense Program, 1961-1969* (New York: Harper and Row, 1971), p. 201.

12. Ibid., pp. 199-203.

13. McGeorge Bundy, "Existential Deterrence and Its Consequences," in *The Security Gamble: Deterrence Dilemmas in the Nuclear Age*, Douglas MacLean, ed. (Totowa, NJ: Rowman & Allanheld, 1984), p. 10.

14. There are numerous examples of this conclusion. See, for example, York, op. cit., pp. 188-212; and, McGeorge Bundy, William J. Crowe, Jr., and Sidney D. Drell, *Reducing Nuclear Danger* (New York: Council on Foreign Relations Press, 1993), p. 93.

15. Thomas Schelling, prepared testimony, U.S. House of Representatives, Committee on Foreign Affairs, Subcommittee on National Security Policy and Scientific Developments, Hearings, 91st Congress, 1st Session, *Strategy and Science: Toward a National Security Policy for the 1970's* (Washington, D.C: USGPO, 1969), p. 135.

16. Thomas C. Schelling and Morton H. Halperin, *Strategy and Arms Control* (New York: The Twentieth Century Fund, 1961), p. 101.

17. Schelling, *Strategy and Science: Toward a National Security Policy for the 1970's*, op. cit., p. 124.

18. The classic article asserting that the U.S.-led action-reaction dynamic caused the arms race is, George Rathjens, "The Dynamics of the Arms Race," *Scientific American* (April 1969). Reprinted in, *Arms Control: Readings From Scientific American* (San Francisco, CA: W. H. Freeman and Company, 1973), pp. 177-187. That this action-reaction metaphor was key to considerations of senior U.S. officials is attested to in, Robert S. McNamara, *The Essence of Security: Reflections in Office* (New York: Harper and Row, 1968), pp. 58-67.

19. Schelling, *The Strategy of Conflict*, op. cit., pp. 251-252.

20. Ibid., p. 241.

21. Ibid., p. 234. (Emphasis added).

22. Ibid., p. 233.

23. Ibid., p. 241.

24. Herbert Scoville, "Next Steps in Limiting Strategic Arms," *Bulletin of the Atomic Scientists*, Vol. 28, No. 3 (March 1972), p. 11.

25. See, especially, the discussion in, National Conference of Catholic Bishops, "The Challenge of Peace: God's Promise and Our Response," *Origins*, Vol. 13, No. 1 (May 19, 1983).

26. Schelling, *Strategy and Science: Toward a National Security Policy for the 1970's*, op. cit., p. 125.

27. *Dr. Strangelove: A Continuity Script*, available at www.tigersweat.com/movies/strangel.

28. Herman Kahn, "The Arms Race and Some of Its Hazards," in *Arms Control, Disarmament and National Security*, Donald G. Brennan, ed. (New York: George Braziller, 1961), pp. 89-90.

29. Herman Kahn, U.S. House of Representatives, Committee on Foreign Affairs, Subcommittee on National Security Policy and Scientific Developments, Hearings, 91st Congress, 1st Session, *Strategy and Science: Toward a National Security Policy for the 1970's* (Washington, D.C.: USGPO, 1969), p. 154.

30. Quoted in, Kathleen Archibald et al., *Strategic Interaction and Conflict: Original Papers and Discussion* (Berkeley, CA: Institute of International Studies, University of California, 1966), p. 150.

Chapter 4
The Competition for U.S. Policy

"One cannot fashion a credible deterrent out of an incredible action."
-Robert S. McNamara

Which school of thought—Schelling's stable balance of terror or Kahn's U.S. advantage—became the basis for actual U.S. policy? Plausible answers to the question could be neither, both, or the stable balance of terror. U.S. policy never has been an unalloyed reflection of Kahn's recommended U.S. advantage or Schelling's definition of a stable balance of terror. Generally, U.S. policy has reflected selected elements of both simultaneously. From the early 1960s on, however, with some notable exceptions the U.S. acquisition of strategic forces, declarations about deterrence and nuclear weapons, and strategic arms control goals were guided increasingly and stubbornly by the basic tenets of a stable balance of terror.

Posing the above question—Which school was the policy "winner"?—is not to imply necessarily that Schelling and Kahn saw themselves in a direct competition for preeminence in actual U.S. strategic policy, or aspired to so compete. Schelling, in his brilliant text, *Arms and Influence*, wrote that he sought not to advance particular policies, but to "discern a few of the principles that underlie this diplomacy of violence" pertinent across time and place.[1] His development of a strategy of conflict was for the self-declared purpose of advancing "the theory of interdependent decision."[2] He acknowledged that his working assumptions of rational, consistent and "cool headed" decision making were of limited value for recommending actual policies because they, "...could prove to be a good approximation of reality or a caricature," and that, "whether the resulting theory provides good or poor insight into actual behavior is, I repeat, a matter for subsequent judgment."[3]

Alexander George and Richard Smoke offered the same caveat regarding the direct application of abstract deterrence theory to actual policy in *Deterrence in American Foreign Policy: Theory and Practice*, their classic examination of deterrence in history: "Substantively, deterrence theory is seriously incomplete, to say the least, for a normative-prescriptive application."[4] These great, original contributors to deterrence theory fully recognized that the basic tenets of theory alone were an inadequate basis for making specific policy recommendations.

Whether or not Schelling or Kahn saw themselves in competition for policy, the concepts and theories they developed during the Cold War—in company with other brilliant contributors, such as Bernard Brodie, Albert Wohlstetter and Glenn Snyder—constituted the conceptual cores of these two different schools of thought that did compete for primacy in the formulation of U.S. policy.

Deterrence Threats: The Targets for "Assured Destruction"

From the early 1960s to the mid-1970s, U.S. officials publicly discussed nuclear deterrence largely in terms of threatening Soviet cities and industry with "assured destruction," including the destruction of specific percentages of Soviet population and industry. [U.S. nuclear deterrence policy came to be associated with the threat of destroying Soviet cities.] As noted in Chapter 2, the science advisor to Presidents Kennedy and Johnson, Jerome Wiesner, claimed in Congressional testimony that deterrence of the Soviet Union could be established firmly on the basis of a U.S. threat to destroy six of the ten largest Soviet cities.[5]

Actual U.S. force planning was considerably broader than was suggested by such statements. In Secretary of Defense Robert McNamara's Top Secret Draft Presidential Memorandum to President Kennedy dated September 23, 1961, he included 200 "urban/industrial" targets *with an array of selected Soviet military capabilities* in the list of "high priority" targets for U.S. nuclear weapons.[6]

From the early 1970s to the end of the Cold War, official public statements increasingly moved away from discussing U.S. nuclear deterrence strategy in terms of threats to Soviet population and industry alone. By the mid-1980s, U.S. officials observed publicly that U.S. strategy sought to avoid targeting population per se. In 1985, for example, Secretary of Defense Caspar Weinberger stated that, "...our strategy consciously does not target population and, in fact has provisions for reducing civilian casualties."[7] U.S. official public discussions increasingly emphasized threats against a spectrum of Soviet military targets, including the capability to threaten Soviet nuclear forces.[8] Nevertheless, official U.S. pronouncements regarding strategic forces continued to reflect a conscious, strong presumption against the acquisition of offensive and defensive strategic forces sufficient to threaten seriously the Soviet nuclear retaliatory potential. Such an objective was labeled "destabilizing," per Schelling's formula, and U.S. policy consciously limited U.S. forces from becoming so capable.

Damage Limitation: Ballistic Missile Defense

Ballistic missile defense (BMD), so emphasized by Kahn, went through periods of intense favor and equally intense disdain, but there was no serious deployment of BMD during the Cold War. Secretary of Defense McNamara, for example, strongly *opposed* the deployment of the 1960s *Nike-X* BMD program for the defense of U.S. cities against Soviet missile attack. In 1967, however, he announced the Johnson Administration's decision to deploy the *Sentinel* BMD system to help provide effective societal protection against a potential Chinese nuclear attack. In doing so, as will be discussed below, Secretary McNamara simultaneously expressed his commitment for a *stable balance of terror vis-à-vis the Soviet Union*, but made the intellectual case for rejecting it as the basis for U.S.-Chinese relations in favor of the damage-limitation capabilities necessary to defend against a Chinese nuclear attack.

The Nixon Administration entered office well before the *Sentinel* defense against Chinese missiles could be deployed. There was heated public and Congressional debate about the program, with the criticism largely derived from the stable balance of terror desiderata. In response, the Nixon Administration renamed the BMD program *Safeguard* and reoriented it to provide protection *not for cities*, but for U.S. strategic retaliatory capabilities. President Nixon's announcement of this decision was couched wholly in terms of a stable balance of terror. His declared defensive goal followed the balance of terror formula for stable deterrence, namely, BMD protection for U.S. retaliatory capabilities was acceptable but defending U.S. society was not.

Despite the Nixon Administration's reorientation of the BMD program, sharp public and Congressional criticism of *Safeguard* continued; it was argued that the Soviets still would see it as a destabilizing threat to their retaliatory forces. This debate ended in 1972 when the question of U.S. BMD deployment was settled by the U.S.-Soviet Anti-Ballistic Missile (ABM) Treaty. The Treaty effectively limited BMD development, testing, and deployment on the balance of terror-derived arguments that the policy priority was stable mutual deterrence, and that BMD could not provide a useful level of protection, would destabilize mutual deterrence, motivate an arms race, and preclude arms control. In September 1975, the Ford Administration deployed a single *Safeguard* BMD site as then allowed by the ABM Treaty. That solitary deployment, however, could find no plausible rationale, lost support in Congress, and was deactivated in February 1976.

The debate over BMD resurfaced with great gusto in 1983 when President Reagan initiated the Strategic Defense Initiative (SDI), with the long-term goal of providing comprehensive protection of U.S., allied, and possibly Soviet cities, against nuclear missile attack. The SDI, popularly called "Star Wars," brought on another round of sharp public debate about strategic BMD. Despite President Reagan's initiative, the Cold War ended with the ABM Treaty intact and no actual BMD deployment beyond the short-lived single *Safeguard* site deployed during the Ford Administration.

National debates about BMD from the late 1960s to the end of the Cold War typically found the executive branch and Congress taking opposing positions for or against it at different times. The political consensus necessary to sustain deployment never materialized, and the arguments against BMD throughout the period consistently came from the stable balance of terror canon.

Damage Limitation: Air Defense and Civil Defense

During the 1950s and early 1960s, U.S. defensive efforts included the significant deployment of interceptor aircraft and missiles to defend against Soviet strategic bomber attack. During the latter half of the Cold War, however, in line with the balance of terror's mandate of mutual vulnerability, the United States eliminated most of its strategic air defense capabilities. Secretary McNamara's opposition to the deployment of BMD to defend against Soviet missiles left little room for defending against Soviet bombers—to be vulnerable to the former but defend against the latter made no sense. In 1960, the United States deployed 2,700 strategic defensive interceptor aircraft and 4,400 strategic air defense missile launchers to protect U.S. territory from bomber attack. By 1980, the United States had reduced those defensive capabilities to 273 interceptor aircraft and zero defensive missile launchers.[9] U.S. strategic air defense came to be described in Department of Defense publications as providing "...the U.S. with forces for limited day-to-day control of U.S. airspace *in peacetime*," and with "surge" capabilities to "... a) defend against limited attacks, b) raise the uncertainty that must be considered by offensive planners, and c) deny any intruder a free ride in [U.S.] airspace."[10] The provision of defenses for such narrow purposes as the "limited" control of U.S. airspace *in peacetime* and increased "uncertainty" for Soviet offensive planners perfectly fit the role for defenses within the balance of terror narrative.

U.S. civil defense programs for population protection against nuclear attack followed a similar course of decline. During the early 1960s, U.S. annual spending on civil defense reached an apogee of almost $1 billion (in 1982 dollars). By the end of the 1960s, it had declined to under $200 million annually, and settled in at approximately $150 million per year throughout the 1970s.[11] Such a low level of spending had been described by Secretary of Defense McNamara, again with no apparent intended irony, as one which bought "an organization, but [did] not buy a program."[12]

Civil defense to protect the population against attack appeared to be on the verge of gaining favor again in the late 1970s. In 1978, President Jimmy Carter issued Presidential Directive/NSC-41 (PD-41) entitled, *U.S. Civil Defense Policy* (Secret; declassified on June 23, 1980). PD-41 specifically referred to the potential for crisis relocation of urban populations and called on civil defense as an element of the strategic balance to, "… assist in maintaining perceptions of that balance favorable to the U.S." It also called for a U.S. civil defense program to, "…provide some increase in the number of surviving population and for greater continuity of government, should deterrence and escalation control fail.…"[13]

The Director of the Defense Civil Preparedness Agency during the Carter Administration, Bardyl Tirana, testified before a committee of the House of Representatives that: "The President's policy decision supported the Secretary's [of Defense] program recommendation, which was designed to result ultimately in survival of at least two-thirds of the U.S. population in a large-scale, mid-1980s attack, given at least a week in which evacuation plans were executed and other preparations made."[14] This Carter Administration policy direction for civil defense suggested political support for Kahn's agenda of providing protection of the population against nuclear attack, both to contribute to deterrence and to mitigate damage if deterrence failed.

Despite these favorable policy words and the suggestion of political support, U.S. spending on civil defense did not appreciably increase in the years following PD-41.[15] In 1979, Bardyl Tirana reported that, if funded, the average cost for the President's PD-41 civil defense program in years 1980 through 1984 would have been $230 million annually.[16] Nevertheless, the Carter Administration ultimately requested only $108 million for 1980, and Congress provided still less, $99 million. As William Odom, a senior official in the National Security Council during the Carter Administration has since observed, PD-41 raised the visibility of the value of civil defense, but ultimately not spending.[17]

The Balance of Terror Formula for Stable Deterrence: Dominant Norms From the Mid-1960s Onward

As the above brief summary illustrates, in terms of the U.S. strategic capabilities actually deployed during the Cold War, neither Kahn's nor Schelling's school was a decisive "winner" to the full exclusion of the other. U.S. policy embraced some of Kahn's recommendations and some of Schelling's, with the emphasis shifting over time in favor of stable balance of terror guidelines. In general, as the Cold War matured through the 1960s, 1970s, and 1980s, U.S. officials gave limited support to Kahn's recommendations regarding offensive force requirements for deterrence, while Schelling's concept of stable mutual deterrence and the rejection of direct protection for U.S. cities dominated the U.S. acquisition of forces.

Schelling himself discussed how the ideas about deterrence and arms control with which he was closely associated were translated directly into policy beginning in the early 1960s: "A number of participants in the Harvard-MIT seminar took positions in the Kennedy White House, Department of State and Department of Defense; others from RAND and elsewhere, who had been part of this intellectual movement, moved into the government as well. So it is not completely surprising that those ideas became the basis for U.S. policy and were ultimately implemented in the ABM Treaty."[18]

A book detailing the intellectual development of these ideas and their translation into policy, *The Wizards of Armageddon*, reaches essentially the same conclusion: with the 1960 election of President Kennedy, the ideas about nuclear weapons and deterrence developed by Schelling and Brodie and elaborated at the RAND Corporation were brought directly into the Pentagon with the new Secretary of Defense and his chosen senior officials.

The subsequent near-decade-long promulgation and institutionalization of those ideas set them firmly in U.S. thought on the subject: "By the 1970s and especially the eighties, the ideas of these thermonuclear Jesuits would have so thoroughly percolated through the corridors of power—and through their annexes in academia—that, at least among fellow members of the congregation, their wisdom would be taken almost for granted, their assumption worshipped as gospel truth, their insight elevated to an almost mystical level and accepted as dogma."[19]

When viewed from the perspective of the Cold War evolution of U.S. policy and the longevity of ideas, the influence of Schelling's guidance for a stable balance of terror was overwhelming. This influence did not result in his specific force recommendations ever being adopted fully, but Schelling's desiderata for a stable balance of terror—his terms of art, definition of stable deterrence, the requirements for stability and its associated measures of merit for strategic forces—were well-absorbed and established in the policy-making process by a broad cadre of U.S. officials and commentators. That framework has shaped the development of actual U.S. policy since the early 1960s by capturing the language and definitions used in government offices and, more broadly, in national debates and commentary on the subject. Schelling's Cold War deterrence language and concepts have outlived the Cold War itself, and continue to influence contemporary national debates about strategic forces and policy.

John Newhouse, the author of the quasi-official account of the Strategic Arms Limitation Talks (SALT) negotiations during the Nixon Administration, *Cold Dawn: The Story of SALT,* described the two dramatically different schools of thought in religious terms, and rightly concluded that the stable balance of terror school—which he refers to as "assured destruction"—had become preeminent in U.S. policy formulation:

> Debates between the two schools recall those between the Thomists and the essentially Franciscan followers of Duns Scotus. The Thomists prevailed, as have the proponents of assured destruction, who assert, for example, that ballistic-missile defense of population is immoral because it may degrade your adversary's ability to destroy your own cities in a second strike. His confidence undermined, he might then be tempted in a crisis to strike pre-emptively; in short, knowing you are effectively protected from his second-strike assault and fearing your intentions, he may choose to strike first. Thus, stability, a truly divine goal in the nuclear age, becomes the product of secure second-strike

[handwritten annotation in right margin: missile defense is destabilizing]

nuclear offenses on both sides. This offensive capability is known as assured destruction; *it is the supreme dogma of the ascendant branch of the defense and arms-control communities.*[20]

In fact, "assured destruction," with its focus on threatening Soviet cities for deterrent effect, was but one variant of the broader balance of terror formula and, as noted above, U.S. offensive threats came to include a spectrum of possible Soviet targets. Nevertheless, the stable balance of terror approach to deterrence became the "ascendant branch" because Schelling's basic tenets about the goals and functioning of deterrence came to dominate how "stability" was defined, how strategic forces were judged for value, the fundamental goals of strategic arms control, and the jargon used to discuss these subjects in most of the popular media, academic settings, the halls of Congress, and in many offices in the White House, State Department and Pentagon. Schelling's propositions that achieved such power included:

- Confidence in the deterring effect of uncertainty and in the potential for deterrence to be orchestrated to function reliably and predictably.
- The central problem of "instability" as revolving around "reciprocal fears of surprise attack."
- The definition of deterrence "stability" as coming from a mutual balance of terror.
- The categorization of forces as being "stabilizing" or "destabilizing" per their expected contribution to a stable balance of terror and the corresponding presumption against the deployment of defenses for society.
- The definition of arms control goals in terms of facilitating a stable balance of terror.

In particular, from the mid-1960s until the end of the Cold War, there was a powerful consensus across much of the political spectrum that the priority U.S. goal was a stable balance of terror. With some greater license for including targets beyond Soviet cities as the basis for U.S. deterrence threats, this consensus followed Schelling's guidelines. A powerful continuing theme in U.S. strategic policy was that stability could be orchestrated reliably by the maintenance of secure U.S. offensive, retaliatory threats that would compel the Soviet Union to confront uncertainties regarding the potential for U.S. escalation, and by the limitation of purportedly "destabilizing" forces in the U.S. strategic arsenal. In addition, the U.S. goal of strategic arms control came to be accepted as part of that orchestration.

Much of Schelling's carefully-nuanced and deductive discussion of a stable balance of terror was lost in the intense, polemical and occasionally vitriolic U.S. policy debates regarding strategic forces. His careful arguments often were reduced to shorthand "bumper stickers" that came to be accepted as distilled truths about deterrence, the acquisition of strategic forces, and arms control goals. These distilled truths included the propositions that "stable" mutual deterrence:

- Could be made to "work" reliably and predictably;
- Required *mutual* societal vulnerability;
- Was antithetical to significant U.S. offensive counterforce or defensive capabilities to destroy Soviet strategic retaliatory forces; and,
- Constituted a realistic basis for negotiating strategic arms control agreements by offering an equilibrium point of mutual vulnerability that would cap either side's incentives to build strategic arms.

In addition, Schelling's innovative proposition that the "chance" of U.S. escalation could be sufficient for extended deterrence to "work" reliably—even when a deliberate U.S. decision to execute its nuclear threat would not be reasonable—became the linchpin of U.S. and NATO deterrence policy, and remains a powerful norm in U.S. thinking about deterrence.

Uncertainty and Extended Deterrence

By the late 1960s, the expectation that uncertainty would deter Soviet leaders was at the heart of NATO's nuclear deterrence policy and the rationale for NATO's locally-deployed conventional forces; the latter were to serve as a "trip wire," or "plate glass" barrier to Soviet conventional attack. These forces were to provide the visible linkage to the *possibility* of U.S. nuclear escalation that was expected to deter Soviet attack: NATO forces did not need to be so capable as to defeat a concerted Soviet invasion, but they had to be sufficiently robust to provide the linkage to that deterring possibility of nuclear escalation.

Schelling's proposition that extended deterrence could be based on a balance of terror, with locally-deployed conventional forces and the capability for graduated nuclear escalation highlighting the possibility of general nuclear war, dominated U.S. and NATO thinking about extended deterrence. In 1988, for example, Joseph Nye, Harvard professor and an Assistant Secretary of Defense during the Clinton Administration, essentially repeated Schelling's themes when explaining the requirements for extended deterrence: "Extended deterrence does not require elaborate theories of escalation control. So long as a Soviet leader can see little prospect of a quick conventional victory and *some risk of events becoming out of control and leading to nuclear escalation*, the expected costs will outweigh greatly any benefits."[21]

Sir Lawrence Freedman, a leading British voice on these matters, again affirmed Schelling's belief that effective extended deterrence could be based on Soviet uncertainties *as opposed to the logical credibility of a deliberate U.S. decision* of nuclear escalation outlined by Kahn:

> Since 1945 Europe has been at peace. This underlines the point that nuclear deterrence may be a viable policy *even if it is not credible*; the legion of uncertainties means that no one could contemplate aggression with a confident forecast of the full consequences. Despite preparations for nuclear war as if it could be tamed and controlled, it is probably the fear of the whole process getting out of control that is the strongest source of caution in the modern world. The Emperor Deterrence may have no clothes, but he is still Emperor.[22]

The belief that high confidence in deterrence did *not* require Soviet anticipation of deliberate U.S. escalation to general nuclear war, but could rest on Soviet *uncertainty* regarding U.S. behavior, was not limited to academic-sounding statements. During the Cold War, the official *NATO Handbook* similarly read like a paraphrase of Schelling on how deterrence was to work. His *leitmotif* that Soviet uncertainty would create adequate deterrent effect dominated the logic: locally-deployed conventional forces were to provide "tangible evidence" of "the risk of escalation to total nuclear war." NATO's self-declared aim was to support nuclear deterrence by "leaving the enemy in doubt" about the process of escalation.[23]

NATO's reigning policy for much of the Cold War, "Flexible Response," was formally adopted by NATO's Defence Planning Committee in December 1967 as its "overall strategic concept." This policy sounded many of the same themes. The "strategic nuclear forces of the Alliance" were the "backbone of NATO's military capabilities," and for deterrence purposes, "These should be adequate to inflict catastrophic damage on Soviet society even after a surprise nuclear attack..."[24] In addition:

> The deterrence concept of the Alliance is based on:...A flexibility which will prevent the potential aggressor *from predicting with confidence NATO's specific response to aggression, and which will lead him to conclude that an unacceptable degree of risk would be involved regardless of the nature of his attack.*

> ...The conventional forces of the Alliance, land, sea and air, many of which are organically supported by tactical nuclear weapons, are a further essential component of the deterrent. *They should be designed to deter and successfully counter to the greatest extent possible a limited non-nuclear attack and to deter any larger non-nuclear attack by confronting the aggressor with the prospect of non-nuclear hostilities on a scale that could involve a grave risk of escalation to nuclear war.*[25]

NATO forces were to be capable of countering a "limited" conventional attack, and contributing to extended deterrence by compelling the Soviets to confront the deterring possibility that a larger attack on NATO could escalate to nuclear war. "Flexible Response" explicitly acknowledged that NATO could not prevent the destruction of Western societies if the Warsaw Pact chose not to be deterred, but noted in this regard with considerable understatement that, "risks are a necessary corollary of a policy founded on deterrence."[26]

In addition to being pervasive in most academic commentary on the subject and in NATO's official policy declarations, this acceptance of Soviet uncertainty as an adequate mechanism for deterrence affected how senior U.S. Government officials put deterrence into practice. For example, Soviet Premier Nikita Khrushchev directly challenged U.S. Secretary of State Dean Rusk regarding the credibility of the U.S. nuclear umbrella by asking["Why should I believe that you Americans would fight a nuclear war over Berlin?"[27]] Khrushchev had raised the fundamental question about U.S. will and deterrence credibility, the differing answers to which defined the two schools of U.S. thought: if the United States was unwilling to fight a deliberate nuclear war over Berlin, why should the Soviet Union be deterred by the U.S. nuclear threat?

Kahn's rejoinder to this central question would have been that the U.S. extended nuclear escalation threat would be sufficiently credible to deter effectively *if* U.S. cities were defended so that the consequences for the United States of nuclear escalation could be seen as preferable to the consequences of Soviet domination of Western Europe. If U.S. society was defended, the stakes for the United States could then be seen as worth the risk of threatening nuclear escalation because the consequences could be judged less costly than the loss of Europe to Soviet control. For Kahn, the proper U.S. investment in strategic offensive *and particularly defensive forces* would have allowed Secretary Rusk to reply to Khrushchev that the Soviet Premier should believe the U.S. threat because, ultimately, Washington might deliberately accept the risks of escalation. That set of circumstances, said Kahn, would make the U.S. extended deterrent effective because it would appear credible.

Secretary Rusk's actual response to Khrushchev, however, was a reflection of Schelling's view of deterrence, not Kahn's. Rusk moved the question away from the logical credibility of the U.S. threat to escalate and emphasized the uncertainty of U.S. behavior. Khrushchev should be deterred because the United States might irrationally escalate to nuclear war despite the mutually destructive consequences of such a decision. Secretary Rusk tells of this exchange with Khrushchev: "That was quite a question, with Khrushchev staring at me with his little pig eyes. I couldn't call [President] Kennedy and ask, 'What do I tell the son of a bitch now?' So I stared back at him, 'Mr. Chairman, you will have to take into account the possibility we Americans are just [expletive] fools.'"[28] Secretary Rusk had put Schelling's proposition regarding the deterring effect of uncertainty into practice over high stakes and at the highest possible political level.

The proposition that uncertainty deters even affected the conclusions of threat assessments conducted by the U.S. intelligence community. For example, the July 7, 1970 National Intelligence Estimate signed by the Director of Central Intelligence included an assessment of the possible threat of an enemy's covert placement of nuclear weapons on U.S. soil. This threat assessment, entitled *The Clandestine Introduction of*

Nuclear Weapons Into the US, essentially judged the threat to be highly unlikely. Why? Not because the Soviet Union could not do so; Soviet weapons were judged to be quite light (weighing as little as 150 pounds) and transportable. Nevertheless, the *chance* of detection, U.S. escalation, and the consequent possibility of unacceptable damage to the Soviet Union would deter:

> The Soviets would recognize, however, that even if such an effort were successful, it could not prevent US retaliation or reduce it to what they would consider an acceptable level.... the Soviets would have to consider the risk...that discovery would have severe and unpredictable repercussions, possibly including a US pre-emptive attack which would be disastrous for the USSR. For these reasons, we think it highly unlikely that the USSR will attempt to introduce nuclear weapons clandestinely into the US.[29]

Reinforcing Soviet perceptions of the chance of U.S. nuclear escalation, not its logical credibility in Kahn's sense, was at the heart of the Nixon Administration's major strategic policy initiative, particularly for extended deterrence purposes. In 1974, the Nixon Administration announced its decision to plan for the employment of nuclear weapons in a fashion consistent with Schelling's proposition that, in a balance of terror, graduated nuclear escalation threats could add to deterrence credibility by demonstrating U.S. resolve—"rocking the boat" to reinforce Soviet uncertainties. In 1974, National Security Decision Memorandum-242 (NSDM-242, Top Secret; declassified February 20, 1998) called for, "limited employment options which enable the United States to conduct selected nuclear operations...these options should enable the United States to communicate to the enemy a determination to resist aggression, coupled with a desire to exercise restraint."[30] Multiple pre-planned nuclear targeting options had been available "for quite some time" prior to NSDM-242.[31] "In practice," however, those options were only, "at the upper end of the spectrum," involving massive Soviet casualties and thousands of weapons.[32]

NSDM-242 called for graduated nuclear escalation options, including plans to limit an American nuclear strike to a very few weapons. As envisaged by Schelling as early as the late 1950s, and described officially by Secretary of Defense James Schlesinger in 1974, this plan for limited nuclear escalation steps was intended largely to reinforce the credibility of the U.S. extended deterrent threat.[33] NSDM-242 was not superseded with regard to nuclear targeting until President Carter's Presidential Directive-59 (PD-59) of July 1980.[34] And, PD-59 (Top Secret; partially declassified/ released on March 6, 1998) continued to identify limited nuclear escalation options as important for the credibility of extended nuclear deterrence because Soviet capabilities for nuclear counterstrikes cast doubt on the credibility of U.S. assured destruction threats alone.[35]

Schelling's original Cold War proposition was that uncertainty could deter—especially if the risk of escalation could be made manifest to Soviet leaders by U.S. forces deployed abroad, U.S. capabilities for limited nuclear escalation, and "rocking the boat" behavior that demonstrated the chance of escalation. In U.S. policy parlance, the balance of terror tenet that "uncertainty deters" became established as a general truth.

Assured Destruction: Secretary McNamara's Balance of Terror Metric for Strategic Forces

Secretary of Defense McNamara embraced much of the basic stable balance of terror formula—as originally described by Schelling and Brodie—as the basis for U.S. strategic force acquisition policy and official expressions regarding the U.S. strategic deterrence threat. In doing so, he expressed the following as conclusions or beliefs:

- A reliable, predictable deterrent effect could be based on the U.S. threat of U.S. nuclear destruction to Soviet population and industry, i.e., the "assured destruction" threat.
- The priority goal for U.S. strategic forces was deterrence. Significant direct damage-limitation capabilities were not a priority given their unsustainable cost at an acceptable level of effectiveness, their incompatibility with stable mutual deterrence, and the near certainty of an offsetting Soviet offensive reaction.
- There was a predictable, even mechanistic, relationship between the characteristics of U.S. forces and their deterrent effect on Moscow, i.e., deterrence is a function of force structure. The survivable U.S. nuclear threat to Soviet society would provide virtually certain deterrent effect against deliberate attack because the Soviet Union

could anticipate no "gain" in striking first.

- Significant U.S. strategic capabilities for limiting damage to cities would threaten to destabilize mutual deterrence by giving the Soviet Union incentives to strike first to obtain strategic advantage.

- Both sides were driven to acquire strategic forces by the goal of preserving their "assured destruction" retaliatory capabilities. Thus the Soviet Union would react to offset any U.S. damage-limitation initiative that might appear to threaten its presumed assured destruction requirement: "Whatever be their intentions, whatever be our intentions, actions—or even realistically potential actions—on either side relating to the build-up of nuclear forces, be they either offensive or defensive weapons, necessarily trigger reactions on the other side. It is precisely this action-reaction phenomenon that fuels an arms race."[36]

Secretary McNamara's specific claim that the Soviet Union had no rational choice but to accede to the deterring effect and the technical reality of a balance of terror, and that Moscow also subscribed to assured destruction guidelines, reflected the technological determinism that was central to balance of terror thinking. Here was a nuclear *deus ex machina* that ensured the mutual deterrence of deliberate attack. The balance of terror was said to be mutually inescapable, which led McNamara's critics to label his approach to deterrence, "Mutual Assured Destruction," and pejoratively shorten that title to MAD.[37]

McNamara repeatedly defined and endorsed assured destruction as the U.S. retaliatory threat metric along with other elements of the stable balance of terror formula in his now-declassified annual Draft Presidential Memorandums (DPMs) on strategic forces. These DPMs, highly classified at the time, were "recognized and accepted as the principal document for the Secretary's decisions and policies"; when Secretary McNamara was asked if he would write memoirs, he described the DPMs as, "a far better source than any personal memoirs."[38]

Secretary McNamara's acceptance of stable balance of terror guidelines *vis-à-vis* the Soviet Union is evident as early as his 1962 DPM.[39] That he adopted the assured destruction metric within a stable balance of terror as an explicit standard for determining the role and value of strategic forces is clear in his annual strategic forces DPMs from 1963 through 1968.

For example, he observed in the DPM dated January 15, 1968:

> The main objective of our nuclear forces is to deter nuclear attacks on the U.S. Our ability to strike back and destroy Soviet society makes a Soviet decision to strike the U.S. highly unlikely. By choosing to develop and deploy harder-to-attack forces, we can reduce even more the likelihood of such an attack. Unable to destroy most of our nuclear striking power, the Soviets would gain little by striking first.[40]

And:

> Like us, to deter a first-strike nuclear attack, the Soviets maintain the ability to strike back and destroy our society. When they take steps to reduce the damage that we can inflict (e.g., by deploying ABMs), we react to offset these steps. I believe that the Soviets would react in the same way to similar U.S. steps to limit damage to ourselves. [41]

Secretary McNamara's recommended means to deter Soviet attack, and indeed any "rational enemy," was deployment of survivable U.S. retaliatory nuclear forces that could present the Soviet leadership with the prospect of massive societal destruction. This became Secretary McNamara's self-expressed standard for deterrence:

> We deter a rational enemy from launching a first strike against us by maintaining a strong and secure ability to retaliate under any circumstances. We measure our second strike ability in terms of Assured Destruction—the capability to inflict unacceptable damage, calculated under extremely conservative assumptions, on the USSR, even after sustaining a surprise Soviet first strike.[42]

In 1981, the Department of Defense's Historical Office produced a Top Secret report entitled, *History of the Strategic Arms Competition: 1945-1972*, edited by Alfred Goldberg, with contributions by Ernest May, John Steinbruner, and Thomas Wolfe. Now declassified, it points to the centrality of Secretary McNamara's assured destruction metric in U.S. policy:

> *The United States and the Soviet Union had different*

points of departure when rationalizing strategic forces, the U.S. emphasis <u>falling on assured destruction</u>, the Soviet emphasis initially <u>falling on damage limitation</u>. Possessing unmatched strategic offensive power and facing danger of strategic attack as a prospect rather than in reality, Americans developed the notion of deterrence through terror. As Soviet strategic offensive power began to grow, this notion was replaced by the concept of a balance of terror or mutual assured destruction. Thinking about strategic defensive operations quickly narrowed to thinking primarily about means of safeguarding the deterrent forces in case of an enemy first-strike.[43]

And:

Though the United States and the Soviet Union both came to conceive of strategic forces as having the function of war prevention, their views concerning these forces continued to be different, the U.S. emphasizing manifestation of capability for inflicting unacceptable damage on an adversary's homeland, and the Soviets emphasizing manifestation of capability for fighting a war.[44]

The Pentagon's adoption of Secretary McNamara's survivable assured destruction capability as the policy standard for judging the value of U.S. strategic forces fully reflected a stable balance of terror formula for deterrence. It defined the basic U.S. requirement for strategic deterrence as a massive retaliatory nuclear threat to Soviet civilians and industry, and it explicitly excluded as necessary or useful for deterrence any significant U.S. offensive or defensive capabilities intended to help defend U.S. society directly against Soviet nuclear attack, i.e., U.S. damage-limitation capabilities.[45]

In fact, Secretary McNamara endorsed the argument—again derived from Schelling's balance of terror logic—that the Soviet capability to retaliate was an unavoidable and useful condition because Moscow's confidence in its capability to retaliate contributed to "a more stable posture."[46] He also has expressed his belief that the only "plausible" route to the deliberate use of nuclear weapons followed from the potential strategic advantage of a first strike that could eliminate or reduce the other side's capability to retaliate[47]—i.e., Schelling's "reciprocal fear of surprise attack"—and that retaining the manifest capability for assured destruction virtually precluded this only "plausible" route to nuclear use. These beliefs were, of course, central tenets of the "stable" balance of terror framework introduced by Schelling.

For most of a decade, Secretary McNamara routinely recommended to the president strategic force programs that contributed to the U.S. assured destruction threat, and opposed strategic programs that fell outside that gauge, particularly including those for reducing the vulnerability of American population and industry to Soviet attack. By the mid-1960s, a balance of terror not only was a technical fact, but acquiring and orchestrating U.S. strategic forces according to its requirements—largely as prescribed in Schelling's theoretical work—was the lodestar in the official Department of Defense guidelines used to answer the question: How much strategic force capability should the United States acquire?

As such, balance of terror guidelines became formal, official policy parameters for the acquisition of select U.S. offensive capabilities and against the acquisition of defensive strategic forces. This policy guidance sought to ensure the U.S. assured destruction threat as the U.S. side of the balance of terror, and eschewed challenging the supposed Soviet requirement for an assured destruction capability.

Commentators sympathetic to this stable balance of terror/ assured destruction approach to deterrence often claim that U.S. societal vulnerability to Soviet nuclear attack was strictly an objective condition—never a U.S. policy choice—possibly to preclude any notion that such an inherently repugnant condition could be a choice: if inalterable societal vulnerability to nuclear attack simply was a fact of life, there could be no policy choice in the matter, hence no culpability for the choice. The mutual vulnerability of the balance of terror, however, became far more than an objective condition.

The guidelines identified by Schelling for stabilizing and perpetuating the balance of terror became official U.S. Cold War policy for the acquisition of U.S. forces, including: the deployment of the types and number of offensive nuclear capabilities deemed necessary to threaten Soviet society—estimated very conservatively; and, the deactivation and general avoidance of "destabilizing" strategic forces—particularly including those that might be intended to provide U.S. society protection against Soviet nuclear attack.

These staples of the balance of terror formula for stable mutual deterrence became overarching U.S. policy goals and important guidelines for decisions regarding the development, testing, acquisition and deployment of strategic forces, and for establishing U.S. arms control goals. To be sure, mutual societal vulnerability became an objective condition; facilitating and preserving it, however, also became fundamental U.S. policy goals for strategic force sizing, acquisition, and arms control purposes.

Declassified documents covering the 1960s—including Secretary McNamara's progression of classified DPMs on strategic forces from 1961 until 1968—demonstrate conclusively that *he explicitly rejected the logic and strategic force goals recommended by Kahn in favor of those compatible with Schelling's definition of a stable balance of terror with the Soviet Union.* For most of the 1960s, he used assured destruction as the primary, officially-applied metric for strategic capabilities to argue *for* the types of capabilities supporting a stable balance of terror, and *against* those strategic offensive or defensive forces deemed by that standard to be unnecessary, unhelpful and destabilizing.

Secretary McNamara's use of the term "assured destruction" appears to have first entered the strategic force DPMs in 1963. His identification of U.S. nuclear threats to Soviet cities as the basis for deterrence, however, was emphasized as early as his September 23, 1961 DPM (regarding the FY 1963 strategic forces budget) to President Kennedy: "The 200 Urban-Industrial targets and the 150 bomber bases have the highest priority in the sense of required degree of assurance that we can destroy them. The capability to destroy the Urban-Industrial targets is our power to deter attacks on our own cities."[48]

In the 1962 DPM to President Kennedy, Secretary McNamara added that his strategic force recommendations were intended to serve deterrence by giving, "any rational Soviet decision-maker the strongest possible incentives to avoid a nuclear attack on ourselves or our allies." He added that this goal established two related deterrence requirements: the retaliatory capabilities necessary to destroy "Soviet urban society if necessary, in a controlled and deliberate way"; and, to deny the Soviets the prospect of, "achieving a military victory by attacking our forces."[49] Identified here was the U.S. strategic requirement for a survivable U.S. nuclear retaliatory capability to destroy Soviet urban society, i.e., the U.S. side of the mutual balance of terror.

The 1961 and 1962 DPMs also presented Secretary McNamara's explicit rejection of U.S. "first-strike" capabilities intended to reduce the Soviet retaliatory capability, "to the point at which it could not cause severe damage to U.S. population and industry."[50] In the 1961 DPM, he explicitly rejected pursuit of such a policy and related damage-limitation capabilities because he believed they would be too costly, instigate an arms race, and ultimately be insufficiently effective.[51] His 1962 DPM regarding the FY 1964 strategic forces budget reiterated this rejection. Referring to his previous memo of September 1961, Secretary McNamara stated: "I indicated then and I reaffirm now my belief that the 'full first-strike capability'—and I now include the Air Force's variant of it—should be rejected as a U.S. policy objective." He then added to the previous year's reasons for rejecting the goal, "It is neither necessary nor particularly useful."[52]

In 1967, Deputy Secretary of Defense Cyrus Vance emphasized the point in closed testimony before the Senate Committee on Foreign Relations:

> We believe that even if we struck first they would still have the capability to come back and inflict that [unacceptable] amount of damage upon the United States. And we have reviewed, not because we ever intended to do so, the question of whether or not the United States could ever launch a pre-emptive strike on the Soviet Union and receive an acceptable level of damage in return. The Joint Chiefs of Staff and we are all in agreement that we could not do so, even if we struck first.[53]

Throughout Secretary McNamara's tenure at the Pentagon, as reflected in his annual classified DPMs, he explicitly rejected a policy of and capabilities for a "full first strike" or "credible first strike," to include rejection of offensive and defensive forces intended to provide significant, direct damage limitation for U.S. cities against Soviet attack.[54] He concluded early in his tenure that what he defined as an "acceptable" or "reasonable" absolute level of damage limitation was not feasible at tolerable cost.[55] As with Schelling's recommended balance of terror guidelines, U.S. policies and capabilities for protecting U.S. cities from Soviet nuclear attack were out; priority was given instead to the requirement for strategic offensive capabilities to threaten massive retaliation against Soviet society. Deputy Secretary of Defense Vance also confirmed this point in closed testimony. Senator Albert Gore, Sr. stated: "You and Secretary McNamara take the position that the best, most fortuitous balance of terror so far as we are concerned is to pay relatively small attention to defense and maximize our power of assured destruction." Secretary Vance answered: "That is correct, sir."[56]

As mentioned above, Secretary McNamara's 1963 DPM introduced the specific assured destruction levels of offensive nuclear threat to Soviet cities and industry deemed necessary to deter deliberate Soviet attack under "all foreseeable conditions":

> An essential test of the adequacy of our posture is our ability to destroy, after a well planned and executed Soviet surprise attack on our Strategic Nuclear Forces, the Soviet government and military controls, plus a large percentage of their population and economy (e.g., 30% of their population, 50% of their industrial capability, and 150 of their cities). The purpose of such a capability is to give us a high degree of confidence that, under all foreseeable conditions, we can deter a calculated deliberate Soviet nuclear attack. The calculations made to test this ability are our best estimates of the results of possible Soviet calculations of what we could do to them in retaliation if they were to attack us. This calculation of the effectiveness of the U.S. forces is not a reflection of our actual targeting doctrine in the event deterrence fails. I will call this objective "Assured Destruction."[57]

In Secretary McNamara's 1964 DPM, he again defined assured destruction with precision and claimed its *deterrent effect against* "any industrialized nation" with extreme confidence:

> It is generally agreed that a vital first objective, to be met in full by our strategic nuclear forces, is the capability for assured destruction. *Such a capability would, with a high degree of confidence, ensure that we could deter under all foreseeable conditions, a calculated, deliberate nuclear attack upon the United States.* What amounts and kinds of destruction we would have to be able to deliver in order to provide this assurance cannot be answered precisely, but it seems reasonable to assume that the destruction of, say, 25 percent of its population (55 million people) and more than two-thirds of its industrial capacity would mean the destruction of the Soviet Union as a national society. *Such*

a level of destruction would certainly represent intolerable
punishment to any industrialized nation and thus should
serve as an effective deterrent.[58]

Secretary McNamara asserted that assured destruction would
"ensure" effective deterrence under "all foreseeable conditions" because
it represented an "intolerable" cost to Soviet decision makers. Indeed, he
believed that assured destruction would constitute a threat of "intolerable"
cost to any "industrialized nation." This was a powerful promise, following
from the balance of terror guidelines, that the United States had found
the key to effective deterrence of deliberate attack, namely, the nuclear
assured destruction metric within a balance of terror.

Assistant Secretary of Defense Alain Enthoven later emphasized
the relative ease of calculating the requirements for strategic forces per
the assured destruction metric: "Indeed, in sharp contrast to most other
types of military requirements, those for strategic forces lend themselves
to calculation. At least the task presents a problem of finite dimension,
measurable in terms of the number and types of weapon systems required
to do the job under various circumstances."[59]

Secretary McNamara frequently expressed great confidence in
the expected effectiveness of deterrence based on assured destruction.
In his Top Secret DPM dated January 15, 1968, for example, he states
confidently and without caveat: "I believe that our ability to kill from one-
fifth to one-fourth of the Soviet people, including at least two-thirds of the
people and industry in their large cities, is enough to deter the USSR from
launching a first strike against the U.S., even in extreme situations."[60]

Similarly, in the November 9, 1966 DPM, under the heading,
"Adequacy of the Programmed Offensive Forces for Assured Destruction,"
Secretary McNamara stated: "I believe that a clear and unmistakable
ability to inflict 20-30% Soviet fatalities will deter a deliberate Soviet attack
on the U.S. or its Allies."[61] Here he stated with confidence and without
caveat that the assured destruction threat was effective for the deterrence
of direct attacks on the United States and also for the *extended deterrence
goal* of preventing deliberate attacks on U.S. allies.

Although Secretary McNamara insisted that U.S. nuclear forces
would not actually be employed in the fashion suggested by assured
destruction language,[62] he called assured destruction the "essence" of "the
whole U.S. deterrence concept":

The cornerstone of our strategic policy continues to be to deter deliberate nuclear attack upon the United States or it allies. We do this by maintaining a highly reliable ability to inflict unacceptable damage upon any single aggressor or combination of aggressors at any time during the course of a strategic nuclear exchange, even after absorbing a surprise first strike. This can be defined as our assured destruction capability.

It is important to understand that assured destruction is the very essence of the whole deterrence concept....The conclusion, then is clear: if the United States is to deter a nuclear attack on itself or its allies, it must possess an actual and a credible assured destruction capability.[63]

According to Pentagon studies, the specific warhead count necessary for the assured destruction deterrence threat was the U.S. capability, "with high confidence, [to] deliver 400 1-megaton weapons on the Soviet Union in a retaliatory strike."[64] Secretary McNamara identified this level of U.S. threat to Soviet population and industry as the basis for strategic deterrence, *not* as the result of a careful analysis of the likely cost-benefit calculations of the Soviet leadership given its particular values and intentions, but because it represented the "flat of the curve" for threatening societal destruction.[65]

The "flat of the curve" meant that, given the destructive potential of 400 1-megaton weapons against unprotected cities and industry, additional U.S. nuclear weapons beyond that capability would have provided diminishing marginal returns for attacking societal targets. That is, because the destructive potential of 400 1-megaton nuclear weapons against cities and industry was so great, additional nuclear weapons would have been of rapidly decreasing value for destroying additional societal targets, and thus would be "insignificant for deterrence."[66]

In Secretary McNamara's December 6, 1963 DPM on *Strategic Retaliatory Forces*, he presented the chart below under the section heading, "Forces Required for 'Assured Destruction'":

Soviet Fatalities and Industrial Destruction

	Expected Factors			Pessimistic Factors		
	Fatalities			Fatalities		
Number of Minutemen	Mil.	%	Ind'l. Cap. Destroyed (%)	Mil.	%	Ind'l. Cap. Destroyed (%)
0	115	50	57	40	17	30
950	158	69	82	66	29	50
1,000	160	70	87	68	30	51
1,200	164	71	89	73	32	53
1,400	165	72	90	75	33	54

From this chart, Secretary McNamara observed that, "the force of 950 Minuteman missiles already authorized, in combination with the other planned forces should be clearly adequate for 'Assured Destruction,' while a larger force would add very little from this point of view."[67] The chart illustrated that with 950 *Minuteman* missiles, "in combination with the other planned forces," U.S. retaliatory capabilities reached the "flat of the curve" per the assured destruction deterrence metric. Consequently, additional missiles would provide little additional value.

Secretary McNamara's annual Top Secret DPMs to Presidents Kennedy and Johnson included numerous charts identifying the number and type of U.S. strategic forces necessary to destroy specific percentages of Soviet population and industry, so as to meet the assured destruction requirement. He similarly discussed assured destruction-type deterrence threats with regard to China.[68] And, as noted above, Secretary McNamara evaluated the adequacy of U.S. forces for deterrence according to these standards. Frequently this had the practical effect of justifying his *rejection* of strategic programs recommended by one of the military services or by the Joint Chiefs of Staff, but which could be judged unnecessary, useless, wasteful, and/or destabilizing per stable balance of terror guidelines and the assured destruction barometer.

It would be hard to overstate the importance attributed by Secretary McNamara to assured destruction as the standard for guiding the acquisition or rejection of U.S. strategic forces or the inauguration of prospective new U.S. strategic force programs. In the January 15, 1968 Top Secret DPM, Secretary McNamara reviewed U.S. strategic forces for fiscal years 1969-1973. In his discussion of emerging Soviet strategic forces and prospective U.S. strategic force programs, *he made only the preservation of assured destruction the key standard for new capabilities*:

"We should develop new systems *only as options which would restore our Assured Destruction capability* should the greater-than-expected [Soviet] threat occur, realizing that it is not likely to occur."[69]

The Pentagon under Secretary McNamara used this assured destruction metric specifically to help identify the strategic forces to be purchased—their number, characteristics, and the proper mix of those forces—or rejected as unnecessary or not cost-effective for the assured destruction mission. Henry Rowen, Deputy Assistant Secretary of Defense for International Security Affairs from 1961 to 1964, and Assistant Director, U.S. Bureau of the Budget from 1965 to 1966, observed:

> The principal test of adequacy of the U.S. strategic force came to be the ability of our programmed force to produce civil damage, even against a greater than expected threat. The damage criterion settled on by McNamara for determining the size of the strategic force was the destruction of 20-25 percent of the Soviet population and 50 percent of its industrial capacity....The primary purpose of the Assured Destruction capabilities doctrine was to provide a metric for deciding how much force was enough: it provided a basis for denying service and Congressional claims for more money for strategic forces.[70]

Indeed, on the basis of the assured destruction standard, Secretary McNamara repeatedly opposed U.S. Air Force requests for funding for the Advanced Manned Strategic Aircraft (AMSA), the proposed follow-on to the B-52 strategic bomber, while also reducing the number of and the alert rate for the B-52s—all money-saving steps. He could do this prudently, he said, because the very limited contribution of strategic bombers to assured destruction could be achieved with lower numbers of bombers, at lower alert rates, and by adding some new capabilities to the existing B-52s rather than pursuing the new AMSA. He explicitly linked the assured destruction standard to this rejection of a new strategic bomber. For example, in the 1968 DPM, Secretary McNamara stated: "Since the strategic forces are already well-hedged, *we can keep an Assured Destruction capability against greater-than-expected threats without the AMSA*."[71]

Similarly, Secretary McNamara rejected calls by the Air Force civilian and military leadership for 1,400 and 1,950 *Minuteman* ICBM launchers, respectively—450 and 1,000 launchers above his preferred total number of 950 at the time—on the grounds that those additional ICBM launchers were unnecessary for assured destruction and could not contribute usefully to a reliable damage-limitation capability.[72] The 950 Minuteman missiles already authorized could inflict 158 million Soviet fatalities in combination with the other forces and thus, as noted above, were deemed sufficient for "assured destruction."[73]

Assured destruction was not, however, a gauge only for *rejecting* offensive strategic forces. Secretary McNamara supported moving forward with new, multiple, independently-targeted warheads (MIRVs) for U.S. submarine-launched ballistic missiles because they would provide a cost-effective, offensive "hedge" against then-emerging Soviet strategic forces that threatened to degrade the U.S. assured destruction capability, particularly Soviet BMD.[74]

The Balance of Terror, Assured Destruction, and U.S. Damage-Limiting Forces

On the defensive or damage-limitation side, on November 14, 1963, Secretary McNamara reported to President Kennedy that a decision needed to be made, "whether to base our strategic posture primarily on strong offensive forces or to provide the elements of a balanced defense against a nuclear attack."[75] He estimated that the "High Alternate Program" for damage limitation—which included a substantial nationwide fallout shelter system, improved air defense, and BMD for the 22 largest U.S. urban areas—would cost approximately $32 billion over five years; this program would, "increase the population surviving [nuclear attack] to around two-thirds" and provide the capability, "to moderate damage to our industrial structure... An additional $20 billion for a combination of the programs would increase the proportion surviving to around three-fourths against a constant Soviet threat or would provide a comparable level of defense against a somewhat larger attack."[76]

However, Secretary McNamara recommended instead a much more limited strategic defense program, and noted that a fundamental choice in favor of a strategic posture based primarily on strong offensive forces should, "lead to a phased reduction of present [defensive] programs..."[77] The United States subsequently undertook just such a "phased reduction" of these defensive programs from which they never recovered.

Secretary McNamara used the assured destruction standard for deterrence primarily to demonstrate *the absence of a need for significant air defenses, civil defense, and BMD capabilities.* In presenting the case against acquiring significant damage-limitation capabilities to President Kennedy in 1963, Secretary McNamara noted that, "our strategic offensive forces, alone, should deter a calculated Soviet first strike."[78] His annual DPMs reveal that he deemed U.S. air defenses, civil defense, and BMD for cities *unnecessary* under the assured destruction deterrence metric. For example, only in the case of a "thin" ballistic missile defense system intended primarily to defend U.S. strategic retaliatory capabilities, particularly ICBMs—called "hard-point defense" (HPD) at the time—did he find value for U.S. BMD against Soviet attack. By building HPD to protect U.S. ICBMs against a Soviet first strike, *but not to protect U.S. cities*, HPD could help preserve the U.S. assured destruction retaliatory threat against increases in Soviet strategic capabilities without undercutting the Soviet nuclear threat to U.S. society. This role for BMD was wholly compatible with the balance of terror formula for stable deterrence. Indeed, Schelling also identified the potential balance of terror value of BMD for the purpose of defending *not U.S. cities, but retaliatory strategic forces.*[79]

In contrast, the defense of U.S. cities with BMD, air defenses, and civil defense as recommended by Kahn fared very poorly under Secretary McNamara. This was to be expected, as the focus of value for the assured destruction metric was on offensive retaliatory capabilities, and balance of terror guidelines attributed little value and great potential harm to the strategic defense of cities.

Secretary McNamara rejected a policy of substantial U.S. damage limitation against Soviet nuclear attack and, correspondingly, consistently opposed the strong and repeated recommendations by the Joint Chiefs of Staff to deploy the *Nike-X* BMD system for the purpose of protecting U.S. cities against Soviet nuclear missiles.[80] There was no point in deploying *Nike-X*, McNamara said, because given Soviet resources and technical capabilities, Moscow's leaders could and would choose to react to U.S. BMD to negate any meaningful U.S. population defenses; they would have to do so to preserve their own assumed assured destruction requirement. Secretary McNamara believed that this presumed action-reaction dynamic would prevent meaningful U.S. population protection against Soviet nuclear missiles.[81]

Secretary McNamara directly linked any acceptance of a policy and capabilities for substantial U.S. strategic damage limitation to high confidence in effective BMD.[82] Yet, he simultaneously concluded that confidence could not be placed in BMD because of the expected action-reaction dynamic that would drive a further buildup of Soviet strategic offensive forces. Here was the "Catch-22" for U.S. damage limitation posited by Secretary McNamara: effective BMD was a necessary component for the meaningful defense of cities against Soviet attack, but BMD could not be sufficiently effective and affordable over time because the Soviets were expected to react to offset U.S. BMD capabilities. Correspondingly, he recommended that the United States respond to a potential, massive Soviet BMD deployment by expanding U.S. offensive capabilities so as to preserve the U.S. offensive, retaliatory nuclear threat, not by deploying U.S. societal defenses.[83]

Secretary McNamara and President Johnson were so persuaded of the action-reaction cycle, and that BMD initiatives would compel offensive responses, that President Johnson invited Secretary McNamara to present the thesis to Soviet Chairman Aleksei Kosygin and his delegation at the 1967 Glassboro Summit in Glassboro, New Jersey. In what can only be described as an attempted executive tutorial on balance of terror logic, Secretary McNamara explained to Soviet Chairman Kosygin that the United States would react to Soviet BMD capabilities because, "we have to maintain a certain nuclear strength," and that, "you must react to us.... [The] Development of defensive systems will lead to responses by each of us to offset the other."[84]

In full keeping with balance of terror thinking, Secretary McNamara's tutorial was a warning to Kosygin that missile defenses would instigate an action-reaction cycle because both sides would be compelled to protect their offensive assured destruction deterrence threats. BMD, therefore, ostensibly could not be effective, and ultimately could leave both sides worse off. Chairman Kosygin's response to Secretary McNamara reflected no sympathy for the tutorial, criticizing it for taking an "immoral" and "commercial" approach to the issue by preferring offensive forces over defensive forces, and caring more about the cost of weapons than the value of possible saved lives.[85]

The irony here remains striking. At Glassboro, the leadership of a Communist regime long known for its history of utter brutality toward millions of its own subjects criticized the U.S. leadership for taking an "immoral" and cavalier attitude toward the protection of citizens. Members of the U.S. delegation attributed Kosygin's failure to embrace the balance of terror tutorial to primitive thinking on the part of the Soviet leaders; they just could not yet comprehend the elegance of balance of terror thinking.

Secretary McNamara's belief that the Soviet Union possessed the necessary resources and will to react to U.S. damage-limitation initiatives to prevent any meaningful U.S. population protection was an important element in his recommendation against a U.S. policy of substantial strategic damage limitation against Soviet attack. *This was an historic judgment and related decision.* With it the U.S. Department of Defense accepted the condition of U.S. societal vulnerability to Soviet nuclear arms, and chose as a matter of policy *not* to pursue damage-limitation programs to challenge that condition. Such a policy position, in effect, was a conscious decision to acquiesce to the perpetuation of U.S. societal vulnerability and a balance of terror. It is in this sense that the assured destruction metric and the balance of terror were fully conscious U.S. policy choices.

Secretary McNamara's own classified analyses of the potential for U.S. damage limitation showed that scores of millions of Americans could be protected by a combination of U.S. defensive programs, *even in the event of a heavy Soviet nuclear first strike against U.S. cities.* Such programs, however, would be far more costly than the strategic forces corresponding to assured destruction alone. As Secretary McNamara observed using Kahn's term: a "...'credible first-strike capability,' even if feasible...would require very large expenditures on Civil Defense and Continental Air and Missile Defenses."[86]

Pentagon calculations also showed that, even should the United States pursue a costly damage-limitation policy, the Soviet Union did have the capability to deploy additional offensive forces in pursuit of continuing high levels of U.S. societal vulnerability, and that Moscow could add to its offensive capabilities at less cost than the cost of the U.S. damage-limitation programs. If the United States and Soviet Union engaged in such an offensive-defensive competition, the Pentagon estimated that the additional Soviet offensive forces offsetting U.S. defenses would cost considerably less than the U.S. defenses. The Soviet cost advantage in this regard was estimated to be 3:1 at U.S. population survival rates of 80 percent, and possibly 4:1 at levels of U.S. population survival above 80 percent.[87] Consequently, Secretary McNamara believed that the Soviet Union had the will and resources to pursue an offensive-defensive competition, if necessary, to maintain its putative assured destruction requirement, and could do so at a significant cost advantage.

Secretary McNamara stated as early as his 1962 DPM that in this strategic situation only two conditions could make a significant level of U.S. damage limitation feasible *vis-à-vis* the Soviet Union. First, if the Soviets were "so foolish" as to leave their own assured destruction capabilities vulnerable to a U.S. first strike; or, second, if the balance of terror could be extended into a war to deter Soviet leaders from striking at U.S. cities throughout the conflict—that is, if they limited their offensive strikes to avoid U.S. cities by deliberate and coerced choice.[88]

He did not believe that the chances for such Soviet folly or wartime deterrence limitations warranted pursuit of a substantial U.S. damage-limitation policy.[89] The possibility of mutual deterrence working in wartime via reciprocal restraint to limit the targeting of cities, however, opened the possibility that *limited* additional strategic capabilities *beyond* assured destruction could have some damage-limiting value in that particular context. This did not represent a commitment to significant direct damage-limiting capabilities, but a limited role for modest defenses within a continuing balance of terror. Secretary McNamara said in this regard: "In this case we would be counting on our ability to destroy their will, not their ability, to destroy our cities. I believe that the coercive strategy is a sensible and desirable option to have in second-strike circumstances in which we are trying to make the best of a bad situation."[90]

In the absence of Soviet folly or this reciprocal intra-war deterrence, however, Secretary McNamara had no confidence in the value of substantial damage limitation because of his expectation that the Soviet Union could and would prevent a meaningful level of effectiveness from costly U.S. damage-limitation efforts, and do so at a cost advantage. This was, however, only a part of the interrelated and complementary set of reasons for his critical decision to eschew substantial, direct population protection as a realistic goal for U.S. forces and, effectively, to embrace the balance of terror as policy.

In addition, and perhaps most importantly, Secretary McNamara directly rejected Kahn's central thesis that the capability for substantial damage limitation was necessary for *credible* U.S. extended deterrence or as a hedge against the possibility of deterrence failure *vis-à-vis* the Soviet Union. In contrast to this core tenet of Kahn's thinking, Secretary McNamara asserted with regard to such a U.S strategic capability: "It is neither necessary nor particularly useful. The threat of a U.S. first-strike has long since been shown to be ineffective in deterring limited provocations and aggression."[91] Here was a direct rejection of Kahn's basic thesis. Assured destruction, Secretary McNamara believed, could provide the necessary levels of deterrent effect, and Kahn's "credible first-strike capability" could not usefully add to that.

With this belief and related rejection of significant U.S. damage-limitation capabilities, assured destruction could be considered a necessary and generally sufficient standard for deterrence and U.S. forces *if great confidence could be placed in assured destruction deterring reliably and predictably.* Secretary McNamara certainly had that confidence and explicitly said so. By the early 1960s, he frequently expressed certainty or near certainty that assured destruction would deter reliably and predictably. As quoted above, his 1964 DPM states with regard to assured destruction: "Such a capability would, with a high degree of confidence, ensure that we could deter under all foreseeable conditions, a calculated, deliberate nuclear attack upon the United States."[92]

It is in this light that Secretary McNamara judged significant damage-limitation efforts—of considerable expense and what he deemed inadequate absolute effectiveness—to be, "neither necessary nor particularly useful." When the governing beliefs were that deterrence via assured destruction and a stable balance of terror would protect fully, reliably and at modest cost—while expensive defenses could not—the reasonable policy course was self-evident. Who wants to pay for uncertain, expensive defenses when it is believed that a relatively cheap form of deterrence protects, "with a high degree of confidence...under all foreseeable conditions"?

Also contributing to the rejection of substantial damage limitation was the definition or threshold Secretary McNamara established for what would constitute a satisfactory damage-limiting capability: he said that an "impenetrable shield" would be worth virtually any plausible cost,[93] but that U.S. damage-limitation capabilities that would leave approximately 20 percent of the U.S. population as likely prompt fatalities did *not* represent an "acceptable" level of protection.[94]

In 1963, Secretary McNamara reported to President Kennedy that, "Under no circumstances have I been able to get US casualties under 30 million. In fact I have not been able to get them down to 30 million....They can destroy us with a few weapons and we can do the same to them."[95] Similarly, in 1964 he reported to President Johnson that, "the Soviets have the technical and economic capacity to prevent us from assuring *that more than 80 percent* of our population would survive a determined attack, possibly less. They can do this by offsetting any increases in our defenses by increases in their missile forces."[96]

The baseline U.S. population typically used in the calculations presented in the DPMs was 200 or 210 million. An 80 percent survival rate thus equated to approximately 160 million survivors. This meant possibly saving many millions of American lives, yet failing to "keep our fatalities below some tens of millions."[97] More specifically, according to Secretary McNamara: "Against a massive and sophisticated Soviet attack on civil targets, we cannot have high confidence of reducing fatalities below 40 or more millions."[98] Such a level of prospective survivors and fatalities, according to Secretary McNamara, did not warrant a strategic policy commitment to substantial, direct damage limitation.[99] As he concluded in 1968: "Convinced that the Soviets would counter a major U.S. attempt to take away their second strike [i.e., retaliatory] capability, we have chosen not to start a major Damage Limitation program against the USSR."[100]

Of course, the possibility of millions of fatalities must be regarded as "unacceptable" compared to the alternative of peace with no fatalities. A pertinent question of values, however, was whether those damage-limitation measures believed to be feasible at the time for *reducing potential U.S. fatalities* would be worth the effort and expense *in the event of war.* Secretary McNamara's particular answer to this question of values was that the protection possible via damage limitation would *not* be worth the investment necessary because the Soviet reaction could preclude the U.S. capability to sustain a meaningful level of damage limitation given the expected Soviet cost advantage in doing so. That conclusion was at the heart of his expressed preference for a balance of terror over the goal of direct damage limitation.

At the same time, Secretary McNamara identified a level of societal protection and other conditions that he believed *made a U.S. commitment to direct damage limitation the preferred policy choice and priority.* In his DPMs to President Johnson, he endorsed a significant damage-limitation goal and related U.S. defensive capabilities against China, *not a balance of terror*; and he explained the interrelated reasons for this dramatic difference in approaches.[101] Against China, U.S. damage-limitation capabilities, particularly including BMD, could be expected to reduce U.S. fatalities in a nuclear war to fewer than 1 million, with some probability of no deaths;[102] China's "primitive technology" and "poor economy" would likely prevent effective Chinese competition in this regard.[103] Consequently, while a balance of terror with the Soviet Union became the U.S. goal, "against China, conversely, we can buy an effective defense of CONUS [the continental United States] as insurance against a failure of deterrence."[104]

In the case of the Soviet Union, Secretary McNamara's commitment to a balance of terror was driven by his apparent beliefs that the Soviet Union could and would preserve its supposed assured destruction standard at a cost ratio so advantageous that the United States could *not* sustain a worthy level of societal protection. His threshold regarding a worthy level of protection *vis-à-vis* a Soviet attack, and conclusion that such a level could not be sustained affordably, led to the Pentagon's policy of rejecting those damage-limiting programs estimated to be capable of providing *partial* protection for the population even if the Soviet Union sought to offset U.S. defensive efforts as predicted. At the level of societal protection he deemed practicable under these particular circumstances, he opposed the deployment of significant damage-limiting capabilities.

A senior White House official in the Kennedy and Johnson Administrations later illustrated this mode of assessing the value of strategic damage limitation against a demanding standard, stating that with regard to the level of protection necessary to be regarded as acceptable and worth the effort, "...10 million casualties are no different than 100 million casualties."[105] The meaning here was not that there literally is no difference between 10 million casualties and 100 million casualties; the difference, of course, is 90 million fewer casualties. Rather, the official's meaning was that unless damage-limitation capabilities could be expected to reduce fatalities to fewer than 10 million, those capabilities could not be considered sufficiently effective to warrant their acquisition.

McGeorge Bundy later explicitly laid out an even more demanding standard for defense effectiveness, and simultaneously declared that standard unlikely ever to be met: "There is also the problem that thermonuclear weapons impose a radically new calculus of advantage on anyone seeking to neutralize them: *they make it necessary to defeat them all. Anything less is not good enough for safety.*...it is extremely hard to believe we shall ever have a perfect defense against ballistic missiles, including those at sea."[106] In proposing "perfect defense" as the necessary standard for "safety," Bundy ensured that U.S. damage-limitation capabilities could never be considered adequate for deployment.

In short, with his recommendation of U.S. BMD against Chinese missiles, Secretary McNamara identified a threshold for what he believed was a worthy and acceptable level of defense effectiveness. For the Soviet threat there was no comparable threshold—other than an "impenetrable shield"—because he believed that an acceptable level of protection was unsustainable at affordable costs due to the expected action-reaction dynamic.

The following summary of a key, originally-classified 1964 study of damage limitation by the Department of Defense appears under the heading, "General Picture of Damage Limitation By The U.S. and By The

U.S.S.R.":

> Depending on the relative levels of effort on damage limiting by the defense and "damage inflicting" by the offense, the amount of industry and population surviving nuclear attacks can be raised and maintained at levels above the "no defense" posture. For the United States, there is the potential for raising the levels from around 25%-30% surviving up to about 80% surviving for both industry and population, allowing for present indications of poor planning on the part of the Soviets. On the Soviet side, there is the potential for raising the levels from about 40% surviving up to 80% surviving for population and from about 30% surviving to 60% surviving industrial capacity. The lower bounds are set by concentrated U/I [urban and industrial] attacks with no defense measures, the upper bounds by unfavorable cost ratios.[107]

The "upper bounds" of "about 80%" survival for U.S. population and industry was not identified as a ceiling based on technological limits. Rather, it represented a judgment about the level of defense effectiveness regarded as practicable, based on an expectation of Soviet offensive competition to maintain its putative assured destruction goal, and a related cost projection of the relative costs for Soviet offenses and U.S. defenses in that competition. With that mixture of expectations, political judgments and cost projections, "about 80%" survival of U.S. population and industry was deemed likely too costly to sustain and insufficient to justify the defensive efforts necessary to achieve it.

The official embrace of this principle occasionally was expressed in terms that now sound astonishingly stark. For example, in his 1964 DPM, Secretary McNamara recommended the phase-out of 22 specific air defense squadrons because: "Studies made by the North American Air Defense Command indicate that in 1970 the [U.S.] fatalities from a Soviet attack, after withdrawal of these squadrons would be no more than 1.5 to 5 million higher than they would be if the squadrons were retained— i.e., the fatalities might be 48 to 50 percent of the population instead of 47 percent."[108] These studies indicated to Secretary McNamara that the United States should *not* fund those air defense squadrons because the damage-limitation benefit would have been "no more" than 1.5 to 5 million additional U.S. survivors; others might have concluded that the value of reducing U.S. civilian fatalities by 1.5 to 5 million was worth the effort and expense of this increment of U.S. air defense capability. This was not a technical issue per se, but a policy question regarding the prioritization of goals and values.

Secretary McNamara's general rejection of a significant civil defense program reflected a similar type of cost-benefit assessment: "His downgrading of the civil defense program reflected accurately his views on damage limitation. The combination of an inevitably high death rate in the event of a Soviet attack and the high cost of expanding shelters to shield the public *demonstrated convincingly that the number of additional survivors per billion dollars expended would not justify the marginal returns of the investment.*"[109]

Finally, in justifying his rejection of damage limitation Secretary McNamara included one of the central balance of terror tenets: mutual deterrence would be *more stable if the Soviet leadership had confidence in Soviet strategic nuclear retaliatory capabilities.* The condition of U.S. societal vulnerability to strategic attack had come to be considered synonymous with prudent management of a "stable" deterrence strategy. Secretary McNamara has said that as early as 1962 he "wanted Soviet leaders to have confidence" that their forces would "be capable of retaliating effectively";[110] preserving that confidence would help stabilize mutual deterrence. From this perspective, seeking to reduce the Soviet nuclear threat to U.S. cities via damage limitation not only was deemed unnecessary for deterrence, it was considered a danger to deterrence stability. When identifying the basic reasons why damage-limiting programs received an ever lower priority under Secretary McNamara, Assistant Defense Secretary Enthoven included this balance of terror tenet that an effective damage-limiting capability, if possible, would threaten the Soviet retaliatory capability.[111]

Donald Hornig, science advisor to Presidents Eisenhower, Kennedy, and Johnson, identified this supposedly destabilizing effect of defending cities as one of the primary reasons for the U.S. decision not to proceed with the *Nike-X* BMD city-defense program: "To the extent that [*Nike-X*] might threaten to be effective against a Soviet second strike, it would be provocative by suggesting we were aiming at a first strike capability. It would therefore put a premium on a Soviet first strike in the event of a tense international situation."[112] The working principles here reflected the balance of terror canon: deterrence was the priority, and mutual capabilities for nuclear terror were considered critical for "stable" deterrence purposes and thus not to be undermined by threats to Soviet retaliatory capabilities.

The previously Top Secret *History of the Strategic Arms Competition* affirms that the U.S. decision to eschew significant damage limitation reflected a conscious policy choice in deference to "stable" deterrence theory:

> During 1964-1965 the principle was advanced that a meaningful damage-limiting posture was precluded not only because of marginal decrease in what bigger strategic programs could provide, *but because any U.S. effort to achieve such a posture would degrade the Soviet assured destruction threat against the United States*....Thereafter, OSD increasingly narrowed the rationale for strategic forces to the concept of "mutual assured destruction," which downgraded counterforce targeting in favor of the capacity to impose assured second-strike retaliation upon the adversary's society....[113]

In short, in determining the adequacy of U.S. strategic forces, Secretary McNamara rejected as a matter of policy the goal of pursuing substantial, direct U.S. damage-limitation capabilities *not* because reducing damage was determined to be infeasible technically per se. A combination of beliefs and expectations led to this rejection, including those about the functioning of deterrence, the Soviet reaction to U.S. damage-limitation initiatives, the prospective effectiveness and cost of offensive and defensive capabilities, and the cost versus value of pursuing imperfect defenses:

- Deterrence could be made to function reliably and predictably by adjusting the characteristics of the U.S. strategic nuclear arsenal.
- "Assured destruction" was adequate to provide reliable, high-confidence deterrence and extended deterrence.
- The action-reaction dynamic ensured that the Soviet Union would seek to negate U.S. defensive efforts, and it could do so at a significant cost advantage.
- A substantial damage-limitation policy and program would be much more expensive than assured destruction alone,

necessitating extensive air defenses, civil defense, and ballistic missile defense.

- Because the Soviet Union could and would respond to U.S. defensive efforts, even substantial damage-limitation efforts could provide only partial, *inadequate* protection and would place an asymmetric, intolerable cost burden on the United States.
- Substantial damage-limitation programs would "destabilize" deterrence.
- Sustaining stable mutual deterrence was a higher priority than acquiring the partial population protection believed practicable.

In the context of this set of beliefs, judgments, expectations and calculations there was no room for substantial but imperfect U.S. damage-limitation goals or programs. Secretary McNamara reached a fundamental judgment regarding the perceived tradeoff between deterrence and defense in U.S. strategic force acquisition—a tradeoff that was at the heart of balance of terror logic: the value of stable deterrence in the absence of substantial U.S. damage-limitation capabilities was deemed to be the priority over the purportedly destabilizing and very imperfect levels of damage limitation believed to be available via unilateral defensive efforts.

Air Defenses

The rejection of a substantial damage-limitation policy and the related rejection of BMD for U.S. cities against Soviet attack had extremely negative consequences for other U.S. strategic defensive programs. For example, Secretary McNamara showed waning interest in modernizing U.S. air defenses against Soviet bomber attacks, arguing that in the absence of effective U.S. societal defenses against Soviet missile attack there was no sense in defending against Soviet bombers. He reported to President Kennedy that damage-limitation programs had to work together and thus had to be considered in the aggregate: "...the effectiveness of each major element depends critically on the scale of the other elements. A decision to improve our continental air defense force is not consistent with a decision against deploying a ballistic missile defense system."[114]

Correspondingly, the history of the U.S. air defense program reveals its dramatic descent beginning in the 1960s. John Collins, noted

Senior Specialist in National Security at the Library of Congress, charted the reduction of U.S. bomber defenses and linked it directly to, "Assured Destruction policies."[115] Similarly, the Office of Air Force History notes in this regard that under Secretary McNamara, "MAD became so decisive 'as to make those who support[ed] a capable air defense posture almost shrug their shoulders and give up with the futility of it all.'"[116]

The graphics below illustrate the rapid and steep reduction of U.S. air defenses, including both surface-to-air missiles (SAMs) and interceptor aircraft, from the late 1950s through 1980:

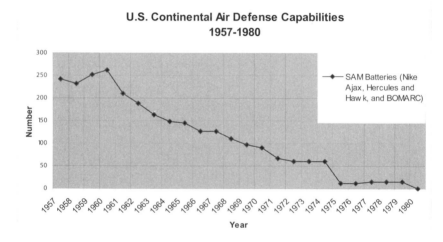

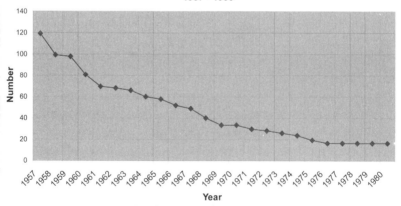

Source of Graphics: Kenneth Schaffel, *The Emerging Shield: The Air Force and the Evolution of Continental Air Defense, 1945-1960* (Washington, D.C.: United States Air Force, Office of Air Force History, 1991), Table 5, pp. 270-271. Note: The interceptor squadron figures are derived from adding the number of equipped interceptor squadrons and the number of interceptor squadrons in the Air National Guard.

Civil Defense

U.S. civil defense spending to protect against nuclear attack similarly declined precipitously following the mid-1960s, and has never recovered. Secretary McNamara identified the potential effectiveness of civil defense for limiting civilian fatalities. For example, his December 6, 1963 DPM to President Johnson on strategic retaliatory forces presented an analysis of U.S. civil defense programs under differing circumstances. In most cases an "augmented" nationwide fallout shelter program costing $4 billion was shown to save between 40 million and 90 million lives in the event of a Soviet nuclear attack.[117] In fact, Secretary McNamara said of civil defense: "A complete fallout shelter system would be the most effective component of a balanced damage limiting program against large attacks....Against a wide range of urban/military attacks, a complete fallout shelter system alone would save 20 to 25 percent of our population and should therefore be a first component of any larger damage limiting program."[118] A classified 1964 study of damage limitation prepared for the Pentagon's Director of Defense Research and Engineering concluded that, "Full fallout shelters are still the best initial investment for saving lives."[119]

Nevertheless, because the overarching policy choice was *not to pursue a substantial damage-limitation capability*, Secretary McNamara rejected U.S. Army proposals for substantially increased spending on civil defense,[120] JCS recommendations for significant civil defense protection for the civilian population,[121] and the JCS-recommended military survival measures program to provide fallout protection for U.S. military personnel to help with post-attack order and recovery.[122] Instead, according to the declassified memorandum for the record of a 1964 meeting with President Johnson, Secretary McNamara, "felt that pushing ahead on civil defense while not pushing ahead with the antiballistic missile might not be of any great value."[123] Correspondingly, he recommended a civil defense program that he himself described as "very austere."[124] Even the modest funding Secretary McNamara requested from Congress for civil defense typically was reduced by Congress without a real fight from the Johnson Administration. This pattern was sustained throughout the Cold War.

Bardyl Tirana, the Carter Administration's Director of the Defense Civil Preparedness Agency, stated in open Congressional testimony in 1979 that against a Soviet "heavy mid-1980s [nuclear] attack on military and urban/industrial targets," a "full crisis relocation" civil defense system could provide population survival rates of "some 80 percent" given a week or more of warning to execute evacuation plans. A "blast shelter system," possibly costing over $60 billion but requiring little warning, could provide a survival rate of up to 90 percent.[125]   Nevertheless, according to Tirana, the absence of serious leadership support for increased spending on civil defense since the early 1960s had the predictable effect:

> Really, since the Cuban missile crisis, in my judgment, funds have been spent to create the illusion of having civil defense when in reality we have virtually none.

> So, if I am asked today, "What is the capability of the nation to protect its citizens from the consequences of nuclear attack?" I would say virtually none.

> If I am asked today, "What do I get for the funds that I have been spending over the last couple of years?" I will tell you that I have maintained in support of state and local government an organization on which one could build an attack preparedness system, but I have not provided in any meaningful way a genuine attack preparedness capability.[126]

Again, there was a well-recognized relationship between the establishment of the stable balance of terror framework as the basic metric for U.S. deterrence policy and the subsequent minimal investment in civil defense. As John Collins commented: "Since emphasis on active defense is nearly nonexistent, official policy now considers civil defense almost pointless."[127]

The following graphic illustrates the dramatic increase in U.S. civil defense spending following the 1950s, and the subsequent decline and minimal U.S. investment in civil defense:

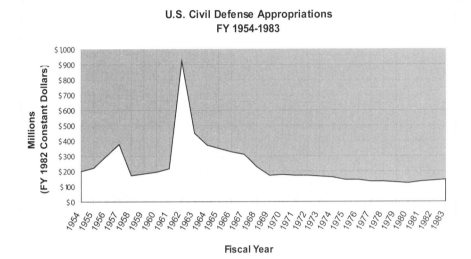

U.S. Civil Defense Appropriations
FY 1954-1983

Fiscal Year

Source: General Accounting Office, *The Federal Emergency Management Agency's Plan for Revitalizing U.S. Civil Defense: A Review of Three Major Plan Components,* GAO/NSIAD-84-11 (Washington, D.C: General Accounting Office, April 16, 1984), p. 51.

Anti-Submarine Warfare

The effect of balance of terror thinking on another U.S. strategic defensive capability—strategic anti-submarine warfare (ASW)—is unclear, as reflected in the Pentagon's strategic forces DPMs. These declassified DPMs do not much address the subject of ASW, other than to observe that the United States had the capability to sink Soviet submarines in a protracted war, but could *not do so promptly*; therefore, the Soviet Union would retain numerous ballistic missiles at sea able to retaliate against many U.S. cities and thus ensure the supposed Soviet assured destruction requirement.[128]

According to unclassified discussions of the subject, the U.S. Navy gave increased priority to strategic ASW during the 1960s and 1970s, as the Soviet ballistic missile-carrying submarine capabilities emerged.[129] It is possible that the Navy's strategic ASW somehow "escaped" the scrutiny and assured destruction-based cuts that hit other strategic defense systems.

What is clear from unclassified sources is that after the mid-1960s, public discussion of strategic ASW by senior Pentagon officials largely disappeared, and U.S. Navy public comments typically focused instead on ASW against Soviet attack submarines ("tactical" ASW), vice Soviet ballistic missile-carrying submarines: "During the middle to late 1960's, damage limitation as a *procurement* policy (criterion for weapons purchases) yielded to the doctrine of assured destruction, and references to strategic ASW all but disappeared from official pronouncements. The logic of deterrence based upon *mutual* assured destruction would both explain and recommend the deemphasis of strategic ASW."[130]

Assured Destruction and Stable Balance of Terror Guidelines: Three No's

Official acceptance of assured destruction and mutual vulnerability as the basis for a stable balance of terror orphaned most, if not all, U.S. programs to provide societal protection against deterrence failure. Some of these programs, including U.S. air defense and civil defense—essential ingredients for any substantial goal of damage limitation against the Soviet Union—had been funded robustly through the early-to-mid 1960s, but declined rapidly thereafter.

By the end of the 1960s, the categorization of defensive systems for U.S. society as unnecessary, useless and "destabilizing" had taken firm root and had the predictable effect. Funding for these damage-limiting strategic capabilities declined dramatically and defensive capabilities evaporated. Funding for BMD technology development continued, but consistent military recommendations for BMD deployment were rejected just as consistently by the Pentagon's civilian leadership. Balance of terror thinking had helped to establish three "no's": no major civil defense or air defense, and no ballistic missile defense deployment programs.

A decade later, Paul Warnke, an Assistant Secretary of Defense under Secretary McNamara and Director of the Arms Control and Disarmament Agency under President Carter, expressed this rejection of U.S. defensive programs on the basis of the stable balance of terror formula:

> …There is now a situation of mutual deterrence.
>
> Now hypothetically, the bringing into being of strategic defenses could destabilize the strategic balance by making impossible the type of retaliatory nuclear strike that would inflict unacceptable damage on the aggressor.

If it were possible for either side to protect its people, its facilities, and its industry—whether by antiballistic-missile systems and air defense or by sheltering its population or evacuating it, and hardening and dispersing its industry— then adequate deterrence no longer would exist.[131]

Balance of terror thinking reigned: the protection of "people" and "industry" was deemed to be inconsistent with a "situation of mutual deterrence." And, according to Warnke, perpetuating deterrence stability based on essentially unmitigated civilian vulnerability was judged preferable even over the hypothetical "bringing into being of strategic defenses" capable of protecting people, facilities and industry. It is difficult to find in history a comparable, deliberate set of policy decisions by government to eschew significant, available preparations for direct defense against an obvious threat.

This overarching approach to deterrence strategy and the corresponding "three no's" in U.S. strategic acquisition policy were reflected in U.S. spending on individual elements of strategic defense, as illustrated in the previous graphics, and on strategic defense forces as a whole. The graphic below shows the dramatic decline in overall U.S. spending for these programs:

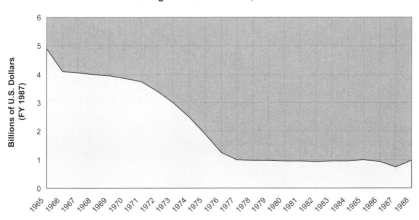

U.S. Defense Activities
Strategic Defensive Forces, 1965-1988

Source: Statement by George Kolt, Director, Office of Strategic Analysis, Central Intelligence Agency, in Joint Economic Committee, Subcommittee on National Security Economics and Subcommittee on Technology and National Security, *Allocation of Resources in the Soviet Union and China,* Part 14, Hearings, 101st Congress, 1st Session (Washington, D.C.: USGPO, 1990), p. 12.

Variations on the Balance of Terror Theme

Secretary McNamara's constant references to assured destruction, and later even occasionally to "MAD" as the basic standard for strategic forces, did not mean that the United States only targeted Soviet cities or that it abandoned *all* strategic damage-limitation goals and capabilities—whether offensive forces to target Soviet nuclear weapons or *limited* defensive capabilities such as air defense and civil defense. The Pentagon did reject major damage-limitation programs designed to protect U.S. society directly against a full Soviet nuclear attack for the reasons listed above, but allowed a narrow window for limited counterforce targeting and some defenses. Rather than the rejection of stable balance of terror guidelines, however, this opening reflected a role for such capabilities well within the formula.

It is important to understand this limited scope and rationale for damage limitation as presented in the pertinent DPMs. Some commentators mistakenly have concluded that because limited provision was made for defensive capabilities and the targeting of Soviet military assets, the United States pursued a credible first-strike policy rather than a policy oriented around a stable balance of terror.[132] The actual history of U.S. policy since the early 1960s clearly does *not* support this conclusion, but it is easy to understand how a cursory examination could yield such an interpretation.

As noted, Secretary McNamara repeatedly stated that assured destruction was a metric for assessing strategic forces for deterrence purposes, *not how the United States would employ nuclear weapons in the event deterrence failed and war with the Soviet Union ensued.* He emphasized that unless the Soviet Union initiated a war with a massive strike against U.S. cities, the U.S. nuclear response should be to facilitate the extension of deterrence into the war via controlled limited strikes, including strikes against Soviet military targets. His self-expressed interest in limited U.S. counterforce capabilities did *not* reflect a "counterforce doctrine" in the sense of positing a strategy to *eliminate* the Soviet capability to threaten U.S. society, "...but rather a statement of policy which we hoped would influence the Soviets, were we and they ever to be involved in a nuclear exchange, to limit severely the initial launches of nuclear weapons in the hope that we would avoid destruction of our societies. I never did believe in a counter-force strategy per se."[133] The goal was to help extend into war the *deterrence* of Soviet strikes against American society. As Secretary of Defense McNamara wrote in a memorandum on the subject for President

Johnson in 1968: "If we failed to deter nuclear war, we would want to be able to follow a policy of limiting our retaliatory strikes to the enemy's military targets and not attacking his cities if he refrained from attacking ours."[134]

The point was to avoid striking Soviet cities, at least in an initial response, so that their continuing presence and vulnerability would provide *a reason for Soviet reciprocity* in the avoidance of striking cities. *Not* destroying Soviet cities was a tactic for *maintaining* deterrence leverage over Soviet decision making during a war, *not* the rejection of mutual deterrence by the United States. This targeting tactic within a balance of terror was to be the basic mechanism for disciplining Soviet nuclear escalation after the initial outbreak of conflict, allowing the possibility for mutual deterrence to limit the destruction of U.S. cities in wartime. It was an extreme form of graduated escalation or "rocking the boat" as described earlier by Schelling.

In addition, U.S. limited offensive and defensive damage-limitation efforts might provide some useful contribution to societal protection *if the initial Soviet strike was accidental or piecemeal or if mutual deterrence could work to contain escalation during war.* Secretary McNamara endorsed modest U.S. offensive counterforce and defensive damage-limitation capabilities for the value they might provide in these narrow contexts.[135]

The goal of this balance of terror variant was not contrary to mutual deterrence; it relied on mutual deterrence. It was to prevent unrestricted nuclear strikes against cities through an extension of the balance of terror into war itself, *and in that constrained context* of mutual deterrence, to destroy Soviet nuclear capabilities to the limited extent possible while also deterring the destruction of U.S. cities. Secretary McNamara indicated that with intra-war deterrence so limiting nuclear strikes against cities, even minor U.S. defenses and offensive capabilities capable of striking Soviet military forces might help to provide some damage limitation for the United States. He continued to support "very austere" civil defense and air defense preparations to help mitigate the consequences of war in this context of a nuclear war limited by mutual deterrence. As noted above, Secretary McNamara emphasized that outside of gross Soviet folly, this combination of intra-war mutual deterrence and modest damage-limitation capabilities was the only avenue he believed had the potential for meaningful U.S. population protection.

Secretary McNamara labeled this balance of terror variant a "coercive strategy" of "second-strike counterforce." It called for neither a "credible first strike" policy or capability, nor substantial, expensive damage-limitation programs. In the context of mutual deterrence serving to limit strikes on cities, McNamara's definition of a meaningful defensive capability was far less demanding, and thus worth pursuing: "I believe that the coercive strategy is a sensible and desirable option to have in second-strike circumstances in which we are trying to make the best of a bad situation. There the only justification it requires is a reasonable possibility that it might work."[136]

As described, this was a hope that even following the initial outbreak of war, deterrence would continue to place limitations on nuclear escalation and targeting, and thereby provide a limited war context wherein modest damage-limiting capabilities could contribute to meaningful protection; this was *not* a "credible first strike" policy. Indeed, according to Secretary McNamara, "In long private conversations with successive Presidents— Kennedy and Johnson— *I recommended, without qualification, that they never initiate, under any circumstances, the use of nuclear weapons.* I believe they accepted my recommendation."[137] For most of the decade, Secretary McNamara's DPMs reflect this explicit rejection of a "first-strike" policy as the basis for U.S. planning or acquisition of strategic capabilities.

Secretary McNamara's limited endorsement of counterforce and damage-limitation programs *vis-à-vis* the Soviet Union can only be seen— and was described officially—as intended to support the "best possible outcome" in a context where *mutual deterrence continued to function during war. Damage limitation* required this functioning of mutual deterrence to have value. In the absence of the balance of terror working to compel targeting restraints during war, Secretary McNamara believed the Soviet Union could and would prevent an "acceptable" level of direct U.S. damage limitation, with "acceptable" defined as discussed above.

This approach to the intersection of deterrence, damage limitation, and the employment of U.S. strategic forces did not stray from reliance on the mutual deterrence of a balance of terror. It remained well within Schelling's narrative and far from Kahn's recommended substantial, direct damage limitation to provide a credible U.S. threat of nuclear escalation and meaningful protection in the event deterrence utterly collapsed. The balance of terror remained the necessary basis for protection against the Soviet nuclear threat to U.S. society.

Consequently, that the United States retained some programs for limited damage limitation, and did not plan to employ strategic capabilities according to assured destruction quotients, hardly indicated U.S. rejection of the balance of terror or even much of a departure from the assured destruction metric. Secretary McNamara's "coercive strategy" was dependent on the balance of terror because, as envisaged, modest levels of offensive and defensive damage limitation could provide no independent, meaningful value apart from it, per his expressed definition of "meaningful."

The Primacy of the Balance of Terror Formula

The overwhelming influence of the stable balance of terror formula is amply demonstrated by the U.S. Government's decades-long policy—beginning in the early 1960s—to curtail, if not eliminate entirely, programs intended to reduce directly U.S. societal vulnerability to Soviet nuclear attack *to the extent thought feasible at the time.* U.S. strategy relied on deterrence and intra-war deterrence as the basic means of protection, and balance of terror metrics defined the type of strategic arsenal considered necessary and adequate for deterrence. Beyond the modest damage-limiting capabilities that might be meaningful if the balance of terror could be made to "work" during war, there remained no room for significant offensive counterforce or defensive damage-limiting capabilities because they were regarded as unnecessary, useless and "destabilizing" of the mutual deterrence that was the overarching goal of U.S. strategic policy.

This was a conscious policy choice to place priority on "stable" mutual deterrence at the expense of the substantial damage-limitation capability believed to be feasible. The balance of terror formula posited that deterrence stability and significant damage limitation were mutually exclusive and, when this apparent tradeoff was confronted, Secretary McNamara's choice was in favor of stable mutual deterrence. It was considered reliable, predictable, effective and more affordable for societal protection than unilateral damage-limitation capabilities and, ironically perhaps, it was less controversial.

This choice was at the heart of the U.S. strategic debates of the mid-to-late 1960s, and was recognized by Secretary McNamara as such.[138] The JCS, Army, and Air Force—in opposition to the "three no's"—pushed for strategic offensive and defensive programs intended to provide the United States with substantial, direct damage-limiting capabilities. The JCS fully understood and recognized the contrary balance of terror orientation of the

DPMs, and frequently registered its principled opposition. For example, its originally Top Secret comments on the draft 1968 DPM included the following:

> The implications of the rationale and the tentative recommendations in the DPM are that the United States has neither the capacity nor intent to acquire the strategic force capabilities, to include damage limiting, required to pursue effectively a complete military strategy. While the principal military objective of the United States with regard to strategic nuclear warfare is to deter an attack upon the United States, our deterrent could fail for a number of reasons. Important among these are miscalculation of intent or resolve, underestimation of military capabilities, or commission of an irrational act. Should deterrence fail, the principal objective is to terminate hostilities under conditions of relative advantage while limiting damage to the United States and minimizing damage to US and allied interests. This latter objective is considered to be as important as deterring nuclear war since, if deterrence fails, we must ensure the continued existence of the nation by safeguarding the survival of our essential political, military, and economic structure.[139]

In line with Kahn's approach to U.S. deterrence strategy, the JCS sought a U.S. nuclear escalation capability made credible for deterrence and extended deterrence by the direct U.S. capability to reduce U.S. fatalities and damage to meaningful levels *in comparison to the level of destruction that otherwise would occur in the event of war.* This was not a strategy choice that *rejected deterrence* in favor of defensive capabilities; rather, it placed considerable priority on the goal of reducing civilian casualties directly in the event deterrence failed and on the acquisition of strategic forces for that purpose.

Accordingly, in language consistent with Kahn's earlier recommendations, an Air Force report to Secretary McNamara read: "The Air Force has rather supported the development of forces which provide the United States a first-strike capability credible to the Soviet Union, as well as to our Allies, by virtue of our ability to limit damage to the United States and our Allies to levels *acceptable in light of the circumstances and the alternatives available.*"[140] In contrast to the balance of terror narrative, proposed here was a principled and coherent strategy of deterrence that *incorporated* direct damage limitation as a priority goal and metric for force acquisition.

Secretary McNamara and his Pentagon staff *instead* consciously adopted assured destruction and a stable balance of terror as the preferred guide to U.S. policy and force sizing. He made explicit in his 1962 DPM that this was the fundamental strategic policy choice to be made, and that his choice was to reject attempts to deploy U.S. forces, "so large and effective" that "the resulting damage to ourselves and our Allies could be considered acceptable on some reasonable definition of the term."[141]

In particular, Secretary McNamara pointed to the U.S. inability to eliminate Soviet nuclear-powered, missile-carrying submarines promptly and the corresponding enduring Soviet capability to destroy many U.S. cities as a reason for this choice. In the 1962 DPM, for example, he said that even after a U.S. first strike against Soviet nuclear forces, "... approximately 100 submarine-launched missiles could be at sea. If these remaining forces were targeted against U.S. cities, they could inflict roughly 50 million direct fatalities in the United States, even with fallout protection. I do not consider this an 'acceptable' level of damage."[142]

In his 1963 DPM to President Kennedy, Secretary McNamara elaborated on the problem further:

> But the same means we are using to achieve a posture of 'Assured Destruction' are available to the Soviets. In particular, as indicated earlier, we expect the Soviets to have, at a minimum, between 185 and 236 ballistic missiles on submarines by 1969. There is also a possibility that a portion of their cruise-missile submarine force could be assigned to targets in the U.S. Although we can have an effective capability to sink enemy attack submarines in a protracted war of attrition at sea, we do not appear to have any realistic prospect of being able to destroy a major part of the Soviet deployed submarine missile force in a sudden attack.[143]

The basic differences between Schelling and Kahn were expressed in practice and in explicit language at the highest levels of U.S. defense policy making: Secretary McNamara—judging a *worthy* level of damage limitation to be unaffordable, impracticable and destabilizing—instead endorsed and sought to facilitate a "stable" mutual balance of terror with the Soviet Union.   In contrast, the JCS and the Air Force—reflecting Kahn—placed priority on the goals of deterrence *and* reducing prospective casualties with U.S. damage-limitation capabilities.   They favored acquisition of offensive *and* defensive forces to strengthen deterrence and to protect the U.S. population directly. The JCS continued without success to press for U.S. adoption of this significant damage-limitation goal and corresponding capabilities well into the Nixon Administration.[144] The U.S. civilian leadership's rejection of the same also continued.

It is a simple matter to question the values and choices Secretary McNamara brought to this historic question: it was *not self-evident* that the U.S. Government should have preferred an approach to deterrence that eschewed protection for scores of millions of citizens because millions of others could not be protected under plausible conditions. The policy choice *not* to acquire capabilities that could protect much of the population made sense *only* if the priority goal was a balance of terror and there was great faith that it would prevent war reliably.

Kahn argued by analogy that the same logic which pointed to a stable balance of terror as the preferred policy guidance would suggest that lifeboats on ships should be eschewed because they could be expensive, only partially effective, leave survivors to die at sea, lower the captain's fear of collisions, and thereby encourage reckless navigation.[145] That logic could indeed be persuasive *if*—to continue with the lifeboat analogy—it also is believed that the prospects for a collision could be made so exceedingly low that preparations to save passengers could be considered a low priority and not worth the expected cost. Similarly, the fundamental question for U.S. strategic policy was whether nuclear deterrence could be considered so reliable that the value of imperfect damage-limitation preparations could be judged a low priority and not worth the expected cost.   Secretary McNamara's position, as with the Cold War balance of terror framework in general, was built on the belief that deterrence could be orchestrated to achieve that high level of reliability.

The preferred course is obvious if there is extreme confidence in a "stable" balance of terror, and thus the choice is believed to be between a policy of deterrence that virtually promises no war and thus no fatalities, or an expensive, "destabilizing" damage-limitation policy thought to increase the probability of a war with millions of fatalities. The route that preserves security with no war and no casualties must appear the prudent choice.

This was the basic character of the question as structured by Secretary McNamara and the balance of terror framework in general.

As Kahn's work, and the Air Force and JCS quotes above suggest, however, different expectations about the reliability of deterrence and the value of imperfect defenses could lead to a far different view of the available choices. If deterrence could *not* be rendered predictably reliable, and thus there existed an *unavoidable and uncontrollable chance of a nuclear war*, then what? According to the calculations presented by and to Secretary McNamara, with no U.S. strategic damage limitation to mitigate the consequences of war, there could have been over 160 million U.S. fatalities. With substantial, expensive damage limitation, however, that number of fatalities might have been reduced by more than 100 million, to 40-50 million fatalities.[146] It was in this very select context that the JCS and Air Force could find considerable value in partial societal protection and consider significant damage-limitation preparations to be the prudent choice and worthy of the cost.

With obvious confidence in the predictable functioning of deterrence in a stable balance of terror, Secretary McNamara instead found inadequate value in the expensive, partial damage limitation considered feasible. High confidence in his assured destruction metric and a stable balance of terror trumped the goal of direct damage limitation because the latter's potential value paled when set against his apparent confidence in and the affordability of stable deterrence and the prevention of war altogether. And, given the belief that damage-limitation capabilities posed a threat to stable deterrence, they could only be regarded as *worse than useless*.

Donald Baucom, staff historian for the U.S. missile defense program, linked Secretary McNamara's opposition to BMD directly to "... his growing conviction that the most effective way to deter nuclear war was to possess an offensive force that could assure destruction of the Soviet Union as a viable society....Therefore, it made no sense to invest in defenses in the mid-1960s because a better return on the dollar could be had by enhancing the ability of offensive forces to penetrate enemy defenses, thereby ensuring deterrence through assured destruction."[147]

This policy position reflected the extreme confidence of U.S. senior civilian officials in their understanding of the opponent and deterrence, and thus their belief that they could manipulate Soviet decision making predictably by controlling the characteristics of the U.S. nuclear arsenal. This belief was the central tenet of the balance of terror theory of deterrence. Intentional mutual vulnerability was a reasonable policy option *if* the theory could be put into policy practice and made to "work" reliably and predictably. However, having put that theory into practice as did Secretary McNamara, if deterrence ever utterly failed or simply was irrelevant to a crisis, the partial levels of physical protection that otherwise could have been available for the U.S. population would have been absent by conscious policy choice. The ensuing nuclear holocaust would have been unmitigated as a result of that conscious policy choice. This was the practical effect of following a deterrence strategy defined by the balance of terror formula and the assured destruction metric. It was a policy decision based on faith in the capability of governments to understand and orchestrate deterrence to prevent nuclear war altogether and without fail, or at least to prevent it from escalating to the mutual destruction of society.

Interestingly, the technical skepticism applied to the potential for creating a worthy damage-limitation capability was *not* applied to expectations regarding the functioning of deterrence, despite the unavoidable fact that the predictable functioning of deterrence requires the fine-tuned and timely orchestration of many unpredictable and un-controllable "moving parts." Naïve confidence in the predictable functioning of a stable balance of terror contrasted sharply with obvious skepticism regarding the prospects for highly-effective damage limitation at the time. The latter skepticism is understandable. The former—unfettered confidence in the predictable, easy functioning of deterrence—reflects a breathtaking lack of appreciation for the complexities involved in the predictable functioning of deterrence. Skepticism so asymmetrically applied in this fashion could lead only to a policy choice in favor of a balance of terror.

As noted above, many mistakenly claim that the U.S. rejection of damage limitation, and particularly BMD, was simply recognition of technical and cost realities, not a policy choice: "The crucial reason was that the mission of full-scale, countrywide missile defense was too difficult to perform in operational terms, and it was also unaffordable. The technology of ABM defense did not allow either country to build a reliable shield over itself even had the large sums needed been devoted to this endeavor. Full-scale ABM defense was simply impossible for both sides...."[148] This interpretation of U.S. decision making that attributes the U.S. rejection of damage limitation to technical issues and cost alone misses most of the actual story.

Secretary McNamara's recommendation against damage limitation for U.S. cities as a policy and acquisition goal clearly was not simply the result of technical realities. It also reflected an interrelated set of beliefs and judgments about the functioning of deterrence, the appropriate prioritization of goals, and the capabilities and character of the Soviet Union. Based on his own account, Secretary McNamara rejected a significant, direct, damage-limitation goal and the acquisition of related strategic capabilities because he believed that: the Soviet Union had an assured destruction metric for its strategic forces and thus would seek to keep U.S. societal vulnerability high; the cost disadvantage for the United States in an offensive-defensive competition (3:1 to 4:1) was intolerable and would yield an imperfect and unworthy level of defense effectiveness; and, the Soviet Union's *confidence* in its own assured destruction threat contributed to the priority goal of a stable balance of terror. Thus, U.S. defensive capabilities would be worse than expensive and partial; they would undermine deterrence. The available declassified record consistently reflects the importance of these expectations and judgments in the U.S. rejection of BMD and damage limitation in general.

As noted, Secretary McNamara emphasized that cost would not be a consideration *if* the United States "could build and deploy a genuinely impenetrable shield," but that, "none of the [BMD] systems at the present or foreseeable state of the art would provide an impenetrable shield over the United States." [149] *By identifying a "genuinely impenetrable" defense as the effectiveness threshold at which cost would not matter, Secretary McNamara set a standard that never could be met and ensured that the offensive-defensive cost ratio would be a critical consideration.*

Armed with the same expectations about the effectiveness and cost of damage-limitation programs, but also with *an alternative set of beliefs and judgments*—about the reliability of deterrence, likely Soviet behavior, and the value of substantial albeit partial defense—the prudent policy choice could have been to place high priority on the goal of direct protection for the U.S. population. This policy choice with regard to priorities and values correspondingly could have led to full acceptance of an integrated deterrence and damage-limitation strategy, with the acquisition of robust strategic defense capabilities judged able to protect scores of millions of lives. As noted, this was Kahn's approach to the subject, and the position reflected in commentary by the JCS, the Air Force, and much of the senior military leadership.

Senior members of Secretary McNamara's Pentagon staff expressed exasperation with the U.S. military's continuing opposition to the stable balance of terror deterrence strategy and its embrace of deliberate American vulnerability to nuclear attack; they complained that this reluctance on the part of the military reflected an inability to comprehend the new realities of nuclear weapons. The charge was that the U.S. military was stuck in primitive thought patterns, and that traditional military professionals had "no clear claim to special wisdom" regarding the new subject of nuclear deterrence and policy.[150] This was part and parcel of the view, discussed in Chapter 3, that stable balance of terror thinking broke with traditional notions of strategy, was avant-garde and scientific, and a new, even revolutionary approach to security that left past "wisdom" behind.

American civilian officials eventually expressed similar exasperation with Soviet military planners who also eschewed the stable balance of terror requirement for mutual societal vulnerability to nuclear attack. Paul Warnke famously remarked that the continuing, "primitive" Soviet policy of strategic damage limitation indicated the need for more U.S. tutorials:

> This kind of [Soviet] thinking is on a level of abstraction which is unrealistic. It seems to me that instead of talking in these terms, which would indulge what I regard as the primitive aspects of Soviet nuclear doctrine, we ought to be trying to educate them into the real world of strategic nuclear weapons, which is that nobody could possibly win. Nor could anybody calculate what the consequences would be in the event of a strategic nuclear exchange.[151]

For Paul Warnke, a civilian official, to speak of Soviet nuclear doctrine as "primitive," and "trying to educate" the Soviet General Staff about the "real world" of nuclear weapons reflected the hubris frequently exhibited by balance of terror enthusiasts. The point here, however, is not to critique the logic, values or ego behind the assured destruction metric and balance of terror-derived policy choices. It is to identify that logic and those values and choices, and to understand how Secretary McNamara came to the historic policy conclusion that the United States should give up the "common defense" mandated in the U.S. Constitution and considered feasible at the time, in deference to a concept of stable deterrence that placed priority on abetting U.S. societal vulnerability. The balance of terror tenets played powerfully in that policy choice.

In summary, Secretary McNamara's own accounting over the course of years makes apparent his acceptance of Schelling's basic balance of terror tenets with respect to mutual deterrence and the Soviet Union, and his translation of those tenets into Department of Defense policy guidance for U.S. strategic force acquisition. That the desiderata for a stable balance of terror captured the intellectual basis for Secretary McNamara's decisions is reflected in numerous primary source documents, most importantly his annual, once highly-classified and authoritative decision documents, the strategic force DPMs. These same documents reveal, however, that while in office Secretary McNamara publicly identified and expressed support for a different acquisition metric and set of goals for U.S. strategic forces *vis-à-vis* the emerging Chinese nuclear threat. As noted above, in the case of China he identified *not* a stable balance of terror, but Kahn's formula of pursuing simultaneously deterrence and direct, unilateral damage-limitation capabilities.

McNamara's Apparent Rejection of a U.S.-Chinese Balance of Terror

As mentioned above, as early as 1964 Secretary McNamara made a clear distinction between the Soviet Union and China with regard to the potential value of a U.S. damage-limiting goal and capabilities.[152] Schelling also made such a distinction.[153]

With respect to China—whose strategic nuclear capabilities and potential were so limited compared to those of the Soviet Union—Secretary McNamara concluded that, in the event of a possible future nuclear war, the United States could limit societal damage so effectively in absolute terms that a significant damage-limitation goal was the appropriate policy priority.[154] The Johnson Administration moved far forward to establish a substantive, direct damage-limitation policy goal against China, including the initiation of the *Sentinel* BMD program for the expressed purpose of defending U.S. cities against a future Chinese nuclear missile attack.

Secretary McNamara announced the deployment of *Sentinel* during a 1967 speech in San Francisco. He explained that deploying a ballistic missile defense system for U.S. cities against the massive Soviet nuclear threat would reflect a "foolish and feckless" policy because the Soviets surely would respond and render it ineffective. Deploying a "thin" system to protect against Chinese attack, however, *would be "prudent" because deterrence could fail,* and against the more modest foreseeable Chinese nuclear missile threat, *ballistic missile defense would be effective and affordable*. He also observed that, in the case of China, effective U.S. missile defense would strengthen confidence in the U.S. extended deterrent in Asia and therefore help ensure that allies could continue to feel secure *without their own nuclear weapons.* It would, therefore, contribute to U.S. nuclear non-proliferation goals.

Secretary McNamara presented the case for significant societal protection against Chinese attack for the purposes of direct damage limitation, making U.S. extended deterrence guarantees credible, and contributing to non-proliferation. As a separate, secondary benefit *Sentinel* would provide the basis for a future possible defense of U.S. ICBMs to protect against increases in Soviet offensive threats *to U.S. assured destruction retaliatory capabilities.*[155]

Secretary McNamara sounded these same themes in his 1968 strategic forces DPM. The Department of Defense projected the effectiveness of U.S. BMD against future Chinese missile attacks involving 10, 25, and 75 ICBMs armed with extremely high-yield nuclear warheads.[156] This now-declassified assessment showed that, in the event of the largest postulated Chinese attack of 75 ICBMs, the projected "thin" U.S. missile defense system by itself would reduce the number of U.S. fatalities by 95 percent—from 20 million fatalities to 1 million. In the other cases presented, the "thin" U.S. defense would reduce U.S. fatalities from as high as 10 million to "fewer than one million U.S. dead, with some probability of no deaths."[157] He also again emphasized that missile defense against China could contribute to the credibility of the U.S. extended deterrent in Asia.

In the case of China, Secretary McNamara's remarks were largely in line with Kahn's approach to U.S. strategic policy and fully contrary to placing priority on a balance of terror. An imperfect U.S. BMD in the case of the Chinese missile threat was judged worth the effort because deterrence might fail and defenses could provide a high level of absolute effectiveness at tolerable cost.

Then Secretary of the Air Force, Harold Brown, who later served as Secretary of Defense in the Carter Administration, also emphasized limited BMD deployment to protect against third party (i.e., non-Soviet) missile threats, and particularly against the emerging Chinese missile threat. He suggested that the United States consider deploying between 100 and 1,000 BMD interceptors for this purpose.[158] The Johnson Administration came to a close with this decision and an intact budgeted program to defend against Chinese missiles.

Additional primary, declassified documents from the period reveal that while Secretary McNamara *provided the intellectual case for deploying limited BMD to protect against Chinese missiles, he personally remained uncommitted to doing so.* Rather, Secretary McNamara felt "very, very strong" political pressure from Congress to deploy some BMD, but told President Johnson that he would wait to deploy even a "thin" system against China.[159]

Nonetheless, the Johnson Administration decided to move forward with *Sentinel* deployment and Secretary McNamara made the pertinent announcement in his 1967 San Francisco speech. Later, he said of that part of the speech in which he endorsed "thin" BMD deployment: "I would like to scrap and remove [it] from the records....The only reason that was in there was...to recognize the political pressure and the fact that the Congress had authorized such a system, appropriated funds for it, and was pushing unmercifully to deploy not the thin system but a thick system."[160]

Thus, Secretary McNamara made the intellectual case for "thin" BMD to protect U.S. cities. In making the case, he identified a clear distinction between the Soviet Union and China: he believed mutual deterrence through a stable balance of terror to be an acceptable basis for strategic force acquisition in the case of the Soviet Union, and judged the sustainable level of damage limitation to be unacceptable. Against the Soviet Union, U.S. forces were to be procured according to the assured destruction metric, thereby facilitating mutual vulnerability and the conditions for a "stable" balance of terror.

In contrast, as noted, Secretary McNamara expressed interest in the goal of *precluding the establishment of a balance of terror relationship with China*: "China's more primitive technology and poorer economy allow us to develop an effective defense against her nuclear attack capability."[161] Here Secretary McNamara argued that deploying defensive capabilities to preclude or limit damage directly was the right priority because insurance against the failure of deterrence was valuable, and an affordable and acceptable absolute level of damage limitation was feasible *vis-à-vis* China.   *can't trust dkmrwl (cultural revolution at the time)*

As already mentioned, the distinction Secretary McNamara made between China and the Soviet Union with regard to U.S. strategic policy provides insight into the thresholds he considered meaningful in deciding the future of U.S. strategic forces and policy in this regard. The apparent keys to understanding this dramatically different approach to strategy included the operative definitions of what would constitute an affordable and acceptable absolute level of defense effectiveness and the expected risk of deterrence failure. When U.S. defenses were projected to be affordable—and provide for one million or fewer U.S. fatalities, "with some probability of no deaths"—and the functioning of deterrence was judged to be less than certain, a policy of direct damage limitation was considered a superior alternative to a mutual balance of terror.

Secretary McNamara rightly is considered responsible for establishing "stable" balance of terror guidelines and the assured destruction metric as the basis for U.S. strategic policy with regard to the Soviet Union. He led the Pentagon in this direction and was deeply involved in the historic policy decision to forego significant damage-limitation capabilities in favor of a deterrence theory built on sustained mutual societal vulnerability. The honor or blame for the institutionalization and perpetuation of that Cold War policy direction, however, must be awarded on a bipartisan basis. While future leaders thoroughly revised Secretary McNamara's assured destruction metric, the basic balance of terror guidelines continued to dominate U.S. strategic policy through Republican and Democratic administrations to the end of the Cold War. In particular, the Nixon Administration not only continued the basic approach established by Secretary McNamara; it reaffirmed, expanded and codified the balance of terror. The next chapter examines this continuing primacy of Schelling's school of thought.

Endnotes

1. Thomas Schelling, *Arms and Influence* (New Haven, CT: Yale University Press, 1966), pp. vi-vii.

2. Thomas Schelling, *The Strategy of Conflict* (Cambridge, MA: Harvard University Press, 1960), p. 16.

3. Ibid., p. 4.

4. Alexander L. George and Richard Smoke, *Deterrence in American Foreign Policy: Theory and Practice* (New York: Columbia University Press, 1974), p. 83.

5. Testimony of Jerome Wiesner in U.S. Senate, Committee on Foreign Relations, Subcommittee on Arms Control, International Law and Organization, *ABM, MIRV, SALT, and the Nuclear Arms Race*, Hearings, 91st Congress, 2nd Session (Washington, D.C.: USGPO, 1970), p. 402.

6. Draft Memorandum for the President, Secretary of Defense [Robert S. McNamara] to the President [John F. Kennedy], Subj: Recommended Long Range Nuclear Delivery Forces 1963-1967, Appendix I, September 23, 1961, p. 5. (Originally classified; sanitized and declassified January 5, 1983); cited hereafter as 1961 DPM. This and other Draft Presidential Memoranda can be found online at the Master OFOI Reading Room, Department of Defense, http://www.dod.mil/pubs/foi/master_reading_ list01.html.

7. Caspar Weinberger, *The Potential Effects of Nuclear War on the Climate: A Report to the United States Congress* (Washington, D.C.: USGPO, 1985), p. 11.

8. James Schlesinger, *Annual Defense Department Report Fiscal Year 1975* (Washington, D.C.: USGPO, March 4, 1974), p. 39.

9. John M. Collins, *U.S.-Soviet Military Balance: 1980-1985* (Washington, D.C.: Congressional Research Service, Spring 1985), CRS 85-89, p. 14. See also, Kenneth Schaffel, *The Emerging Shield: The Air Force and the Evolution of Continental Air Defense, 1945-1960* (Washington, D.C.: United States Air Force, Office of Air Force History, 1991), Table 5, pp. 270-271, available at, https://www. airforcehistory.hq.af.mil/publications/fulltext/emerging-shield.pdf.

10. Donald Rumsfeld, *Annual Defense Department Report FY 1977* (Washington, D.C.: USGPO, January 27, 1976), p. 70 (Emphasis added). See also, John Collins, *U.S.-Soviet Military Balance: Concepts and Capabilities 1960-1980* (New York: McGraw-Hill Publications, 1980), p. 122.

11. For the history of U.S. civil defense spending see, General Accounting Office, *The Federal Emergency Management Agency's Plan for Revitalizing U.S. Civil Defense: A Review of Three Major Plan Components*, GAO/NSIAD-84-11 (Washington D.C.: General Accounting Office, April 16, 1984), Appendix II.

12. Quoted in, Collins, *U.S.-Soviet Military Balance: Concepts and Capabilities 1960-1980*, op. cit., p. 171.

13. Jimmy Carter, Presidential Directive/NSC-41, *U.S. Civil Defense Policy*, September 29, 1978, p. 1. (Secret; declassified on June 23, 1980).

14. Bardyl R. Tirana, in House of Representatives, Committee on Appropriations, Subcommittee on HUD—Independent Agencies, *Department of Housing and Urban Development—Independent Agencies Appropriations for 1980*, Hearings, 96th Congress, 1st Session (Washington, D.C.: USGPO, 1979), p. 488.

15. See, General Accounting Office, *The Federal Emergency Management Agency's Plan for Revitalizing U.S. Civil Defense: A Review of Three Major Plan Components*,

op. cit., Appendix II; Collins, *U.S.-Soviet Military Balance: Concepts and Capabilities 1960-1980*, op. cit., pp. 171-172; and, William E. Odom, "The Origins and Design of Presidential Decision-59: A Memoir" in Henry D. Sokolski, ed., *Getting MAD: Nuclear Mutual Assured Destruction, Its Origins, and Practice* (Carlisle, PA: Strategic Studies Institute, U.S Army War College, Nov. 2004), p. 190.

16. Tirana, loc. cit.

17. Odom, op. cit., in Sokolski, ed., op. cit., p. 189.

18. Schelling, "What Went Wrong With Arms Control?," *Foreign Affairs*, Vol. 64, No. 1 (Winter 1985/86), p. 222.

19. Fred Kaplan, *The Wizards of Armageddon* (Stanford, CA: Stanford University Press, 1983), p. 11.

20. John Newhouse, *Cold Dawn: The Story of SALT* (New York: Holt, Rinehart and Winston, 1973), p. 9. (Emphasis added).

21. Joseph S. Nye, Jr., "The Role of Strategic Nuclear Systems in Deterrence," *The Washington Quarterly*, Vol. 11, No. 2 (Spring 1988), p. 47. (Emphasis added).

22. Lawrence Freedman, *The Evolution of Nuclear Strategy* (New York: St. Martin's Press, 1983), p. 399. (Emphasis added).

23. *NATO Handbook* (Brussels: NATO Information Series, February 1974), p. 16.

24. North Atlantic Military Committee, *Final Decision on MC 14/3*, A Report by the Military Committee to the Defence Planning Committee on Overall Strategic Concept for the Defense of the North Atlantic Treaty Organization Area, MC 14/3 (Final), January 16, 1968, p. 16. Text available at, www.nato.int/docu/stratdoc/eng/a680116a.pdf.

25. Ibid., pp. 9, 10, 16. (Emphasis added).

26. Ibid., p. 16.

27. Dean Rusk, *As I Saw It* (London: W.W. Norton & Company, 1990), p. 228.

28. Ibid. See also, Arnold Beichman, "How Foolish Khrushchev Nearly Started World War III," *The Washington Times*, October 3, 2004, p. B 8.

29. National Intelligence Estimate Number 4-70, *The Clandestine Introduction of Nuclear Weapons Into the US*, NIE-4-70, July 7, 1970, CIA Historical Review Program, Release in Full, Release Date, February 4, 1994, pp. 3-4. (Top Secret; declassified January 31, 1994).

30. Richard Nixon, National Security Council, National Security Decision Memorandum-242, *Policy for Planning the Employment of Nuclear Weapons*, January 17, 1974, p. 2. (Top Secret; declassified February 20, 1998); cited hereafter as NSDM-242.

31. Schlesinger, op. cit., p. 33.

32. See the briefing on September 11, 1974 by Secretary of Defense James Schlesinger, in U.S. Senate, Committee on Foreign Relations, Subcommittee on Arms Control, *Briefing on Counterforce Attacks*, Hearings, 93rd Congress, 2nd Session (Washington, D.C.: USGPO, 1975), p. 37; and, James Schlesinger, in U.S. Senate, Committee on Foreign Relations, *U.S.-U.S.S.R. Strategic Policies,* Hearings, 93rd Congress, 2nd Session (Washington, D.C.: USGPO, 1974), p. 9.

33. Schlesinger, *Annual Defense Department Report Fiscal Year 1975,* op. cit., pp. 37-38; and, Schlesinger, *U.S.-U.S.S.R. Strategic Policies*, op. cit., pp. 8, 12-13.

34. Presidential Directive/NSC-59, *Nuclear Weapons Employment Policy*, July 25, 1980 (Top Secret/Sensitive; partially declassified August 20, 1996); cited hereafter as PD-59. Available at the Jimmy Carter Presidential Library at, http://www.jimmycarterlibrary.org/documents/pddirectives/pd59.pdf;.

35. See the comments by Secretary of Defense Harold Brown in, U.S. Senate, Committee on Foreign Relations, *Nuclear War Strategy*, Hearings, 96th Congress, 2nd Session (Washington, D.C.: USGPO, 1981), pp. 15, 21-23. (Top Secret Hearing; sanitized and printed on February 18, 1981).

36. Speech by Secretary of Defense Robert S. McNamara before United Press International Editors and Publishers, San Francisco, California, September 18, 1967. See, Robert S. McNamara, "Text of McNamara Speech on Anti-Chinese Missile Defense and U.S. Nuclear Strategy," *The New York Times*, September 19, 1967, p. 18.

37. The acronym MAD appears to have been the creation of Donald Brennan, who served as the Director of National Security Studies at the Hudson Institute. See, "When the SALT Hit the Fan," *National Review*, June 23, 1972, pp. 685-692.

38. Alain Enthoven, *Management of Department of Defense Programs*, AIAA Paper, No. 68-796, CASI/AIAA Management in the Fields of Aerospace Meeting, July 8-9, 1968, Montreal, Canada, pp. 3, 4.

39. See, for example, Draft Memorandum for the President, Secretary of Defense [Robert S. McNamara] to the President [John F. Kennedy], Subj: Recommended FY 1964-FY 1968 Strategic Retaliatory Forces, November 21, 1962, p. 9. (Originally classified; sanitized and declassified on January 5, 1983); cited hereafter as 1962 DPM.

40. Draft Memorandum for the President, Secretary of Defense [Robert S. McNamara] to the President [Lyndon B. Johnson], Subj: Strategic Offensive and Defensive Forces, January 15, 1968, p. 5. (Originally classified; sanitized and declassified on January 5, 1983); cited hereafter as 1968 DPM.

41. Ibid.

42. Ibid., p. 8.

43. *History of the Strategic Arms Competition: 1945-1972, Part II*, Alfred Goldberg, ed., with contributions by Ernest R. May, John D. Steinbruner, and Thomas W. Wolfe (Washington, D.C.: Historical Office, Office of the Secretary of Defense, March 1981), p. 818. (Emphasis in original).

44. Ibid., p. 819. (Emphasis in original).

45. For explicit statements along these lines see, Alain Enthoven and K. Wayne Smith, *How Much Is Enough? Shaping the Defense Program, 1961-1969* (New York: Harper and Row, 1971), pp. 174-196, 207-210.

46. Robert S. McNamara, *Blundering Into Disaster: Surviving the First Century of the Nuclear Age* (New York: Pantheon Books, 1986), pp. 45-47. See also, Draft Memorandum for the President, Secretary of Defense [Robert S. McNamara] to the President [Lyndon B. Johnson], Subj: Recommended FY 1965-FY 1969 Strategic Retaliatory Forces, December 6, 1963, p. I-35. (Originally classified; sanitized and declassified on January 5, 1983); cited hereafter as 1963 DPM.

47. Carl Kaysen, Robert S. McNamara, and George Rathjens, "Nuclear Weapons After the Cold War," *Foreign Affairs*, Vol. 70, No. 4 (Fall 1991), p. 100.

48. 1961 DPM, op. cit., p. 6.

49. 1962 DPM, op. cit., p. 5.

50. 1961 DPM, op. cit., p. 4.

51. 1961 DPM, op. cit., p. 5.

52. 1962 DPM, op. cit., pp. 7-9.

53. *Strategic Implications of Antiballistic Missile Defense Deployment*, Hearing, February 7, 1967, in Senate Foreign Relations Committee, *Executive Sessions of*

the Senate Foreign Relations Committee Together With the Senate Armed Services Committee (Historical Series), Vol. 19, 90th Congress, 1st Session, 1967 (Washington, D.C.: USGPO, 2007), p. 41.

54. 1968 DPM, op. cit., p. 5.

55. 1962 DPM, op. cit., pp. 7-8; and, 1963 DPM, op. cit., pp. I-21-I-22.

56. *Strategic Implications of Antiballistic Missile Defense Deployment*, loc. cit.

57. 1963 DPM, op. cit., p. I-5.

58. Draft Memorandum for the President, Secretary of Defense [Robert S. McNamara] to the President [Lyndon B. Johnson], Subj: Recommended FY 1966-FY 1970 Programs for Strategic Offensive Forces, Continental Air and Missile Defense Forces, and Civil Defense, December 3, 1964, p. 4. (Originally classified; sanitized and declassified on January 5, 1983); cited hereafter as 1964 DPM (Emphasis added).

59. Enthoven and Smith, op. cit., p. 176.

60. 1968 DPM, op. cit., p. 8.

61. Draft Memorandum for the President, Secretary of Defense [Robert S. McNamara] to the President [Lyndon B. Johnson], Subj: Recommended FY 1968-FY 1972 Strategic Offensive and Defensive Forces, November 9, 1966, p. 9. (Originally classified; sanitized and declassified on January 5, 1983); cited hereafter as 1966 DPM.

62. 1963 DPM, op. cit., p. I-12; and, 1968 DPM, op. cit., p. 9.

63. Robert S. McNamara, *The Essence of Security: Reflections in Office* (New York: Harper and Row, 1968), pp. 52-53.

64. See, Enthoven and Smith, op. cit., pp. 317-319.

65. Ibid., pp. 207-208.

66. Ibid., p. 67; and, 1964 DPM, op. cit., p. 17.

67. 1963 DPM, op. cit., p. I-14.

68. 1968 DPM, op. cit., p. 10.

69. Ibid., p. 11. (Emphasis added).

70. Henry S. Rowen, "Formulating Strategic Doctrine," Commission on the Organization of the Government for the Conduct of Foreign Policy, Volume 4, Appendix K: *Adequacy of Current Organization: Defense and Arms Control* (Washington, D.C.: USGPO, June 1975), p. 227. See also, Enthoven and Smith, op. cit., pp. 23-24, 170-171, 179, 194-195.

71. 1968 DPM, op. cit., p. 16. (Emphasis added).

72. 1963 DPM, op. cit., pp. I-18, I-22.

73. Ibid., p. I-14; see also, p. I-4.

74. 1968 DPM, op. cit., pp. 11-13.

75. Draft Memorandum From Secretary of Defense McNamara to President Kennedy, November 14, 1963, U.S. Department of State, *Foreign Relations of the United States, 1961-1963*, Vol. 8, National Security Policy (Washington, D.C.: USGPO, 1996), Document 145. This and other FRUS documents can be found online at the Office of the Historian, Bureau of Public Affairs, U.S. State Department, http://www.state.gov/r/pa/ho/frus/index.htm.

76. Ibid.

77. Ibid.

78. Ibid.

79. See his testimony in, House Foreign Affairs Committee, *Strategy and Science: Toward a National Security Policy for the 1970's*, Hearings, 91st Congress, 1st Session

(Washington, D.C.: USGPO, 1969), p. 125.

80. See, for example, Memorandum From the Chairman of the Joint Chiefs of Staff (Wheeler) to Secretary of Defense McNamara, November 23, 1964, U.S. Department of State, *Foreign Relations of the United States, 1964-1968*, Vol. 10, National Security Policy (Washington, D.C.: USGPO, 2001), Document 61; and, Draft Notes of Meeting (with the President, Secretary McNamara, and the Joint Chiefs of Staff in Austin, Texas), December 6, 1966, U.S. Department of State, *Foreign Relations of the United States, 1964-1968*, Vol. 10, National Security Policy (Washington, D.C.: USGPO, 2001), Document 150.

81. See, McNamara, *The Essence of Security*, op. cit., pp. 63-67.

82. 1964 DPM, op. cit., p. 22.

83. McNamara, *The Essence of Security*, op. cit., p. 66.

84. Quoted in, Glenn T. Seaborg, *Stemming the Tide: Arms Control in the Johnson Years* (Lexington, MA: D.C. Heath and Company, 1987), pp. 426-427.

85. See, Memorandum of Conversation, Glassboro, New Jersey, June 23, 1967, *Foreign Relations of the United States, 1964-1968,* Volume 14, Soviet Union (Washington D.C.: USGPO, 2001), Document 231.

86. 1962 DPM, op. cit., p. 10.

87. 1963 DPM, op. cit., pp. 22-23; 1964 DPM, op. cit., pp. 25-26. See also, *Damage Limiting: A Rationale for the Allocation of Resources by the US and the USSR*, prepared for the Director of Defense Research and Engineering, R&E Log No. 64-248, January 21, 1964 (Secret; sanitized and declassified after 12 years), pp. 39-42. This can be found online at http://www.dod.mil/pubs/foi/russia_soviet_union/.

88. 1962 DPM, op. cit., pp. 8-9.

89. Ibid., pp. 8-10.

90. Ibid., p. 9.

91. Ibid.

92. 1964 DPM, op. cit., p. 4.

93. McNamara, *The Essence of Security*, op. cit., pp. 63-64.

94. 1964 DPM, op. cit., pp. 19-22. See also 1962 DPM, op. cit., pp. 8-9.

95. Summary Record of the 517th Meeting of the National Security Council, September 12, 1963, U.S. Department of State, *Foreign Relations of the United States, 1961-1963*, Vol. 8, National Security Policy (Washington, D.C.: USGPO, 1996), Document 141.

96. 1964 DPM, op. cit., p. 4. (Emphasis added).

97. Draft Memorandum for the President, Secretary of Defense [Robert S. McNamara] to the President [Lyndon B. Johnson], Subj: Recommended FY 1967-FY 1971 Strategic Offensive and Defensive Forces, November 1, 1965, p. 4. (Originally classified; sanitized and declassified on January 5, 1983); cited hereafter as 1965 DPM.

98. 1965 DPM, op. cit., p. 20.

99. 1962 DPM, op. cit., p. 8.

100. 1968 DPM, op. cit., p. 5.

101. See, for example, 1965 DPM, op. cit., p. 5; and, 1968 DPM, op. cit., pp. 6, 19.

102. 1968 DPM, op. cit., p. 19.

103. Ibid., p. 6.

104. Loc. cit.

105. *Conference of War and Politics*, sponsored by the Center for International and Strategic Affairs, University of California at Los Angeles, November 16-17, 1979.

106. McGeorge Bundy, "Existential Deterrence and Its Consequences," in *The Security Gamble: Deterrence Dilemmas in the Nuclear Age*, Douglas MacLean, ed. (Totowa, NJ: Rowman & Allanheld, 1984), p. 5. (Emphasis added).

107. *Damage Limiting: A Rationale for the Allocation of Resources by the US and the USSR*, op. cit., p. 58.

108. 1964 DPM, op. cit., p. 31.

109. Lawrence Kaplan, Ronald Landa, and Edward Drea, *History of the Office of the Secretary of Defense, The McNamara Ascendancy, 1961-1965*, Volume V (Washington, D.C.: Historical Office, Office of the Secretary of Defense, 2006), p. 320. (Emphasis added).

110. McNamara, *Blundering Into Disaster: Surviving the First Century of the Nuclear Age*, op. cit., pp. 45-47; 1963 DPM, op. cit., p. I-35.

111. Alain Enthoven, "Reflections on the Development of U.S. Strategic Offensive and Defensive Forces, 1961-1968," in *China-United States Comprehensive Security: Report of a Meeting* (Stanford, CA: Northeast Asia-United States Forum on International Policy, 1982), p. 104.

112. See the testimony of Donald Hornig in U.S. Senate, Committee on Armed Services, *Authorization for Military Procurement, Research and Development, FY 1971*, Hearings, Part 1, 91st Congress, 2nd Session (Washington, D.C.: USGPO, 1970), p. 2296.

113. *History of the Strategic Arms Competition: 1945-1972, Part II*, op. cit., p. 801. (Emphasis added).

114. Draft Memorandum from Secretary of Defense McNamara to President Kennedy, November 14, 1963, Document 145, op. cit.

115. Collins, *U.S.-Soviet Military Balance: Concepts and Capabilities 1960-1980*, op. cit., p. 167.

116. Schaffel, *The Emerging Shield: The Air Force and the Evolution of Continental Air Defense, 1945-1960*, op. cit., pp. 268, 272.

117. 1963 DPM, op. cit., p. I-19.

118. 1964 DPM, op. cit., pp. 21-22.

119. *Damage Limiting: A Rationale for the Allocation of Resources by the US and the USSR*, op. cit., p. 16.

120. 1965 DPM, op. cit., p. 38.

121. See, for example, Memorandum for the Record, LBJ Ranch, Texas, December 22, 1964, U.S. Department of State, *Foreign Relations of the United States, 1964-1968*, Vol. 10, National Security Policy (Washington, D.C.: USGPO, 2001), Document 71; and, Memorandum From the Chairman of the Joint Chiefs of Staff (Wheeler) to Secretary of Defense McNamara, op. cit., Document 61.

122. 1968 DPM, op. cit., p. 5.

123. Memorandum for the Record, LBJ Ranch, Texas, December 22, 1964, op. cit., Document 71.

124. 1964 DPM, op. cit., pp. 65-66.

125. Tirana, in House of Representatives, Committee on Appropriations, Subcommittee on HUD—Independent Agencies, *Department of Housing and Urban Development—Independent Agencies Appropriations for 1980*, op. cit., pp. 486, 490. According to a synopsis of Department of Defense studies during the Carter Administration, "A program of crisis relocation and in-place shelter protection [Program D] would increase the survival rate to 80 percent and would cost approximately $2.3 billion in fiscal years 1980 through 1984. A blast shelter system

[Program F], costing about $60 billion, was expected to save about 90 percent of the population." See, Thomas J. Kerr, *Civil Defense in the U.S.: Bandaid for a Holocaust?* (Boulder, CO: Westview Press, 1983), pp. 158-159.

126. Tirana, in House of Representatives, Committee on Appropriations, Subcommittee on HUD—Independent Agencies, *Department of Housing and Urban Development—Independent Agencies Appropriations for 1980*, op. cit., p. 482.

127. Collins, *U.S.-Soviet Military Balance: Concepts and Capabilities 1960-1980*, op. cit., p. 122.

128. 1963 DPM, op. cit., pp. I-18, I-20.

129. See, John Benedict, "The Unraveling and Revitalization of U.S. Navy Antisubmarine Warfare," *Naval War College Review*, Vol. 58, No. 2 (Spring 2005), pp. 98-99.

130. Bruce G. Blair, "Arms Control Implications of Anti-Submarine Warfare (ASW) Programs," in, *Evaluation of Fiscal Year 1979 Arms Control Impact Statements: Toward More Informed Congressional Participation in National Security Policymaking*, Report Prepared for the U.S. House of Representatives, Committee on International Relations by the Congressional Research Service, Library of Congress (Washington, D.C.: USGPO, 1978), pp. 112-113. (Emphasis in original).

131. Statement of Paul Warnke in, U.S. Senate, Committee on Banking, Housing and Urban Affairs, *Civil Defense*, Hearings, 95th Congress, 2nd Session (Washington, D.C.: USGPO, 1979), p. 4.

132. As claimed in, Keir Lieber and Daryl Press, "The Rise of U.S. Nuclear Primacy," *Foreign Affairs*, Vol. 85, No. 2 (March-April 2006), pp. 42-54.

133. Quoted in, Kaplan, Landa, and Drea, op. cit., p. 315.

134. Draft Memorandum for the President, Secretary of Defense [Robert S. McNamara] to the President [Lyndon B. Johnson], Subj: Strategic Offensive and Defensive Forces, January 15, 1968, p. 9. (Originally classified; sanitized and declassified on January 5, 1983).

135. 1962 DPM, op. cit., p. 9; 1963 DPM, op. cit., pp. I-18 – I-20, I-33, I-34; and 1968 DPM, op. cit., p. 9.

136. 1962 DPM, op. cit., p. 9.

137. Robert S. McNamara, "The Military Role of Nuclear Weapons: Perceptions and Misperceptions," *Foreign Affairs*, Vol. 62, No. 1 (Fall 1983), p. 79. (Emphasis added).

138. 1962 DPM, op. cit., pp. 6-7.

139. Memorandum From the Joint Chiefs of Staff to Secretary of Defense Clifford, August 26, 1968, U.S. Department of State, *Foreign Relations of the United States, 1964-1968*, Vol. 10, National Security Policy (Washington, D.C.: USGPO, 2001), Document 213.

140. 1962 DPM, op. cit., p. 6. (Emphasis added).

141. Ibid., p. 7.

142. Ibid., p. 8. See also, Draft Memorandum From Secretary of Defense McNamara to President Kennedy, November 14, 1963, Document 145, op. cit.

143. 1963 DPM, op. cit., pp. I-18, I-20.

144. The JCS unsuccessfully attempted to include a damage-limitation goal as one of the strategic force "sufficiency" criteria during the Nixon Administration. See, Henry A. Kissinger, Memorandum for the President, June 17, 1969, "June 18 NSC Meeting on U.S. Strategic Posture and SALT," with enclosures (Top Secret, declassified/released on November 7, 2000), Tab A: "Discussion of Issues for Decision," p. 5; Tab D: [NSC Study Summary] "U.S. Strategic Posture: Basic Issues," p. 9, available at, http://www.

gwu.edu/~nsarchiv/NSAEBB/NSAEBB173/SIOP-8.pdf.

145. See, Herman Kahn, *Thinking About the Unthinkable* (New York: Avon Books, 1962), pp. 93-94.

146. 1964 DPM, op. cit., p. 20.

147. Donald R. Baucom, *The Origins of SDI: 1944-1983* (Lawrence, KS: University Press of Kansas, 1992), pp. 20, 23-24.

148. Richard Kugler, *Political Analysis in National Security Affairs* (Washington, D.C.: National Defense University Press, 2006), p. 450. See also, MAJ Andrew Pache, "The Strategy of Nuclear Deterrence: Why MAD Was Sane," *NBC Report: U.S. Army Nuclear and Chemical Agency* (Fall/Winter 2005), p. 47.

149. McNamara, *The Essence of Security: Reflections in Office*, op. cit., pp. 63-64.

150. See, Enthoven and Smith, op. cit., pp. 45, 200-201.

151. See the interview of Paul Warnke in, "The Real Paul Warnke," *New Republic,* March 26, 1977, pp. 22-23. See also the discussion in, Keith B. Payne, *Nuclear Deterrence in U.S.-Soviet Relations* (Boulder, CO: Westview Press, 1982), p. 138.

152. 1964 DPM, op. cit., p. 24.

153. Schelling appears to have been sympathetic to a different approach to China, observing that, "a reasonable case" could be made for, "some defense against Chinese ICBM's." See, Thomas C. Schelling, in House of Representatives, House Foreign Affairs Committee, *Strategy and Science: Toward a National Security Policy for the 1970's*, Hearings, 91st Congress, 1st Session (Washington, D.C.: USGPO, 1969), p. 125.

154. 1968 DPM, op. cit., pp. 6, 19.

155. Speech by Secretary of Defense Robert S. McNamara, "Text of McNamara Speech on Anti-Chinese Missile Defense and U.S. Nuclear Strategy," loc. cit.

156. 1968 DPM, op. cit., p. 19.

157. Ibid.

158. Harold Brown, "Security Through Limitations," *Foreign Affairs*, Vol. 47, No. 3 (April 1969), p. 430.

159. Secretary of Defense McNamara in a Telephone Conversation With the President, January 4, 1967, Editorial Note, U.S. Department of State, *Foreign Relations of the United States, 1964-1968*, Vol. 10, National Security Policy (Washington, D.C.: USGPO, 2001), Document 167. See also the statement by Robert McNamara in, *NOVA, Visions of Star Wars*, Transcript, p. 13; and, Baucom, *The Origins of SDI: 1944-1983*, op. cit., pp. 35-38.

160. Quoted in, Baucom, op. cit., p. 37.

161. 1968 DPM, op. cit., p. 6.

Chapter 5
The Balance of Terror: A Bipartisan Monarch

> *"Wars are not caused by the buildup of weapons. They are caused when an aggressor believes he can achieve objectives at an acceptable price....Our task is to see that potential aggressors, from whatever quarter, understand plainly that the capacity and resolve of the West would deny them victory and that the price they would pay would be intolerable."*
>
> -British Prime Minister Margaret Thatcher

Following Secretary McNamara's departure from office, the subsequent January 9, 1969 DPM of the Johnson Administration by Secretary of Defense Clark Clifford repeated each of the themes regarding strategic forces and mutual deterrence developed by Secretary McNamara. These included: the action-reaction dynamic; the belief that the Soviet Union followed an assured destruction metric; the rejection of a U.S. policy of and programs for "significant" direct damage limitation against the Soviet Union, but the strong endorsement of the same *vis-à-vis* China; extreme confidence in the predictable functioning of deterrence in a balance of terror; and, the use of the assured destruction standard for U.S. strategic forces: "We continue to base the gross size of our strategic nuclear forces on Assured Destruction."[1]

Accordingly, Secretary Clifford continued the rejection of U.S. programs for significant civil defense, air defense, and missile defense consistently recommended by the JCS for protection against Soviet attack. Indeed, his recommended budget for strategic defense for 1970-1974 was almost $19 billion under that recommended by the Joint Chiefs.[2]

In the event of war with the Soviet Union, according to Secretary Clifford the U.S. goal was for the "best possible outcome."[3] But again, this expressed goal was in the context of the rejection of substantial damage-limitation programs and the belief that the action-reaction dynamic precluded the possibility of "significant" damage limitation: "Achieving a significant Damage Limiting capability against the Soviet Union does not appear to be feasible with current technology."[4] Again, meaningful protection for the U.S. population was deemed feasible only through intra-war deterrence, which in turn was considered a possibility via capabilities for controlled and limited nuclear escalation.[5] It was only within this possible wartime functioning of the balance of terror that the Secretary of Defense attributed potential value to the secondary goal of damage limitation. The "best possible outcome" if mutual deterrence *utterly* failed to limit escalation would have been unacceptable societal destruction.

Importantly, this was the first such strategic forces DPM of the decade to include an extensive discussion of U.S. arms control goals. In doing so, it revealed the extent to which balance of terror norms had come to dominate the definition of deterrence and the purpose of arms control. As noted above, Schelling had explained years earlier how arms control could support a stable balance of terror: "Schemes to avert surprise attack have as their most immediate objective the safety of weapons rather than the safety of people....They seek to perfect and to stabilize mutual deterrence—to enhance the integrity of particular weapon systems."[6]

Almost a decade later, in 1969, Schelling rightly was able to point to the profound effect this idea had on actual U.S. acquisition and arms control policy: "This concern with the vulnerability of retaliatory systems is undiminished, and properly so, a decade after it became the primary criterion for the selection of a weapons system itself. It is not much of an exaggeration to say that it has become also the primary criterion for the design of an arms agreement between the United States and the USSR."[7]

In line with Schelling's earlier recommendation and the balance of terror guidelines, Secretary Clifford's 1969 DPM explicitly identified the goals for what came to be the U.S.-Soviet Strategic Arms Limitation Talks (SALT): to "increase the stability of our deterrent," and to help secure the U.S. assured destruction capability.[8]

Correspondingly, there was growing domestic opposition to the Johnson Administration's *Sentinel* BMD program. Criticism came primarily from the same set of judgments and concerns that had led Secretary McNamara earlier to oppose the *Nike-X* BMD system and substantial strategic defenses against the Soviet Union. Commentators and senior advisors to President Johnson with no apparent expertise on Chinese decision making asserted confident knowledge that BMD was unnecessary because deterrence would prevent a Chinese missile attack. For example, Jerome Wiesner, who had served as science advisor to President Kennedy, directly assured President Johnson that, "with respect to Communist China, there is no need for an ABM system. We can rely on normal deterrence"; the President's science advisor, Donald Hornig, agreed.[9]   Spurgeon Keeny, of President Johnson's National Security Council Staff, similarly claimed that there was no reason that U.S. deterrence would not work against China.[10]

In addition, and also in line with Secretary McNamara's generally negative assessment of BMD and damage limitation, *Sentinel's* critics claimed that it would: be expensive; undermine mutual deterrence by appearing to challenge Soviet retaliatory nuclear capabilities; and, compel a Soviet responsive buildup that would render it useless and ignite the arms race. *Sentinel* also suffered from the then-growing public opposition to the Vietnam War and defense spending in general, and fears that its nuclear-armed interceptors posed the threat of a nuclear accident to nearby cities.[11]

Enter the Nixon Administration: A Balance of Terror, the "Best Preventive" of War

The Nixon Administration inherited a controversial *Sentinel* BMD program, and quickly put it on hold pending a Pentagon review. The Nixon Administration's strategic program review, led by Deputy Secretary of Defense David Packard, soon led to a presidential decision that reoriented *Sentinel* to fit easily within established balance of terror guidelines.

Specifically, on March 14, 1969, President Nixon announced the redirection of the U.S. BMD program *to emphasize the defense of U.S. ICBMs against a Soviet first strike rather than the defense of U.S. cities.* The Nixon Administration dubbed this reoriented BMD program *Safeguard.* With it, the United States signaled at least tacit acceptance of the perpetuation of the balance of terror as a condition and a policy goal.

Safeguard was presented *not as a system to help provide a direct damage-limitation capability against Soviet attack, but primarily to help preserve the U.S. nuclear retaliatory capability, and thus a stable balance of terror.* President Nixon was explicit about this reorientation of BMD. At his March news conference announcing *Safeguard*, he stated:

> It is a safeguard of our deterrent system, which is increasing-
> ly vulnerable due to the advances that have been made
> by the Soviet Union....It does not provide defense for our
> cities, and for that reason the sites have been moved away

from our major cities....The only way that I have concluded
that we can save lives, which is the primary purpose of
our defense system, is to prevent war; and that is why the
emphasis of this system is on protecting our deterrent,
which is the best preventive for war.[12]

This reorientation reaffirmed BMD for the purpose of defending U.S.
nuclear forces. It was a BMD role both Schelling and Secretary McNamara
had presented years earlier as potentially contributing to a stable balance
of terror. U.S. BMD that could help deny the Soviet Union the capability to
destroy U.S. retaliatory forces, but *not* offer a significant defense of U.S.
society, would help preserve a stable balance of terror.

The U.S. fear that suggested the need for *Safeguard* was that
Soviet ICBM warheads would increasingly come to pose a first-strike
threat to the U.S. *Minuteman* ICBM force, and thereby put a key part of
the U.S. retaliatory capability in doubt. The Nixon Administration intended
to help counter that threat by protecting U.S. *Minuteman* ICBMs with
Safeguard BMD. Deputy Secretary Packard presented the rationale for
this reorientation of the U.S. BMD program in familiar balance of terror
terms. U.S. defenses were primarily for the protection of U.S. retaliatory
forces—and thus deterrence—not for U.S. cities.

The modified program [*Safeguard*] we talk about puts the
emphasis on the protection of our deterrent...because if we
deployed this system around our cities, the enemy could still
MIRV his missiles, and there is not any way in which you
really gain anything by this course. Furthermore, you give
the impression that you are trying to build up a first strike
capability, and in my view you reduce your deterrence.[13]

President Nixon similarly stated explicitly the reasons he rejected
substantial BMD for city defense in favor of *Safeguard*. These reasons
harkened back almost precisely to Secretary McNamara's earlier rationale
for rejecting a policy of substantial damage limitation. First, President Nixon
identified a high absolute standard for defense adequacy: "it needs to be
a perfect or near perfect system to be credible."[14] Based on that standard
he found the effectiveness of even "massive city defenses" inadequate
and unsupportable. In line with Secretary McNamara's earlier analyses
and priorities, President Nixon indicated that defenses could save 30-40

million lives but, "we would still lose 30 to 40 million."[15] His reasoning as expressed paralleled that of Secretary McNamara's: BMD could save scores of millions of lives, but could nevertheless allow scores of millions of fatalities—in contrast to deterrence, which he described as the "best preventive" of war.

Second, again like Secretary McNamara, President Nixon rejected as "destabilizing" thick city defenses because: "Moving to a massive city defense system, even starting with a thin system and then going to a heavy system, tends to be more provocative in terms of making credible a first-strike capability against the Soviet Union. I want no provocation which might deter arms talks."[16] Here President Nixon adhered closely to the balance of terror staple that "stable" mutual deterrence requires the opponent's confidence in its retaliatory capabilities. Thick city defenses were to be avoided because they would pose a provocative, "destabilizing" challenge to that confidence.

President Nixon and senior members of his administration often criticized MAD sharply.[17] However, in identifying the value of BMD in terms of its capability to defend U.S. ICBMs against a Soviet first strike, and eschewing the goal of substantial, direct protection for cities, U.S. BMD policy fully reflected balance of terror tenets. The protection of U.S. cities was to come from mutual deterrence, not U.S. strategic capabilities to limit damage directly; hence, efforts to acquire a substantial damage-limitation capability were rejected as unnecessary for deterrence, lacking adequate value, and inimical to stable mutual deterrence.

Codifying the Balance of Terror: The 1972 ABM Treaty

President Nixon helped to institutionalize and even codify the balance of terror as policy by establishing severe limitations on BMD as the primary U.S. SALT goal. Many in his administration were far from enthusiastic about balance of terror guidelines. Nevertheless, in the emerging SALT negotiations, the U.S. definition of success included severe BMD limitations. The administration accepted or acceded to the balance of terror narrative that limiting BMD would help stabilize mutual deterrence and stop the action-reaction cycle generally thought to drive the arms race. Limiting or eliminating BMD became a U.S. SALT *leitmotif.*

The continuing U.S. adherence to the balance of terror formula as the basic metric for acquiring strategic forces and for U.S. strategic arms control following the Johnson Administration was most visible in its paralyzing effect on U.S. BMD. The general U.S. SALT principle was to link mutual limits on BMD to mutual limits on offensive forces, primarily ICBM launchers. Because the Nixon Administration identified the value of BMD largely in terms of its potential protection for U.S. ICBMs and stable deterrence, if SALT could effectively limit the Soviet ICBM threat to U.S. ICBMs, then BMD was regarded as largely unnecessary and could be limited strictly or banned.

President Nixon identified U.S. SALT goals precisely in terms of this linkage between limitations on BMD and offensive force limitations: "The United States took the position that our ABM requirements were determined by the extent of the [Soviet] offensive threat to Minuteman; if that threat could be reduced, so could our defensive requirements. This was the principle of defense-offense linkage."[18] If arms control could limit the Soviet threat to U.S. ICBMs, then there was little value to be found in continuing to pursue U.S. BMD deployment.

In testimony before the Senate Armed Services Committee in 1972, Professor William Van Cleave, a member of the U.S. SALT delegation, specifically identified this linkage and the premise that the envisaged role for BMD was the protection of U.S. retaliatory forces: "The U.S. position on ABM limitations continued to be that defensive limitations depended on offensive levels permitted by any agreement. The U.S. might be willing to forego a light area defense in return for an agreement stabilizing the U.S.-USSR strategic balance, but the level of defense of retaliatory systems depended on the level of the threat."[19]

President Nixon's strategic arms control policy thus became a full reflection of stable balance of terror thinking: he presented *Safeguard* BMD protection as largely for the U.S. retaliatory nuclear capabilities enforcing deterrence threats. And, if U.S. retaliatory forces did not need *Safeguard's* protection because arms control constrained the Soviet offensive first-strike threat and thus helped preserve the balance of terror, then BMD could be foregone; there was no room in this construction of the BMD question for the significant defense of cities.

Balance of terror proponents, true to their belief in the action-reaction dynamic, promised that a treaty limiting or, better still, banning BMD would create the necessary condition for a Soviet commitment to halt the buildup of offensive forces: in the absence of U.S. defenses, they claimed, the Soviets would *not need* more offensive capabilities because both sides already had sufficient retaliatory capabilities for mutual deterrence. Both sides had reached a balance of terror equilibrium point and could stop building offensive forces. The logic of the U.S. "defense-offense" linkage was elegant: an ABM Treaty would help preserve the balance of terror equilibrium, and BMD protection for U.S. ICBMs would be unnecessary because arms control could limit the Soviet offensive threat and thus solve the U.S. ICBM vulnerability problem.[20]

President Nixon's SALT goal of linking offensive and defensive capabilities was based on this promise: arms control could codify a stable balance of terror and thus curtail the arms race. He explicitly stated as much:

> The ABM Treaty stopped what inevitably would have become a defensive arms race, with untold billions of dollars being spent on each side for more and more ABM coverage. The other major effect of the ABM Treaty was to make permanent the concept of deterrence through "mutual terror": by giving up defenses, each side therefore had an ultimate interest in preventing a war that could only be mutually destructive.[21]

The text of the treaty itself ultimately included the underlying balance of terror thinking with its confident assertion that the limitation of BMD would have a predictably positive effect on the stability of mutual deterrence and thus reduce motivations for the arms race: "Effective measures to limit anti-ballistic missile systems would be a substantial factor in curbing the race in strategic offensive arms and would lead to a decrease in the risk of outbreak of war involving nuclear weapons."[22]

Arms Control to Help Preserve a Balance of Terror

SALT and the 1972 ABM Treaty had been guided by the goals of preserving the balance of terror and codifying the equilibrium point in armaments thought to exist when both sides were confident and satisfied with their assured destruction deterrents. Secretary of Defense Caspar Weinberger later observed: "The primary U.S. goal in negotiations was to enshrine forever the strategic doctrine of mutual vulnerability. By putting caps on each side's strategic nuclear arsenals and foregoing the deployment of all but the most limited anti-ballistic missile systems, strategic stability was to be enhanced."[23]

In 1972, Henry Kissinger, the immediate architect of the U.S. SALT agenda, explained the ABM Treaty purely in these balance of terror terms: "By setting limits to ABM defenses, the [ABM] treaty not only eliminates one area of dangerous defensive competition, but it reduces the incentives for continuing deployment of offensive systems. As long as it lasts, offensive missiles have, in effect, _a free ride to their targets_."[24] Of course, according to balance of terror tenets, for each side's missiles to have a "free ride to their targets" was positively "stabilizing."

Similarly, Gerard Smith, the Nixon Administration's Director of the Arms Control and Disarmament Agency and chief U.S. negotiator for the ABM Treaty, explained the merit of the ABM Treaty per the balance of terror tenet that defending people would be destabilizing:

> The ABM Treaty was based on a recognition by the superpowers that a nationwide missile defense system could only increase the risk of nuclear war. What's wrong with trying to develop defenses? After all, it is their aim to destroy missiles and not people, to protect rather than to threaten....For years, American and Soviet security has involved a condition of mutual insecurity—like two scorpions in a bottle each unwilling to sting the other lest it be stung to death. If one side came to believe that it was sting proof it could be tempted to attack.[25]

Schelling's "reciprocal fear of surprise attack" was a priority concern and preserving a stable balance of terror to prevent it became the key goal of U.S. arms control. This recalled the fundamental tenet of a stable balance of terror: capabilities to protect people directly were regarded as a threat to mutual deterrence, while preserving those weapons that threatened cities was stabilizing. Correspondingly, the Arms Control and Disarmament Agency explicitly described the Nixon Administration's ABM Treaty limiting defenses as ensuring that, "each country thus leaves unchallenged the penetration capability of the other's retaliatory missile force."[26] There was no ambiguity about U.S. goals. The Nixon Administration consciously codified in treaty and international law this fundamental ingredient of the balance of terror—U.S. and Soviet mutual societal vulnerability to nuclear missile retaliation. Missiles were to have, by conscious binding agreement, a "free ride to their targets."

In SALT the United States ultimately acceded to strict limitations on BMD in exchange for the absence of significant Soviet strategic BMD and *the promise of future arms control limitations* that would constrain the Soviet counterforce threat to U.S. forces and thus help preserve the balance of terror. In parallel with the policy positions expressed by Secretary McNamara during much of the previous decade, the Nixon Administration consciously decided to forego the level of damage limitation considered feasible at the time in declared deference to the conditions believed necessary for a stable balance of terror.

The Nixon Administration's ABM Treaty did not simply signal the end of U.S. BMD deployment. It surely had that effect, but the broader and enduring effect of the treaty was in its additional strict constraints on the *development and testing of future BMD components*. The level of damage limitation potentially afforded by the BMD programs of the time was deemed inadequate by the Johnson and Nixon Administrations, and the ABM Treaty *helped to ensure the perpetuation of that condition* by placing significant constraints on BMD development and testing. The treaty was indeed designed, as President Nixon said, "to make permanent" the balance of terror.

This closing of the books on the prospects for BMD reinforced the U.S. rejection of substantial air defense and civil defense; if there was to be no defense against nuclear missiles, it made little sense to defend against other means of attack. The minimal investment in these capabilities set in motion by Secretary McNamara thus continued. The ABM Treaty's restrictions on BMD and the corresponding continuing minimal efforts behind air defense and civil defense were evidence of the continuing primacy of the balance of terror guidelines in U.S. policy.

Another major effect of the ABM Treaty not identified by President Nixon was that it effectively precluded the United States from deploying BMD against the emerging strategic missiles of third parties such as China. Secretary McNamara earlier had made the intellectual case for pursuing a damage-limitation policy *vis-à-vis* the Chinese even as he rejected such a policy for the Soviet Union. And, the Johnson Administration went forward with the *Sentinel* BMD program ostensibly for that purpose.

Highly-classified documents from the Nixon Administration, now declassified, show that in 1969 Henry Kissinger expressed strong support for limited BMD to protect U.S. society against Chinese or other third party nuclear missile attacks, and recommended against giving up the option in SALT: "I believe we should plan on retaining at least that part of the *Safeguard* ABM program designed to: defend the American people against the kind of primitive nuclear attack or nuclear blackmail which countries such as Communist China may be able to threaten within a decade or so, [and] protect against the possibility of accidental or unauthorized attacks from any source."[27]

Nevertheless, with the 1972 ABM Treaty's severe limitations on BMD development, testing and deployment, the Nixon Administration precluded any significant defenses against Soviet missiles and also severely limited the U.S. potential to defend against Chinese or any other emerging strategic missile threats. As a practical matter, a casualty of the ABM Treaty was not just U.S. BMD to protect society against Soviet missiles, but against virtually any other strategic missile threat; the vulnerability to Soviet missiles enforced by the ABM Treaty for balance of terror purposes meant U.S. vulnerability to other future long-range missile threats as well. The Nixon Administration essentially gave up the U.S. option of defending against third party missiles in pursuit of an ABM Treaty designed to stabilize and codify as law a balance of terror with the Soviet Union.

The Nixon Administration inherited from the Johnson Admin-istration the *Sentinel* program to defend U.S. society against Chinese missiles, then reoriented it to the defense of U.S. retaliatory forces, and finally bartered that *Safeguard* BMD program away for the promise of arms control constraints on the Soviet ICBM threat to *Minuteman*. These choices regarding BMD were at the nexus of the Nixon Administration's strategic policy regarding deterrence, force acquisition and arms control; they reflected the priorities and tenets of the balance of terror.

Schelling helped to introduce the balance of terror conceptual guidelines of eschewing damage limitation for the purpose of stabilizing mutual deterrence, and using strategic arms control to facilitate a "stable" condition of mutual vulnerability. Secretary McNamara and the Johnson Administration elevated those guidelines to U.S. policy, and the Nixon Administration enshrined them in arms control practice and international law.

Strategic arms control negotiations intended to *limit offensive forces* also became consciously subservient to the balance of terror deterrence formula. As Adm. Stansfield Turner, head of the CIA during the Carter Administration, observed regarding the role of arms control: "The key objective of arms control is not control of the number of weapons but a lessening of the likelihood of anyone starting a nuclear war....

The critical step toward that goal is a reduction of the number of weapons that put people on edge by posing the threat of a surprise attack—and those weapons, by and large, are the ICBMs."[28]

Nixon Administration officials claimed to have accomplished this U.S.-envisaged bargain to codify an agreed balance of terror-oriented equilibrium point in offensive forces in exchange for, and on the basis of, agreed strict limits on BMD. This is what they claimed when presenting the ABM Treaty and the related SALT offensive agreement to the U.S. Senate:

> This [ABM Treaty] is a general undertaking of utmost significance. Without a nationwide ABM defense, there can be no shield against retaliation. Both nuclear powers have recognized—and, in effect, agreed to maintain—nuclear deterrence.[29]

> What we are trying to do is to set up a useful device that will hold the situation while we negotiate, hopefully, a matching treaty; that is to match the treaty in the ABM defense field. I think that the measures that we have succeeded in spelling out in this interim [offensive] agreement with the Russians will do just that. There will be a commitment on their part not to build any more of these ICBMs that have concerned us over the years.[30]

> The [ABM] Treaty, by permitting only a small deployment of ABMs, tends to break the offense-defense action-and-reaction spiral in strategic arms competition....In view of the low ABM levels agreed on, it should be possible in the future to agree on mutual reductions in offensive weapons without impairing strategic stability....[31]

The ABM Treaty certainly did provide the envisaged strict limits on strategic BMD, and the United States correspondingly spent the next two decades attempting to realize the expected arms control constraints on Soviet strategic offensive forces—in particular, its large ICBM arsenal which posed a potential threat to U.S. forces. Unfortunately for the United States, literally decades of trying to achieve this arms control goal *did not* produce the anticipated constraints on Soviet offensive forces.

That the United States was *unsuccessful* during the Cold War in achieving the goal of this grand arms control linkage of limitations on offensive and defensive capabilities per a stable balance of terror is beyond question. Soviet strategic offensive nuclear warheads, particularly those with capabilities to attack U.S. ICBM silos, grew in number dramatically following the ABM Treaty—from several hundred during the first year of negotiations to over 5,000 by the mid-1980s.

By the early 1980s there was a strong bipartisan consensus that Soviet ICBM capabilities had grown so powerful that they posed a "first strike" threat to U.S. ICBMs.[32] The official NATO report, *NATO and the Warsaw Pact Force Comparisons*, concluded that the Soviet threat to U.S. ICBMs had matured by the end of the 1970s.[33] The 1983 bipartisan *Report of the President's Commission on Strategic Forces* confirmed that the Soviets, "...now probably possess the necessary combination of ICBM numbers, reliability, accuracy, and warhead yield to destroy almost all of the 1,047 U.S. ICBM silos, using only a portion of their own ICBM force."[34] This, of course, was just the reverse of the arms control linkage claimed by the Nixon Administration and suggested by the balance of terror narrative: codifying stable mutual deterrence *was supposed to* facilitate an end to the need for further offensive buildups. In the absence of BMD both sides were to rest content with their missiles having a "free ride."

Soviet participants in the arms control process noted after the Cold War that they never considered the ABM Treaty as a route to reductions in their strategic offensive capabilities; in fact, they were pleasantly surprised by the U.S. desire for an ABM Treaty because it allowed the Soviet Union to concentrate its resources on the *modernization and strengthening* of its ICBM arsenal.[35]

President Nixon intentionally gave up *Safeguard's* role of protecting U.S. ICBMs on the basis of SALT's promissory note that arms control restrictions on strategic offensive forces could solve the U.S. ICBM vulnerability problem at the source of the threat, i.e., by restricting Soviet ICBMs. Many years of arms control efforts to limit Soviet offensive arms, however, did not produce the desired outcome. In contrast to U.S. behavior, the Soviet Union had moved far forward to acquire the prompt capability to destroy hardened strategic targets such as U.S. ICBMs. Soviet armament decisions obviously were driven by factors *other* than securing a stable balance of terror and resting at that equilibrium point.

John Deutch, Deputy Defense Secretary during the Clinton Administration, Jim Woolsey, Director of the CIA during the Clinton Administration, and Brent Scowcroft, National Security Advisor to Presidents Ford and George H. W. Bush, identified this U.S. arms control intent and failure explicitly:

> Our major effort over 17 years of arms control negotiations on strategic offensive systems has been dedicated to preserving the survivability of our own silo-based ICBMs. To this end we have used, and wasted, much negotiating leverage in trying to get the Soviets to agree to restrictions on their large MIRVed ICBMs. They have noted our concern about survivability and have cheerfully made it worse with their massive investments in the programs we most want to restrict.[36]

Leslie Gelb, chief arms control architect of the Carter Administration's SALT II negotiations, similarly observed in 1979 that: "Arms control has essentially failed. Three decades of U.S.-Soviet negotiations to limit arms competition have done little more than codify the arms race."[37] Secretary of Defense Weinberger similarly summarized the balance of terror thinking behind the earlier Nixon Administration's SALT negotiations, and its frustration: "This view, of course, held that the United States and Soviet Union could remain perfectly safe so long as both populations remained perfectly vulnerable....Needless to say, things did not work out as planned. For not only did the Soviets refuse to buy into our concept of stable deterrence through mutual vulnerability, they also engaged in one of the most dramatic arms buildups in history."[38]

In short, in line with the balance of terror for stable mutual deterrence, President Nixon's 1969 *Safeguard* announcement explicitly reflected a decision *against* substantial BMD protection for U.S. cities, in favor of a "thin" defense to protect U.S. retaliatory capabilities and preserve mutual deterrence. And, his early instructions to the U.S. SALT delegation were to maintain the U.S. potential for a "thin" U.S. BMD capability. However, the actual terms of the ABM Treaty ultimately gave up the possibility even of a "thin" defense of cities and severely restricted the testing and development of future BMD capabilities in the ultimately fruitless pursuit of an offensive arms control agreement that would protect U.S. strategic forces made vulnerable by the Soviet ICBM buildup, notably U.S. ICBMs.

The Congressional hearings on SALT and the ABM Treaty revealed a strong bipartisan consensus in favor of pursuing a "stable" balance of terror at the expense of substantial damage limitation, and in favor of the strategic arms control goal of preserving U.S. retaliatory forces at the expense of even a "thin" BMD. In line with balance of terror thinking, Congressional concerns about BMD at these hearings centered on fears that BMD would destabilize mutual deterrence, ignite the action-reaction driven arms race, and thereby obstruct the preferred arms control route to a secure balance of terror. The Nixon Administration and Congress had absorbed balance of terror norms and applied them as the metric for defining the goal of arms control.

There were very few dissenting voices in Congress or elsewhere to the Nixon Administration's rejection of substantial damage limitation and an arms control agenda that sought significant BMD limitations as the key to preserving the balance of terror. Indeed, the Senate ratified the ABM Treaty in August 1972 by a vote of 88-2. The United States included a Unilateral Statement in the ABM Treaty that illustrated both its goals and the importance attached to this promised linkage between offensive and defensive limitations:

> The U.S. Delegation has stressed the importance the U.S. Government attaches to achieving agreement on more complete limitations on strategic offensive arms, following agreement on an ABM Treaty and on an Interim Agreement on certain measures with respect to the limitation of strategic offensive arms. *The U.S. Delegation believes that an objective of the follow-on negotiations should be to constrain and reduce on a long-term basis threats to the survivability of our respective strategic retaliatory forces....* If an agreement providing for more complete strategic offensive arms limitations were not achieved within five years, U.S. supreme interests could be jeopardized. Should that occur, it would constitute a basis for withdrawal from the ABM Treaty.[39]

Although strategic arms control never provided the hoped-for solution to the problem of U.S. ICBM vulnerability, the United States did not respond as threatened in this Unilateral Statement by withdrawing from the ABM Treaty. Instead, the United States spent over a decade trying to achieve the promised offensive reductions and to identify suitable alternative routes to safeguarding its ICBMs from Soviet ICBM attack, including such gems as placing them on large aircraft, at sea on faux merchant ships, or in deep underground tunnels.[40]

The point here, however, is neither to applaud nor lament U.S. Cold War strategic arms control efforts. It is to show that for successive Democratic and Republican administrations, the goals and metrics of arms control success came to reflect the overarching goal of establishing and sustaining a stable balance of terror.

Why did the Nixon Administration essentially follow the balance of terror policy path established by Secretary McNamara, and further institutionalize the rejection of damage limitation? Did it willingly embrace balance of terror guidelines? The underlying motives within the Nixon Administration appear to have been mixed; rarely is there a single reason for such decisions—even a reason as powerful as an overarching strategic policy orientation. An explanation is suggested by Fred Iklé, Director of the Arms Control and Disarmament Agency during the Nixon Administration:

> While President Nixon and some of his senior advisors, especially Henry Kissinger, recognized that this MAD strategy inherited from the Johnson administration was deeply flawed, they felt the United States could not change course, given, on one side, the pressures by arms control advocates and their Congressional supporters, and, on the other side, the exigencies of the Vietnam War (which had also been inherited from the Johnson administration). So in 1972, Nixon and Brezhnev signed the ABM Treaty prohibiting missile defenses....[41]

While some in the Nixon Administration clearly did embrace balance of terror tenets, others apparently opposed but grudgingly recognized them as politically unbeatable. In either case, the power of those tenets was manifest. Those opposed ultimately abided an approach to arms control and BMD that codified a balance of terror only because they believed that the political context of the time allowed no other options.

There is little doubt that some members of the Nixon Administration strongly favored the deployment of BMD, as had some members of the previous Johnson Administration, as well as members of the later Ford, Carter, Reagan, and initial Bush Administrations. In open testimony before the Senate in 1972, William R. Van Cleave of the U.S. SALT delegation bucked intellectual fashion and expressed deep skepticism of the "action-reaction" thesis and the related belief that the limitation of BMD would lead to effective limits on offensive forces.[42] Donald Brennan, President of the Hudson Institute and an advisor to the Departments of State, Defense, and to the Arms Control and Disarmament Agency, rejected both the balance of terror deterrence strategy and its extension to U.S. arms control objectives:

> I do not believe that any of the critics of BMD have even the beginnings of a plausible program for achieving major disarmament of the offensive forces by, say 1980. Many of them seem committed to support a strategic posture that appears to favor dead Russians over live Americans. I believe that this choice is just as bizarre as it appears; we should rather prefer live Americans to dead Russians, and we should not choose deliberately to live forever under a nuclear sword of Damocles.[43]

Despite these few skeptical, prescient voices regarding the arms control promise of the ABM Treaty, the U.S. strategic arms control process followed the balance of terror road map. Despite the preferences of some in Democratic and Republican administrations—with the exception of the short-lived deployment of a single BMD site in 1975—the ultimate choice of subsequent U.S. governments throughout the Cold War period and the early post-Cold War years was continued strict adherence to the ABM Treaty and the corresponding rejection of strategic BMD deployment. A decade *after* the end of the Cold War, the Clinton Administration continued to describe the ABM Treaty as the "cornerstone of strategic stability" because it provided mutual confidence of each side's vulnerability.[44]

The influence of balance of terror tenets on the U.S. strategic arms control agenda can be seen amply in the ABM Treaty's limitations on BMD development, testing and deployment, the envisaged linkage of offensive and defensive limitations, and in the subsequent series of annual federal government *Arms Control Impact Statements*. These reports, modeled after environmental impact statements, were required of the executive branch by Congressional mandate. They were intended to identify the potential arms control impacts of various U.S. weapons programs. In doing so, they made explicit the fact that, for the United States, strategic arms control was regarded as the handmaiden of the balance of terror. A standard refrain in these statements, for example, was that mutual deterrence and stability, "...constitute the primary objectives of both U.S. strategic force modernization and US arms control policy."[45] Strategic force programs deemed compatible with stable deterrence per balance of terror definitions and metrics also were regarded as compatible with arms control.

Through years of publication, these reports defined U.S. strategic systems as "stabilizing" and thus compatible with arms control, depending largely on whether they would facilitate mutual vulnerability via secure retaliatory nuclear threats. To wit, U.S. strategic missile modernization programs were judged positively if they contributed to the U.S. retaliatory nuclear threat *without also* posing a substantial counterforce threat to Soviet nuclear retaliatory capabilities. The balance of terror categorization of counterforce capabilities as "destabilizing" was standard fare.

Fully in line with the balance of terror formula, these arms control impact statements also posited virtue in U.S. strategic systems if their deployment might encourage the Soviet Union to deploy its own strategic forces in ways that made those forces *invulnerable to* U.S. attack: "By deploying more of their capability at sea, or on mobile ICBMs, they may improve their strategic force survivability, which, in turn, may enhance strategic and crisis stability...."[46] The operative definition of deterrence and stability clearly came from the balance of terror school.

Similarly, discussion of U.S. BMD in these impact statements was grounded in the expressed belief that it was the ABM Treaty and the corresponding absence of significant strategic BMD that promoted stability, or that defenses could be stabilizing *if they magnified the Soviet leadership's uncertainties about Soviet counterforce capabilities.* In the Reagan Administration's *Arms Control Impact Statements*, even the SDI—introduced in 1983 with the goal of seeking comprehensive U.S. defensive capabilities—was presented as contributing to this balance of terror metric for mutual deterrence rather than as transcending the balance of terror.

The *Arms Control Impact Statement* for fiscal year 1986, for example, put the value of missile defenses largely in traditional balance of terror terms: BMD could contribute to deterrence stability by forcing "uncertainties" into prospective Soviet first-strike calculations. Balance of terror concepts were so deeply ingrained that the SDI's prospective impact on stability was assessed primarily according to the uncertainties it would force on Soviet counterforce offensive planning rather than for the protection it was intended to provide to U.S. society. Orchestrating such uncertainties was "the essence of deterrence":

> An effective defense against ballistic missiles would have the potential for enhancing deterrence and stability by increasing attack uncertainties of an aggressor and by reducing or eliminating the utility of a nuclear first strike to an aggressor. In the face of effective defense against ballistic missiles, a potential aggressor could not be certain that any given weapons would penetrate the defensive system and destroy a given military target. It would be very difficult for a potential aggressor to predict likely outcomes of a nuclear attack in the face of such uncertainties, and no aggressor is likely to contemplate initiating a nuclear conflict, even in crisis circumstances, while lacking any confidence in a successful outcome. *This is the essence of deterrence.*[47]

This bow to established deterrence norms, of course, undercut the original rationale for the SDI. Balance of terror proponents always could identify alternative measures as preferable for increasing Soviet counterforce uncertainties.[48] With few exceptions, the U.S. strategic policy and force initiatives of the 1970s and 1980s fit, or ultimately were made to fit, within this reigning balance of terror orthodoxy.

Ronald Reagan's SDI: A Short-Lived Challenge to Balance of Terror Guidelines

President Reagan initiated the SDI with the goal of exploring the potential for providing comprehensive defense against the Soviet ballistic missile threat. This was an explicit rejection of the balance of terror, and President Reagan presented the SDI as such. In his March 23, 1983 speech introducing the SDI, he observed:

> But since the advent of nuclear weapons, [U.S.] steps have been increasingly directed toward deterrence of aggression through the promise of retaliation....What if free people could live secure in the knowledge that their security did

not rest on the threat of instant U.S. retaliation to deter a Soviet attack, that we could intercept and destroy strategic ballistic missiles before they reached our soil or that of our allies? I know that this is a formidable, technical task....But isn't it worth every investment necessary to free the world from the threat of nuclear war? We know it is.[49]

Immediately after this speech, Secretary of Defense Weinberger emphasized that, "The defensive systems the president is talking about are not designed to be partial. What we want to try to get is a system which will develop a defense that is thoroughly reliable and total."[50] The SDI represented a full frontal assault on the balance of terror *sine qua non* of mutual societal vulnerability. Unsurprisingly, it unleashed a torrent of criticism based on the balance of terror canon: such damage limitation was unnecessary, useless and destabilizing, and would spark an action-reaction arms race. Furthermore, it would be a violation of a "sacred" treaty.

White House and Defense Department officials soon began to *de-emphasize* SDI as a comprehensive defense to transcend the balance of terror, and instead focused on an intermediate SDI goal that was wholly in line with balance of terror norms—i.e., protection for deterrence purposes of the U.S. strategic retaliatory arsenal, particularly ICBMs and NATO military assets.[51] Although the long-term goal of societal protection was not abandoned, in 1987 the JCS established operational requirements for a "Phase I" SDI that—according to senior Pentagon officials—was intended to help strengthen deterrence by providing the capability to intercept 40 percent of Soviet ballistic missile warheads, including 50 percent of those Soviet ICBM warheads that posed a particular counterforce threat to U.S. forces.[52] Former Director of the Strategic Defense Initiative Organization, Lt. General George Monahan, noted that the JCS purpose for such a capability was to "blunt" the counterforce potential of a Soviet pre-emptive attack.[53]

A report on the SDI by the Congressional Research Service summarized this Phase I goal in traditional balance of terror terms: "It can be said that the major Phase I deployment objective is to ensure, albeit with less than 100% effectiveness, the survival of an effective U.S. retaliatory force capability."[54] This was, of course, reminiscent of the Nixon Administration's reorientation of the U.S. BMD goal for its *Safeguard* program and fit well within the standard balance of terror metrics for stable deterrence.

This reshaping of the SDI to fit the balance of terror formula also was reflected in the Reagan Administration's handling of the ABM Treaty. In 1985, the Reagan Administration announced a reinterpretation of the ABM Treaty's Agreed Statement D; this new, "broad" reinterpretation would have permitted the development and testing of advanced mobile and space-based BMD elements in ways previously considered prohibited by the treaty. The Reagan Administration's reinterpretation appeared to be a move to loosen the BMD development constraints of this treaty, rightly described by President Nixon as the legal codification of a balance of terror. This move again suggested a possible challenge to balance of terror orthodoxy.

Following sharp Congressional opposition led by Senator Sam Nunn, however, the Reagan Administration quickly retreated on the issue and declared its acceptance of the traditional, more restrictive interpretation of the treaty as a matter of policy.[55] President Reagan could have withdrawn from the treaty upon six months notice as provided for in Article XV, particularly given U.S. Unilateral Statement A and the by-then-manifest vulnerability of the U.S. ICBMs to Soviet attack. Or, he could have taken other appropriate legal steps against the treaty given Soviet noncompliance with its terms. Ultimately, however, he did neither, and essentially left intact the treaty's strict prohibitions on the development and testing of advanced BMD systems.

By emphasizing deterrence as the SDI's rationale, the Reagan Administration brought the SDI into greater compatibility with balance of terror norms, but placed it in competition with other measures and programs that also could be claimed to strengthen "stable" deterrence—including arms control and improvements in strategic offensive forces. As Bruce MacDonald, legislative assistant to Sen. Dale Bumpers, rightly observed in this regard:

> Seeking to strengthen deterrence puts SDI on a crowded playing field, along with the B-2 bomber, the Trident II missile, Midgetman, and the whole panoply of U.S. strategic offensive forces. If the job is to improve U.S. retaliatory capabilities, many of these other programs could do it with greater certainty at less cost, without destroying the ABM Treaty and thereby scuttling the current prospects for offensive arms reductions.[56]

Official discussion of the SDI shifted from a goal that was incompatible with balance of terror deterrence thinking—i.e., the protection of U.S. society from strategic missile attack—to the more acceptable role of contributing to deterrence stability by protecting U.S. retaliatory nuclear forces. That deterrence role, however, placed it squarely in competition with less controversial offensive measures to strengthen deterrence. This dilemma did not augur well for securing a consensus in favor of BMD deployment.

In the late 1980s, officials in the George H.W. Bush Administration continued to emphasize "enhancing deterrence" as SDI's primary goal.[57] The Department of Defense's 1989 report on SDI, *Strategic Defense Initiative: Progress and Promise*, made the case clearly:

> Strategic defenses, by having the capability to destroy ballistic missiles and nuclear warheads before they reach their targets, would reduce the confidence Soviet leaders have in their ability to launch a first strike and destroy the forces we would use to retaliate. Lacking confidence that they could destroy our retaliatory forces, and faced with the threat of enormous damage to their nation if we retaliate, Soviet leaders would not risk an attack.[58]

With the collapse of the Soviet Union, the program was reoriented again and renamed *Global Protection Against Limited Strikes* (GPALS). The U.S. missile defense goal returned to providing defensive protection against limited missile attacks—similar to the goal for the Johnson Administration's *Sentinel* program of the 1960s. Secretary of Defense Richard Cheney noted specifically in the 1992 *Department of Defense Annual Report to the President and the Congress* that GPALS was "focused on protection against limited strikes and would not threaten to undermine existing retaliatory capabilities."[59] Advertising that GPALS would not threaten to undermine "existing retaliatory capabilities" was the hallmark of placing priority on stable balance of terror guidelines *vis-à-vis* the Soviet Union, and now Russia, while defending against lesser missile threats. After 25 years, U.S. BMD goals had returned full circle to those enunciated by Secretary McNamara in his 1967 speech announcing the Johnson Administration's *Sentinel* program.

Despite this progression of U.S. BMD programs spanning multiple *Democratic and Republican administrations, from the 1960s to*

*the end of the Cold War the United States Government deployed and
sustained no strategic BMD to defend against Soviet or any other strategic
ballistic missiles.* Instead, it established and preserved an ABM Treaty
that effectively prevented any significant BMD deployment and greatly
constrained development. The policy, legal, economic, and technical
challenges to moving far from the basic balance of terror formula became
insurmountable as consecutive administrations consciously:

- Decided against acquiring the numbers and types of
  offensive or defensive strategic capabilities needed
  to pose a significant challenge to Soviet retaliatory
  capabilities;
- Deactivated most of the U.S. air defense capability;
- Agreed by binding treaty to strict limits on the development, testing and deployment of strategic BMD; and,
- Rejected the funding necessary for a civil defense
  program with a serious intention or capability to protect
  the American population against nuclear attack.

U.S. vulnerability—not just to Soviet attack, but to virtually any strategic
attack—was a consequence of this policy direction.

Evident in this consistent policy choice was an enduring consensus
around the balance of terror-derived propositions that mutual deterrence
based on mutual vulnerability was the priority goal for strategic force
acquisition and arms control. Whether select officials in any particular
presidential administration embraced balance of terror norms, accepted
them grudgingly, or found them utterly lacking in merit, U.S. policy
overwhelmingly conformed to them.

MIRV, MX, Trident II, and Counterforce

The strength of the balance of terror guidelines in Democratic and
Republican administrations was obvious not only by the enduring, strict
limitations on BMD and other damage-limitation measures, but also in the
debates over strategic offensive forces and policy initiatives from the late
1960s to the end of the Cold War. During that period, the most prominent
offensive force debates addressed the emerging U.S. capability to arm
strategic missiles with multiple and separately-targeted nuclear warheads
(Multiple Independently-Targeted Reentry Vehicles, or MIRVs), and the

deployment of a large, new U.S. ICBM—the MX or *Peacekeeper*. Balance of terror norms ultimately affected each of these programs significantly.[60]

The potential advantage of MIRV technology for a stable balance of terror was that it could place multiple nuclear warheads on U.S. strategic missiles, and thus help ensure that Soviet counterforce and BMD capabilities could not prevent the United States from posing its nuclear retaliatory threat. MIRVs allowed the United States to deploy redundant nuclear warheads for this purpose without increasing the actual number of missile launchers. By the mid-1960s, Secretary McNamara presented the value of MIRV capabilities in this light.[61]

The potential problem of MIRVs from a balance of terror perspective, however, was that U.S. MIRV capabilities could pose an offensive threat to Soviet ICBMs on the ground *if* the U.S. offensive warhead numbers, accuracy and yield were of sufficient counterforce lethality. With most of the Soviet strategic arsenal residing in its ICBMs, balance of terror proponents in Congress, the press, and academia expressed great concern that U.S. MIRV capabilities would "destabilize" the balance of terror by threatening Soviet nuclear capabilities. U.S. MIRVs might threaten the "free ride" for Soviet missiles "to their targets."

Ted Greenwood, in his detailed review of the U.S. MIRV debate, identified this policy challenge to MIRV derived from balance of terror norms:

> It was not MIRV as a hedge against ABM deployment or MIRV as an efficient and effective countervalue [i.e., targeting cities] weapon that attracted criticism. It was, rather, MIRV as an effective counterforce [i.e., targeting military forces] weapon that could either threaten or be perceived as threatening the destruction of Soviet land-based missiles. Without the accuracy improvements of the past and the expectation of future improvements, MIRV systems could not have been seen as a destabilizing force for the strategic balance.[62]

Members of Congress, led by Senator Edward Brooke, put considerable pressure on the Nixon Administration to avoid the combination of accuracy and yield that could give U.S. MIRVed missiles a significant counterforce capability against Soviet ICBMs. Senator Brooke waged a long political campaign based entirely on the assured destruction metric and balance of terror guidelines to pass legislation to restrict the development or prevent the deployment of MIRVed warheads.[63] The Nixon Administration ultimately agreed to support MIRV weapons that would help penetrate Soviet defenses and cap the number of missile launchers, *but would not significantly threaten Soviet silos.*

The Nixon Administration added a fourth "no" to Secretary McNamara's earlier three "no's" against significant BMD, air defense, and civil defense. This fourth "no" was against the acquisition of sufficient prompt, offensive counterforce capabilities to pose a significant "first-strike" threat to Soviet retaliatory capabilities. U.S. officials presented this fourth "no" purely in balance of terror terms, i.e., the United States should not threaten Soviet confidence in its assured destruction capability for fear of creating mutual deterrence "instability." This decision and its underlying rationale were identified clearly in a 1969 letter to Senator Brooke by Dr. John Foster, an innovative nuclear weapons scientist and then Director of Defense Research and Engineering in the Pentagon:

> Our development of MIRV is, in essence, a reaction on our part to Soviet ABM activity....Faced with these Soviet defense measures, our deterrent capability could erode seriously without a countering move on our part. Our counter, as you are aware, is our MIRV program....Our own MIRV systems are not efficient against missile silos; they are designed for, and intended for use against defended urban/industrial type targets. They are not 'first-strike' weapons.[64]

In 1970 Congressional testimony, Dr. Foster made clear that the United States could develop the MIRV capability necessary to pose a significant threat to Soviet ICBM silos, *but consciously chose as a policy decision not to do so for stability reasons, per the balance of terror guidelines*:

> →...it is technologically feasible, in my opinion, for the United States to develop sufficient accuracy that with multiple vehicles sometime in the future we would be able to attack silos in the Soviet Union. However, we had a program of investigation along these lines and last year I canceled it. My purpose was to make it absolutely clear to the Congress

and, hopefully, to the Soviet Union, that it is not the policy of the United States to deny the Soviet Union their deterrent capability.[65]

In line with the stable balance of terror canon, the United States chose to eschew such capabilities. The result of that decision was still evident almost 15 years later when, in contrast to considerable Soviet capabilities to threaten U.S. hardened strategic targets, the United States had quite limited, prompt counterforce strategic capabilities: "Only the 550 MIRVed Minuteman III missiles in the U.S. ICBM force have relatively good accuracy, but the combination of accuracy and yield of their 3 warheads is inadequate to put at serious risk more than a small share of the many hardened targets in the Soviet Union."[66] Professor William R. Van Cleave, who, as noted, served on the U.S. SALT I delegation and later as a key advisor to presidential candidate Ronald Reagan, described U.S. Cold War strategic policy as designed to provide protection for U.S. society against Soviet nuclear attack "to the extent feasible," through mutual "self-restraint." He concluded that, "...counterforce and damage limiting were eschewed as major US objectives and strategic force planning criteria in order to exercise a self-restraint that was to induce Soviet reciprocity."[67] This induced "reciprocity" of mutual deterrence was the mechanism the U.S. Government relied upon to protect U.S. society, *not* direct damage-limiting capabilities. This was true by choice, not chance.

Even in the context of the manifest Soviet drive to acquire significant, prompt counterforce capabilities, the United States continued to avoid comparable capabilities that might pose a threat to Soviet forces. This was demonstrated amply in the most visible strategic offensive acquisition debate of the mid-1970s through mid-1980s—the political fight over deployment of the new U.S. MX or *Peacekeeper* ICBM. The MX ultimately was deployed in 1986 following a decade of sharp debate; this was accomplished, however, in a way that reflected fully the power of the stable balance of terror formula.

The MIRVed *Peacekeeper* ICBM was recognized as having the necessary lethality to threaten Soviet ICBM silos. This made it a target for those who believed such capabilities to be destabilizing and inconsistent with stable mutual deterrence. This assessment of the MX became the main feature of opposition to the new missile. It was reflected in Senator

Daniel Moynihan's expressed belief that mutual deterrence "stability" was "the utterly essential consideration" with regard to the MX and, correspondingly, by his opposition to the MX because it, "could strike at and 'take out' the missiles of the Soviet Union." This capability, observed Senator Moynihan, was "incompatible with the [deterrence] doctrine" and would be, "the makings of ruin."[68]

Adm. Stansfield Turner similarly opposed the MX on these instability grounds: "...the MX—added to the capability of our existing ICBM's— would give us the potential for a surprise attack on Soviet ICBM's, it would make the Russians nervous, their finger, too, would have to be on the trigger."[69] Adm. Turner argued strongly that instead of deploying "war-fighting" capabilities such as the MX, "...we must recommit ourselves to a doctrine of assured retaliation, relying principally on submarine-based missiles, bombers, and cruise missiles, and rejecting MX as unsuited to our needs."[70]

The Carter Administration's plan for the MX was to deploy 200 missile launchers. This was a lower number than the Air Force originally sought and reflected a compromise with Congressional MX critics who shared Senator Moynihan's and Adm. Turner's concern about stability.[71] Subsequently, when the Reagan Administration inherited the MX program, it too was sensitive to concerns about MX deployment causing deterrence "instability."

At least partially in deference to the "stability" requirement to preserve Moscow's confidence in its nuclear retaliatory capabilities, the Reagan Administration reduced MX launcher numbers further still, from the Carter Administration's compromised numbers of 200, to 100, and ultimately, to 50. At this low level of MX deployment, the Reagan Administration sought to assure Congress and the Soviet Union that MX would threaten only a limited set of Soviet hardened targets for deterrence purposes, and *could not pose a significant threat to Soviet retaliatory capabilities.*[72] The call was for a limited level of MX counterforce capability that could contribute to deterrence *without* posing a destabilizing threat to the Soviet retaliatory capability. This balancing act from the heart of the balance of terror narrative on deterrence strategy and acquisition policy clearly shaped the Reagan Administration's considerations of MX deployment.

The addition of a *limited* counterforce requirement to the U.S. deterrence metric in the 1970s and 1980s was obvious in the decision to deploy the MX ICBM in such modest numbers. In 1990, the final year of the Cold War, the U.S. Navy began deployment of another new strategic ballistic missile with counterforce capabilities, the *Trident II*. Although not deployed in significant numbers during the Cold War, it also reflected the general U.S. acceptance of limited counterforce capabilities for deterrence purposes.

Democratic and Republican officials advanced several deterrence-related reasons for staying within balance of terror guidelines but moving away from Secretary McNamara's expressed definition of assured destruction by adding limited, prompt counterforce capabilities to U.S. strategic deterrence requirements. First, some counterforce capabilities were said to be required to pose a threat to the Soviet military and political control assets that Moscow was thought to value highly. As Secretary Brown observed in 1983: "It is important for U.S. forces to be able to threaten retaliation against the assets that the Soviet leaders appear to prize, which are not only their urban industrial facilities but their nuclear and conventional forces and the hardened shelters that protect their political and military control centers, as well as their own lives."[73]

In addition, as noted already, the Soviet Union had increased dramatically its own MIRVed ICBM counterforce capabilities during the 1970s. By the mid-1980s, U.S. officials believed that the resultant signif-icant Soviet advantage in prompt counterforce potential would under-mine mutual deterrence stability.[74] The 1983 *Report of the President's Commission on Strategic Forces* pointed specifically to the need to rectify this imbalance, at least in part, and to be capable of threatening what "Soviet leaders most value" in recommending MX and *Trident II* counterforce capabilities:

> A one-sided strategic condition in which the Soviet Union could effectively destroy the whole range of strategic targets in the United States, but we could not effectively destroy a similar range of targets in the Soviet Union would be extremely unstable over the long run. Such a situation could tempt the Soviets, in a crisis, to feel they could successfully threaten or even undertake conventional or limited nuclear aggression in the hope that the United States would lack a fully effective response....our strategic forces must be modernized, as necessary, to enhance to an adequate degree their overall survivability and to enable them to engage effectively the targets that Soviet leaders

most value.[75]

The deterrence requirement for survivable strategic forces presented in this statement had long been recognized. The need for limited U.S. counterforce capabilities for deterrence purposes was a revision of Secretary McNamara's declared assured destruction standard for deterrence, but it did not challenge the basic balance of terror.

Finally, perhaps most indicative of the enduring consensus behind the balance of terror formula for deterrence stability — if *not* for the original definition of assured destruction—U.S. officials and official reports identified MX and *Trident II* counterforce capabilities as important for stable deterrence *because of their potential to motivate the Soviet Union to take greater measures to ensure that its strategic forces could not be destroyed.*[76] This perfect reflection of balance of terror thinking was prevalent, and was reflected in remarks by Richard DeLauer, Under Secretary of Defense for Research and Engineering during the Reagan Administration:

> By placing some Soviet ICBM's and C3 [command, control, and communications] facilities at risk, we encourage the Soviets to divert some of their resources to the defense and survivability of those forces and facilities. Soviet expenditures of this type are not threatening, in fact, we regard them as stabilizing and welcome actions in the ICBM area...Forcing the Soviets to invest in survivable systems not only enhances stability but also reduces Soviet incentives for a surprise attack against the U.S. If their forces are not vulnerable, they will have less incentive to use them in a crisis.[77]

The treatment of *Safeguard*, SALT, MIRV, MX, the SDI, and *Trident II* demonstrated a strong and enduring political consensus on the basic parameters of U.S. strategic policy. By the end of the 1980s, Democratic and Republican administrations had *short-lived* excursions in favor of significant damage limitation and concluded that Secretary McNamara's original simple measure of assured destruction was an inadequate standard for U.S. strategic deterrence, opening the door for *limited* U.S. counterforce capabilities. However, these developments respectively did not long endure or did not depart from Schelling's basic balance of terror guidelines, and the presumption against significant BMD, air defense and civil defense deployment remained intact.

U.S. Strategic Policy Initiatives and Balance of Terror Norms

This evolution of U.S. deterrence strategy and acquisition policy was evident in two major strategic policy initiatives of the period, the Nixon Administration's National Security Decision Memorandum-242 (NSDM-242) of 1974, and the Carter Administration's Presidential Directive/ NSC-59 (PD-59) of 1980. These called for the adoption of deterrence requirements per a definition of assured destruction that differed from Secretary McNamara's but—as suggested above—did *not* transcend stable balance of terror guidelines.

In 1974, NSDM-242—known informally as the "Schlesinger Doctrine" after then Secretary of Defense James Schlesinger—revised McNamara's assured destruction deterrence metric. Secretary Schlesinger moved the discussion beyond the assured destruction of Soviet population and industry to include the threatened "destruction of the political, economic, and military resources critical to the enemy's postwar power, influence, and ability to recover at an early time as a major power" and, as noted above, more options for graduated nuclear escalation.[78]

Broadening the set of targets in the Soviet Union to be threatened for deterrence purposes and increasing the planning and capabilities for graduated nuclear escalation options was a move away from the earlier definition of assured destruction, *but did not connote the rejection of a stable balance of terror.* Rather, this more expansive threat was intended to strengthen the salience and credibility of the U.S. nuclear escalation threat within the context of an overarching stable balance of terror.[79]

Mutual deterrence remained the priority goal of U.S. strategic policy; there continued to be *no* commitment to the deployment of BMD, air defense or civil defense to protect U.S. society directly if mutual deterrence utterly failed. As Secretary of Defense Schlesinger stated in 1975 with reference to the U.S. strategic posture: "...with the ABM Treaty—we have recognized *the difficulty* of implementing a full-scale damage-limiting posture....While [the U.S. strategic posture] contains *some* counterforce capability, neither that capability nor the improvements we are proposing for it should raise the specter in the minds of the Soviets that their ICBM force is in jeopardy...our decided preference [is] that neither side attempt to acquire such a capability."[80] The U.S. goal of stable mutual deterrence and Soviet confidence in its capability to threaten U.S. society continued to hold sway.

Shortly thereafter, on August 24, 1977, the Carter White House issued Presidential Directive/NSC-18 (PD-18). PD-18 included a call for a thorough review of U.S. nuclear policy, and resulted in a series of presidential directives that reinforced the movement of U.S. policy beyond the classic assured destruction metric,[81] but within continued adherence to basic stable balance of terror desiderata.

By all appearances, President Carter entered office committed to a minimal version of Secretary McNamara's original assured destruction gauge and to sustaining a balance of terror. In his 1979 State of the Union address, President Carter appeared to define deterrence in terms of the minimal nuclear firepower necessary to threaten Soviet cities: "...just one of our relatively invulnerable Poseidon submarines—comprising less than 2 percent of our total nuclear force of submarines, aircraft, and land-based missiles—*carries enough warheads to destroy every large-and-medium sized city in the Soviet Union.* Our deterrent is overwhelming, and I will sign no agreement unless our deterrent force will remain overwhelming."[82]

Prior to President Carter's inaugural, during an initial meeting with the Joint Chiefs of Staff, President-elect Carter startled the Chiefs by asking about the possibility that 200 ICBMs could be adequate for the strategic balance.[83] And, reportedly he attempted unsuccessfully to secure an arms control commitment from Moscow to scale back Soviet air defense and civil defense programs per the classic requirements for a stable balance of terror.[84] President Carter clearly had absorbed assured destruction as the strategic metric and the stable balance of terror narrative.

Toward the end of the Carter Administration, however, the initiatives set in motion by PD-18 pointed some elements of U.S. strategic policy further away from Secretary McNamara's definition of assured destruction and even briefly suggested movement away from stable balance of terror guidelines.[85] As previously noted, Presidential Directive/NSC-41 (PD-41) called for the U.S. civil defense program to provide an improved basis for "carrying out eventual national recovery...should deterrence and escalation control fail," including "some increase" in U.S. population survival, and "greater continuity of government."[86]

The 1980 Amendment to the Federal Civil Defense Act of 1950 similarly called for the U.S. civil defense program to: "Enhance the survivability of American people and leadership in the event of nuclear war, thereby improving the basis for recovery and reducing the vulnerability to attack, enhance deterrence, and reduce the possibility that the United States might be susceptible to enemy coercion in times of increased tension."[87] This certainly echoed some of Kahn's earlier themes.

William Odom of the Carter Administration's National Security Council, has noted that those in the Carter White House did not believe that fighting and winning a nuclear war was possible in any meaningful sense—but that efforts should be made nonetheless to provide protection for American citizens because deterrence could fail:

> By late 1979 and early 1980, directives and guidance were in place on all of the key fronts that had to be addressed if the United States was serious about dealing with the advent of the failure of nuclear deterrence. No one working on these issues, as far as I could tell, suffered illusions about fighting and winning a nuclear war. No one seemed to take that as the primary aim. In my case, the rationale was plain. A modicum of effort was necessary in order to prepare for failure of deterrence. This was the barest minimum a responsible president could afford to do.[88]

President Carter's Presidential Directive/NSC-53 (PD-53) complemented PD-41. It directed that "the nation's telecommunications must provide for....Continuity of government during and after a nuclear war or natural disaster," and "recovery of the nation during and after a nuclear war or natural disaster."[89]

Critics responded sharply, however, per the established balance of terror formula and Secretary McNamara's old definition of the assured destruction metric. They charged that increased civil defense could not provide meaningful protection given the certain Soviet response, would "destabilize" deterrence, and would hinder arms control.[90] Congress responded by rejecting real increases and leaving the actual amount appropriated for civil defense at previous minimal levels, without much apparent fight from the Carter Administration.[91] As short-lived as President Carter's initiative was, here at least was an official shot at the balance of terror principle that significant strategic capabilities for protecting society had to be eschewed as incompatible with stable deterrence.[92] The apparent lack of full confidence in the reliability of mutual deterrence, and related attribution of value to significant if imperfect defenses for people via civil defense, was a challenge to the standard formula for a stable balance of terror.

In 1980, the Carter Administration issued PD-59. Secretary of Defense Brown said that U.S. nuclear retaliation could be directed selectively or comprehensively against, "...what the Soviets consider most important to them,"[93] which could include: Soviet military forces, conventional and nuclear; the military and political control apparatus ("their power structure"); military industry; and, the economic base.[94] PD-59 directed that U.S. strategic offensive forces be capable of targeting a spectrum of Soviet targets, including Soviet strategic nuclear forces, for the purpose of limiting damage to the United States from Soviet nuclear attack.[95] In contrast to the original language of assured destruction, PD-59 stipulated that for deterrence purposes the United States needed to be capable of threatening what the Soviet leadership truly valued, and that included hardened military and political control targets.

Some officials in the Carter White House working these policy initiatives were well aware that they were rejecting the purist's definition of assured destruction as an adequate deterrence standard and challenging the balance of terror categorization of defensive capabilities as unnecessary, useless and destabilizing.[96] PD-59 weathered an intense storm of criticism from commentators and former officials who could not countenance a definition of deterrence outside of the original, 1960s-era assured destruction/balance of terror framework.[97] They labeled PD-59 "destabilizing" because the targeting of Soviet military forces supposedly would move the Soviets toward pre-emption in a crisis and heighten the arms race; moreover, it allegedly was a rejection of stable mutual deterrence in favor of a nuclear "war-fighting" doctrine.

Secretary Brown responded to criticism that PD-59 was a dramatic policy shift away from past U.S. approaches to deterrence strategy by observing that "It has never been U.S. policy to limit ourselves to massive counter-city options in retaliation, nor have our plans been so circumscribed. For nearly 20 years, we have explicitly included a range of employment options—against military as well as non-military targets—in our strategic nuclear employment planning."[98] Indeed, as already mentioned in Chapter 4, Secretary McNamara had distinguished between assured destruction as the metric for acquiring strategic forces, and how U.S. forces might be employed in wartime to preserve some deterrence limits. He included some counterforce targeting in the latter as part of what he labeled a "coercive" retaliatory strategy.

Secretary Brown's explicit adoption of limited strategic counterforce capabilities as *a necessary part of U.S. deterrence capabilities was not* a rejection of a stable balance of terror, but it certainly was another step—following NSDM-242—away from Secretary McNamara's simple assured destruction standard for strategic force acquisition. The resulting firestorm of criticism—and the fact that PD-59 came toward the end of the Carter Administration—helped to limit the implementation of these policy initiatives, particularly acquisition of the strategic capability for societal defense. For example, as noted above, U.S. spending on civil defense had been at very modest levels through the 1970s, largely on the balance of terror grounds that civil defense would be unnecessary, useless and destabilizing.[99] Despite the goals expressed in PD-41 and the 1980 Amendment to the Federal Civil Defense Act, funding remained essentially flat. In 1980, Secretary of Defense Harold Brown noted in pertinent Senate testimony that there was no new, substantial damage-limitation capability for society any more than there had been under Republican initiatives: "We are not building millions of shelter spaces for our population: none of those things that you would expect are being done in the United States. You hear talk about things, but you don't see action along those lines. That has been true in administrations of all political colorations."[100]

Neither NSDM-242 nor PD-59 led to a major redirection of U.S. capabilities in favor of the substantial, direct damage-limitation capabilities that might have challenged the basic balance of terror formula for mutual deterrence. Graduated escalation options and limited counterforce targeting capabilities held no promise for extracting the United States from that formula—and were not meant to do so, according to the witness of the pertinent senior officials of the time. Instead, both policy initiatives were intended to expand Secretary McNamara's simple assured destruction metric to strengthen U.S. nuclear deterrence within a stable balance of terror. As Secretary of Defense Brown observed in 1979:

> Assured destruction is necessary for nuclear deterrence, but it is not, in my judgment, sufficient as a strategic doctrine or as a sole basis for determining the characteristics of our strategic forces....it would be imprudent to place the United States in a position in which uncontrolled escalation would be the only course we could follow. Massive retaliation may not be appropriate, nor will its prospect be sufficiently credible in all circumstances to deter the full range of actions we seek to prevent. Effective deterrence requires forces of sufficient size and flexibility to attack selectively a range

of military and other targets, yet enable us to hold back a significant and enduring reserve. The ability to provide measured retaliation is essential to credible deterrence.[101]

From the mid-1960s to the mid-1970s, however, Secretary McNamara's simple assured destruction/balance of terror metrics and the pursuit of strategic arms control to facilitate a stable balance of terror constituted the intellectual core of U.S. strategic policy in most public discourse. These interrelated concepts had taken firm root in Congressional, academic and journalistic commentary: a stable balance of terror was the accepted goal of U.S. deterrence strategy, acquisition policy, and U.S. strategic arms control goal efforts, and Secretary McNamara's simple assured destruction standard was widely believed to be synonymous with deterrence. This combination was said to provide reliable, predictable mutual deterrence at modest strategic force requirements and cost. Subsequent policy initiatives that departed from the 1960s assured destruction guidelines—such as NSDM-242 and PD-59—were criticized as unnecessary, useless and destabilizing.

Because Secretary of Defense Schlesinger and Secretary of Defense Brown spoke of U.S. limited counterforce capabilities and multiple U.S. escalation options, critics charged that NSDM-242 and PD-59 were rejections not just of Secretary McNamara's simple assured destruction metric, but rejections of mutual deterrence altogether in favor of nuclear "war-fighting" doctrines. The 1960s narrative had become so closely associated with deterrence and U.S. strategic policy that any departure from script was deemed an assault on deterrence in favor of "war-fighting": a stable balance of terror was thought to have been achieved and the equilibrium point for stable deterrence and successful strategic arms control was in hand. This mutually advantageous context had to be preserved against allegedly retrograde policy challenges such as NSDM-242 and PD-59, which threatened to upset deterrence stability and the related arms control process. Keeping nuclear war as mutually horrific as possible was easy and essential to deterrence stability and the supposed arms control equilibrium point. Limited escalation options, it was said, might reduce the mutual horror, and thus degrade mutual deterrence. Limited U.S. counterforce capabilities were deemed unnecessary for deterrence and would inspire "destabilizing" Soviet fears of surprise attack, spark another round of action-reaction arms racing, and destroy the basis for arms control, namely, mutual deterrence at the balance of terror equilibrium point.[102]

A typical critique appearing in *The New York Times* in 1980 charged: "Deterrence once meant reluctance to attack for fear of being unacceptably damaged. Assured 'second strike' capability—200 protected nuclear weapons—was considered an adequate deterrent. But military tradition and nationalist competition require superiority and winning, not deterring. Thus, an unwinnable race was started for military advantage, ignoring overkill limits."[103] The push for graduated escalation options and limited counterforce capabilities intended to strengthen deterrence was instead attributed to the pursuit of "winning" strategies, "military superiority," "hynernationalism," and, "nostalgia for a replay of World War II." [104]

In fact, neither NSDM-242 nor PD-59 merited any such criticism. As mentioned, they moved U.S. policy modestly away from the old assured destruction metric and continued full acceptance of a stable balance of terror as the basis for U.S. strategic policy. In each case, with the exception of the Carter Administration's fleeting policy commitment to significant civil defense, the reliable functioning of deterrence remained the only plausible basis for direct protection of the U.S. population against strategic attack. U.S. societal vulnerability to nuclear attack remained *intentionally unchallenged* by any significant U.S. BMD, air defense or civil defense capabilities, and modifications of U.S. offensive targeting options were for deterrence and possibly limited defensive purposes *within a functioning balance of terror*. Indeed, senior U.S. officials, including Secretary Schlesinger, went to great lengths to emphasize that they were not advocating a U.S. force posture capable of "threatening the Soviet deterrent" through offensive or defensive capabilities.[105]

Without serious, comprehensive damage-limitation programs—including civil defense, air defense, and BMD—meaningful, planned protection of U.S. cities and NATO Europe was still entirely dependent upon mutual deterrence. Simply adding some limited counterforce requirements to the assured destruction standard could not fundamentally alter the U.S. commitment to a stable balance of terror; nor could the addition of limited escalation options. These were expected to help deter Soviet attacks against cities during war and to highlight the dangers of the escalation process to help deter the Soviets from attack altogether. They could not and were not intended to deliver significant damage limitation *apart from the continuing functioning of mutual deterrence*. Great deference continued to be paid to preserving mutual vulnerability and capping damage-limitation capabilities to avoid the "reciprocal fear of surprise attack," and to the notion that arms control should be aimed at facilitating a balance of terror. Hence, U.S. policy remained consistent with balance of terror tenets, if not with Secretary McNamara's assured destruction metric.

The Defense Department's *History of the Strategic Arms Competition* rightly observes that the rationale for supposedly "war-fighting" U.S. policy developments actually remained squarely within the realm of mutual deterrence: "...second-strike counterforce operations against carefully segregated military targets seemed conceptually to offer the best hope of *preserving some constraints, maintaining intrawar deterrence,* and reducing the weight of societal damage in a nuclear conflict."[106]

Senior Department of Defense official Henry Rowen summarized the purposes behind the "Schlesinger Doctrine" in precisely these terms: "to help the credibility of deterrence and to help keep conflict at a low level if it were to occur. However, in contrast to the early 1960's, the objectives of limiting damage to the U.S. by having the capacity to deny physically the Soviets the ability to kill U.S. civilians has been rejected."[107]

Secretary of Defense Harold Brown similarly made this point with remarkable clarity in his fiscal year 1980 annual Department of Defense report: *"In the interests of [deterrence] stability, we avoid the capability of eliminating the other side's deterrent,* insofar as we might be able to do so. In short, we must be quite willing—as we have been for some time—to accept the principle of mutual deterrence, and design our defense posture in light of that principle."[108] And, similarly, as he stated in January 1981, "... the absence of a widely deployed ABM system makes for stability."[109]

Contrary to the popular, superficial criticism of the time, neither NSDM-242 nor PD-59 challenged the central tenets of mutual deterrence via a stable balance of terror, i.e., the notion that mutual deterrence could reliably and predictably be orchestrated on the basis of Soviet rationality, uncertainty and mutual vulnerability to nuclear retaliation. Both initiatives transcended Secretary McNamara's simple definition of assured destruction, but such variations fit easily within an enduring balance of terror framework.

Colin Gray rightly identified these departures from previous assured destruction orthodoxy as variants of the balance of terror:

> Indeed, U.S. ["war fighting"] nuclear strategy is a sophisticated variant of the "competition in risk taking" described so eloquently by Thomas Schelling more than twenty years ago. Today, preeminently, the United States plans to punish the Soviet state and its executive

instruments rather than its captive, or acquiescent, society. The official U.S. concept of deterrence [still] depends on the idea that a Soviet leadership, anticipating severe damage to its most cherished values, will be deterred from choosing to fight.[110]

President Nixon criticized "MAD," and claimed that his initiative for limited escalation options was a shift away from MAD.[111] This was true in the narrow sense that NSDM-242 posited requirements beyond the simple 1960s assured destruction metric. But neither the changes to policy during his tenure, nor any coming during the subsequent Cold War years, altered the minimal deployment of damage-limitation measures and U.S. societal vulnerability, or challenged for long the central tenets of the balance of terror. They and the related "four no's" resisted any successful challenge as the fundamental basis for U.S. deterrence strategy and force acquisition.

An early Top Secret Nixon Administration White House study on the U.S. strategic posture reflected this policy consensus around the balance of terror and its generally negative effect on the appraisal of U.S. damage-limitation capabilities:

> There is agreement that we would want such a [damage limitation] capability if we could have it without sacrificing the attainment of other national objectives. There is disagreement about whether this is possible. One view holds that this is possible, *that we could buy more damage limiting capability without threatening the Soviet deterrent and thus without provoking an offsetting Soviet reaction.* The other view, held by most of the Steering Group, is that the Soviets, using pessimistic assumptions about our capabilities and intentions, would certainly react, perhaps even overreact, and largely offset the U.S. damage limiting initiatives.[112]

As portrayed, neither side of this debate advocated "threatening the Soviet deterrent" via comprehensive U.S. defenses.

In summary, the fact that NSDM-242 and PD-59 were criticized mistakenly as the rejection of mutual deterrence in favor of "nuclear war-fighting" illustrated the degree to which the simple assured destruction metric and balance of terror norms had become synonymous with deterrence. The United States defense community debated NSDM-242 and PD-59 in the 1970s and 1980s as if they were major policy shifts; in fact they represented revisions to the assured destruction standard but did not call into question the stable balance of terror foundation of U.S. policy. Balance of terror norms enjoyed a powerful political consensus and, in adherence to those norms, the political process beat back the few actual challenges of the era—including President Reagan's original conceptualization of the SDI, and the occasional, short-lived displays of interest in civil defense. The fate of the U.S. civil defense office immediately following the end of the Cold War reflects the reality of the continuing power of the balance of terror guidelines:

> Since the end of the Cold War, America's programs (except those designated to protect key government leaders) to provide shelter, food, and water in the case of a nuclear exchange have essentially disappeared. Although an Office of Civil Defense existed within the Federal Emergency Management Agency (FEMA) to coordinate these programs, the office was quietly closed during the mid-1990s.[113]

U.S. Damage-Limitation Goals: *"Insofar as We Can" and "To the Extent Practicable"*

The continued rejection of significant damage-limiting programs undercut the practical meaning of typical official statements that U.S. strategic goals included direct wartime damage limitation: "To protect ourselves and our Allies from the destructive consequence of nuclear wars, *insofar as we can*."[114] And, "In the event deterrence fails, our forces must be capable… of preventing Soviet victory and securing *the most favorable possible outcome* for U.S. interests."[115] Official wording consistently sounded the same theme: if deterrence failed and nuclear war were to occur, a priority U.S. goal would be to limit damage, "*to the extent practicable*," or on terms "*as favorable as possible*."[116] Such phrases have been referenced to suggest that the United States, in fact, was committed to a "first-strike," "war-winning" nuclear strategy during the period. The caveats in these phrases, however, are the key to understanding their meaning.

Such expressions clearly were meant to convey the point that, if deterrence failed, there would be an effort to provide damage limitation for the United States. While undoubtedly true, to identify damage limitation as a meaningful strategic goal if deterrence failed was at best an expression of hope. The realization of that hope was remote indeed given the general U.S. policy direction since the early 1960s to abandon most existing damage-limiting programs and to eschew new capabilities for that purpose on the officially-expressed grounds that meaningful damage limitation was infeasible, intolerably expensive, unnecessary and undesirable. These expressions suggested the reality of preparations for deterrence failure when direct damage limitation, in any meaningful sense, had been eschewed for years: senior officials emphasized that if deterrence failed to prevent or limit war, there could be no meaningful societal damage limitation. U.S. acquisition policy, correspondingly, had been designed explicitly *not to pursue the basis for direct damage limitation*—thus ensuring the absence of whatever level of partial defense that otherwise would have been possible.

Here was the inherent inconsistency in U.S. strategic thought, planning and official expressions: U.S. strategic force acquisition and arms control policies were built around a strategic concept of mutual deterrence that consciously eschewed substantial damage-limitation capabilities as unnecessary, useless and antithetical to the U.S. goal of stable mutual deterrence. Yet, senior U.S. officials in Democratic and Republican administrations continued to assert that a priority U.S. goal in the event deterrence failed would be damage limitation. This claim, of course, could be true in the technical sense while also subject to the vulnerability that the conscious choice to reject damage-limitation measures was not a particularly persuasive basis from which to suggest the reality of serious damage-limitation preparation for deterrence failure.

In the context of overwhelming reliance on mutual deterrence and the corresponding rejection of forces for damage limitation, the claim that damage limitation, nevertheless, would be the priority goal can only be regarded as a confusing half-truth. The unspoken complete truth would have been to add that—despite any expressed damage-limitation goal—if deterrence failed to prevent war and constrain escalation, then no meaningful, direct damage limitation could result; as defined, we had chosen not to seek it. By design, there could be no meaningful measure of damage limitation apart from deterrence.

The Nixon Administration's 1974 *Nuclear Weapons Employment Policy* coinciding with NSDM-242 illustrates the point well.[117] If deterrence failed, damage limitation was the declared goal—including via counterforce strikes. Yet, it also emphasizes that damage limitation could *only* be accomplished through mutual deterrence and the control of escalation, which "requires both sides to show restraint. Such restraint could stem from a combination of self-interest and coercion," namely, the continued functioning of deterrence.

Similarly, in 1980, Secretary of Defense Brown was asked by Senator Charles Percy in closed (since sanitized), Top Secret testimony if the United States had a plan to conduct a pre-emptive nuclear strike: "Do we have a plan? If our intelligence, for instance, gave us 100-percent assurance that there was an intended strike on us unless we did something about it, what would we do? Do we have such a plan to deal with such a hypothetical situation?" Secretary Brown responded: "There are options that cover that situation. [Deleted.]" Almost immediately thereafter, however, Secretary Brown added:

> *We will not have the capability of destroying the Soviet capability to retaliate and destroy us.* We cannot destroy their SSBN's [submarines carrying strategic ballistic missiles]....Actually, as things now stand, if we were to launch a surprise attack, we would catch their bombers, but we couldn't destroy their land-based missiles because we don't have enough warheads able to do that promptly, and we would not even with the MX [deleted] capability.[118]

The U.S. employment of strategic nuclear weapons could not equate to U.S. survival of the process and could not correspond to Kahn's damage-limitation notions or with a "credible first-strike" capability.

U.S. officials and documents could posit a damage-limitation priority in the event deterrence failed, but U.S. preparations would not prevent societal destruction in its absence. To return to the lifeboat analogy used by Kahn, U.S. policy was somewhat akin to shipowners consciously deciding not to buy any, or many, lifeboats because of their cost and inefficiencies, and because of the owners' confidence that the ship would have no collisions. And, to extend the analogy, while the ship owners chose not to prepare for a collision, they simultaneously claimed that— if there ever was a collision—their goal would be to save passengers "insofar as we can." By their own prior actions they would have done much to ensure that "insofar as we can" would likely have little practical meaning. Such a claim could be technically correct, but also meaningless and likely misunderstood.

All analogies are imperfect, but perhaps a more apt analogy than lifeboats—given that deterrence decision making involves both the party issuing threats and the intended audience—is that of urban police and violent criminals. U.S. policy after the mid-1960s was analogous to a city outfitting its SWAT Team with extremely lethal offensive firepower, but with minimal body armor: that lethal firepower surely would deter attacks while body armor would be expensive, imperfect and simply lead criminals to seek less-expensive armor-piercing bullets. In the context of a willful decision to forego the partial protection possibly afforded by body armor, any claim that the city's goal was to limit SWAT Team casualties to the extent possible could be seen as hollow, even cynical.

Nevertheless, by the middle years of the Cold War this was the character of U.S. statements about U.S. damage-limitation goals in the event deterrence failed. Some officials' public declarations *attempted to blend Schelling and Kahn by suggesting the serious priority of both balance of terror guidelines and damage limitation.* However, U.S. acquisition policy from the mid-1960s on revealed the truth about U.S. priorities and goals: by policy choice, direct damage limitation was subordinated to the balance of terror formula which argued against the acquisition of defensive capabilities. Cold War claims that damage limitation would be the priority goal if deterrence failed could hardly be reconciled with the reality of the virtual U.S. abandonment of serious efforts to mitigate damage to the United States directly in the event deterrence actually did fail.

At one point, Secretary McNamara described then current U.S. offensive strategic capabilities as providing the capability to "completely crush" the Soviet Union and achieve "victory" in nuclear war; he hastened to add, however, that the United States would suffer tens of millions of casualties in the process.[119] As noted in Chapter 4, Secretary McNamara had rejected JCS calls for damage-limitation capabilities in part because, he said, such absolute levels of destruction were intolerable. In the context of this operative definition of what could constitute meaningful protection, and the subsequent intentional rejection of measures to mitigate the destruction of American society, any talk of "crushing" the Soviet Union and "victory" was confusing at best.

In summary, mutual deterrence was the chosen means of protection, and U.S. survival had become wholly dependent on deterrence *vis-à-vis* the Soviet Union never utterly failing: if it did fail, many millions of lives likely would be lost, and additional millions of lives that otherwise might have been saved via damage-limitation capabilities would be lost. Throughout the 1970s and 1980s, however, many commentators and senior U.S. officials offered confident assurances that holding close to the assured destruction metric and stable balance of terror guidelines essentially guaranteed deterrence of deliberate attack. This was an important claim because, if true, it meant that the tradeoff involved in pursuing "stable" deterrence at the expense of damage limitation was more apparent than real because the balance of terror, when properly orchestrated, essentially could not fail to deter deliberate attack. That was a powerful, comforting and convenient promise under the circumstances.

Relax, Deterrence is "Existential"

By the late 1960s, government officials—former and serving—academic commentators, and noted members of the pertinent scientific communities did indeed claim widely that the balance of terror essentially *could not fail to deter deliberate attacks*; any sane opponent supposedly would be deterred by the possibility of nuclear escalation to the destruction of cities. These officials and commentators essentially elevated Schelling's initial, nuanced proposition that uncertainty could deter to an iron law of deterrence: deterrence would work, reliably and predictably, against rational opponents because they would be prudent in the face of an uncertain risk of U.S. nuclear escalation. And, because unprotected population centers are highly vulnerable to nuclear weapons, the orchestration of an essentially infallible deterrent was relatively undemanding. Again, a nuclear threat to cities was the common problem, and sustaining that common threat was the sure deterrence solution to the problem: the threat was the sure solution to the threat—how easy.

This view—that the proper orchestration of mutual deterrence essentially guaranteed deterrence—became the basis for optimistic promises offered up by serving and former government officials. For example, McGeorge Bundy, President John Kennedy's National Security Advisor, identified a balance of nuclear terror, the uncertainty of escalation, and sane leaders as *the necessary and sufficient* conditions ensuring the effective functioning of nuclear deterrence. Under these conditions, he considered deterrence to be so reliable and predictable that it was "existential." "Existential deterrence" became a term of art for the infallibility of deterrence to prevent deliberate attack in a stable balance of terror. Mutual deterrence would prevent war and would continue to do so: "As long as each side has thermonuclear weapons that could be used against the opponent, even after the strongest possible preemptive attack, existential deterrence is strong and it rests on uncertainty about what could happen."[120]   And: "In the light of the certain prospect of retaliation there has been literally no chance at all that any sane political authority, in either the United States or the Soviet Union, would consciously choose to start a nuclear war. This proposition is true for the past, the present, and the foreseeable future. For sane men on both sides, the balance of terror is overwhelmingly persuasive."[121]

Why, according to Bundy, could such a high level of confidence be placed in the balance of terror? Because: "In the real world of real political leaders—whether here or in the Soviet Union—a decision that would bring even one hydrogen bomb on one city of one's own country would be recognized in advance as a catastrophic blunder; ten bombs on ten cities would be a disaster beyond history; and a hundred bombs on a hundred cities are unthinkable."[122]

Bundy's supreme confidence in deterrence was not unique. As noted above, Secretary McNamara often expressed near absolute confidence in the combination of assured destruction and the balance of terror for deterrence and extended deterrence: "…we can confront the Soviets with such a clear prospect of defeat, should they initiate a major war against this country and its allies, that we will be able to avoid such a war, while accomplishing our foreign policy objectives."[123]

Paul Warnke, an Assistant Secretary of Defense under Secretary McNamara and Director of the Arms Control and Disarmament Agency under President Carter, offered similar assurances:

> The strategic balance is now characterized by stability, by which I mean that neither side could give serious consideration to initiating a strategic nuclear war because of the certainty that that would provoke a retaliatory response which would destroy the attacker's society. There is now a situation of mutual deterrence.[124]

A former senior State Department official even identified the specific events that could be "permanently ruled out" because of the balance of terror. Confidence in the balance of terror was not limited to the U.S.-Soviet relationship, but could be universal:

> Our conclusion, in its narrowest terms, must be that the deliberate resort to war by a nuclear power against a power capable of effective retaliation is permanently ruled out.... the deliberate resort to major nonnuclear warfare between such powers is also ruled out. And the resort to even such limited warfare as border skirmishes between them is notably inhibited by the danger that it would escalate out of control, ending in nuclear war.[125]

Confidence in the reliable functioning of deterrence and in the understanding of how to make it so remained to the end of the Cold War. In 1992, Harvard's Ashton Carter and Stanford's William Perry (who shortly thereafter became an Assistant Secretary of Defense and Secretary of Defense, respectively) wrote that "core deterrence" had become "securely established" and that, "virtually all plausible varieties of deterrence of such deliberate attack could be underwritten with a fraction of the existing nuclear arsenals."[126]

In making such powerful and confident claims, government officials were extrapolating on themes in the writings of the great academic theorists. Bernard Brodie, for example, seemed to take Kahn to task in this regard, and in doing so reflected his own belief that deterrence could be considered "existential":

> The phrase "if deterrence fails" rolls rather too trippingly off the tongues of some of those many defense specialists whose work requires them to think about what happens in actual combat. Certainly the phrase begs many questions. For the purpose of deciding what our defense posture should be, one has to consider some all-important questions, like: *Why* should deterrence fail? *How* could it fail? How can we keep it from failing? To the last of these questions one should always be able to give a positive answer.[127]

As was essential for proponents of a stable balance of terror, Brodie appears to have believed that there *always could be a positive answer.* Why? Because:

> Unless we are dealing with utter madmen, there is no conceivable reason why in any necessary showdown with the Soviet Union, appropriate manipulations of force and threats of force, certainly coordinated with more positive diplomatic maneuvers, cannot bring about deterrence. That is one respect in which the world is utterly different now from what it was in 1939 or 1914, when deterrence, however effective temporarily, had the final intrinsic weakness that one side or both did not truly fear what we would now call general war.[128]

Brodie claimed that the Cold War balance of terror was not fragile because of, "human inhibitions against taking monumental risks or doing things which are universally detested...."[129] Deterrence apparently worked so easily and predictably because it conformed to universal human characteristics.

Similarly, in describing the functioning of mutual deterrence, Schelling drew an analogy to the behavior of pedestrians to illustrate that mutual deterrence was reliable, predictable, and not necessarily based on mutual hostility: "People regularly stand at the curb watching trucks, buses, and cars hurtle past at speeds that guarantee injury and threaten death if they so much as attempt to cross against the traffic. They are absolutely deterred. But there is no fear. They just know better."[130]

In Congressional testimony in which both Kahn and Schelling participated, Schelling drew another analogy to illustrate how safety and vulnerability can coexist because deterrence will work:

> I think I disagree with Herman that for the rest of this century we should try to rely more on defensive systems than offensive systems....if you rely on offense, it means you learn how to live in a world in which, whether you like it or not, countries have great capacity to hurt each other. Even if you go through occasional periods when that is not so, I think you have to learn to live as we do in our neighborhoods. My neighbor could kill me. I can kill him.

I don't know why we don't kill each other, but I think it is because we got so used to the fact that punishment, if not swift and sure, was at least likely enough that even if you didn't like your neighbor you let him live.[131]

It was convenient and comforting to believe that mutual deterrence could be orchestrated and, once in place, would function naturally—"existentially"—like pedestrians avoiding buses and neighbors not killing one another, to repeat Schelling's analogies. The balance of terror would prevent deliberate Soviet nuclear attack reliably and required a relatively modest effort on our part. We could dismiss Kahn's hard, expensive road to credible deterrence and damage limitation because U.S. nuclear retaliatory threats created their own credibility; the existence of a relatively small number of secure U.S. nuclear weapons made the possibility of U.S. nuclear escalation sufficiently threatening to deter any sane opponent reliably and predictably. Opponents' uncertainty about the prospect for U.S. escalation—not its confident expectation—would suffice to deter.

This proposition offered great relief. It meant that the U.S. decision to set aside serious, direct damage-limitation capabilities carried no real potential downside. There were no predictable tradeoffs involved in placing priority on mutual deterrence at the expense of damage limitation because to give up the deployment of defenses was to give up nothing that could be useful enough to be worth the effort and the related threat to deterrence stability. In contrast, mutual deterrence worked easily, predictably, existentially—with proper management, it was "securely established."

There may have been, however, less protection in the balance of terror than promised by confident assurances of existential deterrence. As postulated, such assurances presumed a near omniscient understanding of how opponents—including future opponents—would think and behave. The assertion of deterrence functioning predictably had become an easy tautology: mutual deterrence would preclude deliberate nuclear attack by any sane opponent because only an insane opponent would undertake such a deliberate attack. When the realities of deterrence are taken into account, however, this comforting and convenient tautology was highly suspect even during the Cold War era; in the security environment of the twenty-first century, it is high-risk guidance for U. S. policy.

Schelling's analogies to pedestrians and neighbors were intended to illustrate how naturally deterrence works; in fact, they illustrate why deterrence cannot be relied upon to function predictably and existentially.

On occasion, pedestrians tragically do walk in front of speeding autos or buses, and occasionally vehicles come over the curb accidentally or on purpose, killing pedestrians who believed they were safe on the curb. In fact, pedestrians are referred to as "vulnerable road users" by transportation experts.[132] Drivers impaired by alcohol often decide to get behind the wheel despite the severe potential costs to themselves and others; in 2006 they killed more than 17,000 people in the United States.[133] Such high-risk behavior is not the norm, but is very familiar.

In addition, some neighbors do deliberately shoot and kill each other. In fact, such incidents, along with internal family tragedies, account for a large proportion of homicides in the United States. Most neighbors are not killers, and most drivers are not grossly negligent; unfortunately, however, the inherent risks of such behavior—and the laws and sanctions put in place by society—have not and will not reliably and predictably prevent it.

The implications of this point for U.S. security in the twenty-first century could be trivial except for the fact that many key contributors to U.S. acquisition and deterrence policies believe that the promise of deterrence in the balance of terror tenets represents an enduring truth, as valid for the future as it was for the past. Despite the dramatic changes in the international landscape since the collapse of the Soviet Union, U.S. strategic policies continue to be governed by a conscious adherence to balance of terror guidelines with a corresponding presumption against damage-limiting capabilities. The "four no's" of U.S. Cold War strategic acquisition policy have outlived the threat and conditions that spawned them. Chapter 6 examines the contemporary application of Cold War balance of terror tenets.

Endnotes

1. Draft Presidential Memorandum, Secretary of Defense [Clark M. Clifford] to the President [Lyndon B. Johnson], Subj: Strategic Offensive and Defensive Forces, January 9, 1969, p. 6 (Originally classified; sanitized and declassified on January 5, 1983); cited hereafter as 1969 DPM. This and other Draft Presidential Memoranda can be found online at the Master OFOI Reading Room, Department of Defense, http://www.dod.mil/pubs/foi/master_reading_list01.html.

2. Ibid., p. 3.

3. Ibid., p. 4.

4. Ibid., p. 2.

5. Ibid., pp. 4-5, 13, 24-26.

6. Thomas C. Schelling, *The Strategy of Conflict* (Cambridge, MA: Harvard University Press, 1960), p. 233.

7. Thomas C. Schelling in, U.S. House of Representatives, Foreign Affairs Committee, *Strategy and Science: Toward a National Security Policy for the 1970s*, Hearings, 91st Congress, 1st Session (Washington, D.C.: USGPO, 1969), p. 123.

8. 1969 DPM, op. cit., pp. 2, 23.

9. Record of Meeting With President Johnson, January 4, 1967, U.S. Department of State, *Foreign Relations of the United States, 1964-1968*, Vol. 10, National Security Policy (Washington, D.C.: USGPO, 2001), Document 166. See also, Robert L. Rothstein, "The ABM, Proliferation and International Stability," *Foreign Affairs*, Vol. 46, No. 3 (April 1968), p. 493.

10. Memorandum From Spurgeon Keeny of the National Security Council Staff to the President's Special Assistant for Science and Technology (Donald Hornig), January 4, 1967, US Department of State, *Foreign Relations of the United States, 1964-1968*, Vol. 10, National Security Policy (Washington D.C.: USGPO, 2001), Document 165.

11. See the discussion in, Donald R. Baucom, *The Origins of SDI: 1944-1983* (Lawrence, KS: University Press of Kansas, 1992), pp. 28-29, 38-39.

12. "The President's News Conference of March 14, 1969," Richard Nixon Library, *Public Papers of President Richard Nixon*, Research Center Book, 1969, March 14, 1969, No. 108-109, available at http://www.nixonlibrary.org/clientuploads/directory/archive/1969_pdf_files/1969_0108.pdf.

13. See U.S. Senate, Committee on Foreign Relations, *Strategic and Foreign Policy Implications of ABM Systems,* Hearings, Part 1, 91st Congress, 1st Session (Washington, D.C.: USGPO, 1969), p. 289; and W.K. Panofsky, "Roots of the Strategic Arms Race: Ambiguity and Ignorance," *Bulletin of the Atomic Scientists*, Vol. 25, No. 1 (January 1969), p. 20.

14. Richard Nixon, quoted in "The President's News Conference of March 14, 1969," op. cit.

15. Ibid.

16. Ibid.

17. Richard Nixon, *The Real War* (New York: Warner Books, 1980), pp. 161-162.

18. Ibid., p. 168.

19. William R. Van Cleave, *Statement on the SALT Agreements Before the Senate Armed Services Committee*, July 25, 1972, prepared text, p. 4; printed in, U.S. Senate, Committee on Armed Services, *Military Implications of the Treaty on the Limitation of Anti-Ballistic Missile Systems and the Interim Agreement on Limitation of Strategic Offensive Arms*, Hearing, 92nd Congress, 2nd Session (Washington, D.C.:

USGPO, 1972), p. 4.

20. See, for example, the testimony of Wolfgang Panofsky in, U.S. Senate, Committee on Foreign Relations, Subcommittee on Arms Control, International Law and Organization, *ABM, MIRV, SALT, and the Nuclear Arms Race,* Hearings, 91st Congress, 2nd Session (Washington, D.C.: USGPO, 1970), pp. 179-180; George Rathjens, "A Breakthrough in Arms Control," *Bulletin of the Atomic Scientists,* Vol. 25, No. 1 (January 1969), p. 5; and, Herbert Scoville, "Next Steps in Limiting Strategic Arms," *Bulletin of the Atomic Scientists,* Vol. 28, No. 3 (March 1972), p. 11.

21. Richard Nixon, *The Memoirs of Richard Nixon* (New York: Grosset & Dunlap, 1978), pp. 617-618.

22. U.S. Arms Control and Disarmament Agency, *Arms Control and Disarmament Agreements: Texts and Histories of Negotiations,* 1980 Edition (Washington, D.C.: USGPO, August 1980), p. 139.

23. Caspar Weinberger, "Strategic Defense Initiative Opponents Show Reluctance for Self-Defense," *ROA National Security Report,* No. 4 (November 1986), p. 2.

24. Statement by Henry Kissinger in, U.S. Senate, Committee on Armed Services, *Military Implications of the Treaty on the Limitation of Anti-Ballistic Missile Systems and the Interim Agreement on Limitation of Strategic Offensive Arms,* Hearings, 92nd Congress, 2nd Session (Washington, D.C.: USGPO, 1972), p. 121. (Emphasis added).

25. Gerard Smith, in, House of Representatives, Committee on Foreign Affairs, *The Role of Arms Control in U.S. Defense Policy,* Hearings, 98th Congress, 2nd Session (Washington, D.C.: USGPO, 1984), Appendix 5, p. 302.

26. U.S. Arms Control and Disarmament Agency, *Arms Control and Disarmament Agreements* (Washington, D.C.: USGPO, 1982), p. 137.

27. Henry A. Kissinger, Memorandum for the President, June 17, 1969, "June 18 NSC Meeting on U.S. Strategic Posture and SALT," with enclosures, Tab A: "Discussion of Issues for Decision," p. 2 (Top Secret; declassified/released on November 7, 2000), in National Security Archive Electronic Briefing Book No. 173, available at http://www.gwu.edu/~nsarchiv.

28. Stansfield Turner, "The 'Folly' of the MX Missile," *The New York Times Magazine,* March 13, 1983, p. 94.

29. Statement by Secretary of State William Rogers in 1972, before the Senate Foreign Relations Committee. Quoted in, *SALT I Reconsidered* (Washington, D.C.: Institute of American Relations, 1979), p. 99.

30. Statement by Gerard Smith, head of the U.S. SALT I delegation in, U.S. Senate, Committee on Armed Services, *Military Implications of the Treaty on the Limitation of Anti-Ballistic Missile Systems and the Interim Agreement on Limitation of Strategic Offensive Arms,* op. cit., p. 100.

31. Statement by Gerard Smith in 1972, before the Senate Armed Services Committee. Quoted in, *SALT I Reconsidered,* op. cit., p. 13.

32. See, for example, the testimonies of Harold Brown, John Deutch, Brent Scrowcroft, and James Schlesinger on the subject in, U.S. Senate, Committee on Armed Services, *MX Missile Basing System and Related Issues,* Hearings, 98th Congress, 1st Session (Washington, D.C.: USGPO, 1983), pp. 3-94.

33. *NATO and the Warsaw Pact Force Comparisons,* 2nd Impression (Brussels: NATO Information Service, 1982), p. 29, Figure 11.

34. *Report of the President's Commission on Strategic Forces* (Washington, D.C.: The White House, April 1983), p. 4.

35. This point is made explicitly by former senior participants in the Soviet strategic force and arms control processes. See William E. Odom's classic text on the Soviet military, *The Collapse of the Soviet Military* (New Haven, CT: Yale University Press, 1998), pp. 71, 85-86.

36. Brent Scowcroft, John Deutch, and R. James Woolsey, "A Small, Survivable, Mobile ICBM," *The Washington Post*, December 26, 1986, p. A23.

37. Leslie Gelb, "A Glass Half Full," *Foreign Policy*, No. 36 (Fall 1979), p. 21.

38. Weinberger, *ROA National Security Report*, op. cit., pp. 2-3.

39. U.S. Arms Control and Disarmament Agency, *Arms Control and Disarmament Agreements: Texts and Histories of Negotiations*, op. cit., p. 146. (Emphasis added).

40. See, Congress of the United States, Office of Technology Assessment, *MX Missile Basing* (Washington, D.C.: USGPO, September 1981).

41. Fred Charles Iklé, *Annihilation From Within: The Ultimate Threat to Nations* (New York: Columbia University Press, 2006), pp. 119-120.

42. Van Cleave, loc. cit.; printed in, U.S. Senate, Committee on Armed Services, *Military Implications of the Treaty on the Limitation of Anti-Ballistic Missile Systems and the Interim Agreement on Limitation of Strategic Offensive Arms*, op. cit., pp. 8, 10.

43. Donald G. Brennan, "The Case for Population Defense," in, Johan Holst and William Schneider, eds., *Why ABM?* (New York: Pergamon Press, 1969), p. 116.

44. See, for example, the statement in, John Holum, Under Secretary of State for International Security and Arms Control, Interview with Jacquelyn Porth, Washington File, Office of International Information Programs, Department of State, October 30, 2000 (transcript).

45. This particular line is repeated in numerous impact statements. See, for example, House of Representatives, Committee on Foreign Affairs, U.S. Senate, Committee on Foreign Relations, Joint Committee Print, *Fiscal Year 1985 Arms Control Impact Statements, Statements Submitted to the Congress by the President Pursuant to Section 36 of the Arms Control and Disarmament Act* (Washington, D.C.: USGPO, 1984), p. 95.

46. House of Representatives, Committee on Foreign Affairs, U.S. Senate, Committee on Foreign Relations, Joint Committee Print, *Fiscal Year 1982 Arms Control Impact Statements, Statements Submitted to the Congress by the President Pursuant to Section 36 of the Arms Control and Disarmament Act* (Washington, D.C.: USGPO, 1981), p. 107.

47. House of Representatives, Committee on Foreign Affairs, U.S. Senate, Committee on Foreign Relations, Joint Committee Print, *Fiscal Year 1986 Arms Control Impact Statements, Statements Submitted to the Congress by the President Pursuant to Section 36 of the Arms Control and Disarmament Act* (Washington, D.C.: USGPO, 1985), pp. 46-47. (Emphasis added).

48. As in, Herbert York, *Race to Oblivion: A Participant's View of the Arms Race* (New York: Simon and Schuster, 1970), pp. 202-203.

49. Ronald Reagan, *Address to the Nation on Defense and National Security*, March 23, 1983, available at, http://www.reagan.utexas.edu/archives/speeches/1983/32383d.htm.

50. Quoted in, Charles Corddry, "Weinberger Says Total Defense Is Sought for U.S.," *The Baltimore Sun*, March 28, 1983, p. 21.

51. See, Bill Keller, "Pentagon Aide Calls Antimissile Plan Central to Military Outlook," *The New York Times*, February 22, 1985, p. 15; William Broad, "Reduced Goal Set

on Reagan's Plan for Space Defense," *The New York Times*, December 23, 1984, p. 1; Secretary of Defense Caspar Weinberger, *Remarks to the Foreign Press Center*, Washington, D.C., December 19, 1984, Transcript; and, Edward Rowny, "SDI: Enhancing Security and Stability," in U.S. State Department, *Current Policy*, No. 1058, April 1988, p. 2.

52. See, for example, Richard Cheney, *Report of the Secretary of Defense to the President and the Congress* (Washington D.C.: USGPO, 1990), p. 35; and, Transcript, Richard Cheney, Secretary of Defense, National Press Club Luncheon Speaker, National Press Club, Washington, D.C., March 22, 1990, pp. 19-1, 20-1. Secretary of Defense Cheney observed publicly that the "Phase 1 requirements designed by the Chiefs" would "allow us to intercept approximately 40 percent of a first wave attack, [and] about 50 percent of all the SS-18s." Quoted from, National Press Club Luncheon, National Press Club, ibid., p. 19-1.

53. From Lt. General Monahan's testimony before the House Armed Services Research and Development Sub-Committee, quoted in, *Defense Daily*, April 5, 1990, p. 2.

54. Steven Hildreth, *The Strategic Defense Initiative: Issues for Phase I Deployment*, CRS IB88033 (Washington D.C.: Congressional Research Service, March 30, 1988), p. 4.

55. See, Sam Nunn, "The ABM Treaty Reinterpretation Issue," *The Washington Quarterly*, Vol. 10, No. 4 (Autumn 1987), pp. 45-57; and, Abraham D. Sofaer, "The ABM Treaty: Legal Analysis in the Political Cauldron," *The Washington Quarterly*, op. cit., pp. 59-75.

56. Bruce MacDonald, "Falling Star: SDI's Troubled Seventh Year," *Arms Control Today*, Vol. 20, No. 7 (September 1990), p. 7.

57. See, for example, White House, Office of the Press Secretary, *Remarks by the President to National Employees of Lawrence Livermore Laboratory*, Lawrence Livermore Laboratory, San Francisco, California, February 7, 1990, p. 2; Strategic Defense Initiative Organization, *Report to the Congress on the Strategic Defense Initiative* (March 13, 1989), pp. 1-1 - 1-9; Richard Cheney, *Report of the Secretary of Defense to the President and the Congress* (Washington D.C.: USGPO, 1990), p. 35; and, Transcript, Richard Cheney, National Press Club Luncheon, National Press Club, op. cit., pp. 19-1, 20-1. A "defensive deterrent posture," including a "true damage limiting capability for the United States should deterrence fail," continued to be endorsed as a long-term objective. See, Stephen Hadley, Assistant Secretary of Defense (ISP) in, *Statement Before the U.S. House of Representatives Committee on Armed Services Defense Policy Panel*, March 22, 1990, p. 3; and, Paul Wolfowitz, *U.S. Senate, Committee on Armed Services, Department of Defense Authorization for Appropriations for Fiscal Years 1990 and 1991,* Part 6, Hearings, 101st Congress, 1st Session (Washington, D.C.: USGPO, 1989), pp. 493-494.

58. Department of Defense, *Strategic Defense Initiative: Progress and Promise*, Undated [but 1989], p. 6.

59. Richard Cheney, *Department of Defense Annual Report to the President and the Congress* (Washington, D.C.: USGPO, February 1992), p. 66.

60. For MIRV, see Ted Greenwood, *Making the MIRV: A Study of Defense Decision Making* (Lanham, MD: University Press of America, 1988), pp. 65, 70, 79, 109, 116, 148. For the MX, see Colin S. Gray, *The MX ICBM and National Security* (New York: Praeger Publishers, 1981).

61. As discussed in, Greenwood, *Making the MIRV: A Study of Defense Decision*

Making, op. cit., p. 54. See also, Draft Memorandum for the President, Secretary of Defense [Robert S. McNamara] to the President [Lyndon B. Johnson], Subj: Strategic Offensive and Defensive Forces, January 15, 1968, pp. 12-13. (Originally classified; sanitized and declassified on January 5, 1983); cited hereafter as 1968 DPM.
62. As discussed in, Greenwood, *Making the MIRV: A Study of Defense Decision Making,* op. cit., p. 116.
63. See, for example, the statement of Senator Edward Brooke in, U.S. Senate, Committee on Foreign Relations, Subcommittee on Arms Control, International Law and Organization, *ABM, MIRV, SALT, and the Nuclear Arms Race,* Hearing, 91st Congress, 2nd Session (Washington, D.C.: USGPO, 1970), pp. 2-9.
64. Quoted in, U.S. Senate, *ABM, MIRV, SALT, and the Nuclear Arms Race,* op. cit., p. 53.
65. See the testimony of Dr. Foster in, ibid., p. 509.
66. *Report of the President's Commission on Strategic Forces,* loc. cit.
67. William R. Van Cleave, "The US Strategic Triad," in, Ray Bonds, ed., *US War Machine* (New York: Crown Publishers, 1983), p. 67.
68. Daniel Patrick Moynihan, *Loyalties* (New York: Harcourt Brace Jovanovich, 1984), pp. 15-16.
69. Turner, loc. cit.
70. Ibid., p. 96.
71. Colin S. Gray, *Nuclear Strategy and National Style* (Lanham, MD: Hamilton Press, 1986), p. 217.
72. See, for example, House of Representatives, Committee on Foreign Affairs, U.S. Senate, Committee on Foreign Relations, Joint Committee Print, *Fiscal Year 1983 Arms Control Impact Statements, Statements Submitted to the Congress by the President Pursuant to Section 36 of the Arms Control and Disarmament Act,* March 1982 (Washington, D.C.: USGPO, 1982), pp. 21-23. This point also was made with regard to 100 missiles by Secretary of State George Shultz and Lt. Gen. Brent Scrowcroft, Chairman of the President's Commission on Strategic Forces [The Scowcroft MX Commission] in their testimony before the Senate in 1983. See U.S. Senate, Committee on Armed Services, *MX Missile Basing System and Related Issues,* Hearings, 98th Congress, 1st Session (Washington, D.C.: USGPO, 1983), pp. 110, 118, and 17-18, respectively. See also, *Report of the President's Commission on Strategic Forces,* op. cit., pp. 3, 6, 14, 18.
73. From Harold Brown's testimony in, U.S. Senate, *MX Missile Basing System and Related Issues,* op. cit., p. 7. See also, *Report of the President's Commission on Strategic Forces,* op. cit., p. 6.
74. See the discussion in, U.S. Department of Defense, *Soviet Military Power: An Assessment of the Threat* (Washington, D.C.: USGPO, 1988), pp. 98-100.
75. *Report of the President's Commission on Strategic Forces,* op. cit., pp. 6, 10.
76. House of Representatives, *Fiscal Year 1982 Arms Control Impact Statements, Statements Submitted to the Congress by the President Pursuant to Section 36 of the Arms Control and Disarmament Act,* loc. cit.; House of Representatives, Committee on Foreign Affairs, U.S. Senate, Committee on Foreign Relations, Joint Committee Print, *Fiscal Year 1984 Arms Control Impact Statements, Statements Submitted to the Congress by the President Pursuant to Section 36 of the Arms Control and Disarmament Act,* April 1983 (Washington, D.C.: USGPO, 1983), p. 26.
77. Richard DeLauer, in U.S. Senate, Committee on Armed Services, *Department of Defense Authorization for Appropriation for Fiscal Year 1983,* Part 7, Hearings, 97th

Congress, 2ⁿᵈ Session, (Washington, D.C.: USGPO, 1982), p. 4196.

78. Richard Nixon, National Security Council, National Security Decision Memorandum-242, *Policy for Planning the Employment of Nuclear Weapons*, January 17, 1974, p. 2. (Top Secret; declassified February 20, 1998).
79. See, Keith B. Payne, "The Schlesinger Shift: Return to Rationality," in, Keith B. Payne, C. Johnston Conover, and Bruce William Bennett, *Nuclear Strategy: Flexibility and Stability* (Santa Monica, CA: The California Seminar on Arms Control and Foreign Policy, March 1979), pp. 3-48.
80. James Schlesinger, *Department of Defense Annual Report FY 1976 and FY 197T* (Washington, D.C.: USGPO, February 5, 1975), pp. I-15 - I-16. (Emphasis added).
81. William E. Odom, "The Origins and Design of Presidential Decision-59: A Memoir" in Henry D. Sokolski, ed., *Getting MAD: Nuclear Mutual Assured Destruction, Its Origins, and Practice* (Carlisle, PA: Strategic Studies Institute, U.S. Army War College, November 2004), pp. 175-196.
82. Jimmy Carter, State of the Union Address, January 25, 1979, available at http://www.jimmycarterlibrary.gov/documents/speeches/su79jec.phtml. (Emphasis added).
83. See, Zbigniew Brzezinski, *Power and Principle: Memoirs of the National Security Adviser 1977-1981* (New York: Farrar, Straus, Giroux, 1983), p. 157. See also, Mark Perry, *Four Stars* (Boston, MA: Houghton Mifflin Co., 1989), pp. 265-266.
84. Henry S. Bradsher, "U.S. Scraps Effort to Curb Soviet Civil Defense as It Seeks to Match It," *Washington Star*, November 22, 1978, p. A4.
85. See, Jimmy Carter, Presidential Directive/NSC-18, *U.S. National Strategy*, The White House, August 24, 1977, (Top Secret; partially declassified/released on May 28, 1999); cited hereafter as PD-18. Available at, http://www.jimmycarterlibrary.org/documents/pddirectives/pd18.pdf.
86. Presidential Directive/NSC-41, *U.S. Civil Defense Policy*, September 29, 1978, p. 1.
87. General Accounting Office, *The Federal Emergency Management Agency's Plan for Revitalizing U.S. Civil Defense: A Review of Three Major Plan Components*, GAO/NSIAD-84-11 (Washington D.C.: General Accounting Office, April 16, 1984), p. 4.
88. Odom, "The Origins and Design of Presidential Decision-59: A Memoir," op cit., p. 192.
89. Jimmy Carter, Presidential Directive/NSC-53, *National Security Telecommunications Policy*, The White House, November 15, 1979, pp. 1-2; cited hereafter as PD-53.
90. See, for example, statement of Paul Warnke in, U.S. Senate, Committee on Banking, Housing and Urban Affairs, *Civil Defense*, Hearings, 95ᵗʰ Congress, 2ⁿᵈ Session (Washington, D.C.: USGPO, 1979), pp. 3-11.
91. See, Thomas J. Kerr, *Civil Defense in the U.S.: Bandaid for a Holocaust?* (Boulder, CO: Westview Press, 1983), pp. 101-132, 169-193.
92. The early Reagan Administration similarly sought to double the approximately $130 million typically spent for civil defense annually, but again Congress cut the actual funding appropriated back to the more modest traditional level suitable, as Secretary McNamara said, for maintaining an organization, but not a program. The erosion of Reagan Administration enthusiasm for promoting significant U.S. civil defense protection against nuclear attack can be seen in a comparison of the 1982 National Security Decision Directive-26 (cited hereafter as NSDD-26) on *U.S. Civil Defense Policy,* with the 1987 National Security Decision Directive-259 (cited hereafter as NSDD-259) on *U.S. Civil Defense.* The 1982 directive states that, "It is

a matter of national priority that the US have a Civil Defense program which provides for the survival of the US population," and directs that the U.S. Civil Defense program will "...provide for survival of a substantial portion of the US population in the event of nuclear attack preceded by strategic warning and for continuity of government, should deterrence and escalation control fail." The 1987 directive, to risk understatement, contains no such language. Both documents are unclassified. See, NSDD-26, dated March 16, 1982 (Full text, unclassified version), and NSDD-259, February 4, 1987, (Full text released on October 16, 1987). Available online at the National Archives Archival Research Catalog (ARC), www.archives.gov/research/arc. NSDD-26: ARC Identifier 198187; NSDD-259: ARC Identifier 198359.

93. See, the testimony by Secretary of Defense Harold Brown in, U.S. Senate, Committee on Foreign Relations, *Nuclear War Strategy*, Hearings, 96th Congress, 2nd Session (Top Secret hearing held on September 16, 1980; sanitized and printed on February 18, 1981). (Washington, D.C.: USGPO, 1981), p. 10.

94. See, the testimony by Secretary of Defense Harold Brown and the "Administration's Responses to Questions Submitted Before the Hearing," in ibid., pp. 10, 16, 25, 29-30.

95. Brown in, U.S. Senate, *Nuclear War Strategy*, op. cit., p. 16.

96. Odom, "The Origin and Design of Presidential Decision-59," op. cit., pp. 182-184.

97. See, for example, Louis Rene Beres, "Tilting Toward Thantos: America's 'Countervailing' Nuclear Strategy," *World Politics*, Vol. 34, No. 1 (October 1981), pp. 25-46.

98. Harold Brown, *Department of Defense Annual Report Fiscal Year 1981* (Washington, D.C.: USGPO, 1980), p. 66.

99. See, Kerr, op. cit., pp. 187-191.

100. Brown, in U.S. Senate, *Nuclear War Strategy*, op. cit., p. 11.

101. Harold Brown, *The Department of Defense Statement on Strategic Military Balance: Military Assessment*, before the U.S. Senate, Committee on Foreign Relations, Hearings, 96th Congress, 1st Session, July 11, 1979, p. 3.

102. This type of criticism was prevalent and is well illustrated in, George Rathjens, "Flexible Response Options," *Orbis*, Vol. 28, No. 3 (Fall 1974), pp. 677-688; Herbert Scoville, "Flexible Madness," *Foreign Policy*, Vol. 14 (Spring 1974), pp. 175-176; and, Daniel Ford, Henry Kendall and Steven Nadis, *Beyond the Freeze: The Road to Nuclear Sanity* (Boston, MA: The Union of Concerned Scientists/Beacon Press, 1982).

103. Seymour Melman, "Limits of Military Power," *The New York Times*, October 17, 1980, p. A-31.

104. Ibid.

105. See, James Schlesinger in, U.S. Senate, Committee on Foreign Relations, *U.S./U.S.S.R. Strategic Policies*, Hearings, 93rd Congress, 2nd Session (Washington, D.C.: USGPO, 1974), pp. 2, 21, 71; James Schlesinger, Remarks to Overseas Writers Association Luncheon at the International Club, Washington, D.C., January 10, 1974; and, James Schlesinger, News Conference at the Pentagon, January 24, 1974, transcript, p. 2.

106. *History of the Strategic Arms Competition: 1945-1972, Part II*, Alfred Goldberg, ed., with contributions by Ernest R. May, John D. Steinbruner, and Thomas W. Wolfe (Washington, D.C.: Historical Office, Office of the Secretary of Defense, March 1981), p. 804.

107. Henry S. Rowen, "Formulating Strategic Doctrine," Commission on the

Organization of the Government for the Conduct of Foreign Policy, Volume 4, Appendix K, *Adequacy of Current Organization: Defense and Arms Control* (Washington, D.C.: USGPO, June 1975), p. 228.

108. Harold Brown, *Department of Defense Annual Report Fiscal Year 1980* (Washington, D.C.: USGPO, 1979), p. 61. (Emphasis added).

109. Quoted in, "Brown Says an Accord Won't Make Teheran Into a 'Buddy' of U.S.," *The New York Times,* January 18, 1981, p. A12.

110. Colin S. Gray, *Nuclear Strategy and Strategic Planning* (Philadelphia, PA: Foreign Policy Research Institute, 1984), p. 41.

111. Nixon, *The Real War*, op. cit., pp. 162-163.

112. Henry A. Kissinger, Memorandum for the President, June 17, 1969, "June 18 NSC Meeting on U.S. Strategic Posture and SALT," with enclosures, copy at NSArchive (Top Secret; declassified/released on November 7, 2000), Tab D: [NSC Study Summary] "U.S. Strategic Posture: Basic Issues," p. 6, in National Security Archive Electronic Briefing Book No. 173, available at, http://www.gwu.edu/~nsarchiv (Emphasis added).

113. Commander Michael Dobbs, "A Renaissance for U.S. Civil Defense?" *Journal of Homeland Security* (July 2001), available at, http://www.homelandsecurity.org/journal/ articles?Dobbs_July01.htm.

114. Kissinger, "June 18 NSC Meeting on U.S. Strategic Posture and SALT," op. cit., Tab D, p. 1. (Emphasis added).

115. Brown, *Department of Defense Annual Report Fiscal Year 1981*, op. cit., p. 68. (Emphasis added).

116. Harold Brown, quoted in, *Evaluation of Fiscal Year 1979 Arms Control Impact Statements: Toward More Informed Congressional Participation in National Security Policymaking*, Report Prepared for the U.S. House of Representatives, Committee on International Relations by the Congressional Research Service, Library of Congress (Washington, D.C.: USGPO, 1978), p. 113. (Emphasis added); and, Brown, *The Department of Defense Statement on Strategic Military Balance: Military Assessment*, op. cit., p. 2. (Emphasis added).

117. Office of the Secretary of Defense, "Memorandum for General Scowcroft," from MG John Wickham, Jr., Military Assistant, Subj: Nuclear Weapons Employment Policy, April 10, 1974 (Top Secret Sensitive; declassified on July 17, 2003), enclosure, *Policy Guidance for the Employment of Nuclear Weapons*, April 3, 1974, pp. 2, 4-5, in National Security Archive Electronic Briefing Book No. 173, available at, http://www. gwu.edu/~nsarchiv.

118. Senator Charles Percy and Secretary of Defense Harold Brown in, U.S. Senate, Committee on Foreign Relations, *Nuclear War Strategy*, op. cit., pp. 18-19. (Emphasis added).

119. Secretary of Defense McNamara, answers submitted for the record in, U.S. Senate, Committee on Armed Services, *Military Procurement Authorization Fiscal Year 1964*, Hearing, 88th Congress, 1st Session (Washington, D.C.: USGPO, 1963), p. 90.

120. McGeorge Bundy, "The Bishops and the Bomb," *The New York Review of Books*, Vol. 30, No. 10 (June 16, 1983), p. 4.

121. McGeorge Bundy, "To Cap the Volcano," *Foreign Affairs*, Vol. 48, No. 1 (October 1969), p. 9.

122. Ibid., p. 10.

123. McNamara, *Military Procurement Authorization Fiscal Year 1964*, loc. cit.

(Emphasis added).

124. Warnke in, *Civil Defense*, op. cit., p. 4.

125. Louis Halle, "Does War Have a Future?" *Foreign Affairs*, Vol. 52, No. 1 (October 1973), p. 23.

126. Ashton Carter, William Perry, John Steinbruner, *A New Concept of Cooperative Security* (Washington, D.C.: Brookings Institution, 1992), p. 1.

127. Bernard Brodie, *Escalation and the Nuclear Option* (Princeton, NJ: Princeton University Press, 1966), p. 74. (Emphasis in original).

128. Ibid.

129. Bernard Brodie, "The Development of Nuclear Strategy," *International Security*, Vol. 2, No. 4 (Spring 1978), p. 69.

130. Thomas Schelling, "What Went Wrong With Arms Control," *Foreign Affairs*, Vol. 64, No. 2 (Winter 1985/86), p. 233.

131. See his testimony in, *Strategy and Science: Toward a National Security Policy for the 1970's*, op. cit., p. 149.

132. Gabriella Boston, "Using Street Smarts," *The Washington Times*, January 14, 2008, p. B4.

133. Reported in, Allen J. DeWalle, "A Sobering Reality," *AAA World*, Vol. 9, No. 2 (March/April, 2007), p. 13.

Chapter 6
Extending Assured Destruction and Balance of Terror Tenets to Twenty-First Century Threats

"Ideas have consequences."
-Richard M. Weaver, University of Chicago

The beliefs about "stable" deterrence that guided U.S. deterrence strategy, strategic arms control, and acquisition policies during the second half of the Cold War remain powerfully in play in contemporary strategic force policy and budget debates. As an article on the subject appearing in *The Christian Science Monitor* concludes regarding the U.S. *post-Cold War* strategic debate: "Strangelovian or not, MAD remains the foundation of the way the U.S. regards nuclear weapons today."[1] This conclusion is not true for many officials with policy responsibility, but it captures the truth about most public commentary on the subject by pundits, academics, journalists, and some leaders in government.

Despite the technical fact that a comparable condition of mutual enmity and vulnerability does not exist with any country today, much of the U.S. security community—broadly defined to include commentators— holds to the concepts, language and beliefs about strategic forces derived from the Cold War balance of terror, particularly including the following:

- Short of an opponent's insanity, deterrence is understood and can be orchestrated to work reliably and predictably to prevent deliberate attack. Consequently, we can prudently avoid taking defensive measures that might be in order in the absence of reliably effective deterrence.
- Nuclear deterrence is "existential" because nuclear weapons promise such horrific destruction that all sane leaderships will be compelled by their rationality to be prudent and cautious: rational equates to deterrable and only "suicidal" leaders could fail to be deterred.
- The *chance* of U.S. nuclear retaliation will deter reliably and predictably. Schelling's "threat that leaves something

to chance" is sufficient for deterrence rather than Kahn's threat that leaves little to chance.

- U.S. strategic force parameters should be derived from deterrence requirements, which can be calculated according to the Cold War formula of counting warheads and potential targets to threaten, i.e., the basic arithmetic of an assured destruction-like metric.
- Damage limitation and counterforce capabilities are incompatible with deterrence. They are for "war-fighting" purposes and will "destabilize" deterrence if deployed.
- The action-reaction dynamic, typically driven by U.S. initiatives, underlies opponents' desires for nuclear capabilities: U.S. inaction with regard to strategic forces thus will reduce or eliminate opponents' motives to acquire nuclear weapons.

Each of these Cold War balance of terror tenets either is demonstrably false or highly suspect for many plausible contexts. Nevertheless, most commentators continue to assert them as enduring, unquestioned truths about deterrence and U.S. strategic policy. Again, as during the Cold War, these tenets serve primarily as the rationale for constraining or precluding U.S. capabilities that do not fall within the formula for deterrence "stability" and arms control. The categorization of systems as being stabilizing or destabilizing remains the same, based on the supposed effects of their technical characteristics on stable deterrence and the action-reaction dynamic.

More than a decade after the collapse of the Soviet Union and the emergence of regional rogue states as primary opponents, for example, an academic commentator and former senior U.S. Government official claimed "the yardstick of strategic stability" still to be the appropriate "standard" for U.S. strategic policy and capabilities.[2] Why this "yardstick" as the appropriate "standard"? Because, "strategic arithmetic is the same as always. And so is human nature."[3] Herein is encapsulated the continuing dominant view: the familiar balance of terror deterrence metrics remain valid because they capture the inalterable verities of "strategic arithmetic" and "human nature."

Appreciation and understanding of Schelling's and Brodie's original nuance, detail and elaborations generally are missing now, as is recognition that the unique conditions of the Cold War were integral to the logic of those metrics and the related prescriptions for policy and forces. What remains, typically, are "bumper sticker" dictums about "stability" from the Cold War balance of terror formula. These are extended to the contemporary scene without much, if any, consideration given to their applicability in the geopolitical context of the twenty-first century. They remain enormously powerful as baseline gauges for judging the value of U.S. strategic forces and policy, particularly in journalistic commentary and Congressional debates regarding the U.S. acquisition of strategic forces.

Schelling's propositions about "crisis instability" and the "reciprocal fear of surprise attack" that so shaped the language of the balance of terror and its formula for "stability" are thoroughly ingrained as basic truths about deterrence. Commentators apply them when recommending deterrence policies and preparations for the United States and other countries, including for example, Israel: "Israel will need to choose wisely between 'assured destruction' and 'nuclear war-fighting.' ...If Israel were to opt for nuclear deterrence based upon counterforce capabilities, its pertinent enemies could feel especially threatened. This could heighten the prospect of nuclear aggression against Israel and of subsequent nuclear war."[4] U.S. Cold War "stable" deterrence theory and balance of terror tenets remain powerful at home and have become an intellectual export.

Particularly apparent in domestic commentary is the direct and uncritical application of Cold War deterrence concepts and language to contemporary U.S.-Chinese relations, as if the dramatic differences in time, place, opponent and circumstances are unrelated to the applicability of those concepts and language: "Just as the danger of mutual nuclear annihilation—or mutual assured destruction (MAD), as it was labeled then—helped prevent war between the United States and the Soviet Union during the Cold War, so too will nuclear deterrence cool tensions between the United States and China."[5]

Relax: Nuclear Deterrence Still Works Universally, Reliably and Predictably

Noted commentators and senior officials continue to have widespread confidence that they know how to orchestrate offensive retaliatory threats to prevent attack reliably, predictably, even near universally. They refer to balance of terror "stability" tenets as the basis for their contemporary recommendations about U.S. requirements for deterrence and the acquisition of strategic forces. Doing so represents the extension of a

50-year-old school of thought about deterrence into new and dramatically different post-Cold War conditions.

Whether the old "truths" derived from that school of thought—geared as it was to the Soviet Union and unique conditions of the Cold War—remain coherent in this new epoch is a question that deserves, but typically does not receive, serious consideration. Far more typical is the simplistic repetition of old, formulaic lines and adages about deterrence, uncertainty, "stability" and arms races, without apparent consideration of how different opponents and changing conditions may have eroded whatever coherence those lines and adages may have had during the Cold War.

Continuing faith in the predictable functioning of deterrence, for example, is common fare across a broad spectrum of "hawks," "doves," Republicans, Democrats, civilians and the military. Many from each group replay the Cold War deterrence articles of faith that the functioning of deterrence can be understood, orchestrated mechanistically, and predicted with confidence based on the characteristics of U.S. forces and the sanity of the opponent. From these meager beginnings, commentators in and out of government continue to claim confident knowledge about how deterrence will function, and that they thus can identify the optimal character of U.S. strategic forces and policies:

> Deterring Russia, as well as China and other states that have acquired nuclear weapons remains a justifiable function of U.S. nuclear weapons policy. But several thousand U.S. nuclear warheads are not needed to discharge that mission; a few hundred would suffice....Nor are large numbers of nuclear weapons needed to ward off potential nuclear threats from rogue states or non-state actors. Some worry that proliferators such as Iran and North Korea may prove to be undeterrable. This is unlikely to be the case, since the leadership of even a rogue state can be expected to value its own survival. A dramatically reduced U.S. arsenal would still provide more than enough weapons to deter such a threat.[6]

Such confident, detailed promises represent pretensions of a near omniscient ability to predict the decision making and behavior of many different decision makers in diverse circumstances. They are possible only courtesy of the balance of terror tenets that posit a predictable, mechanistic relationship between force characteristics and deterrent effect—the opponent has little input into the process other than to be controlled predictably by U.S. threats and the demands of reason.

Now, as during the Cold War, faith in the U.S. capability to make deterrence "work" reliably against any sane opponent is presented as the basis for concluding that we need not fear threats that we otherwise might fear and, correspondingly, that we need not take *defensive measures* that we otherwise might feel compelled to take. Such conclusions are offered confidently without any apparent examination of the opponent or the prospective circumstances of the presumed contest of wills. Universal principles regarding how opponents will think and behave continue to be offered up as truisms. "Existential deterrence" continues to provide a justification for *not fearing, not defending, and generally not doing*.

The question of importance typically left unaddressed is the soundness of past deterrence truisms in new conditions that are far removed from those of the Cold War. The confidence in deterrence that typified the Cold War is presumed to apply to China and to rogue states as if the dramatic changes in opponent and context are irrelevant. A noted *New York Times* journalist, for example, claims confidently: "What deters them today is what will always deter them—the certainty that if they attack us with weapons of mass destruction their regimes will be destroyed. In other words, what is protecting us right now from the most likely rogue threat...is classic deterrence."[7]

A reported account of George W. Bush Administration officials also reflects this continuing confidence in deterrence: "In private, [Bush] administration officials dismissed the threat the [North Korean] missile might pose...asserting that the logic of deterrence that worked throughout the cold war would do just fine. The North Koreans know, they said, that a missile attack on the United States would result in the vaporization of Pyongyang."[8]

A former Reagan Administration official recommends Cold War practice as the guide for contemporary efforts to deter nuclear terrorism: "The same logic could be adapted today to nuclear terrorism. Instead of focusing on preventive efforts to resist nuclear terrorist attack, we should focus on the kind of retaliation—what game theorists call 'optimal threats'—that would constitute deterrence for ideologically or religiously sanctioned terrorism."[9] Again, the goal of defending against the threat is subordinated to establishing severe U.S. retaliatory threats to deter. In this case, the threats suggested for deterrence purposes are the contemporary equivalent of Secretary McNamara's simple assured destruction: the "retaliatory obliteration of the *umma*" (the *umma* being the totality of the community of Muslims) or possibly the destruction of "Muslim holy sites."[10] Here the subordination of U.S. defensive efforts to wholly speculative offensive deterrence threats is offered up as reasonable guidance without any apparent recognition of the possibility that the deterrent effect of such threats is unpredictable, and that there could be significant regrets involved in perpetuating the Cold War's policy of eschewing direct defensive efforts in deference to offensive deterrence.

A comparable promise that "deterrence works" against rogues is presented by a former staff member of the Office of the Director of National Intelligence.[11] Why does it work? Purportedly because: "There is plenty that each of these rogue states holds dear that the United States can threaten," and "No regime, no matter how aggressive and risk-inclined, would be so foolish as to attack the United States, a move that would yield little advantage, and thereby incur an attack's clear consequence—utter destruction."[12] Here is the balance of terror's logic and promise that "they wouldn't dare" in full bloom and recast as universally applicable against contemporary threats. What could be more comforting or convenient than to believe it is possible to predict rogue decision making with such confidence?

Former President Clinton expressed similar confidence in the continuing reliable and predictable functioning of offensive deterrence threats, including *vis-à-vis* a potentially nuclear-armed Iran: "Deterrence still works, just like it did between us and the Soviet Union. So if Iran had a nuclear weapon, the main thing it would do is cast a pall over the Middle East. But they'd have to think a long time before they used it, because they'd be toast if they used it."[13] This notion—that U.S. nuclear retaliatory threats essentially guarantee deterrence against nuclear attack—survived the Cold War fully intact as the expressed expectation of many senior U.S. officials. In 1996, for example, Secretary of Defense William Perry stated that, "no rogue nation today has ICBMs; only the established nuclear powers have ICBMs. And, if these powers should ever pose a threat, our ability to retaliate with an overwhelming nuclear response will serve as a deterrent. Deterrence has protected us from the established nuclear arsenals for decades, and it will continue to protect us."[14] Similarly, in 1994, Deputy Secretary of Defense John Deutch stated even more emphatically in public testimony that, "*deterrence is ensured* by having a survivable [nuclear] capability to hold at risk what potentially hostile leaders value, and we will maintain that capability."[15] Embedded in such confident assertions about deterrence is an implicit claim of certain knowledge regarding how foreign leaders will think and behave—what they will and will not "dare."

Well-known and respected commentators continue to assert without much or any reservation that they *know* how contemporary and future opponents will think and behave, and thus can claim with confidence that offensive U.S. deterrence threats will continue to prevent attack on the United States. Why so? Because: "The credibility of an overwhelming U.S. response (nuclear or conventional) that would severely punish the state would be extremely high. It would seem that nothing could be gained by such an [opponent's] attack and much could be lost."[16]

It is noteworthy that, in the absence of any apparent examination of a specific opponent or circumstance, commentators believe they can predict with confidence how opponents will perceive U.S. threats, the level of credibility opponents will attribute to those threats, and how opponents will calculate costs and benefits. Such confident assertions abound with regard to the contemporary functioning of deterrence: it will now prevent rogues from a specialized electromagnetic pulse (EMP) attack;[17] additionally, the familiar formula of the opponent's uncertainty plus U.S. retaliatory capabilities will deter them from transferring nuclear weapons to terrorists, "since no cooperating state could be sure that the United States would not learn its identity, much the same deterrence applies."[18] Left unsaid is how these commentators have come by such intimate knowledge of how numerous foreign leaders will think and behave in response to U.S. deterrence threats. But, of course, if confident claims about deterrence are derived from the inalterable truths of "strategic arithmetic" and "human nature," how can there be any doubt?

The balance of terror supposedly taught us that a universal rationality compels all prospective opponents to behave in like manner— they will be deterred via nuclear threats as long as the familiar formula is followed. British scholar Professor Lawrence Freedman states simply, "the unimaginable consequences of [nuclear weapons] use still acts as a powerful inhibition."[19]

In *The Spread of Nuclear Weapons,* noted academic and former president of the American Political Science Association, Professor Kenneth Waltz, takes the argument that nuclear threats deter reliably to its logical extreme, applies it universally, and concludes that the "spread" of nuclear weapons to many new states, if done within balance of terror guidelines, *may be welcomed*: "...with more nuclear states, the world will have a promising future....The gradual spread of nuclear weapons is more to be welcomed than feared."[20]

True to the balance of terror tenet that deterrence is the sure mechanical effect of a properly orchestrated nuclear threat, Waltz asserts that the specific motivations and characteristics of the opponent are immaterial to the reliable functioning of nuclear deterrence. The spread of nuclear weapons—even to eccentric, perplexing leaders such as North Korea's Kim Jong II—holds the promise of creating multiple stable balances of terror, and thus benefiting world peace: "The history of the cold war shows that what matters is not the character of the countries that have nuclear weapons but the fact that they have them. Differences among nuclear countries abound, but for keeping the peace what difference have they made?"[21] And: "In a nuclear world any state will be deterred by another state's second-strike [retaliatory] forces. One need not become preoccupied with the characteristics of the state that is to be deterred or scrutinize its leaders." [22] This is a comforting conclusion; it means that nuclear weapons, arrayed according to the balance of terror formula, can deliver stable balances of terror throughout regions that otherwise might be prone to war. Whereas some see nuclear proliferation as the priority security threat, Waltz sees this silver lining because the old deterrence formula will continue to work.

Given the international furor over the North Korean and Iranian nuclear programs, how does Waltz reach the conclusion that nuclear proliferation can be welcomed? It is a logical extrapolation from his familiar balance of terror starting points: "Not much is required to deter....Because the use of nuclear weapons could lead to catastrophe for all of the parties involved, nuclear weapons create their own credibility. No one wants to risk their being used against them. Much of the nuclear literature is devoted to the problem of credibility, a problem easily solved."[23] Obvious in such claims is Waltz's belief that he can predict the parameters of decision making and behavior of all pertinent, prospective opponents.

He essentially repeats the premise that uncertainty within a balance of terror can deter easily, reliably, predictably and, with the exception of insanity on the part of the opponent, universally. This view leads Waltz logically to embrace nuclear proliferation if kept within balance of terror guidelines, and to the continued rejection of U.S. damage-limitation capabilities. Repeating the favored Cold War narrative, Waltz contends that the United States need not and should not seek to defend against emerging nuclear capabilities; he asks rhetorically, "Why should anyone want to replace stable deterrence with unstable defense?"[24] Herein is Secretary McNamara's Cold War-era conclusion applied without variance to the contemporary scene: "destabilizing" defenses can be eschewed on the promise that deterrence will work reliably and predictably.

Waltz repeats the set of balance of terror beliefs and reaches their logical conclusion: Because prudence and caution will be the common leadership response to the possibility of societal destruction, mutual nuclear deterrence can be made to work easily and universally in the context of such threats. Barring "madness," new nuclear powers will have the same prudent, cautious reaction to the possibility of nuclear escalation, and thus can be deterred easily, reliably and predictably. Consequently, the spread of nuclear weapons need not be feared; it can be welcomed because "stable" nuclear deterrence can be made to work all around. And, of course, effective deterrence is to be preferred over the partial levels of defense that may be feasible. In a full replay of Secretary McNamara's Cold War logic, Waltz contends that sustaining nuclear deterrence is cost-effective compared to damage-limitation efforts because the latter suffer from a cost disadvantage in an offensive-defensive competition.[25]

Waltz takes the fundamental question of Cold War strategic policy—whether the United States should place priority on a deterrence strategy that embraces U.S. societal vulnerability, or on a strategy which incorporates substantial, direct U.S. damage limitation—and reaffirms the U.S. Cold War choice for the twenty-first century. He does so on the basis of beliefs about deterrence, defense and "rational" behavior identified by Schelling fifty years ago and subsequently put into policy practice by Secretary McNamara. The difference, of course, is that Schelling and Secretary McNamara elaborated their positions in the context of the Cold War superpower standoff, while Waltz extends the same to all contemporary hostile regional powers and settings.

Waltz is not alone in this confidence that nuclear deterrence can counter the potential threats posed by today's nuclear proliferation reliably and predictably. Another eminent academic commentator similarly argues that, "there is reason to believe that we could readily manage a nuclear Iran."[26] What is that reason? U.S. nuclear deterrence works: "Anyone who attacks the United States with nuclear weapons will be attacked with many, many more nuclear weapons....Tehran could not rule out the possibility that others with more and better nuclear weapons would strike Iran first, should it provoke a crisis or war."[27] Another frequent commentator concurs, with specific reference to China, North Korea and Iran: "Capability does not necessitate use. Each of these countries would almost surely be deterred from attacking the United States by the certainty that swift retaliation would follow even a failed or thwarted attack."[28] And another: "...the obnoxious nature of the Iranian regime (or other rogue regimes) does not negate the underlying realities of deterrence. The United States has an enormous nuclear arsenal and the delivery systems to launch retaliatory strikes with pinpoint accuracy."[29]

The notion remains that the "realities of deterrence" are that sane opponents will be prudent and cautious—and thus deterrable—because that is the predictable response of a rational opponent to our nuclear threat. This now-aged balance of terror tenet continues as a baseline assumption in recent works intended to update thinking about deterrence,[30] and in the reported opinion of senior intelligence officials:

> For the past several years, U.S. intelligence analysts have doubted hawkish U.S. and Israeli rhetoric that Iran is dominated by "mad mullahs"—clerics whose fanatical religious views might lead to irrational decisions. In the new NIE [National Intelligence Estimate], the analysts forcefully posit an alternative view of an Iran that is rational....Asked if this meant the Iranian regime would be "deterrable" if it did obtain a [nuclear] weapon, a senior official responded, "That is the implication."[31]

Obvious in this confidence that rogue states predictably will weigh costs and benefits, and reliably will agree to be deterred is the now-familiar Cold War dictum that the combination of opponents' rationality, a lethal U.S. threat, and the *possibility* of its execution deters universally. These are the familiar "underlying realities of deterrence" that supposedly continue to have universal application. An editorial in *The New York Times* on the subject explicitly makes the claim: "One advantage of deterrence is that it induces responsible behavior by enemies as a matter of their own self-interest. Even dictators tend to put certain basic interests above all else— pre-eminently their survival in power....Aggression becomes unattractive if the price is devastation at home and possible removal from power.... *The logic of deterrence transcends any particular era or enemy.*"[32]

Those who are confident that highly lethal U.S. threats and the possibility of their execution ensure the reliable, predictable effectiveness of deterrence offer a wide-ranging set of policy recommendations following from that confidence. As the above discussion illustrates, it is the basis for the conclusion—heard with increasing frequency—that nuclear proliferation by states such as Iran and North Korea need not pose a significant threat to U.S. or allied security. Deterrence purportedly can be made to work against these and other states so concern about new nuclear threats should be tempered. French President Chirac expressed just such a view *vis-à-vis* Iranian nuclear proliferation: "I would say that what is dangerous about the situation is not the fact of [Iran] having the nuclear bomb. Having one or perhaps a second bomb a little later, well, that's not very dangerous.... Where will it drop it, this bomb? On Israel? It would not have gone 200 meters into the atmosphere before Tehran would be razed."[33]

The logical corollary of this continuing expressed confidence in offensive nuclear deterrence threats is the related conclusion—also heard with increasing frequency—that the United States need not pursue proactive military measures to address the threat of nuclear proliferation for fear that deterrence will fail to provide protection.[34] When deterrence is expected to work reliably and predictably to contain a threat, there is no need to take military action to prevent it.

Some commentators have even identified the supposed reliable effectiveness of offensive deterrence threats *vis-à-vis* states as the specific reason for concluding that Israel should agree to a Palestinian state. Why? Because: "...the only way for Israel to achieve security is to reach a final peace agreement involving the establishment of a Palestinian state (because states can be more easily deterred than independent groups like Hamas)."[35] Again, U.S. Cold War deterrence theory and experience is the basis for the export of deterrence advice.

These many continuing confident assertions that deterrence threats of nuclear retaliation can be made to work predictably, easily and near universally are not based on any apparent close examination of the many states and leaders included in such claims. There is little or no examination of specific opponents' perceptions, intentions, determination, values, risk tolerances or goals as the basis for confident claims regarding how they will judge credibility, risk, and costs and benefits, in determining their response to U.S. deterrence threats. Supposed universal truths based on "strategic arithmetic" and "human nature" need no such validation. Rather, these confident assertions regarding post-Cold War deterrence follow the Cold War era's faith that we can rely on universal principles and a mechanistic formula for "existential deterrence," and that we can implement that formula consistently.

As a result, commentators offer up the same *punitive* U.S. nuclear threats that were thought to ensure reliable deterrence of the Soviet Union as the answer to contemporary nuclear threats. How to deter the contemporary North Korean leadership? Easy. Follow guidelines from the past:

> Here, the president can take a page from President John F. Kennedy in the Cuban missile crisis. In 1962, as the Soviet Union was emplacing nuclear-tipped missiles in Cuba....Kennedy issued an unambiguous warning to Nikita Khrushchev. "It shall be the policy of this nation," he announced, "to regard any nuclear missile launched from Cuba against any nation in the Western Hemisphere as an attack by the Soviet Union on the United States requiring *a full retaliatory response* upon the Soviet Union." Khrushchev knew that meant a nuclear war.[36]

Rogue state leaders, it is suggested, would even refrain from transferring nuclear capabilities to terrorists for fear of such U.S. Cold War-style threats: "The United States would threaten unacceptable retaliation were a state to provide the seeds of a terrorist attack; unable to use terrorists for clandestine delivery, rogue states would be returned to the grim reality of massive retaliation."[37]

We now are to believe that a U.S. threat of nuclear retaliation will deter reliably the eccentric dictator of North Korea, Kim Jong II, or Iran's quixotic millenarian President Ahmadinejad who claims that as a "true believer" he is supernaturally protected and assured of "victory," is "privy to God's intentions and actions," and was "surrounded by a halo of light" when speaking at the United Nations in 2005.[38]

Continued expressions of faith in the old deterrence formula are comforting and convenient. They provide the basis for concluding that the United States can reliably prevent nuclear attack and that the force requirements needed to provide this certain deterrent effect are relatively easy to meet. Better still, reliable deterrence precludes requirements for strategic damage-limitation capabilities and offensive counterforce capabilities. Schelling's easy deterrence formula and Secretary McNamara's policy choices survived the Cold War unscathed.

Balance of Terror Tenets and Contemporary Ballistic Missile Defense

As the above comments by Waltz and others illustrate, the claim that nuclear deterrence can be made to work predictably, easily and near universally continues to be used to argue *against* the deployment of U.S. damage-limitation capabilities, particularly including U.S. ballistic missile defense (BMD). The belief that BMD is *not* of practicable value, in part because deterrence will work to prevent attacks, faithfully repeats Secretary McNamara's Cold War position; it now is extended as an enduring truth pertinent to contemporary threats. U.S. Ambassador Jonathan Dean, for example, repeats this familiar argument against U.S. BMD with the assertion that deterrence remains the "main insurance" against missile attack from "any source" and that, "Deterrence will remain a reliable defense against possible rogue missile attack on the United States....they know their regimes would be wiped out if they actually launched a missile attack on the United States."[39] The senior editor of the *Bulletin of the Atomic Scientists* similarly assures readers that there still is no need for missile defense because U.S. deterrence will work: "NATIONAL MISSILE DEFENSE STILL MAKES LITTLE SENSE, mainly because there is no threat. What nation is going to attack the United States, the sole remaining superpower as the cliché has it, with a missile that bears a return address?"[40] The message—that because deterrence will work there is "no threat" necessitating defenses— is as attractive and powerful now as it was during the Cold War.

Senior U.S. political leaders also express continuing confidence in deterrence and, therefore, question the possible need for BMD: "It is almost inconceivable that North Korea would ever launch a missile at the U.S., because regime survival is their number-one priority, according to the Intelligence Community. The one way they will guarantee their own destruction is to launch a ballistic missile at the U.S."[41] Another asks rhetorically: "Name me a time in the last 500 years when a leader of a nation state has said, 'I know I face virtual annihilation if I take the following action, but I'm going ahead and I'm going to do it anyway.'"[42] Again, because deterrence is expected to work, BMD is deemed unnecessary.

Former senior U.S. arms control officials typically continue to argue against contemporary U.S. BMD with the familiar claim that deterrence will work, so BMD is unnecessary:

[Rogue states] do have home addresses, and their leaderships have always preferred to survive....Ballistic missile defenses, moreover, are virtually irrelevant to this situation, since no rogue states would risk the long and easily detectable development process (including nuclear weapons tests and ballistic missile tests) required to acquire the capability to deliver nuclear arms by long-range ballistic missile and thereby invite preemptive attack. A state, even a rogue state, is governed by a regime that has a built-in incentive to survive.[43]

This particular confident assertion about what rogue states will *not* dare is unmistakably *incorrect*: North Korea has indeed already risked "the long and easily detectable development" processes for long-range missiles and nuclear weapons. A North Korean nuclear test took place on October 9, 2006, and North Korea tested long-range missiles in 1998, and again in 2006.

This expression that rogue states have "home" or "return addresses," and thus deterrence will work, is an oft-repeated metaphor. It means that because the United States would know from whose territory a missile was launched, rogue leaders will be deterred from launching for fear of U.S. retaliation. With reference to rogue states, such assertions as, "...none would be so foolish as to risk total destruction by launching one, as such missiles clearly carry a return address"[44] or, "...just about the least likely threat we face is from a North Korean nuclear ICBM with a return address that invites that country's destruction,"[45] have gained currency as the reason why BMD is as "unnecessary" in the twenty-first century as it was during the Cold War. Why unnecessary? Because deterrence will work: universally, reliably and predictably.

A senior official from the Reagan Administration's Department of Defense similarly now argues against the U.S. need for BMD to counter North Korean missiles because deterrence purportedly will prevent a North Korean missile attack: "They've got to know we would blow them off the face of the Earth."[46] A letter to President George W. Bush signed by 49 retired U.S. generals and admirals—including former Chairman of the JCS Admiral William Crowe—also argued against U.S. BMD deployment on the basis of confidence that deterrence will work: "U.S. technology, already deployed, can pinpoint the source of a ballistic missile launch. It is, therefore, highly unlikely that any state would dare to attack the U.S. or allow a terrorist to do so from its territory with a missile armed with a weapon of mass destruction, thereby risking annihilation from a devastating U.S. retaliatory strike."[47] Again, implicit in such claims is the authors' confidence in their ability to predict how foreign leaders will perceive risk, make decisions and behave—what they will and will not "dare."

Noted U.S. commentator and scientist Richard Garwin offers an extremely skeptical assessment of the value of a proposed U.S. BMD program to defend against Iranian missiles, and then proceeds to recommend instead that, "the United States should put its primary effort into making sure that deterrence by the promise of retaliation is effective as it tries to persuade Iran not to acquire nuclear weapons or missiles...."[48] Garwin's obvious presumption here is that Iranian decision making is so well understood and subject to control that the United States can, in fact, make "sure that deterrence" via retaliatory threat "is effective." Prudent skepticism regarding the capability for missile defense is replaced by an amazing lack of skepticism regarding the U.S. capability to deter predictably an opaque foreign leadership.

Also, in full repetition of Cold War arguments, contemporary commentators continue to assert not only that U.S. BMD is unnecessary because deterrence will protect, but also that BMD is dangerous because it would destabilize deterrence. They continue to highlight its supposed "destabilizing" character:

> If you combine sharply reduced numbers of nuclear weapons and increasingly effective defenses, one way of looking at the result is that it creates an increased temptation for launching a first strike in a crisis. Why? Because conservative military planners can think of desperate situations in which one side might hope to destroy as much as possible of the other side's nuclear forces before they can be launched, and then rely on defenses to soak up the remainder.[49]

MIT Professor Noam Chomsky similarly contends that a U.S. BMD system that "might seem workable" is dangerous: "Both U.S. planners and potential targets regard missile defense as a first-strike weapon."[50] These warnings against contemporary U.S. BMD repeat exactly Schelling's Cold War tenet that the "reciprocal fear of surprise attack" would destabilize mutual deterrence, and that U.S. BMD should be avoided because it would cause such instability.

The contemporary conclusion flowing from this concern is the same as that reached during the Cold War—that is, the United States should give up the level of societal protection possibly afforded by BMD in favor of the "effective" deterrence thought to be available *in the absence of BMD*: "Although it is true that even a defense of unknown or low effectiveness could limit damage, this benefit would likely be more than offset by the increased risk of an ICBM attack that an NMD [national missile defense] deployment may produce."[51]

During the Cold War, as discussed in Chapter 4, Secretary McNamara presented the intellectual case for *rejecting* balance of terror guidelines for U.S. strategic forces pertinent to China, and thus for significant damage-limitation capabilities against China.   In contrast, in a   complete   turnaround   of   the   Johnson   Administration's   policy, contemporary commentators now use the balance of terror formula as a reason for rejecting or truncating U.S. BMD capabilities *vis-à-vis* China. In effect, today's "stable" deterrence critique of BMD argues that in deference to a "stable" balance of terror the United States should *not* seek to counter the Chinese capability to threaten U.S. cities with nuclear attack. This position, derived directly from Cold War deterrence tenets, simply substitutes contemporary China for the Cold War's Soviet Union; now, Washington should eschew or limit damage-limitation capabilities against China because priority should be placed on the effective "stable" deterrence thought to be available *in the absence of significant BMD*.

Senior U.S. officials in the Clinton Administration, for example, assured China that U.S. defenses would not be designed to defend against Chinese long-range missiles.[52] The U.S. Department of State's Senior Advisor for Arms Control assured China that the United States was "satisfied" with a "stable deterrent relationship,"[53] and that U.S. BMD would *not* be "aimed at China" because, "We believe deterrence works in the context of the U.S.-China relationship....even a limited NMD system aimed at the North Korean threat could also significantly erode China's deterrent capability against the U.S."[54] The underlying theme, of course, is that U.S. vulnerability to Chinese missiles simply is part of a reliable "stable deterrence" formula and thus the United States need not, and *should not*, seek to "erode" the Chinese capabilities to strike U.S. cities. This repeats the Cold War balance of terror dictum, quoted in Chapter 1, "that vulnerability contributed to peace, and invulnerability contributed to war."[55]

Now, as during the Cold War, the underlying presumptions are that stable deterrence can protect reliably and effectively, and that deterrence is incompatible with U.S. damage-limitation capabilities. Thus the United States should eschew defensive capabilities for societal protection in deference to the pursuit of stable *mutual* deterrence; hence, until defenses can protect *perfectly*, they must be subordinated to the deterrence stability supposedly ensured by mutual vulnerability: "The hard reality of the situation is that, absent a perfect shield, the logic of MAD will remain an integral part of strategic arithmetic....the safety of the US populace depends at least in part on allowing them to remain vulnerable to Armageddon."[56] Again, this supposedly is the enduring truth of "strategic arithmetic."

In a full replay of Secretary McNamara's Cold War argument, no real downside or tradeoff is acknowledged in this prioritization of offensive threat over defense because it is believed that "deterrence works" reliably and predictably. As an editorial in the *Chicago Tribune* asserts, BMD can still be eschewed with no regret because, "the U.S. already has an effective protection...namely deterrence. The main reason the Chinese would not obliterate Los Angeles is that they know we could obliterate their entire country. For half a century, the balance of terror has served to keep the missiles in their silos."[57]

During the Cold War, despite the Soviet Union's own building and modernizing of a strategic BMD site around Moscow, Soviet spokesmen repeated back to American audiences familiar balance of terror adages against BMD in obvious appreciation of their political effect for limiting or curtailing U.S. BMD initiatives. So too, contemporary Chinese officials now obviously seek to move the United States away from BMD by directing the same Cold War balance of terror language and adages at U.S. audiences.

After China's deployment of literally hundreds of offensive missiles capable of targeting much of Asia, Chinese officials now self-servingly play back to American and Japanese audiences the supposed "destabilizing" effect of defenses against those missiles. For example, the Chinese Foreign Ministry's spokesperson recently observed that potential U.S. and Japanese missile defenses would negatively "impact stability and the strategic balance."[58] Commentators cite the "grave concerns" of Chinese officials about the "first strike" incentives U.S. BMD would cause because it could, "neutralize China's fewer than two dozen single-warhead ICBMs that are capable of reaching the United States."[59] The use here of familiar, benign-sounding balance of terror language takes the edge off of what is claimed—that U.S. and allied cities *should be vulnerable* to Chinese nuclear missile attack for the sake of "balance" and "stability." It is no exaggeration to note that at least some of the Chinese spokespersons who now give voice to these long-familiar balance of terror idioms learned them from the talking points of domestic critics of U.S. BMD and similarly appreciate their paralyzing effect on U.S. BMD programs.

If balance of terror tenets are to serve as the lodestar for U.S. policy *vis-à-vis* China, of course, the United States must resist any aspirations to "neutralize" Chinese nuclear missiles threatening U.S. cities. That U.S. vulnerability allegedly contributes to "stable" deterrence. Before now repeating with China the U.S. Cold War policy course, however, it would seem reasonable to conduct a thorough re-examination of the coherence and wisdom of balance of terror tenets against contemporary threats and conditions. BMD critics who continue to argue on behalf of those tenets provide no evidence of having done so.

The contemporary U.S. BMD debate also continues to reflect the familiar Cold War-era assertion that an action-reaction dynamic—led by U.S. actions—explains opponents' incentives to acquire nuclear weapons. As during the Cold War, the recommendation that follows is that U.S. rejection of BMD will reduce or eliminate those incentives. During the Cold War, many U.S. academic commentators and some public officials routinely and confidently predicted an unbeatable Soviet offensive reaction to U.S. BMD and, in contrast, Soviet offensive force *moderation* if the United States did *not* pursue BMD. Now the same action-reaction dynamic is said to apply globally, to include the reactions of Russia, China, Pakistan, India and North Korea.[60]

A former senior Defense Department official, for example, warns that while the United States cannot perfect missile defense technology, "even if it were possible, the program would motivate a response from adversaries that would inevitably offset the defense."[61] Another former official echoes the same sure prediction based on the old action-reaction theme: U.S. missile defenses surely would be followed by an opponent's expansion of its offensive missile capabilities to overwhelm those defenses; North Korea would do the same in response to Japanese defenses and China would do the same in response to Taiwanese defenses.[62]

The normally staid *Business Week* predicts with similar certainty that in response to U.S. missile defense, "China...is bound to expand its arsenal. It certainly won't stand by and let its small retaliatory capability be blunted by our defense system."[63] A joint publication by traditional domestic

BMD opponents—the Federation of American Scientists, the Natural Resource Defense Council, and the Union of Concerned Scientists—similarly asserts that U.S. missile defense, "will almost certainly spur China to compensate by building more missiles, both to overwhelm the defense and to make this capability evident to the United States."[64] Even North Korea is predicted to follow with certainty this action-reaction cycle: "North Korea can be expected to step up the development and production of long-range ICBMs, inevitably with multiple warheads."[65] Worse yet, according to a former State Department official, U.S. BMD would instigate a worldwide crisis of armament: "With China increasing its missiles, India and Japan, and then Pakistan, would follow suit, inciting a worldwide arms race."[66]

Prominent national security journalists still present the action-reaction thesis as if it were an enduring truth, one labeling it the "first law of nuclear politics" and claiming that, "in the world of missiles, missile defenses, nuclear physics and nuclear politics, action-reaction is still the norm."[67] In repetition of past claims, opponents' contemporary strategic initiatives are attributed to an action-reaction dynamic triggered by some prior U.S. stimulus, including China's 2007 testing of a missile capable of destroying satellites in orbit.[68] More than a year *after* that Chinese test, the United States destroyed one of its own satellites which posed an environmental hazard if left to descend from orbit on its own. Nevertheless, the subsequent commentary reliably repeated the old action-reaction thesis: the United States was pursuing a "capacity to wage war in space. And that, it seems likely, will prompt others to keep pace."[69]

This ultimately condescending view of opponents, besides often confusing the sequence of events, concedes them no internal motivation in defining their own doctrine and force requirements: they supposedly mimic or try to "keep pace" with U.S. actions, and hardly would pursue strategic initiatives at all if not for the need to respond to U.S. provocations. It is all about us. Once again with regard to BMD, it is said that U.S. deployment would motivate opponents to buy missiles; but, if we do not attempt to deploy defenses, it is argued, opponents will not need to increase their offensive capabilities and arms control efforts can succeed. Continuing expressions of action-reaction often wax with hyperbole: "The cost of this defense will not simply be measured in dollars. It may include an end to further nuclear arms reductions with Russia, and increased Chinese effort to expand its nuclear forces in response to the defense...and an eventual collapse of global arms control and nonproliferation efforts."[70]

This general action-reaction argument against BMD remains unchanged from the 1960s: U.S. BMD deployment will necessarily compel others to increase their offensive missile capabilities so as to overcome U.S. defenses. Also unchanged from the 1960s are commentators' confident assertions that by prompting an action-reaction cycle, U.S. BMD will "destroy the arms reduction process" and make "inevitable the next round of arms escalation."[71] Apparently the future force acquisition decisions of opponents are as fully transparent to these commentators as is the future susceptibility of their decision making to U.S. deterrence threats.

Some senior U.S. political leaders continue to express this belief that U.S. BMD will ignite this action-reaction dynamic—leading Russia and China to increase their missile capabilities, and to missile proliferation among rogue states. It was predicted that U.S. withdrawal from the ABM Treaty to deploy missile defense:

> ...could result in more nuclear weapons on Russian soil, increase the risk of proliferation of these weapons, lead Russia and others to develop, deploy and even sell countermeasures to our defenses, cause China to increase their nuclear arsenal, *all that and no doubt more*....If China believes our NMD [National Missile Defense] system is designed to negate its nuclear deterrent, it could increase its nuclear forces far beyond what it would otherwise do. This could lead India and Pakistan to reciprocate. We should be very cautious about taking a step that could result in many more nuclear weapons in China, prompting a buildup in India and Pakistan....[72]

In short, contemporary critics of BMD offer the same balance of terror narrative against BMD that Schelling made familiar in the late 1950s, that Secretary McNamara instituted as policy guidelines in the 1960s, and that President Nixon codified in the 1970s. As in the past, these arguments are predicated on the confident belief that how opponents think and behave is transparent and predictable; to wit, deterrence can be orchestrated to work, while U.S. BMD deployment would destabilize deterrence, instigate an action-reaction arms race, and preclude future success in arms control.

Balance of Terror Tenets and Contemporary U.S. Offensive Force Initiatives

Balance of terror tenets also continue to affect contemporary U.S. acquisition decisions about offensive forces. For example, the George W. Bush Administration included in its 2004 defense budget request a cost and feasibility study for a new nuclear capability; in 2005, it proposed a separate program to create *non-nuclear*, strategic ballistic missiles by replacing nuclear warheads on select long-range ballistic missiles with conventional warheads. Both of these proposals essentially were rejected by Congress, in large measure on the strength of old Cold War balance of terror dictums and metrics applied against these new capabilities.

The nuclear feasibility study—despite a relatively modest $45 million projected price tag through fiscal year 2005—became the most controversial nuclear weapons initiative of the decade. The study was intended to examine the prospects for modifying an existing nuclear weapon to be capable of threatening to destroy opponents' hard and deeply-buried bunkers.[73] The Department of Defense estimates that potential opponents have 10,000 such facilities, 2,000 of which serve a "major strategic function."[74] Reportedly, many of these *cannot be threatened* by non-nuclear weapons and some cannot be threatened by "one or a few" existing U.S. nuclear weapons.[75]

This proposed penetrating weapon was dubbed the Robust Nuclear Earth Penetrator (RNEP). The Bush Administration's interest in studying the feasibility of RNEP centered on its potential value for deterrence: An opponent with deeply-buried facilities, such as North Korea, might be more willing to provoke the United States severely if it believed that it could evade the threat of U.S. retaliation by escaping to its deeply-buried "sanctuaries." Ambassador Linton Brooks, then head of the National Nuclear Security Administration, emphasized this deterrence point: "What we're doing is trying to preserve options, that if a future president decides we need some capability to deter, we'll have the technical wherewithal to do it." And: "We want, in some hypothetical future confrontation with a hypothetical generic dictator, to make it absolutely clear that he doesn't have an invulnerable sanctuary."[76]

Congressional opposition to the proposed RNEP development study, however, led to funding problems that ultimately killed the initiative. Opposition to RNEP in Congress followed the familiar presumption against

U.S. strategic capabilities categorized as "war-fighting" per the balance of terror formula and the cause of an "action-reaction" arms race.[77] This opposition, of course, mirrored Secretary McNamara's 1960s arguments against counterforce offensive capabilities. Rather than threatening an action-reaction cycle with Russia, however, some in Congress opposed a U.S. nuclear initiative such an RNEP because they believed that it would motivate nuclear proliferation *among rogue states* that otherwise would forego nuclear weapons: "How we determine the future of the United States nuclear weapons policy will go a long way to determining whether we control nuclear proliferation or expand it."[78] Movement *away* from nuclear weapons by nuclear powers is expected to encourage states which otherwise might aspire to nuclear weapons to remain non-nuclear; those so convinced saw RNEP as movement in the wrong direction.

A *Washington Post* editorial against RNEP combined the basic deterrence instability and the action-reaction critiques prominent in the Congressional debate: "The administration insists it wants only to pursue research on the new nukes. But even this research will, at a minimum, multiply the incentives for rogue states and rival powers to build nuclear arsenals of their own....At worst, the administration will succeed in making nuclear war easier and more tempting...."[79]

The Republican chairman of the House subcommittee with considerable authority over U.S. nuclear capabilities—i.e., Water and Energy—led the opposition to RNEP largely on the basis of this supposed action-reaction effect. The RNEP study, he contended, would undermine U.S. nuclear non-proliferation objectives by sending, "...the wrong signal to the rest of the world...encouraging other countries' nuclear weapons initiatives."[80] This type of language goes beyond the Cold War "four no's" by adding that even U.S. nuclear *feasibility studies* must be eschewed because they would motivate nuclear proliferation.

This appeal to the action-reaction dynamic mirrors Secretary McNamara's position during the Cold War. It simply substitutes rogue states for the Soviet Union; rogue states now will be motivated by U.S. initiatives to pursue nuclear capabilities that they otherwise would not have sought: "The more the [nuclear weapons] asymmetry is diminished, the more likely it is that nonproliferation can achieve the status of an acceptable international regime."[81]

In addition, contemporary commentators similarly applied the old assured destruction-type metric against counterforce offensive capabilities in their assessment of RNEP and, on this basis, concluded that RNEP also would be unnecessary for a strategy of deterrence:

> The new weapons concepts advanced to date seem to have little to do with deterrence of a nuclear (or other WMD) attack on the United States or its allies. Instead, they appear to be geared toward a warfighting role, which could ultimately undermine rather than enhance U.S. security....Would an identifiable regional power initiate an unprovoked WMD attack on the U.S. homeland based on the conclusion that the United States did not have the "appropriate" nuclear weapons? It seems very unlikely.... Any lack of U.S. capability to attack hard and deeply buried targets or other weapons storage facilities would probably play no role in the aggressor's decision because the aggressor would be aware that the United States has many other retaliatory options.[82]

Again, without any apparent examination of the decision making and behavior of opponents, confident assertions about how they would think and behave abound. These assertions posit opponents who will conveniently be deterred by U.S. threats *in the absence* of the proposed U.S. capability. What is the basis for offering such seemingly profound conclusions about how unspecified opponents in unspecified circumstances will make decisions? Nothing beyond the authors' speculation which, in turn, simply follows the balance of terror and assured destruction narrative. With this uncanny understanding of how potential opponents will think and behave, these commentators assert confident knowledge of what will and will not contribute to deterring opponents and causing an arms race. On this basis they concluded that RNEP could offer nothing of value for deterrence and would be so potentially "destabilizing" that even a feasibility study should not go forward. The question here is not whether these commentators applied traditional assured destruction/balance of terror measures to contemporary deterrence questions—clearly they did; the question is whether any credence should be attributed to confident conclusions so derived.

Conventional Strategic Missiles

The George W. Bush Administration's initiative to replace nuclear warheads with conventional weapons on select long-range ballistic missiles suffered a similar fate in Congress, at least in part because the same long-familiar balance of terror definitions and adages were brought to bear against it. The advantage identified for placing conventional weapons on long-range ballistic missiles was the expected U.S. capability to strike very rapidly at fleeting distant targets with a non-nuclear weapon vice a nuclear weapon.[83]

Opponents of this proposed non-nuclear strategic capability repeated a version of the "crisis instability" rationale for Cold War opposition to significant U.S. nuclear counterforce capabilities. For example, an academic commentator raised the red flag of "crisis instability" against U.S. conventional strategic missiles—specifying that they could motivate China to launch nuclear missiles or compel smaller powers to use their WMD against the United States.[84] The most salient points of opposition to the proposal for non-nuclear strategic missiles were summarized in a 2006 report by the Congressional Research Service (CRS). This summary reflects the continuing power of this balance of terror tenet; it simply accepts "crisis instability" as a reality to be recognized and a metric to be applied: "Most analysts *recognized*, during the Cold War, that long-range land-based ballistic missiles could prove destabilizing in a crisis...."[85] In this summary, it is argued that if a non-nuclear missile were launched:

> ...a nation who was not an intended target, such as Russia, might choose to respond quickly, rather than to wait for more information. The same could be true for the adversaries who are the intended targets of U.S. ballistic missiles. If the United States hoped to destroy a nation's military forces or weapons of mass destruction at the start of a conflict, before they could be used against U.S. troops, the other nation might choose to use these weapons even more quickly during a crisis, before it lost them to the U.S. attack.[86]

This critique, in fact, distorts Schelling's concepts of "stability" and "crisis instability." The balance of terror tenet that a secure U.S. nuclear retaliatory capability provides reliable deterrence against severe provocation by rational opponents suggests that we should *not* anticipate the "crisis instability" response pointed to in these critiques: the opponent should instead be deterred reliably by the U.S. nuclear deterrent from launching its weapons against the United States. Why then did critics of this program—who also typically make confident claims about deterrence "working" reliably—object to this particular capability on the argument that it would cause "crisis instability"? Did they examine closely the goals, fears, decision making and behavioral patterns of contemporary opponents and thereby discover that, *despite the great risk and uncertainties*, opponents in this case would be provoked to attack by the new U.S. non-nuclear strategic missiles? No, their conclusions and recommendations are innocent of any apparent assessment of any contemporary opponent.

Rather, the criticism of this contemporary program includes the familiar Cold War narrative that prompt counterforce weapons are dangerously "destabilizing." As the CRS study quoted above illustrates, contemporary commentators applied this same dictum as an enduring truth to the post-Cold War proposal for a prompt U.S. non-nuclear, offensive missile capability; from this they declared it to be "destabilizing" absent much, or any, apparent examination of contemporary opponents, threats or conditions.

Knowing Deterrence: The Formula for U.S. Strategic Force Requirements

Also inherited from the Cold War and pervasive today is the confident belief in the continuing validity of the past methodology for "knowing" deterrence requirements and, with that, U.S. strategic force requirements. Deterrence is deemed to be orchestrated with confidence by acquiring the level of survivable offensive capability necessary and adequate to threaten designated targets; this is "strategic arithmetic"—involving the number of survivable weapons necessary to threaten designated enemy targets, whether they be cities, military forces, political centers, or other physical assets.

As was the case during the Cold War, the level of U.S. offensive capability identified in this manner as necessary for deterrence is likely to include more or fewer weapons depending on the number and types of targets designated as significant for deterrence purposes. Fewer, soft, unprotected targets—such as cities—can equate to a deterrence requirement for fewer nuclear weapons. More numerous, hardened and protected targets—including military targets—can equate to increased requirements. In either case, the logic and formula are clear: Possessing the forces necessary to threaten the selected targets is equated to having "the deterrent." Consequently, the adequacy requirements for deterrence and U.S. strategic forces in general are deemed to be calculable via this simple "strategic arithmetic."

Secretary McNamara's assured destruction metric was the archetype of this target-based approach to determining "how much is enough" for deterrence. Secretary McNamara designated a relatively vulnerable set of targets—cities and industry—as the basis for calculating his simple assured destruction standard. Preserving the strategic forces necessary to meet that standard and later, more expansive, variations became the fundamental guideline for identifying U.S. strategic force requirements and for acquisition policy in general. The question of how to deter was reduced to this formula of possessing redundant capabilities to threaten the chosen targets. The requirements for deterrence and, by extension, U.S. strategic force requirements, came to be defined in this manner. Armed with this formula, Secretary McNamara and many others issued definitive-sounding statements with regard to what was and was not necessary to ensure continuing stable deterrence.

Commentators no longer use the label "assured destruction" routinely. The preferred phrases now include, *inter alia,*[87] "unacceptable damage" and "unacceptable retaliation"; as noted in Chapter 5, the targets considered important for deterrence evolved over time. Nevertheless, what remains in public debate is this familiar target-based formula that equates U.S. deterrence requirements with numbers of weapons and targets, and overall strategic force requirements with "how much is enough" as determined by this deterrence formula. Deterrence and overall U.S. strategic force requirements are reduced to a matter of identifying the necessary "package of capabilities."[88] This methodology and linkage are a balance of terror legacy that continues to dominate contemporary popular discussions of U.S. deterrence and strategic force requirements.

Former Deputy Secretary of Defense and Director of Central Intelligence John Deutch, for example, continues to employ this traditional formula to identify U.S. deterrence requirements and thus, "a sense of how much smaller the U.S. nuclear arsenal could be."[89] He calculates the number of U.S. nuclear weapons sufficient for the "complete destruction of any opponent's interests or sanctuary" to be "less than 1,000 warheads in total," and concludes that a U.S. strategic arsenal of this size "would be enough."[90] The goal is to force any opponent, "to consider the possibility of U.S. nuclear retaliation" of such severity.[91]

As in the past, this target-based formula for calculating deterrence and strategic force requirements provides commentators with an apparently precise basis for defining the force numbers necessary and sufficient for deterrence and U.S. strategic force acquisition. Numbers and types of forces that do *not* correspond with the posited offensive targeting requirement for deterrence, such as significant damage-limitation capabilities, simply are outside of the formula and typically continue to be deemed unnecessary, useless and/or destabilizing. When U.S. deterrence and strategic force requirements are defined in this fashion, the conclusion could not be otherwise.

Following Secretary McNamara's example in this regard, contemporary commentators use this methodology to identify the necessary level of U.S. strategic capability. For example, a 2005 report published by the Arms Control Association uses this target-based approach to conclude that no more than 500 deployed U.S. nuclear weapons and 500 reserve nuclear weapons now are sufficient for deterrence, and that no additional or new U.S. nuclear capabilities are necessary.[92] Other commentaries use the same mechanistic, target-based approach to identify the precise deterrence requirements for nuclear weapons. The explicit use of this Cold War balance of terror formula and the simple assured destruction metric to define U.S. post-Cold War nuclear requirements is obvious in the following:

> No sane adversary would believe that any political or military advantage would be worth a significant risk of the destruction of his own society. As noted earlier, the delivery of one hundred U.S. warheads would be sufficient to destroy the society and economy of Russia or China, and as few as ten detonations could kill more people than have ever been killed in any country in any previous war. *Thus ten to one hundred survivable warheads should be more than enough to deter any rational leader* from ordering an attack on the cities of the United States or its allies.[93]

Similarly, a prominent scientist who worked on the U.S. Manhattan Project and continues to comment on U.S. deterrence requirements uses the methodology to recommend "a few hundred" nuclear weapons,[94] while a former senior member of the Clinton Administration's National Security Council concludes that "having 100 nuclear warheads... will deter others from using nuclear, biological, or chemical weapons or from even engaging in conventional attacks."[95]

These continuing target-based recommendations repeat the familiar Cold War formula and are offered without any apparent investigation of the different values, perceptions, goals, wills, vulnerabilities, and concerns of the opponents and likely circumstances in question, or any questioning of the validity of this mechanistic target-based formula for identifying U.S. deterrence and strategic force requirements in the twenty-first century. This familiar Cold War methodology is comforting and convenient: it supposedly allows the otherwise very challenging question of "how much is enough" for deterrence to be answered with apparent mathematical precision on the basis of simple "strategic arithmetic." As during the Cold War, with limited effort it facilitates definitive-sounding conclusions regarding an adequate strategic arsenal.

Knowing Deterrence: Terrorists Are "Undeterrable"

As noted, contemporary commentators continue to have confidence in the relatively easy and predictable deterrence of rational state leaders; ironically, that same faith leads them to have an equally pessimistic view of how deterrence will function *vis-à-vis* terrorist organizations. A result of continued adherence to a target-based formula for deterrence is the oft-heard refrain that terrorists and their organizations *cannot be deterred.* Why not? This is so because terrorist organizations do not have state-like characteristics—with obvious cities, citizens, or territory to threaten per se. This new enemy does not fit the old target-based formula for deterrence or the familiar profile of the "rational" opponent embedded in the balance of terror tenets, so the *a priori* conclusion that deterrence cannot be effective against terrorists has become popular. This conclusion typically is offered up *without any apparent* recognition of the ample available history illustrating how terrorists, past and present, have been deterred on occasion:[96] "In today's war waged on world order by terrorists, nuclear weapons are the ultimate means of mass devastation. And non-state terrorist groups with nuclear weapons are conceptually outside the bounds of a deterrent strategy and present difficult new security challenges."[97] In 2006, President George W. Bush made a similar observation: "The terrorists have no borders to protect, or capital to defend.

They cannot be deterred—but they will be defeated."[98]

The old balance of terror practice of equating deterrence to the capability to threaten physical targets within an opponent's territory does not fit this new type of enemy, so deterrence supposedly is of little or no value. Confidence in the old formula that purportedly tells when and how deterrence will function remains so ingrained that when the opponent does not fit the familiar formula the applicability of deterrence itself is denied rather than the old approach adapted to new opponents and circumstances.

Knowing Deterrence: Conventional Weapons Are Enough

Another new, post-Cold War twist on the old target-based formula for defining "how much is enough" follows from the increase in the lethality of conventional forces over the past two decades. Because deterrence is equated to the requirements necessary to threaten the destruction of selected targets, and conventional weapons are becoming much more lethal against most targets, noted commentators began in the early 1990s to suggest that the deterrence requirement for nuclear weapons was receding. In 1994, for example, Paul Nitze, a highly-regarded expert and senior official in Republican and Democratic administrations stated:

> ...the United States should consider what might seem at first glance a step backward: converting its principal strategic deterrent from nuclear weapons to a more credible deterrence based at least in part upon 'smart' conventional weapons....Can they adequately carry out their combat missions? If so, will that fact deter aggression as effectively as nuclear weapons appear to have done? I believe the answers to these questions are, in general, positive and that a strategic conventional military option may become practical for many strategic missions previously thought of as a nuclear preserve....From a policy perspective, there *should be a conscious decision by the government to pursue the conversion of our strategic deterrent from nuclear to conventional weapons.*[99]

Similarly, in 1996, two retired senior military leaders issued a joint statement declaring that, "the roles of nuclear weapons for purposes of security have been sharply narrowed in terms of the security of the United States....In the world environment now foreseen, they are not needed against non-nuclear opponents. Conventional capabilities can provide a sufficient deterrent and defense against conventional forces and in combination with defensive measures, against the threat of chemical or biological weapons."[100] One added that the proper U.S. deterrent to rogue *nuclear weapons* is the threat, "we can destroy you with our conventional capabilities."[101] When the formula for deterrence is reduced to the "package of capabilities" necessary to threaten the opponent, whether the instrument of the threat is nuclear or non-nuclear presumably is irrelevant as long as the appropriate targets can be threatened.

Noted civilian experts often make a similar formulaic argument: "In most cases, if a regional power attacked a U.S. ally, the United States could respond with an overwhelming conventional attack that could severely damage the attacker's forces and infrastructure, perhaps causing its government to collapse, even without resorting to nuclear weapons. This in itself is likely to be a sufficient deterrent."[102] The balance of terror formula that measured deterrence requirements via a target-based calculation of assured destruction continues to provide the basis for confident conclusions about when, how, against whom, and with what instruments of threat deterrence will work. Because non-nuclear forces now may be lethal against most types of targets, or soon could be, the United States supposedly can forego new nuclear weapons and eliminate most or even all existing nuclear capabilities without degrading deterrence.[103]

If U.S. strategic deterrence requirements truly can be equated to the "package of capabilities" necessary to threaten the destruction of an opponent's designated targets, and *if* U.S. conventional weapons can threaten those same targets with the same expected deterrent effect, the logic of this position would be coherent, even persuasive. Despite the many assertions that presume each of these propositions to be true, both remain largely unexamined.

Knowing Deterrence: Uncertainty Deters and Ambiguity Is "Good For Deterrence"

The thesis that the chance of U.S. nuclear escalation—and an opponent's uncertainty about the chance—can provide adequate deterrent effect was the key to Schelling's expressed confidence in the balance of terror, especially for its extended deterrence purposes. This thesis—that a "threat that leaves something to chance" can deter reliably—was Schelling's conceptual innovation that allowed confidence in the extended deterrent effect of U.S. threats even if the execution of those threats would be catastrophic for the United States. The threat of nuclear escalation, despite the likely intolerable consequences for the United States if executed, was expected to deter reliably because it was believed that rational opponents, including Soviet leaders, would not dare risk U.S. escalation. As noted in Chapter 2, Kahn and Schelling split over the question of whether extended deterrence could be based on this uncertainty.

Following the Cold War, many senior U.S. officials continued to accept as a near universal principle the proposition that an opponent's uncertainty concerning U.S. escalation could provide an adequate basis for U.S. deterrence. In 1998, for example, U.S. Secretary of Defense William Cohen observed: "We think that the ambiguity involved in the issue of the use of nuclear weapons contributes to our own security, keeping any potential adversary who might use either chemical or biological [weapons] unsure of what our response would be. We think that it is a sound doctrine. It was adopted certainly during the Cold War, but modified and reaffirmed following the end of the Cold War."[104] More recently, a senior official of the George W. Bush Administration reportedly affirmed and even elevated the supposed value of ambiguity for deterrence: "The essence of deterrence strategy is having some element of ambiguity."[105]

Throughout the 1990s, U.S. policy toward China over Taiwan officially was referred to as one of "strategic ambiguity." Consistent with this approach, in late 1995, Assistant Secretary of Defense Joseph Nye was asked by Chinese officials how Washington would respond to a Chinese military threat to Taiwan. Secretary Nye's reply was a classic reflection of Schelling's Cold War proposition that uncertainty can deter: "We don't know what we would do, and you don't because it's going to depend on the circumstances."[106] There remains considerable confidence in the value of uncertainty for sustaining the deterrence of China without stimulating Taiwan toward independence.[107]

The expectation that uncertainty can deter reliably and universally is reflected in Waltz's view of nuclear proliferation discussed above. The *chance* of U.S. nuclear escalation is expected to deter rogue nuclear attacks on the United States and U.S. allies, and even to deter rogues from transferring WMD, whether or not the credibility of the U.S. threat is reinforced by U.S. protection against attack as recommended by Kahn.

During the Cold War, Schelling's original proposition that uncertainty could be compatible with deterrence under proper circumstances was truncated to the general truth that "uncertainty deters." In the immediate post-Cold War era, it was truncated further still to the generalized policy "bumper sticker" that "ambiguity" of threat and commitment "is good for deterrence": Ambiguity in the expression of U.S. intentions and deterrence commitments is deemed "a sound doctrine" for deterrence. Senior U.S. leaders have continued to recommend it as a basic approach to deterrence: "The United States *should maintain a declaratory policy of purposeful ambiguity* and should not foreswear nuclear retaliation against enemies who use biological or chemical weapons against U.S. territory, force, or allies."[108]

Republican and Democratic administrations have made conscious use of ambiguous language in the declaration of U.S. deterrent threats since the end of the Cold War. For example, President George H.W. Bush's January 15, 1991 letter to Saddam Hussein, then President of Iraq, stated the following: "...the United States will not tolerate the use of chemical or biological weapons or the destruction of Kuwait's oil fields and installations. Further, you will be held directly responsible for terrorist actions against any member of the coalition. The American people would demand the strongest possible response. You and your country will pay a terrible price if you order unconscionable acts of this sort."[109] What and how "terrible" that "price" might be, and how it would be inflicted apparently was left open to Saddam Hussein's interpretation. If uncertainty deters, ambiguity of threat presumably need not degrade the intended deterrent effect.

Similarly, on December 23, 1990, then Secretary of Defense Richard Cheney made public threats clearly meant for Saddam Hussein following a meeting with Egyptian President Hosni Mubarak: "And, were Saddam Hussein foolish enough to use weapons of mass destruction, the US response would be absolutely overwhelming and it would be devastating. He has to take that into consideration, it seems to me, before he embarks upon a course of using those kinds of capabilities."[110] In this case, the threat was a U.S. response to Iraqi WMD use that would be "overwhelming" and "devastating"—implying the possibility of U.S. nuclear use. The exact meaning, however, is left unspecified.

The Clinton Administration subsequently used this same formulation of a "devastating" and "overwhelming" response in its public expressions of U.S. strategic deterrent threats, as has the more recent

Bush Administration. For example, the Bush Administration's 2006 *National Strategy for Combating Terrorism* uses the following pertinent language: "We will make clear that terrorists and those who aid or sponsor a WMD attack would face the prospect of an overwhelming response to any use of such weapons."[111] Again, ambiguous language leaves it to the terrorists and their sponsors to interpret what would be a U.S. "overwhelming response," when and how it might be inflicted, and whether their employment of WMD would be worth that price.

Armed with the presumption that uncertainty deters, there is no reason to expect a degradation of deterrent effect from a lack of specificity in U.S. commitments and threats; moreover, it provides many advantages. Ambiguous or imprecise language affords the United States "wiggle room" in terms of its commitment to execute a specific response to the proscribed provocation. Threats can be made, if done imprecisely, without committing to a specific action. Consequently, if uncertainty truly deters, ambiguity may facilitate the desired deterrent effect with limited accountability for the United States; ambiguity can suggest a deterrent threat that inspires uncertainty and deterrent effect but which cannot be "called" because the threat is left unspecific and imprecise. This makes the practice of deterrence much more convenient and comfortable for the threatener—deterrence can be achieved with limited accountability. This advantage is enormously attractive and entails no downside *if* the deterrent effect sought is available in the context of uncertainty and ambiguity.

It is worth noting here that South Korean and Japanese public reactions to the North Korean 2006 nuclear test included the desire for assurance regarding the U.S. extended nuclear deterrent and an *explicit* U.S. statement of that nuclear deterrence commitment. Japanese Defense Minister Fumio Kyuma reportedly spoke of strengthening the U.S. extended nuclear deterrent: "The strongest deterrence would be when the United States explicitly says, 'If you drop one nuclear bomb on Japan, the United States will retaliate by dropping 10 on you.'"[112] Hardly an ambiguous threat. This suggests that allies who feel threatened by nuclear neighbors may *not* be assured by U.S. extended deterrence commitments that contain significant ambiguity. Even if uncertainty can be expected to deter reliably—a proposition that will be addressed in the next chapter—the price of U.S. *ambiguity* may be the lack of assurance it provides allies.

Conclusion

The balance of terror theory of "stable" deterrence that became the basis for U.S. deterrence strategy and strategic acquisition policy in the 1960s, and was codified into law under President Nixon with the 1972 ABM Treaty, has had a lasting legacy. The basic tenets of that Cold War formula have survived the Cold War era. They are regarded widely as enduring truths and continue to be applied to contemporary questions of deterrence and strategic force acquisition. These tenets include the following:

- U.S. deterrence can be orchestrated with confidence to work reliably against rational opponents.
- The *chance* of U.S. escalation can deter because rational opponents will not dare to provoke that escalation.
- Deterrent effects are calculable and can be manipulated with precision via changes in U.S. forces.
- Forces can be categorized as "stabilizing" or not, depending on their consistency with a balance of terror.
- U.S. societal defenses and counterforce capabilities are inconsistent with deterrence—they are destabilizing.
- Deterrence requirements can be calculated according to the number and type of weapons needed to threaten an opponent's designated targets.
- U.S. strategic force requirements *in toto* are determined by the calculation of U.S. deterrence requirements.
- The tradeoff of foregoing damage-limitation capabilities is acceptable because deterrence can be made to "work" reliably, while damage-limitation capabilities are unnecessary, imperfect and destabilizing.
- Action-reaction explains arms racing and U.S. actions drive rogue proliferation incentives—therefore U.S. nuclear "inaction" is the necessary basis for non-proliferation.
- Because uncertainty can deter, ambiguity in threat and commitment can provide adequate deterrent effect.

    This interrelated set of beliefs and judgments continues to be reflected in most contemporary public, journalistic, "blogged" and Congressional discussions of deterrence, arms control, nuclear forces,

BMD, and U.S. strategic force requirements; it also shapes perceptions of the threat represented by nuclear and missile proliferation.

There appears to be little understanding today of the original rationale for these beliefs and judgments. Only simplified conclusions remain: deterrence is existential; "rational" equates to deterrable; deterrence requirements can be calculated precisely; nuclear-armed states can be deterred reliably; ambiguity is good for deterrence; U.S. BMD and counterforce weapons are unnecessary and "destabilizing"; and, U.S. nuclear and defensive initiatives will drive opponents to proliferation while U.S. inaction will beget opponents' inaction. These "bumper sticker" conclusions are wielded in contemporary debate with little apparent cognizance of where they came from or why they were afforded credence by some thoughtful individuals during the Cold War. Their pertinence in the very different strategic environment of the twenty-first century remains largely unexamined and unchallenged, as might be expected of purported enduring truths that provide so much comfort and convenience.

As we think about deterrence in the twenty-first century a critical question is whether the Cold War theory that gave birth to these surviving "truths" is coherent and whether the truths hold up in a dramatically changed post-Cold War strategic environment. That is the subject of Chapters 7 and 8.

Endnotes

1. Peter Grier, "The New Nuclear 'Theology,'" *The Christian Science Monitor*, May 8, 2001, p. 1.
2. Leon Fuerth, "Return of the Nuclear Debate," in *Contemporary Nuclear Debates*, Alexander Lennon, ed. (Cambridge, MA: The MIT Press, 2002), p. 187.
3. Ibid., p. 189.
4. Louis Rene Beres and Isaac Ben-Israel, "Deterring Iran," *The Washington Times*, June 11, 2007, p. A17.
5. Keir Lieber and Daryl Press, "Superiority Complex," *The Atlantic*, Vol. 300, No. 1 (July/August 2007), p. 86.
6. Wolfgang Panofsky, "Nuclear Insecurity: Correcting Washington's Dangerous Posture," *Foreign Affairs*, Vol. 86, No. 5 (September/October 2007), pp. 113-114.
7. Thomas Friedman, "Who's Crazy Here," *The New York Times*, May 15, 2001, p. 25.
8. David E. Sanger, "Don't Shoot. We're Not Ready," *The New York Times*, June 25, 2006, p. 1.
9. John B. Roberts, "Deterrence Needed: Preventing Islamofascist Attack," *The Washington Times*, November 3, 2006, p. A19.
10. Ibid.
11. Elbridge Colby, "Restoring Deterrence," *Orbis*, Vol. 51, No. 3 (Summer 2007), pp. 413-428.
12. Ibid., pp. 418-419.
13. Quoted in, Sebastian Rotella, "At Davos Forum, Every Topic Is Fair Game for Bill Clinton," *The Los Angeles Times*, January 28, 2005, p. A-3.
14. Quoted in, Bill Gertz, "Perry: Missile Defense Unnecessary," *The Washington Times*, April 26, 1996, p. A-6.
15. See, Testimony in U.S. House, Committee on Foreign Affairs, *U.S. Nuclear Policy,* Hearings, 103rd Congress, 2nd Session (Washington, D.C.: USGPO, 1995), p. 36. (Emphasis added).
16. Roger Speed and Michael May, "Dangerous Doctrine," *Bulletin of the Atomic Scientists*, Vol. 61, No. 2 (March/April 2005), p. 43.
17. Nick Schwellenbach, "The EMP(ty) Threat," *The Washington Times*, November 11, 2005, p. B2.
18. Speed and May, op. cit., p. 44.
19. Lawrence Freedman, *Deterrence* (Malden, MA: Polity Press, 2004), pp. 120-121.
20. Kenneth N. Waltz, "More May Be Better," in, Scott D. Sagan and Kenneth N. Waltz, *The Spread of Nuclear Weapons* (New York: W.W. Norton, 2003), pp. 44-45.
21. Kenneth N. Waltz, "Waltz Responds to Sagan," in, ibid., p. 117.
22. Kenneth N. Waltz, "Nuclear Myths and Political Realities," *American Political Science Review*, Vol. 84, No. 3 (September 1990), p. 737.
23. Waltz, "More May Be Better," op. cit., pp. 22, 26.
24. Waltz, "Waltz Responds to Sagan," in, op. cit., p. 153.
25. Ibid., p. 147.
26. Barry R. Posen, "We Can Live With a Nuclear Iran," *The New York Times*, February 27, 2006, p. A19.
27. Ibid.
28. Joseph Cirincione, "A Much Less Explosive Trend," *The Washington Post*, March

10, 2002, p. B-3.

29. Ted Galen Carpenter, "Iran's Nuclear Program: America's Policy Options," *Policy Analysis*, Cato Institute, No. 578 (September 20, 2006), p. 10.

30. See, for example, James H. Lebovic, *Deterring International Terrorism and Rogue States* (New York: Routledge, 2007), pp. 28-29.

31. David Ignatius, "The Myth of the Mad Mullahs," *The Washington Post*, December 5, 2007, p. A29.

32. "In Defense of Deterrence," *The New York Times*, September 10, 2002, p. A24. (Emphasis added). This argument is ubiquitous. See also, Jonathan Rauch, "Containing Iran," *The Atlantic*, Vol. 298, No. 1 (July/August 2006), pp. 33-34; and, Paul Starobin, "Experts Consider Ability to Deter Iran," *Global Security Newswire*, May 19, 2006, available at, www.nti.org/d_newswire/issues/print.asp?story_id=C7E7270-0202-4436-A427-26; and, Janne Nolan and Mark Strauss, "The Rogues' Gallery," *World Affairs*, Vol. 4, No. 1 (Winter/Spring 1997), pp. 21-38.

33. Quoted in, Elaine Sciolino and Katrin Bennhold, "Chirac Unfazed by Nuclear Iran, Then Backtracks," *The New York Times*, February 1, 2007, p. 1.

34. Patrick Morgan makes this argument about Iraq in, "Deterrence and the Contemporary Situation in the Middle East," *Special Policy Forum*, No. 46, The Nautilus Institute, October 30, 2002, available at, http://www.nautilus.org/archives/fora/Special-Policy-Forum/46_Morgan.html. See also, Waltz, "Waltz Responds to Sagan," in, op. cit., pp. 148-153.

35. Nicholas D. Kristof, "Spanish Lessons for Israel," *The New York Times*, July 23, 2006, p. 10.

36. Graham Allison, "Deterring Kim Jong II," *The Washington Post*, October 27, 2006, p. A-23. (Emphasis in original). See also, Michael A. Levi, "Deterring Nuclear Terrorism," *Issues in Science and Technology*, Vol. 20, No. 3 (Spring 2004), pp. 70-71; and, Caitlin Talmadge, "Deterring a Nuclear 9/11," *The Washington Quarterly*, Vol. 30, No. 2 (Spring 2007), pp. 21-32.

37. Levi, ibid., p. 70.

38. Quoted in, A. Savyon and Y. Mansharof, "The Doctrine of Mahdism: In the Ideological and Political Philosophy of Mahmoud Ahmadinejad and Ayatollah Mesbah-e Yazdi," Middle East Media Research Institute, *Inquiry and Analysis Series*, No. 357, May 31, 2007, available at, http://memri.org/bin/latestnews.cgi?ID=IA35707.

39. Jonathan Dean, "The Front Lines of Defense: Prevention Part A: Deterrence and Diplomacy," in, *The Last 15 Minutes: Ballistic Missile Defense in Perspective*, Joseph Cirincione and Frank von Hippel, eds. (Washington, D.C.: Coalition to Reduce Nuclear Dangers, 1996), pp. 24-25.

40. Mike Moore, "Missile Defenses, Relabeled," *Bulletin of the Atomic Scientists*, Vol. 58, No. 4 (July/August, 2002), p. 22. (Emphasis in original).

41. See the discussion in, Carl Levin, *Remarks of Senator Carl Levin on National Missile Defense, National Defense University Forum Breakfast on Ballistic Missile Defense*, May 11, 2001, p. 4. Also available at, www.senate.g0v/~levin/newsroom/release.cfm?id=209421.

42. Joseph Biden, quoted in, Steven Mufson, "Sen. Biden Attacks Missile Defense Plans as Costly, Risky," *The Washington Post*, September 11, 2001, p. 4.

43. Thomas Graham, "Sixty Years After Hiroshima, A New Nuclear Era," *Current History*, Vol. 104, No. 681 (April 2005), p. 148.

44. Craig Eisendrath, "Missile Defense System Flawed Technically, Unwise Politically," *Philadelphia Inquirer*, May 23, 2001.

45. Sen. Joseph Biden, "Why Democrats Oppose Billions More on Missiles" (Letter to the editor), *The Wall Street Journal*, July 31, 2006, p. A11.

46. Lawrence Korb, quoted in, William Finn Bennett, "Hunter Pushes for Beefed Up Missile Defense Systems," October 10, 2006, available at, www.nctimes.com/articles/2006/10/11/news/top_stories.

47. *Forty-Nine Generals and Admirals Call for Missile Defense Postponement*, March 26, 2004, text available at, Nuclear Age Peace Foundation, www.wagingpeace.org/articles/2004/2004/03/26_generals_admirals_postponement_print.

48. Richard L. Garwin, "Evaluating Iran's Missile Threat," *Bulletin of the Atomic Scientists*, Vol. 64, No. 2 (May/June 2008), p. 42.

49. Leon Fuerth, "Tampering With Strategic Stability," *The Washington Post*, February 20, 2001, p. 23; see also, Theodore Postol, quoted in, Scott Peterson, "Back to the Future: New US-Russia Arms Race," *The Christian Science Monitor*, June 16, 2004, p. 1.

50. Noam Chomsky, *The Resort to Force* (2004), p. 4, available at, http://www.tomdispatch.com/.

51. George Lewis, Lisbeth Gronlund, and David Wright, "National Missile Defense: An Indefensible System," in, Joseph Cirincione et al., *Nuclear Tensions in a New Era* (Washington, D.C.: Carnegie Endowment for International Peace, 2000), p. 32. See also, MAJ Andrew Pache, "The Strategy of Nuclear Deterrence: Why MAD Was Sane," *NBC Report: U.S. Army Nuclear and Chemical Agency* (Fall/Winter 2005), p. 47.

52. See, "Excerpts from Gore's Remarks on Bush, the Presidential Race and the Issues," *The New York Times*, June 14, 2000, p. A20.

53. Quoted in, John Pomfret, "Taiwan May Get Antimissile Technology," *The Washington Post*, July 9, 2000, p. A19.

54. Presentation by the Honorable John Holum, Senior Advisor for Arms Control and International Security, U.S. Department of State, *Conference on International Reactions to U.S. National and Theater Missile Defense Deployments*, Stanford University, March 3, 2000, p. 5.

55. Quoted in, "Kissinger Looks at the Future of NATO," *Congressional Record*, September 6, 1979, p. E4292.

56. Peter Grier, "The New Nuclear 'Theology,'" *The Christian Science Monitor*, May 8, 2001, p. 1.

57. Steve Chapman, "Why China Fears Missile Defense…And Why We Should Too," *Chicago Tribune*, July 16, 2000, p. 17.

58. Quoted in, Edward Lanfranco, "China Warns U.S., Japan Against Missile Defense," *The Washington Times*, June 6, 2007, p. A12.

59. See the discussion in, Hui Zhang, "Action/Reaction: U.S. Space Weaponization and China," *Arms Control Today*, Vol. 35, No. 10 (December 2005), available at, www.armscontrol.org/act/2005_12/Dec-cvr.asp?. See also, Li Bin, Zhou Baogen, and Liu Zhiwei, "China Will Have to Respond," *Bulletin of the Atomic Scientists*, Vol. 57, No. 6 (November/December 2001), pp. 25-28.

60. See the discussion in, Levin, op. cit., pp. 3-4.

61. Jan Lodal, "Pledging 'No First Strike': A Step Toward Real WMD Cooperation," *Arms Control Today*, Vol. 31, No. 2 (March 2001), p. 6.

62. Philip Coyle, "The Limits and Liabilities of Missile Defense," *Current History*, Vol. 105, No. 694 (November 2006), pp. 391-394.

63. Stan Crock, "It's Rocket Science—And That's Not Good," *Business Week*, May

14, 2001, p. 64.

64. See, Bruce Blair et al., *Toward True Security: A U.S. Nuclear Posture for the Next Decade* (Cambridge, MA: UCS Publications, June 2001), p. 10.

65. Walter Pincus, "The First Law of Nuclear Politics: Every Action Brings Reaction," *The Washington Post*, November 28, 1999, p. B-2.

66. Eisendrath, op. cit.

67. Pincus, loc. cit.

68. See, for example, Hans Kristensen, "Chinese Anti-Satellite Weapons Experiment: What Now?," Federation of American Scientists Strategic Security Blog, January 19, 2007. Available at, http://www.fas.org/blog/ssp/2007/01/chinese_antisatellite_weapon_t.php.

69. Steven Lee Myers, "Look Out Below: The Arms Race in Space May Be On," *The New York Times*, March 9, 2008, p. 3.

70. Theodore A. Postal, "The Target Is Russia," *Bulletin of the Atomic Scientists*, Vol. 56, No. 2 (March/April 2000), p. 31.

71. James Carroll, "The Paradox of Missile Defense," *The Boston Globe*, June 5, 2007, p. A11. See also, Jonathan Schell, "The Folly of Arms Control," *Foreign Affairs*, Vol. 79, No. 5 (September/October 2000), pp. 24, 46.

72. Levin, op. cit., p. 1. (Emphasis added).

73. For details of the program see, Jonathan Medalia, *"Bunker Busters": Robust Nuclear Earth Penetrator Issues, FY2005-FY2007*, Congressional Research Service Report for Congress, RL32347 (February 21, 2006); and, Jonathan Medalia, *"Bunker Busters": Sources of Confusion in the Robust Nuclear Earth Penetrator Debate*, Congressional Research Service Report for Congress, RL325599 (September 22, 2004).

74. See the discussion in, National Research Council of the National Academies, *Effects of Nuclear Earth-Penetrator and Other Weapons* (Washington, D.C.: The National Academies Press, 2004), p. S-1.

75. See the discussion in, ibid., p. S-3.

76. Quoted in, Michael Killian, "Debate Rages on Plan to Develop New Nukes," *Chicago Tribune Online Edition*, September 11, 2004, available at, http://story.news.yahoo.com/news?tmpl=stroy&u=/chitribts/debateragesonplantodevelopnewnukes. See also, the comments by Assistant Secretary of Defense J.D. Crouch, quoted in, Tom Squitieri, "Bush Pushes for Next Generation of Nukes," *USA Today*, July 7, 2003, p. 1; Medalia, *"Bunker Busters": Sources of Confusion in the Robust Nuclear Earth Penetrator Debate*, op. cit., p. 8; and, Bryan L. Fearey et al., "An Analysis of Reduced Collateral Damage Nuclear Weapons," *Comparative Strategy*, Vol. 22, No. 4 (October-November 2003), pp. 305-324.

77. See, Linton Brooks, "The Future of the Nuclear Enterprise," *Comparative Strategy*, Vol. 26, No. 4 (July-September 2007), pp. 365-370.

78. Senator Dianne Feinstein, quoted in, Carl Hulse, "House Retreats From Bush Nuclear Plan," *The New York Times*, July 15, 2003, p. A18. See also Jonathan Medalia, "Water Power: Why Congress Zeroed 'Bunker Buster' Appropriations," *Comparative Strategy*, Vol. 26, No. 3 (May-June 2007), p. 238.

79. "No More Nukes," *The Washington Post*, May 26, 2003, p. 28.

80. David Hobson, "Forward Thinking on Nuclear Policy," *The Washington Times*, January 10, 2005, p. 14.

81. Carl Kaysen, Robert McNamara, and George Rathjens, "Nuclear Weapons After the Cold War," *Foreign Affairs*, Vol. 70, No. 4 (Fall 1991), p. 109.

The Great American Gamble

82. Speed and May, op. cit., pp. 40, 43.

83. See, the testimony of General James Cartwright, Commander of the U.S. Strategic Command, in U.S. Senate, Committee on Armed Services, Subcommittee on Strategic Forces, *Global Strike Plans and Programs in Review of the Defense Authorization Request for Fiscal Year 2007*, March 29, 2006, text available through LexisNexis.

84. See, Hans Kristensen, "U.S. Strategic War Planning After 9/11," *Nonproliferation Review*, Vol. 14, No. 2 (July 2007), pp. 383-385.

85. Amy F. Wolf, *Conventional Warheads for Long-Range Ballistic Missiles: Background and Issues for Congress*, February 13, 2006, Congressional Research Service, Order Code RL33067, pp. 25-26. (Emphasis added). See also, Hans M. Kristensen, "The Role of U.S. Nuclear Weapons: New Doctrine Falls Short of Bush Pledge," *Arms Control Today*, Vol. 35, No. 7 (September 2005), p. 18.

86. Wolf, loc. cit.

87. See, for example, Kaysen, McNamara, and Rathjens, op. cit., p. 108; and, Levi, op. cit., p. 70.

88. As stated by the Commander in Chief of the U.S. Strategic Command, Gen. Eugene Habiger, in U.S. Senate, Committee on Armed Services, *Statement of General Eugene E. Habiger*, March 13, 1997, p. 4 (Prepared Text).

89. John Deutch, "A Nuclear Posture for Today," *Foreign Affairs*, Vol. 84, No. 1 (January/February, 2005), pp. 52-53.

90. Ibid.

91. Ibid., p. 52.

92. S. Drell and J. Goodby, *What Are Nuclear Weapons For?* (Washington, D.C.: Arms Control Association, April 2005), pp. 14-15, available at, www.armscontrol.org/pdf/USNW_2005_Drell-Goodby.pdf.

93. Steve Fetter, "Nuclear Strategy and Targeting Doctrine," in, *The Nuclear Turning Point*, Harold A. Feiveson, ed. (Washington, D.C.: The Brookings Institution Press, 1999), p. 57. (Emphasis added).

94. Panofsky, op. cit., p. 114.

95. Morton Halperin et al., "Parsing the Nuclear Posture Review," *Arms Control Today*, Vol. 32, No. 2 (March 2002), pp. 19-20. See also, Bruce G. Blair, "Trapped in the Nuclear Math," *The New York Times*, June 12, 2000, p. A29.

96. See, "Special Issue: Deterring Terrorism," *Comparative Strategy*, Vol. 26, No. 5 (2007), pp. 371-493.

97. George P. Shultz, William J. Perry, Henry A. Kissinger, and Sam Nunn, "A World Free of Nuclear Weapons," *The Wall Street Journal*, January 4, 2007, p. 15. See the similar statement by then Director of National Intelligence, John Negroponte in, U.S. Senate, Senate Select Committee on Intelligence, *Current and Projected National Security Threats to the United States*, Hearing, 109th Congress, 2nd Session (Washington, D.C.: USGPO, 2007), pp. 15-16.

98. President George W. Bush, Commencement Address at the U.S. Military Academy at West Point, May 27, 2006, available at, www.whitehouse.gov/news/releases/2006/05/20060527-1.html.

99. Paul Nitze, "Is It Time to Junk Our Nukes? The New World Disorder Makes Them Obsolete," *The Washington Post*, January 16, 1994, p. C1. (Emphasis added).

100. Gen. Andrew Goodpaster, former Supreme Allied Commander, Europe, and Gen. Lee Butler, former Commander in Chief, U.S. Strategic Command, *Joint Statement on Reduction of Nuclear Weapons Arsenals: Declining Utility, Continuing*

Risks, December 4, 1996, The Stimson Center: Eliminating Weapons of Mass Destruction, p. 1.

101. Gen. Lee Butler, National Press Club Speakers Series, *Generals Goodpaster and Butler*, December 4, 1996, Transcript, pp. 9-10.

102. Speed and May, op. cit., p. 44.

103. See, for example, Panofsky, op. cit., p. 109.

104. Quoted in, Martin Sieff, "U.S. Rejects German's Suggestion on Nukes," *The Washington Times*, November 24, 1998, p. A-13. See also, Charles Aldinger, "U.S. Rebuffs German Call on NATO Strategy," *Excite*, November 23, 1998, at nt.excite.com/news/r/981123/13/international-nato.

105. Quoted in, Colum Lynch, "U.S. Official Is Faulted for Nuclear Weapons Claim," *The Washington Post*, November 1, 2007, p. A17.

106. See, Martin L. Lasater, "A U.S. Perception of a PLA Invasion of Taiwan," in Peter Kien-hong Yu, ed., *The Chinese PLA's Perception of an Invasion of Taiwan* (New York: Contemporary U.S.-Asia Research Institute, 1996), p. 252. See also, Press Briefing by Deputy Press Secretaries Barry Toiv and David Leavy, August 13, 1999, Transcript released by the Office of the White House Press Secretary, http://www.pub.whitehouse.gov/urires/I2R?urn:pdi://oma.eop.gov.us/1999/13/8.text.1; and, Press Briefing by National Security Advisor Sandy Berger, National Economic Advisor Gene Sperling, and Press Secretary Joe Lockhart, Sky City Hotel, Auckland, New Zealand, September 11, 1999, Transcript released by the Office of the White House Press Secretary, http://www.pub.whitehouse.gov/urires/I2R?urn:pdi://oma.eop.gov.us/1999/9/12/7.text.1.

107. See, for example, Demetri Sevastopulo and Andrew Ward, "Clinton Backs 'Ambiguity' on Taiwan Policy," *Financial Times*, August 3, 2007, available at, http://www.ft.com/cms/s/fd5cc702-4153-11dc-8f37-0000779fd2ac.html.

108. William J. Perry, Madeleine Albright et al., *An American Security Policy: Challenge, Opportunity, Commitment*, National Security Advisory Group, July 2003, p. 19. (Emphasis added).

109. This passage is from the letter Secretary James Baker gave to Tariq Aziz during their meeting in Geneva just prior to the 1991 war. See, *Weekly Compilation of Presidential Documents*, Vol. 27, No. 3 (January 21, 1991), p. 44, available at http://bushlibrary.tamu.edu/research/papers/1991/9101/201.html.

110. Secretary of Defense Richard Cheney in, *Public Statements of Richard B. Cheney, Secretary of Defense*, 1990, Vol. IV (Washington, D.C.: Historical Office, Office of the Secretary of Defense, 1990), p. 2547.

111. The White House, *National Strategy for Combating Terrorism,* September 2006, p. 14.

112. "North Korea's Nuclear Threat/Reinforcing Alliance With U.S. Helps Bolster Nuclear Deterrence," *The Daily Yomiuri* (Internet version), March 23, 2007.

Chapter 7
End of the Line: "Rational" Opponents Are Predictably "Deterrable"

"Sometimes I've believed as many as six impossible things before breakfast."
-The Queen, *Alice's Adventures in Wonderland*

Confidence in the reliability of deterrence based on a presumed "rational" opponent and a mechanistic relationship between strategic forces and deterrent effect is predicated on very specific expectations about how and why opponents will make decisions and behave.[1] In a properly orchestrated balance of terror, opponents are expected consistently to choose to be prudent and cautious in the face of uncertainty and thus deterred from deliberate, severe attack; moreover, they are expected to expand their own offensive strategic capabilities, as necessary, to offset U.S. damage-limitation capabilities and thus to preserve their own retaliatory deterrence threat.

As Chapter 6 illustrates, these expectations about how opponents will make decisions and behave continue to inform contemporary recommendations regarding U.S. strategic policy and forces. As was the case during the Cold War, they backstop recommendations generally *against* the U.S. development and acquisition of strategic forces, particularly including damage-limitation capabilities.

Many who are confident in such expectations of how foreign leaders will make decisions and behave typically are unburdened by any apparent assessment of opponents' actual past or present behavior and decision making. The pertinent modes of behavior are presumed to be inevitable for any "rational" opponent. This presumption allows the avoidance of any serious examination of opponents or contexts because any "sane" opponent will think and behave as expected and, consequently, deterrent effect can be predicted with confidence.

McGeorge Bundy's description of how deterrence was expected to operate within the balance of terror reflects this confidence and presumption, and the resultant direct policy conclusion that deterrent effect can be orchestrated reliably, predictably and relatively easily:

The terrible and unavoidable uncertainties in any recourse to nuclear war create what could be called "existential deterrence," where the function of the adjective is to distinguish this phenomenon from anything based on strategic theories or declared policies or even international commitments.

...Now that both strategic arsenals are redundantly destructive and amply survivable, we can say with still more confidence that existential deterrence is strong, and that its strength is essentially independent of most changes in deployment. Because no one can predict how these arsenals might be used, because these uncertainties create an enormously powerful existential deterrent, and because this reality is essentially unaffected by any changes except those that might truly challenge the overall survivability of the forces on one side or the other, it makes no sense to base procurement decisions on refined calculations of the specific kinds of force that would be needed for a wide variety of limited nuclear responses.... But at current levels of survivable strength and accuracy, to maintain such options is relatively easy; to let the pursuit of special capacities to "kill hard targets" drive procurement is wrong.[2]

Thomas Schelling made the same presumption of "rational" modes of decision making and behavior in his elaboration of the balance of terror framework, but also recognized that this presumption could provide only a "caricature" of how opponents actually would think and act. He warned that this caricature might or might not be valid, and should *not* be used alone as the basis for actual policy guidance. Another preeminent scholar on deterrence theory and practice, Alexander George, voiced the same warning: "A critical problem with this strategy is that it rests on the assumption of pure rationality on the part of the opponent, and on his ability to recognize and act upon his self-interest. Of course, this assumption is inadequate—you must know the other side well enough to understand, in the particular case, the political, psychological, and cultural aspects of rationality."[3] George's point here is deeper than simply suggesting that opponents might be irrational; it is that their interpretation of *what is rational or sensible* could be affected significantly by their unique political, psychological and cultural makeup, and thus expectations of a universal rationality leading predictably to specified behaviors may be miscast.

This important caveat, however, is virtually nowhere to be found in past or contemporary assertions about "existential deterrence," or in the continuing use of balance of terror tenets to buttress specific conclusions about deterrence policy and related recommendations against the U.S. acquisition of forces. The functioning of deterrence supposedly is so integral to rational decision making that it swamps other factors; there is no need for caveats.

As Chapter 6 illustrated, balance of terror tenets continue to be applied mechanistically in contemporary debates to reach long-familiar conclusions and recommendations: U.S. counterforce capabilities and BMD are useless, unnecessary and "destabilizing"; uncertainty deters, so the ambiguity of U.S. commitments and threats "is good for deterrence"; and, *new* U.S. strategic programs will initiate an action-reaction cycle and prevent arms control progress, and thus must be avoided. It is all very familiar to those schooled in the Cold War debates.

Professor Waltz's logical extension of balance of terror tenets to the contemporary scene as discussed in Chapter 6 leads him and others to the logical conclusion that nuclear proliferation can expand the geographic scope and number of participants in "stable" balances of nuclear terror. Consequently, there is no overriding reason to seek to prevent nuclear proliferation or to acquire damage-limitation capabilities in response to it. As during the Cold War, the balance of terror tenets provide comforting, convenient, and relatively inexpensive answers to questions of deterrence and security.

What's the Matter With That?

There are many problems with the application of Cold War balance of terror tenets to contemporary security questions. First, there are internal contradictions in these tenets so severe that policy recommendations based on them must be suspect. Second, they are inconsistent with much of the actual historical evidence of how states behave. Third, they are demonstrably incompatible with the contemporary security environment vice that of the Cold War. And, fourth, they are built on wholly misplaced confidence in our ability to predict in detail how opponents will think and behave. Particularly unwarranted is the critical and convenient presumption at the heart of the tenets, i.e., given the proper orchestration of threats, a universal rationality leads inevitably to the predictable functioning of U.S. deterrence strategies.

There are numerous internal contradictions in the balance of terror tenets. This does not necessarily mean that each must be mistaken on every occasion. It does mean that some cannot now, and never could, be valid simultaneously. This is not a trivial conclusion; the balance of terror tenets that have been so important in U.S. assessments of deterrence and strategic force requirements tend to be employed together as a set to close off all argument—as is illustrated by past and contemporary assertions that damage limitation is simultaneously unnecessary, useless and destabilizing. In fact, it cannot logically be each of these simultaneously.

1. Internal Contradiction: The Opponent Is Both Prudent and Reckless; Deterrence Is Both Existential and Fragile; Damage Limitation Is Both Useless and Destabilizing.

Balance of terror-derived points of opposition to U.S. acquisition of offensive and defensive damage-limitation capabilities include:

- They are *useless and unnecessary* because U.S. deterrence will work predictably as uncertainty compels any rational opponent to prudence and caution; and,
- They "destabilize" deterrence by motivating opponents to strike first.

These two familiar balance of terror tenets typically are presented in tandem: damage-limitation capabilities not only provide no added value, but promise to upset the primary goal of deterrence stability. To apply them in this combined fashion, however, requires an internal contradiction: it requires an opponent who, on the same matter, avoids risks *and* willingly takes great risks. Some commentators continue to employ these two mutually contradictory balance of terror tenets in their opposition to U.S. defensive capabilities within virtually the same breath.[4]

Strategic defenses cannot be both "unnecessary" because the opponent is sure to be prudent and thus deterred reliably and predictably by secure U.S. retaliatory nuclear forces, and "destabilizing" because they will cause the opponent to risk everything by striking first recklessly against those secure U.S. retaliatory forces. Whether or not the United States complements its strategic retaliatory capabilities with damage-limiting measures, striking first against truly survivable U.S. forces would be the most significant step toward ensuring the very catastrophe that supposedly would reliably deter attack in the first place, i.e., the prospect of devastating U.S. nuclear retaliation.

If fear and uncertainty regarding the possibility of severe U.S. nuclear retaliation in fact deters rational opponents reliably, it is illogical to expect that the same opponents will deliberately provoke U.S. retaliation by striking first. The deterrent effect of uncertainty on the opponent's decision making cannot logically be both *so decisive* that deterrence is "existential" and damage limitation is without added value, and *so fragile* that the addition of damage-limiting capabilities to secure U.S. retaliatory capabilities will be "destabilizing" because the opponent will then embrace the great gamble of striking first. An opponent cannot be prudent and thus reliably "deterrable" and, simultaneously, highly imprudent and willing to strike first in a potentially suicidal roll of the dice. To assert that damage-limitation capabilities are both "unnecessary" because deterrence will work, and also "destabilizing" because deterrence is fragile, is to posit an opponent who simultaneously is deterred reliably by the fear of destruction and yet also is motivated to strike first *despite* the near certainty of destruction following such a strike.

Some opponents may be risk-averse in the face of uncertainty and thus reliably deterred; others may be willing or even eager risk-takers and consider striking first against the United States regardless of cost. If the United States deploys its retaliatory forces survivably, to the extent that we anticipate the prudent opponent who is deterred reliably by the *possibility* of severe U.S. retaliation, the familiar "instability" critique against U.S. counterforce and defensive capabilities cannot logically apply. To the extent that we anticipate an opponent who willingly accepts or even embraces great risk, we should *not* expect deterrence to perform reliably. In such cases, U.S. damage-limitation capabilities may be of great value depending on their potential levels of effectiveness.

If opponents are manifestly vulnerable to U.S. retaliatory threats, and *uncertainty* deters reliably as envisaged in the balance of terror formula, then the same "rational" opponent *cannot* be expected to be deterred reliably by the possibility of U.S. retaliation and, at the same time, be undeterred from provoking that retaliation by striking first. The addition of some U.S. strategic counterforce and/or defensive capabilities to secure

U.S. retaliatory forces logically would neither reduce the deterring fear of U.S. retaliation, nor provide an opponent with the incentive to launch a first strike against the United States. *If the logic of deterrence holds*, then the cautious, prudent opponent will choose *not* to strike for fear of the consequences because those consequences remain the same and striking first can only ensure their realization.

Schelling's proposition that U.S. damage-limiting forces could cause deterrence instability originally had a coherent logic specific to the Cold War context. Schelling posited that Soviet leaders might logically risk national destruction by striking first if motivated to do so by fear *and the possibility of securing a material strategic advantage*. His belief that the "reciprocal fear of a surprise attack" could "destabilize" deterrence stemmed from his proposition that one or both sides *could be tempted to strike first not simply to avoid striking second, but if doing so appeared to hold the potential to mitigate the damage they otherwise would suffer in a conflict*. His expressed concern in this regard was that the deployment of damage-limitation capabilities might introduce the material basis for one or both sides to anticipate the possibility of realizing a strategic advantage by striking first. It was on the strength of this proposition and concern that damage-limiting capabilities became typecast as "destabilizing."

Schelling's Cold War concern that damage-limiting capabilities might introduce "instability" into an otherwise stable balance of terror in these very specific conditions was coherent. In each case, it assumed a similarly prudent opponent: Striking first in the very narrow conditions specified by Schelling could be considered prudent because it could be thought to hold out the possibility of a *net* advantage. Schelling's coherent proposition, however, has since been recast and truncated by commentators into the adage that *any* U.S. strategic capability that might threaten an opponent's military forces is "destabilizing" because it will motivate the opponent to strike first. This "dumbing down" of Schelling's original point not only misses his original logic, but is implausible in the contemporary context in which regional foes and rogue states cannot logically hope to have strategic capabilities that inspire expectations of gaining a net material advantage by striking first against the United States. In the absence of this aspiration to secure such a strategic advantage, according to Schelling, there is no crisis instability because there is no "fundamental basis for an attack" and, "…the incentives to strike *at all* will be reduced."[5]

If the logic of deterrence actually functions as envisaged in balance of terror tenets, whether or not the United States has damage-limiting capabilities, an inescapable U.S. retaliatory threat precludes the possibility of "crisis instability" *vis-à-vis* contemporary opponents who do not have the strategic capability necessary to anticipate a possible first-strike net advantage. Neither China nor North Korea, nor prospectively Iran, for example, could plausibly anticipate that striking first against survivable U.S. retaliatory strategic capabilities could be a route to a strategic advantage over not striking. Chinese, North Korean, or Iranian leaderships deterred by lethal U.S. retaliatory capabilities and the risk of escalation cannot logically also be inspired by U.S. damage-limitation capabilities to strike first because the consequences for them of doing so would be comparably catastrophic, and striking first would be the likely guarantee that they would suffer those consequences.

Even during the Cold War, a Jekyll-to-Hyde change in Soviet decision making would have been required for U.S. damage-limitation capabilities to transform a Soviet leadership deterred reliably by uncertainty into a Soviet leadership that preferred the gamble of striking first in pursuit of a material net strategic advantage. Barely plausible in the context of the Soviet Union's strategic capabilities, this notion of deterrence "instability" being driven by U.S. damage-limitation capabilities is incoherent against contemporary foes.

When considering U.S. strategic requirements and acquisition policy for deterrence purposes it is important to understand that an opponent may characteristically be risk-averse, risk-tolerant, risk-insensitive, or somewhere in between. Risk tolerance may shift along this continuum over time and in different contexts, but contemporary commentary that confidently labels U.S. damage-limitation capabilities simultaneously unnecessary—because deterrence "works"—and "destabilizing" ought to be recognized as requiring an opponent that, correspondingly, is prudent and imprudent simultaneously.

2. Internal Contradiction: Certainty Miraculously Follows From Uncertainty.

During the Cold War, Schelling pointed to a series of potentially uncontrollable factors in decision making and behavior to buttress his point that uncertainty should deter: "Where does the uncertain element in the decision come from? It must come from somewhere outside of the threatener's control. Whether we call it 'chance,' accident, third-party influence, imperfection in the machinery of decision, or just processes that we do not entirely understand, it is an ingredient in the situation that neither we nor the party we threaten can entirely control."[6] It is the ineradicable possibility of an escalation process that can proceed beyond any deliberate control that is expected to compel prudence, caution and deterrence of all rational leaders. They are expected to be deterred from provoking an escalation process that could proceed beyond control and carry the risk of their own possible destruction. Commenting on this critical point, Schelling emphasized:

> ...the notion that some of the most momentous decisions of government are taken by a process that is not entirely predictable, not fully "under control," not altogether deliberate. It implies that a nation can get even into a major war somewhat inadvertently, by a decision process that might be called "imperfect" in the sense that the response to particular contingencies cannot exactly be foretold by any advance calculations, that the response to a particular contingency may depend on certain random or haphazard processes, or that there will be faulty information, faulty communication, misunderstanding, misuse of authority, panic, or human or mechanical failure....And it takes no cynic to recognize that two governments may misjudge each other's commitments...even an orderly government with responsible, comparatively cool-headed leaders is necessarily an imperfect decision system, especially in crises.[7]

Professor Richard Ned Lebow, a well-known academic who studies the nexus between history and deterrence theory, concludes that there are three general types of escalation "sequences" that lead to war in crises: pre-emption; loss of control; and miscalculated escalation.[8] According to Lebow, for example, two of those sequences—loss of control and miscalculation—were particularly apparent in the outbreak of World War I. These two types of sequences identified by Lebow encompass Schelling's list of factors that can drive an unintended escalation process beyond control and culminate in a nuclear war at least initially unwanted and unintended by any leader.

Confidence in the deterrent effect of an opponent's fear and uncertainty that the United States *might* behave in an uncontrolled, even irrational fashion, was the basis for Schelling's claim that an opponent's fear of *deliberate* U.S. escalation was unnecessary for extended deterrence. The reliable deterring effect of this uncertainty was Schelling's rejoinder to Kahn's contention that effective U.S. extended deterrence threats could follow *only* from Soviet expectation of a *deliberate* U.S. decision to escalate and, correspondingly, that the United States must have damage-limitation capabilities to provide that necessary credibility. To this centerpiece of Kahn's thinking Schelling replied:

> The credibility of a massive American response is often depreciated: even in the event of the threatened loss of Europe the United States would not, it is sometimes said, respond to the fait accompli of a Soviet attack on Europe with anything as "suicidal" as general war. But that is a simple-minded notion of what makes general war credible. What can make it exceedingly credible to the Russians— and perhaps to the Chinese in the Far East—is that the triggering of general war can occur whether we intend it or not.[9]

Schelling's innovative proposition that the opponent's fear of an out-of-control escalation process will deter reliably was key to the stable balance of terror desiderata for U.S. strategic acquisition and arms control policies. Deterrence could be made to work reliably via a balance of terror, and thus giving up U.S. damage-limitation capabilities in favor of a "stable" balance of terror was reasonable—defensive capabilities were unnecessary. The deterrent effect of uncertainty has become a truism that continues to be repeated as the basis for confidence that U.S. nuclear retaliatory threats will deter all rational state leaders. And—so the argument is repeated—because deterrence will work, the United States can eschew damage-limitation capabilities without regret and, according to Waltz, can even welcome nuclear proliferation.

The inherent uncertainties in an escalation process are expected to have this powerful, decisive effect on decision making and to ensure the functioning of deterrence. Ignored in this central tenet, however, is the fact that *the same uncertainties expected to deter must also render unpredictable* an opponent's decision-making process and behavior in response to U.S. deterrence threats. The problem with Schelling's innovative proposition that is so central to balance of terror tenets is that it *posits an unerring consistency of prudent leadership and decision making in response to the unavoidable uncertainties of leadership decision making.* The unavoidable uncertainties of decision making and behavior inexplicably fix themselves: in an intense, escalating crisis they somehow miraculously disappear, leaving only the opponent's consistent prudent behavior, and thus the reliable and predictable functioning of deterrence.

This proposition accepts the unavoidable reality of uncertainties in decision making and thus of an escalation process, yet simultaneously posits certainty with regard to how opponents will make decisions and behave in response to those uncertainties. In effect, crisis decision making is said to include an unavoidable degree of uncertainty and unpredictability, with the exception of how opponents will respond to our deterrence threats; here they are certain to be prudent, cautious and "deterrable." No explanation is offered or available as to why an opponent's decision making in response to U.S. deterrence threats should somehow uniquely be free of the inherent uncertainties and lack of predictability affecting all other leadership decision making.

The same irreducible imponderables of leadership decision making and behavior that Schelling highlights to emphasize why opponents *should* choose prudence and caution, and thus be deterred, *must instead render uncertain whether they will in fact do so.* Again, with balance of terror tenets, it is as if a miracle happens: the inherent uncertainties of crisis decision making and behavior inexplicably no longer apply and we can be confident that opponents reliably and consistently will choose to be deterred.

In sum, the basic balance of terror proposition that uncertainties abound in leadership decision making and behavior is sound. The very existence of these uncertainties, however, points *not toward a single consistent "rational" mode of opponent decision making—i.e., prudence and caution in the face of uncertainty and thus the reliable working of deterrence—but toward the potential for multiple, unpredictable decisions and behaviors,* including surprising decisions to provoke and run great risk. The irreducible uncertainties in decision making and leadership behavior do not ensure the predictable functioning of deterrence; they preclude it.

3. Internal Contradiction: Who "Rocks the Boat"?

A third internal contradiction in the balance of terror tenets is found in the critical proposition that U.S. threats can deter reliably in the absence of Kahn's desired strategic advantage because the United States can "rock the boat"—to use Schelling's apt metaphor—to fan the flames of an opponent's fear of the emerging potential for catastrophe. Partial steps of U.S. escalation supposedly can underscore and make persuasive for U.S. deterrence purposes the potential for catastrophe if the opponent does *not* initially choose to be cautious. Graduated U.S. escalation steps are expected to contribute to the deterring effect of the opponent's uncertainties regarding where the process of escalation might lead by helping to make the "threat that leaves something to chance" loom ever larger in the opponent's decision making.

As discussed in Chapter 5, the expected deterrence value of limited and flexible escalation steps was the expressed rationale behind important U.S. policy initiatives such as the 1974 "Schlesinger Doctrine" and NATO's Flexible Response doctrine. The deterrent effect of uncertainty, buttressed by graduated escalation options and "rocking the boat," was the route proposed by Schelling and accepted in U.S. policy as a way to extend deterrence in the absence of Kahn's preferred formula of U.S. strategic advantage and an imbalance of terror.

The internal contradiction in this "rocking the boat" mechanism for magnifying the expected deterring effect of uncertainty is in the wholly different effects that fear and uncertainty inexplicably are expected to have on U.S. leaders and opponents. The uncertainties regarding the outcome of an escalation process expected to deter opponents from provocation and escalation are *not*, for some reason, also expected to deter U.S. leaders from promoting an escalation process. Instead, rational U.S. leaders are expected to embrace escalation steps in order to frighten rational foreign leaders. Yet, there is no logical basis for positing that U.S. leaders would be undeterred from "rocking the boat"—an action that would unleash many uncertainties regarding the outcome of such a step—while opponents would reliably be deterred by the same uncertainties.

U.S. leaders may be in control of their initial escalation steps, but neither they nor their opponents would be in positive control of the escalation process thereafter. If the fear of uncertainty deters rational leaders, why logically should we expect U.S. leaders to be free from its effect? Why expect U.S. leaders to be at liberty to start an uncertain and possibly uncontrollable process of escalation by "rocking the boat," but simultaneously expect opponents to be deterred by the uncertainties of the process? Kahn's answer to this question was that the United States could be in such an advantageous position *if* the United States *was protected* from the unacceptable consequences of an escalation process; thus, he emphasized the value of damage-limitation capabilities. In contrast, the balance of terror tenets emphasize the U.S. deterrence strategy of graduated escalation measures while offering *no alternative, logical basis* for U.S. leaders to be at liberty to "rock the boat." This is not simply a matter of expecting U.S. leaders to be courageous; it is to posit that U.S. leaders somehow are free to undertake imprudent actions that others cannot take because their rationality prevents it.

In the absence of Kahn's recommended strategic advantage, on what basis can we expect U.S. leaders to be less susceptible to the fears expected to compel other rational leaders to be cautious and deterred? Are we to expect U.S. leaders to be more risk- and cost-tolerant than opponents? Should we believe that U.S. leaders will care *less* than opponents about the potential destruction that might follow from an out-of-control escalation process? Or, are we to assume that U.S. leaders will care so much *more* than their opponents about the stakes involved in a crisis that they will be willing to run *greater risks* and accept greater costs to secure their favored outcome? Any one of these conditions might pertain in very select circumstances, but there is no reason to assume *a priori* that U.S. leaders will have such perspectives in a contest of wills. Again, as if by a miracle, U.S. leaders are expected to be less susceptible than opponents to the fears expected to deter rational decision makers reliably and predictably.

Kahn's U.S strategic advantage via strategic defense may or may not be practicable and may or may not actually provide greater freedom of action for U.S. leaders. But, at least Kahn identifies a coherent reason *why* U.S. leaders could be expected to prevail in an escalating contest of wills. The balance of terror tenets provide no basis for such a belief—other than the self-serving presumption that all opponents of the United States will be more cautious and less willing to tolerate "boat rocking" than their U.S. counterparts. In fact, in the absence of some form of strategic advantage, U.S. leaders should be expected to be at least as cautious of "boat rocking" as are their opponents, and may often be more so.

Some have suggested that the feigning of irrationality could help fill this logical gap—that *by deliberately striking a pose of irrationality* the U.S. leadership could put the opponent in the disadvantageous position of being the *more afraid of an escalation* process: an apparently irrational United States would, by definition, pose an unpredictable, uncontrolled threat.[10] In the past, some U.S. leaders appear to have pursued this approach to deterrence, as is illustrated in Chapter 4 by Secretary of State Dean Rusk's recounting of his encounter with Soviet Premier Nikita Khrushchev on the subject of U.S. extended deterrence credibility.

President Nixon explained to aide H.R. Haldeman that he wanted the image of a "madman" for deterrence and coercion purposes: "I call it the Madman Theory....I want the North Vietnamese to believe I've reached the point where I might do anything to stop the war. We'll just slip the word to them that, 'for God's sake, you know Nixon is obsessed about communism. We can't restrain him when he's angry—and he has his hand on the nuclear button'—and Ho Chi Minh himself will be in Paris in two days begging for peace."[11]

A strategy of feigned irrationality may have some value. It cannot, however, fill the logical gap of expecting without reason U.S. leaders to provoke escalation by "rocking the boat" while also expecting opponents to stand back for fear of escalation. Striking a pose of "irrationality" may fan an opponent's fears, but *it cannot provide a U.S. leadership with any greater confidence that the escalation process it unleashes by "rocking the boat" would proceed to an acceptable conclusion.* U.S. leaders posing as "madmen" would know that they are posing. In the absence of a logical basis for actual confidence, there is no reason to expect that the U.S. leadership would be more willing to risk escalation than its opponent. Indeed, an opponent might not respond benignly to U.S. escalation steps and apparent irrationality; that combination could instead lead an opponent to a more provocative course of action than otherwise would be the case in the belief that *conciliation* would provide no predictable relief from an irrational U.S. leadership.

With regard to the hostile and potentially hostile states of the twenty-first century, are we to assume in future possible crises with regional powers such as China, North Korea, Iran or Syria that U.S. leaders will be more risk- and cost-tolerant than opponents, care less about the potential destruction that might follow from an escalation process, or be more willing to run great risk and accept great cost to secure favored U.S. outcomes? It is far from self-evident that any of these conditions will apply reliably, and assuming it to be so hardly constitutes a reasonable basis for U.S. deterrence strategy and strategic force requirements.

Indeed, a U.S. problem for the twenty-first century is that, on occasion, opponents will be the more cost-tolerant, willing gamblers or will care more about the outcome of a crisis. They will be more capable of "rocking the boat" to deter Washington if they choose than vice versa. During the Cold War, senior U.S. official Fred Iklé observed that opponents armed with nuclear weapons and "schooled in the uses of terror" could be much more capable of appearing menacing and reckless than U.S. leaders. Such an opponent "could lay iron hands on the deepest emotions and fears of a great many people in the West. He could make them believe that the horrors of nuclear destruction were about to become real."[12] Iklé's concern here, of course, was that leaders "schooled in the uses of terror" and armed with nuclear weapons could have this coercive leverage over the United States rather than vice versa.

U.S. post-Cold War relations with North Korea illustrate the advantage just such an opponent may have to "rock the boat" and thereby put intolerable pressure on the United States, even if that opponent is armed with few or no nuclear weapons. Former Secretary of Defense William Perry and former Assistant Secretary of Defense Ashton Carter have described the 1994 confrontation with North Korea over its nuclear weapons program, noting that the United States came to the brink of war to stop North Korea from acquiring nuclear weapons.

According to then Secretary Perry and Assistant Secretary Carter, the "likely result" of a U.S. "surgical strike" against North Korea would be "a spasmodic lashing out" by North Korea, including the possibility that North Korea's 11,000 long-range artillery pieces "could rain destruction on the South Korean capital of Seoul, only 40 miles away."[13] At the time, North Korean leader Kim Il Sung threatened to turn "Seoul into a sea of flames"[14] and General Gary Luck, Commander in Chief of U.S. Forces in Korea, reported that a conventional war on the Korean Peninsula would cause at least a million fatalities—including 80,000-100,000 U.S. soldiers—and cost up to $1 trillion. General Luck described that scenario in stark terms: "Bottom line: Unbelievable hardships would occur."[15]

This combination of factors understandably affected the U.S. willingness to "rock the boat" in a way that might precipitate war. According to Secretary Perry and Assistant Secretary Carter, while they were willing to risk war at the time, "Since we fully understood the dangers of a war with North Korea, we proceeded in a manner that would avoid that war, if possible."[16] One summary account of the crisis described the effect of Kim Il Sung's manipulation of threats: "[Secretary] Perry concluded that he had to take the wild threats of total war issued regularly by North Korea's press agency at face value. Perry understandably decided that without confidence about what Kim might be willing to risk in conflict with the United States, it would be unwise to view his threats as mere bluff."[17] Kim Il Sung may have "rocked the boat" and affected U.S. options and behavior in the crisis.

There was little doubt at the time that the United States had the strategic nuclear capability to threaten nuclear assured destruction on North Korea, and that North Korea did not have a comparable capability against the United States. Nevertheless, the threat that North Korean leader Kim Il Sung highlighted for U.S. leaders was that of a bloody conventional war that would inflict heavy costs on the United States and an even greater cost on America's ally, South Korea.

In this case from 1994, we have an apparent example of the *possibility* of escalation having had at least some deterring effect. The problem for the United States in this example, of course, is that it appears that Kim Il Sung may have manipulated risk to his advantage against the preeminent nuclear superpower. A North Korean expatriate who writes on military matters and is known as "the unofficial spokesman for North Korea," summarizes this point by observing that, "this military giant [United States] is afraid of fighting [a] war with the tiny poor country that has not a single nuclear capable warship."[18]

"Rocking the boat" may be a useful tactic for enhancing the credibility of threats, as envisaged by Schelling. The United States, however, cannot count on the benign outcome of an escalation process it initiates any more than can an opponent, and that outcome may be as intolerable for the United States as it is for the opponent, or more so. Again, it is convenient to believe that the United States can take steps that other rational leaders must be deterred from undertaking; opponents, however, are not always so accommodating.

Without some powerful factor affecting U.S. or enemy decision making that is external to the balance of terror formula, there is no logical reason to expect U.S. leaders to take graduated escalation steps because they should be as susceptible as opponents to the caution inspired by uncertainty and "boat rocking." On occasion they may be more so, as was suggested by Fred Iklé in 1985, and seemingly illustrated by actual events in 1994.

Internal Contradictions:
Necessary for Comforting Conclusions

Ignoring the internal contradictions of Cold War balance of terror tenets permits the comforting conclusion that opponents will be deterred by U.S. nuclear retaliatory threats reliably and predictably in the absence of Kahn's strategic advantage: all rational opponents will be deterred predictably as we desire because the uncertainties of escalation will compel them to be prudent and cautious. Happily we do not need to do much to ensure this deterrent effect beyond posing lethal retaliatory threats and avoiding defenses. And, we can buttress this deterring effect of uncertainty by pursuing limited escalation steps as necessary—compelling sane opponents to stand back for fear of an uncontrolled escalation process.

The balance of terror path to these comforting and convenient conclusions requires overlooking or dismissing the internal contradictions described above. Indeed, the motto underlying these balance of terror tenets should be "Expect a Miracle." It simply is illogical to claim that an opponent's behavior will simultaneously be risk-averse and risk-tolerant; that the inherent uncertainties of decision making and behavior can reliably and predictably beget prudent reactions to our threats; and that, in the absence of some intervening factor, the escalation potential of U.S. "boat rocking" will predictably be feared *more* by opponents than it is by U.S. leaders. Balance of terror tenets offer no basis for accepting these incoherent propositions other than the vapid tautology that only irrational *opponents would not respond to our deterrence threats rationally, i.e., as prudently and cautiously as fits our need.*

Commentators continue to voice the balance of terror tenets that U.S. damage-limitation capabilities are unnecessary because deterrence can be orchestrated to work reliably, and that they are "destabilizing" because they could tempt an opponent to strike first and upset deterrence stability. These long-familiar balance of terror dictums dismiss the potential value of damage-limitation capabilities in principle without providing any logical basis for believing that deterrence can be made to work as described and as necessary to justify the dismissal. Indeed, by eschewing damage-limitation capabilities balance of terror tenets stand against the one factor Kahn insists would give U.S. leaders the strategic advantage necessary to prevail in a contest of wills.

Does Not History Prove That the Combination of Uncertainty and Severe Retaliatory Threats Deters Rational Opponents Reliably?

Even given the incoherence in the balance of terror formula described above, a frequent, understandable rhetorical question is: Doesn't the fact that the Cold War did not end in nuclear holocaust "prove" that deterrence works as advertised, and that the balance of terror tenets provide continuing useful guidance? The answer to this oft-repeated question is "no."

The peculiar context of the Cold War may have been optimal for expecting deterrent effect from a "threat that leaves something to chance," largely because Cold War conditions did make any acute crisis in Western Europe extremely dangerous and the potential for disastrous escalation tangible regardless of initial intentions:

- Each side paid close attention to the other, and each was relatively familiar with the other.
- Those in leadership positions were known, and channels of mutual communication existed.
- Each side had easily identified physical targets that could be held at risk for deterrence purposes.
- The acts to be deterred and the culpable parties were considered easily identifiable.
- The European boundary between the two blocs was well-defined and was the world's most highly militarized zone, increasing the probability that any sizable, violent conflict would escalate.
- The stakes of any actual war were very high for each side, reducing the prospects that either could conciliate following the outbreak of war and thus highlighting for both the need to avoid war altogether.
- Both sides deployed nuclear weapons locally in the region, adding the potential for local escalation to turn nuclear in any violent conflict.
- Neither superpowers' strategic culture licensed cavalier gambling in the face of threats to survival.
- Neither saw war with the other as an internally- or externally-driven imperative.

- After Stalin's death neither side's decision making was likely to follow unchecked the possibly eccentric thinking of an individual.

Even these optimal conditions, however, could not render the fear of escalation and uncertainty a wholly reliable basis for confidence in the deterrence of high-risk provocations. In 1962, for example, at a time of significant U.S. strategic nuclear advantage, Soviet Premier Nikita Khrushchev was undeterred by the uncertainties associated with pursuing the highly risky step of moving nuclear missiles to Cuba. This reckless Soviet move against a far superior nuclear power set in motion an escalation process that included dangerous misperceptions, misinformation, and missteps in decision making and behavior. Then Secretary McNamara has since observed that the Cuban Missile Crisis, "...was a dramatic demonstration of fallibility—of the degree to which all parties were captives of misinformation, misjudgment and miscalculation."[19] His conclusion is that the world came "within a hair breath of nuclear war," and that we avoided nuclear war in this crisis because: "We lucked out."[20]

Little more than a decade later, Soviet leader Leonid Brezhnev was undeterred by the uncertainties involved in pursuing a high-risk course in the volatile Middle East prior to and during the 1973 Yom Kippur War. Soviet actions included support for the Arab states' preparation for war and a direct confrontation with the United States during the war—including a blunt Soviet "ultimatum" to President Nixon threatening direct Soviet military intervention. The United States responded by putting its forces worldwide on a high level of readiness, and putting pressure on Israel to desist in its combat operations.[21]

The point here is *not* to suggest that Khrushchev or Brezhnev was unconcerned about the prospect for nuclear war with the United States. Rather, it is that Khrushchev was undeterred by the great uncertainties involved in orchestrating a high-risk gambit that escalated into a dangerous nuclear confrontation; he had a higher priority than avoiding the risk of that gambit. Brezhnev, in turn, was undeterred by the uncertainties and risks involved in helping to unleash a regional war in an explosive region and then crudely transforming that war into an escalating confrontation with the United States. He had a higher priority than avoiding such risks. Soviet leaders could not predict the outcome of the crises they were willing to foment; they were, nonetheless, undeterred from doing so by the uncertainties.

Whether by "luck" or design, superpower nuclear war obviously did not occur in 1962 or 1973. The material point for this discussion, however, is not that nuclear war was avoided; it is that the uncertainties of escalation did *not* deter Soviet leaders from choosing the high-risk path of brinkmanship and escalation that could have culminated in nuclear war. The logic of the balance of terror rests on the proposition that, in the face of survivable nuclear retaliatory capabilities, opponents will be deterred from willingly provoking a high-risk escalation process in recognition of the fact that numerous decision-making and behavioral factors are inherently beyond their control and could drive that process to a nuclear culmination point and their own annihilation. This key balance of terror tenet, however, does not comport well with a "real-world" case in which, according to Secretary McNamara, escalation to nuclear war was avoided by luck.

Some might protest that the 1962 and 1973 cases described above involved leaders who made mistakes and had poor judgment, but did not consciously take great risks; thus, in that sense deterrence did not fail. Perhaps Khrushchev did not recognize in advance the possibility that moving nuclear weapons to Cuba was a risky gambit.[22] Perhaps Brezhnev did not anticipate that a sharp Soviet military ultimatum to Nixon could provoke further escalation. This interpretation of Soviet behavior seems far-fetched in both cases, particularly with regard to the Cuban Missile Crisis. At the time Khrushchev said, "Why not throw a hedgehog at Uncle Sam's pants?" and, "They can attack us and we shall respond. This may end in a big war."[23]

Even the interpretation that Soviet leaders unwittingly initiated escalation processes, however, does not provide coherence to the balance of terror's confidence in the predictable functioning of deterrence. With this interpretation, Soviet leaders *unwittingly* set in motion an escalating crisis that could have been driven to a horrific conclusion by factors beyond deliberate human control. To acknowledge that leaders *knowingly* can initiate an uncontrollable escalation process that could end in their nuclear destruction destroys the veracity of balance of terror tenets; to acknowledge that leaders *can take those steps unwittingly* hardly validates the expectation that deterrence will function reliably and predictably.

The conclusion that leaders can stumble into high-risk decision making certainly appears to be accurate on occasion, and deterrence can be fragile as a consequence. As Professor Robert O'Neill has observed: "Many of those who initiate wars either do not understand what they are doing or fail to realize the size of the gamble they are taking."[24] It appears, for example, that Argentina's decision to invade and occupy the British Falkland Islands in 1982 was made with little expectation that British Prime Minister Margaret Thatcher would respond forcefully, including deployment into the region of British forces with nuclear weapons aboard.[25] The head of Argentina's junta leadership at the time, General Leopoldo Galtieri, said after the war: "Though an English reaction was considered a possibility, we did not see it as a probability. Personally, I judged it scarcely possible and totally improbable."[26]

There are numerous earlier historical examples of leaderships *deliberately* lighting or embracing the powder keg of escalation despite recognition that their own futures were at great risk. Apparently rational leaders who act imprudently in this sense effectively demonstrate the error embedded in the balance of terror tenets. In these cases, leaders have had no way of knowing that the crisis would *not* escalate beyond prudent control and yet were undeterred from igniting or abetting them. Russia's decision to enter World War I in 1914 was deliberate, for example, but was taken in desperation with little or no optimism about the likely outcome.

Similarly, British historian Sir Michael Howard has characterized German decision making in 1914 as involving a level of gambling that looks "very much like madness."[27] Historian Holger Herwig quotes the Prussian War Minister General Erich von Falkenhayn as observing on August 4, 1914 that, "even if we go under as a result of this, still it was beautiful." Professor Herwig goes on to observe, "These almost surrealistic words, uttered by the Prussian war minister in the wake of the July Crisis, in many ways encapsulate the mood that prevailed among Germany's political and military elite as July yielded to August 1914."[28]

In March 1936, Adolf Hitler ordered the German remilitarization of the Rhineland despite full recognition of the high risk and strong opposition from within his own military. Hitler later acknowledged that, "a retreat on our part would have spelled collapse… The forty-eight hours after the march into the Rhineland were the most nerve-wracking of my life. If the French had then marched into the Rhineland we would have had to withdraw with our tails between our legs…."[29]

The Japanese attack on Pearl Harbor in 1941 similarly was seen by senior Japanese leaders as a prospectively fatal roll of the dice undertaken deliberately but with great trepidation. Japanese leaders were aware of the massive U.S. potential for war, even a war on two fronts, but believed that the great risks involved in the attack on Pearl Harbor were necessary to address what General Hideki Tojo described as the immediate "crisis for self-existence."[30] Prominent World War II historian, Louis Morton, concludes his examination of Japanese decision making with the following:

> In the final analysis, the Japanese decision for war was the result of the conviction, supported by the economic measures imposed by the United States and America's policy in China, that the United States was determined to reduce Japan to a position of secondary importance. The nation, Tojo and his supporters felt, was doomed if it did not meet the challenge. In their view, Japan had no alternative but to go to war while she had the power to do so. She might lose, but defeat was better than humiliation and submission. "Japan entered the war," wrote a prince of the Imperial family, "with a tragic determination and in desperate self-abandonment." If it lost, "there will be nothing to regret because she is doomed to collapse even without war."[31]

The belated British declaration of war following the German invasion of Poland in 1939 also was done deliberately, but with the expectation of great cost. Indeed, the British declared war despite the fear that the, "...bombing of London and the great cities would lead to casualties on the order of hundreds of thousands or even millions within a few weeks. We thought of air warfare in 1939 rather as people think of nuclear warfare today."[32]

In these cases there were plausible reasons for the willingness of leaders to take the path to a prospectively catastrophic war despite recognition of the grave uncertainties and fears. The involved leaderships often believed that the value to be protected or gained could not be compromised and that any tolerable alternative course of action also involved great risk—even survival risks; nevertheless, a "least miserable" course had to be chosen. Prudence born of the fear of escalation has been overshadowed frequently by such considerations. Leaders under great pressure deliberately and rationally can choose paths that involve potentially fatal risks—not always because they want to, but because they believe they have no tolerable alternatives.

This brief historical excursion demonstrates that *fear of escalation, including the possibility of nuclear escalation, has been insufficient* to deter apparently rational leaders from initiating significant provocations and running the risk of catastrophe. These unarguable points have direct implications for the integrity of the balance of terror tenets and for the familiar assertion that the propositions about deterrence embedded in those tenets are justified by the absence of a strategic nuclear war throughout the Cold War. The centerpiece of those tenets—that uncertainty and fear of escalation will deter reliably—is in demonstrable error.

The balance of terror tenets themselves do not permit the pertinent measure of deterrence "success" to be the absence of the employment of nuclear weapons since 1945. For confidence that deterrence will prevent nuclear attack reliably and predictably opponents must be deterred from igniting an escalation process that could *be driven to a nuclear culmination point by those same uncontrollable factors that are presumed to compel uncertainty and fear of escalation.* Given the potential for a crisis to escalate beyond the control of either side and to the employment of nuclear weapons, the prevention of escalation processes with that potential must be included in any definition of deterrence success per the balance of terror tenets. By this necessary standard, the balance of terror tenets are indeed invalidated by historical evidence; there have been numerous crises before and since 1945 that either escalated beyond deliberate control or could have done so. History affords *no* confidence that deterrence can "work" reliably in the sense demanded by the balance of terror formula.

As quoted above, McGeorge Bundy believed that in a "stable" balance of terror any choice but prudence and caution would be "unthinkable." This is the heart of confidence in nuclear deterrence per that formula. Bundy's belief, however, tells us much more about his worldview and the worldview implicit in the balance of terror tenets than about any universally-shared modes of rationality and behavior. Bundy was decisively impressed by the understandable fear of an escalation process that could lead to one or more nuclear strikes on cities. His definition of rationality and what is "thinkable," however, tells us nothing certain about how opponents will think and behave.

As mentioned above, Bundy's implicit tautology is that all rational opponents will be deterred by severe retaliatory nuclear threats to cities because only irrational opponents would *not* be deterred by those threats. Subsumed in this definition of what is "rational" and "thinkable" is an expected set of values, risk tolerance, norms, calculations, judgments and decision making; it assumes that above all other possible goals and motivation, "rational" leaders must always place highest value on avoiding, or at least minimizing, the risk of an escalation process that could end in the destruction of their cities and economic infrastructure. This comforting deterrence tautology and the definition of rationality ignore the demonstrable variation in human reasoning and judgment, as well as variation in the range of possible "rational" interpretations of—and responses to— threats, risk, stress and uncertainty. It falsely claims ownership of the definition of "rational." Unfortunately, what was deemed "unthinkable" by Bundy may be "thinkable" or even welcomed by other leaders also capable of rational decision making.

As discussed in Chapter 6, academic commentators opine that questioning the reliability of deterrence in this way constitutes "impugning the rationality of U.S. adversaries"[33]—as if opponents behaving unpredictably in the face of our nuclear deterrent is possible only if those opponents are ignorant or irrational: "In a nuclear world, to act in blatantly offensive ways is madness. Under the circumstances, how many generals would obey the commands of a madman?"[34] And, "Of all the possible external forces, what could affect state behavior more strongly than nuclear weapons? Who cares about the 'cognitive' abilities of leaders when nobody but an idiot can fail to comprehend their destructive force?"[35]

Yet, the prospect for unexpected and even shocking decision making and behavior cannot be precluded by an opponent's rationality or intellect. A truly irrational opponent could indeed respond in shocking, unpredictable ways. Prudence, caution and conciliation in the face of even very severe retaliatory threats and uncertainty, however, cannot be deemed the *only* possible course of action by a rational decision maker and, thus, inevitable for all such opponents. Expecting prudent, cautious behavior to be inevitable from all rational opponents—and elevating that expectation to the logical lodestone of U.S. deterrence strategy—reflects an ethnocentric definition of what constitutes "rational," misplaced certainty in the predictability of opponents and, thus, misplaced confidence in the reliability and predictability of deterrent effect.

The Importance of Cognition, Personality, Perceptions, Goals and Culture

Perceptions of risk, expectations of cost, risk tolerances, and responses to stress, uncertainty and risk can vary widely among different leaderships in different circumstances without any psychopathology or "idiocy." The operative definition of "rational" can be shaped by the priorities and perceptions of the decision maker, which in turn can be shaped by: the unique characteristics of personality, perspective, attention and culture; the particular set of available alternatives perceived at the time; the stakes at risk; and, the decision maker's emotions, health and age.[36] How else might one explain that 90 percent of coronary patients reportedly do not switch to a healthier lifestyle even following bypass grafting; that 25 million Americans still use tobacco and over 1 million new smokers join their ranks annually; that 15 percent of adult American drivers report driving under the influence of alcohol during the course of a year; and, that more than half of young drivers knowingly engage in extremely high-risk behaviors while driving?[37] The definition of "rational" decision making and behavior must include approaches to the calculation of risk and benefit that seem preposterous to a prudent outside observer.

In addition, recent cognitive studies suggest what parents and the automobile insurance industry have long understood: That portion of the brain which governs judgment, sets priorities, and controls impulses does not fully mature until age 25 or so. As one commentator observes: "Allstate [a major U.S. insurance company] says, we now know through science… that the brains of teenagers are not physically wired to make good decisions. They are wired in many ways to take risks."[38] There also may be a genetic disposition to engage in risky behavior.[39] Even when the brain matures, decision making often cannot be explained or anticipated by a universally-applicable definition of what constitutes informed, "rational" decision making because values and perceptions can be driven by unique factors of personality, culture and context.

Cognitive studies reveal, moreover, that the brain functions in ways that can work against the well-informed, universal "rationality" presumed in the balance of terror tenets. For example, people of all ages "misremember" factual information at a significant rate immediately after its presentation, and the rate of error increases rapidly. This may help explain why forensic scientists find eyewitness accounts of events so faulty. In addition, "myths" can be established as accepted truths by repetition, *independent of the authority of their sources*. Once established, they are extraordinarily difficult to dislodge—particularly among those who want to believe them— and they serve as rules of thumb that bias the brain's interpretation of new information.[40] The point here is that leaders acting on "myths" and biased information about an opponent can easily make profound mistakes that affect the functioning of deterrence in ways that may appear "irrational," but can be attributed to unexceptional cognitive processes. It may be hoped that good staff work and governmental checks and balances in decision making always will protect against behavior that follows from myths and biases, but that hope frequently clashes with reality.

As Professor Brad Thayer has observed, recent developments in the understanding of cognition do *not* support the basic proposition of a universal rationality leading inevitably to prudent behavior by decision makers confronting severe deterrence threats:

> As a result of advances in evolutionary psychology, we now know that the human mind is heavily influenced by the environment and body. How the brain interprets actions and makes decisions is complicated, imperfect, greatly depends upon emotions, and varies among humans. There is tremendous variation in the human brain, with the result that threats that work in most circumstances will not work in all and that the appreciation of consequences, upon which rational deterrence theorists depend, cannot be assumed.
>
> Accordingly, it is fundamentally naïve and dangerous to assume a similar outcome (e.g., that nuclear deterrence will obtain) in all situations when there is variation in people (e.g., leaders), even when the consequences are great, as it is when nuclear weapons are involved. This finding has enormous implications for nuclear deterrence theory: The rational deterrence model's assumption of a universal rationality in the face of a nuclear deterrent threat is irredeemably flawed.[41]

In addition, emotions play a significant role in all "rational" decision making, and a person's emotional reaction to a given set of conditions is extremely difficult to predict even by that person. More challenging still is the prediction of how emotions will affect the decision making of unfamiliar foreign leaderships in future stressful conditions.[42]

The reliable transmission of information within or between governments necessary for the predictable functioning of deterrence also may be distorted by the effect of emotions—not because leaders are irrational, but because the human brain has been "wired" to avoid negative stimulation. As an unclassified Department of Defense study entitled,

Recent Findings in the Biosciences, concludes:

> What gets called 'emotion' is, in effect, the experience of the neurophysiologic condition of the brain. Dozens of neurotransmitters—and new ones are being discovered all the time—wash the brain in response to social stimuli.... the neurophysiology of negative stimulation can be so unpleasant that people will avoid interacting with people who produce such stimuli, even though it may be essential to their job for them to have such interaction. The consequences of this for restricting or withholding negative but vital information may obviously be very serious.[43]

Deterrence cannot be expected to function reliably and predictably as the inevitable result of rationality when leaders naturally seek to avoid unwanted news and the individuals who bring it; accordingly, individuals with the responsibility to inform their leaderships may be loath to bring them unwanted news. This type of leadership aversion to unwanted "bad" news and the desire of staffs to avoid bringing unwanted news is not simply theoretical; it can be seen in the behavior of the Kaiser and the Tsar and their respective courts in August 1914, in Joseph Stalin's response to the German invasion in 1941 and, more recently, in Saddam Hussein's behavior in 1991 and 2003.

The balance of terror cannot work *predictably* as envisaged in the context of a leadership misinformed by silence or a web of lies. A credible description of Saddam Hussein's modus operandi in this regard, and its effect on those expected to keep him informed, illustrates this point well:

> As time passed, Saddam developed a reputation of punishing the bearers of bad news. Not surprisingly, lying became endemic throughout the Iraqi government and the military. In time, rumors began circulating among senior officials that summary execution awaited anyone contradicting the dictator. Officers were aware of the story of the brigadier general who spent over a year in prison for daring to suggest that American tanks might be superior to those of the Iraqi army. Unable or unwilling to risk speaking the truth, most of those around Saddam fed him a regular diet of lies and half truths.[44]

We can believe the logic of the balance of terror tenets and posit that all rational leaders will indeed prudently follow their best interest as we think they should, and thus be deterred by our nuclear retaliatory threats. We can hope that our belief will be sustained by actual leadership behavior. But rational decision makers can and do choose high-risk behaviors that appear contrary to external "rational" judgments about their best interest, even when there seems to be only one "rational" choice.   It was in recognition of this absence of an inevitable, universally-rational mode of behavior in response to deterrence threats that the American Group for the Advancement of Psychiatry observed early in the Cold War: "It rests on certain dubious psychological assumptions."[45]

Schelling acknowledges that the assumption of a "rational" opponent as defined is an inadequate "approximation to reality" and may not, in fact, provide a useful basis for anticipating an opponent's actual behavior in response to a deterrent threat.   Rather, he suggests that the value in the assumption is that it may establish a "bench mark" in understanding how opponents may respond—excursions from which may then be explored.[46] The balance of terror tenets, however, narrow the definition of that "rational bench mark" to opponents' prudence and caution in the face of our severe nuclear retaliatory threat when, in fact, rational calculations understood properly and more broadly may lead some opponents to behavior that is not captured by that self-serving and comforting definition.

The manifest variation in the decision making and behavior separating Britain's Neville Chamberlain and Germany's Adolf Hitler illustrates this point. They were contemporaries and capable of rational decisions, but with very different perceptions of risk and risk-taking propensities. Chamberlain was the architect of Britain's policy of appeasing Germany; Hitler, on the other hand, disdained caution, willingly acted against prudent advice in the face of uncertainty, and embraced risks that deterred others. Bernd Freytag von Loringhoven, a young military aide to General Heinz Guderian, was an eyewitness to Hitler's decision making: "The Fuhrer would accept advice from nobody, [and was] convinced he was infallible, both in political and military matters....The destiny of Germany only interested him insofar as he confused it with his own.... the German people were simply a means to an end."[47]

Hitler reveled in his willingness to charge forward where no one else would dare go: "As the political leader, however, who wants to make history, I must decide upon one way, even if sober consideration a thousand times tells me that it entails certain dangers and that it will not lead to a completely satisfying end."[48] And: "Neither threats nor warnings will prevent me from going my way. I follow the path assigned to me by Providence with the instinctive sureness of a sleepwalker."[49] Hitler once confided after tasting bitter military setbacks in the Soviet Union that he "had no idea" of the strength of the Soviet military power arrayed against him, but that had he known of that strength earlier, "I would have taken the decision to invade anyhow...."[50] Schelling's "threat that leaves something to chance," the key to the logical integrity of the balance of terror tenets, is unlikely to elicit a similarly prudent, cautious response predictably from leaders as different as Neville Chamberlain and Adolf Hitler.

Professor Waltz repeats the notion that prudent behavior is the rational response to retaliatory nuclear threats and thus defends his expectation of the predictable functioning of deterrence with the assertion and rhetorical question quoted above. Reflecting Schelling's theoretical framework, Waltz asks: "In a nuclear world, to act in blatantly offensive ways is madness. Under the circumstances, how many generals would obey the commands of a madman?" The conclusion Waltz reaches is at the heart of the balance of terror framework and the minimal force requirements it establishes for deterrence: "A low probability of carrying a highly destructive attack home is sufficient for deterrence. A force of an imprecisely specifiable minimum capacity is nevertheless needed."[51] Yet, the "blatantly offensive" behavior Waltz dismisses as "madness"— and thus impossible for rational leaders—occasionally has been the reality, and generals *have dutifully obeyed.* Unfortunately, the destructive retaliatory potential of nuclear weapons clearly does *not* preclude the possibility of opponents acting in "blatantly offensive ways."

Another vivid historical illustration of the significance of differing leadership characteristics in this regard is captured by the exchange between Cuban and Soviet leaders during the 1962 Cuban Missile Crisis. We now know what we did not even suspect at the time: Fidel Castro and Che Guevara encouraged the Soviet leadership to launch a nuclear attack against the United States, using the Soviet missiles stationed in Cuba. Castro and Guevara demanded that the Soviets use their nuclear weapons—with a willingness to accept Cuban national martyrdom as the price of destroying capitalism.[52] Soviet Vice Premier Mikoyan's response to these Cuban demands illustrates the significance for deterrence of the possible differences in rational leadership decision making. Mikoyan said, "We see your willingness to die beautifully, but we do not believe it is worth dying beautifully."[53] The deterrence calculations of the Soviet leadership were very different from those of an imprudent, incautious Cuban leadership. Both apparently were rational, but the Soviet and Cuban leaderships had different priorities, and only the former appears to have been deterrable on that occasion. The depth of Castro's willingness to run great risks may be illustrated further by his reported subsequent request to the Soviets in 1981 to *reintroduce* nuclear weapons to Cuba.[54]

There are many possible reasons other than irrationality or ignorance for such Cuban perspectives and behavior. One possible explanation lies in the tradition of self-sacrifice in Cuban culture and nationalism. A.L. Bardach, a prominent expert on Cuban culture, describes it as one, "...that abhors surrender, rejects compromise and finds a measure of redemption in suicide." And: "...Cuban nationalism from time immemorial is studded with the rhetoric of self-sacrifice, from the 1854 chant of *Cuba Libre o Muerte* ('A Free Cuba or Death') to the post-Castro slogan *Patria o Muerte* ('Country or Death'). Indeed, 'La Bayamesa,' the Cuban national anthem, declares, '*Que morir por la Patria es vivir*'—'To die for the homeland is to live.'"[55]

The point here, however, is not whether this characteristic of Cuban culture and nationalism helps to explain the Cuban leadership's high-risk behavior during the Cuban Missile Crisis; it is that during the Cuban Missile Crisis the Cuban leadership appears to have had a higher priority than avoiding the risk of provoking an escalation process possibly leading to Cuban national destruction. It was far from prudently cautious in the face of a well-recognized, severe retaliatory threat. In 1962, an ultimately deterrable Soviet leadership was in control of the missiles and nuclear weapons. In the future, leaders willing or eager to "die beautifully" may be in control.

Similarly, even after the atomic destruction of Hiroshima, the Japanese War Minister Korechika Anami sought to continue the war to a cataclysmic ending as the only honorable course, even given the possible destruction of Japan. He actively conspired against the Emperor's efforts to conclude the war. In deference to the demands of honor, the War Minister said, "Would it not be wondrous for this whole nation [Japan] to be destroyed like a beautiful flower?"[56] In this case it appears that for the Japanese War Minister, preserving the Japanese cultural value of honor and sacrifice was a higher priority than avoiding the risk of Japan's societal destruction.

The point here, again, is not whether the traditional priorities of self-sacrifice and honor in Japanese military culture help to explain War Minister Anami's high-risk behavior at the end of World War II; it is that, at the time, some senior members of the Japanese leadership appear to have had a higher priority than avoiding the risk of societal destruction. They appear to have accepted that possible outcome over surrender. Their behavior was far from prudent in the face of a severe threat that had been made evident not simply by the United States cleverly "rocking the boat," but via the atomic destruction of Hiroshima. In 1945, an ultimately prudent Japanese emperor maintained control of Japanese decision making despite serious internal efforts to intervene.

The 1973 Yom Kippur War is an even more striking demonstration of rational leaders willing to tempt fate in ways that are irreconcilable with "rational" decision making per the balance of terror tenets. On October 6, 1973, Egypt and Syria launched a massive, well-coordinated, surprise assault against Israel, despite the fact that Israel was widely believed by that time to have a nuclear retaliatory capability. Avner Cohen makes the point succinctly: "The Arabs were not deterred from waging the 1973 war by the knowledge that Israel was in possession of nuclear weapons...."[57] This was not a border skirmish, but a massive Arab armored attack that Egyptian President Anwar Sadat initiated *in the hope that it would* "precipitate" superpower intervention.[58] Israel reportedly put its nuclear weapons on alert during the conflict.[59] This event is a devastating contradiction of the proposition that the possibility of unleashing an escalation process that could culminate in nuclear destruction will deter rational leaders from acting "in blatantly offensive ways." Leaders will do so when they believe themselves compelled by overwhelming internal or external demands.

For American leaders convinced that prudence in the face of great risk must lead inevitably to cautious behavior, the Arab decision to strike against a putative nuclear-armed opponent was inexplicable. Secretary of State Henry Kissinger observed that, despite ample information about Arab troop movements, "no one believed" they would launch an attack because, "Our definition of rationality did not take seriously the notion of [Egypt and Syria] starting an unwinnable war to restore self-respect."[60]

Another example involving Israel occurred eighteen years later. During the 1991 Gulf War, Saddam Hussein launched dozens of missiles against Israel. A former Iraqi senior military official, General Abderrazzak Al-Ayubi, publicly confirmed a particularly high-risk gambit as an element in these Iraqi missile attacks: "...that Iraq targeted [Israel's] Dimona nuclear complex with Scud missiles during the 1991 Gulf War."[61]

Conventional wisdom is that Saddam Hussein attacked Israel, which was not a belligerent in the 1991 war, for the *very purpose of inciting Israeli retaliation* and thereby possibly fracturing the allied coalition confronting Iraq. Here was a non-nuclear power engaged in what can only be described as a "blatantly offensive" and high-risk provocation of a putative nuclear power, possibly seeking not to discourage but *to encourage its retaliation.* The central balance of terror proposition that universal rationality and prudence in the face of a nuclear retaliatory threat ensures the deterrence of such high-risk behavior is here again contradicted by actual leadership behavior.

Additional Historical Illustrations

There are many additional pre-nuclear and nuclear-age examples of leaders taking "blatantly offensive" initiatives against opponents despite the *possibility* of setting off an escalating crisis to their own destruction. For example, on November 25, 1950, China deployed 170,000 troops directly against the U.S. Eighth Army operating in North Korea. The United States had discounted the possibility of Chinese intervention in the mistaken belief that Mao Zedong and Soviet leader Joseph Stalin would be deterred from intervention by the possibility of igniting a global conflict with the United States. Mao, however, apparently saw no acceptable alternative to war: he believed U.S. intervention in Korea was part of a larger U.S. plan to encircle and ultimately attack China from the Korean Peninsula, across the Taiwan Strait, and from French Indochina.[62] Stalin, rather than being deterred from endorsing the attack as expected, stated to Mao: "If a war [with the United States] is inevitable, then let it be waged now."[63] U.S. expectations to the contrary, the fear of unleashing a dangerous escalation process did not deter Mao or Stalin at a time of considerable U.S. nuclear advantage—not because they were irrational, but because each perceived the situation as compelling his high-risk actions.

In August 1958, Mao again defied the reassuring, narrow definition of "rational" embedded in balance of terror tenets by intentionally initiating a military crisis in the Taiwan Strait. He ordered a massive shelling of the small island of Quemoy *for the purpose of eliciting U.S. nuclear threats.* Mao hoped to buttress his request for nuclear capabilities from the Soviet Union by *inciting U.S. nuclear threats.* He ultimately reassured Khrushchev at the time that he did not actually intend for a nuclear war on that occasion, but pointed to the certainty of a future nuclear war with the United States over Taiwan. Mao told Russian leaders that he was willing for China to, "take the full consequences of this [nuclear] war," if the Soviet Union helped China with the necessary preparations: "Mao then wrote to Khrushchev confirming that he would be only too happy for China to fight a nuclear war with America alone. 'For our ultimate victory,' he offered, 'for the total eradication of the imperialists, we [i.e., the Chinese people, who had not been consulted] are willing to endure the first [U.S. nuclear] strike. All it is is a big pile of people dying.'"[64] Some contemporary Chinese statements continue to proclaim a readiness for nuclear war with the United States if the latter were to intervene over the issue of Taiwanese independence, even if U.S. intervention were non-nuclear.[65]

Mao made public and private statements that reflected a shockingly callous disregard for prospective Chinese nuclear war casualties and again contradict "rationality" as narrowly defined in balance of terror tenets. He reportedly described the prospective loss of hundreds of millions of Chinese lives in a nuclear war with the United States as, "no great loss."[66] Other statements by Mao on the subject similarly reflected a perspective apparently detached from concern about any level of human loss: "America's atom bombs are too few to wipe out the Chinese. Even if the U.S. atom bombs…were dropped on China, blasted a hole in the Earth or blew it to pieces, this might be a big thing for the solar system, but it would still be an insignificant matter as far as the universe as a whole is concerned."[67] The tolerance he showed for the horrific famines his policies unleashed on the Chinese people reinforce this appreciation that his highest priority was not the avoidance of massive Chinese casualties and suffering. The level of societal destruction potentially inflicted by nuclear weapons was "unthinkable" to McGeorge Bundy, but appears to have been quite "thinkable" to Mao. While Mao's decision making and behavior could be reckless and inhumane, it was not "irrational" per se; he followed a specific logic that linked his actions and goals. But, he certainly appears to have held to a set of values and judgments far outside the narrow definition of "rational" informing the balance of terror tenets.

An additional nuclear-age example involving China and the Soviet Union is the 1969 series of spring and summer border clashes. This was, according to previously classified State Department assessments in the National Archives, an "exceptionally violent turn" in Sino-Soviet relations that was triggered when "Chinese forces fired on Soviet border troops patrolling *Zhenbao* (*Damanski*), an island on the Ussuri River."[68] The Chinese goal in the battle was, "to contest [the Soviet] presence" on the border.[69] There was serious concern within the U.S. State Department at the time about the potential for escalation. The validity of this concern was borne out by the massing of Soviet forces on the border and the Soviet inquiry regarding how the United States would react if the Soviet Union launched a pre-emptive strike on Chinese nuclear weapons facilities.[70] Again, the risk of escalation involved in provoking a nuclear power did not deter the provocation.

A final and more recent example is Iraq's torching of Kuwaiti oil installations during the 1991 Gulf War. Iraq did so despite Secretary of State James Baker's presentation of President George H.W. Bush's direct retaliatory threat to the Iraqi Foreign Minister, as quoted in Chapter 6: "... that the United States would not tolerate the use of chemical or biological weapons or the destruction of Kuwait's oil fields and installations....The American people would demand the strongest possible response. You and your country will pay a terrible price if you order unconscionable acts of this sort."[71] Saddam Hussein apparently would not risk the use of chemical or biological weapons against the backdrop of this deterrent threat, but he was willing to risk burning Kuwaiti oil installations despite the same U.S. retaliatory threat. [72]

It is a convenient and comforting hope that such willing acceptance of risk will be deterred reliably and predictably by an opponent's rationality, uncertainty and prudence in the face of severe U.S. retaliatory threats. But this hope is in fundamental conflict with a more sober understanding of human decision making and behavior, and with much of the actual historical record before and after the advent of nuclear weapons. As one of America's foremost historians Professor Donald Kagan has concluded: "...*on countless occasions* states have acted to defend or foster a collection of beliefs and feelings that ran counter to their practical interests and have placed their security at risk, persisting in their course even when the costs were high and the danger evident."[73]

Preferring Comforting Theory Over Inconvenient History

The many examples cited above are outside the definition of "rational," deliberate decision making and behavior necessary for coherence of the balance of terror framework. How then did these experiences *not* foreclose the sanguine proposition that a narrowly-defined, universal rationality and sensibility promises an easy deterring effect from uncertainty? Typically, the most egregious of these historical examples simply were dubbed illogical or irrational; that is the only interpretation available to maintain the balance of terror tautology and coherence of the accepted deterrence framework. Indeed, at the time, U.S. officials dismissed Khrushchev's reckless behavior triggering the Cuban Missile Crisis as simply "illogical."[74] If a rational, informed leader could behave so incautiously, then confidence that retaliatory nuclear threats would deter sane leaders predictably could not be sustained. That confidence is too convenient and too comforting to be abandoned simply because actual events repeatedly contradict the definition of rationality upon which it is based.

Other than in 1945, not one of the historical cases cited above led to nuclear destruction, however risky the escalation process. As mentioned above, however, the absence of nuclear employment since 1945 is a wholly inadequate basis for concluding confidently that deterrence will "work" predictably and reliably into the future as envisaged. The definition of deterrence "working" per the balance of terror logic *must* include the deterrence of crisis behavior that could ignite an uncontrollable escalation process culminating in nuclear war. Simply because a military crisis and escalation process has not yet proceeded to the full nuclear culmination point in the recent past does not mean that there can be no such future event because all pertinent leaders must be prudent as defined. The past would provide the basis for confidence in this regard only in the absence of this litany of occasions for escalation.

Fortunately, the combustible combination has not yet emerged of a risk-tolerant, reckless, ruthless, misinformed, miscalculating, distracted, desperate, or gravely mistaken opponent who is driven decisively by a felt imperative to act and who is armed with nuclear weapons. The absence of that particular "combustible combination" over a few decades hardly validates confidence in its continuing absence because a universal rationality and the threat of nuclear retaliation ensure prudence and caution. That explanation is comforting and self-serving, but cannot stand given the numerous historical examples of imprudent and incautious behavior in the face of implicit or explicit survival threats, including those from nuclear arms. *The relatively small number of states possessing nuclear weapons and the discipline imposed on most of those states by the Cold War's bipolar structure undoubtedly helped in the past few decades to preclude that combustible combination from emerging and leading to nuclear war. Those past helpful governors, however, are going and gone, respectively.*

As the above brief discussions of historical cases illustrate, there is a wide spectrum of leadership motives and behaviors that could, in the future, trigger imprudent, incautious behavior and an escalating crisis, even at the risk of nuclear retaliation. This spectrum includes: overriding leadership goals that are believed to demand great risk-taking or sacrifice; decision making that does not take into account reasonable calculations of expected cost; and, leadership mistakes and errors in perception or judgment, including those based on health problems or faulty, incomplete or distorted information.[75] These types of factors can be seen in:

- Hitler's absolute goals of a "reckoning" with France, *Lebensraum* ("living space") in the Soviet Union, and self-glorification.
- Mao's response to his own exaggerated interpretation of the U.S. threat to China in 1950; his 1958 goal of eliciting U.S. nuclear threats and expressed acceptance of massive Chinese casualties in a nuclear war over Taiwan; and, his 1969 challenge to Soviet positions on the Sino-Soviet border.
- Khrushchev's desire in 1962 for a shortcut to a stronger strategic nuclear position *vis-à-vis* Washington.
- The Cuban leadership's apparent ideological zealotry and embrace of martyrdom in its calls for a nuclear war in 1962.
- Sadat's need in 1973 to reestablish Egyptian honor and an improved basis for negotiations with Israel.
- The Argentine junta's misreading of British will in 1982.
- Saddam Hussein's apparent goal of using missile attacks to incite Israeli retaliation in 1991, and thereby advancing a wartime political goal.

The perception of an opponent's weakness also can invite provocation, crisis and escalation: British appeasement of Germany in 1938 over Czechoslovakia contributed to Hitler's underestimation of Britain's likely response to his later attack on Poland ("Our enemies are little worms, I got to know them in Munich").[76]

All of these goals and motivations appear to have been part of actual leadership decision making that inspired crises and the potential for an escalation process that could have transcended supposedly "rational" boundaries regardless of initial intentions. Such powerful and disparate motivations may be unknown or only partially transparent to outside observers and wholly beyond their influence. They may be unseen, unexpected and uncontrolled triggers to crises and escalation.

John Stoessinger's conclusion regarding the causes of war following his detailed analysis of historical case studies is insightful when considering the supposed predictability of deterrent effect imposed by rationality: "The case material reveals that perhaps the most important single participating factor in the outbreak of war is misperception. Such distortion may manifest itself in four different ways: in a leader's image of himself; a leader's view of his adversary's character; a leader's view of his adversary's intentions toward himself; and finally, a leader's view of his adversary's capabilities and power."[77] The potential weight of such factors in decision making and their possible opaqueness to outside observers preclude any confidence in the old promises of easy, "existential" deterrence based on rationality and the proper alignment of nuclear threats.

There is sufficient historical evidence since 1945 to conclude without reservation that, contrary to the centerpiece of the balance of terror's logic, *the inherent risks and uncertainties of nuclear escalation do not reliably and predictably prevent deliberate or unwitting leadership behavior that could ignite a deadly escalation process.* We can hope that one day a universal rationality and sensibility will drive leaders inevitably to an overriding prudence and caution in the face of severe risk as is demanded by the balance of terror tenets, but it is important to distinguish between hopes and expectations.

Hope as the Basis for Expectations

The important distinction to be recognized here is between the understandable *hope* for reliably prudent, cautious opponents, and the unwarranted expectation that all rational opponents must be so. Kahn well understood this distinction. *Some* of Schelling's comments during the Cold War suggest his acknowledgement that he was dealing more in the *hope* that leaders would learn to be prudent and cautious than the legitimate expectation of such thought and behavior:

- "If you rely on offense [for deterrence], it means you learn how to live in a world in which, whether you like it or not, countries have great capacity to hurt each other." [78]
- "I think it would be wise to learn to govern our relations even with adversaries in the expectation that usually, at least

on and off, but perhaps usually and maybe always, very severe destruction can be done by either of us to the other. We must learn to govern our motives, our understanding and our relations, rather than to rely on our hardware."[79]

- "Once a country becomes the owner of nuclear weapons, it is imperative that they learn to deal with them responsibly.... Part of the learning process is learning to be deterred."[80]

Schelling's recognition of the need for such learning suggests his recognition that the day had not yet arrived. We can *hope* fervently that such learned governing will take place universally. And, of course, as Schelling observes, it indeed "would be wise" for all leaders to become so learned. In fact, it would be miraculous.

Following a comprehensive examination of deterrence-related historical case studies, Professor Lebow concludes: "These case histories suggest the pessimistic hypothesis that those policy makers with the greatest need to learn from external reality appear the least likely to do so."[81] Careful study of states and terrorist organizations that exhibit "high-intensity aggressive ideologies" and lack a commitment to "rational" prudence yields an even more pointed conclusion: "...there are still widespread views that progressing 'modernity' will produce more 'rational' international behavior, with an end to ideologies and contraction in ideology-generated violence. But such hopes have no basis other than wishful thinking."[82]

Nevertheless, seemingly knowledgeable commentators continue to claim that U.S. deterrence strategy should be based on the balance of terror expectation that prudent and cautious enemy responses to U.S. threats will follow reliably and predictably from learned prudence and universal, well-understood values. For example, in a lengthy discussion of contemporary deterrence requirements Nobel Laureate Roger Myerson observes:

> ...to get a sense of what people are likely to do in any given situation, it is generally a good idea to think about what their interests are and to assume that they will act to pursue those interests. Our adversaries' interests may be different from our own, but we generally share at least some common interests, such as avoiding the costs of destructive conflict.[83]

Here Myerson gives explicit voice to the familiar balance of terror hope that we can "think about" and thereby reliably understand opponents' highest values—which will be the shared "common interests" of avoiding "destructive conflict"—and that deterrence can be orchestrated accordingly. Myerson's expectations of intuitive insight into the opponent's decision making calculus and of an opponent who reliably shares interest in the avoidance of "destructive conflict" allow the conclusion that U.S. deterrence efforts should work nearly effortlessly. We can threaten the "destructive conflict" they most want to avoid; therefore we can deter. Unfortunately, these comforting expectations are historically, politically and psychologically naïve.

Balance of terror tenets elevate *hope* for the particular type of opponent decision making that is most susceptible to U.S. deterrence strategy to its confident expectation, and build on that sanguine expectation the standards for strategic force adequacy and measures of merit for the proper deterrence threat. This is a conveniently circular and self-serving strategic logic: all rational opponents are expected to behave in the fashion necessary to ensure that the easy deterrence strategy and minimal force requirements we prefer are adequate to deter them predictably and reliably. Despite such comforting hopes some, and perhaps many, leaders will continue to miscalculate or be driven by powerful and diverse motives to accept great risk—and the functioning of deterrence will be uncertain.

The hope that the possibility of severe consequences will compel leaders to "learn to govern" their motives and behave prudently and cautiously is as understandable as it is unrealistic, and therefore inade-quate as the basis for deterrence strategy. Even if that happy day were to arrive, the reliable functioning of deterrence would remain vulnerable to the possibility that factors beyond the control of prudent, cautious decision makers could drive an escalation process to a nuclear culmination point. The possibility of *deliberate* escalation could, in principle, be ameliorated by the hoped-for universal "learning" but even if prudence and caution were to abound there would remain the "chance" of unintended escalation— as Schelling rightly emphasizes. This "chance" will cease only when leaders are *incapable* of making rash judgments, miscalculating, being inattentive, making mistakes, and being poorly informed or misinformed, i.e., when the lion lays down with the lamb and both survive the occasion.

The comforting and convenient belief that all "rational" opponents will be deterred reliably by our severe retaliatory threats is folly because many different types of factors can motivate an opponent's seemingly high-risk decision making, and some of those factors are likely to be unique to that opponent and wholly unfamiliar to us. Because an opponent's decision making and behavior cannot be deduced reliably from universal principles with precision, confident predictions about when, if, or how deterrence will operate against unspecified or unfamiliar leaders, over unpredictable stakes, in unknown or unfamiliar contexts, can only be speculative guesses. Gordon Craig and Alexander George emphasize that, "a grave and fatal error may be committed" in expecting deterrence to unfold in a predictably rational way because: "Not all actors in international politics calculate utility in making decisions in the same way. Differences in values, culture, attitudes toward risk-taking, and so on vary greatly. There is no substitute for knowledge of the adversary's mind-set and behavioral style, and this is often difficult to obtain or to apply correctly in assessing intentions or predicting responses."[84] Great confidence in the mechanistic linkage of severe threats to predictable deterrent effect ignores this fair warning.

The uncertainty surrounding the functioning of deterrence may be higher or lower depending on the details of the engagement and the success of our efforts to understand the opponent and context. But, deterrence cannot be as predictable and reliable as was believed widely to be the case during the Cold War. This is *not because opponents should be considered irrational*, but because in the absence of considerable empathy for, and understanding of the opponent and the circumstances, and how those circumstances will affect an opponent's decision making, we are unlikely to have the basis to predict confidently how our deterrence threats will affect an opponent's behavior.

Even with empathy and understanding, deterrent effect cannot be entirely predictable. U.S. threats of nuclear retaliation cannot be expected to check all of the plausible motivations for an opponent's deliberate nuclear or non-nuclear attack, or prevent all of the possible avenues to deterrence failure. In the contemporary era, the obstacles to the *predictable* functioning of deterrence contradict the sanguine expectations embedded in balance of terror tenets: the list of provocations and opponents we now hope to deter has expanded; the contexts within which we hope to deter are far more variable, as are the stakes involved; and, our familiarity with many contemporary and potential opponents is limited. We may be ignorant of an opponent's decision making process, the identity or character of the decision makers, and the potentially unique and key factors that drive an opponent's decision making. Some opponents will seek to hide such pertinent information to help reduce their vulnerability to our strategies for deterrence and coercion; authoritarian, closed societies are particularly well-suited to do so.

Because an opposing leadership's unfamiliar or perhaps hidden perceptions, beliefs and behaviors can determine the functioning of deterrence, identifying practicable strategies for deterrence has become a far more complicated process than simply posing a severe retaliatory threat and expecting the opponent's rationality and uncertainty to produce the awaited prudence and caution. Very specific types of opponents are required for that "easy" deterrence strategy to be plausible:

- Opponents who understand and fear the U.S. deterrent threat sufficiently to subordinate *whatever else* might motivate their behavior to that threat.
- Opponents capable of taking in and assessing information about the external world in a fashion that is sufficiently accurate to support reasonable cost-benefit calculations.
- Opponents capable of linking means to ends in their decision making (i.e., they perform cost-benefit calculations and understand when tradeoffs must be made).
- Opponents with whom we can communicate, and who are attentive to and understanding of our intentions, interests and commitments.
- Opponents able to communicate with and control their own subordinates.
- Opponents who operate in a political system that allows individually rational cost-benefit calculations to establish corresponding state policies which, in turn, determine actual state behavior.

Assuming such an opponent into place during the Cold War, and thus concluding that the Soviet Union would not precipitate a nuclear conflict, may have seemed reasonable. Even during that era, however, a lethal surprise would likely have been the outcome of any East-West crisis that escalated. While U.S. and NATO strategy envisaged deterrence of a "rational" and thus prudent, cautious foe via graduated escalation options, Warsaw Pact plans reportedly included extremely heavy nuclear and chemical strikes against NATO from the outset of a war, even if NATO employed only conventional forces.[85] It is difficult to imagine a greater mismatch than the Warsaw Pact war plans and Western expectations of deterrence "crisis management" with a "rational" foe: "NATO forces were positioned to blunt westward land thrusts from the Warsaw Pact [while] nuclear strikes and landings on Europe's western coast, [Warsaw] Pact planners felt, were keys to early victory."[86]

During the Cold War, Bernard Brodie lamented that so few people studied Soviet decision making, and he scorned the "spinning of military theories" based on the image of a Soviet leadership with "no biases other than those we share."[87] Brodie emphasized that the Soviet leadership "... has very special ways of looking at things—in other words, [it has] strong biases, some of which are fundamentally different from our own."[88]

However mistaken our expectations about the Warsaw Pact may have been during the Cold War, to risk understatement, the characteristics of opponents and conditions listed above as necessary for deterrence to operate predictably are not universal over time and cannot be assumed *vis-à-vis* the diverse set of contemporary and potential foes. We cannot be confident that the communication or lethality of our deterrent threats will be understood and decisively shape the decision making of opposing leaders who may be willing martyrs or desperate gamblers, or who are incommunicado, ignorant, self-destructive, self-absorbed, foolish, inattentive, distracted, or ultimately motivated by absolute, intangible goals.

Unfortunately, we are insufficiently familiar with the myriad of possible opponent perceptions, beliefs and behaviors to predict with confidence how or whether deterrence will work. Given the wide range of *unfamiliar* motives and behaviors that could unleash escalating crises, it is unreasonable to expect the functioning of deterrence to be so predictable. The unavoidable implication of this set of observations is that there is an ever-present and likely incalculable potential for the surprising failure of deterrence to prevent deliberate attacks or an escalation process that culminates in nuclear use. The uncertainties surrounding deterrence may be reduced via efforts to understand the opponent and context, but confident assertions about deterrence performing reliably and predictably, however tenuous during the Cold War, are without merit in the contemporary environment.

During the Cold War, the metaphor of "two scorpions in a bottle" was used to help describe the dynamics of deterrence. This metaphor conveyed the idea of captive participants whose sole preoccupation was to avoid the other's deadly stinger. A more apt metaphor now, however, is a congested automobile race with no authorities or binding rules, but numerous hostile participants who define the goal of the race differently, may be distracted or attentive, and may jealously guard and aggressively take space, signal incomprehensibly, and drive autos which are of varying power and mechanical reliability. Prudence is only reasonable, of course, and those most concerned about their own physical safety will be the most hopeful that caution, decorum and "rules of the road" will prevail. Nevertheless, deliberate high-risk behavior, "road rage," unwitting error, and high-speed collisions are likely.

Precision Prediction

A noted journal boasts a "Doomsday Clock" that supposedly counts down the precise minutes to nuclear doomsday; the editors occasionally adjust it with worldwide fanfare to show that the planet is a few minutes closer to, or further from, midnight and a nuclear catastrophe.[89] The journal boasts that the adjustment of the "Doomsday Clock" is done in consultation with "18 Nobel laureates."[90] The problem with such dramatic timekeeping, however, is that the journal's "keepers of the clock"—no matter how prize-worthy— cannot knowledgeably offer fine-grained prediction about the imminence of nuclear war. This is so because many possible proximate causes of great risk-taking and escalation are wholly unrecognized or visible only in part; the timing of a deliberate or an unwitting path to crisis and escalation is unpredictable; and, a crisis once unleashed may escalate beyond deliberate control. In truth, the "keepers of the clock" do not and cannot know whether it should be set at five minutes or five hours to midnight, or how it subsequently should be adjusted. The lack of precision truly feasible may be recognized: according to Kennette Benedict, editor of the journal that hosts the "Doomsday Clock," it originally was set "at seven minutes to midnight because that's where it would look best in a design sense."[91]

A review of past issues of the journal reveals that there was no change in the "Doomsday Clock" immediately prior to the Chinese attack on U.S. forces in Korea in 1950, the Cuban Missile Crisis in 1962, or the Yom Kippur War in 1973. In 1969, at the time of the violent Sino-Soviet border clashes which precipitated the Soviet inquiry to the United States about a pre-emptive strike against Chinese nuclear facilities, the journal actually had set the clock *back* three minutes, as if the prospects for nuclear war had become more remote. In fact, the movement of the clock seems to be affected *only* by developments in the areas of nuclear testing and formal arms control. Whether these developments have much, if anything, to do with the probability and timing of war is questionable; what is unquestionable is that there are many other potentially significant factors, and those who set the clock cannot have an adequate level of knowledge about them to adjust it with any accuracy.[92]

The point here is not about the "Doomsday Clock" per se. It is that prediction is a particularly inexact business when the subject involves processes as potentially complex, idiosyncratic and opaque as the possible roads to war, and whether or not deterrence will work as hoped.

So What?: The End of the Comforting, Convenient Balance of Terror Lines

Critics of the balance of terror formula have voiced multiple reasons over the years for their opposition to that formula. These include: Kahn's classic critique of it as an inadequate and even dangerous guide for U.S. deterrence strategy and forces; its willful rejection of serious preparation for deterrence failure; and, a more general moral opposition to U.S. nuclear threats to cities.[93]

These well-trod points of opposition to balance of terror tenets are understandable. More fundamental, however, are the internal incoherence of those tenets and their frequent contradiction by the actual historical record of leadership decision making and behavior. Continued adherence to incoherent and unrealistic expectations about opponents' prospective decision making and behavior represents a significant danger. In this case, it can lead to strategies and force acquisition guidelines that eschew damage-limitation capabilities and may be useless for deterrence, yet foster the expectation that deterrence will function reliably and predictably. The resultant mismatch between our strategies, forces, and the real threats we face may be worse than was the now-apparent mismatch between NATO's expectations and Warsaw Pact war plans. That did not end in catastrophe; however, the future may not be so forgiving of a U.S. deterrence strategy and related force metrics which are based on the confident expectation that all rational opponents will be deterred by our preferred strategy and arsenal.

Nevertheless, as illustrated in Chapter 6 above, the balance of terror tenets survived the Cold War and continue to play heavily in contemporary debates on U.S. strategic forces, both offensive and defensive. There is continuing, unchallenged and often unabated confidence that:

- Deterrence can be made to work reliably and predictably against rational opponents because universal modes of rational thought compel state leaders inevitably to be prudent and cautious in the face of uncertainty and U.S. retaliatory nuclear threats;
- Damage-limitation capabilities continue to be unnecessary and destabilizing;
- We can know the specific requirements for orchestrating predictably the deterrence of all rational state leaders, and those force requirements can be defined in terms of a minimal quantity and their "stabilizing" or "destabilizing" characteristics;
- The "action-reaction" dynamic drives opponents' motivations to acquire nuclear weapons and thus can be mitigated by U.S. "inaction"; and,
- Arms control measures can facilitate "stability" predictably by orchestrating U.S. forces per balance of terror desiderata.

Acceptance of those tenets in the United States continues to influence the types of strategic forces deemed adequate, necessary and "stabilizing." It shapes the contemporary U.S. debate on security questions as diverse and important as the seriousness of the threat posed by the proliferation of nuclear weapons, and the potential value of U.S. nuclear, advanced conventional, and damage-limitation capabilities. When nuclear deterrence continues to be considered universally "existential" per the balance of terror tenets, for example, WMD proliferation can be considered manageable and damage-limitation capabilities can be said to offer relatively little unique value.

No confidence, however, should be attributed to these balance of terror tenets in light of their logical incoherence, incompatibility with the historical record, and demonstrably naïve expectations of leadership decision making and behavior. U.S. deterrence strategies buttressed by the threat of nuclear retaliation may "work," fail, or be irrelevant to an opponent's crisis decision making and behavior. And, U.S. deterrence threats can have no predictable effect on a crisis that is driven to its culmination point by factors beyond deliberate control. Deterrence effect cannot be orchestrated predictably, and is not the inevitable consequence of any particular technical/force relationship. Predictable deterrent effect would require a world that neither exists nor appears to be taking shape: a world in which all pertinent leaders have "learned" to be prudent and cautious in the face of severe threats, and in which crises once unleashed *cannot* be driven decisively by, *inter alia*, ignorance, mistakes, distortion of information, errors in judgment, emotion and personal egos.

The long-familiar balance of terror guidelines are now more likely to mislead than enlighten. There are at least seven implications of this conclusion that deserve attention.

1. Deterrence May Work Unpredictably, Fail, or Be Irrelevant: U.S. Damage-Limitation Efforts May Now Be Useful, Necessary and "Stabilizing"

As noted in Chapter 6, key U.S. political leaders continue to oppose BMD by asserting the familiar balance of terror tenet that damage limitation is unnecessary because deterrence offers complete, sure protection while damage-limitation capabilities do not: "We should try to rely on some mutual deterrence, rather than thinking we can replace it, because, in fact, deterrence works."[94] The supposed impossibility of, and lack of historical precedent for, leaderships willing to risk survival continues to be put forward erroneously as proof of this tenet: "Name me a time in the last 500 years when the leader of a nation has said, 'I know I face virtual annihilation if I take the following action, but I'm going ahead and I'm going to do it anyway.'"[95]

In fact, as discussed above, extreme vulnerability and risk often have not deterred highly provocative choices. Leaders have willingly *accepted the risk* of personal and societal "annihilation," not typically because they aspired to destruction but because they saw no acceptable alternative courses of action. Lawrence Freedman's observation that, "Some [decision makers] might be beyond deterrence but that does not mean they are invariably so,"[96] rings true, but the point is not that leaders should be described as "invariably" *undeterrable*, but that they cannot be described as invariably *deterrable*. Recognition of deterrence fallibility, even in the context of U.S. retaliatory nuclear threats, stands out starkly when a single failure could result in an opponent inflicting thousands to millions of U.S. or allied civilian casualties. Acknowledging that rational leaders "might be beyond deterrence" on occasion is a devastating indictment of the easy confidence in "existential deterrence" posited in balance of terror tenets, and the force guidelines that follow from those tenets.

Consequently, the familiar line that damage-limitation capabilities lack sufficient value to warrant deployment because deterrence will work reliably to prevent attack and any casualties—a staple of Cold War and contemporary debate on the subject—should now be recognized as an anachronism. Continued acceptance of uncontested U.S. societal vulnerability is a much different proposition now when the prospect of deterrence working reliably must be recognized as a hope, not a reasonable expectation.

Full confidence that deterrence works reliably *in the absence of defenses* renders moot any concern about the possible opportunity costs involved in *not* deploying defenses. Recognition that deterrence may unexpectedly fail or be irrelevant, however, changes the manner in which the question of the potential value of damage limitation can reasonably be posed. During the Cold War, as noted in Chapters 4 and 5, U.S. Government officials placed great confidence in the predictable functioning of the stable balance of terror *in the absence of city defenses*. Consequently, they posed the question of U.S. damage limitation as a choice between "destabilizing" defensive capabilities which could provide only partial societal protection at great cost, *or* stable deterrence *without defenses* that would prevent attack at relatively modest cost.

By posing the question in this fashion defenses could easily be judged unnecessary, useless and destabilizing. The certain absolute protection supposedly available via a "stable" balance of terror could reasonably take priority over the partial and "destabilizing" protection then considered feasible via damage-limitation capabilities, with no meaningful tradeoffs or opportunity costs. Defensive capabilities could promise only to limit damage at intolerable expense, while deterrence without defenses promised *absolute* and cost-effective protection; equally important, defensive capabilities supposedly threatened to upset this preferred deterrence strategy. This, of course, was Secretary McNamara's narrative and basis for his prioritization of strategic goals and force metrics during the Cold War. As noted in Chapter 6, Kenneth Waltz essentially applies this same Cold War formulation to the contemporary question of U.S. damage-limitation capabilities, and unsurprisingly reaches the same easy conclusion: "Why should anyone want to replace stable deterrence with unstable defense?"[97] This rhetorical question posed by Waltz is a perfect illustration of the application of Cold War balance of terror logic regarding deterrence and damage limitation to contemporary threats: deterrence supposedly works reliably to provide comprehensive protection, so why embrace damage-limitation goals and capabilities that cannot provide comparable protection and supposedly will upset deterrence?

The contemporary value of damage-limitation capabilities, however, no longer can be dismissed by positing this easy choice between the complete, affordable protection of nuclear deterrence and the partial, "destabilizing" protection available via costly defenses. Structuring the question of damage limitation in this Cold War fashion mistakenly supposes that confidence can be placed in the reliable, predictable functioning of nuclear deterrence, and that U.S. damage-limitation capabilities are known to be "destabilizing." In fact, there is no logical basis for continuing to give credence to either of these familiar balance of terror tenets as general propositions. No one can identify with confidence the acquisition of strategic force capabilities that reliably and predictably will ensure or "destabilize" deterrence in the abstract. Such specific effects are not so predictable.

Deterrence may unexpectedly fail, and U.S. damage-limiting capabilities may be the *only* means for mitigating the catastrophic consequences of nuclear or other WMD attack. The value of limiting the fatalities and destruction potentially afforded by U.S. damage-limitation capabilities—whatever level of defense effectiveness may be available— must now be assessed against the probability that deterrence will fail to prevent attack or escalation. The value of damage-limitation capabilities for the provision of incomplete societal protection may reasonably take first priority when juxtaposed against the uncertainties of deterrence and the potentially horrific consequences of a single failure. And, to complete the point, no one knowingly can claim as a general proposition that U.S. damage-limitation capabilities would come at the cost of "destabilizing" the potentially desirable deterrent effect.

This particular approach to the question of damage limitation is reminiscent of the JCS critique of Secretary McNamara's priorities during the 1960s, and can make significant damage limitation the reasonable, prudent choice of priorities. Why? Because the tradeoff involved in continuing to eschew damage-limitation capabilities could be an *unnecessary* level of U.S. vulnerability to casualties and destruction, with *no corresponding benefit for the functioning of deterrence*. In the past, acceptance of the balance of terror tenets allowed U.S. leaders to dismiss the possible opportunity costs of eschewing damage-limitation capabilities with the easy adage that defenses are useless, unnecessary and destabilizing.

Now, when the alternative of deterrence functioning predictably to prevent war—and thereby reliably preventing any casualties—may *not* exist, the opportunity cost of *not* pursuing damage-limiting capabilities could be exceedingly high. In the context of contemporary limited WMD threats, the possible reduction in societal destruction via damage-limitation capabilities may on occasion be the highest priority, a matter of good government and—for the United States—a fundamental responsibility of the federal government as mandated by the Constitution.

   Of course, the actual value of defenses for any given contingency will be shaped by the nature of the threat, the cost of defenses, their expected effectiveness in reducing casualties and destruction, and the probability that deterrence will work, fail, or be irrelevant in crisis. Now, however, when it is the easy confidence in deterrence that must be dismissed, and the prospective opportunity costs involved in eschewing defenses may loom large, the potential tradeoffs involved in placing priority on the pursuit of "stable" deterrence at the expense of defenses must be faced. The easy Cold War generalizations and adages cannot provide reliable guidance.

2. No More Generalizations About Forces Being "Stabilizing" or "Destabilizing"

There are too many plausible routes to nuclear war and opaque factors potentially driving that decision making for confidence to be placed in the fixed balance of terror categorizations of "stabilizing" or "destabilizing" forces. No one can knowledgeably offer *a priori* generalizations about the particular types of forces that predictably will "stabilize" or "destabilize" the functioning of deterrence. Even during the Cold War it was not possible to anticipate what actual effect, if any, the "reciprocal fears of surprise attack" and supposedly "destabilizing" forces would have had on the potential for war—given the multiplicity of factors that could have driven or restrained the chances for crisis and war.

   Even the most "destabilizing" capabilities, as defined by the balance of terror tenets, for example, will not affect the functioning of deterrence predictably when factors *other than* force structure are decisive in the pertinent decision making. Whether the character of available forces is one of those factors driving decision making and, if so, what the weight of that specific factor is among the many which affect decision making, is unlikely to be knowable in advance with confidence. There is no reasonable basis for continuing confidence in those familiar Cold War lines that one or another type of prospective strategic capability can be categorized generically as "destabilizing" or "stabilizing." During the Cold War such labels were speculative; apart from the Cold War context these familiar, fixed categorizations have little or no meaning.

Further, *if and when* force relationships are of decisive importance to decision making, in the contemporary period there is no apparent, logical basis for anticipating that China or any rogue state could be inspired by Schelling's venerable "reciprocal fear of surprise attack" to strike first at U.S. strategic retaliatory forces. Unless the United States behaves very foolishly by abandoning its secure nuclear retaliatory capabilities, no contemporary opponents' strategic capabilities could inspire plausible visions of gaining strategic advantage via a pre-emptive strike. It would be an act of self-disarmament and self-destruction. That some opponents *nevertheless* might lash out unpredictably, unexpectedly, and against all seeming logic is obvious, but only adds to the point: the old, Cold War definition of U.S. damage-limiting forces as "destabilizing"—according to their expected potential to tip a fragile balance in the direction of the "reciprocal fear of surprise attack"—presumes a predictable, mechanistic linkage of forces to decision making that is unwarranted and, in any event, logically irrelevant *vis-à-vis* today's potential opponents. Contemporary use of the label "destabilizing" continues to suggest deep strategic insight and analysis, but typically is nothing more than a façade for, "I don't like it."

3. No More Generalizations About the Adequacy of Specific Force Numbers to Ensure Deterrent Effect

As illustrated in Chapter 6, in the absence of any reference to a specific opponent or circumstance, commentators schooled in balance of terror tenets continue routinely to claim that a *certain number of strategic weapons* will ensure deterrence because the proper alignment of U.S. weapons to an enemy's designated targets supposedly equates to deterrence: the number of targets deemed necessary to hold at risk—with a few additional factors taken into account—supposedly indicates the number of U.S. strategic weapons necessary and adequate for deterrence. If opponents have 50 or 500 of the designated types of targets, then a secure and redundant capability to threaten retaliation against that number of targets will deter, and thus represents an adequate force level.

According to this familiar methodology, "the" U.S. deterrent is that level of forces which meets the target coverage requirement. Predictions about the functioning of deterrence based on the number and targeting effectiveness of U.S. strategic forces render deterrence a convenient, mechanical question of military force numbers. The many additional factors that can shape decision making and behavior decisively are dismissed because these forces—along with rationality, unchanging "strategic arithmetic," and "human nature"—are expected to ensure the proper functioning of deterrence.

The typical assertions stemming from this balance of terror formula for determining how many and what types of U.S. strategic forces will "ensure" deterrence should be recognized for what they usually are— wholly speculative guesses about a function that is unpredictable on the basis of the alignment of forces and prospective targets. The balance of terror formula that reduces deterrence effect to the number of military forces necessary to destroy select sets of an opponent's targets betrays a certainty that cannot, in fact, exist about the specific linkage between strategic forces and deterrent effect, and assumes a universality about that connection that similarly does not exist.

This thinking is a legacy of the assured destruction and balance of terror notion that predictable deterrence effect equates to the technical fact of target coverage. Under virtually any set of circumstances, however, deterrent effect is not the mechanical effect of aligning the number of U.S. retaliatory weapons with an opponent's targets, and cannot usefully be calculated as such. It is the opponent's unique circumstances, perceptions, calculations, and decision-making calculus which ultimately determine the deterrent effect of U.S. threats. Consequently, as noted above, there are many other factors that can contribute to, and even be decisive in, determining if and how deterrence actually plays out in crises—including a leadership's attention, will, goals, information, health, cost and risk tolerances, the stakes at risk, and communications. The character of U.S. forces, of course, may be a factor in that determination. The number of weapons covering a specific set of targets, however, cannot reasonably serve as the basis for prediction of actual deterrent effect. Warhead and target numbers alone are inadequate, at best, for such prediction because in international crises "all other things" rarely are equal or can be anticipated to be so. Such a reductionist methodology makes for easy calculations, but otherwise is of limited use.

Sir Lawrence Freedman rightly observes that taking multiple factors into account complicates the prediction of deterrent effect, and thus may be "frustrating" for "practitioners":

> It is certainly possible to come up with propositions about when, in particular conditions, certain types of deterrence are more or less likely to work. But the concept requires considerable differentiation, according to the ambition of the task, the numbers of actors involved and the degree of the antagonism. Students of international relations may find this interesting and worthwhile, but practitioners may find it frustrating....[98]

More frustrating still for serious practitioners are the unduly confident assertions that follow from a combination of formulaic speculation and a reductionist methodology which equate predictable deterrent effect to force numbers. Such assertions are worse than "frustrating"—they are likely to be misleading: the authors of these claims cannot appreciate how far or close they are to the truth, and typically do not acknowledge their ignorance. Taking them seriously breeds false confidence that deterrence will work as it "*should*"—based on the arithmetic of force numbers and targets—when, in fact, it may not and the related probabilities cannot be calculated according to "strategic arithmetic." All of the frequent claims that some number of nuclear weapons will ensure deterrence—typically proffered sans any serious assessment of opponents and circumstances— are equally suspect.

Correspondingly, confidence should not be placed in the increasingly frequent assertion that U.S. advanced, *conventional* weapons are adequate for all or most U.S. deterrence needs because their lethality now is sufficient to destroy most enemy targets.[99] Such assertions simply repeat the mistake of believing that deterrent effect can be understood as the inevitable outcome of the proper juxtaposition of weapons and targets, with some number of non-nuclear forces substituting for nuclear weapons to satisfy the formula.

U.S. non-nuclear threats and capabilities frequently may be adequate for deterrence. Whether non-nuclear weapons ever will be sufficiently lethal to substitute for nuclear weapons for the purpose of threatening select types of targets remains an open question. More fundamentally, however, that question is of secondary importance when the formula of equating deterrent effect with the number and types of forces necessary to threaten selected targets is so inadequate. Even if non-nuclear weapons were to pose a fully lethal threat to an opponent's targets, the substitution of non-nuclear weapons for nuclear weapons cannot render deterrence requirements so calculable and predictable because deterrence involves much more than targets and weapons— whether the weapons are nuclear or conventional.

4. No More Generic Claims That Ambiguity Is a "Sound Doctrine" for Deterrence

Ambiguous threats and commitments may be attractive because they leave "wiggle room" for the deterrer. Leaders may expect ambiguous threats to provide deterrent effect without tying them to a commitment to execute a specific deterrent threat if the opponent does not comply. The lack of precision and accountability in this sense may be extremely attractive; this attractiveness, however, *should not be conflated with the truncated balance of terror tenet that uncertainty deters reliably and, therefore, ambiguity is "good for deterrence."*

Ambiguous U.S. threats and commitments may be adequate to deter those opponents for whom an uncertain U.S. threat *is* sufficient to deter. For other opponents, however, ambiguity *may degrade deterrent effect or even incite provocation.*[100] Rather than deter, ambiguity of U.S. threat and commitment may offer an opening that provokes opponents who are highly motivated, desperate, or high-risk gamblers. Soviet leaders typically were not such highly motivated, desperate, or willing gamblers; there may be contemporary and future opponents who are, under some circumstances. For example, Peter Rodman of the Brookings Institution and former Assistant Secretary of Defense, has observed that with regard to the U.S. commitment to Taiwan, the United States must make "its deterrent . . . as unambiguous as possible to ensure [that] China [does] not get the wrong message."[101]

The generalization that ambiguity is "good for deterrence" reflects the balance of terror tenets that uncertainty deters reliably and there is a uniformity in "rational" decision making and behavior. Neither should be assumed in the contemporary threat environment. The goal now, of course, should be to understand particular opponents sufficiently well to identify the level of threat ambiguity or explicitness likely to be necessary to deter. U.S. leaders may choose to place priority on "wiggle room" and ambiguity even when a close reading of the opponent suggests that doing so would degrade deterrent effect. In such cases, U.S. leaders should at least understand that a tradeoff is involved.

5. No More Generic Claims That Terrorist Organizations Are "Beyond Deterrence"

Following the September 11, 2001 terrorist attacks, the question of deterring terrorists came into focus as never before. A common assertion is that terrorists cannot be deterred. This point does not follow from an examination of pertinent historical cases which, in fact, suggest differently;[102] it follows from the balance of terror tenets that equate "rational" opponents with reliable deterrence, and deterrent effect with the offensive forces necessary to threaten selected sets of enemy targets typically associated with nation states. These possible targets include cities, citizens, economic and military centers, and political capitals within sovereign territories. The balance of terror formula cannot easily accommodate terrorists and terrorist organizations because some terrorists are willing to engage in suicide operations—and thus are deemed "irrational"—and because terrorist organizations lack traditional types of state-based targets to threaten. Consequently, terrorist organizations do not fit the old deterrence formula.

This train of thought and logic illustrates the dangers lurking in continued acceptance of the balance of terror tenets. It wrongly suggests that by taking on the accoutrements of statehood, the leadership of an organization can be transformed into a "rational" entity that is reliably and predictably susceptible to deterrence. It also wrongly suggests that if terrorist organizations cannot assume statehood in some fashion, which is often likely to be the case, then deterrence should be set aside.

In fact, deterrence is neither so predictable nor reliable whether the subject of a threat is the leadership of a state or a terrorist organization. A leadership that is highly determined, unfamiliar, risk-acceptant, and cost-tolerant will not be susceptible to punitive deterrence threats predictably, whether it is the leadership of a state or a terrorist organization. Providing the trappings of statehood to such leaders may create traditional targets to threaten but contribute little to the predictable susceptibility of those leaders to deterrence.

In addition, to revise somewhat the point made by Lawrence Freedman quoted above: some terrorist leaders may be beyond deterrence, but that does not mean all invariably are so. An organization which is unfamiliar, highly determined, extremely violent, and lacks traditional state targets does not necessarily equate to an entity which is "beyond deterrence." There are many examples in history of such non-state actors having been deterred and coerced effectively. On September 30, 1985, for example, four Soviet embassy workers in Beirut, Lebanon were kidnapped, with demands made on Moscow for their release. Apparently they were held by the Iranian-sponsored terrorist organization, Hizbollah. According to Russian sources, the Soviet clandestine service immediately began work to identify the individual terrorists and organizations involved and their motivations; it then took strong measures locally to threaten Hizbollah directly, and also threatened its Iranian sponsors with increasingly dire consequences if those kidnapped were not freed.[103] Shortly thereafter, although one captive already had been killed, the three remaining Soviet hostages were released unharmed near the Soviet embassy in a "goodwill" gesture by the terrorists. At the time, then CIA Director William Casey reportedly, "read with fascination a report that three Soviet diplomats who had been kidnapped in Beirut that fall had been released after a month…Casey was persuaded that the Soviets knew the language of Hizbollah."[104]

Israel's long-standing conflict with various terrorist organizations has demonstrated that the latter can call for a cease-fire ("*hudna*") or a more informal "quiet" ("*tahdiya*") under Islamic law when demanded by challenging circumstances:

> The period of the second Intifadah (2000 onwards) was fraught with Israeli attempts to persuade Arafat [then-head of the Palestinian Authority] to desist from encouragement of terrorism. The Israeli threats of retaliation during the first few months of the Intifadah seemed not to have had much credibility in Palestinian eyes. It is however of interest that this changed after the election of Ariel Sharon as Prime Minister and after the terrorist attacks of September 11th in the U.S. According to Israelis who followed the Palestinian scene at the time, Arafat's call of 16 December 2001 to refrain from terrorism was motivated by his final understanding that 9/11 had tipped the scales in Israel's favor: it had caused a fundamental change in the western world's tolerance towards terrorism; Israeli

reactions to Palestinian terrorism would be viewed more sympathetically. …in fact, after Arafat's call of 16 December 2001, the number of weekly terrorist attacks went down from 100 to 79 and then to 40 and even to 20.[105]

Deterrence in such cases may necessitate the creation of hardship, frustration and denied goals rather than reliance on Cold War-style punitive threats. The personal accounts and reflections of urban terrorists who struck Europe with such violent ferocity during the 1970s and 1980s suggest that strong, consistent policing measures put these terrorists under severe psychological pressures—which caused disillusionment and had some deterrent effect. For example, captured German urban terrorist Bommi Baumann—former member of the June 2nd Movement terrorist organization—identified the effect on decision making of police and military operations that kept these urban terrorists isolated, hiding and running:

> We were never successful at keeping sensibility in the group—the pressure from the outside was so great it caught up with you. …The greater the pressure from the outside, the more you stick together, the more mistakes you make, the more pressure is turned inward—somewhere you have to even things out. What did people in at the end were the psychological difficulties inside the group.[106]

A captured Italian urban terrorist who operated under the *nom de guerre*, "Giorgio," offers a similar insight:

> What I'd really like to do is go away. Just leave, take a long, long trip somewhere, get away, body and mind, somewhere different. I am so tired, and when you enter this long tunnel that life has become, you just need to forget the idea of a future. There are no roads out of here. One way out, of course, would be the Revolution. But let's not kid ourselves. More likely, it will be prison. Or worse. You don't think about it, of course, but then you can hardly imagine going on like this for the rest of your life either.... The life we lead does not encourage solidarity, but rather tension, resentment, and constant conflict.[107]

Discerning *how* to deter the specific audience in question, given its unique goals and vulnerabilities, is key. The question for deterrence is not whether the opponent is the leadership of a state or a "non-state actor" terrorist organization per se, but whether the pertinent decision makers can be placed under such pressures and constraints that they choose to desist from their activities—even if only for a season—and whether they have important and identifiable values that the United States can threaten in a fashion that is decisive in their decision making and behavior. The values to be threatened, the instruments of that threat, and the instruments of communication may vary widely depending on the circumstances; they may, in fact, bear little resemblance to our Cold War experience.

As suggested by this discussion, deterrence of non-state terrorist organizations may be based less on Cold War-style *punitive* threats than on measures to frustrate their planning, operations and goals—actions which compel them to move and hide, put pressure on their societal network and state sponsors, demoralize their personnel, and deny their aims. Such direct and indirect deterrence mechanisms are intended to persuade terrorists and their supporters, respectively, to choose alternative courses of action.[108] In some cases, state leaderships or terrorist opponents may indeed be "beyond deterrence" regardless of the punitive threats and denial measures undertaken. Whether or not a terrorist organization will be susceptible to deterrence or coercive pressure, and what form that pressure should take, cannot be determined by an *a priori* generalization that deterrence is unworkable because the opponent does not fit the balance of terror's profile of "rational," or because it lacks the types of targets traditionally linked to deterrence threats.

A close examination of the opposing leadership's motivations and circumstances—apparently undertaken by the Soviets in the 1985 case involving Hizbollah—may yield some helpful clues about the most practicable forms of deterrence. But little about deterrence of a specific terrorist opponent—the necessary threat, its credibility, or how to communicate it—can be understood with confidence in the absence of that examination. As Craig and George concluded in a quote cited above, "There is no substitute for knowledge of the adversary's mind-set and behavioral style." Deterrence theory tells us little in this regard that is useful for policy other than to examine the opponent and context closely for clues as to how best to attempt deterrence.

6. The Question "How Much Do You Know?" Must Precede the Question "How Much Is Enough?"

The balance of terror deterrence formula focuses on the relationship of weapons to targets, and conveniently assumes that opponents' decision making and behavior will be prudent in the manner necessary for that relationship to have the desired deterrent effect. Positing that "rational" opponents are deterrable in this fashion is convenient because it reduces deterrence to the alignment of U.S. offensive forces with an opponent's targets. Because U.S. offensive forces and enemy targets are *relatively* easy to count, deterrence "stability" becomes a relatively simple, tractable problem of "strategic arithmetic."[109]

Much more challenging is understanding an opponent's "mind-set and behavioral style," and anticipating how that unique mind-set and behavioral style will affect the opponent's response to U.S. deterrence threats. When diverse and unfamiliar opponents present numerous uncertainties, seeking to understand the how's and why's of their unique decision making should be the first priority of a deterrence strategy. Why? Because brandishing threats for deterrence purposes is more akin to a Rorschach test than a mechanical, technically-determined process made certain by the opponent's rationality. Information of importance for deterrence purposes includes key and diverse facts about the opponent and the context—including most basically the opponent's identity, values, goals, motivations, determination, susceptibility to U.S. instruments of power, sources of information, perceptions of the United States, evaluation of stakes involved in the contingency, organizational structure and circumstances, and modes of cost-benefit calculation, *inter alia*. As Craig and George conclude, the absence of an investigation into such matters "...can result in the disintegration of even the best deterrence strategy."[110]

We can seek to reduce uncertainties about how deterrence is likely to function by gaining insight into the factors animating the opposing leadership's decision making—including, for example, what the opposing leadership believes are unquestionable truths pertinent to the context. To what and to whom does that leadership pay attention? How and from whom does it receive information? To what extent are its communications subject to distortion and how can that distortion be managed? Is the opponent motivated by absolute goals that make concession intolerable? How does the opponent perceive the threat we hope will deter, and is that threat sufficiently salient to deter? Does the opponent more or less doubt or believe that Washington has the will and capability to inflict its threat and that Washington, in fact, will withhold the said threat if it conciliates to U.S. demands? Strategies of deterrence can stand or fall depending on the unique answers to such questions.

Balance of terror tenets, for example, posit that the U.S. nuclear retaliatory threat to destroy physical targets ultimately can be decisive in the opponent's decision making. If, however, the opponent's highest priority is protecting or promoting *intangible* values—such as national or personal honor, ego, freedom or glory, or spiritual or ideological fidelity—then even a very severe retaliatory threat to destroy physical targets may not be decisive in its decision making. Do we know if the opponent places highest value on tangible targets that can be threatened by the tools available to us, or on intangible values that may be unrelated to any physical targets? Deterrence can and has been affected by these types of factors; its functioning in the future may be more or less surprising depending on how familiar we are with these factors and how they will shape an opponent's response to our deterrence threats.

Our threats are only one side of a multidimensional problem. False confidence and a tremendous opening for making mistakes follow from the expectation that it is possible to understand intuitively how opponents will think and act. Schelling's comment along this line quoted in Chapter 3 reflects the typical confidence in this methodology: "You can sit in your armchair and try to predict how people will behave by asking how you would behave if you had your wits about you. You get, free of charge, a lot of vicarious empirical behavior."[111] On the strength of this "armchair" methodology commentators often assert that "I can't imagine" a designated opponent would "dare" to behave in a particular fashion or would fail to be deterred by some postulated number of U.S. weapons and expression of U.S. threat. Such expectations tell us much about the commentator's values, fears and limited imagination, but nothing certain about an opponent's likely responses to U.S. deterrence threats.

The "armchair methodology" is likely to miss characteristics of opponents that can be decisive in their behavior but are outside of Western observers' cultural framework. For example, some states and terrorist organizations properly categorized as having "high-intensity aggressive ideologies" can have "propensities toward martyrdom and apocalyptic visions...with no risk being too high if top decisionmakers prefer self-destruction to nonrealization of their vision."[112] Such propensities and their possible effects typically are neglected in Western threat estimates because of the "cultural barriers built into the world views that dominate policymaking in the Western world and the United States in particular, which expect nations to be essentially 'reasonable' in a Western, secular way."[113] What are the implications for deterrence of regimes with such high-intensity aggressive ideologies? Intense ideologies "unavoidably produce serious misperceptions of international realities" and, correspondingly, in these cases the "application of stable nuclear deterrence models...constitutes a grave error."[114] Useful assessments of deterrence must take such potential factors into account and cannot be discovered via the balance of terror formula of first principles, intuition and deductive logic.

Kahn and Schelling confronted the same Soviet Union but posited a very different opponent for their respective work. In the absence of serious efforts to understand the unique opponent and context, the "default" opponent conjured up via an intuitive, "armchair" methodology may have little or no connection with reality, but will determine expectations about whether and how deterrence will function.

U.S. policymakers now need to understand the opponent's "mind-set and behavioral style" to the extent possible in order to have an informed basis for anticipating whether that opponent is likely to be susceptible to deterrence pressure and, if so, how best to orchestrate deterrence for any specific purpose. Perfection in this effort will never be possible, but reduction of our ignorance in important ways will be. As Winston Churchill remarked: "However absorbed a commander may be in the elaboration of his own thought, it is sometimes necessary to take the enemy into account."[115] One of those occasions is when considering how deterrence might work against a particular enemy for a particular purpose.

During the Cold War, the priority deterrence question was "how much [force] is enough?" Now, the priority question must be "how much do you know?" A recent study of this question by the National Defense University concluded with a specific list of questions about an opponent and context that must be addressed for deterrence purposes:

- What are the nation's or group's values and priorities? How are these affected by its history and strategic culture?
- What are their objectives in the particular situation?
- What factors are likely to influence their decisionmaking?
- Who makes decisions, how does the leadership think, what is their view of the world and experience with and view of

the United States?

- How do they calculate risks and gains?
- What do they believe their stakes to be in particular situations (stakes may vary depending on the scenario)?
- What is the likely credibility of U.S. deterrence options to this adversary—for both imposing costs and denying gains?
- How inclined is the leadership to risk-taking or risk-aversion?
- How much latitude does the leadership have to either provoke or conciliate?
- What are their alternative courses of action?
- What do they believe the costs and benefits of restraint to be? Do they think they are worse off if they do not take the aggressive action? Do they see any positive benefits in not taking the action in question?
- What do they perceive as America's answers to the questions above—for example, U.S. objectives, stakes, or risk-taking propensity?[116]

Gaining useful understanding along these lines to deter opponents more effectively obviously is a challenging task; it requires observers to step outside of their own culturally-defined beliefs about what is reasonable and what *should be* the opponent's "mind-set and behavioral style," and focus instead on opponents' actual beliefs and worldviews. The deterrence order of the day is understanding opponents' unique modes of decision making without disdaining, demonizing, exaggerating, or presuming what must appear "rational" to them. Presuming such knowledge based on confidence in universal verities and in the absence of serious investigation of opponent and circumstance was a convenient and comforting fallacy of the balance of terror/assured destruction formula.

Former Director of Central Intelligence, George Tenet, makes the pertinent observation that one lesson of the U.S. failure to predict the 1998 Indian nuclear tests was, "…that both the U.S. intelligence and policy communities had an underlying mind-set that Indian government officials would behave as ours behaved....The lesson learned is that sometimes intentions do not reside in secret—they are out there for all to see and hear. What we believe to be implausible often has nothing to do with how a foreign culture might act."[117] The lesson here for deterrence considerations is clear: because deterrence is about shaping opponents' perceptions and decision making, in order to understand deterrence for any specific case one must understand the unique form and ingredients of the opponent's worldview, decision making and behavior to the extent possible. The scope for investigation suggested here is wide—ranging from the opponent's formal authority structure and processes to the cultural norms that affect decision making. As Tenet has noted in this regard: "Relying on secrets themselves divorced from deep knowledge of cultural mind-sets and history, will take you only so far."[118]

Collection of information dedicated to the goal of deterring rogue states and non-state actors will require different emphases than those established by the Cold War's focus on the Soviet Union and its forces. In particular, it may necessitate an ongoing, systematic multidisciplinary effort for this specific purpose—including a renewed emphasis on intelligence collection against state and non-state opponents built on direct, personal contact—complemented by regional experience and area expertise. Some have described this as a need to "revive" U.S. human intelligence (HUMINT) capabilities, including a renewed emphasis on cultural and linguistic expertise.[119] As then Under Secretary of Defense for Intelligence, Stephen Cambone, observed in Senate testimony: "Deterring future adversaries will require a detailed understanding of their goals, motivations, history, networks, relationships, and all the dimensions of human political behavior, on a scale broader and deeper than today's."[120]

This task of understanding opponents to strengthen deterrence certainly requires a new appreciation for what is referred to as "cultural knowledge." A U.S. Army War College publication describes the concept of culture as "fundamental" to understanding "how people think and respond."[121] To understand opponents' cultures is to understand how they "assign meaning to the world around them and define their place in that world....The values, interests, perceptions, and biases of individuals and of the collective society...."[122] The study of culture for deterrence purposes can be dismissed as unnecessary when expectations of opponent decision making are extrapolated from presumptions about how all "rational" decision makers must behave. That "armchair" methodology, however, is likely to mislead in the context of diverse and unfamiliar opponents.

Seeking to buttress deterrence with dedicated intelligence efforts to understand opponents so broadly may seem to be simple common sense; so it is. This "common sense," however, comes against decades of mechanistic assertions that deterrence *can be orchestrated to work reliably and predictably because rational leaders inevitably will think and behave within well-understood boundaries that are compatible with the predictable "working" of U.S. deterrence threats.* Those days—if they ever truly existed—are gone and the priority deterrence requirement is for a detailed understanding of specific opponents in all their uniqueness.

7. No More Claims That Action-Reaction—With the United States in the Lead—Is the "First Law of Nuclear Politics"

As discussed in Chapter 6, action-reaction is the supposed "first law of nuclear politics." The motivation for strategic arms racing is said to be driven by action-reaction cycles, generally sparked by U.S. initiatives. In fact, this "law" is of limited use for anticipating an opponent's armament decisions. Its inadequacies were well-documented during the Cold War by Colin Gray and others;[123] yet it continues to be put to considerable misuse in U.S. policy debates.

Noted independent experts conducted an exhaustive, Top Secret study for the Office of the Secretary of Defense entitled, *History of the Strategic Arms Competition: 1945-1972*. Completed in 1981 and now declassified, that study emphasizes the inadequacy of the action-reaction model to explain actual U.S. and Soviet strategic armament choices during much of the Cold War: "No sweeping generalizations about action-reaction cycles or inexorable Soviet designs or the momentum of science and technology can survive detailed examination of the sequence of events."[124] Instead, the study points to the frequent salience of the idiosyncratic political and budgetary preferences of political leaders and to the effects of domestic and international political events, "the perceptions of which by one party were virtually beyond being influenced by the other party."[125] While the study acknowledges that there were some interactions in U.S.-Soviet armament choices, it concluded that "no consistent pattern can be found."[126] If action-reaction is the "first law of nuclear politics," it is a law that is violated regularly.

The frequent accusation that the United States was responsible for driving the Cold War's supposed action-reaction arms competition also does not withstand scrutiny. In 1977, three researchers from the Graduate Institute of International Studies in Geneva—Jean-Christian Lambelet, Urs Luterbacher, and Pierre Allan—concluded in a rigorous empirical study of the U.S.-Soviet arms competition that *Soviet strategic arms acquisition was largely self-motivated*, not the result of action-reaction cycles led by the United States. Consequently, the authors observed that it was not curtailing U.S. "actions" that would end the arms competition, but changing the character of the Soviet Union: "Our analysis of the U.S-Soviet arms race indicates that while mutual stimulation is at work on both sides the most prominent feature of the race is the importance of self-stimulation in the Soviet Union. To the extent that our results have any validity, the conclusion would therefore be that a genuine peace movement in the Soviet Union is what is most needed to bring the arms race under lasting control."[127] This iconoclastic conclusion—so distant from the usual application of the supposed action-reaction "law"—was validated by subsequent history as reductions in strategic- and intermediate-range nuclear arms via arms control became possible only *after* the dramatic reorientation of Soviet policies under its final set of leaders and with the new leadership of the Russian Federation.

Yet, the entrenched action-reaction line continues that virtually any U.S. strategic initiative will motivate opponents predictably to take corresponding counteractions that they would not otherwise take. The easy solution to this supposed action-reaction process is for the United States to cease taking initiatives that will drive arms race cycles. The political effect of this venerable but demonstrably misleading line continues to be its contribution to arguments for curtailing virtually any U.S. strategic initiative.[128]

During the Cold War, Secretary McNamara expected the Soviet Union to respond to any significant U.S. BMD deployment in order to protect its putative goal of maintaining an assured destruction capability: action-reaction posited a very specific type of Soviet reaction, compelled by this specific, presumably powerful motive—to maintain its side of a "stable" balance of terror in the face of a U.S. BMD challenge. Secretary McNamara's expectation of this action-reaction cycle contributed heavily to his decision to eschew significant damage-limitation protection for U.S. cities. As illustrated in Chapter 6, this powerful balance of terror tenet continues to be offered as a reason for the United States to reject BMD capabilities; added now is the rejection of any *new* U.S. nuclear initiative lest it motivate rogue states to seek nuclear weapons and generally promote nuclear proliferation.

In this case, rogue states rightly are *not* presumed to be driven to protect a nuclear assured destruction capability from the challenge of U.S. damage-limitation capabilities. Instead, they are expected essentially to mimic U.S. armament priorities in a new action-reaction tango. The demonstration of continuing U.S. interest in nuclear weapons supposedly will lead other states to attribute greater value to nuclear weapons and, therefore, to have a greater desire to acquire them than they otherwise would have: "If the nuclear-armed states…consider nuclear weapons as valuable tools of policy and warfare, security establishments in the many countries that are more vulnerable than they will consider [the acquisition of] nuclear weapons more seriously."[129] What is the solution? The United States should "devalue" nuclear weapons: the desire of other countries to acquire nuclear weapons supposedly will be reduced to the extent that the United States moves away from nuclear weapons itself and demonstrates its belief that nuclear weapons *lack* "salience."[130] Belief in this action-reaction dynamic continues to reign and the consistent prescription that follows is for the United States to refrain from developing or deploying new capabilities: replace action-reaction with U.S. inaction and nuclear non-proliferation purportedly will be strengthened.

The practical effect of this contemporary rendition of the action-reaction thesis is that many commentators and members of Congress now oppose any "new" U.S. nuclear capabilities. Any such capabilities, it is feared, would show continued U.S. attribution of value to nuclear weapons which would encourage others to believe that nuclear weapons have value and thus drive the action-reaction cycle. This is the reason, for example, that one U.S. Senator observed about a U.S. nuclear initiative: "My vote depends on whether I think this is a new [U.S.] warhead."[131]

There are unavoidable flaws in applying action-reaction in this contemporary fashion to the control of nuclear proliferation. Perhaps most importantly, the action-reaction thesis appears to explain rogue interest in nuclear capabilities no better than it did Soviet interest during the Cold War.

It was not by accident that the United States and Soviet Union built thousands of nuclear weapons during the Cold War, and that other great powers with fewer resources followed suit with more modest numbers. The United States and its allies quickly concluded that nuclear weapons could serve deterrence purposes against an opponent superior in non-nuclear capabilities. Why should we now expect rogues *not* to appreciate that same value *whether or not the United States has many or none, old or new? Some rogues and terrorists seek nuclear weapons not because they mimic U.S. norms and behavior, but because they see nuclear weapons as uniquely useful tools for prestige, destruction, deterrence and coercion.* As United Nations Secretary General Kofi Annan observed, the possession of nuclear weapons is perceived widely as offering "the best protection" for security.[132] *Nuclear weapons have value in the eyes of those states and terrorists seeking them not because the United States does or does not show interest, but because they obviously are valuable* for select purposes. Ironically, this truth is emphasized even by those who recommend that the United States attempt to convince the world of the reduced "salience" of nuclear weapons: "Nuclear weapons are effective military weapons: with a few missions and relatively little expense, they can defeat even large conventional attacks, especially those attacks that require force projection at a distance....They are in fact partial equalizers against the might of the United States especially."[133] What more need be said about their potential value?

U.S. nuclear "inaction" will not contribute to non-proliferation as envisaged because it is not U.S. strategic force developments that appear to inspire rogue states to acquire their own nuclear arsenals per se. Those decisions instead appear to be uniquely and decisively driven by the leadership's images of personal and national identity, and by emotion, as the conclusion of a recent study on the subject affirms: "...decisions to go or not to go nuclear reflect the psychology of the leaders who make them. In particular, there are discrete decision-making pathways leading from different national identity conceptions, through emotions, to ultimate nuclear choices."[134] Leadership views regarding national identity and local security concerns may loom large in such decision making; mimicking or competing with the U.S. strategic arsenal does not. U.S. action in this regard does not appear to drive rogues' reactions, and U.S. inaction will not deliver rogue inaction: "In sum, if the nuclear weapons states exercise restraint or even seriously pursue disarmament, such actions are unlikely to achieve the non-proliferation objectives that their advocates claim."[135] When contemporary commentators assert that opponents who may want nuclear weapons will instead be motivated to inaction by U.S. example per the old action-reaction line, they apply a Cold War model of arms competition that did not serve well during the Cold War and lacks coherence when applied to contemporary opponents.

U.S. posturing as if nuclear weapons have little value is likely to be seen as a deceptive and self-interested feint by rogues and terrorist leaders who appear to be quite attentive to the manifest reality of their value. For the United States, armed with incomparable conventional military power, it certainly would be convenient were others to reject nuclear weapons in the belief they provide no unique value. Opponents could then not threaten to trump U.S. non-nuclear military advantages with nuclear escalation: U.S. posturing, however, is unlikely to convince those who do not need U.S. instruction on these matters. As the former Indian Army Chief of Staff, General K. Sundarji, famously remarked following the U.S.-led coalition's quick victory over Iraq in 1991: "The Gulf War emphasized once again that nuclear weapons are the ultimate coin of power."[136]

Indeed, it is in part because nuclear weapons have such lethality and potential value for deterrence and coercion that there is intense domestic and international concern about North Korea, and potentially Iran, acquiring them. The United States and its allies betray the reality of the "salience" of nuclear weapons by rightly and continually opposing their acquisition by rogues and terrorist organizations. If nuclear weapons truly lacked unique value, who would care?

In addition, rather than *causing* nuclear proliferation via an action-reaction process, the U.S. nuclear arsenal undoubtedly *makes an essential contribution to nuclear non-proliferation*. This positive correlation between U.S. nuclear capabilities and nuclear non-proliferation may be counterintuitive—and it is inconsistent with the old action-reaction notions as applied today—but it is unquestionable.

On the basis of the U.S. nuclear "umbrella," countries such as Germany, Japan and South Korea have felt secure without their own independent nuclear capabilities. Following the North Korean testing of nuclear weapons in October 2006, the importance of the U.S extended *nuclear* deterrence for non-proliferation was highlighted by numerous and once-unthinkable statements by Japanese officials that *Japan would be forced to reconsider its non-nuclear status if it lost confidence in the U.S. nuclear umbrella*. Remarks by then Director General of the Japan Defense Agency, Akio Kyuma, highlighted the assurance provided by U.S. extended nuclear deterrence and the theme of potential Japanese interest in nuclear weapons in the absence of that assurance: "Japan should have a nuclear deterrent capability. Yet, Japan is not allowed to possess nuclear arms; on the other hand, the United States has them."[137] It is hard to imagine a greater stimulus to nuclear proliferation than decisions by U.S. allies who have had the protection of the U.S. nuclear umbrella to "go nuclear" themselves as a result of their loss of confidence in the U.S. nuclear umbrella.

A similar concern was expressed publicly by former German Defense Minister Rupert Scholz: "We need to ask ourselves how we could react in an appropriate manner to a nuclear threat from a terror state, and if needs be, even by using our own nuclear weapons....without the appropriate guarantees of protection by our partners, the question of our own nuclear deterrent needs to be discussed openly."[138] German Minister of Defense, Franz Josef Jung, reportedly commented that all options should remain open.[139]

A detailed review of specific country case studies by pertinent regional experts underscores the importance for non-proliferation that, "the U.S. nuclear umbrella remains credible....The case studies suggest that the perceived reliability of U.S. security assurances will be a critical factor, if not *the* critical factor, in whether such countries as Japan, Saudi Arabia, South Korea, Taiwan, and Turkey reconsider their nuclear options."[140]

In the contemporary environment, North Korean and Iranian aspirations for nuclear weapons understandably cause U.S. allies great concern and highlight the criticality of U.S. extended nuclear deterrence for non-proliferation. The contemporary application of the action-reaction thesis to the question of nuclear proliferation and the concomitant political pressure against U.S. nuclear capabilities generated by that application ignores this reality; it actually threatens to contribute to nuclear proliferation by undermining a fundamental basis for allied confidence in U.S. security assurances, i.e., the U.S. extended nuclear deterrent.

In short, there now are two significantly different logical propositions hidden behind the common "action-reaction" metaphor inherited from the balance of terror tenets. First, the original Cold War logic attributed the expected reaction to an overwhelming motive to sustain mutual deterrence: the Soviet Union would respond to U.S. damage-limitation capabilities with additional offensive nuclear capabilities in order to preserve its retaliatory nuclear threat. Second, more recent logic posits the motive of states to follow the U.S. lead in their evaluation of nuclear weapons. In both cases, commentators assert that the onus is on the United States to forego new capabilities lest they spark the action-reaction mechanism. In both cases, the logic may seem elegant, but reality is far more complex.

What of the contemporary predictions presented in Chapter 6 that U.S. BMD deployment will create an action-reaction cycle and increase the missile threat to the United States by instigating a "worldwide arms race"? In principle, there is nothing amiss with the observation that some decisions to deploy or upgrade forces seem to be traceable to an action-reaction dynamic. The problem, of course, is that there are numerous *other* factors that drive decisions about the armaments a country will or will not develop and deploy. The Cold War action-reaction model was elevated to a law—applied mechanically, and ultimately used politically—despite the fact that it may be wholly irrelevant to many armament decisions. When numerous factors can determine decisions about force acquisition, confident predictions based on the single action-reaction dynamic are reductionist and very likely to be misleading.

Given the credence typically attributed to the action-reaction "law"—particularly by commentators and in Congressional debate—one might expect it to be reflected consistently in the historical record. Considerable historical evidence, however, contradicts the notion that an action-reaction arms race cycle is in any way inevitable or a "law of nuclear politics." In fact, predictions based on the action-reaction model typically have missed the actual course of events.

The Soviet buildup of offensive missile capabilities following the 1972 ABM Treaty was driven powerfully by factors unrelated to seeking an equilibrium point in the balance of terror, and unaccounted for by the action-reaction model. As discussed in Chapter 5, sanguine U.S. expectations of Soviet moderation following the ABM Treaty, based fully on the action-reaction model, were dashed by reality; the model proved misleading as the basis for prediction. Foregoing missile defense hardly checked the Soviet Union's incentives to expand its missile capabilities. They increased dramatically *following* the ABM Treaty. As Harold Brown, President Carter's Secretary of Defense, concluded in 1979: "Soviet spending...has shown no response to U.S. restraint—when we build, they build, when we cut, they build."[141]   U.S. restraint was followed by Soviet action, the reverse of the future promised by ABM Treaty proponents.

Indeed, according to Colonel General Nikolai Detinov, a key player in Soviet arms control policy throughout the period, the Soviet leadership *never* accepted U.S. "stable deterrence" logic in this regard. Rather, as noted in Chapter 5, Washington's proposal for an ABM Treaty came as a "pleasant surprise" to the Soviets not because it codified a "stable" balance of terror, but *because it allowed Moscow to concentrate resources on its planned buildup of ICBMs.*[142] As William Odom concludes in his unparalleled study of the Soviet military: "Thus the ABM treaty appeared to have allowed a considerably larger number of offensive nuclear weapons in the Soviet arsenal than there would have been without it."[143] Proponents of the ABM Treaty employed the action-reaction arms race model with powerful political effect, but little accuracy.

Nevertheless, in 1983, when President Reagan set in motion the next great missile defense debate with his Strategic Defense Initiative

(SDI), missile defense opponents again predicted with similar certainty the same frightening action-reaction cycle: "The Soviet Union would be certain to respond, by developing countermeasures and increasing its offensive forces to ensure that the U.S. defense could be penetrated."[144] And, again, they asserted that the absence or strict limitation of BMD was necessary for any possible success in offensive force reductions:

> ...limits on missile defenses are the necessary base for negotiated limits on offensive strategic missiles....The ABM Treaty is even more critical today, as the focus of negotiation shifts from limitations to reductions in strategic arms. It is clear that there will be no strategic arms reduction (START) agreement unless the ABM Treaty is maintained, and limits on defenses will be even more essential as the United States and the Soviet Union negotiate subsequent agreements for deeper reductions.[145]

Continuing to present the Cold War action-reaction model as a self-evident "law," former senior officials from the White House, the State Department, and the Department of Defense warned that the SDI ("Star Wars") was wholly incompatible with arms control: "Star Wars, in sum, is a prescription not for ending or limiting the threat of nuclear weapons, but for a competition unlimited in expense, duration and danger."[146] And, "it is possible to reach good agreements, or possible to insist on the Star Wars program as it stands, but wholly impossible to do both."[147]

Subsequent developments, however, proved once again the inadequacy of both the action-reaction model and the confident predictions based on it. On October 5, 1991, in the context of considerable emerging Congressional support for BMD deployment, Soviet President Mikhail Gorbachev announced, "We are ready to discuss U.S. proposals on non-nuclear defensive systems. We propose to study the possibility of creating a joint system to avert nuclear missile attack with ground- and space-based elements."[148]

Shortly thereafter—in 1992—Russian President Boris Yeltsin proposed a cooperative Global Protection System (GPS), focusing on mutual missile defense. At the June 1992 Washington summit, Russian President Yeltsin and President Bush agreed to a START II framework for nuclear force reductions, including the elimination of ICBMs with multiple warheads; *they simultaneously agreed to work cooperatively toward global missile defenses.*

There followed considerable progress toward U.S.-Russian cooperation on missile defense in the unheralded but high-level Ross-Mamedov Talks (named for the senior U.S. and Russian participants, Dennis Ross and Georgei Mamedov). In the context of these talks, Russian officials publicly indicated their willingness to see the ABM Treaty revised or even interpreted as irrelevant to U.S.-Russian missile defense efforts.[149] The Ross-Mamedov Talks made surprising progress toward this goal until brought to an end by a Clinton Administration that was not much interested in strategic BMD deployment. Most importantly for this discussion, this progress was made while Russia and the United States successfully concluded START negotiations that would—for the first time in history—lead to agreed reductions in strategic offensive forces. Literally decades of claims made on the basis of the action-reaction dynamic had warned that such an occurrence was impossible.

Once again, the action-reaction model proved to be the basis for misleading predictions. As was the case following the ABM Treaty, the promises of missile defense opponents based on the model went unrealized, and the actual course of events moved in a dramatically different direction. Reality this time brought simultaneous progress toward cooperation on missile defense and offensive reductions, the reverse of confident predictions throughout the Cold War.

More recently, in December 2001, President George W. Bush announced the planned U.S. withdrawal from the ABM Treaty according to the provisions for doing so under Treaty Article 15. With this move by the White House, and strong Congressional support for BMD, the United States was on an obvious track toward deployment. As in the past, this new U.S. movement toward BMD deployment was greeted with criticism based on the balance of terror adages about action-reaction, "instability," and the certain ruination of arms control. Nevertheless, Russian President Vladimir Putin's response was to observe that U.S. withdrawal from the ABM Treaty, "presents no threat to the security of the Russian Federation" and that the two countries should create a "new framework of our strategic relationship."[150] Simultaneously, the Russian leadership was more than enthusiastic to negotiate a new, binding agreement on offensive force reductions. Within months, the 2002 Moscow Treaty was signed—an agreement that entailed the deepest strategic offensive force level reductions in the long history of strategic arms control negotiations. In the context of the U.S. withdrawal from the ABM Treaty, and obvious

U.S. movement to deploy strategic BMD, the United States and Russia negotiated the most far-reaching strategic offensive force reductions in history.

This set of events truly stood the vintage 1960 action-reaction thesis on end: the overall *political* context of U.S.-Russian relations obviously determined the direction of arms control interactions, *not* a technically-determined action-reaction dynamic. For decades, the inadequacy of the action-reaction model as applied to BMD had become increasingly manifest to those who cared to look. With the simultaneous tracks of the 2002 Moscow Treaty and the Bush Administration's decision to deploy BMD, that venerable model was shown to be worse than inadequate—it was misleading: reality again proceeded in the opposite direction from that suggested by the model and again promised by its proponents.

Why have advocates of the action-reaction thesis as applied to missile defense been mistaken in their predictions so often and for so long? In part, it is because numerous factors drive armament decisions and the simplistic action-reaction formulation does not attempt to account for most of them.[151] It ignores, for example, such basic factors as: competing foreign policy goals and defense requirements; inter- and intra-service rivalries; bureaucratic politics; the specific character and style of political and social systems; electoral politics; resource availability or limitations; organizational momentum; and, technological innovation/limitation. Even highly personal and idiosyncratic factors can drive armament decisions in ways ignored by the action-reaction model. For example, as mentioned in Chapter 1, Adolf Hitler temporarily cancelled the V-2 program on the basis of a bad dream he had about the missile. It took the combined efforts of Albert Speer and Wernher von Braun to get the program back on track.[152]

When these many potentially significant factors are ignored in favor of a simplistic action-reaction model, grossly inaccurate predictions are the likely result. Such factors, singularly and in combination, frequently have produced patterns that bear no resemblance whatsoever to the action-reaction process typically promised by missile defense critics. They can lead to action-inaction, inaction-action, and non-interactive armament decisions. Soviet heavy bomber capabilities, for example, did not develop in accord with the action-reaction model. Neither the significant buildup of U.S. national air defense throughout the 1950s and 1960s, nor its virtual elimination in the 1970s, appears to have driven the Soviet heavy bomber threat in this fashion. There was neither great Soviet strategic bomber buildup to correspond to the U.S. defensive buildup, nor

dramatic change following U.S. reduction of its strategic air defenses—
no action-reaction cycle. In fact, the most obvious Soviet strategic
bomber modernization programs that did occur—the *Bear G* and *H,* and
the *Blackjack*—came after the United States phased *out* much of its
previously-robust strategic air defense capability.

Similarly, as the graphic below illustrates, for almost a decade Soviet
air defense spending was high and modestly increasing while U.S. spending on the strategic bomber program was relatively low and decreasing—
the reverse of an action-reaction dynamic. When U.S. bomber spending
increased significantly in the mid-1980s, Soviet air defense spending
kept within its traditional boundaries. Obviously, spending patterns do
not tell the entire story of acquisition patterns; these spending patterns,
however, certainly do not appear to reflect an action-reaction dynamic.

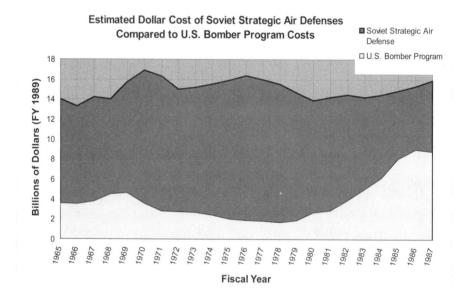

Source: Secretary of Defense Frank C. Carlucci, *Annual Report to the Congress FY 1989* (Washington
D.C.: USGPO, February 18, 1988), p. 49, Chart I.C.2.

There are, of course, logical, plausible and understandable
reasons for these apparent deviations from a simplistic action-reaction
cycle. In 1960, for example, Khrushchev made missiles, not bombers,
the centerpiece of Soviet nuclear strategy. The Soviet Union typically was
considered obsessively concerned with homeland defenses following the

catastrophic German invasion of World War II; it never produced heavy strategic bombers in significant numbers, focusing instead on heavy ICBMs. More recently, the collapse of the Soviet Union and Russia's economic difficulties limited (but did not eliminate) Russia's capability to deploy new offensive missiles regardless of what might be suggested by the action-reaction model. That such factors can be significant contributors to armament decisions, of course, is the point.

On May 1, 2001, President George W. Bush called for a new strategic framework, one allowing the United States, "to build missile defenses to counter the different threats of today's world," while also encouraging "further cuts in nuclear weapons."[153] Commentators subsequently reissued predictions about the arms race sure to follow. They once again pointed with confidence to the action-reaction model as the basis for their predictions, and excluded the many other dynamics that frequently underlie armament decisions. These predictions reflected no greater appreciation of the actual complexity of armament decision making than have similar past predictions, and are no more likely to be accurate.

Are China, North Korea, and other rogues likely to react to U.S. missile defenses by undertaking an offensive-defensive strategic missile competition, as is claimed with such certainty? Any answer, of course, is speculative, and humility should govern all efforts to anticipate future foreign decision making. Nevertheless, there is some basis for expecting that the mechanistic action-reaction model will no more apply here than it has in the past celebrated cases. Two prominent specialists on the Chinese military have concluded that China's force structure decisions cannot be understood via such a crude model: "Rather, an understanding of such variables as domestic political, technological, historical, and cultural factors provide far greater insight and predictive capacity about the drivers that shape China's doctrinal and force structure decisions."[154]

The significance of these variables, of course, is not unique to China. Similarly unique factors generally contribute to many, perhaps most, countries' decision-making processes and acquisition choices, which is why the action-reaction arms race model is so broadly inadequate. The problem is that acknowledging the potential significance of such a broad array of factors suggests the need to examine, understand, and weigh them before making confident predictions; it reduces the ease, convenience and pretense of precision that otherwise is provided by the mechanistic action-reaction model.

It should be noted in this regard that China has long been in the process of improving its ICBM force. For more than a decade it has been clear that China's reported ICBM arsenal of approximately 20 operational DF-5As will be replaced or supplemented with the introduction of new ICBMs.[155] China's ICBM improvement programs, of course, may be affected by U.S. missile defense plans, but multiple reasons for Chinese offensive missile modernization have long been in play. These reasons reportedly include: the natural process of updating old systems with newer systems; the requirement for greater ICBM force survivability and flexibility; and, movement toward a Chinese nuclear doctrine that calls for "limited, counterforce, war-fighting capabilities" as the basis for deterrence and coercion across a wide range of contingencies, including intra-war deterrence.[156] As an examination of the possible linkage between U.S. BMD and Chinese strategic force acquisition concluded: "...it has been difficult to separate Chinese ballistic missile development and deployment efforts aimed at overcoming ballistic missile defenses from China's general strategic modernization program....China is developing new missiles such as the DF-31 and DF-41, but these programs were initiated over a decade ago and were probably not a direct response to NMD [National Missile Defense]."[157]

In short, China appeared well on the road toward modernization of its offensive missile force in the absence of U.S. defenses. Rejecting the possibility of some further Chinese or North Korean offensive reaction to U.S. missile defense obviously is beyond what prudence and evidence can bear. Nevertheless, given the conditions described above, and the manifest inadequacy of the action-reaction model, the most recent crop of related predictions that U.S. BMD must be self-defeating because it can only lead to an unbeatable buildup of Chinese or North Korean offensive missiles and a "worldwide arms race" should be recognized as reductionist speculation and hubris. Self-serving Chinese statements that they will respond in just such a fashion, at least some of which have been well-coached by American missile defense opponents, hardly constitute proof to the contrary.

There undoubtedly will be another national debate concerning the future role and character of U.S. BMD, particularly including the question of overarching U.S. BMD goals. This will not be the first such BMD debate, and our awareness of actual evidence should discipline what now is regarded as a "law." In the past, U.S. officials mistook the logic and elegance of the action-reaction model for validity, and guided U.S. policy on the basis of the mistaken expectations driven by that model.

During the 1960s and early 1970s, it was not yet blatantly obvious just how inadequate was the action-reaction model or how misleading were the confident predictions based upon it. Its inadequacy now is obvious and those factors that render it inadequate—e.g., competing demands, resource limitations, and idiosyncratic leadership preferences—are likely to be just as salient in the future as they have been in the past, perhaps more so. It is time to discard the line that the action-reaction dynamic is any type of "law."

The Director of Central Intelligence, Michael Hayden, recently emphasized the need to understand the unique factors and processes which drive a leadership's decision making when establishing expectations about an opponent's force acquisition. He described this as a "new lesson" following from the CIA's incorrect prewar assessment of Iraqi WMD possession: "You have to lash up [technical expertise] to the people who know how does the Iraqi government make decisions. And who really makes decisions, and why do they make these kinds of decisions? Those have to be combined."[158] That is, you have to understand the unique goals, processes and behavioral norms of the opponent. The absence of any such consideration is why the mechanistic action-reaction model, as applied to the Soviet Union in the past and now applied globally, is likely to be so misleading.

Conclusions

The balance of terror tenets are powerful and enduring, at least in part because they explain in simple terms *the cause* of frightening threats and *point to simple solutions which are relatively easy to implement.* They define opponents and threats in specific ways that permit the easy, predictable control of each: as defined, opponents can be deterred easily and reliably simply by U.S. acquisition of properly threatening strategic forces and the avoidance of forces that are "destabilizing." With the easy, "stable" alignment of a relatively modest number of U.S. offensive nuclear weapons to enemy targets, deterrence supposedly is at risk only with irrational opponents. It is hard to imagine a conceptual framework that places fewer burdens on the United States while offering more comforting assurances about U.S. security.

Similarly, the U.S.-Soviet nuclear arms competition was explained simply and in a fashion that allowed an easy solution—i.e., the arms race supposedly would end when the United States tempered its own actions and deployed only the proper "stabilizing" forces. Both sides would then rest content at the equilibrium point of mutual vulnerability in a "stable" balance of terror. The messy challenge of addressing the fundamental problem of Soviet ideological hostility and military ambitions was unnecessary and better left unmentioned lest one appear "anti-Communist."

The balance of terror tenets provided elegant explanations of, and easy technical solutions to, our most troubling security problems. The general acceptance of these tenets led to a mechanistic determinism that equated arms control success and deterrence "stability" with specific numbers and types of forces—"stability" that could be manipulated predictably by adjusting those forces. An enduring, "stable" balance was believed to be within easy reach, courtesy of the proper orchestration of forces and the expected prudence of all rational leaders.

Acceptance of these balance of terror tenets led to national strategic policy debates over the details of the offensive strategic capabilities most suitable for sustaining mutual deterrence "stability," and whether specific arms control agreements would or would not be "stabilizing." Conspicuously marginalized following the 1960s were great debates over the more fundamental questions: whether the action-reaction "law" could withstand scrutiny; whether the functioning of deterrence could be understood so well that it could be orchestrated in practice and, if so, whether controlling the technical character of the U.S. and Soviet strategic arsenals—unilaterally or cooperatively—actually shaped deterrence "stability"; and, ultimately, whether the goal of damage limitation should be subordinated to the balance of terror tenets.

Despite the powerful political momentum behind the elegant balance of terror tenets, they suffer from internal incoherence and trip over abundant contrary evidence from history, psychology, and recent cognitive studies. To hold, the enemy would have to possess a unique combination of incompatible characteristics: predictably cautious and incautious, risk-averse and risk-tolerant. The inherent uncertainties of decision making and behavior would have to apply to all manner of leaders and decision making, except when they are responding to U.S. nuclear retaliatory threats. Then, happily, they would reliably, predictably choose to be prudent, cautious and deterred. In addition, opponents—including ruthless dictators and ideological zealots—must be *more susceptible* than are U.S. leaders to the fear of uncertainty and possible escalation, thus enabling Washington to "rock the boat" for extended deterrence purposes without Kahn's U.S. strategic advantage to explain the difference.

The balance of terror tenets, internally incoherent during the Cold War, can offer little useful guidance for thinking about deterrence in the contemporary environment. Many of the "truths" inherited from the Cold War are as likely to mislead as to enlighten because opponents' decision making and behavior may be shaped unpredictably by a wide range of factors—including some that are idiosyncratic and opaque—rather than by a universal rationality leading opponents inevitably to prudent, cautious decision making and behavior. Along with Schelling we can *hope* that all leaders everywhere will learn to be prudent and cautious so that our deterrence threats will function more easily and reliably; such hope, however, is neither a strategy nor a prudent basis for strategy.

Nuclear threats, combined with the fear of uncertainty and escalation, cannot be assumed to inspire prudence, caution and conciliation. The United States may *not* be less susceptible than opponents to the fear of escalation. And, defining forces as inherently "stabilizing" or "destabilizing" is an empty exercise when deterrence is not the predictable, mechanistic result of a particular, known alignment of forces. Finally, contemporary motivations for acquiring forces often fall far outside the Cold War's familiar action-reaction model.

Nevertheless, confident assertions and promises continue unabated that deterrence will work predictably; that some specified, minimal number and type of forces assuredly will be adequate for U.S. deterrence purposes; that ambiguity is good for deterrence; that specific types of U.S. forces will be "stabilizing" or "destabilizing" per the old Cold War definitions; that U.S. strategic force initiatives assuredly will spark opponents to an action-reaction arms race; and again, per the old Cold War formula, that U.S. inaction will inspire opponents to benign inaction. Such assertions and promises should now be recognized as hubris, particularly as default expectations lacking any serious examination of the specific mind-sets and behavioral norms of opponents.

In light of the above, Secretary McNamara's reasoning behind the historic U.S. adoption of a balance of terror policy, and corresponding rejection of direct damage limitation, collapses. Deterrence may fail unpredictably—and the only U.S. option may be to defend American society, expeditionary forces, friends and allies as well as possible—in which case the value of defenses could be paramount. Damage limitation would be the priority goal and the prospective reduction in casualties and destruction available via damage-limitation capabilities would likely be worthy of the cost in relative and absolute terms. As illustrated in

Chapter 4, this was the point made by the Joint Chiefs of Staff in response to Secretary McNamara's pertinent DPMs of the 1960s. Little credence should now be attributed to his definitive rejoinder of the time: "stable" deterrence must be the preferred alternative because it surely will provide more reliable, effective and cost-effective protection than damage-limitation capabilities, and defensive capabilities can only "destabilize" deterrence and instigate an unbeatable arms race reaction by the opponent. No ingredient of that particular policy calculation now merits confidence as a generalization *vis-à-vis* most contemporary foes in the contemporary geopolitical environment.

There may be *no* tradeoff involved in placing priority on both deterrence *and* damage limitation; the pursuit of damage-limitation capabilities may have no "destabilizing" effect on deterrence or on an opponent's acquisition of offensive missiles. Similarly, the balance of terror formula that equates predictable deterrent effect with some minimum number of U.S. weapons deemed necessary to threaten some preferred set of the opponent's targets can tell little about whether and how deterrence might function.

No confidence should be attributed to such linkages asserted in the absence of a close examination of specific opponents' mind-sets and behavioral styles in specific contexts. It would have been useful, for example, to understand Soviet motives as described by General Detinov when the United States considered the ABM Treaty in 1972. If so, we might have anticipated that the Treaty would facilitate *more*, not *fewer* Soviet ICBMs. Understanding the specific opponent and context to the extent feasible is the key to improving our capability to deter. Even following such an examination, however, highly confident assertions and predictions are no more suited to deterrence and force acquisition than they are to other extremely complex behaviors by specific individuals whose decision making often is done under great stress, and who may be influenced by many highly variable, obscure and idiosyncratic factors.

With regard to the functioning of deterrence and related U.S. strategic force measures, we live in a world of uncertainties that may be reduced by serious study of opponent and context, but never eliminated. Lingering Cold War expectations that deterrence can be orchestrated to perform predictably and reliably should at last be discarded.

Endnotes

1. This confidence is seen, for example, in Glenn Buchan, "The Anti-MAD Mythology," *Bulletin of the Atomic Scientists*, Vol. 37, No. 4 (April 1981), pp. 13-17.
2. McGeorge Bundy, "The Bishops and the Bomb," *The New York Review of Books*, Vol. 30, No. 1 (June 16, 1983), p. 4. (Emphasis in original).
3. "Speaking With Alexander George About 'Coercive Diplomacy,'" *United States Institute of Peace Journal*, Vol. 4, No. 5 (October 1991), p. 2.
4. Roger Speed and Michael May, "Dangerous Doctrine," *Bulletin of the Atomic Scientists*, Vol. 61, No. 2 (March/April 2005), pp. 43-45.
5. Thomas Schelling, *The Strategy of Conflict* (Cambridge, MA: Harvard University Press, 1960), pp. 207, 231. (Emphasis in original).
6. Ibid., p.188.
7. Ibid., pp. 201-202.
8. See, Richard Ned Lebow, *Nuclear Crisis Management: A Dangerous Illusion* (Ithaca, NY: Cornell University Press, 1987), Chapters 1-4.
9. Thomas Schelling, *Arms and Influence* (New Haven, CT: Yale University Press, 1966), p. 108.
10. Schelling, *The Strategy of Conflict*, op. cit., pp. 16-20.
11. H.R. Haldeman, *The Ends of Power* (New York: Times Books, 1978), p. 82.
12. Fred Charles Iklé, "Nuclear Strategy: Can There Be a Happy Ending?" *Foreign Affairs*, Vol. 63, No. 4 (Spring 1985), p. 822.
13. Ashton B. Carter and William J. Perry, "Nuclear Over North Korea: Back to the Brink," *The Washington Post*, October 20, 2002, p. B-1.
14. As quoted by Secretary Perry in, U.S. Senate, Committee on Foreign Relations, *North Korea Nuclear Agreement,* Hearings, 104th Congress, 1st Session (Washington, D.C.: USGPO, 1995), p. 16.
15. Quoted in, Steve Coll and David B. Ottaway, "New Threats Create Doubt in U.S. Policy," *The Washington Post*, April 13, 1995, p. A-26.
16. Carter and Perry, loc. cit.
17. Coll and Ottaway, op. cit., p. A-27. See also, Samuel S. Kim, *North Korean Foreign Relations in the Post-Cold War World* (Carlisle, PA: U.S. Army War College, Strategic Studies Institute, April 2007), pp. 84-86.
18. Kim Myong Chol, "Kim Jong Il's Military Strategy for Reunification," *Comparative Strategy*, Vol. 20, No. 4 (2001), p. 404.
19. Quoted in, "Nobody Needs Nukes," *The New York Times*, February 23, 1993, p. 21.
20. Robert McNamara, "For the Record," *The Washington Post*, June 18, 1998, p. A-24.
21. See the lengthy first-person discussion by Adm. Elmo R. Zumwalt, former Chief of Naval Operations, in, *On Watch* (New York: Quadrangle/The New York Times Book Co., 1976), pp. 432-449. The text of Brezhnev's letter to Nixon, previously classified, is now available. See, Letter from Soviet Secretary Leonid Brezhnev to President Richard Nixon, October 24, 1973, National Archives, Nixon Presidential Materials Project, Henry A. Kissinger Office Files, Box 69, Dobrynin/Kissinger, Vol. 20 (October 12-November 27, 1993). Available at www.gwu.edu/~nsarchiv/NSAEBB98/octwar-71.pdf.
22. Lebow, op. cit., p. 131.

23. Quoted in, Aleksandr Fursenko and Timothy Naftali, *One Hell of a Gamble: Khrushchev, Castro and Kennedy, 1958-1964* (New York: W.W. Norton and Company, 1997), pp. 171, 241.
24. Robert O'Neill, "The Use of Military Force: Constant Factors and New Trends," *The Changing Strategic Landscape*, Part 2, Adelphi Papers, No. 236 (London: International Institute for Strategic Studies, 1989), p. 3.
25. See the discussion in, Keith B. Payne, *Deterrence in the Second Nuclear Age* (Lexington, KY: University Press of Kentucky, 1996), pp. 114-115. See also, United Kingdom, Ministry of Defence, CBRN Policy, *Operation CORPORATE 1982: The Carriage of Nuclear Weapons by the Task Group Assembled for the Falklands Campaign*, available at, http://www.rna-10-area.co.uk/files/corporate-nuclear.pdf.
26. Quoted in, Oriana Fallaci, "Galtieri: No Regrets, No Going Back," *Times* (London), June 12, 1982, p. 4.
27. Michael Howard, "The Great War: Mystery or Error?" *The National Interest*, No. 64 (Summer 2001), pp. 82-83.
28. Holger Herwig, "Germany," in, *The Origins of World War I*, Richard F. Hamilton and Holger H. Herwig, eds. (Cambridge, UK: Cambridge University Press, 2003), p. 150.
29. Quoted in, Paul Schmidt, *Hitler's Interpreter* (New York: Macmillan, 1951), p. 320.
30. Quoted in, Louis Morton, "Japan's Decision for War," in *Command Decisions*, Kent Greenfield, ed. (Washington, D.C.: USGPO, 1990), p. 122.
31. Ibid., p. 124.
32. Harold Macmillan, *Winds of Change, 1914-1939* (London: Macmillan, 1966), p. 575.
33. James Lebovic, *Deterring International Terrorism and Rogue Threats* (New York: Routledge, 2007), p. 29.
34. Kenneth N. Waltz, "More May Be Better," in, Scott D. Sagan and Kenneth N. Waltz, *The Spread of Nuclear Weapons* (New York: W.W. Norton & Company, 2000), p. 28. See also, Lawrence Freedman, *Deterrence* (Malden, MA: Polity Press, 2004), p. 29; and, George Lewis, Lisbeth Gronlund, and David Wright, "National Missile Defense: An Indefensible System," *Foreign Policy*, No. 117 (Winter 1999-2000), pp. 128-129.
35. Kenneth N. Waltz, "Waltz Responds to Sagan," in, Sagan and Waltz, op. cit., p. 132.
36. See, for example, John Stoessinger, *Why Nations Go to War* (New York: St. Martin's Press, 1993), p. 213; Donald Kagan, *On the Origins of War* (New York: Doubleday, 1995), pp. 8, 569; Bert E. Park, M.D., *Ailing, Aging, Addicted* (Lexington, KY: University Press of Kentucky, 1993), passim; Richard Ned Lebow, *Between Peace and War* (Baltimore, MD: Johns Hopkins University Press, 1981), pp, 220-231; Jonathan Clemente, "In Sickness, In Health," *Bulletin of the Atomic Scientists*, Vol. 63, No. 2 (March/April 2007), pp. 38-44; and, Elinor Ostrom, "A Behavioral Approach to the Rational Choice Theory of Collective Action: Presidential Address, American Political Science Association, 1997," *American Political Science Review*, Vol. 92, No. 1 (March 1998), pp. 1-22.
37. As reported in Alan Deutchman, "Change or Die," *Fast Company*, No. 94 (May 2005), pp. 52-62; Betsy Hart, "Driving Anxieties," *The Washington Times*, December 30, 2007, p. B1; and Kevin Freking, "Midwest Has Worst Drunk Driving Rates," AP, April 23, 2008, available at, http://news.aol.com/health/story/ar/_a/midwest-has-worst-

drunk-driving-rates/2008042309.

38. Hart, loc. cit.

39. See the brief discussions in, Lee Bowman, "Teen Brains Not Wired to Decide: Don't Mature Until Mid-20s," *The Washington Times*, March 30, 2007, p. A9; Anne Munoz-Furlong, "What Were You Thinking?" *Food Allergy News*, Vol. 14, No. 6 (August-September 2005), pp. 1, 9; Jennifer Harper, "Long Reach to Maturity," *The Washington Times*, February 7, 2006, p. A3; and, Amy Harmon, "That Wild Streak? Maybe It Runs in the Family," *The New York Times*, June 15, 2006, available at, www.nytimes.com/2006/06/15/health/15gene.html?.

40. For a useful summary of these studies, see Shankar Vedantum, "Persistence of Myths Could Alter Public Approach," *The Washington Post*, September 4, 2007, p. A3. In particular, see, Norbert Schwarz et al., "Metacognitive Experiences and the Intricacies of Setting People Straight: Implications for Debiasing and Public Information Campaigns," *Advances in Experimental Social Psychology*, Vol. 39 (2007), pp. 127-161.

41. Bradley Thayer, "Thinking About Nuclear Deterrence Theory," *Comparative Strategy*, Vol. 26, No. 4 (July-September 2007), p. 312.

42. See, for example, the discussion in, Gabriella Boston, "One's Inner Crystal Ball Often Misleads When Trying to Predict What Lies Ahead," *The Washington Times*, March 11, 2007, pp. D1, D4. See also, Rose McDermott, "The Feeling of Rationality: The Meaning of Neuroscientific Advances for Political Science," *Perspectives on Politics*, Vol. 2, No. 4 (December 2004), pp. 691-706.

43. Office of the Secretary of Defense, 2002 Summer Study, *Recent Findings in the Biosciences: Implications for DoD*, [Briefing], p. 17.

44. Kevin Woods et al., *Iraqi Perspectives Project: A View of Operation Iraqi Freedom From Saddam's Senior Leadership* (Norfolk, VA: U.S. Joint Forces Command, 2006), p. 8.

45. American Group for the Advancement of Psychiatry, Committee on Social Issues, *Psychiatric Aspects of the Prevention of War*, Report No. 57 (September 1964), p. 268.

46. Schelling, *The Strategy of Conflict*, op. cit., pp. 3-4, 16.

47. Bernd Freytag von Loringhoven, *In the Bunker With Hitler* (New York: Pegasus Books, 2007), p. 88.

48. Adolf Hitler, *Hitler's Secret Book*, Introduction by Telford Taylor (New York: Bramhall House, 1986), p. 40.

49. Adolf Hitler, Speech, Munich Exhibition Halls, March 14, 1936. Quoted in, Max Domarus, *Hitler: Speeches and Proclamations 1932-1945, The Chronicle of a Dictatorship, Vol. II, 1935-1938* (Wauconda, IL: Bolchazy-Carducci Publishers, 1992), p. 790.

50. Quoted in, Donald P. Steury, "Intelligence in Recent Public Literature," *Studies in Intelligence*, Vol. 50, No. 1 (March 2006), unclassified portions of classified edition available at, http://www.cia.gov/csi/studies/vol50no1/9_BK_What_Stalin_Knew_htm.

51. Waltz, "More May Be Better," in, Sagan and Waltz, op. cit., p. 22.

52. See the discussion in, Keith B. Payne, *The Fallacies of Cold War Deterrence and a New Direction* (Lexington, KY: University Press of Kentucky, 2001), pp. 50-52.

53. Quoted in Enrique Krauze, "The Return of Che Guevara," *The New Republic*, Vol. 218, No. 6 (February 9, 1998), p. 34.

54. Juan O. Tamayo, "Castro Requested Soviet Missiles in 1981, Book Says," *Miami Herald*, September 19, 2005, p. 1.

55. "Cuba at the Crossroads," *The Washington Post*, February 12, 2006, p. 7.

56. Quoted in David McCullough, *Truman* (New York: Simon and Schuster, 1992), p. 459. See also, Payne, *Deterrence in the Second Nuclear Age*, op. cit., p. 111.

57. Avner Cohen, *Israel and the Bomb* (New York: Columbia University Press, 1998), p. 342.

58. See, R. Ernest Dupuy and Trevor N. Dupuy, *The Encyclopedia of Military History* (New York: Harper and Row, 1977), p. 1235; and, Karl P. Mueller et al., *Striking First* (Santa Monica, CA: RAND Corp., 2006), p. 210.

59. See the discussion in, Mark Clark, "Nuclear Deterrence for Small Nuclear Powers," in, *American National Security: Essays in Honor of William R. Van Cleave*, Bradley Thayer, ed. (Fairfax, VA: National Institute Press, 2007), p. 41.

60. Henry Kissinger, *Years of Upheaval* (Boston, MA: Little Brown and Company, 1982), p. 465.

61. *Agence France Presse*, International News Section, "Iraq Tried to Hit Israeli Nuclear Plant During Gulf War," February 25, 1997.

62. See the case study in, Payne, *The Fallacies of Cold War Deterrence and a New Direction*, op. cit., pp. 1-2, 11.

63. See, Alexandre Mansourov, "Stalin, Mao, Kim, and China's Decision to Enter the Korean War, September 16 - October 15, 1950: New Evidence From the Russian Archives," *Cold War International History Project Bulletin*, Nos. 6-7 (Winter 1995-1996), p. 101.

64. See, Jung Chang and Jon Halliday, *Mao: The Unknown Story* (New York: Alfred Knopf, 2005), pp. 413-414.

65. See, for example, the statements by Major General Zhu Chenghu, Dean of China's National Defense University, quoted in, Danny Gittings, "General Zhu Goes Ballistic," *The Wall Street Journal*, July 18, 2005, p. A13; Alexandra Harney, Demetri Sevastopulo, and Edward Alden, "Top Chinese General Warns US Over Attack," *Financial Times*, July 15, 2005, p. 5; and, Joseph Kahn, "Chinese General Threatens Use of A-Bomb if U.S. Intrudes," *The New York Times*, July 15, 2005, p. A8.

66. Li Zhisui, *The Private Life of Chairman Mao* (New York: Random House, 1994), p. 125.

67. Chang and Halliday, op. cit., p. 415.

68. See, *The Sino-Soviet Border Conflict, 1969: U.S. Reactions and Diplomatic Maneuvers, A National Security Archive Electronic Briefing Book*, William Burr, ed., June 12, 2001, available at, www.gwu.edu/~nsarchiv/NSEBB/NSAEBB49/index2.html.

69. Ibid.

70. Ibid.

71. President George H.W. Bush's letter delivered to Iraqi Foreign Minister Tariq Aziz is reprinted in, U.S. *Department of State Dispatch, Persian Gulf*, No. 2, January 14, 1991, p. 25.

72. See the discussion in, Payne, *Deterrence in the Second Nuclear Age*, op. cit., pp. 81-87.

73. Donald Kagan, "Honor, Interest, and the Nation-State," in *Honor Among Nations*, Elliot Abrams, ed. (Washington, D.C.: Ethics and Public Policy Center, 1998), p. 1. (Emphasis added).

74. As described in, Stephen Cimbala, *Nuclear Weapons and Strategy: U.S. Nuclear Policy for the Twenty-First Century* (New York: Routledge, 2005), p. 103.

75. See the discussion in, Payne, *The Fallacies of Cold War Deterrence and a New*

Direction, op. cit., especially chapter 3.

76. Quoted in, Max Domarus, *Hitler: Speeches and Proclamations 1932-1945, The Chronicle of a Dictatorship, Vol. III, 1939-1940* (Wauconda, IL: Bolchazy-Carducci Publishers, 1997), p. 1663.

77. Stoessinger, op. cit., p. 214.

78. Thomas C. Schelling, U.S. House of Representatives, Foreign Affairs Committee, *Strategy and Science: Toward a National Security Policy for the 1970s*, Hearings, 91st Congress, 1st Session (Washington, D.C.: USGPO, 1969), p. 149.

79. Ibid.

80. Quoted in, Michael Spence, "Game-Theory Guru," *Hoover Digest*, No. 2 (Spring 2007), pp. 146-147.

81. Richard Ned Lebow, "The Deterrence Deadlock: Is There a Way Out?" in Robert Jervis, Richard Ned Lebow, and Janice Stein, *Psychology and Deterrence* (Baltimore, MD: Johns Hopkins University Press, 1985), pp. 182-183.

82. Yehezkel Dror, "High-Intensity Aggressive Ideologies as an International Threat," *The Jerusalem Journal of International Relations*, Vol. 9, No. 1 (March 1987), p. 159.

83. Roger B. Myerson, *Force and Restraint in Strategic Deterrence: A Game-Theorist's Perspective* (Carlisle, PA: Strategic Studies Institute, U.S. Army War College, November 2007), pp. 21-22.

84. Gordon Craig and Alexander George, *Force and Statecraft: Diplomatic Problems of Our Time*, Third Edition (New York: Oxford University Press, 1995), p. 188.

85. See, for example, Lothar Rühl, "Offensive Defence in the Warsaw Pact," *Survival*, Vol. 33, No. 5 (September/October 1991), pp. 442-450; Beatrice Heuser, "Warsaw Pact Military Doctrines in the 1970s and 1980s: Findings in the East German Archives," *Comparative Strategy*, Vol. 12, No. 4 (October-December 1993), pp. 437-458; Beatrice Heuser, "Victory in a Nuclear War? A Comparison of NATO and WTO War Aims and Strategies," *Contemporary European History*, Vol. 7, No. 3 (November 1998), pp. 311-327; and, Matthias Uhl, "Storming on to Paris: The 1961 Buria Exercise and the Planned Solution of the Berlin Crisis," in, *War Plans and Alliances in the Cold War*, Vojtech Mastny, Sven Holtsmark, and Andreas Wenger, eds. (Oxford: Routledge Press, 2006), pp. 46-71.

86. Julian Isherwood, "Warsaw Pact Planned to Nuke Its Way Across Europe," *Armed Forces Journal International*, Vol. 30, No. 1 (June 1993), p. 15.

87. Bernard Brodie, "What Price Conventional Capabilities in Europe?" *The Reporter*, Vol. 28 (May 23, 1963), p. 28.

88. Ibid.

89. In the January-February 2007 issue of *Bulletin of the Atomic Scientists*, for example, the hands of the clock were advanced two minutes, from the seven minutes to midnight of the November-December 2006 issue, to five minutes to midnight. This change was the cover story of the January-February 2007 issue.

90. "The Clock," *Bulletin of the Atomic Scientists*, Vol. 63, No. 6 (November/ December, 2007), p. 5.

91. Quoted in, Carl Bialik, "Countdown Clocks Offer a Lot of Drama, But Little Information," *The Wall Street Journal*, June 29, 2007, p. B1.

92. For a rare critique of the veracity of doomsday clock-setting see, Marybeth Hicks, "Atomic Scientists Need to Stop Clock," *The Washington Times*, February 4, 2007, pp. D1, D3, D4.

93. These points are nicely summarized in, Roger W. Barnett, "Robert McNamara's Strange Legacy: Mutual Assured Destruction," in Bradley A. Thayer, ed., *American*

National Security Policy: Essays in Honor of William R. Van Cleave (Fairfax, VA: National Institute Press, 2007), pp. 19-26.

94. Senator Joseph R. Biden, Jr., *U.S. Foreign Policy in the 21st Century: Defining Our Interests in a Changing World*, Speech, September 10, 2001, available at, http://biden.senate.gov/newsroom/details.cfm?id=227895&&.

95. Joseph Biden, quoted in, Steven Mufson, "Sen. Biden Attacks Missile Defense Plans as Costly, Risky," *The Washington Post*, September 11, 2001, p. 4.

96. Lawrence Freedman, *Deterrence* (Malden, MA: Polity Press, 2004), p. 99.

97. Waltz, "Waltz Responds to Sagan," loc. cit.

98. Freedman, op. cit., p. 117.

99. Wolfgang Panofsky, "Nuclear Insecurity: Correcting Washington's Dangerous Posture," *Foreign Affairs*, Vol. 86, No. 5 (September/October 2007), pp. 113-114; and, Speed and May, op. cit., p. 44.

100. This point was made with regard to U.S.-Soviet relations in, Michael Altfeld, "Uncertainty as a Deterrence Strategy: A Critical Assessment," *Comparative Strategy*, Vol. 5, No. 1 (1985), pp. 1-26.

101. Quoted in, Demetri Sevastopulo and Andrew Ward, "Clinton Backs 'Ambiguity' on Taiwan Policy," *Financial Times*, August 3, 2007, available at http://www.ft.com/cms/s/fd5cc702-4153-11dc-8f37-0000779fd2ac.html.

102. See, for example, "Special Issue: Deterring Terrorism," *Comparative Strategy*, Vol. 26, No. 5 (October-December 2007), pp. 371-493.

103. Andrei Shoumikhin, *Soviet Responses to Terror Attacks, September-October 1985* (Fairfax, VA: National Institute for Public Policy, February 2005), pp. 1-7.

104. Bob Woodward, *Veil: The Secret Wars of the CIA, 1981-1987* (New York: Simon & Schuster, 1987), p. 416.

105. Shmuel Bar, *Deterring Non-State Terrorist Groups—Palestinian Groups—Fatah and Hamas (2000-2006)* (Fairfax, VA: National Institute for Public Policy, November 2006), p. 14; and, Shmuel Bar, *Warrant for Terror* (Lanham, MD: Rowman & Littlefield Publishers, 2006), p. 78.

106. Bommi Baumann, *How It All Began (Wie Alles Anfing): The Personal Account of a West German Urban Guerrilla* (Vancouver: Arsenal Pulp, 2000), p. 108. Many thanks to Gary Geipel for bringing this material to my attention. See, Gary Geipel, "Urban Terrorists in Continental Europe After 1970: Implications for Deterrence and Defeat of Violent Nonstate Actors," *Comparative Strategy*, Vol. 26, No. 5 (October-December 2007), p. 464.

107. Antony Shugaar, *Memoirs of an Italian Terrorist: Giorgio* (New York: Carroll & Graf, 2003), pp. 60, 163, quoted in, Geipel, loc. cit.

108. The classic, early discussion of the distinction between deterrence by "denial" and deterrence by punitive threat can be found in, Glenn Snyder, *Deterrence and Defense: Toward a Theory of National Security* (Princeton, NJ: Princeton University Press, 1961), p. 15.

109. Leon Fuerth, "Return of the Nuclear Debate," in, *Contemporary Nuclear Debates*, Alexander Lennon, ed. (Cambridge, MA: The MIT Press, 2002), p. 189.

110. Craig and George, op. cit., p. 189.

111. Thomas Schelling, quoted in Chapter 3 above, from, Kathleen Archibald, ed., *Strategic Interaction and Conflict: Original Papers and Discussion* (Berkeley, CA: Institute of International Studies, University of California, 1966), p. 150.

112. Dror, op. cit., p. 161.

113. Ibid., p. 154.

114. Ibid., p. 172.
115. Quoted in, Robert Debs Heinl, *Dictionary of Military and Naval Quotations* (Annapolis, MD: U.S. Naval Institute, 1996), p. 102.
116. Elaine Bunn, "Can Deterrence Be Tailored?" *Strategic Forum*, No. 225, Institute for National Strategic Studies, National Defense University (January 2007), p. 3. This list is derived from, Payne, *The Fallacies of Cold War Deterrence*, op. cit., pp. 104-107.
117. George Tenet (with Bill Harlow), *At the Center of the Storm: My Years at the CIA* (New York: HarperCollins, 2007), pp. 45-46.
118. Ibid.
119. American Foreign Policy Council, *Confronting Iran: U.S. Options* (Chicago, IL: McCormick Tribune Foundation, 2007), pp. 11-12.
120. Stephen Cambone, Under Secretary of Defense for Intelligence, *Prepared Statement Before the Senate Armed Services Committee*, April 17, 2004, p. 5, available at, http://armed–services.senate.gov/testimony.cfm?wit_id=1146.
121. See, Sheila Miyoshi Jager, *On the Uses of Cultural Knowledge* (Carlisle, PA: Strategic Studies Institute, U.S. Army War College, November 2007), p. 5.
122. Ibid., p. 6.
123. See, Colin S. Gray, *The Soviet-American Arms Race* (Farnborough, Hants, England: Saxon House, 1976), pp. 12-57. See also, Gray's later, *House of Cards: Why Arms Control Must Fail* (Ithaca, NY: Cornell University Press, 1992).
124. *History of the Strategic Arms Competition: 1945-1972, Part II*, Alfred Goldberg, ed., with contributions by Ernest R. May, John D. Steinbruner, and Thomas W. Wolfe (Washington, D.C.: Historical Office, Office of the Secretary of Defense, March 1981), p. 811.
125. Ibid., p. 768.
126. Ibid., p. 810.
127. Jean-Christian Lambelet, Urs Luterbacher, and Pierre Allan, "Dynamics of Arms Races: Mutual Stimulation vs. Self-Stimulation," *Journal of Peace Science*, Vol. 4, No. 1 (1979), p. 64.
128. See, for example, Stephen Schwartz, "Don't Know Much About History," *Bulletin of the Atomic Scientists*, Vol. 57, No. 4 (July/August 2001), p. 11.
129. Michael May, "What Are Nuclear Weapons For?" *Physics and Society*, Vol. 36, No. 4 (October 2007), p. 2, available at, http://aps.org/units/fps/newsletters/2007/october/may.cfm; see also, Wolfgang Panofsky, op. cit., p. 113; and, The Stanley Foundation, *Nuclear Weapons, Energy, and Proliferation: Pressures on the Global Community* (Muscatine, IA: The Stanley Foundation, September 2006), pp. 32-33.
130. May, "What Are Nuclear Weapons For?", loc. cit.
131. Senator Diane Feinstein, quoted in, William Matthews, "Senators Question U.S. Nuclear Warhead Project," *DefenseNews.com*, April 18, 2007, available at, http://www.defensenews.com/story.php?=2695738&c=america.
132. As quoted in, William Broad and David Sanger, "Restraints Fray and Risks Grow as Nuclear Club Gains Members," *The New York Times*, October 15, 2006, available at, http://www.nytimes.com/2006/10/15/world/asia/15nuke.html.
133. May, "What Are Nuclear Weapons For?" op. cit., p. 3; see also, Panofsky, op. cit., p. 113.
134. Jacques Hymans, *The Psychology of Nuclear Proliferation: Identity, Emotions, and Foreign Policy* (Cambridge, UK: Cambridge University Press, 2006), p. ix.
135. Ibid., p. 223.

136. Quoted in, Selig Geoffrey Kemp, *India and America After the Cold War* (Washington, D.C.: Carnegie Endowment for International Peace, 1993), p. 20.

137. "JDA Director General Kyuma's Remark Tolerating Passage of Nuclear-Armed Vessel May Make Three Nonnuclear Principles Lose [Their] Validity," *Naha Ryukyu Shimpo* (Morning Edition), November 25, 2006, p. 3.

138. Quoted in, Kate Connolly (in Berlin), "Germany 'Needs a Nuclear Arsenal of Its Own,'" January 27, 2006, available at, http://www.flois.gov/portal/server.pt/gateway/PTARGS_0_33391_246_203_0_43/http%3.

139. Report by Helmut Stoltenberg, "Dispute Over Military Options—Bundestag Again Debated How to Proceed Against Iranian Nuclear Program," Berlin ddp, Independent News Agency, January 26, 2006, in Open Source Center, "German Bundestag Disputes Military Options Against Iran," EUP20060126085012.

140. Kurt Campbell and Robert Einhorn, in "Avoiding the Tipping Point: Concluding Observations," in, Kurt Campbell, Robert Einhorn, and Mitchell Reiss, eds., *The Nuclear Tipping Point* (Washington, D.C.: Brookings Institution Press, 2004), p. 321. (Emphasis in original).

141. Secretary of Defense Harold Brown, Statement on February 27, 1979, in *Outlook and Budget Levels for Fiscal Years 1979 and 1980*, Hearings Before the Committee on the Budget, House of Representatives, 96th Congress, 1st Session (Washington, D.C.: USGPO, 1979), p. 492. See also, Arms Control and Disarmament Agency, *The Soviet Propaganda Campaign Against the U.S. Strategic Defense Initiative* (Washington, D.C.: Arms Control and Disarmament Agency, 1986), p. 8.

142. See, William E. Odom, *The Collapse of the Soviet Military* (New Haven, CT: Yale University Press, 1998), p. 71.

143. Ibid.

144. Matthew Bunn, *Foundation for the Future: The ABM Treaty and National Security* (Washington, D.C.: Arms Control Association, 1990), p. 6.

145. Ibid., p. 7.

146. McGeorge Bundy, George F. Kennan, Robert S. McNamara, and Gerard Smith, "The President's Choice: Star Wars or Arms Control," *Foreign Affairs*, Vol. 63, No. 2 (Winter 1984/85), p. 273.

147. Ibid., p. 277.

148. "Full Text of Statement Made by President Mikhail Gorbachev on Soviet Television on 5 October," TASS, 2054 GMT, October 5, 1991, in FBIS, *Daily Report: Soviet Union*, October 7, 1991, pp. 2-3.

149. See the discussions of these talks in, Stephen Hadley, "The Global Protection System: Concepts and Progress," *Comparative Strategy*, Vol. 12, No. 1 (January-March 1993), pp. 3-6; Robert Joseph, *Testimony of Robert G. Joseph Before the Senate Committee on Governmental Affairs, Subcommittee on International Security, Proliferation, and Federal Services*, April 28, 1999 (mimeo); Strategic Defense Initiative Organization, *1993 Report to the Congress on the Strategic Defense Initiative* (January 1993), pp. 1-5 - 1-12; Senator Thad Cochran, *Stubborn Things: A Decade of Facts About Ballistic Missile Defense* (Washington, D.C.: U.S. Senate, Committee on Governmental Affairs, Subcommittee on International Security, Proliferation, and Federal Services, September 2000), pp. 5-10; Henry Cooper, "Cooperative Defense, Collective Security," *San Diego Union-Tribune*, May 13, 2001, p. G1; and, Keith B. Payne, Linda Vlahos, Willis Stanley, "Evolving Russian Views on Defense: An Opportunity for Cooperation," *Strategic Review*, Vol. 21, No. 1 (Winter

1993), pp. 61-72. On September 24, 1992, at a conference in Washington, D.C., Russian Deputy Foreign Minister Mamedov began a dinner speech by telling the American audience, including many senior officials, that with regard to a cooperative global protection regime, "We are almost there."

150. Quoted in, "U.S. Quits ABM Treaty," *CNN.com*, December 14, 2001, available at, http://archives.cnn.com/2001/AllPolitics/12/13/rec.bush.abm. Some Russians, including former senior officials, responded promptly and positively to President George W. Bush's speech on May 1, 2001 with a call for the renewal of U.S.-Russian strategic cooperation. See, for example, the long commentary by former Foreign Minister Andrey Kozyrev in, "ABM—This is Our Chance," *Moscow Moskovskiye Novosti*, No. 18 [1092], May 1-14, 2001, p. 5. President Putin's initial response to President Bush's strategic framework conveyed the potential for cooperation, not a renewed arms race: "In my opinion this creates a good basis for a positive dialogue. We will see in the future what the result of the dialogue would be." Quoted in, Martin Nesirky, "Putin Welcomes Bush's Defense Policy as 'Good Basis,'" *The Washington Times*, May 5, 2001, p. A5. See also, Peter Baker, "Moscow Dispatch, Starstruck," *The New Republic*, May 28, 2001, pp. 15-16.

151. For an early and still useful discussion of this point see, Gray, *The Soviet-American Arms Race*, op. cit., pp. 12-55.

152. See the discussion in, Payne, *The Fallacies of Cold War Deterrence and a New Direction*, op. cit., p. 70.

153. "Text of President Bush's Speech," *The New York Times on the Web*, May 1, 2001, available at, http://www.nytimes.com/aponline/national/01.

154. Bates Gill and James Mulvenon, "The Chinese Strategic Rocket Forces: Transition to Credible Deterrence," in, National Intelligence Council, Federal Research Division, Library of Congress, *China and Weapons of Mass Destruction: Implications for the United States, Conference Report*, November 5, 1999, CR 99-05 (April 2000), p. 12.

155. Ibid., pp. 35, 46-48.

156. Ibid., pp. 47-55. Thomas Schelling has noted that the vulnerability of Chinese offensive missiles could spur a Chinese missile buildup, "with or without [U.S.] missile defense." Quoted in Fareed Zakaria, "Misapprehensions About Missile Defense," *The Washington Post*, May 7, 2001, p. 19.

157. Center for Nonproliferation Studies, *Archived Material, China's Opposition to US Missile Defense Programs* (2000), available at, http://cns.miis.edu/research/china/chinamd.htm.

158. Central Intelligence Agency, Press Release, April 17, 2007, *Transcript of Interview of CIA Director Michael V. Hayden by C-SPAN's Brian Lamb*, Aired: April 15, 2007. Excerpt from transcript available at, https://www.cia.gov/cia/public_affairs/press_release/2007/pr041707.htm. Also reported in, Walter Pincus, "Hayden Works to Absorb New Hires at CIA," *The Washington Post*, April 15, 2007, p. A-9.

Chapter 8
What Is New and Different? What Difference Does It Make for Deterrence and Defense?

"Facts are stubborn things; and whatever may be our wishes, our inclinations, or the dictates of our passions, they cannot alter the state of facts and evidence."

-John Adams

Expectations about opponent decision making and behavior embedded in the balance of terror tenets are derived from supposedly universal boundaries set by rationality and, therefore, are believed to pertain across time and place. These expectations foster confident predictions about deterrence *vis-à-vis* all "rational" opponents. The problem with such confident predictions, of course, is that the particular worldview of the theory's American architects—their values, judgments and priorities—is projected onto the opponent and actually sets the boundaries of what are then said to be the dictates of "rational" decision making and behavior, i.e., prudence and caution in the face of material threat. This problem is obvious in the "armchair" methodology recommended by Schelling, namely, the values, judgments and priorities of the one in the "armchair" become the bench mark for expectations about opponents' decision making and behavior.

Those who continue to employ the balance of terror tenets, metrics and terms of art do not appear to appreciate the extent to which their expectations of the opponent are a reflection of their own cultural norms and the particular conditions of the Cold War. Several very specific conditions of the Cold War, for example, are necessary for the expectations about opponents reflected in the propositions that secure, retaliatory threats of nuclear annihilation can deter predictably, and that damage-limiting capabilities should be eschewed per the traditional requirements for "stable" deterrence.

Those Cold War conditions essential to the logic of such balance of terror staples generally are absent in the contemporary geopolitical context, and those staples correspondingly have lost coherence. This is not simply to suggest tautologically that in the absence of a Cold War there can be no Cold War balance of terror. Rather, it was the combination of Western cultural norms and the specific conditions of the Cold War that gave birth to the supposedly universal and timeless tenets of the balance of terror; yet, in most cases those Cold War conditions no longer exist. Correspondingly, most of the deterrence concepts, strategic force metrics, and terms of art that continue to dominate the U.S. strategic debate, in fact, now have little or no meaning.

Comparable Intentions, Resources and Capabilities

Balance of terror tenets presume, for example, that the sides involved have comparable intentions, and comparable financial, military and technological resources—at least to the extent that each is expected to seek, establish and sustain secure offensive retaliatory nuclear capabilities for mutual deterrence purposes. It was supposed that neither side could achieve a sustainable, damage-limitation capability *worth the price* because both would have the necessary resources and intention to deny the other that capability.

The presumption of comparable intent and resources in this sense was at the heart of the Cold War's supposed action-reaction "law," and the related proposition that societal defenses could *not* provide sufficient sustained effectiveness to warrant their deployment: the Soviet Union surely could and would enhance its retaliatory capabilities in response to U.S. defenses and thereby prevent the United States from achieving a damage-limitation capability worth buying.

As discussed in Chapter 4, Secretary McNamara believed the Soviet Union to have the motivation and the resources necessary to offset U.S. damage-limitation measures at a competitive cost advantage. The expectation of an unavoidable and cost-effective Soviet offensive counter to U.S. damage-limitation programs contributed to Secretary McNamara's adoption of a balance of terror policy *vis-à-vis* the Soviet Union and the perpetuation of that policy by subsequent administrations. Societal vulnerability to nuclear attack came to be seen as an unavoidable condition with this underlying assumption of comparable resources and intentions.

This presumption also was a necessary ingredient in the balance of terror tenet that there existed a "stable" equilibrium point in the accumulation of strategic arms at which each side could and would *rest content* in its deterrent capabilities—unless spurred on by the "action-reaction" dynamic. SALT, as noted in Chapter 5, was expected to limit those supposedly "destabilizing" systems that would spark that dynamic, and lock in a "stable" balance of terror at that equilibrium point in armaments. That expectation proved to be a frustrated U.S. hope rather than a plausible reality. Nevertheless, the U.S. strategic arms control edifice was built on the belief that each side would seek, establish, sustain *and be content* at an equilibrium point in armaments corresponding to a "stable" balance of terror.

In short, the balance of terror tenets presume conditions in which the antagonists learn to be content and are unable to transcend a balance of terror. The presumption of comparable resources in this sense may have been a useful rule of thumb with regard to the two Cold War superpowers; the presumption of comparable intentions was not. The absence of shared intentions was the basis for the Soviet buildup of strategic forces during the 1970s and 1980s that led to Defense Secretary Harold Brown's famous conclusion also noted in Chapter 7: "When we build, they build; when we stop building, they nevertheless continue to build."[1]

In contrast to the Cold War assumption of comparable resources and intentions, the contemporary geopolitical environment includes highly asymmetric alignments of power, resources and intentions separating the United States from regional opponents. For example, the asymmetry in technological and financial resources available to the United States and its regional foes today is breathtaking. As the graphic below illustrates, *the contemporary U.S. defense budget alone* is approximately fifty times greater than the entire gross domestic product (GDP) of the Democratic People's Republic of Korea (DPRK), twenty-five times greater than Syria's GDP, and approximately double Iran's GDP.

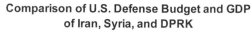

Comparison of U.S. Defense Budget and GDP
of Iran, Syria, and DPRK

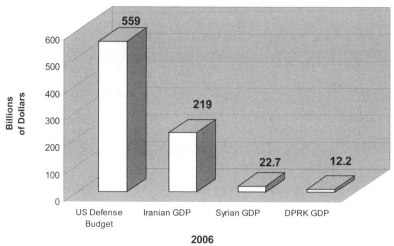

Source: For statistics on the United States, Iran, and Syria see, International Institute for Strategic Studies, *The Military Balance 2007* (London: Routledge, 2007), pp. 28, 224, 243. For statistics on the DPRK see, Dick K. Nanto and Emma Chanlett-Avery, *The North Korean Economy: Overview and Policy Analysis*, CRS RL32493 (Washington, D.C.: Congressional Research Service, April 18, 2007), p. 4.

With such asymmetries in available resources, Cold War expectations of an opponent's successful and cost-effective offsetting reaction to U.S. damage-limitation programs no longer can be considered inevitable. Regional rivals may be incapable of *establishing* and *sustaining* a secure, reliable offensive nuclear retaliatory capability against the United States even should they desire to do so in the face of serious U.S. defenses. Given the limited resources available to contemporary opponents, that goal may be too far-fetched to animate such intentions, regardless of the possible cost-exchange ratio involved.

Reminiscent of the Johnson Administration's embrace of comprehensive strategic damage-limitation goals and capabilities *vis-à-vis* China, the United States may now prefer to defend the American population against plausible limited threats because the level of protection now feasible may be sustainable and worth the price. Indeed, the contemporary asymmetries in resources separating the United States from regional foes are even greater than the asymmetry between the United States and China in the mid-1960s when Secretary McNamara's

Draft Presidential Memorandum recommended that the United States *could and should pursue an effective damage-limitation policy in its strategic relations with China, not a balance of terror*:

> A light anti-ballistic missile system using [deleted] defense at a small number of cities, offers promise of a highly effective defense against small ballistic missile attacks of the sort the Chinese Communists might be capable of launching within the next decade....It appears likely that such a defense would remain highly effective against Chinese capabilities at least until 1980, even if the presence of this defense did not, in the first place, deter them from developing a strong ICBM capability.[2]

At the time of Secretary McNamara's 1967 announcement of the U.S. *Sentinel* BMD program for this purpose, the U.S. defense budget was slightly greater than the Chinese GDP ($73 billion versus $70 billion, respectively).[3]

Given the contemporary asymmetries in resources, the cost-exchange ratio considered so important during the Cold War is likely to be much less important than the ability of the United States to afford the absolute cost for the level of protection deemed feasible and worthy. Rogues are not the Soviet Union; they are not engaged in an action-reaction competition with the United States to protect an assured destruction nuclear capability, as was the Cold War assumption *vis-à-vis* the Soviet Union. They may simply be incapable of engaging in such a sustained competition even if they are so inclined and there is a favorable cost-exchange ratio. The underlying Cold War presumption of comparable intentions and resources per the balance of terror just does not fit the contemporary context.

In addition, the presumption of comparable intentions and resources was integral to the Cold War's focus on "crisis instability" as the plausible route to war—Schelling's "reciprocal fear of surprise attack": each side supposedly fearing the opponent's first strike and therefore anticipating the possibility of gaining *meaningful strategic value* by striking first itself. From this feared chain of perceptions and "crisis instability" came the generic categorization of strategic damage-limitation capabilities as "destabilizing," and the prescription of eschewing such capabilities as the technical "fix" for that worrisome "instability." Again, the focus on this dynamic and corresponding categorization of strategic defensive forces as "destabilizing" may have been logical with the Cold War's condition of a rough comparability of U.S. and Soviet resources, but it makes little sense apart from that condition. As discussed in Chapter 7, contemporary foes can hardly anticipate a strategic advantage by striking first at U.S. retaliatory forces. Schelling's logic of "crisis instability" cannot apply to contemporary foes under contemporary conditions, and the assessment of U.S. strategic forces should no longer proceed as if it does.

Despite the dramatic asymmetries in resources now separating the United States from contemporary regional rogue states such as North Korea, Iran, and China, and the striking differences between U.S. relations with those states and the U.S.-Soviet Cold War relationship, commentaries on U.S. BMD typically still reflect the Cold War presumption of comparable intentions and resources. As a result, they dutifully follow through with the familiar balance of terror tenets: defenses must be self-defeating and "destabilizing," incapable of providing meaningful damage limitation, and inevitably spawning an unbeatable action-reaction cycle. Everything has changed except the formulaic application of Cold War balance of terror measures of merit and terms of art, and the predictable results.

Comparable Stakes at Risk and Room for Deterrence to Work

The balance of terror tenets also presumed the specific Cold War conditions in which the superpowers had no overriding goals and values that compelled war. That is, deterrence had room to work because bargaining was possible: neither superpower was driven inescapably by internal or external imperatives to strike the other in order to preserve or advance a supreme value.

The priority U.S. Cold War objective, for example, was never victory through nuclear war; it was long-term "containment" to facilitate the Soviet Union's collapse under the weight of its own internal contradictions. And, in 1956, Soviet premier Khrushchev replaced the previous dominant Soviet ideological dogma of the "inevitability" of a conclusive East-West war with the new line of "no fatal inevitability of war" and the establishment of "peaceful coexistence" as a "fundamental principle" for overcoming the capitalist West by means short of general war.[4] The conditions of the Cold War *did not demand that the Soviet Union or the United States confront the dilemma of choosing between pursuing a general war or an alternative course that would entail intolerable loss*; there was "room" for deterrence to operate. Even the internal collapse of the Soviet Union did not push

Soviet leaders to war. Mutual deterrence may not have been "easy" but in those conditions at least it was possible in principle.

The Soviet leadership had the option of choosing to place a higher priority on *not risking a nuclear war* than on the conquest of Western Europe or Japan because conquest was not regarded as an inalterable imperative, at least for the near term. The United States, in turn, could choose to place higher priority on *not* risking a nuclear war than on the liberation of the "captive nations" of Eastern Europe because the latter was not the immediate, overriding imperative for the United States. Neither side judged the protection of a supreme interest or the advancement of an inalterable, absolute goal as compelling a deliberate decision to wage war against the other, despite the risk.

Professor Robert Jervis emphasized the Cold War balance of terror tenet that the fear of nuclear escalation helped to ensure prudence, caution, and ultimately, deterrence: "Because force cannot be easily controlled or compartmentalized, the fear of nuclear war does deter the other side from much more than nuclear attack. Irrational as it may be, the chance of devastation has made our world unusually safe."[5] Elsewhere he was more circumspect, noting that in a balance of terror, "if decision makers are 'sensible' peace is the most likely outcome."[6]

Jervis' observation that if leaders are "sensible" in a balance of terror then "peace is the most likely outcome" should be true when peace is seen as a tolerable option—when the choice of war *is not compelled by some overriding imperative*, or when peace is self-evidently the most attractive course because it *does not seem to carry intolerable consequences*. In these cases, if leaders are "sensible" then deterrence *should* work as described by Jervis because leaders logically should prefer the option that avoids survival risks and entails no intolerable consequences. But note that in such cases the "working" of deterrence does not follow simply from the presence of severe threats and "sensible" leaders. An additional factor must be at play: even in the presence of such threats and leaders the "no war" choice must be tolerable, and thus provide the room necessary for deterrence to "work." During the Cold War, it was not simply that mutual nuclear deterrence compelled each side to be so constrained; there were no overshadowing domestic or external imperatives that compelled either side to choose to gamble on war as the necessary or least miserable option.

In short, the stakes at risk in the Cold War standoff were comparable in the sense that neither superpower's respective goals and priorities demanded a desperate roll of the dice—the absence of war was tolerable. In this condition, the deterrence of deliberate attack at least had the opportunity to "work" because the parties involved did not see the resort to war to defend or promote some supreme value as a higher priority than peace: deterrence has room to work when leadership decision making is *not driven by an imperative and timeline that demands war,* and the avoidance of war has no competition as the most obviously "sensible" option.

In the future, if an opponent's goals include an overwhelming imperative to initiate hostilities or otherwise provoke the United States, and its value hierarchy does not permit it to subordinate that goal to the pragmatic desire to avoid risk, there will be no room for deterrence to work as envisaged in the balance of terror tenets. Benign endings may be difficult to see and impossible to choose when a leadership is faced with multiple intolerable alternatives.

Unfortunately, international relations do not always permit deterrence to operate; leaders do not always perceive the availability of tolerable *and* peaceful options. In many actual cases, leaders rightly or wrongly do not see available room for tolerable inaction—only death-defying, high-risk action. The conditions they confront provide *only* high-risk choices and the leadership's unenviable task is to choose from among them. Unfortunately, the choice presumed to be available in the balance of terror tenets, i.e., a peaceful option that also offers tolerable consequences, often does not exist.

The outbreak of World War I, for example, revealed a combination of perceived imperatives and unwitting moves that drove the decision making in Russia, Germany, and Austria to its fatal conclusion. Similarly, Japanese leaders were driven to attack Pearl Harbor by desperation and the perception of no tolerable alternatives. And, as mentioned in Chapter 7, Castro and Che may have been motivated to advocate a nuclear strike on the United States in 1962 by the romance of martyrdom and an ideological zealotry that included faith in a conclusive ideological war.

In 416 B.C., Athens gave the islanders of Melos the choice of facing annihilation or ending Melian neutrality in the Second Pelopon-nesian War. The former choice was daunting, of course, but the latter choice represented an intolerable loss of long-standing Melian freedom. The islanders chose to resist Athens and trust "in fortune."[7] The Athenians consequently carried out their threat.

It is, of course, near certain that the Cold War's nuclear balance of terror encouraged mutual appreciation of the value of placing priority on the avoidance of war; nuclear threats probably helped to create the necessary "room" for deterrence to "work." But that is a far different point from the belief that mutual nuclear deterrence prevented the possibility of deliberate nuclear war. Mutual nuclear threats were able to help prevent war in part because neither side confronted an overriding internal or external imperative to accept the risks of war for fear of intolerable consequences of continued peace.

The balance of terror tenets simply cannot accommodate the historically familiar condition in which leaders believe that the risk of action is extreme, but inaction also is intolerable because some supreme value is at risk and must be served. Inaction or conciliation may be the prudent, "sensible" choice, but the stakes at risk and attendant circumstances do not always allow such an easy choice.

In the contemporary environment, for example, the Chinese political leadership appears to believe that preventing the independence of Taiwan is a matter of national survival,[8] and necessary for continued Communist Party rule in China. The recourse to war, even nuclear war, may be seen as a high-risk, but necessary, part of China's response *to the potentially intolerable problem* of U.S. support for Taiwan in the event of a crisis there. Some Chinese military leaders have expressed China's readiness to initiate a nuclear war with the United States if necessary to preclude U.S. support for Taiwanese independence.[9]

China sees its nuclear capabilities, at least in part, as intended to deter the United States from supporting Taiwan in the event of a crisis, thus giving China a free hand to act militarily against Taiwan as necessary.[10] Chinese sources refer to this as a capability for "nuclear 'counter-intimidation' to retain freedom of action in a conventional conflict."[11] Chinese leaders may see little room for their own prudence if a crisis were to erupt over the question of Taiwan, yet expect U.S. prudence given Chinese capabilities to threaten the nuclear destruction of U.S. cities. At least some in the Chinese military appear to expect that the United States would be *more susceptible* to coerced conciliation than China would be under these circumstances.[12] If such expectations were to contribute to Chinese decision making, then U.S. demonstrative "rocking the boat" and courageous-sounding expressions may contribute little to the deterrence of China. The old mechanistic balance of terror notions about how deterrence *should* operate may be irrelevant in the context of such perceived asymmetries in the stakes at risk.

The implications for the functioning of deterrence and the U.S. deterrence requirement for strategic forces that follow from this discussion represent another significant departure from Cold War "stability" requirements and metrics: even assuming that the logic of deterrence is in play, comparable levels of societal vulnerability cannot be relied upon to enforce comparable levels of prudence and caution when the perceptions of the stakes involved in a contingency can be so asymmetrical. There is no apparent, logical "equilibrium point" of mutual vulnerability that can enforce comparable deterrence effect and mutual deterrence "stability" when the perceptions of interest and will are dramatically different. Long-familiar balance of terror language and concepts simply do not apply in such cases.

Similarly, Iran's prospective acquisition of nuclear weapons, combined with the leadership's stridently-expressed desire for the elimination of Israel, may create the conditions wherein Israel can have little confidence that deterrence has the necessary room to work reliably. Iran's President Mahmoud Ahmadinejad has been described as a "radical millenarian" with "ties to a messianic cult, the Hojjatieh Society whose goal is to hasten the return of the 12th or 'Hidden' Imam, Mohammed ibn Hasan, in 'occultation' since the 9th century, by creating the preconditions for his return. The preconditions are war and cosmic chaos."[13] Moving history in this direction is said to be Ahmadinejad's highest priority.[14] Given his apparent motivations and linkage of religious fidelity to calls for Israel to be "wiped off the map,"[15] there may be insufficient room in Iranian decision making for the "logic of deterrence" to preserve the peace reliably, despite the risks of war. Indeed, the potential chaos from war may work in the opposite direction.

Some contemporary terrorist organizations also are motivated by transcendent goals that can include serving the supposedly-divine mandate of inflicting mass casualties. Their acts of destruction purportedly have "sacred significance"—"Here we have individuals who are 'killing in the name of God.'"[16] A 1998 declaration of a religious "fatwa" signed by five terror leaders, including al Qaeda's Osama bin Laden and Ayman Al Zawahiri, claims "religious inspiration": "The ruling to kill the Americans and their allies—civilians and military—is an individual duty for every Muslim who can do it in any country."[17]

Senior al Qaeda figure Suliman Abu Ghaith similarly has identified the taking of revenge against the United States as a religious duty, and specifies the scope and method of that revenge in terms of the U.S. fatalities that must be inflicted to serve that goal:

> We have not reached parity with them. We have the right to kill 4 million Americans—2 million of them children—and to exile twice as many and wound and cripple hundreds of thousands [more]. Furthermore, it is our right to fight them with chemical and biological weapons, so as to afflict them with the fatal maladies that have afflicted the Muslims because of the [American] chemical and biological weapons.[18]

The charge that the United States has employed chemical and biological weapons against Muslims is utter nonsense, but the call for revenge for supposed wrongs as a matter of religious practice is obvious.

For those so motivated, what room may exist for the grudging cooperation required for punitive deterrence to operate? Rejecting a supposedly transcendent task because of a calculation of great temporal risk may be considered an affront to the sacred—which itself may be considered the course of greatest risk, and certainly more risky than provoking the United States. In such cases, the specific time and place may be variable but setting aside the goal because of a physical risk posed by the United States may not be a tolerable option.

Israeli analyst Anat Berko has held extensive interviews with failed/captured suicide bombers and their dispatchers which have led her to a conclusion that tends to confound Western secular deterrence theory. They often are motivated to undertake suicidal missions by the expectation of being rewarded with the forgiveness of sins and the eternal pleasures of paradise: "Secular Jews and Christians view such things as slightly ridiculous, but religious Muslims relate to them with the utmost seriousness. For them, paradise and its pleasures seem completely realistic and, for many of those whom I interviewed, were a determining factor in their decision to carry out a suicide bombing attack."[19] The spiritual motivation behind at least some grisly terrorist bombings of innocents is unmistakable.[20] Apparently, suicide bombers have been seen to have "joyful" facial expressions just prior to detonating their explosives and themselves—presumably in anticipation of soon entering paradise.[21] Again, there may be no room here for punitive deterrence threats to function predictably.

Following the 1991 Gulf War, Saddam Hussein was driven in two directions by two competing imperatives. He apparently believed that he needed the image of power provided by WMD to help ensure his security against regional foes, particularly Iran; he also needed to relinquish WMD to avoid U.S. threats. Saddam Hussein faced two intolerable alternatives, as often is the case in actual international relations: manifestly give up the image of WMD and the security he believed that provided against local threats, or retain the image and face the U.S. threat. Saddam apparently chose the appearance of possessing WMD to help deter Iranian attack over yielding to U.S. demands that Iraq blatantly give up WMD. His solution was a high-risk scheme of WMD deception that ultimately failed to serve his purposes and contributed to his downfall; it also allowed no room for the success of U.S. threats.[22]

Such opponents and conditions are well outside those envisioned in the balance of terror tenets—in which avoiding high-risk brinkmanship or actions is an option and the obvious, "sensible" choice because there is *relative physical safety* in doing so. In contemporary cases, the presumption of this opportunity for deterrence to function may not hold because the available choice may not be between obviously tolerable and obviously intolerable alternatives: inaction and caution may be judged impossible or the *least tolerable of options*, despite the high risk of action and confrontation. These decision making dilemmas do not equate to "irrationality" and may be pertinent to the decision making of any leadership, including that of rogue states and terrorist organizations.

Confidence that deterrence is reliable because "they wouldn't dare" run the risk of U.S. retaliation can make sense in principle only when the opponent believes that *not daring* is an acceptable choice. The severity of the U.S. threat may be irrelevant if the alternative of "not daring" is seen as carrying intolerable consequences. The assumption that opponents see a tolerable, benign alternative to war is convenient for us and our deterrence objectives—*but it may not apply in contemporary and future cases for reasons that are evident in history, and are well beyond our control.* It would be historically naïve and heroically optimistic to presume that future conditions always will be so conducive to the functioning of deterrence. As has often occurred in the past, for some opponents there will be conditions in which a high-risk gambit is judged to be the "least miserable" course of action because all other alternatives, including inaction, are intolerable.

Comparable Values and Goals at Risk

The balance of terror tenets also require the Cold War presumption that opponents have similar values. This presumption may seem strange given the great differences in the U.S. and Soviet political and economic systems, and in their differing views about basic human rights. However, the comparable U.S. and Soviet value necessary for a stable balance of terror was much more basic; it concerned the value attributed to the targets to be held at mutual risk for deterrence purposes.

A fundamental expectation underlying the balance of terror tenets was that the goal of avoiding the destruction of some set of physical targets would be decisive in the decision making of both leaderships; their choices were expected to be governed by the goal of avoiding or minimizing the nuclear threat to their material assets at risk—whether cities or other tangible, physical targets.

As discussed in Chapters 4 and 5, during the Cold War U.S. declared nuclear deterrence threats evolved to include cities, industry, military targets and the opposing leaders themselves. The details changed but the threats were of necessity tied to some *select sets of physical, material targets*; preserving those targets and the values attached to those targets was fully expected to be a higher priority for Soviet leaders than any plausible incentive they might have to strike first. The only possible exception to this was if "the reciprocal fear of surprise attack" meant that striking first could better protect those same targets and values.

This presumption underlying the balance of terror tenets that supreme value is attached to physical, tangible assets may have been appropriate *vis-à-vis* the Soviet Union. U.S. deterrence threats obviously did not fail catastrophically *vis-à-vis* the Soviet leadership during the Cold War, perhaps because Soviet priority values ultimately *were material and tangible*—as Marxist-Leninist ideology demanded—and were threatened effectively by U.S. retaliatory nuclear capabilities. Soviet leaders expressed the ideological themes of Marxism-Leninism and identified themselves as scientific "materialists" focused on appropriate temporal goals, not on intangible, transcendent goals. The Soviet Union disdained forms of spiritual devotion and often punished it as criminal.[23] Nuclear retaliatory threats by the United States may have been particularly well-suited to threaten that which Soviet leaders valued most, namely, physical and tangible targets.

If so, it was a useful coincidence because Secretary McNamara's assured destruction deterrence metric was hardly tailored intentionally to the particular value hierarchy of the Soviet leadership. Assured destruction targeted that which U.S. strategic forces could most easily threaten, to wit, Soviet industry and population:

> The idea was that as long as the Soviets knew that we could retaliate, that would deter them. McNamara's whiz kids calculated that the Soviets would be sufficiently deterred if we could kill 30 percent of their population and destroy half of their industrial capacity....It all appeared scientific and precise, but in fact it had little to do with any formulation of how much would be enough to deter the Soviets. It was the output of a computer program designed by Alain Enthoven 'laying down' 1-megaton bombs against Soviet cities and calculating, at various points, how much additional damage one additional bomb would do.[24]

Balance of terror tenets, however, cannot accommodate an opponent who is *willing* "to die beautifully" (as Soviet Vice Premier Mikoyan said of the Cuban leadership during the 1962 Cuban Missile Crisis) to advance an intangible or transcendent goal. Confidence in any balance of terror-style, punitive threat requires the expectation of an opponent who is unwilling "to die beautifully" for a cause that is more important than the preservation of those assets held at risk by U.S. forces. Contemporary assertions of the reliable, predictable functioning of traditional deterrence strategies continue to posit, explicitly or implicitly, materialist opponents who fit this convenient mold.[25]

Some opponents, however, may place highest priority on intangible, transcendent values, including those that cannot obviously be put at risk by the U.S. threat to destroy physical targets no matter how lethal the threat. Worse yet from a deterrence perspective, as in the past some contemporary opponents may hold in highest regard transcendent values and goals that they believe can *be advanced* only through high-risk actions and the destruction of physical, tangible targets. If intangible or transcendent goals and values are at the center of conflict with the United States, we should not expect that the opponent's decision making will be compatible with the balance of terror tenets which place the protection of tangible targets as the ultimate priority in enemy decision making. Again, this is not a question of an opponent's rationality; it is a question of the salience of U.S. threats to an enemy's highest values. These values, of course, could include intangibles such as honor and religious martyrdom. Balance of terror tenets, again, cannot accommodate opponents ultimately motivated by such goals and values because they may rationally welcome "dying beautifully" to protect or promote their intangible, highest values.

The Clinton Administration's Director of Central Intelligence, R. James Woolsey, has noted the willingness of contemporary opponents to accept great cost to forward their goals: "There's nothing in those beliefs that puts a constraint on dying horribly while killing massively."[26] Woolsey points to the stark implications for familiar punitive strategies of deterrence *vis-à-vis* such opponents and concludes: "There are days when I miss the Soviets when I think of al-Qaida and Hezbollah. The Soviets were a difficult enemy but one we could deter and contain."[27]

Contemporary opponents may seem eccentric, bizarre or "irrational" by Western cultural standards. For example, as mentioned above, Iranian President Ahmadinejad reportedly attributes a high priority to creating the chaotic conditions necessary for the return of the "Hidden Imam," and "there does not seem to be much of a barrier in the religious views of Iran's leaders to the sort of mass casualties that a nuclear weapon would create."[28] Shoko Asahara, the notorious cult leader and terrorist who reportedly masterminded a sarin chemical attack on the Tokyo subway in 1995, apparently believed and taught his followers that mass killings could be *beneficial* for the victim because it could reduce their accumulation of negative karma and thus allow them to rise to a higher plane of existence than otherwise would be the case. This apparently became an easy justification for murder within his organization and externally.[29]

Such motivations and values are perplexing to Western observers. They are not, however, the only problem for balance of terror tenets in this regard. Some foreign decision makers appear to be both motivated to shocking aggression and to believe that they are protected against risk by divine or supernatural power. Their calculation of risk may be affected by their confidence in such protection—a factor again unaccounted for in the balance of terror tenets. During the 1991 Gulf War, for example, Saddam Hussein apparently believed the advice of soothsayers who foretold of his success against the U.S.-led coalition.[30] Iranian President Ahmadinejad claims special knowledge underlying his confidence that the United States "would not dare" to strike Iran, in part because, "I believe in what God says," to wit, "God says that those who walk in the path of righteousness will be victorious. What reason can you have for believing God will not keep this promise?"[31]

The potential combination of intense, transcendent motivations and the expectation of protection and safety in the face of uncertainty and risk represents a fundamental flaw in the expectation that "rational" opponents surely will act prudently and cautiously to avoid apparent threats to their tangible targets. To question that expectation and conclude that deterrence may not function predictably per the balance of terror tenets is simply to follow available evidence. It is not cultural arrogance, as Professor Waltz charges when dismissing concerns that deterrence may be an uncertain business *vis-à-vis* some contemporary opponents: "Many Westerners write fearfully about a future in which Third World countries have nuclear weapons. They seem to view the people of these nations in the old imperialist manner, as 'lesser breeds without the law.' As ever with ethnocentric views, speculation takes the place of evidence."[32]

This discussion of contemporary deterrence uncertainties has nothing in common with "old imperialist" notions; it does, however, contend strongly against old Cold War notions that there is a uniform, universal hierarchy of values and a set definition of "rational" behavior that can ensure opponents' prudence and caution in response to U.S. deterrence threats. And, it does so on the basis of abundant and mounting evidence. To point out the possibility for perplexing decision making based on a diversity of highest values and the associated potential uncertainty in the functioning of deterrence simply is to acknowledge reality; "ethnocentric" is the claim that all "rational" decision makers must hold to the Western values and norms embedded in the balance of terror tenets.

Those who become expert in a particular foreign culture or region note how easy it is to disdain or refuse to believe the values that other cultures and leaderships cherish because they do not fit within familiar Western enlightenment boundaries. For example, Professor B.R. Myers, an academic specialist on North Korea, notes the ease of misunderstanding North Korean decision making because: "Americans tend to dismiss North Korea's official culture as too ludicrous to warrant careful monitoring."[33] To risk understatement, disdaining opponents in this fashion cannot serve well the goal of understanding them for deterrence purposes.

There is a related long tradition in Western democracies of initially dismissing unfamiliar foreign values, goals and decision making as "irrational." This is how many American and British observers responded when confronted by the perplexing decision making and goals of Hitler,

Khrushchev, Mao and, more recently, Saddam Hussein. Professor Douglas Macdonald of Colgate University draws an extremely important conclusion in this regard that is essential to contemporary considerations of deterrence: "Moderate rationalists steeped in bargaining over flexibly defined interests have difficulty understanding the rigidity of historical 'necessity' or moral imperatives in the totalitarian mindset. Policy advice that flows from such misunderstanding is therefore fatuous, if not dangerous."[34] Balance of terror tenets certainly reflect the intellectual roots of "moderate rationalists steeped in bargaining" and the attendant tendency to dismiss as irrational that which is unfamiliar or unacceptable.

This Western tradition was demonstrated by U.S. officials when they expressed just such an opinion of the Pakistani and Indian decisions to test nuclear weapons in 1998.[35] More recently, the U.S. State Department's spokesman said of the Iranian Government's dogged pursuit of a nuclear capability in the face of international opposition, "this regime clearly doesn't get it."[36] More likely, the Iranian leadership does "get it" but we fail to "get" them. It is easier to dismiss as "irrational" the goals and decision making of foreign leaders of which we disapprove and consider eccentric than to understand them on their own terms.

John Agresto, former President of St. John's College in New Mexico, served in Iraq in 2003 and 2004 as the senior advisor for the Coalition's Provisional Authority to the Iraqi Ministry of Higher Education. Upon returning to the United States he observed that a fundamental U.S. problem was misunderstanding the nature and role of religion in Iraq, largely because it was so far from the familiar secular Western worldview: "We have so tamed and, in a sense, marginalized religion in the West that we consistently underestimate its ferocity and strength....We don't understand either killing for God or dying for God. But others do."[37]

In fact, intangible goals and the potential for virtue in accepting great cost—including martyrdom—have been present in Western culture.[38] We do not disdain or consider "irrational" Patrick Henry's ringing statement at the 1775 revolutionary convention of Virginia: "I know not what course others may take, but as for me, give me liberty or give me death," or young Nathan Hale's final words before being hanged by the British for espionage in 1776: "I only regret that I have but one life to lose for my country." We celebrate their courage, sacrifice and patriotism. The goal of their sacrifice was far different from that of contemporary opponents— they did not kill innocents in the process—but their willingness to accept self-sacrifice was no less salient.

Princeton University's renowned Middle East expert, Bernard Lewis, has noted the challenge of deterring contemporary opponents via Cold War-type nuclear threats when their highest values, according to Lewis, include transcendent goals associated with a Manichean struggle:

> Would the same constraints, the same fear of mutual assured destruction, restrain a nuclear-armed Iran from using such weapons against the U.S. or against Israel?...

> A passage from the Ayatollah Khomeini, quoted in an 11th-grade Iranian schoolbook, is revealing. "I am decisively announcing to the whole world that if the world-devourers [i.e., the infidel powers] wish to stand against our religion, we will stand against their whole world and will not cease until the annihilation of all of them. Either we all become free, or we will go to the greater freedom which is martyrdom. Either we shake one another's hands in joy at the victory of Islam in the world, or all of us will turn to eternal life and martyrdom. In both cases, victory and success are ours."

> In this context, mutual assured destruction, the deterrent that worked so well during the Cold War, would have no meaning. At the end of time [according to the apocalyptic vision] there will be general destruction anyway. What will matter will be the final destination of the dead—hell for the infidels, and heaven for the believers. For people of this mindset, MAD is not a constraint; it is an inducement.[39]

Former Iranian President Akbar Hashemi Rafsanjani observed in 2001 that in the event "the Islamic world" possesses nuclear weapons, "the use of even one nuclear bomb inside Israel will destroy everything. However, it will only harm the Islamic world. It is not irrational to contemplate such an eventuality."[40] Traditional threats to national targets may deter Iranian leaders, but such a statement by a supposed "moderate" leader in Iran suggests a cost tolerance for nuclear war that is nearly incomprehensible to most Westerners and a value structure centered on the "Islamic world." Such statements may be dismissed as bluster or posturing—"too ludicrous to warrant careful monitoring." Instead, however, they may reflect a conception of values, goals, stakes and cost-benefit calculations that lies outside the convenient value hierarchies presumed in the balance of terror tenets.

Former President Jimmy Carter expresses continuing faith in deterrence in this regard: "I think it would be almost inconceivable that Iran would commit suicide by launching one or two missiles of any kind against the nation of Israel."[41] Statements by some Iranian leaders, however, suggest that they and President Carter may not share similar definitions of what is "inconceivable." President Carter equates a leadership that is *not suicidal* to a leadership that is deterrable, and thus concludes that the Iranian leadership is deterrable. Some senior U.S. military leaders express the same logic and language to reach the same reassuring conclusion in general.[42] Why, according to retired U.S. Army Gen. Robert Gard, is deterrence sure to prevent a North Korean ballistic missile attack? Because, "I've not noticed any suicidal tendencies on the part of [North Korean leader] Kim Jong II."[43]

The problems with this frequent and reassuring formulation, however, are twofold: first, very few U.S. commentators have any expertise to offer useful psychological evaluations of foreign leaders, including their "suicidal tendencies" or lack thereof; second, and more importantly, the formula that non-suicidal equates to reliably deterrable does not capture the possibility that leaderships which indeed are *not* suicidal may also *not* be deterrable in all circumstances. Being suicidal and choosing to accept great risk and possible sacrifice in pursuit of a highly-valued goal or cause are *not* the same. Rational decision makers can choose to accept risk and great sacrifice in pursuit of the value they believe their sacrifice will serve, not because they prefer death. Abraham Lincoln deeply mourned the death and destruction of the U.S. Civil War, of which he was the "final casualty"; yet, he ultimately believed that preserving the Union was worth the sacrifice. This simple distinction between suicidal and sacrificial thinking and behavior is lost on those who assert that only those who are suicidal may prove to be beyond deterrence.

The strategic goals of the former al Qaeda leader in Iraq, the late Abu Musab al-Zarqawi, illustrate the challenge of deterring opponents who are motivated by transcendent values and for whom strategic compromise may be intolerable: "We do not wage our jihad in order to replace the Western tyrant with an Arab tyrant. We fight to make God's word supreme, and anyone who stands in the way of our struggle is our enemy, a target of our swords."[44] Zarqawi's goal included two demands: the removal of all non-Muslims from Muslim lands, and the global establishment of *sharia* law and "Islamic justice."[45]

Zarqawi's description of his goals suggests contemporary deterrence questions to consider: if opponents' goals follow from the belief that their mission is a divine calling, what temporal risk may be too great and what sacrifice would be too high to pay in its service? And, correspondingly, what room may there be for the grudging cooperation, prudence, and caution required for punitive deterrence threats to prevent them from carrying out their mission?

That no risk or possible sacrifice may be too great suggests why the presumption of comparable values and goals embedded in the balance of terror tenets may be far removed from some contemporary deterrence challenges, and why posing a lethal retaliatory threat against opponents' lives or other physical targets may not provide predictable deterrent effect. Smart defensive measures and barriers placed in the way of such opponents may make their missions too difficult or too likely to fail, and lead them to decide on another time, manner, or place to strike, hence, deterrence by denial. Neither punitive nor denial deterrence measures, however, are likely to have *predictable* deterrent effect against opponents so motivated.

That intangible temporal or transcendent values can take priority over prudence and risk-avoidance in leadership decision making is not controversial. They appear to have played a powerful role in past decisions regarding war and peace. Indeed, Professor Donald Kagan's monumental historical survey, *On the Origins of War*, emphasizes how frequently throughout history a leadership's consideration of honor or other intangible factor has been decisive in decisions for war and a related willingness to court disaster.[46] As if to confirm Kagan's thesis, Chinese President Hu Jintao has stated that China would use force against Taiwan if a change in the status quo there were to cause him to "lose face,"[47] and Saddam Hussein attributed his ultimate decision to invade Kuwait in 1990 to a crude insult he claims the leader of Kuwait, Emir Al Sabah, directed toward Iraqi women.[48]

Of course, one or a few eccentric statements by opposing leaders cannot alone constitute a sufficient basis for even tentative conclusions regarding how they may think and behave in response to U.S. deterrence threats. Such statements as those presented above, however, may serve as red flags that the opposing leadership's decision making may not meet the comforting and convenient balance of terror expectations. The "rational" opponent envisaged—one so predictably prudent and "deterrable"—may not usefully serve as the default bench mark; the goal, thus, should not be to ignore, dismiss, or rationalize such statements in an effort to make opponents conform to comforting expectations of "deterrability." As has been the case in the past, we should expect that some present and future opponents will hold intangible or transcendent goals in highest esteem, and that in such cases severe U.S. punitive threats to their temporal, physical targets may not prove decisive in that opponent's decision making because prudent avoidance of severe physical threats may not be their highest priority. Their hierarchy of values may provide no such opportunity for punitive deterrence to operate.

This conclusion does not "impugn" the rationality or intelligence of opponents.[49] To the contrary, it recognizes that some leaders the United States may want to deter—whether leaders of states or terrorist organizations—may quite rationally pursue goals and values that are perplexing to Western observers and outside those envisaged in balance of terror tenets. Those tenets certainly reflect the Western academic tradition—particularly apparent in the fields of political science and international relations—of focusing on "material and strategic interaction" while excluding "from the start the possibility that religion could be a fundamental organizing force in the international system."[50] In such cases, the long-familiar Cold War claims about the functioning of deterrence must be suspect.

Finally, the balance of terror tenets reflect the state-centric structure of the Cold War. Recall that the envisaged mechanism for deterrence is two state leaderships in control of national forces choosing to behave prudently to avoid the mutual risk of nuclear retaliation against national targets. Deterrence was expected to follow reliably from "rational" state leaderships seeking as their highest priorities the preservation of state-based targets. As the former Commander of the U.S. Strategic Command, Adm. Hank Chiles rightly observed: "Our deterrence strategy is founded on the theory that an adversarial state or coalition group will act according to the logic of national or group self-interest."[51]

Again, this conceptualization of deterrence may have fit well the state-centric Cold War conditions from which it was derived. Contemporary threats, however, include non-state, terrorist/criminal organizations such as al Qaeda, whose loose, transnational linkage of regional cells are neither state-based nor organized according to a state-based hierarchy of authority and power. These organizations may have no fixed territory or subjects per se; they do not fit within the familiar concept of a state or even a state-like entity with a defined leadership hierarchy that will make decisions to preserve the national values threatened by U.S. strategic forces for predictable deterrent effect. Familiar, state-based opponents surely remain to be deterred, but mercurial or acephalous decision-making structures of rogue states and terrorist organizations have taken on much greater salience for the United States since the end of the Cold War.

In the context of such opponents, to what extent should deterrence continue to be defined per the Cold War's balance of terror tenets? And, to what extent should U.S. strategic force initiatives continue to be assessed by the metrics and terms of art derived from those tenets? The answer is self-evident. The central presumptions of how and why deterrence should function, the road to conflict, the key concepts of "existential deterrence," "stability," "stabilizing" or "destabilizing" forces, and the "action-reaction" model of arms acquisition are largely unrelated to these contemporary conditions and opponents who may lack state-based authority, decision-making institutions, familiar tangible values and vulnerabilities, and who may be motivated by perplexing, transcendent imperatives.

No Intolerable Third Party Strategic Threats

Balance of terror tenets also assume a particular Cold War condition with regard to the number of significant threats facing the United States. Following the late 1960s, the United States was willing to leave uncontested its vulnerability to Soviet nuclear attack in expressed deference to the balance of terror; it also abandoned the Johnson Administration's *Sentinel* BMD program intended to provide comprehensive strategic defense against China. Throughout the remainder of the Cold War there was no sustained U.S. Government consensus that a third party strategic threat was sufficiently "clear and present" to render the state of essential U.S. defenselessness intolerable and therefore warrant significant deployment of strategic damage-limitation capabilities. No intolerable third party threat took precedence over the mutual vulnerability demanded by a U.S.-Soviet balance of terror.

This focus may help to explain the seemingly inexplicable. According to *The 9/11 Commission Report*, on September 11, 2001 *the Northeast Air Defense Sector of the North American Air Defense Command could call on only two alert air defense sites with only two "ready" interceptors each for defense*:

Notwithstanding the identification of these emerging threats, by 9/11 there were only seven alert [air defense interceptor] sites left in the United States, each with two fighter aircraft on alert....On 9/11, all the hijacked aircraft were in NORAD's Northeast Air Defense Sector (also known as NEADS), which is based in Rome, New York. That morning NEADS could call on two alert sites, each with one pair of ready fighters; Otis Air National Guard Base in Cape Cod, Massachusetts, and Langley Air Force Base in Hampton, Virginia. Other facilities, not on "alert," would need time to arm the fighters and organize crews.[52]

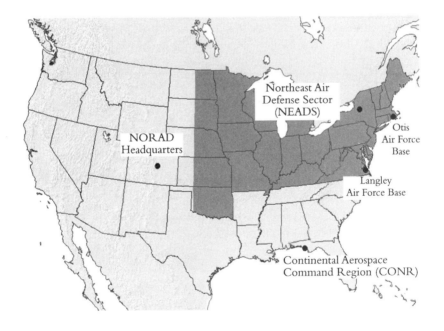

Source: *The 9/11 Commission Report: Final Report of the National Commission on Terrorist Attacks Upon the United States* (New York: W.W. Norton & Company, July 2004), p. 15.

Amazingly, some of those U.S. military aircraft dispatched in response to the attack apparently were unarmed.[53] As noted in Chapter 1, there is little wonder that the paucity of U.S. air defense capabilities, according to *The 9/11 Commission Report*, "...led some

NORAD commanders to worry that NORAD was not postured to protect the United States."[54]   That, of course, might be considered an understatement: the decision to de-emphasize most U.S. strategic defensive capabilities and to leave the United States largely vulnerable had been made almost four decades earlier, and essentially sustained thereafter.   The supposed "stabilizing" benefits of mutual vulnerability to strategic attack and presumption against societal defenses had not been overshadowed by concern about a third party threat during or following the Cold War; thus on 9/11, the U.S. strategic position essentially remained unchanged with regard to minimal preparations for civil defense and air defense, and the absence of deployed BMD.

The events of 9/11 illustrated as nothing else could how balance of terror tenets that mandate societal vulnerability and expect deterrence to function predictably do *not* address contemporary geopolitical conditions wherein there are multiple sources and modes of strategic threat.   U.S. deterrence strategies may "work" against one opponent as expected, but not against another; in other cases they may simply be irrelevant to an opponent's decision making.   Yet, the absence of strategic defenses essentially means vulnerability to all.

When considering the risks of continued vulnerability, contemporary threats posed by terrorist groups that have declared war against the United States must be included.[55] The unclassified July 2007 National Intelligence Estimate from the National Intelligence Council, *The Terrorist Threat to the US Homeland*, concludes that al Qaeda plots to strike the United States, "...with the goal of producing mass casualties, visually dramatic destruction, significant economic aftershocks, and/or fear among the US population....We assess that al-Qai'da will continue to try to acquire and employ chemical, biological, radiological, or nuclear material in attacks and would not hesitate to use them if it develops what it deems is sufficient capability."[56]

The 9/11 attacks demonstrated the risk of continuing to leave U.S. societal vulnerability uncontested in obedience to the Cold War balance of terror tenets that damage-limiting capabilities are useless and "destabilizing."   That risk *vis-à-vis* more familiar state-based threats was illustrated again when North Korea tested multiple ballistic missiles on July 4, 2006, including an ICBM capable of carrying a nuclear payload; by North Korea's subsequent nuclear test conducted on October 9, 2006; and, by its international trafficking in ballistic missiles, including those to Iran.[57]

During much of the Cold War, U.S. deterrence strategy reflected the belief that reliable deterrence of the Soviet strategic threat could be "ensured" via a "stable" balance of terror, and that third party strategic threats were immature or similarly deterrable. Hence, the risk of virtually uncontested U.S. societal vulnerability was deemed an acceptable tradeoff for the deterrence "stability" it was believed to provide *vis-à-vis* the Soviet Union. That conscious choice to forego damage-limitation capabilities entails a tradeoff of much greater risk when deterrence cannot reasonably be considered reliable, and when a growing number of state and non-state actors—some relatively unfamiliar—have self-expressed hostility toward the West and possess or aspire to possess weapons of mass destruction. The calculations of acceptable risks and tradeoffs embedded in the Cold War balance of terror tenets must change with the emergence of multiple strategic threats and the manifest uncertainty of deterrence.

Mutual Familiarity and Positive Control

The expectations embedded in the balance of terror tenets also are coherent *only* in the context of *antagonists who are mutually familiar.* The participants must be sufficiently knowledgeable about each other to communicate suitable, comprehensible threats to the pertinent decision makers reliably, with minimal distortion of the message. There must be considerable uncertainty about the effectiveness of expressed deterrence "redlines" in the absence of a level of familiarity that allows answers to these questions: Against whom should threats be directed? What types of threats should be made? And, how should such threats be communicated?

This level of familiarity at least was thought to characterize the U.S.-Soviet Cold War relationship. For all of the hostility and suspicion that divided the U.S. and Soviet leaderships, they appear to have been sufficiently familiar with one another to communicate. The wartime alliance against Hitler undoubtedly helped in that regard. The transparent political process in the United States leaves little doubt about who serves in senior leadership positions and, while the Soviet political process was more opaque—particularly in periods of leadership transition—from Lenin to Gorbachev there generally was confidence about who constituted the leadership. In addition, the two powers had established the precedent of summitry as wartime allies prior to the Cold War, and these occasions for communicating directly continued during most of the Cold War.

Unfortunately, to risk understatement, mutual familiarity is limited or absent *vis-à-vis* at least some contemporary opponents. Saddam Hussein, for example, had little understanding of the United States, apparently drawing on Hollywood movies as a primary source of information.[58] The lack of U.S. familiarity with rogue states in general is reflected in statements by U.S. Government experts regarding Syria—a problem that is even more pronounced *vis-à-vis* terrorist organizations:

> I have always felt, based on service in Syria in three different decades, that our knowledge of the internal workings of a regime such as this is very limited.[59]

> We as a government know very little about the internal workings of the Syrian regime. This is something we are going to have to put more assets into no doubt.[60]

> ...it is a very opaque system in Syria.[61]

In the absence of a reasonable degree of familiarity and reliable communication, strategies of deterrence will be matters of luck more than informed planning.

Finally, balance of terror tenets presume that each side has reliable control over the forces at its disposal. If U.S. deterrence threats are communicated to the opposing leadership, but "rogue" elements within a country or non-state organization have competing control over the military instruments of power, then U.S. deterrence threats may not be communicated to the needed audience with predictable effect. Again, despite their many differences, the United States and the Soviet Union had traditions and institutions for centralized political control over the instruments of military power. Not all states, much less terrorist organizations, are likely to enjoy such structured and confident leadership control.

These conditions of mutual familiarity and centralized control of forces are necessary for the internal coherence of the balance of terror tenets. Each may have been present in U.S.-Soviet relations during the Cold War, at least to the degree necessary for deterrence to prevent nuclear war. The question to consider now, however, is the degree to which these conditions can be expected to pertain *vis-à-vis* contemporary and future opponents.

The answer to that question is not encouraging. It is obvious, for example, that the degree of U.S. familiarity with some rogue states such as North Korea, the "Hermit Kingdom," or Syria is limited; it also is limited in important ways *vis-à-vis* China. And, familiarity is even more tentative with non-state terrorist organizations.[62] Opposing leaderships may not be identifiable or unified; their control over the use of force we would like to deter may be fragile; and, their foreign policy imperatives may leave little maneuver "room" for deterrence to operate. In such cases, the expectations central to balance of terror tenets about how "rational" leaders *must* behave and how deterrence *must* function if the proper threat is in place are as likely to be more misleading than enlightening.

Detection, Attribution and Accountability

The conditions of the Cold War also facilitated the expectation that the United States would recognize if an attack had occurred, by whom, and with what. Armed with such knowledge, the United States could identify the culpable opponent and implement its retaliatory deterrence threats. The balance of terror formula is predicated on these expectations of confident attack detection and attribution: if an attack cannot be recognized as such—and the culpable party properly recognized—then punitive retaliatory threats can have little direction.

The United States focused enormous attention on identifying the location and number of Soviet strategic nuclear weapon launchers, and providing the basis for early warning and tracking if an attack were launched. While there may have been some room for argument, the general notion was that a Soviet strategic nuclear attack could be recognized as such, and the perpetrator known. That the Soviet Union was the only plausible culprit in this regard for many years obviously was helpful. These conditions were the basis for presuming threats of nuclear retaliation could be targeted against the expected culprit with predictable deterrent effect.

Yet, what if the identity of the attacker cannot be determined with confidence—or the source of the weapons, the nature of the attack, or perhaps *even that an attack has in fact taken place*? Under such conditions, against whom might the United States effectively direct a punitive threat? What should be the nature of the threat, and when and how should it be communicated? How much confidence can be attributed to deterrence if it must be based on the indiscriminate broadcast of a generic threat to a generic audience of "usual suspects"? And, more to the point, how credible may U.S. retaliatory threats be if there are multiple possible culprits and/ or an attack can be masked as a naturally-occurring event? Might not an opponent who is highly motivated to strike and eager to find a reason to believe that it might escape U.S. retaliation find the desired opening to act in such circumstances? Doubts about the U.S. capability to recognize or attribute an attack could be just such a "green light."

In the contemporary environment there may be little basis for confidence in the attribution of attack, particularly with regard to biological weapons (BW) threats and limited nuclear threats. Dr. Jay Davis, founding Director of the Department of Defense's Defense Threat Reduction Agency, offers the following troubling conclusion in this regard:

> As a technologist and operator, I keep a standing mental list of the five hardest technical problems of which I am aware. Nuclear forensics and biological forensics each make that list. There is no assurance that we can work backwards from the effects of these horrific events to uniquely determine a perpetrator....What I suggest is a process that can lead us to knowledge of what is possible, and a way to structure our work so that we will have the largest possible credibility if we must attempt this daunting task.[63]

BW is particularly lethal and well-suited to *covert* employment. The casualties inflicted by the employment of biological weapons could approach or exceed those from a nuclear attack: "The [U.S.] Office of Technology Assessment calculated that 100 kilograms of anthrax spread over Washington could kill from one to three million people if disseminated effectively under the right environmental conditions. In contrast, a one-megaton nuclear warhead would kill from 750,000 to 1.9 million people."[64] Naturally-occurring biological pandemics can be comparable to a major WMD strike in terms of casualties and social disruption. The "Spanish flu" pandemic of 1918-1919 killed up to 40 million people globally, including 675,000 Americans. Those numbers are greater than the numbers of World War I fatalities suffered globally and by the United States, respectively.

Yet, detection and accountability based on confident identification of the culprit and the origins of a deliberate BW attack reportedly may *not* be possible.[65] It may even be difficult in practice to distinguish between an opponent's employment of a biological agent and a naturally-occurring health disaster: "A virus's strength can be altered to increase its efficiency. A particularly powerful strain of an endemic pathogen [disease-producing agent such as bacteria and viruses] could simply be blamed on a chance natural mutation."[66] And, "A biological agent attack is unlikely to generate any visible signatures, and the first evidence of a biological attack is likely to be the onset of disease. Thus, it might be days or even weeks before the consequences of a biological attack become evident. It might be impossible to determine that an outbreak resulted from an intentional act."[67]

With BW in particular there could be multiple possible culprits in an attack—including terrorists acting independently or with witting or unwitting state sponsors. Those states known or believed to possess a biological weapons program, according to a study by the Congressional Research Service, are: China, Cuba, Egypt, Iran, Israel, North Korea, Russia and Syria.[68] How and against whom would U.S. leaders communicate threats to deter an attack that may not be recognized as such, or be traceable to its source? In such cases, the familiar balance of terror confidence in the functioning of deterrence simply cannot apply.

Even if a biological attack is recognized as such, and the agent employed in an attack traced to a particular supplier state, that state could have been an unwitting accomplice in the attack, i.e., BW could have been stolen or misappropriated by state operatives acting independently of their leadership. Could a punitive retaliatory threat against the state be appropriate in such a case, or have the desired deterring effect? Rather than retaliating against a possibly unwitting state accomplice, might the United States instead need its cooperation in the hunt for information about the biological agent, its distribution, and the possible terrorist network involved?[69] These plausible contemporary conditions hardly provide fertile ground for balance of terror type punitive threats to work predictably.

This problem also poses potentially severe challenges to the traditional U.S. goal of extended deterrence. What credibility can U.S. extended deterrence threats have if there is significant uncertainty about an attack and its perpetrator? On what level of confidence in attribution and culpability would the United States be willing to threaten to retaliate against plausible perpetrators in response to an attack on an ally? The ally attacked may have very different perspectives about the level of evidence necessary to warrant U.S. threats of retaliation for the attack. When U.S. capabilities for attack recognition, detection and attribution may be so limited, the balance of terror's basic expectations about how deterrence will operate stretch credulity.

New U.S. Deterrence Goals and Priorities in a New Geopolitical Environment

During the Cold War, deterring the strategic threat posed by the Soviet Union was, understandably, the central focus of U.S. and NATO concern and attention. Secretary McNamara's assured destruction metric and U.S. arms control policies focused almost exclusively on sustaining a stable balance of terror with the Soviet Union. In the contemporary geopolitical environment, however, the immediacy of the Russian threat has sub-sided—whether temporarily or for the long term is unclear—and a diversity of new regional and transnational threats has emerged. In 1993, R. James Woolsey, the Director of Central Intelligence, characterized this change in the threat environment well: "We have slain a large dragon. But we live now in a jungle filled with a bewildering variety of poisonous snakes. And in many ways, the dragon was easier to keep track of."[70]

The continuity and centrality of the Soviet threat has been replaced by a kaleidoscope of opponents, threats and potential threats. U.S. deterrence goals and priorities correspondingly have become more varied both in the target audiences and the scope of actions to be deterred. The new priorities for deterrence do not suggest any lessening of its importance or ease in its practice; they do suggest less reliability and predictability in the functioning of deterrence than was believed to be available via a "stable" balance of terror. Rogue states and non-state actors (NSAs), including terrorist organizations, now take center stage in posing WMD threats to be deterred. Russia continues to be a factor, but more as a threat that may return to deterrence center stage depending on the path chosen by Kremlin leaders. The future of China in this regard is of concern, particularly with the future of Taiwan as a continuing flashpoint.

In this new, dynamic, multithreat environment, the formulation and conduct of deterrence policy faces a triple challenge: the expanded set of contemporary opponents to be deterred; the expanded range of their actions that must be deterred; and, the potential for political changes in Russia to (re-)establish the need to deter a peer nuclear power as an immediate objective.

New Opponents and Unprecedented Threats to Be Deterred

U.S. declared goals now include a wide range of possible opponents and threats: the familiar deterrence and extended deterrence of state-based nuclear and WMD attack; the deterrence of any Chinese attempt to solve the Taiwan question militarily; the deterrence of North Korean aggression or transfer of nuclear weapons or plans to a terrorist organization; and, *inter alia*, the deterrence or dissuasion of continued Iranian development of nuclear weapons. In addition, 9/11 foreshadowed the significance of deterring non-state organizations that have relatively modest resources, manpower and training—but in some cases aspire to nuclear weapons— and have used biological weapons.[71] The target audiences now include rogue state leaderships—including those about which we know relatively little with regard to form and function—and NSAs which may have unfamiliar and transitory leadership structures and whose goals, intentions, values, motivations, sources of information, health, capabilities and modes of decision making may be obscure and intentionally hidden.

One characteristic of this contemporary era is the unprecedented potential and apparent intention of relatively small, non-state terrorist/ criminal organizations to inflict large numbers of casualties on undefended, technically-advanced societies, particularly with potential biological or nuclear weapons.[72] Since the 1990s, terrorist organizations appear to have become increasingly motivated to employ WMD for the specific purpose of inflicting mass casualties.[73] The publicly expressed views of the CIA on this subject are that, "The newer breed of international terrorist, who seeks revenge more than carefully defined political objectives, is interested in inflicting mass casualties" as the strategic goal.[74] A contemporary challenge is to identify any feasible approach to punitive deterrence when an opponent is motivated to inflict mass casualties as a goal in itself and may attach transcendent value to doing so.

FBI Director Robert Mueller has stated that terrorist organizations such as al Qaeda seek nuclear capabilities and suggested that the economics of supply and demand may lead to terrorist acquisition of a nuclear weapon: "Several rogue nations—and even individuals—seek to develop nuclear capabilities...it is indeed a seller's market in the so-called atomic bazaar."[75] In 2001, al Qaeda reportedly was discovered to have an "aggressive" anthrax program ongoing in Afghanistan, and in 2003 senior al Qaeda leader, Ayman al-Zawahiri, reportedly cancelled a cyanide attack against the New York subway system, ominously telling plotters, "we have something better in mind."[76]

Referring to such opponents, former CIA Director George Tenet observed that they "desperately want" nuclear weapons because:

...if they manage to set off a mushroom cloud, they will make history. Such an event would place al-Qa'ida on a par with the superpowers and make good Bin Ladin's threat to destroy our economy and bring death to every American household. Even in the darkest days of the cold war, we could count on the fact that the Soviets, just like us, wanted to live. Not so with terrorists. Al-Qa'ida boasts that while we fear death, they embrace it.[77]

As the number and type of pertinent opponents increase—including some with transcendent motivations and WMD—the potential for punitive deterrence threats to fail unexpectedly and catastrophically also increases. This is so given the relative lack of mutual familiarity and understanding between the United States and some opponents; the bewildering array of opponents' goals, values and threats; the significant potential asymmetry in stakes and values at risk; and, the many opportunities for distortion in communications. In contrast to the Cold War's *relative* continuity of opponent, threat and conditions, the broad spectrum of opponents in the contemporary era offers more openings for conflicting goals and values, unfamiliar imperatives, distorted communications, and the lack of mutual familiarity to prevent the reliable functioning of deterrence. A particular challenge for contemporary U.S. deterrence policy and a factor contributing to the uncertainty of its functioning is the requirement imposed by contemporary conditions *to know so much about so many diverse opponents, e.g., the goals, values and decision-making processes of rogue states and terrorist organizations.*

Confident generalizations and assertions of universal principles provide little value when there is a broad spectrum of opponents and deterrence goals, and the considerable variation in opponent and circumstance will shape the functioning of deterrence. The value of traditional deterrence theory in this environment is limited largely to underscoring the need to understand the unique opponent and specific circumstances of possible deterrence engagements. Lawrence Freedman rightly observes in this regard that deterrence theory, "...provides little reliable guidance for policy other than to suggest that close attention is paid to the specifics of a situation rather than a reliance on vague generalizations."[78] This again highlights the deterrence value of understanding opponents on their own terms to the extent possible, and to the value of U.S. damage-limiting capabilities that may help save U.S. and allied lives in the event of deterrence failure or irrelevance—the probability of which for any given contingency is not subject to precise calculation.

The goal of deterring rogue states and terrorist organizations also introduces important, new deterrence twists. For example, if the declared U.S. objectives *vis-à-vis* rogue states and terrorist organizations are regime change and their elimination, respectively, what benefit may the opponent see in compliance with U.S. demands ("redlines")? Under these conditions, the U.S. goal is not to cooperate with the opponent to the extent necessary for the functioning of punitive deterrence; the goal is regime change, or the killing or capturing of terrorists, with little or no apparent opportunity for the implicit or explicit grudging cooperation envisaged in the balance of terror tenets. The functioning of punitive deterrence threats requires an expectation on the part of the opponent that there *is value in compliance*—i.e., the United States will refrain from the execution of its expressed threat if the opponent obeys. This point is *not* about the credibility of U.S. *threat execution*—a subject which dominated the debate between Schelling and Kahn—but the credibility of the U.S. promise *not to* act if the opponent complies with U.S. redlines. This was a type of credibility little discussed by Schelling or Kahn; it may now be as significant as the credibility of threat execution. This possible friction between the necessary cooperative element in punitive deterrence and U.S. tactical goals *vis-à-vis* contemporary rogue states and terrorists takes us far from the conditions of the Cold War and the familiar logic of deterrence.

In addition to new target audiences, addressing a broader range of threats has become a priority deterrence goal. These threats include, for example, the use of biological weapons by rogue states and potentially by terrorist organizations; the transfer of nuclear or other WMD from rogue states to terrorist organizations; and, deterrence of rogue state escalation to WMD use against forward-deployed U.S. and allied forces. Attempting to deter the transfer of WMD from rogue states to terrorist organizations poses particularly unprecedented challenges.

In 2004, U.S. Assistant Secretary of State James Kelly testified before the Senate Foreign Relations Committee that North Korean officials explicitly stated that North Korea has, "…nuclear weapons, will not dismantle them, *and might transfer* or demonstrate them."[79] In October 2006, President George W. Bush emphasized the U.S. goal of deterring the North Korean transfer of nuclear weapons: "The North Korean regime remains one of the world's leading proliferators of missile technology, including transfers to Iran and Syria. The transfer of nuclear weapons or material by North Korea to states or non-state entities would be considered a grave threat to the United States, and we would hold North Korea fully accountable for the consequences of such action." [80] This goal of deterring a rogue state from transferring nuclear weapons to other rogues or to terrorist organizations is a useful example of high-priority twenty-first century deterrence objectives.

Tailoring Deterrent Effect for New Goals and Priorities

As with all deterrence strategies, deterring nuclear transfer and related nuclear terrorism activities in an informed fashion requires an understanding of how to deter specific opponents from specific acts under specific conditions. Contemporary opponents to be so deterred are diverse and may include a chain of decision-making centers linked only loosely to each other. Consequently, an initial intelligence/analytical priority is to identify as accurately as possible the important participants in these chains and assess whether they are or can be made susceptible, directly or indirectly, to the deterrence tools available to the United States for this purpose. This is "tailored deterrence."

Who are the critical "links" in the pertinent networks, and can we deter and coerce one or more of them to prevent nuclear transfer and terrorism? There may be a string of important and connected target audiences—including, *inter alia*, state and non-state decision makers, supporting technical groups, intelligence services and free-lancing personnel, financial channels, transportation providers, and terrorist operatives. These potentially different audiences for U.S. deterrence threats are likely to have different levels of importance to the function U.S. leaders want to deter; different vulnerabilities to exploit; different channels of communication; and, are likely to require different tools of deterrence. Their susceptibility to deterrence pressure will vary; so too will U.S. knowledge of, access to, and opportunities for, communication.

Pertinent deterrence mechanisms may be categorized per the traditional distinction of "punitive" threats, i.e., communicating the painful consequences that would follow the opponents' actions if they persist, or "denial" threats that communicate the intolerable difficulties opponents will face in attempting to carry out their plans and their likely inability to realize their goals if they do so. Measures to capture terrorists or otherwise prevent transfer and defend against nuclear terrorism may not be for the purpose of deterrence per se; nevertheless, they may provide useful concomitant punitive and denial deterrent effect via the fears they inspire and the challenging conditions they create for targeted audiences. The fear of being captured or killed may serve as a *punitive* threat, and the expectation of serious operational challenges with the prospect of mission failure may lead an opponent to another course, or to postpone its action until success seems more likely—i.e., deterrence by *denial*.

The potential value of denial deterrence against terrorist threats is suggested by senior Defense Department official Ryan Henry: "Terrorists place a higher value on the completion of their mission than on their own lives. A potential deterrent strategy is to convince them that they will not successfully accomplish their task. We must spend more time understanding a terrorist network's 'value chain,' to determine those assets and capabilities it needs to successfully complete its mission."[81] Armed with sufficient understanding, the United States can seek to "intercept" that terrorist "value chain" to impose cost and/or deny benefit and thereby hopefully deter.[82]

There is some anecdotal evidence suggesting that denial deterrence holds promise.[83] For example, an al Qaeda leader in Iraq, Abu-Tariq, wrote in 2007 that U.S. pressure on al Qaeda's personnel and operations had reduced the number of al Qaeda terrorists in his sector from 600 to "20 or less" because "many of our fighters quit and some joined the deserters...."[84] He adds that for some al Qaeda terrorists, "their activities are frozen due to their present conditions plus their families' conditions."[85] As this example illustrates, denial deterrent effect from defensive/preventive measures can follow from opponents' beliefs that their goals and operations involve such a risk of failure or hardship that postponement or an alternative course of action is chosen.[86]

An extensive set of case studies examining past efforts by states to deter and coerce NSAs demonstrates that both denial and punitive deterrence strategies may be effective against extremely violent and eccentric NSAs. In practice, the deterrence of terrorists and their sponsors often has been the initially unintended concomitant effect of a state's efforts to defeat or destroy the NSA.[87] Manifest state efforts to isolate, capture, incarcerate and kill terrorists have had the effect of demoralizing terrorist cells, effectively degrading their internal cohesion while reducing their will and opportunities to strike.[88] An example of punitive and denial deterrent effect from such defensive measures may be seen in a conclusion offered by Israeli military officials: "Terrorists who head out to carry out rocket attacks know that they are exposed and unprotected and there is no doubt that this acts as a deterrent. Ultimately this also leads to a drop in the number of attacks."[89]

NATO's 1999 air strikes against the assets of Serbian leader Slobodan Milosevic's business associates appear to have had coercive effect,[90] as have financial sanctions such as those implemented by the United States against Iranian, Syrian, and North Korean organizations and individuals linked to WMD proliferation.[91] The Israeli practice of destroying homes of Palestinian terrorists also appears to have had some useful deterrent effect.[92] Additionally, threats by extra-legal forces to family members of drug lord Pablo Escobar apparently helped to deter attacks on Colombian officials.[93] This brief listing of past deterrence practice is not to suggest that such actions are appropriate for the United States; rather, it is to point to the array of military and non-military threats—direct and indirect—that have had some noticeable deterrent effect on NSAs in the past. For each target audience a different combination of punitive threats and denial measures may be necessary and practicable.

As noted above, a contemporary challenge is the possible lack of reliable capabilities to detect the actions to be deterred and to identify the specific, pertinent audiences accountable for the purpose of deterring them.[94] Confident information about those involved in nuclear transfer networks and nuclear terrorism may be difficult or impossible to acquire in a timely fashion.[95] To the extent that there is insufficient "forensic" information to make such distinctions, the United States may be compelled to fall back on generic threats broadcast to generic audiences. This possible lack of information necessary to tailor punitive threats and denial measures heightens the prospective uncertainties of contemporary deterrence strategies.

An important related question concerns the chosen standard for U.S. threat credibility: the standard used to determine the adequacy of threat credibility will be at the heart of the task of deterring nuclear transfer. The different definitions of adequate credibility reflected in Kahn's and Schelling's work again are pertinent. As discussed in Chapter 6, there is considerable momentum behind the standard of imposing "uncertainty" on the opponent as the basis for deterrence credibility, possibly because "uncertainty" is a relatively easy standard to meet (a *chance* of detection, attribution and U.S. threat execution).

During the Cold War, as discussed in Chapter 4, Soviet fear of the *possibility* of U.S. nuclear escalation was expected to prevent Soviet covert movement of nuclear weapons into the United States. The CIA's NIE-4-70

[Declassified: January 31, 1994], *The Clandestine Introduction of Nuclear Weapons Into the US* allowed that, "Nuclear weapons with weights of up to a few thousand pounds *could be brought across US borders by common means of transport without great difficulties* but not without some risk."[96] Nevertheless, Soviet clandestine nuclear introduction was judged to be unlikely because Soviet planners would fear *the possibility of U.S. detection and escalation,* and thus the chance of unacceptable damage to the Soviet Union; therefore, the "chance" of detection and severe consequences were considered likely to deter.[97]

The Soviets were not often desperate or willing gamblers. There are audiences in the prospective nuclear transfer chains, particularly including terrorists, who may well be so. Such audiences may see U.S. uncertainty and ambiguity as an opening to be exploited, and a higher standard of credibility will be necessary for deterrence. Again, the need to understand the specific opponent and context for deterrence purposes is apparent. The goal is to understand to the extent feasible the credibility of U.S. threats from the enemy's perspective, and identify the combination of punitive threats and denial measures likely to be decisive in the decision making of the target audiences, or to understand that such a level of credibility is unlikely to be possible. This is a challenging task, especially when the targeted audiences and their actions may not be detectable in a timely fashion or with great confidence.

Strategic Communication for Deterrence

Deterrence by design involves understanding and shaping the target audience's beliefs about the difficulties and/or likely consequences associated with the actions we want to deter; unless redlines and threats are effectively communicated and understood by the opponent, deterrence strategies can work only by happenstance. Deterrence of unique threats—such as nuclear transfer or nuclear and biological terrorism— can be discussed separately in a conceptual manner, but cannot be pursued in isolation from other U.S. deterrence goals and practices or from broader U.S. foreign policy goals and behavior. U.S. diplomatic statements and actions intended to add credibility to specific deterrence threats are likely to mean much or little depending on how the target audience has read the broader context and history of U.S. behavior.

A former senior Defense Department official has proposed that the United States deter North Korea from transferring nuclear weapons by issuing strongly-worded, unambiguous threats of U.S. nuclear retaliation in the event "a nuclear weapon of North Korean origin explodes on American soil or that of an U.S. ally...."[98] The United States can make such deterrence-related declarations; those declarations may have the intended deterrent effect if they are heard, understood and believed. That is the goal of strategic communication.

There are multiple avenues for the distortion, misunderstanding and disbelief of U.S. efforts to communicate national will and threat. These avenues may have been set years in advance by events wholly unrelated to the U.S. deterrence goal at hand. Saddam Hussein's disdainful view of the United States prior to the 1991 Gulf War, for example, apparently was established in large measure by the U.S. withdrawal from Vietnam and its subsequent withdrawal from Lebanon in 1983.[99] Whatever deterrence messages the U.S. Ambassador to Iraq, April Glaspie, may have intended to deliver to Saddam Hussein in 1990, they were interpreted by Saddam against a backdrop that did not provide much room for the functioning of deterrence.

The point here is that strategic communication for the purpose of deterrence is a complex art form ideally tailored to each audience, time and goal, and put into motion as early as possible *vis-à-vis* that audience. But what the opponent believes ultimately is determined by *its interpretation of that to which it pays attention—which may not easily be anticipated.*

Reviewing how pertinent opponents have been deterred or coerced in the past may provide useful insight with regard to threat and communication. For example, the United States appears to have coerced a rare apology from North Korean leader Kim Il Sung following the 1976 murders by North Korean border guards of two U.S. soldiers who were trimming a poplar tree located in a joint security area. North Korean pronouncements immediately thereafter accused the United States of orchestrating the event as a provocation. The subsequent strong U.S. communication of displeasure included new, daily B-52 training sorties along the demilitarized zone. Within days the North Koreans became much more conciliatory and Kim Il Sung expressed regret over the "incident."[100] This case, while far from the question of nuclear transfer, does provide historical evidence of a U.S. mode of behavior and communication that appears to have effectively coerced a particularly challenging audience.

This brief discussion of contemporary deterrence goals suggests that pressing deterrence requirements include the intelligence, policing and analytic work necessary to identify and understand target audiences as specifically as possible so as to tailor deterrence strategies and communications as accurately as possible, and to strengthen the reality and the perception of U.S. capabilities for detection, attribution/ accountability, prevention and damage limitation. These are challenging tasks that U.S. institutions may not be well-prepared to pursue: the balance of terror tenets do not suggest the deterrence need for such targeted understanding of opponents or for prevention and damage limitation; all rational opponents are expected to respond prudently and cautiously to avoid U.S. nuclear retaliatory threats.

The Cold War's Continuity Versus Contemporary Fluidity

The Cold War was characterized by a remarkable degree of continuity and concentration of the major security threats faced by the United States. The bipolar organization of much of the world included no small threat to the United States, but one with considerable continuity in its basic features and corresponding consistency in U.S. expectations about the deterrence solution. Efforts to establish and "lock in" a "stable" deterrence balance of terror were pursued for the long term because enduring features of the threat environment meant that enduring value was expected to be found in definitions of strategic forces as adequate, "stabilizing" or "destabilizing" per their compatibility with a balance of terror.

The contemporary threat environment, however, appears to be far more dynamic than was that of the Cold War; it may be more analogous to other historical periods in which the parameters of threat changed quickly.[101] The outlines of dramatic changes are obvious in some contemporary developments: the rise of hostile regional rogue powers, NSAs, and Chinese military and economic power, as well as the spread of WMD to otherwise minor powers. The future of Russia could unfold in a dramatically hostile or benign direction, and additional discontinuities not now apparent are likely to emerge to our surprise. As often is remarked in this regard, who in the summer of 2001 anticipated that the United States itself soon would be attacked by an NSA and, as a consequence, would be fighting against an eccentric, obscure Afghan quasi-government called the Taliban?

Putative North Korean nuclear capabilities and Iranian movement toward acquisition of nuclear weapons have the potential to trigger a "cascade" of nuclear proliferation among other states in the region.[102]

Rapid and radical governmental change in currently friendly and allied states, including an existing nuclear power such as Pakistan, could alter the U.S. security calculus in the region dramatically. Finally, the character of the threats posed by NSAs—including terrorist organizations—could become much more severe if those organizations secure additional personnel, funding, technical and logistical support from state sponsors, and acquire WMD.

Mohamed ElBaradei, Director General of the International Atomic Energy Agency, has "estimated that up to 49 nations now know how to make nuclear arms," and that the intentions of those countries regarding nuclear weapons are, "based on their sense of security or insecurity, and could therefore be subject to rapid change."[103] In such a dynamic geopolitical environment, there is no possible formula for deterrence that can define an enduring, adequate set of U.S. forces to be "locked in." Strategies for deterrence will vary according to the dynamic circumstances of opponent and context, as will the corresponding types of threats and supporting forces. Contemporary conditions are the antithesis to those that were the basis for Secretary McNamara's assured destruction formula and balance of terror tenets; the capability to adapt and "tailor" U.S. deterrence strategies and forces to a wide spectrum of circumstances now is paramount.

In a threat environment of shifting opponents and conditions, following any fixed standard for deterrence and strategic capabilities could leave U.S. planning and forces well out of sync with those necessary for deterrence or helpful in the event of deterrence failure. In a direct reversal of the balance of terror tenet that a minimal, adequate and "stable" strategic force equilibrium can be identified and established, a key to deterrence in a highly fluid environment is the capability and freedom to adapt deterrence strategies, planning, and supporting capabilities to the shifting and diverse demands of that environment. Answers to even the most basic questions may no longer be taken for granted. To wit, what threat—if any—is likely to deter? Is communication possible? How does the opponent define rational behavior under given circumstances? Can the perpetrator of an attack be identified? It is a mistake to continue to think and discuss deterrence in Cold War balance of terror terms—to believe that forces can be generically "stabilizing" or "destabilizing" or that some modern variant of the assured destruction metric can provide predictable deterrent effect and serve usefully as the enduring force goal to be "locked in" via arms control. There is no balance of terror-type formula that can be expected to apply generally, work predictably, and provide definitions for those forces and types of threats that can be deemed adequate, "stabilizing" or "destabilizing." This conclusion is antithetical to past confidence in the set formula for "stable" deterrence.

The old balance of terror formula is advantageous in that it provides easy, precise and enduring guidance for identifying "how much is enough" for deterrence, as well as which forces supposedly would be "stabilizing" or "destabilizing." The problem is that the conclusions thus derived are of unknown integrity. They suggest precision that does not exist because whether or how deterrence will apply—if it will work as desired, or what forces would be adequate to "ensure" it—much less whether a particular type of force will prove "stabilizing" or "destabilizing," is not predictable with precision and confidence. The contemporary environment of multiple and variable threats, unfamiliar opponents, and diverse circumstances only exacerbates these inherent causes of deterrence uncertainty. What may reasonably now be said with confidence is that U.S. threats and supporting strategic forces that may provide the desired deterrent effect will change and vary depending on the particulars of audience and context.

So What?

During the Cold War, the continuities of the threat, the expected comparability of interests and values, and confidence that decision makers would behave "prudently" per the supposed demands of rationality, largely spared us the difficult challenge of seeking detailed understanding of unique opponents and circumstances. Contemporary conditions compel taking up that task. Operating with limited understanding does not mean that deterrence threats must fail; nor are they certain to "work" with greater understanding. But, it should help.

In addition, the contemporary diversity of opponents, circumstances and threats suggests the need for a spectrum of U.S. force options and flexibility in deterrence planning. These may better enable us to adapt deterrence strategies to the variability of opponents, threat conditions and stakes. Deterrence strategies and strategic force standards in the contemporary, fluid environment demand flexibility in application, humility in prediction, and preparation for deterrence failure or irrelevance. Colin Gray illustrates the historic precedent in this regard: "... England no sooner had learned which grand strategy to apply in order to beat the Dutch in the seventeenth century than the enemy changed—to France—and yesterday's strategic assumptions no longer worked."[104] Whatever conclusions may be reached about the value of particular forces for deterrence following a careful examination of foes and circumstances, it is critical to recognize that the prospective answers will represent a snapshot in time. The threat conditions that may point to the value or lack of value of certain levels and types of capabilities for deterrence will change, with corresponding changes in the appropriate U.S. threats and forces necessary to support deterrence. The key ingredients now are flexibility and adaptability in planning and force deployment.

A problem, however, with positing flexibility, adaptability, and the availability of numerous threat options as the key deterrence measure of merit for U.S. strategic forces is that these standards suggest virtually unlimited force requirements for numerous plausible opponents and circumstances. This, again, is the antithesis to Secretary McNamara's assured destruction cap on U.S. requirements. In principle, the conclusion that a broad spectrum of forces and the capability to adapt to different threats and circumstances should be helpful. In practice, however, policymakers must work within limited budgets and structured processes, and pursue their deterrence strategies within those limitations. Unable to purchase all the forces that might potentially be useful for deterrence they must ascertain which forces are likely to be *most* valuable for U.S. deterrence needs and allocate their limited resources accordingly.

Finding Limitations for Contemporary Deterrence Force Requirements

Secretary McNamara's mechanistic assured destruction formula was a fully speculative metric by which to judge the adequacy of U.S. strategic forces for deterrence. It provided, however, *an easily calculable rationale for identifying those forces to be labeled necessary or (more often) unnecessary for deterrence.* Assured destruction was an elegant and effective standard for limiting possible force requirements, and was highly valued as such. As elaborated in Chapter 4, former senior Pentagon official Henry Rowen observed: "The primary purpose of the Assured Destruction capabilities doctrine was to provide a metric for deciding how much force was enough: it provided a basis for denying service and Congressional claims for more money for strategic forces."[105]

In the contemporary environment there is no comparable, easily-calculable metric for limitations because U.S. strategic force requirements for deterrence must include consideration of a wide spectrum of opponents and contingencies, and may shift abruptly as new threats emerge and old threats decline or re-emerge. That does not mean, however, that there is no basis now for bounding the strategic force requirements associated with contemporary deterrence goals. Defining such boundaries coherently can follow from the prioritization of deterrence goals per the intelligence and analytical efforts needed to understand opponents and the "how's" associated with U.S. deterrence goals. Generic formulas for limitation— such as assured destruction and its variants—can be replaced by the priorities suggested by the identification of the opponents and threats deemed both most important and susceptible to deterrence, and the corresponding tailoring of deterrence to those threats. The need in this regard is for an ongoing net assessment of threats and deterrence requirements to address these questions:

- What priority should be attached to which opponents and threats?
- Which deterrence goals are most important?
- Which opponents are likely to be susceptible to deterrence and in what fashion?
- Which U.S. strategic forces, correspondingly, are of highest priority for deterrence purposes?

Answers to these questions will not be fixed; high-confidence conclusions may not often be readily apparent. Even when competently done, such assessments are unlikely to provide a basis for the confident expectation that deterrence will function reliably and predictably *à la* the Cold War notion of "existential deterrence." That problem, however, is inherent in any deterrence strategy or approach to defining the necessary force requirements. There are too many unknowns and potentially unknowable variables that may come into play. Nevertheless, boundaries of strategic force requirements may be discernible via efforts to understand opponents for deterrence purposes and to prioritize threats accordingly.

Requirements for standing, deployed U.S. forces also may be limited to the extent that the U.S. military production infrastructure can respond flexibly and promptly to the demands suggested by shifting conditions. The United States will not need to deploy all the types and quantities of forces that might be of value for deterrence if it has a defense industrial infrastructure that can respond in a timely way to those emerging threats deemed to be likely priorities and susceptible to deterrence.

This potential U.S. capacity to adapt its deterrence and acquisition strategies to shifting conditions is now the important deterrence measure of merit for U.S. strategic forces, but it cannot define a fixed numeric standard of adequacy for U.S. strategic forces writ large. Those forces serve *purposes* beyond deterrence that may entail other, separate requirements. Commentators are fundamentally mistaken in four different ways when they use the old target-based formula to specify some set number of U.S. strategic weapons as adequate to "ensure" deterrence, and then proceed to identify that level of capability as the standard of adequacy for U.S. strategic forces in general:

- First, that methodology may tell little to nothing about the actual requirements for deterrence; alone it is utterly inadequate to draw such conclusions.
- Second, deterrence cannot be "ensured" by any set of capabilities because there is no mechanistic linkage between capabilities and deterrent effect.
- Third, U.S. force requirements for deterrence should not be considered fixed—they are as subject to change as is the threat environment itself.
- Fourth, as just noted, whatever level of U.S. strategic capability is judged necessary for deterrence at a given time cannot be the standard of adequacy for U.S. strategic forces in general because those forces serve additional goals beyond deterrence.

This last point is a particularly significant departure from Cold War tradition when deterrence was the priority of priorities: If confidence in stable deterrence required the absence of damage-limitation capabilities, such was the price to be paid for that highest-priority goal. In the twenty-first century deterrence remains important, but on occasion other goals may be equally or even more important, and U.S. strategic force measures of merit must also be informed by these goals.

Contemporary Strategic Force Goals and Metrics Beyond Deterrence

1. Damage Limitation

In the contemporary environment of multiple sources of WMD threat and heightened deterrence uncertainty, the value of strategic forces to support damage limitation directly should be included in the definition of adequacy for U.S. strategic capabilities. This value was anticipated by the Johnson Administration as early as 1964. Secretary of Defense McNamara wrote in his 1964 DPM:

> There remains the possibility of a small nuclear attack on the United States either accidentally or by a nation other than the Soviet Union. Since the next decade will probably see a proliferation of nuclear weapons and strategic delivery systems, and remembering that a single thermonuclear weapon could kill as many Americans as were lost in the entire Second World War, this may become an important problem....Our preliminary conclusion is that a small balanced defense program involving a moderate civil defense effort and a very limited deployment of a low cost configuration of the Nike X [BMD] system (which is technically feasible without commitment to a full-scale deployment) could, indeed, significantly reduce fatalities from such an attack.[106]

Deterrence will work and fail unpredictably in the future, as it has in the past. If and when it fails, the immediate U.S. priority will be the limitation of casualties and damage to the extent possible. Fortunately, some U.S. political leaders now recognize the importance of a commitment to make that a meaningful goal: "The actions we take now could save many thousands of lives and could in many other ways reduce the damage to our country from such an attack....To be sure, no level of all-hazards readiness will prevent the horrendous toll of death, injury, property damage, economic disruption, and political upheaval that would follow a nuclear attack. But proper planning can ease suffering and mitigate losses."[107]

Recent studies demonstrate anew the potential for defensive capabilities to reduce the level of casualties and destruction that might otherwise be inflicted should deterrence fail. The findings from a comprehensive analysis of limited nuclear attacks against U.S. cities are not surprising—the United States presently is ill-prepared for even a "small" nuclear attack: "There is little doubt that a nuclear weapon event will exceed the emergency response system capacity, particularly in the first hours of the event, it is obvious that an expansion of properly trained personnel to meet this glaring deficiency needs to be considered."[108] However, as one of the study's authors concludes, "There actually is quite a bit that we can do [to save lives]. In certain areas, it may be possible to turn the death rate from 90 percent in some burn populations to probably 20 or 30 percent—and those are very big differences—simply by being prepared well in advance."[109] There are numerous practical steps that can be taken to reduce the level of societal vulnerability to limited nuclear attacks.[110]

In this contemporary context, the Cold War proposition that defenses must work near perfectly to be worth the investment seems far-fetched. Indeed, state and federal governments frequently accept or impose considerable costs to improve the safety of homes, the workplace, and most forms of transportation without the unobtainable and thus paralyzing requirement for perfection in doing so.[111]

It would be better, of course, to choose the sure option of deterring attacks and preventing *all* casualties, but that option will not always be available. In some cases feasible damage-limitation measures, if available, will be the only means of added protection and will be judged worth the effort whatever the ratio of their cost to the opponent's offensive capabilities.

Fred Leykam, a respected expert on the threat posed by biological weapons, offers the following conclusion from pertinent analyses in which he has been involved:

> Based on hard scientific data from system testing and urban dispersal modeling, it is clear that significant protection against the threat of [biological] attack is feasible with known technologies at costs that are trivial in relation to the U.S. defense budget and the potential socio-economic impact of an attack. Current programs such as the Autonomous Pathogen Detection System (APDS) and bioaerosol detectors, e.g., biomass change detection, offer a useful capability today and could be expanded significantly with modest additional spending.[112]

The choice no longer can be characterized as between two mutually exclusive alternatives—to wit, the "destabilizing" partial protection afforded by strategic damage-limitation capabilities, *or* the predictable full protection provided by a "stable" balance of terror. When the choice was characterized as such the prudent path seemingly was self-evident. For many plausible contexts, however, that characterization now is nonsense: damage limitation may *not* be "destabilizing," and deterrence may provide *no predictable protection*. The choice now—if indeed a choice needs to be made—is between two imperfect alternatives: uncertain deterrence or imperfect defense. In some cases, a strategy embracing imperfect damage limitation may be the most prudent course because, when deterrence uncomplemented by defenses utterly fails, it "fails deadly." This is why the expectation of deterrence functioning reliably and predictably is so central to its stand-alone value.

When the prospective lethality of threat is high, the reliable functioning of deterrence is questionable, and damage-limitation measures can provide appreciable protection, a strategy that *includes* damage-limitation goals and measures may be the *only* prudent alternative. A number of plausible biological and nuclear contingencies now fit this genre of threat, which is why various forms of damage limitation against mass destruction attacks now are potentially so important. The key questions are:

- Against which threats can the United States provide society with an appreciable level of protection?
- What are the thresholds of effectiveness and cost necessary for U.S. policymakers to deem damage limitation worth the expense?
- What priority is damage limitation?

Another value of manifest damage-limitation measures that goes beyond the direct protection of society is the assurance they may provide to a public under threat of attack. A public's *belief* that its government is taking steps toward its protection can be extremely important to the preservation of public confidence, morale, discipline and order; that public order, in turn, can determine the effectiveness of organized defensive measures and any other organized activity.

This domestic assurance value of damage limitation is not conjecture. It was part of British World War II experience with German air and ballistic missile attacks: "The British people understandably found it extremely difficult, physically and psychologically, to cope with attacks when they knew they were undefended. But they were able to cope, despite sometimes heavy casualties, when they knew they were being defended."[113] Indeed, the public's *perception of government protection* appears to have been key in this regard.[114]

An official British history of this World War II experience concludes that the "remarkable stoicism" demonstrated by the battered British public, "...was due, no doubt...to the wisdom of a governmental policy which did not seek to ignore or understate the hardships of the time, but to alleviate them where it could, and in any case to foster a spirit which could make them bearable."[115] Israel's experience under missile attack during the 1991 Gulf War demonstrated again the psychological value of defensive measures for public calm, and the importance of that value.[116]

Perhaps more importantly, in most plausible contemporary contingencies there now is *no* obvious either/or dilemma compelling a choice *between* deterrence and direct damage-limitation goals. These goals may instead be complementary. As discussed above, damage-limitation measures may contribute usefully to the credibility of U.S. punitive deterrence threats and also to denial deterrent effect. They may be particularly important for the credibility of U.S. extended deterrence when the opponent's strategy is to deter U.S. support for an ally via implicit or explicit nuclear threats to U.S. forces or cities, as certainly appears to be an element in Chinese and North Korean strategy. This potential value of strategic defense for U.S. extended deterrence credibility was one reason the Johnson Administration sought a significant U.S. BMD capability against the "Nth Country" (i.e., non-Soviet) nuclear threat.[117]

In the absence of strategic defense, opponents may believe that the potential downside for the United States is too high for it to carry out its deterrent threats, thus undermining the deterrent effect of those threats. For example, U.S. leaders may not be in a strong position to threaten with credibility severe sanctions against North Korea because of the vulnerability of South Korean civilians to attack.

As described above, given the potential consequences for South Korea of conflict with North Korea, South Korea may be expected to be wary of severe U.S. deterrence threats or actions against North Korea. This is deterrence capital potentially available to North Korea based on

South Korean vulnerability.   In this context, North Korea may lower its
assessment of the credibility of severe U.S. deterrent threats—particularly
as former U.S. leaders publicly point out the constraining effect this
vulnerability has had on U.S. decision making.   Offensive and defensive
damage-limitation capabilities to degrade or deny North Korea the capability
to turn Seoul into a "sea of fire" may be key to the credibility of severe U.S.
deterrence threats posed to North Korea.[118]

Kim Myong Chol, a recognized spokesman for North Korea,
claims that North Korean "ICBMs locked on major metropolitan areas on
the American homeland" will help ensure the deterrence of the United
States.[119]   If severe U.S. threats to North Korea are to provide deterrent
effect, there may be a requirement for extensive U.S. damage-limitation
efforts to minimize the threat to U.S. and allied targets from possible North
Korean missile strikes and artillery barrages, respectively.

One review of North Korean military doctrine and programs
concludes that North Korea allocates its limited resources to "nuclear
weapons, ballistic missiles, [and] artillery (which is really a strategic weapon
vis-à-vis Seoul)," and that U.S. capabilities to counter the effectiveness of
these programs will undermine North Korea's military strategy and thereby
strengthen U.S. deterrence efforts.[120]

This North Korean example illustrates one of the possible constraints on U.S. deterrence threats and how U.S. damage-limitation
measures may help ameliorate those constraints. To the extent that
damage-limitation measures can mitigate U.S. and allied vulnerabilities,
U.S. deterrence threats may have greater credibility and effect because
opponents such as North Korea have lower expectations that U.S. leaders
would be paralyzed by U.S. and allied vulnerabilities.

Perhaps ironically, to the extent that U.S. damage-limitation
capabilities are important for the credibility of the U.S. extended deterrent
and the assurance of allies they are important for non-proliferation
purposes. This possible linkage is antithetical to the now-familiar balance
of terror adages that U.S. damage-limitation capabilities can only undermine U.S. deterrence and arms control goals. Again, Secretary McNamara
pointed to this positive linkage between U.S. BMD and non-proliferation
as a reason to pursue a significant direct damage-limitation capability
against China in 1965.[121]

These points return to the logic behind Herman Kahn's enthusiasm
for U.S. strategic damage-limitation capabilities: the effectiveness of U.S.
deterrence threats, particularly for extended deterrence, can be affected

as much by U.S. vulnerability to being hurt as it is by the U.S. capability to make punitive threats. To the extent that U.S. leaders can issue deterrence threats from an apparent position of limited vulnerability—and, therefore, limited U.S. risk—logically those deterrence threats should appear more credible to opponents and thus be more effective. Kahn made the point simply: "In the absence of enforceable or acceptable adjudication, the side most afraid of a strike will tend to get the worst of the bargain."[122] The deterrence advantage expected by Kahn to follow from U.S. damage-limitation capabilities presumes that opponents will be relatively less willing to provoke the United States when it is they, not U.S. leaders, who are "most afraid of a strike." To the extent that the logic of deterrence pertains to such a contest of wills, this posited linkage between U.S. protection and the credibility of U.S. threats should also apply.

Is this linkage between U.S. damage-limitation measures and more credible U.S. extended deterrence certain? Of course not. The "logic of deterrence" may not govern opponents' decision making or behavior, and U.S. deterrence threats may work or fail regardless of the state of U.S. defensive measures. Reducing U.S. vulnerabilities logically *should* increase U.S. threat credibility, all other things being equal. However, all other things rarely are equal and opponents are not so predictable.

Nevertheless, it is equally true that U.S. damage-limitation capabilities cannot be categorized automatically as "destabilizing"— despite the dreaded "war-fighting" label assigned to them during the Cold War. That familiar and still-frequently repeated balance of terror tenet cannot be sustained anymore than can the equally familiar lines that they are useless for deterrence because "uncertainty" surely will deter and that protection worthy of the name is impracticable.

Indeed, when North Korea pursued obvious preparations to launch missiles in late June 2006, the United States by then had deployed a rudimentary missile defense system. White House National Security Advisor Stephen Hadley said at the time that President Bush was prepared to order an intercept of a North Korean missile, if necessary.[123] U.S. strategic BMD provided a defensive option against the possibility that North Korean missiles might be launched at the United States.

Having a defensive option in place in such circumstances can provide the U.S. public with assurance and possible protection; it also may contribute to a more benign crisis escalation process than otherwise would be the case by mitigating pressure on the United States to strike an opponent's missiles offensively. Here is the possibility of U.S. defensive capabilities helping to prevent traditional notions of "crisis instability" rather than being the cause. Amazingly, commentators who express continuing confidence in deterrence and great concern about the putative "destabilizing" effects of U.S. missile defense simultaneously recommend U.S. pre-emptive, offensive strikes against an opponent's missile sites as the preferred alternative to U.S. missile defense:

> If a hostile emerging missile state acquires intercontinental-range missiles, the United States can deter their use through the threat of overwhelming retaliation. If such a state makes an explicit and credible threat to launch a missile attack against the United States, it may be possible to destroy its missiles before they are launched, in accord with the right of self-defense.[124]

This approach of relying *only* on deterrence or offensive pre-emption could place enormous pressure on the United States to strike first in a crisis. This pressure already is apparent for some U.S. allies. In early 2008, for example, South Korea's newly designated Chairman of the Joint Chiefs of Staff, Gen. Kim Tae-young, stated that the emerging North Korean nuclear threat was compelling South Korea to plan just such pre-emptive, offensive strikes against North Korean nuclear sites, "to prevent North Korea's nuclear weapons from exploding in our territory."[125]

The increased relative value of damage limitation and its possible compatibility with deterrence efforts includes, but is not limited to, BMD. Why should BMD now be considered a *necessary* element of U.S. damage-limitation measures when other threats in addition to missiles loom large? That need is created by those opponents and potential opponents who continue to invest heavily and trade in offensive missile capabilities that pose obvious threats to us and our allies, particularly including North Korea, Iran and China. These state-based missile threats have not been supplanted by the threats posed by NSAs and international terrorism; both have been elevated on the list of twenty-first century threats. As German expert, Michael Rühle, head of NATO's Policy Planning Section, observes in this regard:

> Over the past decades, for example, North Korea has sold upgraded ex-Soviet SCUD missiles to Iran, Libya, Pakistan, and Syria—and perhaps to even more countries.

Today, however, several nations are cooperating on the development, production and testing of missiles. This reduces testing needs, international visibility and costs. Moreover, some countries, including North Korea and Iran, have tested ballistic missiles in the guise of a "peaceful" space launch programme—a politically convenient means to garner support from other countries who would not dare to engage in military cooperation…The result of all this? In 1972, when the ABM Treaty was signed, only 9 countries possessed ballistic missiles. Today, that number has almost tripled. And both North Korea and Iran are likely to have long-range missiles by 2015.[126]

The decision to eschew U.S. strategic BMD made by the Nixon Administration in 1972 now entails real and potentially extreme risks because there are irreducible uncertainties in the functioning of deterrence, and self-described opponents may use offensive missiles of various ranges to deter, coerce and strike, and they may transfer missiles to terrorist organizations. It should be recalled in this regard that the missile threat to the United States does not reside only in ICBMs launched from an opponent's territory. Shorter-range missiles could be launched from offshore against most major U.S. population centers.[127]

The potential for U.S. BMD to provide sustainable societal protection worthy of deployment was limited during the Cold War, given the Soviet potential for massive missile attacks. The value of damage-limitation efforts can be dismissed if history is expected inalterably to "fade to black" in the event of war. But the character and range of threats has changed. Correspondingly, Clinton Administration Secretary of Defense William Perry concluded while in office that *defense against rogue state missile threats* involving, "several dozens of warheads…is quite achievable with present technology, and it's achievable with several tens of billions of dollars, not several hundreds of billions of dollars."[128] In 1996, he noted that the missile defense technologies then in development, "would be quite capable of defending against the much smaller and relatively unsophisticated ICBM threat that a rogue nation or a terrorist could mount any time in the foreseeable future."[129] This language is reminiscent of the Johnson Administration's decision to deploy missile defense *against Chinese missile capabilities*.

Even those typically hostile to U.S. BMD have pointed to the technical feasibility of defense against limited missile threats. As a report by the Arms Control Association noted at the end of the Cold War, "There is little doubt that it is technically possible to protect the United States against a handful of missiles launched by accident, a mad commander, or a Third World country."[130]

It remained for President George W. Bush to announce on December 17, 2002 that the United States, for the first time in three decades, would pursue the sustained deployment of strategic BMD. Five years later, following the North Korean 2006 test launch of missiles, Director of the U.S. Missile Defense Agency, Lt. Gen. Trey Obering, observed that the United States had deployed a capability to defend against a long-range North Korean missile attack: "When North Korea launched short- and long-range missiles last summer, we had, for the first time, the means to defend all 50 states against a possible attack."[131] President Bush's 2002 announcement—and subsequent limited BMD deployment—represents one of the few U.S. departures from the traditional balance of terror formula to be implemented in five decades.

With regional rogue states moving toward nuclear weapons and missiles of increasing range and payload, missile defenses have become an essential element of a U.S. post-Cold War strategy that includes direct damage-limitation goals. Particularly apparent is the need to deploy regional and strategic missile defense capabilities that are sufficiently effective and adaptable to meet missile threats as they emerge. Moving to provide defenses against the North Korean and Iranian missile threats, for example, is key to the strategic goals of being capable of defending against some plausibly undeterrable threats, reducing exploitable vulnerabilities, assuring local publics, and possibly dissuading rogue states from continuing to invest heavily in missiles as a favored weapon. These goals for U.S. BMD are not unprecedented; the Johnson Administration identified precisely the same logic and set of objectives for its planned *Sentinel* BMD program subsequently terminated by the Nixon Administration.

As noted above, civil defense measures also are likely to be essential to a contemporary U.S. strategy that includes damage-limitation goals. There is no recent precedent of U.S. support for serious civil defense programs but, during the Cold War, Secretary McNamara identified civil defense as the single-most cost-effective approach to damage limitation.[132] And, as late as 1968, he recommended a modest level of civil defense as "low cost insurance for our people in the unlikely event of a nuclear attack."[133]   In the contemporary environment, civil defense preparations against limited nuclear and biological attacks—including nuclear terrorism or bioterrorism—could make a valuable difference in the level of societal destruction and casualties.[134] In contrast to Secretary McNamara's Cold War estimate, such an event no longer can be judged "unlikely" with confidence.

As Columbia University Professor Richard Betts has observed: "Some of the [U.S. defensive] responses most likely to cope with the [new] threats in novel ways will not find a warm welcome. The response that should now be the highest priority is one long ignored, opposed, or ridiculed: a serious civil defense program to blunt the effects of WMD if they are unleashed within the United States."[135] Former senior Clinton Administration Department of Defense officials concur. Following a discussion of the contemporary dangers posed by a relatively small nuclear attack on the United States, William Perry and Ashton Carter observe:

> Two capabilities should be fostered by the federal government. First, a new type of fallout shelter program should be promoted by the federal government as a cheap and effective way to minimize the radiation exposure of most people downwind of a nuclear terrorist attack. The Cold War civil defense shelter program was mocked because it could not offer realistic protection against an attack of thousands of warheads from the Soviet Union. Against one or a few terrorist nuclear weapons, however, in-place sheltering is the best way for most people to protect themselves.[136]

The United States would not be alone in this endeavor. South Korea reportedly now is working on, "how to protect domestic communications lines and electronic equipment from the attacks and secure military personnel and civilians from radiological fallout."[137]

Some commentators of a cynical bent have repeated the Cold War argument against BMD that the protection of U.S. society should be rejected because it could embolden a U.S. president to foreign policy adventurism.[138] Such a proposition is folly as a policy guideline: it would leave U.S. society vulnerable to the attacks of imprudent, reckless opponents for the purpose of constraining U.S. presidents. This proposition goes beyond cynicism and should be recognized as such. It recommends the willful vulnerability of the American population for the leverage that vulnerability provides opponents over U.S. decision making and the associated constraints it places on U.S. foreign policy. This U.S. vulnerability to threats is the very condition that some contemporary opponents seek for the coercive leverage it would provide them. The conscious empowerment of opponents suggested by this proposition is a policy goal that no responsible U.S. Government could endorse. Nor is it necessary even on its own cynical terms: it should be recalled in this regard that the United States exhibited considerable prudence during the Cold War when *it had a nuclear monopoly and was itself essentially invulnerable to strategic attack*. As British Prime Minister Thatcher said in this regard: "No country ever used such great power more responsibly or with such restraint."[139]

In summary, in the twenty-first century the absence of significant U.S. damage-limitation goals and measures poses potentially severe risks and tradeoffs that were not part of the Cold War balance of terror narrative. The potential value of strategic damage limitation can no longer be dismissed peremptorily on the basis of the long-familiar balance of terror tenet that defensive measures are useless, unnecessary and "destabilizing." As a baseline generalization, it now is as likely to mislead as it is to enlighten and—if retained as policy guidance—will contribute to continued U.S. vulnerability and opponents' potential leverage over U.S. decision making.

2. Assurance

A political goal beyond deterrence that also should contribute to the measure of U.S. strategic force adequacy is the *assurance* of allies, particularly including the contribution of U.S. strategic forces to extended deterrence. In principle, this goal has a long history of contributing to the U.S. definition of strategic force adequacy. The 1974 "Schlesinger Doctrine," for example, included the standard of "essential equivalence" for U.S. strategic forces, in part to assure allies with regard to U.S. strategic guarantees. The notion was that allied perceptions of U.S. credibility would be strengthened if they viewed U.S. forces as being at least comparable to those of the Soviet Union.[140] As this standard of "essential equivalence" suggests, the adequacy of U.S. strategic forces *to assure allies* may have little or nothing to do with military or deterrence requirements. Assurance involves *allied perceptions* of U.S. commitment and strength, and the related questions of what and how U.S. strategic capabilities can achieve that *political/psychological effect* given allies' particular fears and circumstances. Famed British historian Sir Michael Howard identified this "positive" goal as "reassurance" in a famous 1982 article, and linked "reassurance" to Western publics' perceptions of U.S. power and commitment.[141]

Here again, useful insight regarding the type of U.S. strategic capabilities that might contribute best to (or do least damage to) the goal of assurance may be gained through an effort to understand the fears and perceptions of those key allies for whom the United States has made extended deterrence commitments. The step of asking allies how the United States might best provide the assurance necessary to help them remain secure and confident in their non-nuclear status is obvious but possibly extraordinary. When some Japanese officials were asked this question in 2004, their common response was: "No American has ever asked that question before."[142] If accurate, this should be considered a curious situation. If the United States cares to know the actual requirements for assurance, then asking the pertinent allies the question would seem a reasonable first step.

Some allies have offered more than a glimpse into their thinking on this matter. Sir Michael Howard suggested that early in the Cold War U.S. nuclear superiority may have been important to "reassurance," and that later Soviet achievement of strategic nuclear "parity" or better did cause allied concern in this regard.[143] More recently, allies have been explicit that the U.*S. extended nuclear deterrent* is a key to their assurance and that they link their own nuclear future to the assurance provided by U.S. nuclear weapons. Some Japanese officials reportedly have further elaborated publicly on the characteristics of U.S. nuclear capabilities they consider important for assurance.

A Japanese article on the subject, for example, quotes "a source close to Japan-U.S. diplomatic affairs" as observing that: "Intercontinental ballistic missiles are devastating but inaccurate, and they inflict too many civilian casualties. A nuclear-powered submarine can gradually approach the target, allowing time for diplomatic negotiations while applying military pressure. If the submarine is close enough, it could have the option to launch highly accurate nuclear-tipped cruise missiles."[144] That some allies believe that nuclear-tipped cruise missiles aboard submarines are their preferred means of assurance need not end the discussion, but does warrant consideration in the U.S. calculation of strategic force requirements.

There is an obvious risk in asking allies to weigh in on the question of what assures them; it brings their opinion directly into the definition of U.S. requirements. When this point was made during a 2007 university-sponsored seminar on the subject, a former senior Department of Defense official responded: "We could ask, but then we would have to listen." True. If we ask the question we must be prepared for an answer. Allies may identify forces or force characteristics as important for assurance that U.S. officials otherwise would prefer to avoid. Unfortunately, perhaps, that risk goes along with the long-standing goal of assuring allies. Nevertheless, because the goal is to help provide allies with confidence in U.S. security guarantees—in part to encourage them to remain non-nuclear—their views on the question of U.S. strategic force adequacy and the credibility of U.S. deterrence threats truly matter. The United States cannot reasonably posit this goal as important and then ignore or disdain allied views when their views are the ones that count. The contemporary challenge in this regard is obvious: as WMD spread to regional rogue powers, U.S. allies in rough neighborhoods correspondingly become increasingly concerned about the details of the U.S. extended deterrence commitment and the forces intended to make it credible. This process already is apparent in Asia and the Middle East.

3. Dissuasion

Another political goal beyond deterrence that should be included in the measure of U.S. strategic force adequacy is dissuasion. Dissuasion as a defense policy goal also is not new; it was articulated well by Secretary McNamara in 1965.[145] He identified dissuasion by name as a goal of the Johnson Administration's *Sentinel* BMD system. The notion was that U.S. deployment of BMD could help to *dissuade nuclear proliferation* by undermining the potential value of nuclear weapons; with the exception of the Soviet Union, countries would be *less eager* to acquire nuclear weapons if they could *not* employ them effectively via ballistic missiles. In 1968, Secretary McNamara also identified the possibility that the defense of U.S. ICBMs via limited BMD could "dissuade" the Soviet Union from investing in offensive counterforce strategic systems against U.S. ICBMs.[146]

Dissuasion is the "flip side" of the popular recommendation that U.S. strategic force choices be informed by the expectation that U.S. *restraint would inspire opponents' restraint*, *à la* the action-reaction model. In both cases, the expectation is that U.S. armament choices should be shaped by the goal of affecting opponents' acquisition policies. The difference here is that the more familiar approach is to recommend U.S. *restraint* as the route to securing opponents' restraint. With dissuasion, the contention is that in some cases active U.S. acquisition policies rather than inaction will *discourage* opponents from competition; they will be discouraged by the expectation that U.S. capabilities will prevent realization of their armament goals. The opponent's expected value from arms competition is undercut to such an extent that the opponent decides against competition. This goal of dissuasion again suggests the need to understand the opponent and context. In this case, that understanding is to permit some level of confidence that the opponent's acquisition decisions can be shaped in particular ways by U.S. behavior.

Dissuasion adds a unique temporal dimension to the measures of merit for U.S. strategic forces and the definition of adequacy. Unlike the other goals discussed, the seeds of dissuasion must be sown *in advance* of the manifest appearance of a threat. To discourage opponents from tak-ing the course of armaments competition, by definition, requires the dissuasive effect of U.S. strategic forces when opponents are making acquisition decisions, well before a particular threat appears. If dissuasion works, the feared competition never materializes. This temporal dimension suggests numerous potential problems for ascertaining whether dissua-sion is "working"—the same challenge of "proving a negative" also burdens discussions of deterrence.   But if dissuasion is to have an effect, the disincentives must align in time with opponents' decision making.

To place Secretary McNamara's Cold War dissuasion goal in a contemporary setting, if it is hoped that the U.S. deployment of BMD will contribute to the dissuasion of any particular country's investment in ballistic missiles or expansion of its arsenal, then the reality of the U.S. BMD program and its potential salience for that opponent must be made manifest well before the threat emerges or expands—in time for the opponent to decide not to proceed. BMD that appears after the strategic decision is made will then be in the harder game of "catch up" for dissuasion purposes—trying to reverse an opponent's decision after it has invested the political capital, time, and resources into reaching it. When the goal is damage limitation or deterrence, this early temporal dimension might not be critical; it *is* for dissuasion.

Because opponents' acquisition decisions are driven by many possible factors, the expectation that U.S. initiatives will lead an opponent *in a particular acquisition direction* is vulnerable to the fragility of such specific linkages and predictions. There are, nevertheless, some pertinent examples of dissuasion in operation. The history of U.S. strategic damage-limitation goals and measures, for example, illustrates how U.S. choices with regard to strategic defenses were shaped decisively by *U.S. expectations* that Soviet strategic offensive forces would preclude a U.S. defensive capability worth the cost. U.S. anticipation of Soviet strategic offensive force programs helped to move U.S. decision making away from a significant, direct, strategic damage-limitation goal *vis-à-vis* the Soviet Union. The same Johnson Administration that decided to *forego* a strategy of direct, significant strategic damage limitation against the Soviet Union decided, in contrast, *to pursue* just such a strategy against China *because in that case the goal was regarded as attainable.* This interaction underscores the apparent dissuasive effect that Soviet strategic offensive programs had on U.S. decision making.

Similarly, a previously-classified 1970 CIA study of the Soviet BMD program around Moscow concluded that the Soviet Union decided *not* to complete the full deployment of its BMD systems because of its expectation that U.S. offensive forces could overwhelm it.[147] If true, this interaction suggests that U.S. strategic offensive forces had a dissuasive effect on Soviet willingness to expand its deployment of BMD.

For the future, there are many possible goals for U.S. dissuasion, including discouragement of:

- Rogue states from investing in WMD and missiles;
- The Chinese leadership from pursuing a significant buildup of strategic nuclear weapons; and,
- The Russian leadership from reverting to the former Soviet goal of seeking significant measures of strategic nuclear superiority and counterforce capabilities against the United States.

Whether and how the character of U.S. strategic forces can contribute to such goals is *not* self-evident, and attempted linkages may not "work" predictably anymore than did Cold War efforts to induce Soviet inaction via U.S. inaction. Nevertheless, the potential for dissuasion linkages may yield to examination, and considering how to dissuade opponents and potential opponents via the size and character of U.S. strategic forces is at least as coherent a goal as attempting to induce an opponent's inaction via U.S. inaction—*a self-described element of U.S. strategic policy for decades.* These goals are different sides of the same coin; both seek to use U.S. acquisition decisions to move opponents' decisions in preferred directions. The hoped-for effect is not predictable with confidence in either case. But with due humility, if the pursuit of opponents' inaction via U.S. inaction is regarded as a reasonable metric for U.S. strategic forces, so too should be dissuasion.

Multiple Goals, Strategic Force Sizing, and Measures of Merit for U.S. Strategic Forces

As discussed at length in earlier chapters, the "stable" balance of terror framework facilitated a formula for calculating strategic force adequacy and led to the categorization of particular types of forces as "stabilizing" or "destabilizing." Those categories and measures of merit for judging the adequacy of U.S. strategic forces began and ended with the goals of preserving and exploiting mutual vulnerability for deterrence purposes, and allowed the relatively easy calculation of U.S. strategic force requirements based on offensive force lethality to the chosen targets.

As discussed in Chapter 6, the enduring power of this approach for defining U.S. strategic force requirements and their measures of merit can be seen today in the continuing frequent assertions that a specific number and type of U.S. strategic forces can be known with confidence to be adequate for deterrence, based on the "strategic arithmetic" of counting offensive forces and prospective targets. That Cold War formula for deterrence, however, cannot serve as the basis for determining the adequacy of U.S strategic forces when damage limitation, assurance, and dissuasion are included as priority goals. These goals become pertinent factors in the definition of strategic forces adequacy and can lead to diverse measures of merit for forces. A multiplicity of strategic goals suggests the same requirement for flexibility and a spectrum of strategic capabilities mandated by contemporary deterrence goals because the character of strategic forces suitable to one goal may not correspond with the forces suitable for another. As Michael Howard observed during the Cold War, the types of capabilities that provided "reassurance" to European allies had become decidedly different from the forces experts typically associated with nuclear deterrence or war.[148]

Now, strategic damage-limitation capabilities against a given threat may be the priority and establish requirements beyond the minimal force requirements considered important for deterrence. Similarly, the assurance of an ally in a plausible crisis may necessitate U.S. forces that are separate from deterrent requirements. The strategic force requirements for deterrence, however calculated, cannot define the adequacy of U.S. strategic forces because those forces may also be called on to support these other goals. Consequently, a variety of force measures and requirements may be in play simultaneously. In contrast to the balance of terror/assured destruction formula, in the contemporary environment the U.S. goals of deterrence, assurance, dissuasion and damage limitation lead to the need for a range of capabilities and flexibility to adjust to the variable requirements for deterrence and these other priority U.S. goals.

This answer to the question of strategic force requirements and standards of adequacy is the antithesis of the relatively fixed balance of terror formula. Yet, if strategic requirements can shift in the near term depending on the prioritization of U.S. goals and the character of opponent and context, no narrow set formula for deterrence can be adequate to inform strategic acquisition policy. Asking the traditional "how much is enough" question is akin to asking a carpenter in advance how many nails will be needed for a complex construction project and its many modifications when the building's function and form will have to shift to serve differing priorities in changing external conditions.

In such circumstances, an honest carpenter who lacks the advantage of omniscience will reply that the question itself reflects a misunderstanding of fundamental realities. The number of nails necessary is not so predictable under the circumstances; the immediate expectation may be for many or few nails, but the answer may change throughout construction and indeed throughout the life of the building as it is remodeled to meet changing needs in shifting conditions. What will be critical is the flexibility in skills, tools and resources necessary to adapt the requirements and design to shifting priorities and needs.

Picking some specific number of U.S. strategic weapons as *the* destination for acquisition and arms reduction—and dubbing some types of forces as "stabilizing" or "destabilizing" based on old metrics—remains the popular sport in U.S. strategic force debates. The convenience of doing so—and believing that the answers reached actually have meaning for U.S. strategic requirements—is the primary advantage of the balance of terror tenets. Given contemporary conditions, however, that familiar, convenient sport must now come with the caveat that it can illuminate U.S. deterrence requirements only by happenstance, and excludes any consideration of other priority strategic goals. That admission appears virtually impossible for a strategic community whose thinking about deterrence and strategic forces remains wedded to the continuities, certainties and conveniences of the Cold War's "strategic arithmetic."

Colin Gray makes the extremely insightful point in this regard that the U.S. political process disdains answers to questions regarding defense planning and spending which betray uncertainty and speculation about requirements (and thus the need for considerable flexibility), particularly with regard to the acquisition of strategic forces.[149] Concluding that flexibility is the priority measure of merit because threat conditions are dynamic and uncertain goes against the grain of a rigidly-set acquisition process that demands numeric precision and promises years in advance. It also casts doubt on the wisdom of comforting old expectations of a predictable opponent, and on the value of "locking in" a particular force number as the target for nuclear reductions. This is sure to alienate established participants and institutions involved in the traditional processes of strategic force acquisition, arms control, and the usual calculation of deterrence requirements.

Gray further observes that individuals with governmental responsibilities typically must "pretend" that there is little or no uncertainty in their planning parameters, and proceed as if the future is foreseeable:

> Defence officials and responsible politicians are supposed to know what they are doing. When a Minister talks to the House of Commons, or a senior Pentagon official testifies before a Congressional committee, he or she cannot tell the real story. The truth is that defence planning is guesswork. Instead of saying that, one has to pretend that every dollar, pound, or euro, has been correctly assigned....When you propose to spend this much money, you need to pretend, or perhaps just persuade yourself, that you know what you are doing....*But how can you know*?...Unfortunately for the defence planner, history is resolutely non-linear. It has an uncooperative tendency to produce major and minor irregularities in course.[150]

The problem, of course, is that no one can predict with any confidence the details of future strategic force requirements in a dynamic environment. When precision and promises regarding force requirements are demanded by the political system, so is the pretense to which Gray refers. The beauty of a "stable" balance of terror was that it was believed to make possible an enduring formula for reliable deterrence and force requirements, guaranteed by the objective truths of "strategic arithmetic" and "human nature." No need for pretense. Those who remain wedded to this formula unsurprisingly find fault with the contention that deterrence is uncertain and that the goals of assurance, dissuasion, and damage limitation should be included in the measure of U.S. strategic force adequacy. They insist, for example, that the old formula still works and that the measure of U.S. nuclear weapons "should be limited to deterring other states from using them."[151] The goal should be narrow in scope and singular in purpose. A broader agenda for deterrence and the addition of goals to be supported by U.S. strategic forces is described as "misguided and dangerous," and "dangerous and counterproductive."[152]

Why "dangerous," "misguided," and "counterproductive"? *Opposition* to a broader definition of deterrence and inclusion of additional goals in the measure of strategic forces likely follows from the natural staying power of a well-established formula, and from concern that such changes bring into question the minimal requirements traditionally associated with that formula. The balance of terror/assured destruction formula provided a convenient, if largely incoherent, narrative for opposing *most* U.S. strategic forces, particularly including "counterforce" nuclear weapons and defensive capabilities. Questioning that formula and including diverse goals in the calculation of U.S. strategic force adequacy challenges that minimal agenda.

As if the 1960s never departed, commentators continue to campaign against U.S. damage-limitation capabilities and in favor of restricted definitions of U.S. strategic force requirements on the basis of the familiar balance of terror tenets that deterrent effect is predictable and easily orchestrated because all rational opponents will be cautious, prudent, and thus, reliably deterred. The drive is strong to keep the scope for defining the value of strategic forces narrow and to protect the old requirements formula and terms of art because—in the absence of that narrow scope, formula and nomenclature—the old, easy definitions of adequacy collapse. The problem with those definitions, however, is their basic incompatibility with contemporary realities:

- The measures of merit for strategic forces should include the goals of deterrence, assurance, damage limitation and dissuasion because each, at least on occasion, will be a priority. In many plausible cases wherein deterrence is particularly uncertain and defensive measures are feasible, *damage limitation may be the highest U.S. priority, measurably useful, and even stabilizing.* The labels for these functions may change, and their respective priorities shift, but they will be U.S. goals. How could they *not* be included in considerations of the adequacy of U.S. strategic forces?

- A spectrum of U.S. strategic capabilities and the flexibility to adapt is critical because the threat environment is shifting and opaque, and different U.S. goals suggest different requirements for U.S. strategic forces.
- The measures of merit for nuclear weapons must transcend the narrow goal of deterring nuclear attack because they are pertinent to additional goals—in particular, they may be important for deterring BW threats. Further, some key allies have become increasingly unambiguous about the value they attach to U.S. nuclear capabilities for their assurance and related willingness to remain non-nuclear.

The U.S. agenda with regard to deterrence strategy and strategic forces should not be to protect old verities and adages, especially when contemporary conditions are so far removed from the Cold War environment which spawned them. The strategic conditions of the twenty-first century call for: humility in predicting how opponents will behave, especially with regard to their "deterrability"; defensive hedges against the possibility of surprising behavior and deterrence failure; strategies, acquisition policies, and arms control processes that can adapt flexibly to shifting U.S. strategic priorities and related force requirements; and, dedicated efforts to understand opponents to the extent possible in order to tailor U.S. strategies accordingly, set priorities, and limit the prospects for surprise. The old balance of terror/assured destruction formula, metrics and terms of art work against each of the above.

The following, final chapter further examines the goals of deterrence and assurance with an emphasis on the contemporary debate about U.S. nuclear weapons and U.S. strategic policy development.

Endnotes

1. Quoted in, U.S. Arms Control and Disarmament Agency, *The Soviet Propaganda Campaign Against the US Strategic Defense Initiative* (Washington, D.C.: Arms Control and Disarmament Agency, 1986), p. 8.

2. Draft Memorandum for the President, Secretary of Defense [Robert S. McNamara] to the President [Lyndon B. Johnson], Subj: Recommended FY 1967 - FY 1971 Strategic Offensive and Defensive Forces, November 1, 1965, p. 25 (Originally classified; sanitized and declassified on January 5, 1983); cited hereafter as 1965 DPM. This and other Draft Presidential Memoranda can be found online at the Master OFOI Reading Room, Department of Defense, http://www.dod.mil/pubs/foi/master_reading_list01.html.

3. International Institute for Strategic Studies, *The Military Balance 1967-1968* (London: Institute for Strategic Studies, 1967), pp. 27, 47.

4. See David Rees, *Peaceful Coexistence: A Study in Soviet Doctrine* (Washington, D.C.: International Security Council, 1989), pp. 37-38.

5. Robert Jervis, *The Illogic of American Nuclear Strategy* (Ithaca, NY: Cornell University Press, 1984), p. 12.

6. Robert Jervis, "The Political Effect of Nuclear Weapons: A Comment," *International Security*, Vol. 13, No. 2 (Fall 1988), p. 81.

7. Thucydides, *The Peloponnesian War* (New York: Random House, 1951), pp. 330-337.

8. See, for example, the discussion in, Sheila Miyoshi Jager, *The Politics of Identity: History, Nationalism, and the Prospect for Peace in Post-Cold War East Asia* (Carlisle, PA: U.S. Army War College, Strategic Studies Institute, April 2007), pp. 21-26.

9. See, for example, Danny Gittings, "General Zhu Goes Ballistic," *The Wall Street Journal*, July 18, 2005, p. A13; Joseph Kahn, "Chinese General Threatens Use of A-Bomb If U.S. Intrudes," *The New York Times*, July 15, 2005, p. A8; and, excerpts from "United States Will Suffer Severe Attack," *Chinese Weekly of Extensive Military Knowledge*, quoted in, "Chinese Military Threatens Nuclear War Against the United States Over Taiwan," Association for Asian Research, September 20, 2005, available at, http://asianresearch.org/articles/2718.html.

10. See the detailed discussion in, Mark Schneider, *The Nuclear Doctrine and Forces of the People's Republic of China*, Nuclear Strategy Forum Publication No. 007 (Fairfax, VA: National Institute Press, November 2007).

11. National Intelligence Council, "China's Military Modernization," *Briefing for the Secretary of State's International Security Advisory Board*, January 29, 2008, U.S. Department of State, Washington, D.C., p. 6.

12. The most explicit Chinese statement to this effect remains the 1995 claim by then Deputy Chief of Staff, Lt. General Xiong Guankai that, "…you are not going to threaten us again because, in the end, you care a lot more about Los Angeles than Taipei." Quoted in, Barton Gellman, "U.S. and China Nearly Came to Blows in 1996," *The Washington Post*, June 21, 1996, pp. A1, A20.

13. Joseph Dondelinger, *From the Balkans to Bin Laden, Baghdad and Beyond: Racial, Ethnic, Nationalist, Religious and Cultural Identity Conflict in the 21st Century*, Program 319 (Charlottesville, VA: The Federal Executive Institute, May 2006), p. 123.

14. Mehdi Khalaji, "Apocalyptic Politics: On the Rationality of Iranian Policy," *Policy Focus*, No. 79 (Washington, D.C.: The Washington Institute for Near East Policy,

2008), p. 32.

15. President Mahmoud Ahmadinejad frequently refers to the destruction of Israel as a righteous goal: "Our dear Imam said that the occupying regime [Israel] must be wiped off the map and this was a very wise statement." Quoted in, "Text of Mahmoud Ahmadinejad's Speech," *The New York Times* (nytimes.com), October 30, 2005.

16. Jerrold Post, "Collective Identity: Hatred Bred in the Bone," *Foreign Policy Agenda*, Vol. 12, No. 5 (May 2007), p. 13.

17. Quoted in, Christopher Harmon, *Terrorism Today* (London: Routledge, 2007), p. 2; see also, Jed Babbin, *In the Words of Our Enemies* (Washington, D.C.: Regnery, 2007), pp. 13-15.

18. *In the Shadow of the Lances*, translated in, Middle East Media Research Institute, *Special Dispatch*, No. 388, June 12, 2002, available at, http://memri.org/bin/articles.c gi?Page=archives&Area=sd&ID=SP28802.

19. Anat Berko, *The Path to Paradise: The Inner World of Suicide Bombers and Their Dispatchers* (London: Praeger Security International, 2007), p. 174.

20. See the interview of a terrorist bomber in training in, Aaron Klein, "'Hi, My Name Is Ahmed and I Want to Be a Suicide Bomber,'" *Whistleblower*, Vol. 17, No. 3 (March 2008), pp. 14-16.

21. See Christian Enemark, "Biological Attacks and the Non-State Actor: A Threat Assessment," *Intelligence and National Security*, Vol. 21, No. 6 (December 2006), p. 922.

22. See Kevin Woods et al., *Iraqi Perspectives Project: A View of Iraqi Freedom From Saddam's Senior Leadership* (Norfolk, VA: U.S. Joint Forces Command, 2006), p. 91; and Ronald Kessler, *Terrorist Watch: Inside the Desperate Race to Stop the Next Attack* (New York: Random House, 2007), pp. 144-159.

23. See the discussion in, Kent Hill, *Turbulent Times for the Soviet Church* (Portland, OR: Multnomah Press, 1991), pp. 31-55.

24. Fred Kaplan, *The Wizards of Armageddon* (Stanford, CA: Stanford University Press, 1983), p. 317.

25. See, for example, Elbridge Colby, "Restoring Deterrence," *Orbis*, Vol. 51, No. 3 (Summer 2007), p. 418.

26. Quoted in, Michael Walsh, "Former CIA Director: U.S. Vulnerable to Anthrax Attack," *Arizona Republic*, Nov. 24, 2007, p. A10.

27. Ibid.

28. Khalaji, op. cit., pp. vii, 30-32.

29. See Robert Jay Lifton, *Destroying the World to Save It* (New York: Metropolitan Books, 1999), pp. 65-66; and, Dawn Perlmutter, "Skandalon 2001: The Religious Practices of Modern Satanists and Terrorists," *Anthropoetics*, Vol. 7, No. 2 (Fall 2001/Winter 2002), pp. 12-14.

30. See the discussion in, Keith B. Payne, *The Fallacies of Cold War Deterrence and a New Direction* (Lexington, KY: University Press of Kentucky, 2001), p. 44.

31. Quoted in, "Iran's Ahmadinejad Has 'Proof' US Won't Attack," *Breitbart.com*, September 3, 2007, available at, http://www.brietbart.com/print.php?id.

32. Kenneth N. Waltz, "More May Be Better," in, Scott D. Sagan and Kenneth N. Waltz, *The Spread of Nuclear Weapons* (New York: W.W. Norton & Company, 2000), p. 14.

33. B.R. Myers, "Stranger Than Fiction," *The New York Times*, January 13, 2005, p. 15.

34. Douglas Macdonald, *The New Totalitarians: Social Identities and Radical Islamist*

Political Grand Strategy (Carlisle, PA: Strategic Studies Institute, U.S. Army War College, 2007), p. vii.

35. See the discussion in, Payne, op. cit., pp. 5-6, 13.

36. Sean McCormack, Department of State, daily press briefing, Washington, D.C., January 22, 2007, available at, http://www.state.gov/r/pa/prs/dpb/2007/79119.htm.

37. Quoted in, Marvin Olasky, "The Great Respecting," *World*, Vol. 22, No. 2 (January 20, 2007), p. 48.

38. See, for example, Lucy Baldwin Smith, *Fools, Martyrs, Traitors: The Story of Martyrdom in the Western World* (New York: Alfred A. Knopf, 1997), pp. 117-262.

39. Bernard Lewis, "August 22," *The Wall Street Journal*, August 8, 2006, p. 10.

40. "Rafsanjani's Qods Day Speech (Jerusalem Day)," *Voice of the Islamic Republic of Iran*, Tehran, in Persian, translated by *BBC Worldwide Monitoring*, original broadcast, December 14, 2001.

41. Quoted in, Dan Senor, "The Long Arm of Iran," *The Wall Street Journal*, September 29, 2007, p. 8.

42. See the statement by Gen. John Abizaid in, Ann Scott Tyson, "Security Took 'Turn for the Worse' in Southern Iran," *The Washington Post*, September 18, 2007, p. A14.

43. Quoted in, Thomas Grose, "Science & Society, Missile Defense," *U.S. News & World Report*, Vol. 136, No. 15 (May 3, 2004), pp. 69-70.

44. Quoted in, Clifford May, "Shrinking Superpower?" *The Washington Times*, January 2, 2005, p. B1.

45. Quoted in, Macdonald, op. cit., p. 39.

46. Donald Kagan, *On the Origins of War* (New York: Doubleday, 1995), pp. 8, 569; and, Donald Kagan, "Honor, Interest, and the National State," in, *Honor Among Nations*, Elliot Abrams, ed. (Washington, D.C.: Ethics and Public Policy Center, 1996), pp. 8-9.

47. Quoted in, Edward Cody, "China Easing Its Stance on Taiwan; Tolerance Grows for Status Quo," *The Washington Post*, June 15, 2006, p. 14.

48. As relayed by Saddam Hussein to U.S. interrogator George Piro. See, "Interrogator Shares Saddam's Confessions: Tells 60 Minutes Former Iraqi Dictator Didn't Expect U.S. Invasion," *CBS News*, January 27, 2008, available at, http://www.cbsnews.com/stories/2008/01/24/60minutes/main37494.shtml.

49. As is claimed in, James Lebovic, *Deterring International Terrorism and Rogue States* (New York: Routledge, 2007), pp. 28-29.

50. See, Elizabeth Hurd, *The Politics of Secularism in International Relations* (Princeton, NJ: Princeton University Press, 2008), p. 1.

51. Admiral Hank Chiles, Statement in U.S. Senate, Committee on Armed Services, *Nominations Before the Armed Services Committee*, Hearings, 103rd Congress, 2nd Session (Washington, D.C.: USGPO, 1994), p. 227.

52. *The 9/11 Commission Report: Final Report of the National Commission on Terrorist Attacks Upon the United States* (New York: W.W. Norton & Company, 2004), p. 17.

53. See the statements by Richard Ben-Veniste and Major General Craig McKinley, in National Commission on Terrorist Attacks Upon the United States, public hearing, May 23, 2003, available at, http://www.9-11commission.gov/archive/hearing2/9-11commission_hearing_2003-05-23.htm.

54. *The 9/11 Commission Report: Final Report of the National Commission on Terrorist Attacks Upon the United States*, loc. cit.

55. See John Kelsay, *Arguing the Just War in Islam* (Cambridge, MA: Harvard

University Press, 2007), pp. 134-145.

56. National Intelligence Council, National Intelligence Estimate, *The Terrorist Threat to the US Homeland*, (July 2007), quoted from the "Key Judgments" section, p. 5.

57. See, Statement by John C. Rood, Assistant Secretary of State for International Security and Nonproliferation, House Foreign Affairs Subcommittee on Europe, May 3, 2007, available at, http://foreignaffairs.house.gov/110/roo050307.htm.

58. As relayed by Saddam Hussein to U.S. interrogator George Piro. See, "Interrogator Shares Saddam's Confessions: Tells 60 Minutes Former Iraqi Dictator Didn't Expect U.S. Invasion," op. cit.

59. Theodore Kattouf (former U.S. Ambassador to Syria, 2001-2003), in House International Relations Committee, *Syria Accountability and Lebanese Sovereignty Restoration Act Two Years Later: Next Steps for U.S. Policy*, Hearings, 109th Congress, 2nd Session (Washington, D.C.: USGPO, 2006), p. 28.

60. David Schenker (Syria, Lebanon, Jordan, and Palestinian Affairs Advisor in the Office of the Secretary of Defense, 2002-2006), in House International Relations Committee, *Syria Accountability and Lebanese Sovereignty Restoration Act Two Years Later: Next Steps for U.S. Policy*, op. cit., p. 30.

61. Secretary of State Condoleezza Rice, interview with the CBS News Editorial Board, September 12, 2005, transcript, available at, http://usinfo.state.gov.

62. See Richard Lardner, "U.S. Dissatisfied With Intelligence on Terror Groups," *The Washington Times*, January 23, 2008, p. A13.

63. Jay C. Davis, "The Attribution of WMD Events," *Journal of Homeland Security*, April 2003, available at, http://www.homelandsecurity.org/journal/Articles/Davis. html. See also, Matthew Phillips, "Uncertain Justice for Nuclear Terror: Deterrence of Anonymous Attacks Through Attribution," *Orbis*, Vol. 51, No. 3 (Summer 2007), pp. 429-446.

64. W. Seth Carus, *Bioterrorism and Biocrimes: The Illicit Use of Biological Agents Since 1900* (Washington, D.C.: National Defense University, February 2001), p. 18.

65. See Kathleen C. Bailey, *Doomsday Weapons in the Hands of Many* (Chicago: University of Illinois Press, 1991), pp. 82-87.

66. Dr. Gordon Oehler, Director, Nonproliferation Center, "Continuing Threat From Weapons of Mass Destruction," statement for the record to the Senate Armed Services Committee, March 27, 1996, Appendix C: Biological Agents, available at, https://www.cia.gov/news-information/speeches-testimony/1996/go_appendixc_032796.html.

67. Carus, op. cit., p. 20.

68. Sharon A Squassoni, *Nuclear, Biological, and Chemical Weapons and Missiles: Status and Trends*, CRS Report RL30699 (Washington, D.C.: Congressional Research Service, Library of Congress, January 14, 2005), pp. 5, 12.

69. This same point is made with regard to the possibility of nuclear terrorist attacks in, Ashton Carter, Michael May, and William Perry, "The Day After: Action Following a Nuclear Blast in a U.S. City," *The Washington Quarterly*, Vol. 30, No. 4 (Autumn 2007), p. 29.

70. R. James Woolsey, *Statement Before the Senate Select Committee on Intelligence*, February 2, 1993 (Mimeographed prepared statement), p. 2.

71. For a brief summary of three cases in which non-state actors employed biological weapons see, Enemark, op. cit., pp. 911-930. See also, David Ignatius, "Portents of a Nuclear Al-Qaeda," *The Washington Post*, October 18, 2007, p. 25.

72. Martin Shubik, "Terrorism, Technology, and the Socioeconomic of Death,"

Comparative Strategy, Vol. 16, No. 4 (October-December 1999), pp. 399-414; and Carus, op. cit., pp. 3-17.

73. Brian Jenkins, "Nuclear Terror: How Real?" *The Washington Times*, May 13, 2007, p. B3.

74. Quoted in, Carus, op. cit., p. 33.

75. Quoted in, Jerry Seper, "FBI Director Predicts Terrorists Will Acquire Nukes," *The Washington Times*, June 12, 2007, p. A6.

76. Quoted in, Ignatius, loc. cit.

77. George Tenet (with Bill Harlow), *At the Center of the Storm: My Years at the CIA* (New York: Harper Collins, 2007), p. 279.

78. Lawrence Freedman, *Deterrence* (Malden, MA: Polity Press, 2004), p. 117.

79. See his testimony in, U.S. Senate, Committee on Foreign Relations, *A Report on the Latest Round of Six-Way Talks Regarding Nuclear Weapons in North Korea*, Hearing, 108th Congress, 2nd Session (Washington, D.C.: USGPO, 2004), p. 9. (Emphasis added).

80. The White House, Office of the Press Secretary, *President Bush's Statement on North Korean Nuclear Test*, October 9, 2006, available at, http://www.whitehouse.gov/news/releases/2006/10/20061009.html.

81. Ryan Henry, "Deterrence and Dissuasion in the 21st Century," in, *Implementing the New Triad*, Final Report From a Conference Organized by the Institute for Foreign Policy Analysis and the Fletcher School, Tufts University (Cambridge, MA: Institute for Foreign Policy Analysis, 2006), p. 4.

82. Ibid., p. 3.

83. Anne Sternerson, "Chem-bio Cyber-Class," *Jane's Intelligence Review*, Vol. 19, No. 9 (September 2007), p. 12.

84. "Daily Diary of al-Qaeda Sector Leader Called Abu-Tariq," *WTOP News*, February 14, 2008, available at, http://www.wtopnews.com/docs/abu_tariq_translation.pdf.

85. Ibid. See also, Michael Jacobson, "They Trained. They Plotted. Then They Bailed," *The Washington Post*, March 23, 2008, p. B3.

86. This form of denial deterrence is a U.S. goal. See the discussion in, Steven Aoki, *Statement of Dr. Steven Aoki, Deputy Undersecretary of Energy for Counterterrorism*, before the House Committee on Homeland Security, Subcommittee on Emerging Threats, Cybersecurity, and Science and Technology, October 10, 2007 (Prepared statement provided at the hearing), p. 2.

87. A special issue of *Comparative Strategy* is devoted to case studies involving the deterrence or coercion of NSAs. See, "Special Issue: Deterring Terrorism," *Comparative Strategy*, Vol. 26, No. 5 (October-December 2007), pp. 371-492.

88. Gary Geipel, *Urban Terrorists in Continental Europe After 1970: Implications for Deterrence and Defeat of Violent Non-State Actors* (Fairfax, VA: National Institute for Public Policy, 2007), pp. 52-53.

89. Quoted in, Hanan Greenberg, "IDF Strike Against Qassem Cell Caught on Tape," November 20, 2007, available at, ynetnews.com.

90. Stephen T. Hosmer, *The Conflict Over Kosovo: Why Milosevic Decided to Settle When He Did*, MR-1351-AF (Santa Monica, CA: RAND Corp., 2001), p. 75.

91. See Kurt Guthe, "Plausible Approaches to Deterring Terrorist Use of Biological Weapons: Refining the Discussion," in, Keith B. Payne et al., *Bioterrorism and a Strategy of Concomitant Deterrence* (Fairfax, VA: National Institute for Public Policy, September 2007), p. 66. See also, House of Representatives, House Financial Services Committee, *Weapons of Mass Destruction: Stopping the Funding—The*

OFAC Role, Hearings, 109th Congress, 2nd Session (Washington, D.C.: USGPO, 2006).

92. Doran Almog, "Cumulative Deterrence and the War on Terrorism," *Parameters*, Vol. 34, No. 4 (Winter 2004-2005), p. 4.

93. Willis Stanley, *Colombia and the United States vs. Pablo Escobar, 1989-1993* (Fairfax, VA: National Institute for Public Policy, 2007).

94. See the discussions of nuclear accountability in, Carter, May, and Perry, op. cit., pp. 29-30; and, Phillips, op. cit., pp. 429-434.

95. See the discussion in, U.S. Department of State, International Security Advisory Board, *Report on Discouraging a Cascade of Nuclear Weapons States* (Washington, D.C.: Department of State, October 19, 2007), pp. 22-23.

96. National Intelligence Estimate, Number 4-70, *The Clandestine Introduction of Nuclear Weapons Into the US*, Submitted by the Director of Central Intelligence and Concurred in by the United States Intelligence Board, July 7, 1970, p. 2. (Originally Top Secret; declassified, January 31, 1994), available at, http://www.foia.cia.gov. (Emphasis added).

97. Ibid., pp. 3-4.

98. Graham Allison, "Deterring Kim Jong Il," *The Washington Post*, October 27, 2006, p. A23.

99. See, Lawrence Freedman and Efraim Karsh, *The Gulf Conflict, 1990-1991: Diplomacy and War in the New World Order* (Princeton, NJ: Princeton University Press, 1993), Chapter 2.

100. See the comprehensive discussion of this case in, Richard Mobley, "Revisiting the Korean Tree-Trimming Incident," *Joint Forces Quarterly*, No. 35 (October 2004), pp. 108-115.

101. See the discussion of the extreme fluidity of contemporary developments in, National Intelligence Council, *Mapping the Global Future: Report of the National Intelligence Council's 2020 Project* (Undated, unclassified briefing), pp. 4, 18-19. See also the discussion of past rapid changes in threat conditions in, William Odom et al., *The Emerging Ballistic Missile Threat to the United States*, Report of the Proliferation Study Team (Fairfax, VA: National Institute for Public Policy, February 1993), pp. 19-21.

102. See, for example, the discussion in, U.S. Department of State, International Security Advisory Board, *Report on Discouraging a Cascade of Nuclear Weapons States*, op. cit.; Kathleen McInnis, "Extended Deterrence: The U.S. Credibility Gap in the Middle East," *The Washington Quarterly*, Vol. 28, No. 3 (Summer 2005), pp. 169-186; and, Nicholas Kralev, "'Hegemonistic' Iran Worries Arab States," *The Washington Times*, September 27, 2007, p. A16.

103. Quoted in, William Broad and David Sanger, "Restraints Fray and Risks Grow as Nuclear Club Gains Members," *The New York Times*, October 15, 2006, available at, http://www.nytimes.com/2006/10/15/world/asia/15nuke.html.

104. See, Colin S. Gray, "U.S. Strategic Requirements: What Role for Nuclear Weapons?" in, Keith B. Payne et al., *Rationale and Requirements for U.S. Nuclear Forces and Arms Control*, Volume II (Fairfax, VA: National Institute for Public Policy, January 2001), p. 57.

105. Henry Rowen, "Formulating Strategic Doctrine," in, Commission on the Organization of the Government for the Conduct of Foreign Policy, Vol. 4, Appendix K, *Adequacy of Current Organization: Defense and Arms Control* (Washington, D.C.: USGPO, June 1975), p. 227.

106. Draft Memorandum for the President, Secretary of Defense [Robert S. McNamara] to the President [Lyndon B. Johnson], Subj: Recommended FY 1966-FY 1970 Programs for Strategic Offensive Forces, Continental Air and Missile Defense Forces, and Civil Defense, December 3, 1964, p. 24. (Originally classified; sanitized and declassified on January 5, 1983).

107. Senator Joseph Lieberman, Chairman, Homeland Security and Governmental Affairs Committee, *Opening Statement for Chairman Lieberman*, United States Senate Hearing for the Committee on Homeland Security and Governmental Affairs, titled, "Nuclear Terrorism: Confronting the Challenges of the Day After," April 15, 2008, Washington, D.C., pp. 2-3 (Prepared text).

108. Dr. Cham Dallas, *Impact of Small Nuclear Weapons on Washington, DC: Outcomes and Emergency Response Recommendations*, Written Statement to Accompany Testimony at the United States Senate Hearing for the Committee on Homeland Security and Governmental Affairs, titled, "Nuclear Terrorism: Confronting the Challenges of the Day After," ibid., p. 6.

109. Dr. Cham Dallas, quoted in, "Study Finds U.S. Not Ready for Nuke Hit," *The Washington Times*, March 21, 2007, p. A3. The study referred to is presented in, William C. Bell and Cham Dallas, "Vulnerability of Populations and the Urban Health Care Systems to Nuclear Weapon Attack—Examples From Four American Cities," *International Journal of Health Geographics*, Vol. 6, No. 5 (February 28, 2007), available at, http://www.ij-healthgeographics.com/contents/6/1/5.

110. Dallas, *Impact of Small Nuclear Weapons on Washington, DC: Outcomes and Emergency Response Recommendations*, op. cit., pp. 6-11.

111. Recently, for example, the National Highway Traffic Safety Administration has issued new standards for automobile side-impact protection that will add approximately $33.00 to the cost of an average vehicle, and will prevent an estimated 672 casualties per year. See Cheryl Jensen, "Better Side-Impact Protection Regulations Are in the Works," *The Washington Times*, May 2, 2008, p. G4.

112. Interview with author, Washington, D.C., February 5, 2008.

113. See the discussion in, Robin Ranger, *Timely Defence Against Missiles: Lessons From British Experiences With Air and Missile Defences*, Bailrigg Memorandum, No. 7 (Lancaster, UK: The Centre for Defence and International Security Studies, Lancaster University, 1994), p. 12.

114. Ibid., pp. 10-12.

115. Basil Collier, *The Defence of the United Kingdom* (London: Her Majesty's Stationery Office, 1957), p. 434.

116. See, for example, Moshe Arens, *Broken Covenant* (New York: Simon and Schuster, 1995), p. 212.

117. 1965 DPM, op. cit., p. 22.

118. In 1994, North Korean diplomat Park Young Su threatened South Korea with the phrase: "Seoul is not very far from here. Seoul will turn into a sea of fire." Quoted in R. Jeffrey Smith and Ann Devroy, "U.S. Backs Maneuvers in North Korea," *The Washington Post*, March 20, 1994, p. A1.

119. Kim Myong Chol, "Kim Jong Il's Military Strategy for Reunification," *Comparative Strategy*, Vol. 20, No. 4 (2001), p. 319.

120. Mark Schneider, *Kim Jong Il and Nuclear Deterrence,* Discussion Paper (Fairfax, VA: National Institute for Public Policy, 2005), pp. 2-3.

121. 1965 DPM, op. cit., p. 5.

122. Herman Kahn, *On Escalation: Metaphors and Scenarios* (New York: Frederick

A. Praeger Press, 1965), p. 10.

123. See Rowan Scarborough, "U.S. Puts Faith in Missile Defense," *The Washington Times*, June 24, 2006, p. 1.

124. Union of Concerned Scientists, "Countermeasures," April 11, 2000, available at, http://www.ucsusa.org/publications/report.cfm?publicationID=131.

125. Quoted in Kim Min-seok and Jung Ha-won, "North Nukes on Attack Radar," Seoul JoongAng 1160 (Internet version), March 28, 2008. Transcribed by Open Source Center, Doc ID KPP2008032971089.

126. *Presentation by Michael Rühle, Head of Policy Planning and Speech Writing Section, NATO*, NATO Parliamentary Assembly, 53rd Annual Session, Reykjavik, Iceland, Laugardalshöllin Exhibition Centre, October 6, 2007 (Prepared text), p. 6.

127. As noted in Donald H. Rumsfeld et al., *Report of the Commission to Assess the Ballistic Missile Threat to the United States*, Executive Summary, Pursuant to Public Law 201, 104th Congress (Washington, D.C.: USGPO, July 15, 1998), pp. 20-21.

128. Remarks by Secretary of Defense William Perry at the Regional Commerce and Growth Association of St. Louis, Missouri, September 28, 1995, Federal News Service, pp. 11-12.

129. *Remarks Prepared for Delivery by William J. Perry*, Secretary of Defense, George Washington University, April 25, 1996, News Release No. 241-96, Office of the Assistant Secretary of Defense (Public Affairs), April 26, 1996, p. 4.

130. The Arms Control Association, Background Paper, *New Star Wars Plan: Unnecessary Destruction of the ABM Treaty*, February 1991, p. 1.

131. Lt. Gen. Trey Obering, "Missile Defense Hits Mark," *Defense News*, July 23, 2007, p. 21.

132. Draft Memorandum for the President, Secretary of Defense [Robert S. McNamara] to the President [Lyndon B. Johnson], Subj: Recommended FY 1965-FY 1969 Strategic Retaliatory Forces, December 6, 1963, p. I-21-I-22. (Originally classified; sanitized and declassified on January 5, 1983).

133. Draft Memorandum for the President, Secretary of Defense [Robert S. McNamara] to the President [Lyndon B. Johnson], Subj: Strategic Offensive and Defensive Forces, January 15, 1968, p. 19. (Originally classified; sanitized and declassified on January 5, 1983); cited hereafter as 1968 DPM.

134. Carter, May, and Perry, op. cit., pp. 23-27; and, Payne et al., *Bioterrorism and a Strategy of Concomitant Deterrence*, op. cit., pp. 78-88.

135. Richard Betts, "The New Threat of Mass Destruction," *Foreign Affairs*, Vol. 77, No. 1 (January-February 1998), p. 27.

136. Carter, May and Perry, op. cit., p. 25.

137. Jin Dae-Woon, "Military Works on Nuclear Defense Plans," *The Korea Herald* (internet version), October 27, 2006, from Open Source Center, "ROK Daily: ROK Military Works on Nuclear Defense Plans," KPP20061027971111.

138. See, for example, Herbert York, *Race to Oblivion: A Participant's View of the Arms Race* (New York: Simon and Schuster, 1970), p. 218; and, George Lewis, Lisbeth Gronlund, and David Wright, "National Missile Defense: An Indefensible System," *Foreign Policy*, No. 117 (Winter 1999-2000), p. 30.

139. Margaret Thatcher, *Speech to Congress*, February 20, 1985, Capitol Hill, Washington D.C., available at, http://www.margaretthatcher.org/speeches/displaydocument.asp?docid=105968.

140. See a review of the officially-expressed reasons for essential equivalence in, Keith B. Payne, "The Schlesinger Shift: Return to Rationality," in, Keith B. Payne,

C. Johnston Conover, and Bruce Bennett, *Nuclear Strategy: Flexibility and Stability* (Santa Monica, CA: California Seminar on Arms Control and Foreign Policy, March 1979), pp. 1-48.

141. Michael Howard, "Reassurance and Deterrence," *Foreign Affairs*, Vol. 61, No. 2 (Winter 1982/1983), pp. 309-324.

142. Personal communication with the author.

143. Howard, op. cit., pp. 312-317.

144. Quoted in, "North Korea's Nuclear Threat/Reinforcing Alliance With U.S. Helps Bolster Nuclear Deterrence," *The Daily Yomiuri* (Internet version), March 23, 2007, in, Open Source Center, "Yomiuri: North Korea's Nuclear Threat/Reinforcing Alliance With U.S. Helps Bolster Nuclear Deterrence," JPP20070323969090.

145. 1965 DPM, op. cit., pp. 5, 22.

146. 1968 DPM, op. cit., p. 13.

147. See the discussion of this report in, Robert Burns, "CIA: Russia Tried Own Missile Shield," *Chicago Tribune*, March 10, 2001, available at, file://C:WINDOWS\ Desktop\earlybird\e20010312\e20010312cia.htm.

148. Howard, op. cit., pp. 318-322.

149. Colin S. Gray, "Coping With Uncertainty: Dilemmas of Defence Planning," *The British Army Review*, No. 143 (Autumn 2007), pp. 36-40.

150. Ibid., pp. 36-37.

151. Daryl Kimball, "Of Madmen and Nukes," *Arms Control Today*, Vol. 35, No. 9 (November 2005), p. 3.

152. Wolfgang Panofsky, "Nuclear Insecurity: Correcting Washington's Dangerous Posture," *Foreign Affairs*, Vol. 86, No. 5 (September/October 2007), pp. 112, 113.

Chapter 9
On Nuclear Deterrence and Assurance

"Weakness is provocative."
-Secretary of Defense Donald Rumsfeld

Given the diversity of opponents U.S. leaders now must hope to deter, and the variety of circumstances in which deterrence and assurance will be important goals, a broad spectrum of U.S. strategic capabilities may be necessary. In some plausible cases non-military capabilities will suffice, while in others the immense lethality of U.S. nuclear threats is likely to be required. In some cases *punitive* U.S. threats will not deter because the opponent will accept great risks, but *denying* that opponent a practicable vision of success may deter.

U.S. non-nuclear threats and employment options often are likely to be salient for punitive and denial deterrence. For example, in regional contingencies where U.S. stakes at risk do not appear to involve national survival, or the survival of allies, some opponents are likely to view U.S. nuclear threats as incredible regardless of the character of the U.S. arsenal or the tone of U.S. statements. And, when U.S. priority goals include post-conflict "nation-building" and the reconstruction of a defeated opponent, U.S. advanced non-nuclear threats may be *more credible* because highly discriminate threats will be more compatible with U.S. stakes, interests and the goals of post-conflict reconciliation and reconstruction.[1]

No Deterrence Value for Nuclear Weapons?

As noted in Chapter 6, some contemporary commentators take the plausible cases described above to the extreme and assert that U.S. nuclear weapons now offer little or no added value for deterrence over U.S. non-nuclear capabilities. The rationale for this assertion is derived from the old balance of terror formula: predictable deterrent effect is equated to the U.S. capability to threaten the destruction of a select set of opponents' tangible, physical targets. Consequently, if non-nuclear weapons now can threaten to destroy most or all of that set of targets, then nuclear weapons supposedly no longer are of value for deterrence. The vulnerability of the designated targets, not the specific U.S. instrument of threat, is expected to determine the deterrent effect.

The first of these propositions—that deterrent effect can be equated to target coverage—is fundamentally flawed, as discussed at length in Chapter 7. The second also is highly suspect; it certainly is possible to *hope* that U.S. nuclear weapons no longer are critical for deterrence, just as it is possible to hope that all leaders will learn to be responsible and prudent. To assert confidently that U.S. nuclear weapons no longer are valuable for deterrence purposes, however, is to claim knowledge about how varied contemporary and future leaders in diverse and often unpredictable circumstances will interpret and respond to the distinction between nuclear and non-nuclear threats. Those who make such a claim presume knowledge that they do not and cannot have.

In addition, as discussed in Chapter 8, a popular refrain of some commentators is that U.S. nuclear weapons should be considered useful *only for deterring nuclear attack*.[2] This is not, and has not been, U.S. deterrence policy. The only apparent rationale for this assertion is to buttress the claim that the deterrence value of nuclear weapons is narrow in scope and purpose, and that the commentators' favored steps toward nuclear disarmament could eliminate even that value: if deterring nuclear threats is the *only purpose for U.S. nuclear weapons*, they will then have *no unique value* if others move away from nuclear weapons.

This proposition is logical, but artificially narrow. It misses the other severe non-nuclear threats to the United States and allies that may not be deterred reliably absent U.S. nuclear capabilities, such as threats posed by chemical and biological weapons (CBW). Commentators can claim for political reasons that U.S. nuclear capabilities should be considered pertinent for deterring only nuclear threats, but CBW threats are real and growing and there is no basis to conclude that U.S. non-nuclear capabilities would suffice to deter them. Even if the vision of the complete worldwide elimination of nuclear weapons were to be realized, CBW threats would remain. The most that can be said in this regard is that U.S. nuclear weapons might or might not be necessary for this deterrence goal—hardly a robust basis for making profound policy decisions about the most fundamental security questions.

Thinking through some plausible scenarios may be helpful in this regard. For example, if an opponent were to escalate an intense, ongoing conventional conflict by employing CBW with horrific effect against U.S. forces, civilians or allies, a high-priority U.S. goal would likely be to deter the opponent's subsequent use of CBW. The U.S. deterrence message to the opponent in this case could be that the opponent would suffer exceedingly if it were to repeat CBW use—that the United States would so raise the risks of the conflict for the opponent that it would *choose not to repeat its use of CBW* (even if its initial employment proved useful militarily or politically). This message could be intended to deter a second CBW attack during the crisis at hand and also to send a message to any hostile third parties that they must never consider CBW use against the United States and its allies.

The question in this scenario is whether U.S. *non-nuclear capabilities* alone would constitute an adequate basis for this U.S. deterrence message. As noted above, there is no useful *a priori* answer to this question. Some plausible circumstances, however, suggest the potential unique value of nuclear threats. For example, if a pitched conventional conflict is in progress and the opponent already has been subjected to an intense U.S. campaign of non-nuclear "shock and awe," could the threat of further U.S. non-nuclear fire in response to an opponent's CBW attack be decisive in the opponent's decision making? The United States could threaten to set aside some targeting limitations on its non-nuclear forces for this deterrence purpose. Would such a non-nuclear threat dominate the opponent's calculation of risk, cost and gain? Or, might it look like "more of the same" and have little prospect of being decisive in the opponent's decision making?

The answers to such questions certainly are not so self-evident as to suggest that U.S. nuclear threats would provide no unique added deterrent value. Nuclear weapons may be so much more lethal and distinguishable from non-nuclear threats that, on occasion, they can deter an opponent who would not otherwise be susceptible to control. Strategic nuclear threats have the potentially important advantages of extreme lethality from afar and a relatively obvious firebreak. These could be important qualities to deter CBW first or second use, and to help deter future third party CBW use. Clinton Administration Secretary of Defense Les Aspin rightly pointed to the prospective value of U.S. nuclear weapons for the deterrence of CBW threats given the proliferation of the latter: "Since the United States has forsworn chemical and biological weapons, the role of U.S. nuclear forces in deterring or responding to such non-nuclear threats must be considered."[3]

How and what might constitute an "adequate" U.S. mode of deterrence will depend on the details of the engagement, including opponents' values, vulnerabilities, risk tolerances, perceptions, access to information, and attention. Confident *a priori* assertions that nuclear threats *are sure to make the decisive difference* for deterrence purposes, or that they *can provide no significant added value* betray only the pretense of knowledge regarding how opponents will calculate and behave in the future. Even with a careful assessment of the pertinent details of opponent and context, precise prediction about the linkage of specific threat to deterrent effect is subject to uncertainties.

Nevertheless, a common proposition, initially expressed soon after the Cold War by Paul Nitze (as quoted in Chapter 6), is that the United States may now consider converting its strategic deterrent from nuclear weapons to "smart conventional weapons" because the latter can carry out many of the same "combat missions."[4] Nuclear weapons are said to be of limited and indeed declining value because there are "no conceivable circumstances in which the United States would need to use or could justify the use of nuclear weapons to fight or terminate a conventional conflict with a non-nuclear adversary."[5] As discussed, this proposition ignores the potential value of nuclear weapons for the deterrence of CBW; it also misses the fundamental point that deterrence requirements are *not set by what may be necessary to "fight or terminate" a conflict*.

Linking the assertion that there are few, if any, necessary "combat" roles for nuclear weapons to the conclusion that nuclear weapons lack *deterrence* value is a non sequitur, even if true. Nuclear weapons could be deemed to have no value whatsoever for "combat missions" and remain absolutely key to the deterrence of war and the assurance of allies. Deterrence involves exploiting opponents' fears and sensitivities and may have little or no connection to U.S. preferences for the wartime employment of force for "combat missions." Assurance, in turn, requires the easing of allies' fears and sensitivities, which again may have little or nothing to do with how the United States might prefer to terminate a conflict. Whether U.S. nuclear capabilities are regarded as useful or not "to fight or terminate a conventional conflict" may tell us nothing about their potential value for the political/psychological purposes of assurance and punitive deterrence. Deterrence, assurance, and war-fighting are different functions with possibly diverse and separate standards for force requirements. The potentially different force standards for these different goals should not be confused.

This most basic confusion was apparent during the Congressional discussions of the Robust Nuclear Earth Penetrator (RNEP). As discussed in Chapter 6, RNEP evolved from studies conducted during the Clinton Administration and subsequently was pursued by the Bush Administration *as potentially important for deterrence purposes*.[6] Yet, some Congressional opponents of RNEP pointed to the apparent lack of a "specific military requirement" for RNEP as a basis for their opposition.[7] One prominent member of Congress stated that no "military requirement for a nuclear earth penetrator" has been "articulated to me."[8]

The pertinent questions for RNEP had less to do with any expressed *military requirement* for this niche capability than whether a persuasive case could be made that it would be important for deterrence of significant threats and the assurance of allies. The uniformed military in general may have limited appreciation for a system that, as discussed by political leaders, would be useful as a *withheld* instrument for deterrence. "If I can't use it, what good is it?" is an understandable question. That "use" standard, however, may have limited relevance when the value of a nuclear capability is determined more by opponent and allied perceptions of it than by U.S. employment plans.

The Apparent Value of Nuclear Weapons for Deterrence

Whether or not nuclear weapons are considered useful for "combat missions" or have been asked for by military commanders, a quick review of available evidence points toward their potentially unique value for deterrence and assurance. For example, in the 1991 Gulf War Iraq launched 88 conventionally-armed Scud missiles against targets in Israel and Saudi Arabia; these missile strikes continued until the end of the war. In Israel and the United States there was concern that Iraq would use chemical weapons.[9] The anticipation of such attacks led Israeli citizens to take shelter in specially sealed rooms and to wear gas masks. Although Iraq did not employ chemical or biological warheads, Scud strikes directly inflicted more than 250 Israeli casualties and were indirectly responsible for a dozen deaths, including children, resulting from the improper use of gas masks.[10] U.N. officials have stated that Iraqi bombs and missiles contained enough biological agents to kill hundred of thousands,[11] and U.S. officials have confirmed that *if* Iraq had used available biological weapons the military and civilian casualty levels could have been horrific.[12]

Saddam Hussein was neither a philanthropist nor particularly humane. Why then did he *not* use the available chemical or biological weapons? Was he deterred by the prospect of *nuclear retaliation*? Israeli commentators frequently suggest that the apparent Israeli nuclear threat deterred Iraqi chemical use. In this regard it should be noted that during a CNN interview on February 2, 1991, then U.S. Defense Secretary Dick Cheney was asked about the potential for Israeli nuclear retaliation to Iraqi chemical strikes. Secretary Cheney observed that this would be a decision that "the Israelis would have to make—but I would think that [Hussein] has to be cautious in terms of how he proceeds in his attacks against Israel." The following day, when asked about Secretary Cheney's statement, Israeli Defense Minister Moshe Arens replied, "I think he said that Saddam has reasons to worry—yes, he does have reasons to worry."[13] This reply, and Secretary Cheney's original statement—in which he did not object to the premise of the question about the possibility of Israeli nuclear retaliation, at least to Israeli analysts—was key to deterring Iraqi chemical weapons use.[14]

The possible direct U.S. role in nuclear deterrence in this case should be highlighted.[15] On January 9, 1991, Secretary of State James Baker expressed a severe deterrent threat to Iraqi Foreign Minister Tariq Aziz in Geneva: "Before we cross to the other side—that is, if the conflict starts, God forbid, and chemical or biological weapons are used against our forces—the American people would demand revenge, and we have the means to implement this."[16]

President Bush's strongly worded letter to Saddam Hussein, cited in previous chapters, warned against the use of chemical or biological weapons. It spoke of the "strongest possible" U.S. response and warned that, "you and your country will pay a terrible price" in the event of "such unconscionable acts."[17]

Secretary Cheney also implicitly linked U.S. nuclear threats to Iraqi use of WMD: "The other point that needs to be made, and it's one I have made previously, is that he [Hussein] needs to be made aware that the President will have available the full spectrum of capabilities."[18]

Such statements by then ranking U.S. and Israeli officials, while not explicitly threatening nuclear retaliation, certainly implied the possibility. These threats appear to be a plausible explanation for Iraqi restraint with regard to chemical and biological weapons. Following the 1991 Gulf War, authoritative accounts of Iraqi wartime decision making on this issue emerged. In August 1995, Iraqi Foreign Minister Tariq Aziz reported to Ambassador Rolf Ekeus, a United Nations weapons inspector, that Iraq was deterred from using its WMD because the Iraqi leadership had interpreted Washington's threats of grievous retaliation as meaning *nuclear* retaliation.[19]

Tariq Aziz's explanation has been corroborated by former senior Iraqi military officials, including General Wafic Al Sammarai, then head of Iraqi military intelligence. General Sammarai stated: "Some of the Scud missiles were loaded with chemical warheads, but they were not used. They were kept hidden throughout the war. We didn't use them because the other side had a deterrent force."[20] General Sammarai added, "I do not think Saddam was capable of taking a decision to use chemical weapons or biological weapons, or any other type of weapons against the allied groups, because the warning was quite severe, and quite effective. *The allied troops were certain to use nuclear arms and the price will be too dear and too high.*"[21] Similarly, Iraqi General Hussein Kamal, Saddam Hussein's son-in-law and Iraqi Minister of Military Industries, reportedly stated following his defection from Iraq in 1995 that: "During the Gulf War, there was no intention to use chemical weapons as the Allied force was overwhelming...there was no decision to use chemical weapons for fear of retaliation. They realized that if chemical weapons were used, *retaliation would be nuclear....*"[22] At the time, the fact that some U.S. naval vessels reportedly were deployed with nuclear capabilities aboard may have contributed to this helpful Iraqi view.[23]

In 1995, Brent Scowcroft, President Bush's National Security Advisor during the 1991 Gulf War, revealed publicly that U.S. leaders had decided in fact that the United States would *not* respond to Iraqi WMD use with nuclear weapons. Rather, according to Scowcroft, the United States would have expanded its conventional attacks against Iraqi targets.[24] And President Bush has stated that, "it [nuclear use] was not something that we really contemplated at all."[25] Nevertheless, according to the accounts by Tariq Aziz, General Hussein Kamal, and General Wafic Al Sammarai, the Iraqi leadership *believed* that the United States would have retaliated with nuclear weapons—and the expectations appear to have deterred—as clearly was intended by U.S. officials.

On this occasion, *implicit U.S. nuclear* threats appear to have deterred as hoped; Schelling's proposition regarding the deterring effect of possible nuclear escalation appears to have been demonstrated. The fact that many in the U.S. senior wartime leadership later explained publicly that the United States would *not* have employed nuclear weapons may help to degrade that deterrent effect for the future. A comment by Bernard Brodie *vis-à-vis* the Soviet Union in 1963 may be apropos: If the opponent is under the "apparent conviction" that the U.S. nuclear deterrent is credible, "why should we attempt to shake that conviction?"[26]

Nevertheless, the point here is that the 1991 Gulf War appears to offer evidence that *nuclear* deterrence, on occasion, can be uniquely effective. Saddam Hussein appears to have been confident that he could withstand the pressure of conventional war with the United States— perhaps based upon his relatively dismissive view of the U.S. will to fight a bloody conventional war. When Secretary of State James Baker told Tariq Aziz of the "overwhelming" conventional power that would be "brought to bear" against Iraq, Aziz responded, "Mr. Secretary, Iraq is a very ancient nation. We have lived for 6000 years. I have no doubts that you are a very powerful nation. I have no doubts that you have a very strong military machine and you will inflict on us heavy losses. But Iraq will survive and this leadership will decide the future of Iraq."[27] This prediction proved accurate for a decade.

Of course, the explanations of apparent Iraqi restraint offered by Tariq Aziz, Wafic Al Sammarai, and Hussein Kamal do not close the issue; they do, however, suggest that *nuclear* deterrence was at least part of the answer as to why Saddam Hussein did not use WMD in 1991 when he apparently had the option to do so. These explanations also suggest the profound error of those prominent commentators who asserted with such certainty immediately after the 1991 war that nuclear weapons were "incredible as a deterrent and therefore irrelevant,"[28] and the fragility of similar contemporary claims that U.S. nuclear threats are incredible and thus useless for contemporary regional deterrence purposes.[29]

Prominent American commentators can assert that nuclear weapons are incredible and thus useless in such cases; their speculation about U.S. threat credibility, however, ultimately is irrelevant. For deterrence purposes, it is *the opponent's belief* about U.S. threat credibility that matters, and that cannot be ascertained from the views of American domestic commentators. The 1991 Gulf War appears to demonstrate that Iraqi officials perceived U.S. threats as nuclear and sufficiently credible to deter, and that this *perception was more important* to U.S. deterrence strategy than were actual U.S. intentions. Nuclear deterrence appears to have played a significant role despite the fact that U.S. leaders apparently saw no need to employ nuclear weapons and had no intention of doing so.

There is little doubt that U.S. *nuclear* threats have contributed to the deterrence of additional past opponents who otherwise may have been particularly resistant to U.S. non-nuclear threats. This deterrent effect is a matter of adversary perceptions—which can be independent of our preferences or intentions regarding the use of force. However we might prefer to deter, or plan to employ force, the actual behavior of adversaries on occasion suggests that there can be a difference between the deterring effects of nuclear and non-nuclear weapons. In some past cases, given the adversary's views and the context, it has been "the reality of nuclear deterrence" that has had the desired "restraining effect."[30] In the future, as in the past, the working of deterrence on such occasions may be extremely important.

There is some additional evidence from countries such as North Korea that opponents continue to attribute unique deterrence value to U.S. nuclear weapons. For example, during a 2005 visit by a U.S. Congressional delegation to North Korea, Representative Curt Weldon, then Vice Chairman of the House Armed Services Committee, raised with senior North Korean military and political leaders the U.S. interest in a nuclear capability to threaten hardened and deeply buried targets (i.e., RNEP as discussed above in Chapter 6). According to the after-trip report by Congressman Weldon and other members of the bipartisan delegation, this was the only U.S. military capability that appeared to concern the North Korean leadership and "got their attention,"[31] suggesting its potential deterrence value. North Korean statements regarding U.S. nuclear "bunker burst" capabilities also appear to reveal an unparalleled concern about the possibility of such U.S. nuclear capabilities, thereby suggesting their potential value for deterrence.[32]

Rogues and potential opponents are expending considerable effort on hard and deeply buried bunkers. Some of these bunkers reportedly can be held at risk of destruction *only via nuclear weapons.*[33] During the 1991 Gulf War, some Iraqi bunkers were "virtually invulnerable to conventional weapons."[34] In 1999, concerted NATO air attacks reportedly could not destroy a deep tunnel complex at the Pristina airport in Kosovo. As a British inspector on the ground at the time reported, "On June 11, hours after NATO halted its bombing and just before the Serb military began withdrawing, 11 Mig-21 fighters emerged from the tunnels and took off for Yugoslavia."[35] Similarly, in 1996, senior Clinton Administration officials observed that *only* nuclear weapons could threaten to destroy the suspected Libyan chemical weapons facility located inside a mountain near Tarhunah.[36] Moreover, the U.S. Cold War "legacy" nuclear arsenal apparently has limitations against some protected targets: "Furthermore, the current [nuclear] inventory only has a limited capability for

holding hardened underground facilities at risk. The country's only nuclear earth penetrating weapons…cannot survive delivery into certain
types of terrain in which such facilities may be located."[37]

Adversaries unsurprisingly seek to protect what they value.
And, as Defense Secretary Harold Brown emphasized, U.S. deterrence
threats should be capable of holding at risk those assets valued by the
opponent.[38] Consequently, to the extent that we hope to apply the "logic of
deterrence" to rogue state decision makers, the U.S. capability to threaten
that which they value located within protected bunkers may be important
for deterrence; if North Korean and other rogue leaders demonstrate
the value they attribute to assets via buried and hardened bunkers, the
U.S. capability to hold those types of targets at obvious risk of destruction
may be an important deterrent threat to those leaderships. Highlighting
the potential value of nuclear capabilities to do so hardly connotes a
rejection of deterrence in favor of "war-fighting" as often is claimed; to
the contrary, it reflects an attempt to find plausible deterrence tools suited
to contemporary opponents and conditions. This is precisely the point
made with regard to deterring the Soviet leadership in 1989 by R. James
Woolsey, who subsequently served as the Director of Central Intelligence
in the Clinton Administration:

> …successful deterrence requires being able to hold at risk
> those things that the Soviet leadership most values. The
> nature of the Soviet state suggests that the Soviet leaders
> most value themselves. This emphasizes the importance of
> being able to hold at risk deep underground facilities, such
> as those at Sharapovo, which can only be done effectively
> by an earth-penetrating [nuclear] weapon.[39]

A fundamental deterrence question regarding such U.S. capabilities concerns which set of specific conditions is more likely to provide the
United States with greater leverage: when opposing leaderships have,
or do not have, sanctuaries impervious to U.S. prompt threats? Are
opponents likely to feel greater freedom to provoke the United States
severely when they believe themselves to be *more or less vulnerable*
to U.S. deterrence threats?

There are no *a priori* answers to such questions that can be
assumed to apply across a spectrum of opponents and circumstances.
In contemporary cases, however, as in the past—*if* the complex variety of

conditions necessary for deterrence to work are present and the challenger is risk- and cost-tolerant—then *nuclear* deterrence *may be uniquely decisive* in the challenger's decision making. Moreover, for deterrence to work on those occasions—whether they are few or many—could be of great importance given the potential lethality of emerging WMD threats to the United States. To assert otherwise—that U.S. nuclear weapons now provide *no* unique added value for deterrence—contradicts available evidence and lays claim to knowledge about opponent decision making that domestic commentators do not and cannot have. Such assertions reveal more about what some commentators *wish* to be true than what available evidence suggests should be believed.

There should be no presumption that nuclear threats always will make the difference between effective deterrence or its failure. The capability, however, to threaten an adversary's valued assets with great lethality and from afar—including well-protected targets—may be critical for some U.S. deterrence purposes. Unless future leadership decision making is different from that of the past, in some cases *nuclear* threat options will contribute to deterrence. Given literally decades of experience, the burden of proof lies with those who now contend that nuclear weapons are unnecessary for deterrence; considerable available evidence contradicts such a contention.

The decisions of Britain and France also suggest the continuing value of nuclear weapons for deterrence. Both have reaffirmed their long-term commitments to maintain their nuclear capabilities for deterrence purposes, including deterrence of rogue states and other possible future unexpected contingencies.[40]

Also indicative of the continuing deterrence value of nuclear weapons are Russia's and China's decisions to modernize and expand their nuclear arsenals,[41] and the apparent desire of North Korea, Iran, and possibly Syria to possess nuclear weapons.[42] North Korean officials have pointed to the value of nuclear weapons for deterrence:

> Today's reality verifies that the [North Korean] nuclear deterrent constitutes the one and only means that can prevent war on the Korean peninsula and defend peace in this region....We will strengthen our nuclear deterrent in every way to prevent war and defend peace on the Korean peninsula and in Northeast Asia and will take a decisive self-defensive countermeasure at the necessary time.[43]

North Korea's nuclear weapons program is, "an all-purpose cost-effective instrument of foreign policy...the single most important lever in its asymmetric conflicts and negotiations with South Korea, the United States, and Japan."[44]

So too, Iranian officials reportedly attribute great deterrence value to nuclear weapons. Following Iran's costly war with Iraq in the 1980s, and the subsequent 1991 Gulf War:

> Iranian leaders believed that nuclear weapons were the ultimate instrument of asymmetric warfare. They held that if Iraq had had nuclear weapons [in 1991], the United States would never have attacked it. Hence, in January 1995, Iran signed a contract with Russia for the completion of a nuclear power plant in the city of Bushehr, which... provided Iran with a pretext to begin building a complete fuel cycle, with the aim of producing enriched uranium for nuclear weapons.[45]

The material question is not whether commentators believe nuclear weapons "ought" to have value for deterrence in a normative sense; they *have* demonstrated that value. The question is whether we are willing to accept the risk of deterrence failure on those occasions in which the United States could not threaten nuclear escalation, possibly including threats to some adversaries' highly-valued/protected targets. The added risk of deterrence failure flowing from such an inability surely cannot be calculated *a priori* with precision. It may be non-existent or high depending on the specific circumstances of the contingency. Even if the risk of deterrence failure for this reason is low, however, the possibility would still deserve serious consideration because the consequences of a single failure to deter WMD attack could be measured in thousands to millions of U.S. and allied casualties. And, of course, that risk may not be low.

The Value of Nuclear Weapons for Assurance

Nuclear weapons also appear to have unique value for assurance. Particularly pertinent in this regard are the views of those allies who consider themselves dependent on the U.S. nuclear umbrella for extended deterrence. Former senior military officers from America, Germany, Britain, France and the Netherlands have emphasized the continuing importance of the *nuclear* escalation threat for deterrence: "The first use of nuclear weapons must remain in the quiver of escalation as the ultimate instrument to prevent the use of weapons of mass destruction, in order to avoid truly existential dangers."[46]

Similarly, following the North Korean nuclear test in October 2006, Japanese and South Korean officials emphasized the importance they place on U.S. *nuclear capabilities* for extended deterrence. Former South Korean defense ministers asked that U.S. nuclear weapons removed from South Korea in 1991 be returned, and public sentiment turned strongly in favor of South Korea having a nuclear weapons capability.[47] A South Korean delegation to the United States, led by Defense Minister Yoon Kwang-ung, sought an explicit U.S. public declaration that if North Korea employed nuclear weapons against South Korea, the United States would respond in kind as if the United States itself had been attacked.[48]

A 2006 Japanese study headed by former Prime Minister Yasuhiro Nakasone concluded that, "in order to prepare for drastic changes in the international situation in the future, a thorough study of the nuclear issue should be conducted."[49] Nakasone noted that Japanese security is dependent on U.S. nuclear weapons, but that the future of the U.S. extended deterrent is unclear. As quoted in Chapter 6, Japanese Defense Minister Fumio Kyuma was explicit regarding the nuclear requirements of extended deterrence: "The strongest deterrence would be when the United States explicitly says, 'If you drop one nuclear bomb on Japan, the United States will retaliate by dropping 10 on you.'"[50] There could hardly be a stronger allied statement of the perceived value of U.S. *nuclear* weapons for the continued assurance of allies, or a more explicit *rejection* of U.S. ambiguity in its extended deterrence commitments.

A Japanese commentary on the subject by Kyoto University professor, Terumasa Nakanishi, laments the "Chamberlainization" of the U.S. extended nuclear umbrella for Japan and explicitly links related fears to the potential Japanese need for nuclear weapons:

> With America not indicating that it will shore up its nuclear deterrence toward China and North Korea, if Japan is going to try to put an actual lid on the North Korean nuclear problem, private Japanese citizens, *as "sensible and prudent Japanese,"* should widen and deepen discussion from now on [about] the issue of how Japan can connect its independent national strategy and Japan's own nuclear weapons and nuclear strategy to its foreign policy.[51]

The expressed definition here of what is a "sensible and prudent" course for Japan may be far different from the preferred U.S. definition of the same.

The Iranian drive for nuclear weapons similarly appears to be leading some neighboring Arab states to anticipate *their own need for nuclear weapons*: "Just such a reaction is underway already in the Middle East, as over a dozen Muslim nations suddenly declared interest in starting nuclear-power programs. This is not about energy; it is a hedge against Iran. It could lead to a Middle East with not one nuclear-weapons state, Israel, but four or five."[52]

That officials and commentators in key allied countries perceive great value in U.S. nuclear weapons for extended deterrence suggests strongly that these weapons *do have unique assurance value*. As noted in Chapter 7, there is a direct connection between allied perceptions of the assurance value of U.S. nuclear weapons for extended deterrence and nuclear non-proliferation. There may seem to be an incongruity between the U.S. maintenance of its own nuclear arsenal for deterrence and its simultaneous advocacy of nuclear non-proliferation; a prominent member of the U.S. Congress has likened this seeming incongruity to a drunkard advocating abstinence. However, given the obvious importance of U.S. nuclear weapons for its extended deterrence responsibilities, and the critical role which U.S. extended nuclear deterrence plays in non-proliferation, *there is no incongruity*. Sustaining U.S. capabilities for extended nuclear deterrence is critical for nuclear non-proliferation.

Such allied commentary does not demonstrate directly the value of nuclear weapons for *deterrence*—again, it is U.S. *opponents* who ultimately determine the deterrence value of U.S. nuclear weapons. It is, however, significant evidence of the importance of U.S. nuclear weapons for the assurance of allies via extended deterrence. It also is important to recognize that for North Korea's closest neighbors, including Japan and South Korea, the question of the value of U.S. nuclear weapons is not an academic or theoretical debate about preferred utopian futures. It is a most serious concern among these Asian leaders who undoubtedly understand North Korea at least as well as U.S. commentators. They believe that U.S. nuclear weapons are critical to the deterrence of North Korea and thus their own assurance. These are only perceptions; their perceptions, however, may be particularly well-informed, and both deterrence and assurance fundamentally are about perceptions.

The apparent importance of U.S. nuclear weapons for extended deterrence, assurance, and thus non-proliferation may distress U.S. commentators who would prefer U.S. deterrence threats to be largely or exclusively non-nuclear. Just as deterrent effect ultimately is determined by opponents, however, what does or does not assure allies is not decided by the preferences of U.S. commentators, but by the allies themselves. The United States can decide what priority it places on the assurance of allies, and how it will proceed to support that goal, but only the allies can decide whether they are assured. In the contemporary environment, available evidence suggests strongly that assurance is an important goal and that U.S. *nuclear weapons* are critical to the assurance of key allies to a level they deem adequate.

The United States could decide to withdraw the nuclear umbrella and provide only a non-nuclear commitment. As discussed above, however, it is likely that the U.S. withdrawal of its *nuclear* extended deterrent coverage would create new and powerful incentives for nuclear proliferation among U.S. friends and allies who, to date, have felt sufficiently secure under the U.S. extended nuclear deterrent to remain non-nuclear.[53] This linkage is not speculative; it is voiced by allies who feel increasingly at risk. Extreme care should be exercised before moving in a direction that carries the risk of unleashing a nuclear proliferation "cascade"—such as moving prematurely in the direction of a wholly non-nuclear force structure. As a 2007 report by the Department of State's International Security Advisory Board concludes:

> There is clear evidence in diplomatic channels that U.S. assurances to include the nuclear umbrella have been, and continue to be, the single most important reason many allies have foresworn nuclear weapons. This umbrella is too important to sacrifice on the basis of an unproven ideal that nuclear disarmament in the U.S. would lead to a more secure world....a lessening of the U.S. nuclear umbrella could very well trigger a cascade [of nuclear proliferation] in East Asia and the Middle East.[54]

The Credibility of U.S. Nuclear Threats: Implications for the Arsenal

If we hope to apply the logic of punitive deterrence to an opponent in an acute contingency, then that opponent must attribute *some* credibility to our threats. Whether the intensity of that belief corresponds to Kahn's favored threat that leaves *little* to chance, or to Schelling's threat that leaves *something* to chance, the opponent must anticipate that there is *some probability* that the U.S. threat would be executed.

In the past, militarists and dictators have seen in America's Western and democratic scruples license to provoke the United States. These leaders have included Adolf Hitler, Hideki Tojo, Mao Zedong, Saddam Hussein, and Slobodan Milosevic.[55] Adolf Hitler frequently boasted that he was not limited by "bourgeois scruples" in the manner of liberal democracies, and that this would help ensure his success. Or, as Slobodan Milosevic proudly declared, "I am ready to walk on corpses, and the West is not. That is why I shall win."[56] Obviously, both Hitler and Milosevic misjudged their situations. However, their expectations that Western democratic norms would provide the basis for their victory likely contributed to their willingness to provoke.

This point has implications for the U.S. nuclear arsenal's value for deterrence. In some instances, low-yield, accurate nuclear weapons may contribute to a U.S. deterrent threat that is *more believable* than otherwise would be the case. The U.S. "legacy" nuclear arsenal's generally high yields and limited precision could threaten to inflict so many innocent casualties that some opponents eager to find a rationale for action may seize on the possibility that a U.S. president would not execute an expressed nuclear deterrent threat. Uncertainty regarding the U.S. threat in such cases could work against the desired deterrent effect.

America's aversion to causing "collateral damage" is well-known. Some opponents clearly see proper U.S. concerns about civilian casualties, "nation-building," and winning "hearts and minds" as U.S. vulnerabilities to be exploited. They may disdain as particularly incredible deterrence threats based on the generally high nuclear yields of the U.S. Cold War arsenal given the civilian destruction which high yields could cause. The U.S. desire to minimize unintended destruction, inspire post-conflict support from an opponent's liberated populace, and pursue post-conflict reconstruction may be priorities in the contemporary period that reduce the apparent credibility of Cold War-style assured destruction nuclear threats.[57] In these cases, U.S. non-nuclear and very discriminate nuclear capabilities may be important for U.S. deterrence credibility. During the Cold War—when U.S. survival was at stake and the context involved thousands of nuclear weapons on each side—these types of considerations were likely to have been less pertinent to considerations of credibility. Now, however, they point toward the potential value of advanced non-nuclear and highly discriminate nuclear threat options for deterrence credibility. Some studies done late in the Cold War, and looking 20 years into the future, pointed to the same conclusion.[58]

Consequently, reducing nuclear yields and improving the accuracy of U.S. nuclear forces may be important for contingencies in which nuclear deterrence is critical but new post-Cold War priorities are in play. Again, this suggestion is not, as some commentators charge, a rejection of deterrence in favor of "destabilizing," "war-fighting" nuclear weapons. Such a characterization is to apply loaded Cold War deterrence labels to a context in which they lack *meaning*. The potential value of low-yield, accurate nuclear weapons is fully consistent with their possible deterrent effect.

U.S. strategic policies guided by balance of terror and assured destruction metrics subverted long-standing moral strictures against threatening civilians in favor of the goal of deterrence "stability." In the contemporary era, however, when the stakes at risk for the United States in a regional crisis do not include national survival, and when post-conflict reconstruction and minimization of damage to the opponent and its neighbors may be priority goals, the credibility of the U.S. deterrent may rest *not on how much damage can be threatened* à la assured destruction, but rather on *how controlled is that threatened damage*. Traditional moral considerations and the efficacy of deterrence may now merge.

In short, as the apparent success of nuclear deterrence during the 1991 Gulf War illustrated, perceptions are key to deterrence. Nuclear threats may be important, but high nuclear yields and limited precision *may not* appear to constitute credible threats to opponents who understand U.S. concerns about inflicting "collateral damage," and expect that U.S. "self-deterrence" would provide them greater freedom of action. We should not want the relatively high yields and modest accuracies of the U.S. Cold War legacy nuclear arsenal to give an opportunity for contemporary opponents to view U.S. deterrence threats with disdain.

It does not require much foresight or imagination to conclude that—*to the extent that the logic of deterrence applies*—under plausible circumstances U.S. threats may more readily serve deterrence purposes when U.S. forces can hold enemy sanctuaries at risk with minimal unintended damage. Leaving uncontested an opponent's potential belief that the United States would be incapable of threatening its sanctuaries, or would be "self-deterred" by enlightened scruples from executing its deterrence threats, may contribute to that opponent's felt freedom to provoke the United States. This is not a far-fetched concern. Contemporary rogue states appear eager to exploit both mechanisms in the hope of escaping U.S. deterrence constraints. In this context, capabilities dubbed "destabilizing" by traditional balance of terror categorization— such as precision accuracy and counterforce potential—may be important for deterrence. The old notion that a coherent distinction can be drawn between "stabilizing" forces intended to serve deterrence purposes and "destabilizing" forces for "war-fighting" fits the old formula but does not fit these contemporary circumstances.

Finally, some commentators have opposed U.S. development of nuclear weapons intended to limit "collateral damage" because they claim that U.S. forces designed to do so would be considered by a president to be more "usable," thus "lowering the threshold" to U.S. nuclear employment: "The implication is that, if their resulting collateral damage can be substantially reduced by lowering the explosive power of the warhead, nuclear weapons would be more politically palatable and therefore more 'useable' for attacking deeply buried targets in tactical missions— even in or near urban settings, which can be the preferred locales for such targets."[59]

This critique posits that the United States should forego a capability that may be valuable for deterrence, for fear that a president might employ it cavalierly. Such a tradeoff is at least questionable, particularly given the absence of any history of such cavalier presidential behavior. In addition, because an opponent might consider a U.S. nuclear deterrent threat to be *credible* does not also mean that it is regarded by presidents as easily employable— *as was demonstrated during the 1991 Gulf War.* A president's decision calculus about the actual employment of nuclear weapons is likely to be affected by many factors, particularly including the severity and circumstances of the provocation, other priority U.S. goals, allied considerations, immediate foreign and domestic political circumstances, and personal moral perspectives. The manifest characteristics of U.S. weapons may be more salient to an opponent's *view* of U.S. credibility than it is to a president's view of their "usability." A president's perceptions of "usable" and opponents' views of "credible" need not be conflated.

Can there be confident promises that more "discriminate" U.S. nuclear capabilities would strengthen U.S. deterrence efforts, or make the difference between deterrence working or failing on any given occasion? *No; of course not.* In the absence of a specific examination of opponent and context we are dealing again in speculative generalizations about how deterrence may operate. The particular types of nuclear capabilities necessary to threaten opponents' deeply buried bunkers and other targets, while minimizing the potential for collateral damage, could provide the needed lethality and credibility for deterrence on occasion. However, an opponent also could miss such fine points regarding U.S. nuclear capabilities, or be so motivated that the specific character of the U.S. nuclear threat is irrelevant to its decision making. What can be said is that—unless a close examination of opponents suggests otherwise— these types of specialized nuclear capabilities *cannot reasonably be touted as ensuring deterrence credibility or dismissed a priori as* "destabilizing" and intended for "war-fighting" vice deterrence purposes. In the contemporary environment they may be intended for and well-suited to the political goals of deterrence and assurance.

The Nuclear Disarmament Vision

Throughout the Cold War and post-Cold War years, various groups and individuals have put forth initiatives for the long-term elimination of nuclear weapons or their near-term reduction to small numbers. With the end of the Cold War, many thoughtful people understandably question why the United States should continue to maintain nuclear weapons, particularly if most plausible adversaries can be defeated militarily with conventional forces alone. The point here is that, on some occasions, deterrence and assurance will be the priority goals. Numerous countries— including contemporary opponents and allies—give every indication that they perceive unique value in nuclear weapons for those purposes, whether or not U.S. domestic commentators believe it or want it to be true. Those perceptions alone create the potential value of nuclear weapons for deterring opponents and assuring allies.

A common problem with recent and past nuclear disarmament initiatives is that they emphasize the risks of maintaining U.S. nuclear capabilities, but are silent or wholly superficial in discussing the risks of their elimination. The postulated benefit from U.S. moves toward giving up nuclear capabilities typically is presented in terms of the contribution such a move supposedly would make to the goal of nuclear non-proliferation.[60] U.S. steps toward global nuclear disarmament supposedly will begin the action-reaction process of eliminating those nuclear threats that justify retaining U.S. nuclear weapons for deterrence: no such threat, no such need. Chapter 7 describes the utter inadequacy of the balance of terror's simplistic action-reaction tenet. Whatever the merit of that metaphor for this application, however, the question of nuclear disarmament must include a net assessment—a review of the value of nuclear weapons and the related downside of losing that value.

The burden of proof is on those who now assert that adversaries would be deterred reliably by U.S. non-nuclear capabilities; that allies similarly would be assured reliably by the same; that opponents dutifully would follow the U.S. example; and, that the United States could be confident they had done so. *Considerable evidence points to the contrary in each case.* In 2006, British Prime Minister Tony Blair made this point against those questioning his decision to modernize Britain's nuclear capabilities:

> Those who question this decision need to explain why [nuclear] disarmament by the UK would help our security. They would need to prove that such a gesture would change the minds of hardliners and extremists in countries which are developing these nuclear capabilities. They would need to show that terrorists would be less likely to conspire against us with hostile governments because we had given up our nuclear weapons. They would need to argue that the UK would be safer by giving up the deterrent and that our capacity to act would not be constrained by nuclear blackmail by others.[61]

Blair's critics and their U.S. counterparts who now advocate that the United States embrace the "vision" of nuclear disarmament *have not begun* to offer a plausible net assessment in response to this challenge. Instead, they appear satisfied to assert the old action-reaction/inaction-inaction balance of terror adage—along with the equally dubious claim, also derived from the old formula—that deterrence now can be orchestrated to work reliably with non-nuclear forces alone. Both assertions can be described as reflecting hope over considerable evidence.

There are conditions that should be considered critical milestones for any significant U.S. steps toward nuclear disarmament. The realization of some of those conditions would represent a more dramatic restructuring of international relations than has occurred since the 1648 Peace of Westphalia. This should not preclude creative thinking about prudent steps toward greatly reduced reliance on nuclear weapons, but it certainly should make us wary of embracing the vision of nuclear disarmament as a practicable goal in the absence of such dramatic change.

For example, one of the reasons nuclear deterrence has been valuable is that it appears to have disciplined the behavior of some states that otherwise could not be trusted to behave peaceably. Not all states are trustworthy, and it is those untrustworthy states with hostile designs that often pose security challenges; they are called "rogues" for a reason. In the past, such untrustworthy governments included Hitler's Germany and Stalin's Soviet Union; now they include the governments of Iran, North Korea and Syria. These particular rogue leaderships may come and go but, in the future, there will be comparably untrustworthy leaderships with hostile intent. This is pertinent because there is *no indication* that, in a world of sovereign states, adequate international verification and enforcement measures will be available to backstop nuclear disarmament, much less the elimination of CBW. Most experience points to the contrary.

The Clinton Administration's thoughtful Under Secretary of Defense for Policy, Walter Slocombe, observed rightly in this regard that if "somehow" all of the pertinent powers of the world were to accept the vision of nuclear disarmament, its realization would demand "a verification regime of extraordinary rigor and intrusiveness. This would have to go far beyond any currently in existence or even under contemplation."[62] Secretary Slocombe noted that the challenge to establishing the necessary verification regime should be obvious—it would have to include "certain and timely" procedures for "forcible" international action to ensure compliance.[63] In the absence of a trustworthy authority with much of the power and prerogative of a world government, such a verification and enforcement regime cannot exist. The enduring lack of reliable verification and enforcement—combined with the likelihood that some states will be untrustworthy, armed and aggressive—explains why disarmament visions must remain visions in a world of sovereign states.

There are real risks associated with the possession of nuclear weapons. Great risk also may be expected if the United States and its allies were to give up nuclear weapons in the mistaken belief that untrustworthy, hostile states no longer could pose WMD threats. The same hostility and lack of trust inherent in international relations which creates the need for nuclear deterrence prevents the realization of visionary solutions to end that need.[64]

Other than the occasional, unpromising call for world government,[65] the proponents of nuclear disarmament *have not begun* to suggest how this sturdy barrier to the realization of their vision and like visions in past centuries may be breached while maintaining U.S. security and the security of allies. We all would like to hear and to believe, but no plausible answer is offered.

In his final speech to the U.S. Congress, Winston Churchill warned, "Be careful above all things not to let go of the atomic weapon until you are sure and more than sure that other means of preserving peace are in your hands!"[66] There is no known basis for concluding that those "other means" are at hand or that threats to peace will disappear. Until then, embracing nuclear disarmament seriously as the priority U.S. goal *should be recognized as entailing the serious risk of further vilifying those U.S. forces that may be important to deter future war, assure allies, and help contain nuclear proliferation.*

Balance of Terror Tenets Versus Plausible Deep Nuclear Force Reductions

Not all visions offer a wise path forward. Karl Marx's slogan—"From each according to his ability, to each according to his needs"—was a beautiful vision borrowed from Scripture. Attempts to realize that vision in the Soviet Union instead produced misery for millions and probably set back Russian economic development by half a century.

The vision of zero nuclear weapons appears beautiful.[67] Yet, were the United States to pursue that vision as its priority goal, it could degrade the deterrence of war and the assurance of allies. In contrast, these same risks do not *necessarily* apply to deep reductions in the U.S. strategic nuclear arsenal. Deep nuclear reductions could be consistent with continued support for U.S. strategic goals in a dynamic strategic environment—which is why they could be undertaken prudently in select circumstances.[68]

The continuing undisciplined application of the balance of terror tenets to contemporary questions of strategic forces and policy, as described in Chapter 6, however, will likely *preclude the opportunity* for *prudent deep nuclear force reductions.* As applied, those tenets *work against* the U.S. policies and capabilities that could otherwise help to mitigate the risks associated with deep nuclear reductions and thus help to make them acceptable to U.S. leaders responsible for "the common defense."

The character and size of the U.S. nuclear arsenal should be paced by numerous factors, including:

* The contemporary, highly-dynamic strategic threat environment;
* The relationship of the nuclear arsenal to other national goals, e.g., nonproliferation;
* The goals the nuclear arsenal is intended to serve and their priorities, including assurance and deterrence;
* The potential contributions to those goals by other non-nuclear and non-military means; and,
* Budget and technical realities.

The United States cannot control all of these factors with any predictability, but it can influence some. When the alignment of these conditions presents the opportunity for prudent deep nuclear reductions, that opportunity should be pursued smartly. The Bush Administration's 2002 Treaty of Moscow, for example, contained a two-thirds reduction in the permitted number of operationally-deployed strategic nuclear weapons: from the 6,000 weapons permitted by the 1991 START I Treaty to a range of 1,700-to-2,200 weapons. At the time of the Moscow Treaty, Bush Administration officials publicly identified *the new and more cooperative relationship with the Russian Federation* as enabling such dramatic reductions.[69] The then-emerging improvement in political relations with Russia on a broad scale permitted deep reductions in the U.S. strategic nuclear arsenal. This potential for deep reductions was *not the result of negotiations for that purpose*, but a basic shift in political relations. U.S. officials at the time also stated explicitly that *deeper reductions were possible in the future as conditions permitted.*[70]

What might contribute to the opportunity for further prudent reductions? In 2002, Bush Administration officials included the development of U.S. advanced non-nuclear forces and defensive capabilities as possibly doing so.[71]

Developments in U.S. non-nuclear offensive weapons and damage-limitation capabilities could plausibly contribute to prudent reductions by helping to mitigate the possible risks of deep reductions and by providing non-nuclear offensive and defensive capabilities to perform some duties reserved to nuclear weapons in the past.[72] Significant damage-limitation capabilities, for example, could help to reduce a risk particularly associated with very low nuclear force numbers: they could help to make U.S. security *less vulnerable* to dangerous technical and geopolitical surprises, including deception by countries that had ostensibly agreed to deep reductions and thereby contributed to the freedom felt by the United States to do so.

In addition, the responsiveness of the U.S. nuclear and strategic forces production infrastructure in principle could help mitigate another of the primary risks involved in deep reductions—if the conditions permitting deep reductions shift and reestablish the requirement for an increase in the U.S. arsenal's quantity or quality. The risk of being caught short in a dynamic environment may be eased by retaining a stockpiled reserve of nuclear weapons, *or via the U.S. capability to respond and adapt with new nuclear weapons in a timely way without relying on an inventory of stockpiled weapons*. This latter possibility follows simply from the principle that the United States may not need to have on hand or stockpiled a redundant reserve of nuclear forces *if* they can be produced reliably in a timely fashion: the more reliably, rapidly and credibly the United States can reconstitute forces in a shifting threat environment, the lower the need to rely on existing inventories of stockpiled or deployed weapons. Consequently, the freedom to reduce nuclear weapons deeply ironically may benefit from the U.S. capability to restore nuclear forces as flexibly and rapidly as may be required by changes in the factors that pace U.S. requirements.

In short, the pacing factor most under U.S. control—i.e., the character of U.S. strategic capabilities and nuclear production infrastructure— may help contribute to the realization of deep nuclear force reductions. This could be accomplished by reducing the demand for deployed or stockpiled nuclear weapons, and by mitigating the risks that otherwise could be associated with deep reductions—particularly including risks of surprising behavior by opponents and the need to adjust rapidly to changes in the threat environment.

The continuing, mechanical application of balance of terror idioms and tenets to contemporary questions of U.S. deterrence strategy and strategic policies will *undercut U.S. policies and capabilities that could facilitate the opportunity for further prudent deep nuclear reductions.* Why? First, the balance of terror formula focuses obsessively on calculating *the* number and type of deployed nuclear weapons considered adequate for "stable" deterrence. Long-term linear planning around that number—and setting successively-lower arms control limitations—works against the flexibility to shift and adapt strategy and capabilities as necessary per the threat conditions that pace actual need. If history were fixed or proceeding reliably in a straight line toward greater amity and peace, the lack of flexibility embedded in the balance of terror formula might be acceptable. There is little evidence, however, of such a happy trajectory.

Second, the contemporary action-reaction proposition that a manifest U.S. capability for "new" nuclear weapon production should be rejected because it will drive nuclear proliferation argues against having the type of viable nuclear production infrastructure that could help the United States adjust as necessary to changes in the threat environment *without relying on inventories of deployed or stockpiled weapons*. Similarly, the traditional "instability" arguments now leveled against non-nuclear strategic forces may reduce the potential for the development and deployment of non-nuclear strategic weapons that could permit less reliance on nuclear weapons.

Third, the traditional balance of terror presumption against supposedly "destabilizing" damage-limitation capabilities could keep U.S. vulnerability to the risk of surprise too high for the prudent implementation of much deeper reductions, even if the environment is so conducive. And, at very low numbers the presumption against discriminate, counter-force offensive forces could preclude strategic capabilities important for effective deterrence in plausible circumstances.

In summary, the balance of terror formula and tenets tend to be inconsistent with the flexibility and adaptability of U.S. policy and forces that could contribute to prudent deep nuclear reductions given a permissive threat environment. Sharp opposition to past U.S. policy initiatives for greater flexibility typically followed the balance of terror narrative, including the critiques of the 1974 "Schlesinger Doctrine" (NSDM-242) and Secretary Brown's 1980 "countervailing strategy" (PD-59). And, as is discussed below, the Bush Administration's 2001 Nuclear Posture Review (NPR) endorsed deep nuclear reductions, the possibility for further, deeper nuclear reductions, *and each of the capabilities described briefly above that could facilitate further prudent reductions*. Yet these NPR initiatives ran afoul of the continuing power of the same balance of terror narrative and have largely been stymied as a result.

The 2001 Nuclear Posture Review:
A Self-Conscious Step Toward Prudent Deep Reductions

The Bush Administration's 2001 NPR was a report mandated by Congress to examine the roles and value of U.S. strategic forces in the post-Cold War strategic environment, particularly including nuclear weapons.[73]   It identified several avenues to strengthen deterrence, including the need to understand opponents better so that the United States can "tailor its deterrence strategies to the greatest effect."[74] The NPR correspondingly emphasized the need for a wide spectrum of capabilities—conventional and nuclear, offensive and defensive—to support the tailoring of U.S. deterrence strategies against a diverse set of potential contingencies and opponents.[75]

Senior U.S. officials emphasized that the NPR firmly embraced deterrence as a continuing fundamental U.S. goal,[76] and that it focused on deterring post-Cold War threats including, in particular, those posed by WMD proliferation.[77] Secretary of Defense Rumsfeld's unclassified *Foreword* to the NPR specified that its policy direction was designed to "improve our ability to deter attack" while reducing "our dependence on nuclear weapons" for deterrence and placing greater weight on *non-nuclear* strategic capabilities.[78] Correspondingly, it emphasized the need for flexibility in U.S. strategic force sizing as necessary to meet the needs of a variety of possible future threat conditions, and de-linked the sizing of U.S. nuclear force levels from those of Russia, which *was not considered an immediate threat*.[79] It concluded that the immediate deterrence role for U.S. nuclear weapons could be met with far fewer deployed nuclear forces, and that U.S. nuclear requirements could recede further as advanced non-nuclear weapons and defenses matured.[80]

In addition, Secretary Rumsfeld specified that a potential problem with the extant nuclear arsenal was its combination of relatively modest accuracy and large warhead yields.[81] The NPR pointed to the potential for low-yield, precision nuclear threat options and the ability to hold hard and deeply buried targets at risk to improve U.S. deterrence capability and credibility.[82] Correspondingly, the NPR called for the U.S. capability to "modify, upgrade or replace portions of the extant nuclear force or develop concepts for follow-on nuclear weapons systems better suited to the nation's needs."[83]

Finally, as mentioned above, the NPR concluded that the new relationship with Russia permitted the United States to reduce by approximately two-thirds its deployed strategic nuclear warheads from the START I ceiling of 6,000, [84] and that the requirements for nuclear weapons might be reduced further still as U.S. non-nuclear and defensive capabilities advanced.[85] Senior Department of Defense officials specified that the NPR's sizing of strategic nuclear warheads at 1,700-2,200 did *not* include Russia as an immediate threat.[86] As Undersecretary of Defense Douglas Feith said in open testimony: "We can reduce the number of operationally deployed warheads to this level because… we excluded from our calculation of nuclear requirements for immediate contingencies the previous, long-standing requirements centered on the Soviet Union and, more recently, Russia. This is a dramatic departure from the Cold War approach to nuclear force sizing…."[87] Force sizing instead was calculated to support the *immediate* requirements for deterrence, and to contribute to the additional goals of assuring allies, dissuading opponents, and providing a hedge against the possible emergence of more severe, future military threats or severe technical problems in the nuclear arsenal.[88]

The NPR intentionally moved beyond the balance of terror formula that reduces U.S. strategic nuclear force sizing to the familiar deterrence calculation of U.S. warheads and opponents' targets. This was not unprecedented. As noted in Chapter 8, Secretary of Defense Schlesinger discussed his 1974 "essential equivalence" metric for strategic forces as intended to contribute to allied and enemy *perceptions* of overall U.S. strength.

The NPR also walked away from the balance of terror tenet that societal protection is useless, unnecessary and "destabilizing." Instead, Secretary Rumsfeld tied BMD deployment directly to denial deterrence and improved crisis management options, in addition to providing possible relief against the failure of deterrence: "…active and passive defenses will not be perfect. However, by denying or reducing the effectiveness of limited attacks, defenses can discourage attacks, provide new capabilities for managing crises, and provide insurance against the failure of traditional deterrence."[89] The subsequent formal announcement in December 2002 by President George W. Bush that the United States would deploy strategic BMD against limited offensive missile threats was perhaps the most visible break from long-standing balance of terror policy guidelines.

Finally, the NPR endorsed a "responsive" industrial infrastructure to help provide the basis for flexible and timely adjustment of U.S. strategic capabilities to technological and geopolitical developments. Again, a goal was to ease the requirement for deployed or stockpiled nuclear weapons: as increased reliance could be placed on a responsive industrial infrastructure to allow necessary adjustment to shifting technical or political conditions, there could be less reliance on deployed and non-deployed reserve warheads.[90]

In summary, the NPR established force sizing metrics that took into account U.S. national goals in addition to deterrence. It recognized the potential for deep force level reductions given the new relationship with Russia, and sought to mitigate the risks of those reductions (and possible future, deeper reductions) by establishing a flexible, adaptable approach to force deployments, promoting strategic non-nuclear forces and defenses, and establishing a responsive industrial infrastructure that could reduce reliance on the maintenance of deployed and stockpiled nuclear weapons.

Another Balance of Terror/Assured Destruction Counterreformation: Two Steps Back

Key commentators and members of Congress from both parties were unsympathetic to the NPR and its recommendations, some decidedly so. Responses to the NPR reflected both misunderstanding of its content and the long-familiar points of opposition to *any* strategic policy initiative departing from balance of terror and assured destruction orthodoxy, whether from Democratic or Republican administrations.

As noted, opposition to the NPR mirrored the sharp criticism of both NSDM-242 and PD-59. In each case, criticism followed from the familiar balance of terror/assured destruction formula: Support for multiple U.S. nuclear threat options and the endorsement of modest counterforce strategic capabilities supposedly was the work of nuclear "war-fighting" hawks who rejected deterrence.

Commentators who continued to calculate U.S. strategic force requirements via the Cold War's arithmetic formula dismissed the official claim that Russia was *not included* in the NPR's 1,700-2,200 range of strategic warheads.   They simply could not fathom how the standard deterrence formula of counting U.S. warheads and opponents' targets could result in the range of 1,700-2,200 warheads *unless* Russia continued to be included as the immediate threat to be deterred.[91] As noted above, however, that balance of terror formula was not the NPR's measure; the old metrics simply could not take into account the require-ments stemming from the multiple national goals of assurance, deterrence and dissuasion that were included in the NPR.[92]

In addition, pointing to uncertainty in the functioning of deterrence and recommending damage-limitation measures as a hedge against that uncertainty challenged the core balance of terror tenets. When the NPR recommended a defensive hedge and a spectrum of offensive capabilities—nuclear and non-nuclear—to strengthen deterrence, the old labels of "war-fighting" and "destabilizing" could not be far behind.

Commentators' application of the familiar Cold War formulas and metrics to the NPR's initiatives led inevitably to the erroneous conclusion that the NPR's recommendations reflected a rejection of deterrence in favor of a "destabilizing," "war-fighting" strategy.[93] One commentator's assessment was typical in this regard: "Throughout the nuclear age, the fundamental goal has been to prevent the use of nuclear weapons. Now the policy has been turned upside down. It is to keep nuclear weapons as a tool of war-fighting rather than a tool of deterrence."[94] Precisely the same charge was leveled at NSDM-242 and PD-59, despite the fact that neither they nor the NPR fit such a description.[95]

The NPR's embrace of strategic BMD also predictably brought charges of "instability" and the action-reaction "law" back into play: "Not only did this action destroy the arms reduction process…it made inevitable the next round of arms escalation. Missile defense began as Ronald Reagan's fantasy....The resuscitation of the fantasy of missile defense, and with it the raising from the dead of the arms race, may result in catastrophes in comparison to which [the war in] Iraq is benign."[96]

This narrative on the NPR—derived wholly from the Cold War's balance of terror standards and terms of art—reverberated first within the United States and then abroad. With that, critics could cite each other as authoritative validation of their interpretation and critiques of the NPR.

A similar application of Cold War norms to the NPR was seen in most Congressional commentary and opposition. Consequently, much of the NPR's recommended strategic force program has *not* been pursued. Former senior Pentagon official Tom Scheber has observed in this regard: "*Little progress* has been made on plans to develop and field prompt, conventional global strike [capabilities] and to modernize the nuclear force. In addition, initiatives to modernize the nuclear warhead research and production infrastructure and restore functionality have not progressed substantially."[97]

This opposition was made more enduring and salient than might otherwise have been the case by the Bush Administration's relatively modest efforts to present and explain the NPR publicly. In comparison to previous major initiatives in strategic policy—including NSDM-242 and PD-59—there was considerably less apparent public effort by the White House and Department of Defense to make the case that the new realities of the twenty-first century demanded the approaches to deterrence and strategic forces presented in the NPR.

A critique based on the Cold War's balance of terror orthodoxy was inevitable, even had there been a vigorous effort on the part of officials to present and explain the NPR. That critique has greeted every attempted policy departure from orthodoxy since the 1960s: it constitutes the baseline of accepted wisdom about deterrence and strategic forces for many in the United States. The combination of decades-long familiarity with the idioms and standards of the "stable" balance of terror/assured destruction model, and a limited public effort by the administration to explain the NPR, virtually ensured that the familiar critique based on past terms and definitions would become the accepted public narrative on the NPR. That narrative, in turn, became the basis for Congressional opposition.

In addition, and unsurprisingly, there were extreme-sounding commentaries on the NPR that appeared to be driven by partisan politics. Dr. Helen Caldicott, for example, a co-founder of Physicians for Social Responsibility, provided the following crude, politically-partisan commentary during the lead-up to the 2004 presidential elections: "My prognosis is, if nothing changes and Bush is reelected, within ten or twenty years, there will be no life on the planet, or little."[98] Similarly, a *Los Angeles Times* commentary told of "a hawkish Republican dream of a 'winnable nuclear war'" that threatened a "nuclear road of no return," and that "could put the world on a suicidal course."[99] Another asserted, "with Strangelovian genius" the NPR "puts forth chilling new contingencies for nuclear war."[100] Such descriptions were pure hyperbole, of course, but—presented with the appearance of insight—they were frightening hyperbole.

Leaving such extreme commentary aside, most of the reasoned critique of the NPR was based on standard balance of terror/assured destruction formulas and definitions. This was again apparent during the Congressional debate over RNEP, as discussed in Chapter 6. Congressional critics objected to it as being the "action" that would inspire the "reaction" of nuclear proliferation, and to RNEP's putative "war-fighting" capability, claiming it to be "destabilizing" and contrary to deterrence.

When Cold War measures of merit are applied in such a fashion to a decidedly post-Cold War strategic policy initiative, that initiative can only be deemed unacceptable: the NPR's recommendations were sure to be described as a rejection of deterrence, by definition, because the NPR did not follow the familiar balance of terror formula and related strategic force standards and goals. The critique was understandable on its own terms, but correspondingly missed the greater reality. The NPR's departure from balance of terror orthodoxy did not reflect a rejection of deterrence; it was, instead, an intentional step away from the definition of deterrence and measures of U.S. strategic force adequacy created during and for increasingly distant Cold War conditions.[101] It sought to identify the minimal level of nuclear capability consistent with multiple U.S. strategic goals in a new and dynamic strategic environment. And, in doing so, it recommended a two-thirds reduction in forces and a series of measures to mitigate the risk of such deep nuclear reductions—leaving open the possibility of further nuclear cuts.

The irony here is that the typical critiques of the NPR charged that it was a throwback to Cold War thinking when, in fact, those very critiques sprang from the vintage balance of terror narrative. Commentators responded yet again on the basis of past strategic measures and, unsurprisingly, found the NPR in violation of the definitions, terms and metrics of that old favored Cold War deterrence formula—as if that formula continues to be coherent in conditions so different from those which gave it intellectual life.

The NPR was neither beyond critique nor the final word in "new think" about strategic forces and policy. Useful commentary, however, now can only be based on recognition that our thinking about deterrence, defense, and strategic forces must adapt to the new realities of the twenty-first century. The NPR's drive to help create conditions suitable for prudent nuclear reductions instead was challenged by traditional Cold War standards and idioms that now have little meaning or value.

Still Holding the Horses

There is an anecdote, perhaps true, that early in World War II the British, in need of field pieces for coastal defense, hitched to trucks a light artillery piece with a lineage dating back to the Boer War of 1899-1902.[102] When an attempt was made to identify how gun crews could increase its rate of fire for improved defense, those studying the existing procedure for loading, aiming and firing noticed that two members of the crew stood motion-less and at attention throughout part of the procedure. An old artillery colonel was called in to explain why two members of a five-member crew stood motionless during the process, seemingly doing nothing useful: "'Ah, he said...I have it. They are holding the horses.'"[103] There were, of course, no longer any horses to hold, but the crew went through the motions of holding them nonetheless. The author of this anecdote concludes that the story, "...suggests nicely the pain with which the human being accommodates himself to changing conditions. The tendency is apparently involuntary and immediate to protect oneself against the shock of change by continuing in the presence of altered situations the familiar habits, however incongruous, of the past."[104]

The continued application of the balance of terror tenets as guidelines for U.S. strategic policy is akin to holding on to nonexistent horses. The expectation of well-informed, "rational" (i.e., prudent/cautious) opponents, and the related expectation that the absence of "suicidal" decision making must lead inevitably to the predictable, mechanical functioning of deterrence, are weak reeds upon which to base U.S. policy, as they were during the Cold War. As noted in Chapter 7, Secretary McNamara has since stated that deterrence did not fail catastrophically at the time because, "we lucked out."

Today, it is even more dangerous to expect the functioning of deterrence to be predictable, easily understood, achieved and manipulated. Holding on to such unwarranted expectations virtually ensures that the next failure or irrelevance of deterrence will come as a surprise, and that the United States simultaneously will dawdle in pursuing critical defensive/preventive measures and avoid the hard work necessary to strengthen deterrence to the extent feasible.

The NPR reflected a transformation in thinking about deterrence and strategic forces brought about by the dramatic change in conditions from those of the Cold War. Its basic recommendations were reasonable, prudent steps to align better our strategic policies and forces to the realities of the new era:

- Broadening the range of U.S. strategic goals that define the adequacy of U.S. strategic forces.
- Expanding U.S. deterrent threat options.
- Emphasizing the deterrent role for non-nuclear options.
- Raising concern about the uncertainty of deterrence and the credibility of the inherited Cold War nuclear arsenal for

some contemporary deterrence purposes.

- Seeking an improved understanding of opponents and their intentions, and the flexibility to tailor deterrence to the specific requirements of foe, time and place.
- Moving beyond the balance of terror as the measure of our deterrence and strategic force requirements.
- Placing a new priority on the U.S. capability to limit damage in the event of deterrence failure or irrelevance.

In due course, the fact that continuing faith in fixed Cold War models, terms and metrics has stymied the NPR's implementation will be an historical footnote—one with possibly lasting effect. The important question to consider now, however, is not the fate of the 2001 NPR, but rather the fate of future reviews and efforts to better align U.S. strategic policy and requirements with the reality of multiple and diverse opponents, WMD proliferation, and dynamic threat conditions. Many of the basic contours of U.S. strategic policy goals taken into account by the NPR are likely to endure—particularly including the need to deter multiple threats, assure understandably nervous allies, and provide protection against various forms and sizes of attack, including limited nuclear and biological attacks. Future reviews of U.S. strategic policy will confront the same questions of how U.S. strategies and strategic forces can help support these goals in an unpredictable, dynamic threat environment. The continued application of Cold War strategic orthodoxy to those questions will prevent any plausibly useful set of answers. The balance of terror tenets, as applied, serve largely to buttress a political agenda of stasis that actually works *against* the very steps that could facilitate the realignment of the U.S. nuclear arsenal and policy with contemporary realities—including the potential for prudent, deep nuclear force reductions.

It is time to move on from the enticing convenience and ease of the brilliant and innovative theoretical strategic framework of the Cold War. That framework is traceable to hubris, unwarranted expectations, and the need for convenience and comfort, however false. It is based on hopes that are beyond realization, and conditions that no longer exist. Outside of the unique Cold War standoff that gave it a semblance of coherence, the balance of terror lodestar will be a continuing source of dangerous and confused policy guidance.

Endnotes

1. The increased importance that U.S. officials attribute to these goals is elaborated in, Sharon Behn and Seth Rosen, "U.S. Urged to Focus More on Nation-Building," *The Washington Times*, July 28, 2005, p. 15.

2. Daryl Kimball, "Of Madmen and Nukes," *Arms Control Today*, Vol. 35, No. 9 (November 2005), p. 3, available at, http://www.armscontrol.org/act/2005. See also, Wolfgang Panofsky, "Nuclear Insecurity: Correcting Washington's Dangerous Posture," *Foreign Affairs*, Vol. 86, No. 5 (September/October 2007), pp. 109-110.

3. Les Aspin, *Annual Report to the President and the Congress* (Washington, D.C.: USGPO, January 1994), p. 61.

4. Paul Nitze, "Is It Time to Junk Our Nukes?," *The Washington Post*, January 16, 1994, p. C1.

5. Kimball, loc. cit.

6. See the discussion in Chapter 6, and also statements by Assistant Secretary of Defense, J.D. Crouch, in Tom Squitieri, "Bush Pushes for Next Generation of Nukes," *USA Today*, July 7, 2003, p. 1.

7. See, for example, David Ruppe, "Republican Lawmaker Slams Bush Nuclear Plans," *Global Security Newswire*, February 4, 2005, available at, http://www.nti. org/d_newswire/issues/2005_2_4.html. See also, Jonathan Medalia, *"Bunker Busters": Robust Nuclear Earth Penetrator Issues, FY 2005-FY2007*, Updated February 21, 2006, Library of Congress, Congressional Research Service, RL32347, p. 9.

8. Congressman David Hobson, quoted in, Jim Woolf, "U.S. Drive for Nuclear 'Bunker Buster' Bomb Boosted," *Reuters.com*, February 3, 2005.

9. President George H. W. Bush has stated that, "One of my big worries as commander-in-chief, which was shared by our military, was the fact that he might use chemical weapons. . . .We lived in fear of it." President Bush in *A Gulf War Exclusive: President Bush Talking With David Frost*, Transcript No. 51, January 16, 1996, p. 5. General Norman Schwarzkopf, Commander in Chief of Coalition Forces, and General Walt Boomer, Commander of U.S. Marines, also anticipated Iraqi chemical use. See their statements in, *Frontline*, No. 1408, *The Gulf War, Part II,* January 10, 1996, Transcript, pp. 3-4. See also, Youssef M. Ibrahim, "Israel Expecting Missiles From Iraq in Case of a War," *The New York Times*, January 1, 1991, p. 1.

10. See the discussion in, Moshe Arens, *Broken Covenant* (New York: Simon and Schuster, 1995), p. 201. See also, Senator Arlen Specter, "Statistics on Missile Scud Attacks on Israel," *Congressional Record – Senate,* 5 March 1991, p. S2689.

11. R. Jeffrey Smith, "U.N. Says Iraqis Prepared Germ Weapons," *The Washington Post*, August 26, 1995, p. A1. For a comparison of the lethality of conventional, chemical, biological and nuclear weapons see, Steve Fetter, "Ballistic Missiles and Weapons of Mass Destruction: What Is the Threat? What Should Be Done?" *International Security*, Vol. 16, No. 1 (Summer 1992), p. 27.

12. Presentation by Dr. William Shuler, Deputy for Counterproliferation, Office of the Assistant to the Secretary of Defense for Atomic Energy, December 13, 1995, Seventh Annual SO/LIC Symposium, Washington Sheraton, Washington, D.C.

13. Akiva Eldar, "'Saddam Would Have Reason to Worry,' Says Arens When Asked About Unconventional Weapons," *Ha' aretz*, February 4, 1991, p. 1.

14. As discussed by Shai Feldman of Tel Aviv University's Jaffee Center for Strategic

Studies, and Amatzia Baram of Haifa University in their respective papers presented at the conference, *Regional Stability in the Middle East: Arab and Israeli Concepts of Deterrence and Defense*, hosted by the United States Institute of Peace, June 17-19, 1991, Washington, D.C.

15. See the discussion in, Tim Trevan, "Inside Saddam's Death Lab," *The Sunday Times* (London), February 14, 1999, available at <www.sunday-times.co.uk/news/pages/sti/99/02/4>; Tim Trevan, *Saddam's Secrets: The Hunt for Iraq's Hidden Weapons* (North Pomfret, VT: Harper Collins, 1999), p. 45; and, Keith B. Payne, *Deterrence in the Second Nuclear Age* (Lexington, KY: University Press of Kentucky), pp. 81-87.

16. *Baghdad INA*, January 9, 1991, translated and presented in "INA Reports Minutes of Aziz-Baker Meeting," FBIS-NES-92-009, January 14, 1992, p. 27.

17. Reprinted in *U.S. Department of State Dispatch, Persian Gulf*, No. 2, January 14, 1991, p. 25.

18. *Public Statements of Richard B. Cheney, Secretary of Defense*, Vol. IV (Washington, D.C.: Historical Office, Office of the Secretary of Defense, 1990), p. 2547.

19. Presented in Smith, op. cit., p. A19.

20. *The Gulf War, Part I*, statement by General Wafic Al Sammarai, *Frontline*, No. 1407, January 9, 1996, Transcript, p. 12.

21. See the statements by General Al Sammarai, in *Frontline, The Gulf War, Parts I and II*, January 9-10, 1996. (Emphasis added). Comprehensive background interviews available at, Internet Website www.wgbh.org. See also, Tim Trevan, "Inside Saddam's Death Lab," op. cit.; and Trevan, *Saddam's Secrets: The Hunt for Iraq's Hidden Weapons*, loc. cit.

22. Quoted in, *General Hussein Kamal UNSCOM/IAEA Briefing*, (UNSCOM/IAEA Sensitive) August 22, 1995, Amman, Jordan, transcript available at, http://www.globalsecurity.org/wmd/library/news.iraq/un/unscom-iaea_kamal-brief.htm. (Emphasis added).

23. See, for example, International Institute for Strategic Studies, *The Military Balance: 1990-1991* (London: Brassey's, 1990), pp. 216-218.

24. See the transcript of the statements by Brent Scowcroft, *NBC News Meet the Press*, August 27, 1995, p. 10.

25. *A Gulf War Exclusive: President Bush Talking With David Frost*, loc. cit. Then Secretary of State James Baker also states that President Bush "had also decided that U.S. forces would not retaliate with chemical or nuclear weapons if the Iraqis attacked with chemical munitions." James Baker, *The Politics of Diplomacy* (New York: Putnam, 1995), p. 359.

26. Bernard Brodie, "What Price Conventional Capabilities in Europe?" *The Reporter*, Vol. 28 (May 23, 1963), p. 28.

27. Statements by James Baker and Tariq Aziz, *Frontline, The Gulf War, Part 1*, No. 1407, January 9, 1996, Transcript, p. 9, cited in, Payne, *Deterrence in the Second Nuclear Age*, op. cit., p. 136.

28. Carl Kaysen, Robert McNamara, and George Rathjens, "Nuclear Weapons After the Cold War," *Foreign Affairs*, Vol. 70, No. 4 (Fall 1991), p. 102.

29. Kimball, loc. cit.

30. As concluded by Richard Ned Lebow and Janice Gross Stein, *We All Lost the Cold War* (Princeton, NJ: Princeton University Press, 1994), p. 356.

31. Congressman Curt Weldon, "Congressional Delegation to North Korea Trip

Report," (Presentation, Nuclear Strategy Forum, cited with permission), Washington, D.C., February 22, 2005.

32. See, for example, the review of North Korean statements on the subject in the report by Mark Schneider, *Kim Jong Il and Nuclear Deterrence* (Fairfax, VA: National Institute for Public Policy, 2005), pp. 13-19.

33. Medalia, op. cit., p. 1. See also the extended discussion of this subject in, Kurt Guthe, "Implications of a Dynamic Strategic Environment," in, Keith Payne et al., *Rationale and Requirements for U.S. Nuclear Weapons and Arms Control, Volume II* (Fairfax, VA: National Institute for Public Policy, 2001), pp. 64-69.

34. General Accounting Office, *Operation Desert Storm: Evaluation of the Air Campaign*, GAO/NSIAD-98-134 (Washington, D.C.: USGAO, June 1997), p. 198.

35. Tim Ripley, "Kosovo: A Bomb Damage Assessment," *Jane's Intelligence Review*, Vol. 11, No. 9 (September 1999), p. 11.

36. Harold Smith in, *Remarks by Dr. Harold Smith Before the Defense Writers Group*, April 23, 1996, pp. 1-4 (as transcribed by the Office of the Assistant Secretary of Defense for Public Affairs).

37. Bryan Fearey, Paul White, John St. Ledger, and John Immele, "An Analysis of Reduced Collateral Damage Nuclear Weapons," *Comparative Strategy*, Vol. 22, No. 4 (October/November 2003), p. 312. See also the similar statement by Secretary of Defense Donald Rumsfeld in, Ann Scott Tyson, "'Bunker Buster' Casualty Risk Cited," *The Washington Post*, April 28, 2005, p. A7.

38. See the statement by Harold Brown in, U.S. Senate, Committee on Armed Services, *MX Missile Basing System and Related Issues*, Hearings, 98th Congress, 1st Session (Washington, D.C.: USGPO, 1983), pp. 6-7.

39. R. James Woolsey, "U.S. Strategic Force Decisions for the 1990s," *The Washington Quarterly*, Vol. 12, No. 1 (Winter 1989), p. 82.

40. See, for example, *The Future of the United Kingdom's Nuclear Deterrent*, Presented to Parliament by the Secretary of State for Defence and the Secretary of State for Foreign and Commonwealth Affairs by Command of Her Majesty, Cm 6994 (Her Majesty's Stationery Office: December 2006); and, *Speech by French President Jacques Chirac on Nuclear Deterrence*, at the L'Ile Longue submarine base in Finistere on January 19, 2006, available via the French Embassy in the United States at, info-france-usaWWW-Text.

41. For reviews of Russian and Chinese post-Cold War nuclear force and policy developments, see respectively, Mark Schneider, *The Nuclear Forces and Doctrine of the Russian Federation*, Nuclear Strategy Forum, No. 003 (Fairfax, VA: National Institute Press, 2006); and, Mark Schneider, *The Nuclear Doctrine and Forces of the People's Republic of China*, Nuclear Strategy Forum, No. 007 (Fairfax, VA: National Institute Press, November 2007).

42. It appears that Syria received North Korean assistance in the attempted covert construction of a nuclear reactor "not intended for peaceful purposes." White House spokeswoman Dana Perino, quoted in "U.S. Details Reactor in Syria," *The Washington Post*, April 25, 2008, p. A12.

43. Statement by a spokesman of the North Korean Foreign Ministry, March 31, 2004, Korean Central News Agency, April 1, 2004, Open Source Center, Document KPP20040401000030.

44. Samuel S. Kim, *North Korean Foreign Relations in the Post-Cold War World* (Carlisle, PA: U.S. Army War College, Strategic Studies Institute, April 2007), p. 87.

45. As observed by Kamram Taremi, a researcher at the Center for Graduate

International Studies, University of Tehran, in, "Beyond the Axis of Evil: Ballistic Missiles in Iran's Military Thinking," *Security Dialogue*, Vol. 36, No. 1 (March 2005), pp. 102-103.

46. Klaus Naumann, John Shalikashvili, The Lord Inge, Jacques Lanxade, and Henk van den Breeman, *Towards a Grand Strategy for an Uncertain World: Renewing Transatlantic Partnership*, Center for Strategic and International Studies, 2007, p. 94, available at, http://www.csis.org/media/csis/events/080110_grand_strategy.pdf.

47. See Dana Linzer and Walter Pincus, "U.S. Detects Signs of Radiation Consistent With Test," *The Washington Post*, October 14, 2006, p. A14; and, Reuters, "S. Koreans Want Nuclear Weapons Due to North—Survey," October 12, 2006, available at, http://asia.news.yahoo.com/061012/3/2r7t9.html.

48. "S. Korea Presses U.S. Over 'Umbrella'," *The Washington Times*, October 21, 2006, p. A2.

49. Quoted in, "North Korea's Nuclear Threat: Is U.S. Nuclear Umbrella Effective?" *The Daily Yomiuri*, March 20, 2007, available at, www.opensource.gov/portal/server. pt/gateway. See also, "Nakasone Proposes Japan Consider Nuclear Weapons," *Japan Times*, September 6, 2006; and, Tim Johnson, "Nuclear Taboo Slowly Giving Way," *Miami Herald*, September 24, 2006, p. 1.

50. Quoted in, "North Korea's Nuclear Threat/Reinforcing Alliance With U.S. Helps Bolster Nuclear Deterrence," *The Daily Yomiuri* (Internet version), in English, March 23, 2007.

51. Terumasa Nakanishi, "U.S., North Korea Moving Toward Normalizing Diplomatic Ties; Japan Must Discuss Nuclear Deterrence, Prepare for 'Worst-Case Scenario,'" *Seiron*, December 1-31, 2007, pp. 222-233, translated and printed in, Open Source Center, *Japan: Pundit Says Japan Should Discuss Nuclear Deterrence, Worst-Case Scenario*, JPP20071106015003, available at, https://www.opensource.gov/portal/ server.pt/gateway/PTARGS_0_0_200_51_43/http. (Emphasis added).

52. Joseph Cirincione, "Cassandra's Conundrum," *The National Interest*, No. 92 (November/December 2007), pp. 16-17.

53. See the discussion in, U.S. Department of State, International Security Advisory Board, *Report on Discouraging a Cascade of Nuclear Weapons States* (Washington, D.C.: United States Department of State, October 19, 2007), pp. 22-23.

54. Ibid., p. 23.

55. See the discussion in, Keith B. Payne, *The Fallacies of Cold War Deterrence and a New Direction* (Lexington, KY: University Press of Kentucky, 2001), pp. 61-73.

56. Quoted in, Josef Joffee, "A Peacenik Goes to War," *The New York Times Magazine*, May 30, 1999, *The New York Times on the Web*, "Archives," p. 1.

57. Some former senior officials have concluded that the United States must place greater priority on "nation-building" and post-conflict "reconstruction." See, Behn and Rosen, loc. cit. The new U.S. Army Field Manual reportedly "puts nation-building as a military task alongside combat operations." Sara Carter, "Army Manual Stresses Nation Building," *The Washington Times*, March 3, 2008, p. A1.

58. See, for example, The Commission on Integrated Long-Term Strategy (Chaired by Fred Iklé and Albert Wohlstetter), *Discriminate Deterrence* (Washington, D.C.: USGPO, 1988), p. 2.

59. Sidney Drell et al., "A Strategic Choice: New Bunker Busters Versus Nonproliferation," *Arms Control Today*, Vol. 33, No. 2 (March 2003), p. 9.

60. See, for example, George P. Shultz, William J. Perry, Henry A. Kissinger, and Sam Nunn, "A World Free of Nuclear Weapons," *The Wall Street Journal*, January 4,

2007, p. 15.

61. In, *The Future of the United Kingdom's Nuclear Deterrent*, op. cit., p. 5.

62. See the testimony of Walter B. Slocombe, Under Secretary of Defense for Policy, Department of Defense, *The Future of Nuclear Deterrence*, Hearing, before the Subcommittee on International Security, Proliferation, and Federal Services of the Committee on Governmental Affairs, United States Senate, February 12, 1997, p. 6 (Prepared text).

63. Ibid.

64. The limitations on the international system created by the inherent lack of trust within the system is an overarching theme in, Kenneth N. Waltz, *Man, the State and War* (New York: Columbia University Press, 1954).

65. See, for example, Walter Cronkite, "Cronkite Champions World Government," *The Washington Times*, December 3, 1999, p. A2; and, The United Methodist Church, Council of Bishops, *A Pastoral Letter to All United Methodists In Defense of Creation: The Nuclear Crisis and a Just Peace* (1986), p. 71.

66. Winston Churchill, quoted in a speech by British Prime Minister Margaret Thatcher to a joint meeting of the U.S. Congress, February 20, 1985, available at, http://www.margaretthatcher.org/speeches/displaydocument.

67. See, for example, Shultz, Perry, Kissinger, and Nunn, loc. cit.; George P. Shultz, William J. Perry, Henry A. Kissinger, and Sam Nunn, "Toward a Nuclear-Free World," *The Wall Street Journal*, January 15, 2008, p. 13; and, Ambassador Max Kampelman, "A Serious Look at Our World," *Comparative Strategy*, Vol. 25, No. 2 (April-June 2006), pp. 153-155.

68. For an aged but still useful examination of the question of deep nuclear reductions see, Francis Hoeber, *How Little Is Enough? SALT and Security in the Long Run* (New York: Crane, Russak & Company, 1981), pp. 20-39.

69. See, for example, United States Department of Defense, *Statement on Nuclear Posture Review*, No. 113-02, March 9, 2002, available at, http://www.defenselink.mil/news/Mar2002/b03092002_bt113-02.html.

70. *Statement of the Honorable Douglas Feith, Undersecretary of Defense for Policy*, Senate Armed Services Committee, *Hearing on the Nuclear Posture Review*, February 14, 2002, p. 7 (Prepared text).

71. Ibid.

72. These points are elaborated in, Kurt Guthe, *A Different Path to Nuclear Arms Reduction*, Discussion Paper (Fairfax, VA: National Institute for Public Policy, December 27, 2007), pp. 1-4.

73. See Keith B. Payne, "The Nuclear Posture Review and Deterrence for a New Age," *Comparative Strategy*, Vol. 23, No. 4/5 (October-December 2004), pp. 411-420; and, Keith B. Payne, "The Nuclear Posture Review: Setting the Record Straight," *The Washington Quarterly*, Vol. 28, No. 3 (Summer 2005), pp. 135-151.

74. Donald H. Rumsfeld, "Adapting U.S. Strategic Forces," *Department of Defense Annual Report to the President and the Congress 2002*, Chapter 7, p. 4, available at, www.defenselink.mil/execsec/adr2002.html_files/chap7.htm.

75. Rumsfeld, op. cit., p. 2; *Statement of the Honorable Douglas Feith, Hearing on the Nuclear Posture Review*, op. cit., pp. 3, 5, 7; and, Assistant Secretary of Defense for International Security Policy, J.D. Crouch, *Special Briefing on the Nuclear Posture Review*, January 9, 2002, available at, http://www.defenselink.mil/transcripts/2002/t01092002_t0109npr.html.

76. *Statement of the Honorable Douglas Feith, Hearing on the Nuclear Posture*

Review, op. cit., pp. 3-5; Crouch, *Special Briefing on the Nuclear Posture Review*, op. cit.; and, John Gordon, *Statement Before the Senate Armed Services Committee*, February 14, 2002, pp. 2-5 (Prepared text).

77. Donald H. Rumsfeld, *Foreword to the Nuclear Posture Review Report*, Submitted to Congress on December 31, 2001, available at, http://www.defenselink.mil/news/Jan2002/d20020109npr.pdf.

78. Ibid.; and, *Statement of the Honorable Douglas Feith, Hearing on the Nuclear Posture Review*, op. cit., p. 5.

79. Tom Scheber, Keith Payne, and Kurt Guthe, *The 2001 Nuclear Posture Review: Sizing the Nuclear Force* (Fairfax, VA: National Institute for Public Policy, November 2007), p. 1.

80. *Statement of the Honorable Douglas Feith, Hearing on the Nuclear Posture Review*, op. cit., p. 7; Rumsfeld, "Adapting U.S. Strategic Forces," op. cit., p. 3; and, Keith B. Payne, Deputy Assistant Secretary of Defense for Forces Policy, Office of the Secretary of Defense, *Nuclear Posture Briefing to the Defense Science Board*, February 20, 2003.

81. Quoted in, Julian Borger, "Bunker Bomb Will Bust Test Ban," *Guardian*, March 11, 2002, p. 12. See also, Linton F. Brooks, *Statement Before the Senate Armed Services Subcommittee on Strategic Forces*, April 4, 2005, pp. 2-3 (Prepared text).

82. Tom Scheber, Office of the Secretary of Defense, *The ABCs of the NPR*, (Unclassified briefing, 2003).

83. Rumsfeld, "Adapting U.S. Strategic Forces," op. cit., p. 5; see also, *Statement of the Honorable Douglas Feith, Hearing on the Nuclear Posture Review*, op. cit., p. 4.

84. *Statement of the Honorable Douglas Feith, Hearing on the Nuclear Posture Review*, op. cit., pp. 5-6.

85. Ibid., p. 7.

86. Ibid., pp. 5-6; and, Rumsfeld, *Foreword to the Nuclear Posture Review Report*, op. cit.

87. *Statement of the Honorable Douglas Feith, Hearing on the Nuclear Posture Review*, op. cit., p. 6.

88. Rumsfeld, "Adapting U.S. Strategic Forces," op. cit., pp. 5-6; *Statement of the Honorable Douglas Feith, Hearing on the Nuclear Posture Review*, op. cit., pp. 3, 5; Keith B. Payne, *The Nuclear Posture Review: Key Organizing Principles*, (Unclassified Department of Defense Briefing on the NPR), July 30, 2002, p. 9; Gordon, op. cit., pp. 7-8; and, Scheber, Payne, and Guthe, op. cit., pp. 3-6.

89. Rumsfeld, *Foreword to the Nuclear Posture Review Report*, op. cit.

90. Scheber, Payne, and Guthe, op. cit., p. 6.

91. Richard Sokolsky, "Demystifying the US Nuclear Posture Review," *Survival*, Vol. 44, No. 3 (Autumn 2002), p. 141; Morton Halperin, "Parsing the Nuclear Posture Review," *Arms Control Today*, Vol. 32, No. 2 (March 2002), pp. 19-20; and, David McDonough, *The 2002 Nuclear Posture Review: The 'New Triad,' Counterproliferation, and U.S. Grand Strategy*, Centre of International Relations, University of British Columbia, Working Paper, No. 38 (August 2003), p. 35.

92. As described in, Scheber, Payne, and Guthe, op. cit., pp. 3-5.

93. See, for example, Roger Speed and Michael May, "Dangerous Doctrine," *Bulletin of the Atomic Scientists*, Vol. 61, No. 2 (March/April 2005), pp. 38-49; David McDonough, *Nuclear Superiority: The 'New Triad' and the Evolution of Nuclear Strategy*, Adelphi Paper No. 383 (New York: Routledge, 2006), pp. 63-84; and, Lawrence Freedman, *Deterrence* (Malden, MA: Polity Press, 2004), pp. 2, 24, 84.

94. Ivo Daalder, quoted in Michael Gordon, "Nuclear Arms: For Deterrence or Fighting?" *The New York Times*, March 11, 2002, p. A1.

95. See, for example, Seymour Melman, "Limits of Military Power," *The New York Times*, October 17, 1980, p. 31.

96. James Carroll, "The Paradox of Missile Defense," *Boston Globe*, June 5, 2007, p. A11; see also, David Rupp, "Democratic Senator Says Bush Policies Increase Risk of Nuclear Abyss," *Global Security Newswire*, January 29, 2004, available at, http://www.nti.org/d_newswire/issues/2004_1_29.html#8944A21C.

97. Tom Scheber and Keith Payne, *Examination of U.S. Strategic Forces Policy and Capabilities* (Fairfax, VA: National Institute for Public Policy, February 2008), p. 4. (Emphasis in original).

98. As quoted in, "Nuclear Weapons 'Immoral,' Say Religious, Scientific Leaders," *Los Angeles Times*, March 9, 2004, available at, www.oneworld.net.

99. Robert Scheer, "Commentary: A Nuclear Road of No Return: Bush's Bid for New Kinds of Weapons Could Put the World on a Suicidal Course," *Los Angeles Times*, May 13, 2003, p. B13.

100. William Arkin, "Secret Plan Outlines the Unthinkable," *Los Angeles Times (latimes.com)*, March 10, 2002, available at, http://www.latimes.com/news/opinion/la-op-arkinmar10.story.

101. Crouch, *Special Briefing on the Nuclear Posture Review*, op. cit.

102. This anecdote is recounted by Elting Morison in, *Men, Machines, and Modern Times* (Cambridge, MA: The M.I.T. Press, 1966), pp. 17-18.

103. Ibid., p. 18.

104. Loc. cit.

Index

About the Author

Dr. Keith B. Payne is president of the National Institute for Public Policy, a non-profit research center he co-founded in 1981. He also is professor and head of the Graduate Department of Defense and Strategic Studies at Missouri State University (Washington, D.C. area campus). He previously taught for twenty-one years in Georgetown University's graduate National Security Studies Program and was awarded the Vicennial Medal by Georgetown University. Dr. Payne is the Chairman of the Policy Panel of the U.S. Strategic Command's Senior Advisory Group, Co-Chair of the Nuclear Strategy Forum, and a member of the Department of State's International Security Advisory Board. He serves as a Commissioner on the Nuclear Posture Commission created by the U.S. Congress in 2008. Dr. Payne was Deputy Assistant Secretary of Defense for Forces Policy from 2002 to 2003 and, prior to assuming that position, was the Co-Chair of the Deterrence Concepts Advisory Group, Office of the Secretary of Defense. He received the Department of Defense Medal for Distinguished Public Service in 2003.

Dr. Payne has served as a consultant to the White House, Arms Control and Disarmament Agency, and Department of Defense, and as a member of the Department of State's Defense Trade Advisory Group. He lectures widely on international security issues at universities and governmental offices in the United States, Europe, Asia, and the Middle East. Dr. Payne is the author of approximately one hundred published articles appearing in leading U.S., European, and Japanese journals and newspapers, and is the author or co-author of seventeen previous books and monographs, including *Deterrence in the Second Nuclear Age* (1996) and *The Fallacies of Cold War Deterrence* (2001). He has testified on numerous occasions before Congressional committees on the subjects of deterrence strategy, strategic forces and policy, and arms control. His work has been translated into German, Spanish, Japanese, Portuguese, and Russian.